The Official Guide to the *TOEFL*® Test
Using the Digital Resources

本书的练习题目为托福实考真题，但是屏幕界面和显示方式与实考略有区别。在参加托福考试时，考生会发现实考中题目在屏幕上出现的方式略有不同。

安装

扫描下方二维码获取学习资源，步骤如下：

1. 打开微信或书加加 APP，扫描下方二维码。
2. 扫码后，点击页面下方的 "绑定"，即可将学习资源绑定在你的微信或书加加账号中。
3. 绑定后，点击 "下载到本地"，此时会显示两种下载方式：
   - 将下载链接发送到你的邮箱（官方推荐）
   - 将下载链接复制到电脑端的浏览器
4. 在收到的邮件中点击 "点击下载"，或在浏览器中打开复制好的下载链接，此时会弹出一个二维码，请使用微信或书加加 APP 重新扫码，再次验证。
5. 验证成功后，即可下载学习资源文件夹。文件夹中包括音频和书中 4 套题目的电脑版做题软件，所有文件均适用于 Windows 系统和 Mac 系统。

* 本书采用 "一书一码" 形式，**每个二维码仅限绑定一个微信账号或书加加账号**，绑定后仅供账号所有者使用，转让无效。

* 为了最佳的使用体验，请使用电脑下载和使用学习资源。

* 如有疑问，请拨打咨询电话 010-62605588。

主菜单（导航界面）

安装后屏幕显示如下：

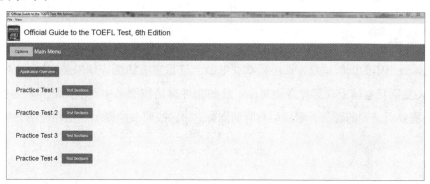

在电脑上进行托福考试模拟练习

在主菜单（导航界面）中，可以选择 Practice Test 1、2、3 或 4，然后选择"Reading"、"Listening"、"Speaking"或"Writing"进行不同部分的测试。要注意每一部分都可以进行多次测试。

在每部分测试开始之前，屏幕上会显示本部分的答题指导。屏幕上的计时器会显示本部分测试的剩余时间。如果你认为计时器妨碍做题，可以将其隐藏。

如果在考试中需要休息，请点击顶部的 Main Menu 键，就会回到主菜单（导航界面）。当你准备好继续做题时，再次打开之前做的那部分考试，选择 Continue 键。你回答的题目不会丢失；重新开始做题时，你将会从接下来的题目开始答题。休息期间计时器会停止计时；重新开始答题时，计时器会立刻继续计时。尽量减少休息时间，因为在托福实考中，即使在休息时间计时器也不会停止计时。

回答问题

在阅读和听力部分，点击选项前对应的椭圆或遵循指示回答问题。一些问题可能需要点击多个选项。在选定某个或某些答案后，选择 Next 键进入下一道题。在阅读部分，还可以点击 Previous 键返回到前面检查答案。

在口语部分，考生需在听到开始回答的指示后，将自己对每道题的回答录进录音设备。答题时间结束后停止录音。

在写作部分，考生需在规定时间内将自己对每道题的回答写在相应位置上。

在回答完一个部分的所有问题后，点击 Next 键，结束本部分的测试。

播放音频文件

听力、口语和写作部分都需要听录音。音频控制条可以在屏幕底部找到。录音结束后，点击 Next 键开始回答问题。

你的成绩

在主菜单（导航界面）中，选择你已经完成的任一测试部分。对于阅读和听力两部分，考生可获得题目回答正确的比例。选择 Review 键，阅读和听力部分的每道题都可以查看正确答案和解析。口语部分可以查看每道题的要点、回答范例和评分者对范例的点评。按指示听回答范例。根据要点、回答范例和评分者的点评来评估自己在口语部分的表现。写作部分可以查看话题要点、范文和评分者对范文的点评。根据话题要点、范文和评分者的点评来评估自己在写作部分的表现。

完成书中习题及模拟测试题

也许，你会选择做书中的纸版试题，而不喜欢在电脑上进行实考演练。如果是这样，你仍然需要听录音。把"Audio"文件夹复制到电脑上，选择音频文件，这些文件都是按照书中对应的题目序号标序的。做书中的测试题时，会遇到需要听录音的题目，题目中有听筒图标 🎧。按照书中提示点击相应的音频序号。

The Official Guide to the TOEFL iBT® Test

托福考试官方指南

美国教育考试服务中心 编著

SIXTH EDITION

QUNYAN PRESS

·北京·

图书在版编目(CIP)数据

托福考试官方指南 / 美国教育考试服务中心编著
. -- 北京：群言出版社，2021.3
书名原文：The Official Guide to the TOEFL iBT
Test, Sixth Edition
ISBN 978-7-5193-0628-1

Ⅰ.①托… Ⅱ.①美… Ⅲ.①TOEFL－自学参考资料
Ⅳ.①H310.41

中国版本图书馆CIP数据核字（2021）第006544号

版权登记：图字01—2020—7328

Educational Testing Service

The Official Guide to the TOEFL® Test, Sixth Edition

ISBN 978-1-260-47035-2

责任编辑：孙平平
封面设计：大愚设计+李　倩

出版发行：群言出版社
地　　址：北京市东城区东厂胡同北巷1号（100006）
网　　址：www.qypublish.com（官网书城）
电子信箱：dywh@xdf.cn　qunyancbs@126.com
联系电话：010-62418641　65267783　65263836
经　　销：全国新华书店

印　　刷：三河市航远印刷有限公司
版　　次：2021年3月第1版　2021年3月第1次印刷
开　　本：889mm×1194mm　1/16
印　　张：43.75
字　　数：876千字
书　　号：ISBN 978-7-5193-0628-1
定　　价：168.00元

Contents

Contents

5 Writing Section 187

6 Authentic *TOEFL iBT*® Practice Test 1 215

7 Authentic *TOEFL iBT*® Practice Test 2 313

Contents

1

About the TOEFL iBT® Test

Read this chapter to learn

➤ The main features of the *TOEFL iBT*® test
➤ What kind of questions are on the test
➤ How you can use this book to help you prepare for the test

这本《托福考试官方指南》旨在帮助英语学习者了解并准备托福考试。在准备考试的过程中，考生可同时培养学术环境所需的各种技能，从而在事业和生活中取得成功。

Getting Started

阅读以下关于托福考试的相关细则、考试要求以及分数评估等重要信息，开始托福考试的准备工作。

全世界的本科、硕士和博士学习项目都要求学生展示他们用英语交流的能力，并以此作为录取要求。

托福考试通过模拟大学课堂和学生日常交流环境，为考生提供机会展现有效沟通的技能。考试中使用的语言反映了真实的英语环境，包括课堂授课、课堂讨论以及实验室研究。教授会用同样的语言与学生讨论专业课或各种概念；学生在学习小组或在大学日常生活中——例如在书店买书——也使用同样的语言。本书的阅读文章均选自真实的教科书和课程资料。

TOEFL® Scores Can Help You Go Anywhere

托福考试着重测试考生使用英语的水平，而并非他们掌握的语言知识。托福考试秉承公平、客观的评分原则，其测试结果的有效性和可靠性能够验证考生是否具备了成功应对学术环境的必要的英语能力。

正因如此，五十多年来，托福考试一直都是全世界最著名的学术英语考试。180多个国家（包括澳大利亚、加拿大、新西兰、美国、英国，以及欧洲和亚洲的其他国家）的11,000多所大学和机构承认托福成绩，所以考生的托福考试成绩可在世界范围内得到认可。

托福考试在180多个国家中的ETS资质认证的、安全的考试中心举行。已有三千五百多万人通过参加托福考试实现了他们的梦想。

Who Creates the *TOEFL®* Test?

托福考试由美国教育考试服务中心（Educational Testing Service，简称ETS）开发和管理。美国教育考试服务中心是世界最大的教育评估和研究机构，旨在提高教育的质量和公平性。提供公平、有效和可靠的评估是ETS存在的关键。

Who Is Required to Take the *TOEFL®* Test?

如果你的第一语言或者母语不是英语，那么你希望申请就读的大学很可能会要求你参加一项英语水平测试。不过，你应当事先查询一下所申请大学的具体入学要求。

How Is the *TOEFL®* Test Used in the Admissions Process?

你所申请的院校将对你的托福考试分数及其他情况进行综合评估，以确定你是否具备进入某一专业学习的必要的学术知识和语言能力。通常，你攻读的专业以及是研究生还是本科生，将决定你申请大学所需要达到的托福分数。

Is There a Minimum Acceptable Score?

各大院校有各自的托福考试最低分数线。各院校的最低分数线不同，主要依据如下因素：申请者要攻读的专业、所申请的学历类别（本科生还是研究生）、申请者能否承担助教工作，以及该院校是否可以为考生提供第二语言（英语）学习上的帮助等。

How to Use This Book

本书/线上资源为考生提供了详细的指导、练习和备考建议，以帮助考生在托福考试中取得好成绩。

- 第1章对托福考试进行了概括性论述，介绍了评分信息、托福考试各部分在屏幕上的界面形式，并提出了一些参加考试的常识性建议。

- 第2、3、4、5章对托福考试各部分的不同题型进行了深入讨论。其中每一章节还包含一些习题和对正确答案的解释说明，从而帮助考生迅速了解每一章节要测试的语言交流技能。

- 第6、7、8、9章是4套完整的托福真题，方便考生自测。

- 第10章是写作手册，指导考生用英文进行写作，内容包括语法、用法、写作技巧、写作风格以及结构和内容的展开。另外，本章也探讨了不同类型的文章，就如何通过修订、编辑和校对改进文章给出建议，并提供了词汇表。

- 可下载的线上资源提供第6到9章的4套真题的电脑实考版。除此之外，还包含与4套真题配套的所有听力材料的音频文件。欲知更多有关使用线上资源的信息，请见本书前几页中的使用说明。

考生可以通过本书熟悉托福考试的形式、时间长度及考试界面。考生还可以通过托福考试在线测试 www.ets.org/toeflpractice 练习更多模拟试题，感受托福实考。托福考试在线测试的功能可以帮助你：

- 体验真实的托福考试场景
- 体验和实际考试相同的屏幕显示
- 通过大量练习为实考做准备
- 获得听、说、读、写四项技能的即时评分与反馈

托福考试在线测试有助于考生熟悉在托福考试过程中屏幕上出现的各种工具的使用方法，以及在限定时间的情况下如何回答问题。这本《托福考试官方指南》将帮助考生了解成功通过考试以及将来在大学课堂上所需要掌握的各种语言技能。

通过本书和线上资源的练习，以及托福考试在线测试，考生能够确定在各种语言技能中自己最薄弱的环节是什么。然后，遵循各章节中的语言技能指导，改进这些薄弱环节。考生还应充分利用其他材料作为本书练习题的补充。

由于托福考试旨在评估考生在今后学习时要用到的实际语言技能，因此考生提高这些语言技能的最好方法是参加一个专门的英语辅导班，重点集中在对以下技能的培养：

- 运用四种语言技能进行交流，尤其是口语
- 综合运用各种语言技能（如：听、读、说；听、读、写）

即便是不准备参加英语辅导班的考生也应当练习托福考试中所要求的语言技能。换句话说，提高考试成绩的最佳方法就是提高自身各项语言技能。本书的每一章节都为考生提供了如何将学习内容与考试中的问题有机结合在一起的相关解释与指导。也许考生想要提高托福考试阅读部分的分数，那么，提高阅读技能的最好办法就是经常阅读，并且涉猎不

同专业领域（如自然科学、社会科学、艺术、商务等）和不同体裁的文章。互联网是这类阅读材料最好的来源之一，各类书籍、期刊、杂志也是不错的选择。另外，多读学术性文章最有助于提高阅读成绩，这类文章可以在各类大学课程中找到。

此外，考生还可以尝试以下一些练习：

- 快速浏览文章段落，找出文章关键信息（日期、数据、术语）。
- 扩大词汇量，可以通过识字卡来记忆单词。
- 不要试图仔细阅读每一个单词、每一个句子，而应练习快速阅读文章，对段落大意有总体印象即可。
- 挑选文章中一些不熟悉的词汇，通过上下文（前后句）猜这些单词的含义。
- 挑出文章中所有的代词（例如，he, him, they, them等），找出这些代词在文章中所指代的名词。
- 练习基于文章的隐含内容，做出推理并得出结论。

All About the *TOEFL iBT* ® Test

托福考试由阅读、听力、口语和写作四部分测试组成。整个考试时间共计约3个小时。所有的考试题目都在一天内完成。

Key Features

- 托福考试测试听、说、读、写四种语言能力，这些能力对于有效交流非常重要；侧重考查考生在学术环境中有效使用英语的能力。

- 托福考试反映了语言的实际应用情况。它利用综合性试题，考查考生的多种语言技能，反映真实的学术环境。综合性考题要求考生：

  ○ 读、听，然后说——就某个问题作出回答
  ○ 听，然后说——就某个问题作出回答
  ○ 读、听，然后写——就某个问题作出回答

- 托福考试代表了语言学习和教学的最好实践。英语学习过去着重语言知识（尤其是语法）的学习，学生不具备外语交流能力也能取得高分。如今，老师和英语学习者都认识到了利用英语交流的重要性，因此在许多英语培训中，综合运用多种英语技能的课堂活动受到普遍欢迎。

Format

- 托福考试通过互联网进行机考，在全球开设众多安全稳定的考点。

- 每个部分都有如何回答该部分问题的指导。没有计算机使用方面的讲解。

- 托福考试并非计算机自适应考试，试题测试考生应具备的全部能力。

- 在整个考试过程中，允许考生做笔记。考试结束时，为确保考试安全，在考生离开考试中心前，所有笔记将被收回并销毁。

- 在听力和口语部分，你可能会听到一些非美式英语的口音，比如英国口音或澳大利亚口音。欲了解样本，请登录www.ets.org/toefl/ibt/about/content/。

- 在口语部分，考生佩戴防噪音耳机，并对着麦克风作答。考生的回答经数字化录音，然后被发送至ETS进行评分。

- 经ETS培训并认证的评分人对口语部分的回答进行评分。

- 在写作部分，考生必须将回答输入计算机，输入的内容被发送至ETS进行评分。

- 经ETS培训并认证的评分人和人工智能（AI）评分会对口语和写作部分的作答提供一个完整的对考生能力的准确描述。

- 考试结束后，考生可以查看非官方的阅读和听力分数。口语和写作部分的评分只能在考试结束后进行，无法实时提供。

- 考试成绩将以线上和邮寄的方式发送。

下表显示了每个部分可能的题目数量和测试时间；每个部分的测试时间会根据各部分试题数量不同而有所不同。托福考试在阅读或者听力部分包含加试题目。这些加试题目由ETS进行测试实验，不计入考生成绩。

Test Format

Test Section	Number of Questions	Timing
Reading	3–4 passages, 10 questions per passage	54–72 minutes
Listening	3–4 lectures, 6 questions each 2–3 conversations, 5 questions each	41–57 minutes
BREAK	10 minutes	
Speaking	4 tasks: 1 independent and 3 integrated	17 minutes
Writing	1 integrated task	20 minutes
	1 independent task	30 minutes

Toolbar

考试中每一部分的工具栏将帮助考生顺利地完成考试。以下是托福考试中听力和阅读部分工具栏的实例。在工具栏的左上角总是显示着当前正在进行的考试是哪一个部分。

阅读部分的工具栏有一些重要特征：

在回答问题时，考生可以查看整篇文章。对于某些问题，考生需要点击View Text键来查看整篇文章。

点击Review键考生可以查看自己所有的答案。这样，考生可以返回到任何一道题目并更正自己的答案。考生也可以查看自己漏答的题目。

在回答阅读部分的问题时，考生可以随时点击Back键，返回到之前的问题。

下面是听力考试中工具栏的模式：

- 考生可以随时查看正在解答的是哪道题以及该部分的剩余时间。点击Hide Time（隐藏时间）键可以随时隐藏时钟。
- Volume键：声音控制键，可以在听录音时调整声音的大小。
- Help键：点击该键可以得到相关帮助。但使用Help键时计时不会停止。
- Next键：点击此键将进入下一道试题。
- 一旦点击了Next键，再点击OK键，即已确认了所选答案。在听力部分，点击OK键之后，考生将无法再查看做过的试题。

Reading Section

Academic Reading Skills

阅读部分测试考生理解大学水平的学术课文与文章的能力。在全世界众多学术领域中，考生需要具备阅读并理解教科书和其他一些用英语写成的学术资料的能力。以下是学术阅读的三个目的。

获取信息：
- 有效地浏览课文，寻找关键事实和重要信息
- 提高阅读效率和速度

基本理解：
- 理解中心论题、主题思想、主要观点、重要事实和细节、语境中的词汇意义以及代词指代[1]
- 对文章所暗示的内容作出推论[2]

理解文章内容和结构：
- 认知文章的结构和写作目的
- 理解观点之间的相互关系
- 为了记忆主要观点和重要细节，将信息整理成分类图表或概要
- 推断整篇文章中的各个观点是如何相互关联的

Description

Reading Section Format

Length of Each Passage	Number of Passages and Questions	Timing
Approximately 700 words	3–4 passages 10 questions per passage	54–72 minutes

Reading Passages

托福考试的每篇阅读文章大多节选自大学程度的教科书，涉及某个学科或主题。节选材料尽可能地保持了文章原貌，以衡量考生阅读学术材料的能力。

阅读文章涵盖各种不同科目的内容。如果考生对某个主题不熟悉，不必担心，回答问题所需的信息全部包含在文章当中。

---

1. 代词指代：文章中代词所实际指代的名词。
2. 作出推论：理解文章中虽然作出强烈暗示但并没有明确陈述的观点或思想。

阅读文章可划分为三种基本类型：

- 解释说明型（exposition）[3]
- 立论型（argumentation）[4]
- 历史题材型（historical）

通常，一篇文章会对关于其主题的信息从不同的角度或观点进行阐述。这一点是考生应在阅读过程中特别注意的。通常题目中至少会有一道题考查考生是否理解全文的结构。常见的文章结构大致有以下几种：

- 分类（classification）
- 比较/对比（compare/contrast）
- 原因/结果（cause/effect）
- 问题/解决方法（problem/solution）

在文章问题出现之前，考生应当把整篇文章通读或下拉着浏览一遍。一旦问题出现在屏幕上，文章就被移至屏幕的右侧，问题则在左侧（见下图）。

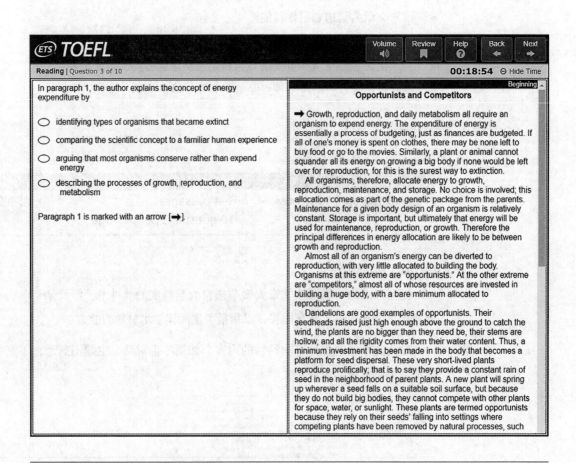

---

3. 解释说明型：解释某个主题。
4. 立论型：针对某个主题阐述一种观点，并提供支持该观点的证据。

在回答阅读部分的问题时，考生不需要知道任何特殊的背景知识，但文章会对一些较难的单词或短语给出解释。点击设有超链接的单词，此词的解释和定义就会出现在屏幕左下方。

本部分测试时间为54~72分钟，考生应在规定时间内读完文章并回答问题。

Reading Question Formats

阅读部分包括4种题型：

- 传统的单项选择题，即题目带有4个选项，只有1个正确答案。
- 多项选择题，即题目有多个选项，正确答案也不止一个（例如，4个选项中有2个是正确答案）
- 题目带有4个选项，只有1个正确答案，要求考生在文章中最合适的位置"插入一句话"（insert a sentence）。
- "深入理解"类（Reading to learn）题目有4个以上的选项，而且有不止1个正确答案。

Features

Reading to Learn Questions

此类问题测试考生认知文章的组织结构、理解位于文章不同部分的事实和观点之间关系的能力。

考生要对信息进行分类，将给出的文本选项放到分类表格或总结中（见下一页的示例）。总结类题目每题最高2分；表格类题目根据正确答案的数量，有的最高可得2分，有的最高可得3分。在这种题型中，选对部分选项也可得分。

Reading to Learn—Category Chart Question Example

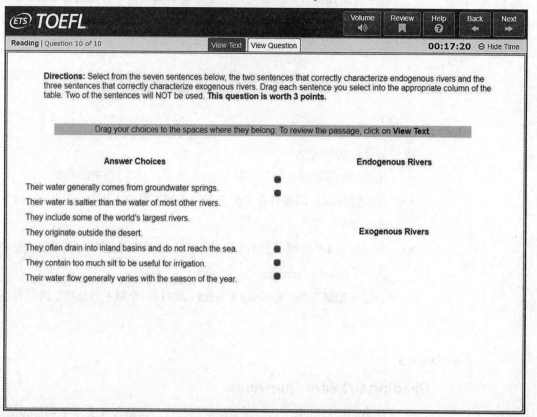

Reading to Learn—Prose Summary Question Example

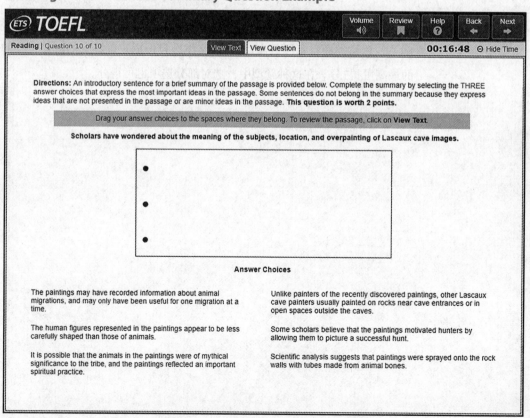

Glossary Feature

考生可以点击某些具有特殊标记的词汇和短语，查看这些术语的定义或解释。在下面的示例中，考生可点击"shamans"一词，查看该词的定义。

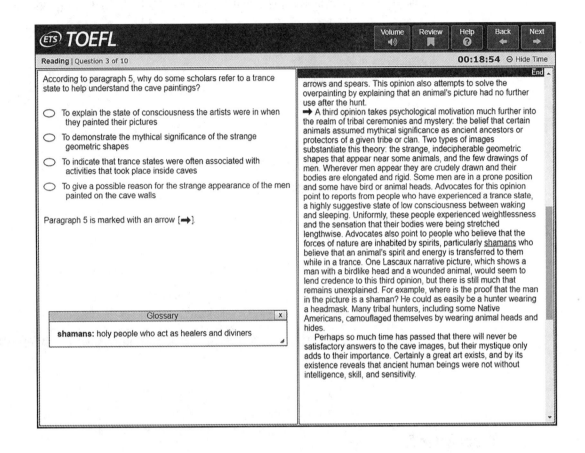

Listening Section

Academic Listening Skills

听力部分测试考生理解口语的能力。在学术环境中，考生必须能够听懂讲座和对话。学术听力通常出于下述三个目的之一：

为基本理解而听

- 理解主题思想、重要观点以及与主题思想有关的重要细节（没有必要理解所有的细节）

为语用理解而听[5]

- 识别说话者的态度和确定程度
- 识别说话者讲述内容的功能或目的

衔接和综合[6]信息

- 识别听力信息的结构
- 理解材料观点之间的关系（例如，比较/对比、原因/结果或者程序步骤）
- 根据听力材料中暗示的信息，作出推论[7]并得出结论
- 衔接对话和讲座中的信息片段
- 识别讲座和对话中的主题转换（例如，话题转换[8]和插入语[9]），识别讲座中的引论和结论

Description

托福考试中的听力材料包括学术讲座和长对话，其语调听起来非常自然。在整个听力测试过程中，考生可以做笔记，回答问题时可能会用到这些笔记。

Listening Section Format

Listening Material	Number of Questions	Timing
3–4 lectures, each 4–5 minutes long, about 500–750 words	6 questions per lecture	41–57 minutes
2–3 conversations, each about 3 minutes long, about 12–25 exchanges	5 questions per conversation	

5. 语用理解：理解说话人的目的、态度、确定程度，等。

6. 综合：把对话或讲座中的两个或多个部分的信息结合起来。

7. 作出推论：理解文章中虽然作出强烈暗示，但并没有明确陈述的观点或思想。

8. 话题转换：附带的评论，即说话者暂时离开主题，但随后又回到主题。

9. 插入语：与主题有关的评论，但打断了信息或思想的叙述流畅性（例如："现在请注意，这是一个考点。"）

Academic Lectures

托福考试所选的讲座材料均真实反映了课堂上的听说情景。在一些讲座中，教授满堂灌输，偶尔有学生提问或提出意见；在另外一些讲座中，教授可能会通过提问题鼓励学生参与讨论。考试时，伴随讲座一起出现在屏幕上的图片将有助于考生了解到底是一个人还是几个人在讲话。

A Lecture Where the Professor Is the Only Speaker

A Lecture Where the Professor and the Students Both Speak

Conversations in an Academic Setting

托福考试中的听力对话场景可能是学生与教授或助教在办公室的交谈，或者是学生和大学工作人员之间有关服务方面的对话。办公室对话的内容通常与学术内容或课程要求有关。服务对话的内容是关于非学习的校园活动，如缴纳公寓住宿费、课程报名或者在图书馆询问信息。学生对话可以是关于课程项目或校园活动。

计算机屏幕上显示的图片有助于考生想象对话的情景以及图中各人物的角色。

Conversation Example

Listening Question Formats

听力材料播放完之后，开始回答问题。考生首先看到并听到问题，然后才能看到选项。

听力部分包含四种题型：

- 单项选择题，即4个选项中有1个正确答案
- 多项选择题，有不止1个正确答案（例如，4个选项中有2个正确答案，或5个选项中有3个正确答案）
- 排序题，即排列事件的先后顺序，或排列某个过程的步骤
- 搭配题，即将一些对象或者文本与图表中的分类进行搭配，或在单元格里打对勾

Chart Question Example

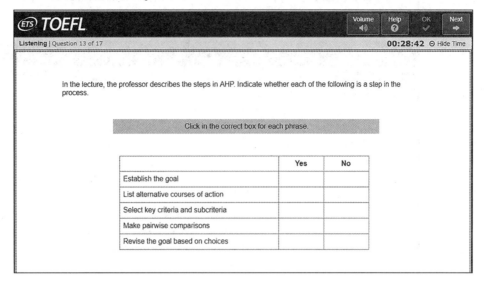

Features

- 允许记笔记。考试结束后，出于安全考虑，在考生离开考试中心前，所有笔记将被收回并销毁。

- 多项选择题旨在考查考生是否理解说话者的态度、确定程度或者说话的目的。这类题目要求考生倾听语调和其他提示性信息，并判断说话者如何看待所讨论的话题。

- 有些题目会重新播放讲座或对话中的某个部分。在这类题目中，考生将再次听到对话或讲座的某个部分，然后回答问题。

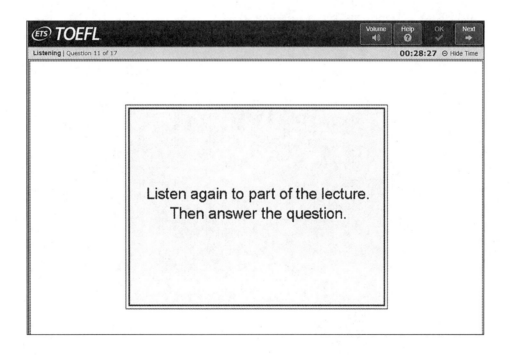

下例所示题目考查考生对说话者讲述内容的目的的理解。

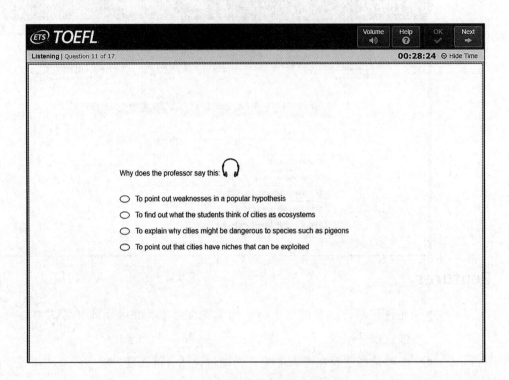

Speaking Section

Academic Speaking Skills

考生应该能够在课堂内外成功地用英语与人交谈。口语部分考查考生在学术环境和校园生活中有效交谈的能力。

在课堂中，考生必须：

- 回答问题
- 与其他学生讨论学术问题
- 对在课上阅读的教材和听到的内容进行综合分析与总结
- 在讨论中表达自己对某个话题的观点

在课堂外，考生必须：

- 参与日常交谈
- 表达意见
- 在书店、图书馆和住宿办公室等场合与他人交流和沟通

Description

口语部分大约持续17分钟，共有4道试题。

- 第一题是独立口语任务，题目内容涉及考生熟悉的话题，要求考生依据自己的想法、观点和个人经历作答。
- 另外三道题是综合口语任务。回答这类试题时，考生必须综合利用多种语言技能。其中的两项任务要求考生首先读、听，然后联系阅读文章和听力材料中的信息用口语作答。另外一项任务要求考生先听，再进行口头回答。考生可以记笔记，并利用这些笔记回答口语问题。

与托福考试的其他测试部分一样，口语部分也通过计算机作答。考生利用带有麦克风的头戴式耳机回答所有口语题目。考生对着麦克风讲话的声音将被录下来。回答经数码技术处理后被传送至ETS，然后由经过认证的评分人和自动评分系统评分。

Speaking Task Types

Task Type	Task Description	Timing
Independent Task		
1: Paired Choice	This question asks the test taker to make and defend a personal choice between two contrasting behaviors, ideas, or courses of action.	Preparation time: 15 seconds Response time: 45 seconds
Integrated Tasks		
	Read/Listen/Speak	
2: Fit and Explain Campus Situation	• A reading passage (80–110 words) presents a campus-related issue. • A listening passage (60–80 seconds) comments on the issue in the reading passage. • The question asks the test taker to summarize the speaker's opinion within the context of the reading passage.	Preparation time: 30 seconds Response time: 60 seconds
3: General/Specific Academic Course Topic	• A reading passage (80–110 words) broadly defines a term, process, or idea from an academic subject. • An excerpt from a lecture (60–90 seconds) provides examples and specific information to illustrate the term, process, or idea from the reading passage. • The question asks the test taker to combine and convey important information from the reading passage and the lecture excerpt.	Preparation time: 30 seconds Response time: 60 seconds
	Listen/Speak	
4: Summary Academic Course Topic	• The listening passage is an excerpt from a lecture (90–120 seconds) that explains a term or concept and gives concrete examples to illustrate that term or concept. • The question asks the test taker to summarize the lecture and demonstrate an understanding of the relationship between the examples and the overall topic.	Preparation time: 20 seconds Response time: 60 seconds
TOTAL		**17 minutes**

Writing Section

Academic Writing Skills

在要求用英语写作的所有学术领域中，考生必须能够用清晰、有条理的方式陈述自己的观点。写作部分考查考生在学术领域中的写作能力。

- 通常，考生需要用课上学到的知识写论文或作文。这要求考生将课堂讲座内容与阅读教材或其他材料相结合，这种类型的写作被称为综合写作。在这种写作题型中，考生必须：

  - 对听到和看到的材料做笔记，在写作前利用这些笔记组织信息
  - 准确地从原文材料中总结、释义和引用信息
  - 写出听到的信息与读到的信息之间是如何联系的

  例如，考生需要将课堂上教授的观点与指定阅读材料中作者的观点进行比较。考生必须能够成功地从两种材料中提取信息，并解释其中的异同。

- 考生还必须会写表达并支持自己观点的论文，这种类型被称为独立写作。在这种写作题型中，考生需要依据自身的知识和经历表达并支持一种观点。

  例如，题目可能要求考生就一个有争议的问题写一篇论文。考生可利用个人经历支持自己的观点。

  在所有的写作题型中，考生最好做到：

- 确定一个主题思想，以及支持该思想的重要观点
- 计划如何组织论文（例如，利用提纲）
- 利用推论、例证和细节展开论述
- 使用有条理的方式表达信息
- 运用有效的连接词（过渡词组）来连接观点，帮助读者理解思路的脉络
- 运用语法和词汇有效表达
- 准确地使用语法和词汇；恰当地使用习惯用语
- 遵循拼写、标点和格式的惯例

Description

写作部分的时间为50分钟，考生需要完成两道写作题目（见下表）。考生将作文输入计算机后，系统会将其发送至ETS，并由经过认证的评分人及自动评分系统评分。

Writing Task Types

Task Type	Task Description
Task 1 Integrated Writing: Read/Listen/Write	• Test takers read a short text of about 250–300 words (reading time, 3 minutes) on an academic topic. • Test takers may take notes on the reading passage. • The reading passage disappears from the screen during the lecture that follows. It reappears when test takers begin writing so they can refer to it as they work. • Test takers listen to a speaker discuss the same topic from a different perspective. The listening passage is about 250–320 words long (listening time, about 2 minutes). • The listening passage provides additional information that relates to points made in the reading passage. Test takers may take notes on the listening passage. • Test takers write a summary in connected English prose of important points made in the listening passage, and explain how these relate to the key points of the reading passage. Suggested response length is 150–225 words; however, there is no penalty for writing more as long as it is in response to the task presented. • Response time: 20 minutes
Task 2 Independent Writing: Writing from Knowledge and Experience	• Test takers write an essay that states, explains, and supports their opinion on an issue. An effective essay will usually contain a minimum of 300 words; however, test takers may write more if they wish. • Test takers must support their opinions or choices rather than simply list personal preferences or choices. • Typical essay questions begin with statements such as: — Do you agree or disagree with the following statement? Use reasons and specific details to support your answer. — Some people believe X. Other people believe Y. Which of these two positions do you prefer/agree with? Give reasons and specific details. • Response time: 30 minutes

About Test Scores

Score Scales

托福考试提供四项语言技能的分数：

Reading	0–30
Listening	0–30
Speaking	0–30
Writing	0–30
Total Score	**0–120**

总分是四项技能得分的总和。

Rating of Speaking and Writing Responses

Speaking

考生对口语部分四道题目的回答经数码技术处理后，被传送至ETS。每位考生的回答由四名经过认证的的评分人及自动评分系统评分。根据第180~183页的评分标准，评分人对每道题目的回答在0~4分范围内。四道题目的总得分将被转换为0~30分的标准分。

评分人根据下列要素对回答进行评分：

- 表述能力：语言表达清晰吗？好的回答应该清晰、流畅，发音标准，停顿自然，并且采用自然的语调模式。

- 语言运用：考生在表达思想时是否有效地使用了语法和词汇？评分人评估考生是否能够掌握基本的和复杂的语言结构，并恰当地使用词汇。

- 话题展开：考生回答问题的全面性以及陈述观点的连贯性如何？在综合口语任务中，考生综合与总结信息的能力如何？好的回答通常会用到规定的全部或大部分时间，观点之间的联系以及前后观点的衔接清晰易懂。

需要注意的是，评分人并不期待考生的回答完美无缺。即使是高分的回答也可能在上述三方面偶尔犯错或出现小问题。

Writing

所有写作题目的回答也被送至ETS，根据第193~194页以及第203~204页的评分标准，由两名经过认证的评分人及自动评分系统在0~5分的范围内进行评分。两道题目的平均分将被转换为0~30分的标准分。

- 综合写作的得分取决于作文的质量（文章的组织结构、词汇和语法的适当性和准确性），以及内容的完整性和精确性。

- 独立写作的得分取决于文章整体质量：论点的展开和组织、词汇和语法的适当性和准确性。

需要注意的是，评分人一般会认为考生的作文是第一手写出的文章，他们并没有期望考生写出经过深入研究、深思熟虑的文章。因此，即便作文中有某些错误，仍可得高分。

Score Reports

托福考试的成绩单为考生提供了有价值的内容，全面反映考生能否融入英语环境，并取得学业成就等信息。成绩单包括下列内容：

- 每个测试部分的得分
- 总分

考生的成绩单还包括对考生考试表现的反馈信息。对于阅读和听力部分，考生表现被描述为高级、中级或初级水平；对于口语部分，考生表现被描述为高级、中高级、中低级和中低级以下；对于写作部分，则被描述为高级、中高级、中低级、基础和基础以下。此外，还分别介绍每个分数段的考生所具备的英语知识和能力。

Score Requirements

各院校和机构有各自的托福考试分数线，考生应该咨询所报考的机构，确定其对托福成绩的要求。有关接受托福成绩的大学和机构列表，以及各机构通报给ETS的成绩要求，请登录www.toeflgoanywhere.org查询。

MyBest® Scores

2019年8月1日之后发送的所有托福考试成绩报告，无论考试日期是什么时候，都会自动包括所选考试日期的MyBest®分数与传统分数。这个新功能体现了考生两年内参加的历次考试每个分项的最高有效分数的总和，以展示考生最好的整体测试表现，如下图：

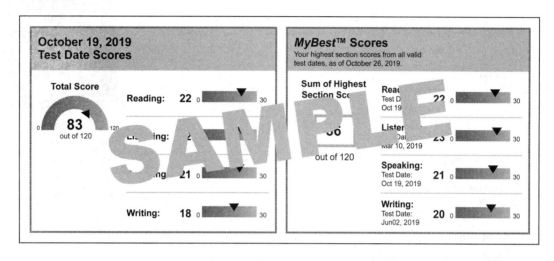

- 考试结束后6天左右，考生会收到一封电子邮件，告知可登录托福官网账户查询成绩。在成绩出来的2天内，考生可以下载并打印成绩单的PDF副本。

- 如果选择接收纸质成绩单，将在考试结束11天内为考生邮寄。美国境内寄送成绩单需要7到10天，其他地点可能需要更长的时间。

- 官方成绩单会在考试结束11天内直接发送给您指定的成绩接收方。

Sample *TOEFL iBT®* Score Report

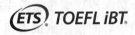

TOEFL iBT.

Test Taker Score Report

Name: Setiadi, Atin
Last (Family/Surname) Name, First (Given) Name, Middle Name

Email: asetiadi@ets.org

Gender: F   **Appointment Number:** 0000 0000 0036 5909

Date of Birth: October 13, 1992   **Test Date:** October 19, 2019

A. Setiadi
73, Jalan Cilaki
BANDUNG 40115
INDONESIA

Inst. Code	Dept. Code
00000	00
00000	00
00000	00
00000	00

Country of Birth: Indonesia
Native Language: Bahasa
Test Center: STN22222C
Test Center Country: United States

Security Identification

ID Type: Passport   **ID No.:** 23645   **Issuing Country:** Indonesia

THIS IS A PDF SCORE REPORT, DOWNLOADED AND PRINTED BY THE TEST TAKER.

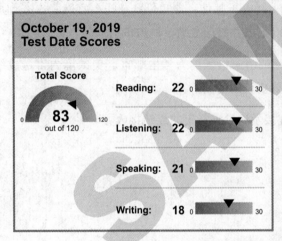

**October 19, 2019
Test Date Scores**

Total Score

83 out of 120
0 — 120

Reading: **22** 0 — 30
Listening: **22** 0 — 30
Speaking: **21** 0 — 30
Writing: **18** 0 — 30

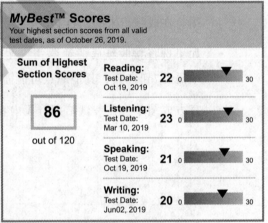

***MyBest*™ Scores**
Your highest section scores from all valid test dates, as of October 26, 2019.

Sum of Highest Section Scores

86 out of 120

Reading: Test Date: Oct 19, 2019   **22** 0 — 30
Listening: Test Date: Mar 10, 2019   **23** 0 — 30
Speaking: Test Date: Oct 19, 2019   **21** 0 — 30
Writing: Test Date: Jun02, 2019   **20** 0 — 30

A total score is not reported when one or more sections have not been administered.
*Expired scores are not included in **MyBest**™ calculations.*

01 - 07

Sample *TOEFL iBT®* Score Report

 **TOEFL iBT.**

Test Taker Score Report

THIS IS A PDF SCORE REPORT, DOWNLOADED AND PRINTED BY THE TEST TAKER.

Setiadi, Atin
Date of Birth: October 13, 1992

Appointment Number: 0000 0000 0036 5909
Test Date: October 23, 2019

SCORE RANGES

Total Score	0–120
Reading	**0–30**
Advanced	24–30
High - Intermediate	18–23
Low - Intermediate	4–17
Below Low - Intermediate	0–3
Listening	**0–30**
Advanced	24–30
High - Intermediate	18–23
Low - Intermediate	4–17
Below Low - Intermediate	0–3
Speaking	**0–30**
Advanced	25–30
High - Intermediate	20–24
Low - Intermediate	16–19
Basic	10–15
Below Basic	0–9
Writing	**0–30**
Advanced	24–30
High - Intermediate	17–23
Low - Intermediate	13–16
Basic	7–12
Below Basic	0–6

INSTITUTION CODES

The Institutions and Department code numbers shown on the front page are the ones you selected before you took the test.

Dept.	Where the Report Was Sent
00	Admissions office for undergraduate study
01, 04–41, 43–98	Admissions office for graduate study in a field other than management (business) or law according to the codes selected when you registered
02	Admissions office of a graduate school of management (business)
03	Admissions office of a graduate school of law
42	Admissions office of a school of medicine or nursing or licensing agency
99	Institution or agency that is not a college or university

For additional information about TOEFL iBT scores, score ranges, and how to improve your skills, visit www.ets.org/toefl/ibt/scores.

General Skill-Building Tips

对于英语学习者而言，培养托福考试所考查能力的最好方式是参加能够提供以下指导的英语培训：

- 阅读、口语、听力和写作能力的培训，重点是口语能力
- 培养综合能力（例如，培养听、读和说的综合能力，或听、读和写的综合能力）

除了本书附录所列的针对技能提高的建议之外，ETS也为考生提供了下列提示，这些提示对老师也同样有帮助。

Reading Tips

对于英语学习者来说，提高英语阅读技能最好的办法就是经常阅读，尤其是大学教材或其他涉及诸如自然科学、社会科学、艺术和商务领域等主题的学术型文章。通过互联网、杂志和期刊可以阅读到大量学术文章。

Reading to Find Information

- 快速浏览文章，找出关键事实（日期、数字和术语）和信息。
- 经常进行阅读练习，提高阅读速度和效率。

Reading for Basic Comprehension

- 练习快速浏览文章，获取文章中心思想。
- 略读一遍文章之后，再仔细精读，记下中心思想、主要观点和重要事实。
- 从文章中挑选一些不熟悉的词汇，查词典确认其含义。

Check Your English Reading Skills

TOEFL® Practice Online gives you the experience of taking the real *TOEFL iBT*® test. It includes *real* past test questions, scores, and performance feedback within 24 hours, and offers full tests, half tests, or Speaking-only test options. **www.ets.org/toefl/shoptestprep**

Reading to Learn

- 确认文章类型（例如，原因/结果、比较/对比、分类、问题/解决方案、描述、叙述）以及文章结构。
- 整理文章中的信息：
  - 列出文章提纲，区别主要观点和次要观点。
  - 如果文章有信息分类，那么，绘制一个图表，将信息放到恰当的类别中。

在托福考试中，考生无须自己绘制这样的表格，题目中会提供表格和答案选项，考生只需将正确的选项填入表格中。练习这种能力有助于考生总结和归类信息。

Listening Tips

英语学习者可以通过经常听英语来提升听力技能。看英文电影、电视节目和录像视频，收听英文广播，都是培养听力技能的绝佳机会。此外，听各种学术内容可以提高学术听力。讲座和报告的录音带、CD、DVD以及播客音频也非常有用，考生可以在图书馆、书店或互联网上找到。带有听力原文的听力材料效果更佳。推荐几个网站，都是很好的听力资源，分别是www.npr.org，www.bbc.co.uk/radio，www.bbc.co.uk/learningenglish，以及http://learningenglish.voanews.com/。

Listening for Basic Comprehension

- 扩充词汇量。
- 对于不熟悉的单词，试着通过上下文语境猜测其意思。
- 听的时候专注于材料的内容和大意，不要受说话人讲话风格和方式的干扰。
- 预测说话人将要说的话，从而将注意力集中在听力材料上。
- 主动向自己提问（例如，教授所要表达的主要观点是什么？）
- 注意听取提示话题转换或临时岔开话题的单词或短语。

- 听讲座或对话中的一部分，写出要点提纲。不要试图写下你听到的每个单词，只需要记录关键点和重要细节。写完之后，再听一遍，检查已经记下的内容，并补充之前未注意的要点。以此逐渐增加所听部分的长度，并进行总结。
- 听一遍对话或讲座。写一个句子，总结大意。再听一遍，检查你之前写下的句子，并补充关键细节。

Notes

阅读部分考查考生识别意译的能力。意译的能力在综合写作和听力的考查中也很重要。

听力部分不考查考生总结归纳的技能，但是训练好这种技能有助于完成口语和写作的综合任务。

Listening for Pragmatic Understanding

- 思考一下每位说话人在陈述或提问时想要达到的目的。说话人是在道歉、抱怨还是在提建议？例如，当说话人说"房间里很冷"的时候，他/她是否不只是在评价房间的温度？是否在暗示某人做些事情来改变房间温度？当说话人陈述"我肯定你对那个有想法"时，他/她是否在间接暗示他人分享各自的想法？
- 注意说话人的确定程度：说话人对信息究竟有多确定？说话人的语气是否能为他/她的确定性提供一些暗示？
- 注意听说话人的话题转换。
- 看电视或喜剧电影。注意说话人在表达意思时所使用的语调和重音。

Listening to Connect and Synthesize Ideas

- 思考一下讲座稿的谋篇布局。注意听清听力材料中的标志词，它们会标明文中的引言、主要步骤或观点、例子、结论。
- 识别材料中各观点之间的关系，可能包括因果、对比、过程中的步骤。
- 注意听那些能表示观点之间关系的词汇。
- 在听录音材料时，可以经常将录音暂停，预测下文将出现的信息和观点。
- 在听录音时或是听完录音后，就所听到的内容写一个提纲。

Speaking Tips

练习口语的最佳方式是和以英语为母语的人交流。如果你并不居住在讲英语的国家，那么可能很难找到以英语为母语的人。某些国家有说英语的辅导老师或者助教，他们可以帮助学生锻炼谈话能力和总体交流能力。尽可能地找他们说话，这一点至关重要。你也可以找到线上辅导老师或对话搭档与你练习口语。另一种练习口语的方式是参加英语俱乐部，与俱乐部成员们用英语讨论电影、音乐和旅行。如果你所在的地区没有英语俱乐部，开办一家，并邀请外教加入。

Independent Speaking Task

- 列举一些你熟悉的话题，练习讲述这些话题。
- 描述一个个人选择或偏好，并用详细的理由阐述。
- 表达一个想法，清晰地陈述观点，并用清楚、详细的理由进行论证。
- 提出一个建议，并解释为什么那是最好的方法。
- 练习就话题进行1分钟的计时回答。

Integrated Speaking Tasks

- 找一本每章之后都附有问题的课本，练习口头回答这些问题。

- 阅读一篇短文章（大约100~200词），写一个只包含文章主要观点的提纲，然后利用该提纲口头总结文章的内容。

- 针对文章涉及的同一话题，找一些听力和阅读材料，这些材料可以包含相似或者不同的观点（互联网和图书馆是搜集资料的好地方）。针对听力和阅读材料记笔记或者写提纲：
  - 对书面和口语材料中的信息进行口头总结，确保利用不同的单词和语法结构进行改述。
  - 对阅读和听力材料中的信息进行口头综述，并解释它们是如何相互联系的。
  - 针对阅读和听力材料中阐述的思想和信息表达自己的观点，并解释它们是如何相互联系的。

All Speaking Tasks

- 尝试每天运用一个新词或新短语。

- 做一个1分钟录音，内容是以英语为母语的人的讲话。（可以请你认识的朋友帮忙录制，也可以从互联网、电视、广播等直接获取录音。）重复播放录音两遍，熟悉说话人的节奏和语音语调。然后播放第三遍，尝试大声地跟读。也许你不能正确地说出所有单词，但这种练习可以帮助你熟悉英语母语者的重音和语调模式。

- 使用以上方法（Speaking Tips）备考托福时，在回答之前先用15秒的时间思考你将要说的话。写下几个关键词和观点，但不要试图写下你要说的全部内容。（评分人能够发觉照读的回答并会对此判低分。）

- 在听英语母语者说话时，注意那些起意义连接作用的单词和表达。然后将这些单词和表达运用到你的说话中，用来引入新的信息、连接各个观点、说出重要的话或想法。这有助于他人听懂你所说的内容。（例如，"on the one hand"，"what that means is"，"one reason is"，"another difference might be".）

- 记录自己的进步，请英语老师或辅导人员通过口语评分标准对你的回答进行评分。（口语评分标准见第180~183页。）

Check Your English Speaking Skills

TOEFL® Practice Online gives you the experience of taking the real *TOEFL iBT*® test. It includes *real* past test questions, scores, and performance feedback within 24 hours, and offers full tests, half tests, or Speaking-only test options.
www.ets.org/toefl/shoptestprep

Writing Tips

Integrated Writing Tasks

- 找一本每章后面附带题目的教材，练习书面回答这些题目。

- 阅读一篇大约300~400词的文章，列出包含文章主要观点和重要细节的提纲，利用提纲对全文信息和观点进行总结。总结应该简练，仅包含主要观点和重要细节。确保利用不同的词汇和语法结构进行释义。

- 在互联网或者图书馆中寻找针对同一话题的听力和阅读材料。这些材料可以包含相似或者不同的观点。对书面和口语表达部分记笔记，并做到以下几点：

- ○ 对书面和口语表达部分的信息和观点进行总结。

- ○ 对信息进行综合，论述阅读和听力材料之间的联系。解释这些观点如何相似、某个观点如何扩展成另一个观点，或者观点之间如何不同或矛盾。

Paraphrasing

改述是指用自己的话重述原文的某些信息。在托福考试中，如果考生只是复制阅读文章的词句，作文将被判零分。利用下述技巧，大量练习改述单词、短语、句子和整个段落：

- 学会轻松地找到同义词。从一篇阅读文章中挑选10~15个单词，在不查词典或同义词、反义词词典的情况下，快速想出它们的同义词。

- 只利用笔记对阅读文章进行释义。如果没有记笔记，在不看原文的情况下写出改述。然后将你的改述与原文进行对照，检查其准确性，并确保使用了不同的词汇和语法结构。

Independent Writing Tasks

- 列举一些熟悉的话题，然后练习针对这些话题写作。
- 就每一个话题陈述自己的观点或倾向，然后用证据支持。
- 针对每一个话题至少练习写一篇文章。确保利用30分钟时间构建、写作并检查每篇文章。
- 在写作之前，思考并列出所有与话题或题目有关的观点，这一步也被称作"构思"。
- 确定一个中心思想，用几个主要观点支持该思想，并计划如何传达这些内容（例如，通过提纲组织这些观点）。
- 写出一个中心论点，用论点展开对文中观点的论述。
- 利用恰当的说明和细节展开论述。但是请记住，不能使用完全是背诵下来的理由或例子，这不会被作为考生自己的写作来考评。

All Writing Tasks

- 扩充词汇量和习惯用语的知识，恰当地使用这些知识。
- 熟识语法结构，以便在写作时能自然地运用。

- 学习拼写、标点符号和文章结构的知识（例如，如何分段）。
- 系统有序地表达信息，展示思想的一致性和连贯性。
- 利用信号词和词组，例如on the one hand或者in conclusion，为文章构建清晰的结构。
- 在练习过程中，问自己以下问题：
  - 我完成题目了吗？
  - 我的写作思路清晰吗？
  - 我犯语法错误了吗？
  - 我用词准确吗？
  - 我清楚、连贯地组织想法了吗？
  - 我有效地利用时间了吗？
- 记录自己的进步，请英语老师或辅导人员通过写作评分标准对你的文章进行评分。（写作评分标准见第193~194页以及第203~204页。）

Check Your English Writing Skills

Are you ready for test day? *TOEFL*® Practice Online gives you the experience of taking the real *TOEFL iBT*® test. It includes real past test questions, scores, and performance feedback within 24 hours, and offers full tests, half tests, or Speaking-only test options. **www.ets.org/toefl/shoptestprep**

Note

Teachers: It is a good idea for English programs to use the *TOEFL*® Speaking and Writing rubrics (pages 180–183, 193–194, and 203–204) to measure students' abilities and evaluate their progress. This helps test takers build their skills for the TOEFL test.

Test Preparation Tips from ETS

当考生提高了语言技能并做了大量练习后，就为参加托福考试作好了准备。下面是ETS推荐的一些好的备考策略：

- 认真遵守每部分的考试说明，以免浪费时间。

- 只有在非常必要的情况下才点击Help键进行考试说明查询，因为启用Help键时不会停止计时。

- 不要惊慌，把注意力集中在正在做的试题上，不要去想如何回答其他题目。考生可通过不断练习培养这种习惯。

- 避免在一个问题上花过多时间。如果看到问题，经过一段时间的思考仍无法回答，尽可能将可供选择的多个选项一一排除，然后选择最合适的选项。在阅读部分，考生可以通过点击Review键重新查看已做过的题目。但最好在做完所有的题目之后再点击此键，以便集中注意力，节约时间。

- 合理安排时间。合理安排时间能使考生有足够的时间回答每个问题。考生应当注意每个部分和每道题的时间限制，给每个问题分配足够的时间，这样就不会在考试临近结束时慌张了。如果考生愿意，可以将时钟隐藏起来。然而，定时查看时钟，了解自己的进度不失为一个好办法。在听力和阅读部分结束前5分钟，时钟会自动提醒考生，在独立写作和综合写作部分也是如此。

Questions Frequently Asked by Test Takers

Test Benefits

Why should I take the TOEFL® test?

No matter where in the world you want to study, the *TOEFL*® test can help you get there. You will be eligible for admission to virtually any institution in the world, including the top colleges and universities in the United States, Canada, the United Kingdom, Australia, and New Zealand. See the Destination Search at **www.ets.org/toefl**.

The TOEFL test gives you more flexibility on when, where, and how often you take the test, and more practice tools and feedback than any other English language test in the world.

Test takers who are well prepared for the TOEFL test can feel confident that they are also well prepared for academic success.

What makes the TOEFL® test better than other English language tests?

The *TOEFL*® test assesses a test taker's ability to integrate English skills and to communicate about what he or she reads and hears. These are the skills you will actually use in an academic classroom.

The test also measures speaking more fairly than other tests. Each Speaking response is evaluated by four different raters, which is more objective and reliable than other tests that use only one interviewer from a local test site.

Who else benefits from the test?

Admissions officials and faculty at colleges and universities, as well as administrators of certification and licensing agencies, receive better information on an applicant's English communication skills.

Registration

How and when do I register for the test?

Online registration is the easiest method. You can also register by mail or by phone. See **www.ets.org/toefl** for details. Registration is available three to four months before the test date. Register early, as seats can fill up quickly.

Where and when can I take the TOEFL® test?

The test is given on fixed dates, more than 50 times a year, via the Internet at secure test centers. The ETS testing network, with test centers in more than 180 countries, is the largest in the world. Go to **www.ets.org/toefl** for a list of locations and dates.

How much does the TOEFL® test cost?

The price of the test varies by country. Please check the *TOEFL*® program website at **www.ets.org/toefl** for the test fees in your country.

Test Preparation

Are sample questions available?

Yes. The *TOEFL iBT*® Free Practice Test, on the *TOEFL*® website at **https://www.ets.org/toefl/test-takers/ibt/prepare**, provides free unlimited access to one full-length *TOEFL iBT*® test, including answer keys for the Reading and Listening questions as well as sample responses with rater commentary for the Speaking and Writing questions. Practice for each section of the test with free sets of *TOEFL iBT*® questions from previous tests are also available on the website.

Can I take a practice test and get a score?

Yes. Practice tests can be purchased at *TOEFL*® Practice Online, at **www.ets.org/toefl/shoptestprep**. This site features practice tests that include exclusive *TOEFL iBT*® practice questions covering all four skills: Reading, Listening, Speaking, and Writing, with scoring provided by certified ETS raters.

Scores and Score Reports

How do I get my scores?

Scores are posted online approximately six days after the test date and then mailed to the institutions you selected. All *TOEFL iBT*® score reports, regardless of the test administration date, automatically include *MyBest*™ Scores along with the traditional scores from your selected test date. *MyBest*™ Scores (also known as superscores) reflect the combination of your highest section scores from all valid test dates in the last two years, and the sum of those section scores.

Included with your registration fees are:

- one online score report for you and one printed score report if requested
- up to four official score reports that ETS will send directly to the institutions or agencies that you select before you take the test

Can I order additional score reports?

Yes. For a small fee, you can send score reports to as many institutions as you choose. See **www.ets.org/toefl** for details.

How long are scores valid?

ETS will report scores for two years after the test date.

Will institutions accept scores from previous tests?

Check with each institution or agency directly.

Test Delivery

What skills are tested on the TOEFL iBT® Test?

The test is given in English, has four sections on reading, listening, speaking, and writing, and takes about three hours.

Section	Time Limit	Number of Questions
Reading	54–72 minutes	27–40
Listening	41–57 minutes	28–39
Break	10 minutes	
Speaking	17 minutes	4 tasks
Writing	50 minutes	2 tasks

Can I take only one section of the test?

No. The entire test must be taken to receive a score.

Which computer keyboard is used?

The *TOEFL iBT*® test uses a standard English-language computer keyboard (a QWERTY keyboard). This type of keyboard takes its name from the first six letters in the top row of the keyboard, below the numbers. If you haven't used this kind of keyboard before, practice on one before test day to become familiar with it. In some countries, the common keyboard used is configured to QWERTY, and a template is provided to each test taker to help with locating the few keys that are in a different location.

Reading Section

Read this chapter to learn

- The 10 types of *TOEFL®* test Reading questions
- How to recognize each Reading question type
- Tips for answering each Reading question type
- Strategies for preparing for the Reading section

托福考试阅读部分由3~4篇文章构成，每篇文章的字数约为700词，每篇文章后有10道题。考试时间为54~72分钟。在阅读部分，你可以（在阅读文章之前）先浏览一遍问题，只要在限定时间内完成题目即可。

Reading Passages

托福考试阅读部分的文章摘自大学程度的教科书或已发表的文章，一般都是对某一学科或主题的介绍性内容。由于托福考试的主要目的是评估考生对学术性文章的理解程度，因此托福考试阅读部分对摘录原文进行了尽可能少的改写。

托福考试阅读文章涉及多种不同的学科。如果考生不了解一篇文章所涉及的主题也没有关系，因为回答问题所需要的所有信息都会在文章中出现。按照出题人的命题意图，所有的托福阅读文章可以分为三种基本类型：（1）解释说明型文章；（2）立论型文章；（3）历史题材型文章。

通常一篇文章会对关于其主题的信息从不同的角度或观点进行阐述。这一点是考生应在阅读过程中特别注意的，因为通常题目中至少会有一道题考查考生是否理解全文的结构。常见的文章结构大致有以下几种：

- 分类
- 比较/对比
- 原因/结果
- 问题/解决方法

托福阅读文章的字数为700词左右，但每篇文章的长度可能会有所不同。有些文章可能会稍多于700词，而有些文章可能会稍少于700词。

Reading Questions

阅读部分考查考生寻找基本信息的能力、进行推理的能力以及理解文章内容的能力。托福阅读题目共有10种类型，具体分类如下：

TOEFL® Reading Question Types

Basic Information and Inferencing questions

1. Factual Information questions (2 to 5 questions per set)
2. Negative Factual Information questions (0 to 2 questions per set)
3. Inference questions (1 to 2 questions per set)
4. Rhetorical Purpose questions (1 to 2 questions per set)
5. Vocabulary questions (1 to 2 questions per set)
6. Reference questions (0 to 2 questions per set)
7. Sentence Simplification question (0 or 1 question per set)
8. Insert Text question (1 question per set)

Reading to Learn questions (1 per set)

9. Prose Summary
10. Fill in a Table

下面的部分将对每一种类型的题目进行逐一讲解。考生将从中学会如何识别考题类型。同时，本书对每种类型的题目都有详细举例和讲解。考生将从中学会解答每种阅读题目的方法。

Basic Information and Inferencing Questions

Type 1: Factual Information Questions

这种题型要求考生识别出文章明确阐述的事实信息。这些事实信息问题主要集中于事实、细节、定义或者作者阐述的其他信息。这种题型会要求考生辨识仅在文章某一部分提到的具体信息，一般不会问及整篇文章的主旨。通常情况下，其相关信息在文章中可能只是一句或两句话。

How to Recognize Factual Information Questions

事实信息类问题经常采取以下提问方式：

- According to the paragraph, which of the following is true of X?
- The author's description of X mentions which of the following?
- According to the paragraph, X occurred because . . .
- According to the paragraph, X did Y because . . .
- According to the paragraph, why did X do Y?
- The author's description of X mentions which of the following?

Example

PASSAGE EXCERPT: "…Sculptures must, for example, be stable, which requires an understanding of the properties of mass, weight distribution, and stress. Paintings must have rigid stretchers so that the canvas will be taut, and the paint must not deteriorate, crack, or discolor. These are problems that must be overcome by the artist because they tend to intrude upon his or her conception of the work. For example, in the early Italian Renaissance, bronze statues of horses with a raised foreleg usually had a cannonball under that hoof. This was done because the cannonball was needed to support the weight of the leg. In other words, the demands of the laws of physics, not the sculptor's aesthetic intentions, placed the ball there. That this device was a necessary structural compromise is clear from the fact that the cannonball quickly disappeared when sculptors learned how to strengthen the internal structure of a statue with iron braces (iron being much stronger than bronze) … "

According to paragraph 2, sculptors in the Italian Renaissance stopped using cannonballs in bronze statues of horses because

Ⓐ they began using a material that made the statues weigh less
Ⓑ they found a way to strengthen the statues internally
Ⓒ the aesthetic tastes of the public had changed over time
Ⓓ the cannonballs added too much weight to the statues

Explanation

The question tells you to look for the answer in the excerpted paragraph, which in this case is paragraph 2. You do not need to skim the entire passage to find the relevant information.

Choice A says that sculptors stopped putting cannonballs under the raised legs of horses in statues because they learned how to make the statue weigh less and not require support for the leg. The passage does not mention making the statues weigh less; it says that sculptors learned a better way to support the weight. Choice C says that the change occurred only because people's taste changed, meaning that the cannonballs were never structurally necessary. That directly contradicts the passage. Choice D says that cannonballs added weight to the statues. This contradicts the passage, which says that the cannonball was needed to support the weight of the leg of the statue. Choice B correctly identifies the reason the passage gives for the change: sculptors developed a way to strengthen the statue from the inside, making the cannonballs physically unnecessary.

Type 2: Negative Factual Information Questions

这类问题要求考生根据文章明确陈述的信息，确定哪些信息是真实的，哪些信息是不真实的或者是原文所没有提及的。回答此类问题时，首先需要找到相关信息在原文中出现的位置，然后确定四个选项中的哪三个选项是真实的，这样剩下的那个选项自然就是不真实的了。注意，对于此类问题，正确答案是那个不真实的选项。

How to Recognize Negative Factual Information Questions

考生可以很容易辨认出否定事实信息类问题，因为在该类题目中会出现大写的"NOT"或"EXCEPT"。例如：

- According to the passage, which of the following is NOT true of X?
- The author's description of X mentions all of the following EXCEPT . . .

Tips for Negative Factual Information Questions

- 通常情况下，否定事实信息类问题比事实信息类问题要求考生回顾更多的原文信息。三个在原文中曾被提及的选项可能分布在一个段落或几个段落当中。

- 否定事实信息类问题的正确选项要么直接与原文中的一处或多处信息相矛盾，要么在原文中没有被提及。

- 解答完否定事实信息类问题后，考生要检查自己的答案，以确保自己精确理解了题目要求。

Example

PASSAGE EXCERPT: "The United States in the 1800s was full of practical, hardworking people who did not consider the arts—from theater to painting—useful occupations. In addition, the public's attitude that European art was better than American art both discouraged and infuriated American artists. In the early 1900s there was a strong feeling among artists that the United States was long overdue in developing art that did not reproduce European traditions. Everybody agreed that the heart and soul of the new country should be reflected in its art. But opinions differed about what this art would be like and how it would develop."

According to paragraph 1, all of the following were true of American art in the late 1800s and early 1900s EXCEPT:

(A) Most Americans thought art was unimportant.
(B) American art generally copied European styles and traditions.
(C) Most Americans considered American art inferior to European art.
(D) American art was very popular with European audiences.

Explanation

Sometimes in Negative Factual Information questions, it is necessary to check the entire passage in order to make sure that your choice is not mentioned. However, in this example, the question is limited to one paragraph, so your answer should be based just on the information in that paragraph. Choice A is a restatement of the first sentence in the paragraph: since most Americans did not think that the arts were useful occupations, they considered them unimportant. Choice B makes the same point as the third sentence: ". . . the United States was long overdue in developing art that did not reproduce European traditions," which means that up to this point in history, American art did reproduce European traditions. Choice C is a restatement of the second sentence in the paragraph: American artists were frustrated because of "the public's attitude that European art was better than American art. . . ." Choice D is not mentioned anywhere in the paragraph. Because you are asked to identify the choice that is NOT mentioned in the passage or that contradicts the passage, the correct answer is choice D.

Type 3: Inference Questions

这类问题主要考查考生对文章中一个观点或立场的理解程度，而这种观点或立场是作者在文章中强烈暗示但并没有明确阐明的。例如，如果文章陈述了一个事件的结果，那么推论类问题很可能问考生其原因是什么；如果文章出现了一个对比，那么推论类问题很可能问考生其对比的基础是什么。解答这类问题时，考生不仅需要理解作者所写出句子的字面意思，还必须搞清楚这些句子之间的逻辑暗示。

How to Recognize Inference Questions

推论类问题的题干中经常会出现infer、suggest或者imply这类单词。例如：

- Which of the following can be inferred about X?
- The author of the passage implies that X . . .
- Which of the following can be inferred from paragraph 1 about X?

Tips for Inference Questions

- 首先要确定所选择的答案与文章的主要观点不矛盾。
- 不要仅仅因为一个选项看上去是重要的或是正确的，就将其作为正确答案。正确答案一定是能从文章中推论出来的。
- 作出选择后，考生应能够明确指出相关信息在原文中出现的位置，从而印证自己的答案是正确的。

Example

PASSAGE EXCERPT: "… The nineteenth century brought with it a burst of new discoveries and inventions that revolutionized the candle industry and made lighting available to all. In the early-to-mid-nineteenth century, a process was developed to refine tallow (fat from animals) with alkali and sulfuric acid. The result was a product called stearin. Stearin is harder and burns longer than unrefined tallow. This breakthrough meant that it was possible to make tallow candles that would not produce the usual smoke and rancid odor. Stearins were also derived from palm oils, so vegetable waxes as well as animal fats could be used to make candles …"

Which of the following can be inferred from paragraph 1 about candles before the nineteenth century?

(A) They did not smoke when they were burned.
(B) They produced a pleasant odor as they burned.
(C) They were not available to all.
(D) They contained sulfuric acid.

Explanation

In the first sentence from the excerpt, the author says that "new discoveries and inventions" made "lighting available to all." Candles are only kind of lighting discussed in the passage. If the new discoveries were important because they made candles available to all, we can infer that before the discoveries, candles were not available to everyone. Therefore choice C is an inference about candles we can make from the passage. Choices A and B can be eliminated because they explicitly contradict the passage ("the usual smoke" and "rancid odor"). Choice D can be eliminated because sulfuric acid was first used to make stearin in the nineteenth century, not before the nineteenth century.

Type 4: Rhetorical Purpose Questions

修辞是有效地进行口头或书面表达的一门艺术。在事实信息类问题中，考生被考查的是识别作者在文章中陈述了什么信息。而在修辞目的类问题中，考生将被考查的是理解作者为什么在文章中某个特别位置或者以某种特殊的方式陈述一个特别的信息。修辞目的类问题考查考生是否理解一句话或一个段落在与文章的其他部分相联系时所起的修辞性作用。

有时候这类问题要求考生确定一个段落与另一个段落之间的联系。例如，文章的第二段可能给出例子来支持第一段中的一个论断，而答案的选项可能是针对整篇文章以总结性的语言出现的（例如，a theory is explained and then illustrated），也可能是针对文章中的一个具体细节出现的（例如，The author explains the categories of adaptation to deserts by mammals and then gives an example.）。

修辞目的类问题也可能考查作者提到某一条特别信息的原因（例如：Why does the author mention "the ability to grasp a pencil"？正确答案：It is an example of a motor skill developed by children at 10 to 11 months of age.），或者是考查作者引用某一个人的例子的原因。

How to Recognize Rhetorical Purpose Questions

修辞目的类问题经常以下列方式进行提问：

- The author discusses X in paragraph 2 in order to . . .
- Why does the author mention X?
- Why does the author compare X to Y?

Tips for Rhetorical Purpose Questions

- 首先要知道一些经常用来描述各种修辞目的的单词或词组的具体含义："definition"，"example"，"to illustrate"，"to explain"，"to contrast"，"to refute"，"to note"，"to criticize"，"function of"。
- 修辞目的类问题通常不会考查整篇阅读文章的结构，而是常常关注句子或段落之间的逻辑联系。

Example

PASSAGE EXCERPT: "... Sensitivity to physical laws is thus an important consideration for the maker of applied-art objects. It is often taken for granted that this is also true for the maker of fine-art objects. This assumption misses a significant difference between the two disciplines. Fine-art objects are not constrained by the laws of physics in the same way that applied-art objects are. Because their primary purpose is not functional, they are only limited in terms of the materials used to make them. Sculptures must, for example, be stable, which requires an understanding of the properties of mass, weight distribution, and stress. Paintings must have rigid stretchers so that the canvas will be taut, and the paint must not deteriorate, crack, or discolor. These are problems that must be overcome by the artist because they tend to intrude upon his or her conception of the work. For example, in the early Italian Renaissance, bronze statues of horses with a raised foreleg usually had a cannonball under that hoof. This was done because the cannonball was needed to support the weight of the leg ... "

Why does the author discuss the "bronze statues of horses" created by artists in the early Italian Renaissance?

Ⓐ To provide an example of a problem related to the laws of physics that a fine artist must overcome

Ⓑ To argue that fine artists are unconcerned with the laws of physics

Ⓒ To contrast the relative sophistication of modern artists in solving problems related to the laws of physics

Ⓓ To note an exceptional piece of art constructed without the aid of technology

Explanation

You should note that the sentence that first mentions "bronze statues of horses" begins "For example . . ." The author is giving an example of something that was introduced earlier in the paragraph. The paragraph overall contrasts how the constraints of physical laws affect the fine arts differently from applied arts or crafts. The fine artist is not concerned with making an object that is useful, so he or she is less constrained than the applied artist. However, because even a fine-arts object is made of some material, the artist must take into account the physical properties of the material. In the passage, the author uses the example of the bronze statues of horses to discuss how artists had to include some support for the raised foreleg of the horse because of the physical properties of the bronze. So the correct answer is choice A.

Type 5: Vocabulary Questions

　　词汇类问题要求考生确定文章中个别单词或短语的具体意思（一个单词可能会有多个意思，但是在阅读文章中只有一个意思与原文相符）。单词的意思必须符合原文的意思。在这里需要指出的是：并没有一个必然会考到的"词汇表"。通常情况下，被考到的单词或短语对于理解文章的一个大的或重要的部分起到至关重要的作用。在托福考试中，不常见的、专业的或是具有特殊意义的词汇是有具体解释的。如果点击文章中有超链接的单词，这些单词的解释就会出现在一个方框中。在本书中，单词的释义均列在文章结尾处。当然，词汇类问题中考查到的词汇是没有任何解释的。

How to Recognize Vocabulary Questions

词汇类问题是很容易辨认的。在文章中被考到的单词或短语会被用阴影标示出来。问题的提问形式如下：

- The word "X" in the passage is closest in meaning to . . .
- The phrase "X" in the passage is closest in meaning to . . .
- In stating X, the author means that . . .

> **Tips for Vocabulary Questions**
>
> - 注意此类问题并不仅仅是考查一个单词的基本意思，而是考查该词在文章上下文中的意思。不要仅仅因为某个选项符合该单词的某一个正确意思就将其作为正确答案。要理解作者在文章上下文中使用了哪一个词义。
> - 将所选择的单词或短语放入原文进行检验，以确认这个句子在全文中仍是有意义的。

Examples

PASSAGE EXCERPT: "In the animal world the task of moving about is fulfilled in many ways. For some animals locomotion is accomplished by changes in body shape . . ."

The word "locomotion" in the passage is closest in meaning to

(A) evolution
(B) movement
(C) survival
(D) escape

Explanation

Locomotion means "the ability to move from place to place." In this example, it is a way of restating the phrase "the task of moving" in the preceding sentence. So the correct answer is choice B.

PASSAGE EXCERPT: "Some poisonous snake bites need to be treated immediately or the victim will suffer paralysis . . ."

In stating that the victim will "suffer paralysis" the author means that the victim will

(A) lose the ability to move
(B) become unconscious
(C) undergo shock
(D) feel great pain

Explanation

In this example, both the words tested from the passage and the possible answers are phrases. *Paralysis* means "the inability to move," so if the poison from a snake bite causes someone to "suffer paralysis," that person will "lose the ability to move." The correct answer is choice A.

Type 6: Reference Questions

指代类问题考查考生辨认文章中单词间指代关系的能力。通常这种关系是代词与其先行词之间的关系，有时也考查其他语法的指代关系（如which或this）。

How to Recognize Reference Questions

指代类问题与词汇类问题很相似。在文章中会有一个单词或短语用阴影标示出来。被标示的词汇经常是一个代词。然后考生会被问到：

- The word "X" in the passage refers to . . .

四个选项都是来自于文章中的单词或短语，但只有一个选项是被阴影标示出的单词或短语所指代的内容。

> **Tips for Reference Questions**
> - 如果考查的是一个代词的指代问题，考生要确保所选答案与被标示的代词具有数（单数或复数）和人称（第一人称、第二人称、第三人称）的一致性。
> - 将所选答案替代句中被标示的单词或短语，检验它是否违反语法规则，是否能使句子表达通顺。

Examples

PASSAGE EXCERPT: "... These laws are universal in their application, regardless of cultural beliefs, geography, or climate. If pots have no bottoms or have large openings in their sides, they could hardly be considered containers in any traditional sense. Since the laws of physics, not some arbitrary decision, have determined the general form of applied-art objects, they follow basic patterns, so much so that functional forms can vary only within certain limits ..."

The word "they" in the passage refers to

- (A) applied-art objects
- (B) the laws of physics
- (C) containers
- (D) the sides of pots

Explanation

This is an example of a simple pronoun-referent question. The highlighted word *they* refers to the phrase "applied-art objects," which immediately precedes it, so choice A is the correct answer.

Often, the grammatical referent for a pronoun will be separated from the pronoun. It may be located in a preceding clause or even an earlier sentence.

PASSAGE EXCERPT: "... The first weekly newspaper in the colonies was the *Boston Gazette*, established in 1719, the same year that marked the appearance of Philadelphia's first newspaper, the *American Mercury*, where the young Benjamin Franklin worked. By 1760 Boston had 4 newspapers and 5 other printing establishments; Philadelphia, 2 newspapers and 3 other presses; and New York, 3 newspapers. The distribution, if not the sale, of newspapers was assisted by the establishment of a postal service in 1710, which had a network of some 65 offices by 1770, serving all 13 colonies ..."

The word "which" in the passage refers to

(A) distribution

(B) sale

(C) newspaper

(D) postal service

Explanation

In this example, the highlighted word is a relative pronoun, the grammatical subject of the relative clause "which had a network of some 65 offices . . ." The relative clause is describing the postal service, so choice D is the correct answer.

PASSAGE EXCERPT: ". . . Roots anchor the plant in one of two ways or sometimes by a combination of the two. The first is by occupying a large volume of shallow soil around the plant's base with a *fibrous root system,* one consisting of many thin, profusely branched roots. Since these kinds of roots grow relatively close to the soil surface, they effectively control soil erosion. Grass roots are especially well suited to this purpose. Fibrous roots capture water as it begins to percolate into the ground and so must draw their mineral supplies from the surface soil before the nutrients are leached to lower levels . . ."

The phrase "this purpose" in the passage refers to

(A) combining two root systems

(B) feeding the plant

(C) preventing soil erosion

(D) leaching nutrients

Explanation

In the example, the highlighted words are a phrase containing a demonstrative adjective (*this*) and a noun (*purpose*). Because a fibrous root system can keep soil in place, it can be used to stop erosion, and grass roots are a fibrous root system. The sentence could be reworded as "Grass roots are especially well suited to preventing soil erosion," so choice C is the correct answer.

Type 7: Sentence Simplification Questions

这类问题要求考生选出一个句子，其句意要与原文中某个句子的主要意思相同。并不是每一篇文章都设有这种题目，一篇文章一般最多只会有一道此类题目。

How to Recognize Sentence Simplification Questions

所有简化句子类问题都是一样的。在文中会有一个句子用阴影标示出来，然后在题目中考生将会被问到：

- Which of the following best expresses the essential information in the highlighted sentence? Incorrect answer choices change the meaning in important ways or leave out essential information.

Example

PASSAGE EXCERPT: "... Although we now tend to refer to the various crafts according to the materials used to construct them—clay, glass, wood, fiber, and metal—it was once common to think of crafts in terms of function, which led to their being known as the "applied arts." Approaching crafts from the point of view of function, we can divide them into simple categories: containers, shelters, and supports. There is no way around the fact that containers, shelters, and supports must be functional. The applied arts are thus bound by the laws of physics, which pertain to both the materials used in their making and the substances and things to be contained, supported, and sheltered. These laws are universal in their application, regardless of cultural beliefs, geography, or climate. If a pot has no bottom or has large openings in its sides, it could hardly be considered a container in any traditional sense. Since the laws of physics, not some arbitrary decision, have determined the general form of applied-art objects, they follow basic patterns, so much so that functional forms can vary only within certain limits. Buildings without roofs, for example, are unusual because they depart from the norm. However, not all functional objects are exactly alike; that is why we recognize a Shang Dynasty vase as being different from an Inca vase. What varies is not the basic form but the incidental details that do not obstruct the object's primary function ..."

Which of the following best expresses the essential information in the highlighted sentence? Incorrect answer choices change the meaning in important ways or leave out essential information.

Ⓐ Functional applied-art objects cannot vary much from the basic patterns determined by the laws of physics.

Ⓑ The function of applied-art objects is determined by basic patterns in the laws of physics.

Ⓒ Since functional applied-art objects vary only within certain limits, arbitrary decisions cannot have determined their general form.

Ⓓ The general form of applied-art objects is limited by some arbitrary decision that is not determined by the laws of physics.

Explanation

It is important to note that the question says that *incorrect* answers change the original meaning of the sentence or leave out essential information. In this example, choice D changes the meaning of the sentence to its opposite; it says that the form of functional objects is arbitrary, when the highlighted sentence says that the forms of functional objects are *never* arbitrary. Choice B also changes the meaning. It says that the functions of applied-art objects are determined by physical laws. The highlighted sentence says that the *form of the object* is determined by physical laws but the function is determined by people. Choice C leaves out an important idea from the highlighted sentence. Like the highlighted sentence, it says that the form of functional objects is not arbitrary, but it does not say that it is physical laws that determine basic form. Only choice A makes the same point as the highlighted sentence and includes all the essential meaning.

Type 8: Insert Text Questions

在这一类问题中，题目给出一个新的句子，然后考查此句子在文章中最合适的位置。考生不仅需要了解这篇文章的逻辑，还要了解句与句之间的语法联系（比如代词的指代）。每篇阅读对应的一套题目中有且仅有一道此类题目。

How to Recognize Insert Text Questions

这类问题在托福考试中较容易识别。在文章中，考生将看到四个黑色的方块。这些方块分布在句首或句末。四个方框有时都出现在一个段落里，有时分布在一段的末尾和下一段的开头。然后考生将会被问到：

Look at the four squares [■] that indicate where the following sentence could be added to the passage.

[You will see a sentence in bold.]

Where would the sentence best fit? Click on a square [■] to add the sentence to the passage.

考生要做的是点击其中的一个方块并将这个句子插入文章。下面展示的是托福实考中这类问题的界面形式。

Look at the four squares [■] that indicate where the following sentence could be added to the passage.

All three of them have strengths and weaknesses, but none adequately answers all the questions the paintings present.

Where would the sentence best fit? Click on a square [■] to add the sentence to the passage.

Scholars offer three related but different opinions about this puzzle. ■ One opinion is that the paintings were a record of the seasonal migrations made by herds. ■ Because some paintings were made directly over others, obliterating them, it is probable that a painting's value ended with the migration it pictured. ■ Unfortunately, this explanation fails to explain the hidden locations, unless the migrations were celebrated with secret ceremonies. ■

Tips for Insert Text Questions

- 托福考试中，试着将这个句子放在这些方块所处的每个位置。考生可以随意放置和替换这些句子无数次。

- 注意要插入原文的句子的结构和逻辑关系。尤其注意逻辑连接词——这些词可以提供重要信息以帮助考生找出这个句子的最佳位置。

- 常用的连接词：

On the other hand	Further, or Furthermore	Similarly
For example	Therefore	In contrast
On the contrary	In other words	Finally
As a result		

- 确保被插入原文的句子与其前后句在逻辑上的衔接，以及代词与其所指代的名词的一致性。

这类问题在纸版考试中的形式是各不相同的。请看下面的例子。这是本书中练习和模拟题的形式。虽然形式稍有不同，但考生需要完成的任务是一样的：指出句子最适合放在段落中的位置。

Example

PASSAGE EXCERPT: "Scholars offer three related but different opinions about this puzzle. **(A)** One opinion is that the paintings were a record of the seasonal migrations made by herds. **(B)** Because some paintings were made directly over others, obliterating them, it is probable that a painting's value ended with the migration it pictured. **(C)** Unfortunately, this explanation fails to explain the hidden locations, unless the migrations were celebrated with secret ceremonies. **(D)**"

Directions: Look at the part of the passage that is displayed above. The letters **(A)**, **(B)**, **(C)**, and **(D)** indicate where the following sentence could be added.

All three of them have strengths and weaknesses, but none adequately answers all of the questions the paintings present.

Where would the sentence best fit?

Ⓐ Choice A
Ⓑ Choice B
Ⓒ Choice C
Ⓓ Choice D

Explanation

In this example, choice A is the correct answer. The new sentence makes sense only if it occurs in the first position, after the first sentence. In that place, "All three of them" refers back to "three related but different opinions." The information in the sentence is a commentary on all three of the "opinions"; the opinions are related, but none is a complete explanation. Logically, this evaluation of all three opinions must come either as an introduction to the three opinions, or as a conclusion about all three. Only the introductory position is available, because the paragraph does not include all three opinions.

Reading to Learn Questions

理解文章内容和结构类题有两种题型：文章总结题（Prose Summary）和表格填写题（Fill in a Table）。这类问题对考生的要求远远超出基本信息题的要求。正如考生所看到的，基本信息题主要考查考生在句子层面上对文中具体信息的理解或定位能力。这类题考查的问题将会涉及以下方面：

- 确认文章的结构和写作目的
- 在头脑中将文中信息整理出一个框架
- 区分文中的主要观点和次要观点，重要信息和非重要信息
- 理解各种修辞写作手法的应用，例如原因—结果关系、对照—对比关系、论点和论据关系等

换句话说，这些问题要求考生展示出对文章的整体理解，而不仅仅是对其中具体细节的理解。

这类题要求考生不仅能够理解每个信息点，还能把文章主要观点和支持该观点的信息整合成一个框架或结构，像"文章总结"或"表格填写"这类题目。回答正确就表明考生已经把握了文章的主要观点、结构、采用这种结构的原因以及文章内部关系的本质等要点。了解文章的整体思路对理解原文的含义非常重要，因为这能够使考生记住文章中的重要信息并可以在其他新的情景下应用这些信息。如果考生头脑中有了文章的整体构架，那么就可以在大脑中重新组织文章中的主要观点和支持性信息。这样，考生就可以对全文有一个全面的理解。在托福考试中，每篇文章都会有一道这类问题，即"文章总结"类题或者是"表格填写"类题，但两者不会在一篇文章中同时出现。

Type 9: Prose Summary Questions

这类题型考查考生对文章主要观点及相对重要信息的理解和辨识能力。做题时，考生要在排除文中次要信息和未提及的信息后，选出文章的主要观点。正确答案会综合文章中的主要观点。同时，由于正确答案综合了文章的各个观点，所以不会与文中的任何一句话

完全相符。要选出正确答案，考生需要在头脑中形成文章的一个整体结构框架，并记清文章主要观点和其他重要信息。理解文中哪些是相对重要的信息，对于解答此类问题非常重要。

　　文章总结题会给出6个选项，要求考生从中选出3个最能概括文章内容的选项。在评分方面，文章总结题与基本信息题不同，后者每道题只得1分，而前者每道题2分。根据考生选对的选项数目，考生得分在0~2分之间。具体来讲就是：如果一道题没有选对答案或只选对1个选项，不得分；如果一道题选对2个选项，得1分；如果一道题选对了3个选项，得2分。考生每道题所选答案的顺序不影响得分。

Example

Because the Prose Summary question asks you to show an understanding of the different parts of the passage, it is necessary to read the entire passage. Parts of the following passage have already been used to illustrate other question types.

APPLIED ARTS AND FINE ARTS

Although we now tend to refer to the various crafts according to the materials used to construct them—clay, glass, wood, fiber, and metal—it was once common to think of crafts in terms of function, which led to their being known as the "applied arts." Approaching crafts from the point of view of function, we can divide them into simple categories: containers, shelters, and supports. There is no way around the fact that containers, shelters, and supports must be functional. The applied arts are thus bound by the laws of physics, which pertain to both the materials used in their making and the substances and things to be contained, supported, and sheltered. These laws are universal in their application, regardless of cultural beliefs, geography, or climate. If a pot has no bottom or has large openings in its sides, it could hardly be considered a container in any traditional sense. Since the laws of physics, not some arbitrary decision, have determined the general form of applied-art objects, they follow basic patterns, so much so that functional forms can vary only within certain limits. Buildings without roofs, for example, are unusual because they depart from the norm. However, not all functional objects are exactly alike; that is why we recognize a Shang Dynasty vase as being different from an Inca vase. What varies is not the basic form but the incidental details that do not obstruct the object's primary function.

　　Sensitivity to physical laws is thus an important consideration for the maker of applied-art objects. It is often taken for granted that this is also true for the maker of fine-art objects. This assumption misses a significant difference between the two disciplines. Fine-art objects are not constrained by the laws of physics in the same way that applied-art objects are. Because their primary purpose is not functional, they are only limited in terms of the materials used to make them. Sculptures must, for example, be stable, which requires an understanding of the properties of mass, weight distribution, and stress. Paintings must have rigid stretchers so that the canvas will be taut, and the paint must not deteriorate, crack, or discolor. These are problems that must be overcome by the artist because they tend to intrude upon his or her conception of the work. For example, in the early Italian Renaissance, bronze statues of horses with a raised foreleg usually had a cannonball under that hoof. This was done because the cannonball was needed to support the weight of the leg. In other words, the demands of the laws of physics, not the sculptor's aesthetic intentions, placed the ball there. That this device was a necessary structural compromise is clear from the fact that the cannonball quickly disappeared when sculptors learned how to strengthen the internal structure of a statue with iron braces (iron being much stronger than bronze).

Even though the fine arts in the twentieth century often treat materials in new ways, the basic difference in attitude of artists in relation to their materials in the fine arts and the applied arts remains relatively constant. It would therefore not be too great an exaggeration to say that practitioners of the fine arts work to overcome the limitations of their materials, whereas those engaged in the applied arts work in concert with their materials.

An introductory sentence for a brief summary of the passage is provided below. Complete the summary by selecting the THREE answer choices that express the most important ideas in the passage. Some sentences do not belong in the summary because they express ideas that are not presented in the passage or are minor ideas in the passage. **This question is worth 2 points.**

> **This passage discusses fundamental differences between applied-art objects and fine-art objects.**

-
-
-

Answer Choices

A Applied-art objects fulfill functions, such as containing or sheltering, and objects with the same function have similar characteristics because they are constrained by their purpose.

B It is easy to recognize that Shang Dynasty vases are different from Inca vases.

C Fine-art objects are not functional, so they are limited only by the properties of the materials used.

D Renaissance sculptors learned to use iron braces to strengthen the internal structures of bronze statues.

E In the twentieth century, fine artists and applied artists became more similar to one another in their attitudes toward their materials.

F In all periods, fine artists tend to challenge the physical limitations of their materials while applied artists tend to cooperate with the physical properties of their materials.

Explanation

Correct Choices

Choice A: Applied-art objects fulfill functions, such as containing or sheltering, and objects with the same function have similar characteristics because they are constrained by their purpose.

Explanation: As the introductory sentence states, the passage is mainly a contrast of applied-art objects and fine-art objects. The main point of contrast is functionality: applied-art objects are functional, whereas fine-art objects are not. The first part of the passage explains the consequences of functionality for the materials and "basic forms" of applied-art objects. The second part of the passage explains the consequences of not being functional to the materials and forms of fine-art objects. A good summary of the passage must include the definition of "applied-art objects" and the major consequence (objects with the same function will follow similar patterns), so choice A should be included.

Choice C: Fine-art objects are not functional, so they are limited only by the properties of the materials used.

Explanation: Because the passage contrasts applied-art objects and fine-art objects, a good summary should include the basic difference. Including choice C in the summary provides the basic contrast discussed in the passage: applied art objects are functional; fine-art objects are not. Fine-art objects are not as constrained as applied-art objects because they do not have to perform a function.

Choice F: In all periods, fine artists tend to challenge the physical limitations of their materials, while applied artists tend to cooperate with the physical properties of their materials.

Explanation: The last paragraph of the passage presents a further consequence of the basic contrast between applied-art objects and fine-art objects. This is the difference between the attitude of fine artists toward their materials and the attitude of applied artists toward their materials. A good summary will include this last contrast.

Incorrect Choices

Choice B: It is easy to recognize that Shang Dynasty vases are different from Inca vases.

Explanation: Although this statement is true, it is not the main point of the first paragraph or of the passage. In fact, it contrasts with the main point of the paragraph: objects that have the same function are all similar. The last sentence of the first paragraph says that the Shang Dynasty vase and the Inca vase are different in "incidental details," but the "basic form" is the same. Including choice B in the summary misrepresents the passage.

Choice D: Renaissance sculptors learned to use iron braces to strengthen the internal structures of bronze statues.

Explanation: Choice D summarizes the information in sentences 9, 10, and 11 of paragraph 2. Within the context of the passage, this information helps you understand the meaning of the limitations that materials can impose on fine artists. However, remember that the directions say to choose the statements that express *the most important ideas in the passage*. The example is less important than the general statements of difference. If choice D is included, then choice A or C or F would be left out, and the summary would be missing an essential point of contrast between fine arts and applied arts.

Choice E: In the twentieth century, fine artists and applied artists became more similar to one another in their attitudes toward their materials.

Explanation: This choice should be excluded because it is not supported by the passage. It is a misreading of paragraph 3, which says that the difference in attitude between fine artists and applied artists has not changed. Obviously, a choice that contradicts the information or argument in the passage should not be part of your summary.

Type 10: Fill in a Table Questions

在表格填写题中，考生会见到一个根据文中信息制作的、并留出部分空白项的表格。考生需要在备选答案中挑出正确选项，并将正确选项拖入表格中的相应位置。

表格题考查考生将文中主要观点和其他重要信息抽象出来并填入表格正确位置的能力。也就是说，考生先要找出并确定文章的要点，然后将其填入正确位置。

和文章总结题一样，要正确解答这类考题，考生必须在头脑里形成一个文章的整体框架，并记清文章主要观点和其他重要信息。

要做到这一点就要求考生能够理解文章中各种修辞写作手法的作用，比如原因—结果关系、对照—对比关系、论点和论据关系等。

在头脑中构建文章整体架构时，一定要记住：如果考生要构建一个水平较高的提纲的话，那么文章的主要观点一定要包含其中。正确答案选项通常体现在一个稍微详细的大纲里。相对次要的细节和例子通常不会在这种大纲中出现，因为它们只会被用来支持那些更重要、更高一级的主题。主要观点/重要信息和次要信息的区别也可以被认为是核心和非核心信息的区别。

设有表格题的文章通常有不止一个核心观点，因为此类文章经常包括不止一个观点。这类文章有以下几种典型的结构：对照—对比、问题—解决方法、原因—结果、论点切换（如理论、假设）等等。

正确答案体现了文章的主要观点和重要的支持性信息。通常这些答案不会和文章中具体的某一句话一致，它们更像是基于文中信息或对文中信息的转述而提取的抽象概念。对于那些能够记住或容易判断出相关信息位置的考生来说，正确答案是很容易确定的。

错误答案可能包含了文中没有提到的话题，或者与表格中的类别不直接相关的信息；它们同样可能是基于文中提到的信息做出的明显错误的推断或总结。注意：错误的选项同样可能会含有与文章中的原词或原句相匹配或相似的单词或短语。

Table Rules

表格题经常会有2或3栏/行表格，包括4个或5个正确答案选项。

备选答案总会多于正确答案，一些备选答案为干扰选项。

每个备选答案在表格中只能使用一次，如果一个备选答案对应表格中的多个选择栏或者不对应任何选择栏，那么在表格中会标有both或neither字样。

Scoring

表格题的得分标准要求考生不但要选出正确选项，而且还要将其填入表格中的正确位置。根据选出正确答案的多少，考生会得到不同的分数。

有4个正确答案的最多可获得2分；有5个正确答案的最多可得3分。题干中会标出特定表项的分值。

在总分为2分的表格中，不选或选出1个或2个正确答案，不得分；选出3个正确答案，得1分；选出全部4个正确答案，得2分。

在总分为3分的表格中，不选或选出1个或2个正确答案，不得分；选出3个正确答案，得1分；选出4个正确答案，得2分；选出全部5个正确答案，得3分。

Note: The passage used for this example is the same one that was used above for the Prose Summary example question. In an actual test, you will not receive both a Prose Summary question and a Fill in a Table question about the same passage.

Directions: Complete the table below to summarize information about the two types of art discussed in the passage. Match the appropriate statements to the types of art with which they are associated. **This question is worth 3 points.**

TYPES OF ART	STATEMENTS
The Applied Arts	**Select 3** • • •
The Fine Arts	**Select 2** • •

Statements

- A An object's purpose is primarily aesthetic.
- B Objects serve a functional purpose.
- C The incidental details of objects do not vary.
- D Artists work to overcome the limitations of their materials.
- E The basic form of objects varies little across cultures.
- F Artists work in concert with their materials.
- G An object's place of origin is difficult to determine.

Correctly Completed Table

Directions: Complete the table below to summarize information about the two types of art discussed in the passage. Match the appropriate statements to the types of art with which they are associated. **This question is worth 3 points.**

TYPES OF ART	STATEMENTS
The Applied Arts	**Select 3** B Objects serve a functional purpose. E The basic form of objects varies little across cultures. F Artists work in concert with their materials.
The Fine Arts	**Select 2** A An object's purpose is primarily aesthetic. D Artists work to overcome the limitations of their materials.

Explanation

Correct Choices

Choice A: An object's purpose is primarily aesthetic. (Fine Arts)

Explanation: This is an example of a correct answer that requires you to identify an abstract concept based on text information and paraphrases of text information. In paragraph 2, sentence 5, the passage states that the primary purpose of Fine Arts is not function. Then, in paragraph 2, sentence 11, the passage mentions a situation in which a sculptor had to sacrifice an aesthetic purpose due to the laws of physics. Putting these statements together, the reader can infer that fine artists, such as sculptors, are primarily concerned with aesthetics.

Choice B: Objects serve a functional purpose. (Applied Arts)

Explanation: This is stated more directly than the previous correct answer. In paragraph 1, sentences 1, 2, and 3 make it clear how important function is in the applied arts. At the same time, paragraph 2 states that Fine Arts are not concerned with function, so the only correct place for this statement is in the Applied Arts category.

Choice D: Artists work to overcome the limitations of their materials. (Fine Arts)

Explanation: This is stated explicitly in the last paragraph of the passage. In that paragraph, it is made clear that this applies only to practitioners of the fine arts.

Choice E: The basic form of objects varies little across cultures. (Applied Arts)

Explanation: In paragraph 1, sentence 5, the passage states that certain laws of physics are universal. Then in sentence 7, that idea is further developed with the statement that functional forms can vary only within limits. From these two sentences, you can conclude that because of the laws of physics and the need for functionality, the basic forms of applied-art objects will vary little across cultures.

Choice F: Artists work in concert with their materials. (Applied Arts)

Explanation: This is stated explicitly in the last paragraph of the passage. In that paragraph, it is made clear that this applies only to practitioners of the applied arts.

Incorrect Choices

Choice C: The incidental details of objects do not vary.

Explanation: This idea is explicitly refuted by the last sentence of paragraph 1 in reference to the applied arts. That sentence (referring only to applied arts) states that the incidental details of such objects do vary, so this answer cannot be placed in the Applied Arts category. This subject is not discussed at all in reference to fine-art objects, so it cannot be correctly placed in that category either.

Choice G: An object's place of origin is difficult to determine.

Explanation: This answer choice is implicitly refuted in reference to applied arts in the next-to-last sentence of paragraph 1. That sentence notes that both Shang Dynasty and Inca vases are identifiable as such based upon differences in detail. By inference, then, it seems that it is not difficult to determine an applied-art object's place of origin. Like the previous incorrect answer, this idea is not discussed at all in reference to fine-art objects, so it cannot be correctly placed in that category either.

Strategies for Preparing for the Reading Section

考生在熟悉了托福考试阅读部分的10种题型后，现在要做的就是阅读完整的文章以提高做题能力。在接下来的几页中，考生可以用ETS专门为托福设计的6篇文章进行练习。文章后并没有标出题目类型，考生需要自己判断出题目类型并思考怎样才能把题做对。在每套题目之后会有正确答案及相关答案的解释说明。

除了做这些练习外，这里还有一些帮助考生提高托福阅读能力的建议：

提高阅读技巧最好的方法是大量阅读各种类型的文章（自然科学、社会科学、艺术、商业等）。网络是这些文章的最好来源之一，当然，书刊同样也很有帮助。一定要养成定期阅读学术类文章（即大学课程中用到的那种类型的文章）的习惯。

下面是一些针对备考托福阅读文章的三种命题目的的建议。

1. Reading to find information

- 浏览文章，找出并标记重要事实（时间、数量、术语）和信息。
- 不断练习以提高阅读效率和流畅性。

2. Reading for basic comprehension

- 扩充词汇量，可以利用词汇记忆卡片。
- 不要试图读懂每个词、每句话，而要练习迅速通读全文，把握文章段落主旨。
- 培养并提高通读和识别主要信息的能力。
- 通读一段文字之后，再次仔细阅读并记下主要观点、主要信息和重要事实。
- 挑出文中一些不熟悉的单词并试着通过上下文语境猜测它们的意思。
- 挑出所有代词（例如，he，him，they，them等），并确定它们在文中所指代的名词。
- 练习通过对文章的整体把握，进行推断和总结。

3. Reading to learn

- 确定文章类型（分类、原因/结果、对照/对比、问题/解决方法、描述、叙述等）。
- 对文章信息进行如下总结：
  - 拟定文章大纲，区别主要信息和次要信息。
  - 如果文章属于信息分类型文章，制作一个表格并将信息填入适当的位置。（记住：在考试中，不需要制作这样的表格。因为考试会提供一个有备用选项的表格，考生必须将正确答案填入表格中。）这种练习可以帮助考生养成信息分类的习惯并在做题时轻松回答问题。
  - 如果文章描述某一过程的先后顺序或步骤，那就需要按照这些先后步骤或叙述过程来拟定大纲。
- 利用表格和大纲对文章进行总结。
- 转述文中的各个句子，既而转述整个段落。注意：托福考试阅读部分考查考生辨识转述的能力。这种能力对托福考试中的综合写作和口语部分也是很有帮助的。

Reading Practice Sets

PRACTICE SET 1

THE ORIGINS OF CETACEANS

It should be obvious that cetaceans—whales, porpoises, and dolphins—are mammals. They breathe through lungs, not through gills, and give birth to live young. Their stream-lined bodies, the absence of hind legs, and the presence of a fluke[1] and blowhole[2] cannot disguise their affinities with land-dwelling mammals. However, unlike the cases of sea otters and pinnipeds (seals, sea lions, and walruses, whose limbs are functional both on land and at sea), it is not easy to envision what the first whales looked like. Extinct but already fully marine cetaceans are known from the fossil record. How was the gap between a walking mammal and a swimming whale bridged? Missing until recently were fossils clearly intermediate, or transitional, between land mammals and cetaceans.

Very exciting discoveries have finally allowed scientists to reconstruct the most likely origins of cetaceans. In 1979, a team looking for fossils in northern Pakistan found what proved to be the oldest fossil whale. The fossil was officially named *Pakicetus* in honor of the country where the discovery was made. *Pakicetus* was found embedded in rocks formed from river deposits that were 52 million years old. The river that formed these deposits was actually not far from an ancient ocean known as the Tethys Sea.

The fossil consists of a complete skull of an archaeocyte, an extinct group of ancestors of modern cetaceans. Although limited to a skull, the *Pakicetus* fossil provides precious details on the origins of cetaceans. The skull is cetacean-like but its jawbones lack the enlarged space that is filled with fat or oil and used for receiving underwater sound in modern whales. *Pakicetus* probably detected sound through the ear opening as in land mammals. The skull also lacks a blowhole, another cetacean adaptation for diving. Other features, however, show experts that *Pakicetus* is a transitional form between a group of extinct flesh-eating mammals, the mesonychids, and cetaceans. It has been suggested that *Pakicetus* fed on fish in shallow water and was not yet adapted for life in the open ocean. It probably bred and gave birth on land.

Another major discovery was made in Egypt in 1989. Several skeletons of another early whale, *Basilosaurus*, were found in sediments left by the Tethys Sea and now exposed in the Sahara desert. This whale lived around 40 million years ago, 12 million years after *Pakicetus*. Many incomplete skeletons were found but they included, for the first time in an archaeocyte, a complete hind leg that features a foot with three tiny toes. Such legs would have been far too small to have supported the 50-foot-long *Basilosaurus* on land. *Basilosaurus* was undoubtedly a fully marine whale with possibly nonfunctional, or vestigial, hind legs.

An even more exciting find was reported in 1994, also from Pakistan. The now extinct whale *Ambulocetus natans* ("the walking whale that swam") lived in the Tethys Sea 49 million years ago. It lived around 3 million years after *Pakicetus* but 9 million years before *Basilosaurus*. The fossil luckily includes a good portion of the hind legs. The legs were strong and ended in long feet very much like those of a modern pinniped. The legs were certainly functional both on land and at sea. The whale retained a tail and lacked a fluke, the major means of locomotion in modern cetaceans. The structure of the backbone shows, however, that *Ambulocetus* swam like modern whales by moving the rear portion of its body up and down, even though a fluke was missing. The large hind legs were used for propulsion in water. On land, where it probably bred and gave birth, *Ambulocetus* may have moved around very much like a modern sea lion. It was undoubtedly a whale that linked life on land with life at sea.

1. Fluke: The two parts that constitute the large triangular tail of a whale
2. Blowhole: A hole in the top of the head used for breathing

Directions: Now answer the questions.

PARAGRAPH 1

It should be obvious that cetaceans—whales, porpoises, and dolphins—are mammals. They breathe through lungs, not through gills, and give birth to live young. Their streamlined bodies, the absence of hind legs, and the presence of a fluke[1] and blowhole[2] cannot disguise their affinities with land-dwelling mammals. However, unlike the cases of sea otters and pinnipeds (seals, sea lions, and walruses, whose limbs are functional both on land and at sea), it is not easy to envision what the first whales looked like. Extinct but already fully marine cetaceans are known from the fossil record. How was the gap between a walking mammal and a swimming whale bridged? Missing until recently were fossils clearly intermediate, or transitional, between land mammals and cetaceans.

1. Fluke: The two parts that constitute the large triangular tail of a whale
2. Blowhole: A hole in the top of the head used for breathing

1.   Which of the following can be inferred from paragraph 1 about early sea otters?

(A) It is not difficult to imagine what they looked like.
(B) There were great numbers of them.
(C) They lived in the sea only.
(D) They did not leave many fossil remains.

PARAGRAPH 3

The fossil consists of a complete skull of an archaeocyte, an extinct group of ancestors of modern cetaceans. Although limited to a skull, the *Pakicetus* fossil provides precious details on the origins of cetaceans. The skull is cetacean-like but its jawbones lack the enlarged space that is filled with fat or oil and used for receiving underwater sound in modern whales. *Pakicetus* probably detected sound through the ear opening as in land mammals. The skull also lacks a blowhole, another cetacean adaptation for diving. Other features, however, show experts that *Pakicetus* is a transitional form between a group of extinct flesh-eating mammals, the mesonychids, and cetaceans. It has been suggested that *Pakicetus* fed on fish in shallow water and was not yet adapted for life in the open ocean. It probably bred and gave birth on land.

2. The word "precious" in the passage is closest in meaning to

   (A) exact
   (B) scarce
   (C) valuable
   (D) initial

4. The word "It" in the passage refers to

   (A) *Pakicetus*
   (B) fish
   (C) life
   (D) ocean

3. *Pakicetus* and modern cetaceans have similar

   (A) hearing structures
   (B) adaptations for diving
   (C) skull shapes
   (D) breeding locations

PARAGRAPH 4

Another major discovery was made in Egypt in 1989. Several skeletons of another early whale, *Basilosaurus*, were found in sediments left by the Tethys Sea and now exposed in the Sahara desert. This whale lived around 40 million years ago, 12 million years after *Pakicetus*. Many incomplete skeletons were found but they included, for the first time in an archaeocyte, a complete hind leg that features a foot with three tiny toes. Such legs would have been far too small to have supported the 50-foot-long *Basilosaurus* on land. *Basilosaurus* was undoubtedly a fully marine whale with possibly nonfunctional, or vestigial, hind legs.

5. The word "exposed" in the passage is closest in meaning to

   (A) explained
   (B) visible
   (C) identified
   (D) located

6. The hind leg of *Basilosaurus* was a significant find because it showed that *Basilosaurus*

   (A) lived later than *Ambulocetus natans*
   (B) lived at the same time as *Pakicetus*
   (C) was able to swim well
   (D) could not have walked on land

PARAGRAPH 5

An even more exciting find was reported in 1994, also from Pakistan. The now extinct whale *Ambulocetus natans* ("the walking whale that swam") lived in the Tethys Sea 49 million years ago. It lived around 3 million years after *Pakicetus* but 9 million years before *Basilosaurus*. The fossil luckily includes a good portion of the hind legs. The legs were strong and ended in long feet very much like those of a modern pinniped. The legs were certainly functional both on land and at sea. The whale retained a tail and lacked a fluke, the major means of locomotion in modern cetaceans. The structure of the backbone shows, however, that *Ambulocetus* swam like modern whales by moving the rear portion of its body up and down, even though a fluke was missing. The large hind legs were used for propulsion in water. On land, where it probably bred and gave birth, *Ambulocetus* may have moved around very much like a modern sea lion. It was undoubtedly a whale that linked life on land with life at sea.

7. Why does the author use the word "luckily" in mentioning that the *Ambulocetus natans* fossil included hind legs?

   (A) Fossil legs of early whales are a rare find.

   (B) The legs provided important information about the evolution of cetaceans.

   (C) The discovery allowed scientists to reconstruct a complete skeleton of the whale.

   (D) Until that time, only the front legs of early whales had been discovered.

8. Which of the sentences below best expresses the essential information in the highlighted sentence in the passage? Incorrect choices change the meaning in important ways or leave out essential information.

   (A) Even though *Ambulocetus* swam by moving its body up and down, it did not have a backbone.

   (B) The backbone of *Ambulocetus*, which allowed it to swim, provides evidence of its missing fluke.

   (C) Although *Ambulocetus* had no fluke, its backbone structure shows that it swam like modern whales.

   (D) By moving the rear parts of their bodies up and down, modern whales swim in a different way from the way *Ambulocetus* swam.

PARAGRAPHS 1 AND 2

Extinct but already fully marine cetaceans are known from the fossil record. **(A)** How was the gap between a walking mammal and a swimming whale bridged? **(B)** Missing until recently were fossils clearly intermediate, or transitional, between land mammals and cetaceans.

(C) Very exciting discoveries have finally allowed scientists to reconstruct the most likely origins of cetaceans. **(D)** In 1979, a team looking for fossils in northern Pakistan found what proved to be the oldest fossil whale.

9. **Directions:** Look at the part of the passage that is displayed above. The letters **(A)**, **(B)**, **(C)**, and **(D)** indicate where the following sentence could be added.

    This is a question that has puzzled scientists for ages.

    Where would the sentence best fit?

    (A) Choice A
    (B) Choice B
    (C) Choice C
    (D) Choice D

10. **Directions:** An introductory sentence for a brief summary of the passage is provided below. Complete the summary by selecting the THREE answer choices that express the most important ideas in the passage. Some answer choices do not belong in the summary because they express ideas that are not presented in the passage or are minor ideas in the passage. **This question is worth 2 points.**

    This passage discusses fossils that help to explain the likely origins of cetaceans—whales, porpoises, and dolphins.

    -
    -
    -

Answer Choices

[A] Recent discoveries of fossils have helped to show the link between land mammals and cetaceans.

[B] The discovery of *Ambulocetus natans* provided evidence for a whale that lived both on land and at sea.

[C] The skeleton of *Basilosaurus* was found in what had been the Tethys Sea, an area rich in fossil evidence.

[D] *Pakicetus* is the oldest fossil whale yet to be found.

[E] Fossils thought to be transitional forms between walking mammals and swimming whales were found.

[F] *Ambulocetus's* hind legs were used for propulsion in the water.

PRACTICE SET 1 ANSWERS AND EXPLANATIONS

1. **(A)** This is an Inference question asking for information that can be inferred from paragraph 1. Choice A is the correct answer because paragraph 1 says that sea otters are unlike early mammals whose appearances are *not* easy to imagine. By inference, then, the early appearance of sea otters must be easy (or not difficult) to imagine.

2. **(C)** This is a Vocabulary question. The word being tested is *precious*. It is highlighted in the passage. The correct answer is choice C, "valuable." Anything that is precious is very important and therefore valuable.

3. **(C)** This is a Factual Information question asking for specific information that can be found in the passage. Choice C is the correct answer. Paragraph 3 describes the differences and similarities between *Pakicetus* and modern cetaceans. Sentence 3 of that paragraph states that their skulls are similar. The other three choices describe differences, not similarities.

4. **(A)** This is a Reference question. The word being tested is *It*. That word is highlighted in the passage. This is a simple pronoun-referent item. Choice A, "*Pakicetus*," is the correct answer. The word *It* here refers to a creature that probably bred and gave birth on land. *Pakicetus* is the only one of the choices to which this could apply.

5. **(B)** This is a Vocabulary question. The word being tested is *exposed*. It is highlighted in the passage. The correct answer is choice B, "visible." *Exposed* means "uncovered." A skeleton that is uncovered can be seen. *Visible* means "can be seen."

6. **(D)** This is a Factual Information question asking for specific information that can be found in the passage. Choice D is the correct answer because it is the only detail about the skeleton of *Basilosaurus* mentioned in paragraph 4, meaning that it is significant. Choice A is true, but it is not discussed in the detail that choice D is, and does not represent the significance of the discovery. Choice C is not mentioned, and choice B is not true.

7. **(B)** This is an Inference question asking for a conclusion that can be drawn from the passage. Paragraph 5 explains that this discovery provided important information to scientists that they might not have been able to obtain without it. Therefore you can infer that the discovery was a "lucky" one. The passage offers no support for the other choices. Therefore choice B is the correct answer.

8.　**C** This is a Sentence Simplification question. As with all of these questions, a single sentence in the passage is highlighted:

> The structure of the backbone shows, however, that *Ambulocetus* swam like modern whales by moving the rear portion of its body up and down, even though a fluke was missing.

Choice C is the correct answer because it contains all of the essential information in the highlighted sentence. Choice A is not true because *Ambulocetus* did have a backbone. Choice B is not true because the sentence says that the backbone showed how the *Ambulocetus* swam, not that it was missing a fluke. Choice D is not true because the sentence states that *Ambulocetus* and modern whales swam in the same way.

9.　**B** This is an Insert Text question. You can see the four possible answer choices in paragraphs 1 and 2.

> Extinct but already fully marine cetaceans are known from the fossil record. **(A)** How was the gap between a walking mammal and a swimming whale bridged? **(B)** Missing until recently were fossils clearly intermediate, or transitional, between land mammals and cetaceans.
>
> **(C)** Very exciting discoveries have finally allowed scientists to reconstruct the most likely origins of cetaceans. **(D)** In 1979, a team looking for fossils in northern Pakistan found what proved to be the oldest fossil whale.

The sentence provided is "This is a question that has puzzled scientists for ages." The correct place to insert it is at choice **(B)**.

The sentence that precedes choice **(B)** is in the form of a rhetorical question, and the inserted sentence explicitly provides a response to it. None of the other sentences is a question, so the inserted sentence cannot logically follow any one of them.

10. **A** **B** **E** This is a Prose Summary question. It is completed correctly below. The correct choices are A, B, and E. Choices C, D, and F are therefore incorrect.

Directions: An introductory sentence for a brief summary of the passage is provided below. Complete the summary by selecting the THREE answer choices that express the most important ideas in the passage. Some answer choices do not belong in the summary because they express ideas that are not presented in the passage or are minor ideas in the passage. **This question is worth 2 points.**

This passage discusses fossils that help to explain the likely origins of cetaceans—whales, porpoises, and dolphins.

> A Recent discoveries of fossils have helped to show the link between land mammals and cetaceans.
> B The discovery of Ambulocetus natans provided evidence for a whale that lived both on land and at sea.
> E Fossils thought to be transitional forms between walking mammals and swimming whales were found.

Answer Choices

A Recent discoveries of fossils have helped to show the link between land mammals and cetaceans.

B The discovery of *Ambulocetus natans* provided evidence for a whale that lived both on land and at sea.

C The skeleton of *Basilosaurus* was found in what had been the Tethys Sea, an area rich in fossil evidence.

D *Pakicetus* is the oldest fossil whale yet to be found.

E Fossils thought to be transitional forms between walking mammals and swimming whales were found.

F *Ambulocetus*'s hind legs were used for propulsion in the water.

Correct Choices

Choice A, "Recent discoveries of fossils have helped to show the link between land mammals and cetaceans," is correct because it represents the major idea of the entire passage. The bulk of the passage consists of a discussion of the major discoveries (*Pakicetus*, *Basilosaurus*, and *Ambulocetus*) that show this link.

Choice B, "The discovery of *Ambulocetus natans* provided evidence for a whale that lived both on land and at sea," is correct because it is one of the major discoveries cited in the passage in support of the passage's main point, that land mammals and cetaceans are related.

Choice E, "Fossils thought to be transitional forms between walking mammals and swimming whales were found," is correct because like choice A, this is a statement of the passage's major theme as stated in paragraph 1: these fossils were "clearly intermediate, or transitional, between land mammals and cetaceans." The remainder of the passage discusses these discoveries.

Incorrect Choices

Choice C, "The skeleton of *Basilosaurus* was found in what had been the Tethys Sea, an area rich in fossil evidence," is true, but it is a minor detail and therefore incorrect.

Choice D, "*Pakicetus* is the oldest fossil whale yet to be found," is true, but it is a minor detail and therefore incorrect.

Choice F, "*Ambulocetus*'s hind legs were used for propulsion in the water," is true, but it is a minor detail and therefore incorrect.

PRACTICE SET 2

DESERT FORMATION

The deserts, which already occupy approximately a fourth of the Earth's land surface, have in recent decades been increasing at an alarming pace. The expansion of desertlike conditions into areas where they did not previously exist is called **desertification**. It has been estimated that an additional one-fourth of the Earth's land surface is threatened by this process.

Desertification is accomplished primarily through the loss of stabilizing natural vegetation and the subsequent accelerated erosion of the soil by wind and water. In some cases the loose soil is blown completely away, leaving a stony surface. In other cases, the finer particles may be removed, while the sand-sized particles are accumulated to form mobile hills or ridges of sand.

Even in the areas that retain a soil cover, the reduction of vegetation typically results in the loss of the soil's ability to absorb substantial quantities of water. The impact of raindrops on the loose soil tends to transfer fine clay particles into the tiniest soil spaces, sealing them and producing a surface that allows very little water penetration. Water absorption is greatly reduced; consequently, runoff is increased, resulting in accelerated erosion rates. The gradual drying of the soil caused by its diminished ability to absorb water results in the further loss of vegetation, so that a cycle of progressive surface deterioration is established.

In some regions, the increase in desert areas is occurring largely as the result of a trend toward drier climatic conditions. Continued gradual global warming has produced an increase in aridity for some areas over the past few thousand years. The process may be accelerated in subsequent decades if global warming resulting from air pollution seriously increases.

There is little doubt, however, that desertification in most areas results primarily from human activities rather than natural processes. The semiarid lands bordering the deserts exist in a delicate ecological balance and are limited in their potential to adjust to increased environmental pressures. Expanding populations are subjecting the land to increasing pressures to provide them with food and fuel. In wet periods, the land may be able to respond to these stresses. During the dry periods that are common phenomena along the desert margins, though, the pressure on the land is often far in excess of its diminished capacity, and desertification results.

Four specific activities have been identified as major contributors to the desertification process: overcultivation, overgrazing, firewood gathering, and overirrigation. The cultivation of crops has expanded into progressively drier regions as population densities have grown. These regions are especially likely to have periods of severe dryness, so that crop failures are common. Since the raising of most crops necessitates the prior removal of the natural vegetation, crop failures leave extensive tracts of land devoid of a plant cover and susceptible to wind and water erosion.

The raising of livestock is a major economic activity in semiarid lands, where grasses are generally the dominant type of natural vegetation. The consequences of an excessive number of livestock grazing in an area are the reduction of the vegetation cover and the trampling and pulverization of the soil. This is usually followed by the drying of the soil and accelerated erosion.

Firewood is the chief fuel used for cooking and heating in many countries. The increased pressures of expanding populations have led to the removal of woody plants so that many cities and towns are surrounded by large areas completely lacking in trees and shrubs. The increasing use of dried animal waste as a substitute fuel has also hurt the soil because this valuable soil conditioner and source of plant nutrients is no longer being returned to the land.

The final major human cause of desertification is soil salinization resulting from over-irrigation. Excess water from irrigation sinks down into the water table. If no drainage system exists, the water table rises, bringing dissolved salts to the surface. The water evaporates and the salts are left behind, creating a white crustal layer that prevents air and water from reaching the underlying soil.

The extreme seriousness of desertification results from the vast areas of land and the tremendous numbers of people affected, as well as from the great difficulty of reversing or even slowing the process. Once the soil has been removed by erosion, only the passage of centuries or millennia will enable new soil to form. In areas where considerable soil still remains, though, a rigorously enforced program of land protection and cover-crop planting may make it possible to reverse the present deterioration of the surface.

Directions: Now answer the questions.

PARAGRAPH 1

The deserts, which already occupy approximately a fourth of the Earth's land surface, have in recent decades been increasing at an alarming pace. The expansion of desertlike conditions into areas where they did not previously exist is called **desertification**. It has been estimated that an additional one-fourth of the Earth's land surface is threatened by this process.

1. The word "threatened" in the passage is closest in meaning to

   Ⓐ restricted
   Ⓑ endangered
   Ⓒ prevented
   Ⓓ rejected

PARAGRAPH 3

Even in the areas that retain a soil cover, the reduction of vegetation typically results in the loss of the soil's ability to absorb substantial quantities of water. The impact of raindrops on the loose soil tends to transfer fine clay particles into the tiniest soil spaces, sealing them and producing a surface that allows very little water penetration. Water absorption is greatly reduced; consequently, runoff is increased, resulting in accelerated erosion rates. The gradual drying of the soil caused by its diminished ability to absorb water results in the further loss of vegetation, so that a cycle of progressive surface deterioration is established.

2. According to paragraph 3, the loss of natural vegetation has which of the following consequences for soil?

   Ⓐ Increased stony content
   Ⓑ Reduced water absorption
   Ⓒ Increased numbers of spaces in the soil
   Ⓓ Reduced water runoff

PARAGRAPH 5

There is little doubt, however, that desertification in most areas results primarily from human activities rather than natural processes. The semiarid lands bordering the deserts exist in a delicate ecological balance and are limited in their potential to adjust to increased environmental pressures. Expanding populations are subjecting the land to increasing pressures to provide them with food and fuel. In wet periods, the land may be able to respond to these stresses. During the dry periods that are common phenomena along the desert margins, though, the pressure on the land is often far in excess of its diminished capacity, and desertification results.

3. The word "delicate" in the passage is closest in meaning to

   Ⓐ fragile
   Ⓑ predictable
   Ⓒ complex
   Ⓓ valuable

4. According to paragraph 5, in dry periods, border areas have difficulty

   Ⓐ adjusting to stresses created by settlement
   Ⓑ retaining their fertility after desertification
   Ⓒ providing water for irrigating crops
   Ⓓ attracting populations in search of food and fuel

PARAGRAPH 6

Four specific activities have been identified as major contributors to the desertification process: overcultivation, overgrazing, firewood gathering, and overirrigation. The cultivation of crops has expanded into progressively drier regions as population densities have grown. These regions are especially likely to have periods of severe dryness, so that crop failures are common. Since the raising of most crops necessitates the prior removal of the natural vegetation, crop failures leave extensive tracts of land devoid of a plant cover and susceptible to wind and water erosion.

5. The word "progressively" in the passage is closest in meaning to

   Ⓐ openly
   Ⓑ impressively
   Ⓒ objectively
   Ⓓ increasingly

6. According to paragraph 6, which of the following is often associated with raising crops?

   Ⓐ Lack of proper irrigation techniques
   Ⓑ Failure to plant crops suited to the particular area
   Ⓒ Removal of the original vegetation
   Ⓓ Excessive use of dried animal waste

PARAGRAPH 9

The final major human cause of desertification is soil salinization resulting from overirrigation. Excess water from irrigation sinks down into the water table. If no drainage system exists, the water table rises, bringing dissolved salts to the surface. The water evaporates and the salts are left behind, creating a white crustal layer that prevents air and water from reaching the underlying soil.

7. According to paragraph 9, the ground's absorption of excess water is a factor in desertification because it can

   Ⓐ interfere with the irrigation of land
   Ⓑ limit the evaporation of water
   Ⓒ require more absorption of air by the soil
   Ⓓ bring salts to the surface

PARAGRAPH 10

The extreme seriousness of desertification results from the vast areas of land and the tremendous numbers of people affected, as well as from the great difficulty of reversing or even slowing the process. Once the soil has been removed by erosion, only the passage of centuries or millennia will enable new soil to form. In areas where considerable soil still remains, though, a rigorously enforced program of land protection and cover-crop planting may make it possible to reverse the present deterioration of the surface.

8. Which of the sentences below best expresses the essential information in the highlighted sentence in the passage? Incorrect choices change the meaning in important ways or leave out essential information.

   Ⓐ Desertification is a significant problem because it is so hard to reverse and affects large areas of land and great numbers of people.
   Ⓑ Slowing down the process of desertification is difficult because of population growth that has spread over large areas of land.
   Ⓒ The spread of deserts is considered a very serious problem that can be solved only if large numbers of people in various countries are involved in the effort.
   Ⓓ Desertification is extremely hard to reverse unless the population is reduced in the vast areas affected.

P
A
R
A
G
R
A
P
H

7

(A) The raising of livestock is a major economic activity in semiarid lands, where grasses are generally the dominant type of natural vegetation. **(B)** The consequences of an excessive number of livestock grazing in an area are the reduction of the vegetation cover and the trampling and pulverization of the soil. **(C)** This is usually followed by the drying of the soil and accelerated erosion. **(D)**

9. **Directions:** Look at the part of the passage that is displayed above. The letters **(A)**, **(B)**, **(C)**, and **(D)** indicate where the following sentence could be added.

    This economic reliance on livestock in certain regions makes large tracts of land susceptible to overgrazing.

    Where would the sentence best fit?

    (A) Choice A
    (B) Choice B
    (C) Choice C
    (D) Choice D

10. **Directions:** An introductory sentence for a brief summary of the passage is provided below. Complete the summary by selecting the THREE answer choices that express the most important ideas in the passage. Some answer choices do not belong in the summary because they express ideas that are not presented in the passage or are minor ideas in the passage. **This question is worth 2 points.**

    Many factors have contributed to the great increase in desertification in recent decades.

    -
    -
    -

    Answer Choices

    A Growing human populations and the agricultural demands that come with such growth have upset the ecological balance in some areas and led to the spread of deserts.

    B As periods of severe dryness have become more common, failures of a number of different crops have increased.

    C Excessive numbers of cattle and the need for firewood for fuel have reduced grasses and trees, leaving the land unprotected and vulnerable.

    D Extensive irrigation with poor drainage brings salt to the surface of the soil, a process that reduces water and air absorption.

    E Animal dung enriches the soil by providing nutrients for plant growth.

    F Grasses are generally the dominant type of natural vegetation in semiarid lands.

PRACTICE SET 2 ANSWERS AND EXPLANATIONS

1. **B** This is a Vocabulary question. The word being tested is *threatened*. It is highlighted in the passage. To threaten is to speak or act as if you will cause harm to someone or something. The object of the threat is in danger of being hurt, so the correct answer is choice B, "endangered."

2. **B** This is a Factual Information question asking for specific information that can be found in paragraph 3. The correct answer is choice B, "reduced water absorption." The paragraph explicitly states that the reduction of vegetation greatly reduces water absorption. Choice D, "reduced water runoff," explicitly contradicts the paragraph, so it is incorrect. The "spaces in the soil" are mentioned in another context: the paragraph does not say that they increase, so choice C is incorrect. The paragraph does not mention choice A.

3. **A** This is a Vocabulary question. The word being tested is *delicate*. It is highlighted in the passage. The correct answer is choice A, "fragile," meaning "easily broken." *Delicate* has the same meaning as *fragile*.

4. **A** This is a Factual Information question asking for specific information that can be found in paragraph 5. The correct answer is choice A: border areas have difficulty "adjusting to stresses created by settlement." The paragraph says that "expanding populations," or settlement, subject border areas to "pressures," or stress, that the land may not "be able to respond to." Choice B is incorrect because the paragraph does not discuss "fertility" after desertification. Choice C is also incorrect because "irrigation" is not mentioned here. The paragraph mentions "increasing populations" but not the difficulty of "attracting populations," so choice D is incorrect.

5. **D** This is a Vocabulary question. The word being tested is *progressively*. It is highlighted in the passage. The correct answer is choice D, "increasingly." *Progressively* as it is used here means "more," and "more" of something means that it is increasing.

6. **C** This is a Factual Information question asking for specific information that can be found in paragraph 6. The correct answer is choice C, "removal of the original vegetation." Sentence 4 of this paragraph says that "the raising of most crops necessitates the prior removal of the natural vegetation," an explicit statement of answer choice C. Choice A, "lack of proper irrigation techniques," is incorrect because the paragraph mentions only "overirrigation" as a cause of desertification. No irrigation "techniques" are discussed. Choices B and D, failure to plant suitable crops and use of animal waste, are not discussed.

7. **D** This is a Factual Information question asking for specific information that can be found in paragraph 9. The correct answer is choice D, "bring salts to the surface." The paragraph says that the final human cause of desertification is salinization resulting from overirrigation. The paragraph goes on to say that the overirrigation causes the water table to rise, bringing salts to the surface. There is no mention of the process as "interfering" with or "limiting" irrigation, or of the "amount of air" the soil is required to absorb, so choices A, B, and C are all incorrect.

8. **A** This is a Sentence Simplification question. As with all of these questions, a single sentence in the passage is highlighted:

> The extreme seriousness of desertification results from the vast areas of land and the tremendous numbers of people affected, as well as from the great difficulty of reversing or even slowing the process.

The correct answer is choice A. That choice contains all of the essential information in the highlighted sentence and does not change its meaning. The only substantive difference between choice A and the tested sentence is the order in which the information is presented. Two clauses in the highlighted sentence, "the great difficulty of reversing . . . the process" and "the tremendous numbers of people affected," have simply been reversed; no meaning has been changed, and no information has been removed. Choices B, C, and D are all incorrect because they change the meaning of the highlighted sentence.

9. **B** This is an Insert Text question. You can see the four possible answer choices in paragraph 7.

(A) The raising of livestock is a major economic activity in semiarid lands, where grasses are generally the dominant type of natural vegetation. **(B)** The consequences of an excessive number of livestock grazing in an area are the reduction of the vegetation cover and the trampling and pulverization of the soil. **(C)** This is usually followed by the drying of the soil and accelerated erosion. **(D)**

The sentence provided, "This economic reliance on livestock in certain regions makes large tracts of land susceptible to overgrazing," is best inserted at choice **(B)**. The inserted sentence refers explicitly to relying on "livestock in certain regions." Those regions are the ones described in the sentence preceding choice **(B)**, which states that raising livestock is "a major economic activity in semiarid lands." The inserted sentence then explains that this reliance "makes large tracts of land susceptible to overgrazing." The sentence that follows choice **(B)** goes on to say that "The consequences of an excessive number of livestock grazing in an area are . . ." Thus the inserted sentence contains references to both the sentence before choice **(B)** and the sentence after choice **(B)**. This is not true of any of the other possible insert points, so choice **(B)** is correct.

10. **A** **C** **D** This is a Prose Summary question. It is completed correctly below. The correct choices are A, C, and D. Choices B, E, and F are therefore incorrect.

Directions: An introductory sentence for a brief summary of the passage is provided below. Complete the summary by selecting the THREE answer choices that express the most important ideas in the passage. Some answer choices do not belong in the summary because they express ideas that are not presented in the passage or are minor ideas in the passage. **This question is worth 2 points.**

Many factors have contributed to the great increase in desertification in recent decades.

A Growing human populations and the agricultural demands that come with such growth have upset the ecological balance in some areas and led to the spread of deserts.

C Excessive numbers of cattle and the need for firewood for fuel have reduced grasses and trees, leaving the land unprotected and vulnerable.

D Extensive irrigation with poor drainage brings salt to the surface of the soil, a process that reduces water and air absorption.

Answer Choices

A Growing human populations and the agricultural demands that come with such growth have upset the ecological balance in some areas and led to the spread of deserts.

B As periods of severe dryness have become more common, failures of a number of different crops have increased.

C Excessive numbers of cattle and the need for firewood for fuel have reduced grasses and trees, leaving the land unprotected and vulnerable.

D Extensive irrigation with poor drainage brings salt to the surface of the soil, a process that reduces water and air absorption.

E Animal dung enriches the soil by providing nutrients for plant growth.

F Grasses are generally the dominant type of natural vegetation in semiarid lands.

Correct Choices

Choice A, "Growing human populations and the agricultural demands that come with such growth have upset the ecological balance in some areas and led to the spread of deserts," is correct because it is a recurring theme in the passage, one of the main ideas. Paragraphs 5, 6, 7, and 9 all provide details in support of this statement.

Choice C, "Excessive numbers of cattle and the need for firewood for fuel have reduced grasses and trees, leaving the land unprotected and vulnerable," is correct because these are two of the human activities that are major causes of desertification. The causes of desertification is the main theme of the passage. Paragraphs 6, 7, and 8 are devoted to describing how these activities contribute to desertification.

Choice D, "Extensive irrigation with poor drainage brings salt to the surface of the soil, a process that reduces water and air absorption," is correct because it is another of the human activities that are a major cause of desertification, the main theme of the passage. Paragraph 6 mentions this first, then all of paragraph 9 is devoted to describing how this activity contributes to desertification.

Incorrect Choices

Choice B, "As periods of severe dryness have become more common, failures of a number of different crops have increased," is incorrect because it is a supporting detail, not a main idea of the passage.

Choice E, "Animal dung enriches the soil by providing nutrients for plant growth," is incorrect because it is contradicted by paragraph 8 of the passage.

Choice F, "Grasses are generally the dominant type of natural vegetation in semi-arid lands," is incorrect because it is a minor detail, mentioned once in passing in paragraph 7.

PRACTICE SET 3

EARLY CINEMA

The cinema did not emerge as a form of mass consumption until its technology evolved from the initial "peepshow" format to the point where images were projected on a screen in a darkened theater. In the peepshow format, a film was viewed through a small opening in a machine that was created for that purpose. Thomas Edison's peepshow device, the Kinetoscope, was introduced to the public in 1894. It was designed for use in Kinetoscope parlors, or arcades, which contained only a few individual machines and permitted only one customer to view a short, 50-foot film at any one time. The first Kinetoscope parlors contained five machines. For the price of 25 cents (or 5 cents per machine), customers moved from machine to machine to watch five different films (or, in the case of famous prizefights, successive rounds of a single fight).

These Kinetoscope arcades were modeled on phonograph parlors, which had proven successful for Edison several years earlier. In the phonograph parlors, customers listened to recordings through individual ear tubes, moving from one machine to the next to hear different recorded speeches or pieces of music. The Kinetoscope parlors functioned in a similar way. Edison was more interested in the sale of Kinetoscopes (for roughly $1,000 apiece) to these parlors than in the films that would be run in them (which cost approximately $10 to $15 each). He refused to develop projection technology, reasoning that if he made and sold projectors, then exhibitors would purchase only one machine—a projector—from him instead of several.

Exhibitors, however, wanted to maximize their profits, which they could do more readily by projecting a handful of films to hundreds of customers at a time (rather than one at a time) and by charging 25 to 50 cents admission. About a year after the opening of the first Kinetoscope parlor in 1894, showmen such as Louis and Auguste Lumière, Thomas Armat and Charles Francis Jenkins, and Orville and Woodville Latham (with the assistance of Edison's former assistant, William Dickson) perfected projection devices. These early projection devices were used in vaudeville theaters, legitimate theaters, local town halls, makeshift storefront theaters, fairgrounds, and amusement parks to show films to a mass audience.

With the advent of projection in 1895–1896, motion pictures became the ultimate form of mass consumption. Previously, large audiences had viewed spectacles at the theater, where vaudeville, popular dramas, musical and minstrel shows, classical plays, lectures, and slide-and-lantern shows had been presented to several hundred spectators at a time. But the movies differed significantly from these other forms of entertainment, which depended on either live performance or (in the case of the slide-and-lantern shows) the active involvement of a master of ceremonies who assembled the final program.

Although early exhibitors regularly accompanied movies with live acts, the substance of the movies themselves is mass-produced, prerecorded material that can easily be reproduced by theaters with little or no active participation by the exhibitor. Even though early exhibitors shaped their film programs by mixing films and other entertainments together in whichever way they thought would be most attractive to audiences or by accompanying them with lectures, their creative control remained limited. What audiences came to see was the technological marvel of the movies; the lifelike reproduction of the commonplace motion of trains, of waves striking the shore, and of people walking in the street; and the magic made possible by trick photography and the manipulation of the camera.

With the advent of projection, the viewer's relationship with the image was no longer private, as it had been with earlier peepshow devices such as the Kinetoscope and the Mutoscope, which was a similar machine that reproduced motion by means of successive images on individual photographic cards instead of on strips of celluloid. It suddenly became public—an experience that the viewer shared with dozens, scores, and even hundreds of others. At the same time, the image that the spectator looked at expanded from the minuscule peepshow dimensions of 1 or 2 inches (in height) to the life-size proportions of 6 or 9 feet.

Directions: Now answer the questions.

PARAGRAPH 1

The cinema did not emerge as a form of mass consumption until its technology evolved from the initial "peepshow" format to the point where images were projected on a screen in a darkened theater. In the peepshow format, a film was viewed through a small opening in a machine that was created for that purpose. Thomas Edison's peepshow device, the Kinetoscope, was introduced to the public in 1894. It was designed for use in Kinetoscope parlors, or arcades, which contained only a few individual machines and permitted only one customer to view a short, 50-foot film at any one time. The first Kinetoscope parlors contained five machines. For the price of 25 cents (or 5 cents per machine), customers moved from machine to machine to watch five different films (or, in the case of famous prizefights, successive rounds of a single fight).

1. According to paragraph 1, all of the following were true of viewing films in Kinetoscope parlors EXCEPT:

   Ⓐ One individual at a time viewed a film.
   Ⓑ Customers could view one film after another.
   Ⓒ Prizefights were the most popular subjects for films.
   Ⓓ Each film was short.

PARAGRAPH 2

These Kinetoscope arcades were modeled on phonograph parlors, which had proven successful for Edison several years earlier. In the phonograph parlors, customers listened to recordings through individual ear tubes, moving from one machine to the next to hear different recorded speeches or pieces of music. The Kinetoscope parlors functioned in a similar way. Edison was more interested in the sale of Kinetoscopes (for roughly $1,000 apiece) to these parlors than in the films that would be run in them (which cost approximately $10 to $15 each). He refused to develop projection technology, reasoning that if he made and sold projectors, then exhibitors would purchase only one machine—a projector—from him instead of several.

2. The author discusses phonograph parlors in paragraph 2 in order to

   (A) explain Edison's financial success

   (B) describe the model used to design Kinetoscope parlors

   (C) contrast their popularity to that of Kinetoscope parlors

   (D) illustrate how much more technologically advanced Kinetoscope parlors were

3. Which of the sentences below best expresses the essential information in the highlighted sentence in the passage? Incorrect answer choices change the meaning in important ways or leave out essential information.

   (A) Edison was more interested in developing a variety of machines than in developing a technology based on only one.

   (B) Edison refused to work on projection technology because he did not think exhibitors would replace their projectors with newer machines.

   (C) Edison did not want to develop projection technology because it limited the number of machines he could sell.

   (D) Edison would not develop projection technology unless exhibitors agreed to purchase more than one projector from him.

PARAGRAPH 3

Exhibitors, however, wanted to maximize their profits, which they could do more readily by projecting a handful of films to hundreds of customers at a time (rather than one at a time) and by charging 25 to 50 cents admission. About a year after the opening of the first Kinetoscope parlor in 1894, showmen such as Louis and Auguste Lumière, Thomas Armat and Charles Francis Jenkins, and Orville and Woodville Latham (with the assistance of Edison's former assistant, William Dickson) perfected projection devices. These early projection devices were used in vaudeville theaters, legitimate theaters, local town halls, makeshift storefront theaters, fairgrounds, and amusement parks to show films to a mass audience.

4. The word "readily" in the passage is closest in meaning to

Ⓐ frequently
Ⓑ easily
Ⓒ intelligently
Ⓓ obviously

PARAGRAPH 4

With the advent of projection in 1895–1896, motion pictures became the ultimate form of mass consumption. Previously, large audiences had viewed spectacles at the theater, where vaudeville, popular dramas, musical and minstrel shows, classical plays, lectures, and slide-and-lantern shows had been presented to several hundred spectators at a time. But the movies differed significantly from these other forms of entertainment, which depended on either live performance or (in the case of the slide-and-lantern shows) the active involvement of a master of ceremonies who assembled the final program.

5. According to paragraph 4, how did the early movies differ from previous spectacles that were presented to large audiences?

Ⓐ They were a more expensive form of entertainment.
Ⓑ They were viewed by larger audiences.
Ⓒ They were more educational.
Ⓓ They did not require live entertainers.

PARAGRAPH 5

Although early exhibitors regularly accompanied movies with live acts, the substance of the movies themselves is mass-produced, prerecorded material that can easily be reproduced by theaters with little or no active participation by the exhibitor. Even though early exhibitors shaped their film programs by mixing films and other entertainments together in whichever way they thought would be most attractive to audiences or by accompanying them with lectures, their creative control remained limited. What audiences came to see was the technological marvel of the movies; the lifelike reproduction of the commonplace motion of trains, of waves striking the shore, and of people walking in the street; and the magic made possible by trick photography and the manipulation of the camera.

6. According to paragraph 5, what role did early exhibitors play in the presentation of movies in theaters?

   Ⓐ They decided how to combine various components of the film program.

   Ⓑ They advised filmmakers on appropriate movie content.

   Ⓒ They often took part in the live-action performances.

   Ⓓ They produced and prerecorded the material that was shown in the theaters.

PARAGRAPH 6

With the advent of projection, the viewer's relationship with the image was no longer private, as it had been with earlier peepshow devices such as the Kinetoscope and the Mutoscope, which was a similar machine that reproduced motion by means of successive images on individual photographic cards instead of on strips of celluloid. It suddenly became public—an experience that the viewer shared with dozens, scores, and even hundreds of others. At the same time, the image that the spectator looked at expanded from the minuscule peepshow dimensions of 1 or 2 inches (in height) to the life-size proportions of 6 or 9 feet.

7. The word "It" in the passage refers to

   Ⓐ the advent of projection

   Ⓑ the viewer's relationship with the image

   Ⓒ a similar machine

   Ⓓ celluloid

8. According to paragraph 6, the images seen by viewers in the earlier peepshows, compared with the images projected on the screen, were relatively

   Ⓐ small in size

   Ⓑ inexpensive to create

   Ⓒ unfocused

   Ⓓ limited in subject matter

PARAGRAPH 3

(A) Exhibitors, however, wanted to maximize their profits, which they could do more readily by projecting a handful of films to hundreds of customers at a time (rather than one at a time) and by charging 25 to 50 cents admission. **(B)** About a year after the opening of the first Kinetoscope parlor in 1894, showmen such as Louis and Auguste Lumière, Thomas Armat and Charles Francis Jenkins, and Orville and Woodville Latham (with the assistance of Edison's former assistant, William Dickson) perfected projection devices. **(C)** These early projection devices were used in vaudeville theaters, legitimate theaters, local town halls, makeshift storefront theaters, fairgrounds, and amusement parks to show films to a mass audience. **(D)**

9. **Directions:** Look at the part of the passage that is displayed above. The letters **(A)**, **(B)**, **(C)**, and **(D)** indicate where the following sentence could be added.

   When this widespread use of projection technology began to hurt his Kinetoscope business, Edison acquired a projector developed by Armat and introduced it as "Edison's latest marvel, the Vitascope."

   Where would the sentence best fit?

   (A) Choice A
   (B) Choice B
   (C) Choice C
   (D) Choice D

10. **Directions:** An introductory sentence for a brief summary of the passage is provided below. Complete the summary by selecting the THREE answer choices that express the most important ideas in the passage. Some answer choices do not belong in the summary because they express ideas that are not presented in the passage or are minor ideas in the passage. **This question is worth 2 points.**

   The technology for modern cinema evolved at the end of the nineteenth century.

   -
   -
   -

   Answer Choices

   A Kinetoscope parlors for viewing films were modeled on phonograph parlors.
   B Thomas Edison's design of the Kinetoscope inspired the development of large-screen projection.
   C Early cinema allowed individuals to use special machines to view films privately.
   D Slide-and-lantern shows had been presented to audiences of hundreds of spectators.
   E The development of projection technology made it possible to project images on a large screen.
   F Once film images could be projected, the cinema became a form of mass consumption.

PRACTICE SET 3 ANSWERS AND EXPLANATIONS

1. Ⓒ This is a Negative Factual Information question asking for specific information that can be found in paragraph 1. Choice C is the correct answer. The paragraph does mention that one viewer at a time could view the films (choice A), that films could be viewed one after another (choice B), and that films were short (choice D). Prizefights are mentioned as one subject of these short films, but not necessarily the most popular one.

2. Ⓑ This is a Rhetorical Purpose question. It asks why the author mentions "phonograph parlors" in paragraph 2. The correct answer is choice B. The author is explaining why Edison designed his arcades like phonograph parlors; that design had been successful for him in the past. The paragraph does not mention the phonograph parlors to explain Edison's financial success, so choice A is incorrect. The paragraph does not directly discuss the situations described in choices C and D, so those answers too are incorrect.

3. Ⓒ This is a Sentence Simplification question. As with all of these questions, a single sentence in the passage is highlighted:

> He refused to develop projection technology, reasoning that if he made and sold projectors, then exhibitors would purchase only one machine—a projector—from him, instead of several.

    The correct answer is choice C. That choice contains all of the essential ideas in the highlighted sentence. It is also the only choice that does not change the meaning of the sentence. Choice A says that Edison was more interested in developing a variety of machines, which is not true. Choice B says that the reason Edison refused to work on projection technology was that exhibitors would never replace the projectors. That also is not true; the highlighted sentence implies that he refused to do this because he wanted exhibitors to buy several Kinetoscope machines at a time instead of a single projector. Choice D says that Edison refused to develop projection technology unless exhibitors agreed to purchase more than one projector from him. The highlighted sentence actually says that Edison had already reasoned or concluded that exhibitors would not buy more than one, so choice D is a change in essential meaning.

4. Ⓑ This is a Vocabulary question. The word being tested is *readily*. It is highlighted in the passage. *Readily* means "easily," so choice B is the correct answer. The other choices do not fit in the context of the sentence.

5. Ⓓ This is a Factual Information question asking for specific information that can be found in paragraph 4. The correct answer is choice D. Early movies were different from previous spectacles because they did not require live actors. The paragraph states (emphasis added):

> "But the movies differed significantly from these other forms of entertainment, which depended on either *live performance* or (in the case of the slide-and-lantern shows) the active involvement of a master of ceremonies who assembled the final program."

So the fact that previous spectacles depended on live performances is explicitly stated as one of the ways (but not the only way) that those earlier entertainments differed from movies. The other answer choices are not mentioned in the paragraph.

6. **(A)** This is a Factual Information question asking for specific information that can be found in paragraph 5. The correct answer is choice A, "They decided how to combine various components of the film program," because that idea is stated explicitly in the paragraph:

"Early exhibitors shaped their film programs by mixing films and other entertainments together."

The other choices, while possibly true, are not explicitly mentioned in the paragraph as being among the exhibitors' roles.

7. **(B)** This is a Reference question. The word being tested is *It*. That word is highlighted in the passage. Choice B, "the viewer's relationship with the image," is the correct answer. This is a simple pronoun-referent item. The sentence says that "It" suddenly became "public," which implies that whatever "It" is, it was formerly private. The paragraph says that "the viewer's relationship with the image was no longer private," so that relationship is the "It" referred to here.

8. **(A)** This is a Factual Information question asking for specific information that can be found in paragraph 6. The correct answer is choice A. The paragraph says that the images expanded from an inch or two to life-size proportions, so "small in size" must be correct. The paragraph does not mention the other choices.

9. **(D)** This is an Insert Text question. You can see the four possible answer choices in paragraph 3.

(A) Exhibitors, however, wanted to maximize their profits, which they could do more readily by projecting a handful of films to hundreds of customers at a time (rather than one at a time) and by charging 25 to 50 cents admission. **(B)** About a year after the opening of the first Kinetoscope parlor in 1894, showmen such as Louis and Auguste Lumière, Thomas Armat and Charles Francis Jenkins, and Orville and Woodville Latham (with the assistance of Edison's former assistant, William Dickson) perfected projection devices. **(C)** These early projection devices were used in vaudeville theaters, legitimate theaters, local town halls, makeshift storefront theaters, fairgrounds, and amusement parks to show films to a mass audience. **(D)**

The inserted sentence fits best at choice **(D)** because it represents the final result of the general use of projectors. After projectors became popular, Edison lost money, and although he had previously refused to develop projection technology, now he was forced to do so. To place the sentence anyplace else would interrupt the logical narrative sequence of the events described. None of the sentences in this paragraph can logically follow the inserted sentence, so choices **(A)**, **(B)**, and **(C)** are all incorrect.

10. **C** **E** **F** This is a Prose Summary question. It is completed correctly below. The correct choices are C, E, and F. Choices A, B, and D are therefore incorrect.

Directions: An introductory sentence for a brief summary of the passage is provided below. Complete the summary by selecting the THREE answer choices that express the most important ideas in the passage. Some answer choices do not belong in the summary because they express ideas that are not presented in the passage or are minor ideas in the passage. **This question is worth 2 points.**

The technology for modern cinema evolved at the end of the nineteenth century.

C   Early cinema allowed individuals to use special machines to view films privately.

E   The development of projection technology made it possible to project images on a large screen.

F   Once film images could be projected, the cinema became a form of mass consumption.

Answer Choices

A   Kinetoscope parlors for viewing films were modeled on phonograph parlors.

B   Thomas Edison's design of the Kinetoscope inspired the development of large-screen projection.

C   Early cinema allowed individuals to use special machines to view films privately.

D   Slide-and-lantern shows had been presented to audiences of hundreds of spectators.

E   The development of projection technology made it possible to project images on a large screen.

F   Once film images could be projected, the cinema became a form of mass consumption.

Correct Choices

Choice C, "Early cinema allowed individuals to use special machines to view films privately," is correct because it represents one of the chief differences between Kinetoscope and projection viewing. This idea is discussed at several places in the passage. It is mentioned in paragraphs 1, 3, 4, and 6. Thus it is a basic, recurring theme of the passage and, as such, a "major idea."

Choice E, "The development of projection technology made it possible to project images on a large screen," is correct because this is a major idea that is treated in paragraphs 3, 4, 5, and 6. This development was essentially the reason that the cinema did "emerge as a form of mass consumption."

Choice F, "Once film images could be projected, the cinema became a form of mass consumption," is correct because it represents the primary theme of the passage. It is explicitly stated in the passage's opening sentence; then the remainder of the passage describes that evolution.

Incorrect Choices

Choice A, "Kinetoscope parlors for viewing films were modeled on phonograph parlors," is incorrect because, while true, it is a minor detail. The Kinetoscope parlors are described in paragraph 2, but the fact that they were modeled on phonograph parlors is not central to the "evolution" of cinema.

Choice B, "Thomas Edison's design of the Kinetoscope inspired the development of large-screen projection," is incorrect because it is not clear that it is true, based on the passage. While it may be inferred from paragraph 3 that the Kinetoscope inspired the development of large-screen projection, it seems more likely that the pursuit of greater profits is what really inspired large-screen-projection development. Since this answer is not clearly supported in the passage, it cannot be considered a "main idea" and is incorrect.

Choice D, "Slide-and-lantern shows had been presented to audiences of hundreds of spectators," is incorrect because it is a minor detail, mentioned only once in paragraph 4 as part of a larger list of theatrical spectacles.

PRACTICE SET 4

AGGRESSION

When one animal attacks another, it engages in the most obvious example of aggressive behavior. Psychologists have adopted several approaches to understanding aggressive behavior in people.

The Biological Approach. Numerous biological structures and chemicals appear to be involved in aggression. One is the hypothalamus, a region of the brain. In response to certain stimuli, many animals show instinctive aggressive reactions. The hypothalamus appears to be involved in this inborn reaction pattern: electrical stimulation of part of the hypothalamus triggers stereotypical aggressive behaviors in many animals. In people, however, whose brains are more complex, other brain structures apparently moderate possible instincts.

An offshoot of the biological approach called *sociobiology* suggests that aggression is natural and even desirable for people. Sociobiology views much social behavior, including aggressive behavior, as genetically determined. Consider Darwin's theory of evolution. Darwin held that many more individuals are produced than can find food and survive into adulthood. A struggle for survival follows. Those individuals who possess characteristics that provide them with an advantage in the struggle for existence are more likely to survive and contribute their genes to the next generation. In many species, such characteristics include aggressiveness. Because aggressive individuals are more likely to survive and reproduce, whatever genes are linked to aggressive behavior are more likely to be transmitted to subsequent generations.

The sociobiological view has been attacked on numerous grounds. One is that people's capacity to outwit other species, not their aggressiveness, appears to be the dominant factor in human survival. Another is that there is too much variation among people to believe that they are dominated by, or at the mercy of, aggressive impulses.

The Psychodynamic Approach. Theorists adopting the psychodynamic approach hold that inner conflicts are crucial for understanding human behavior, including aggression. Sigmund Freud, for example, believed that aggressive impulses are inevitable reactions to the frustrations of daily life. Children normally desire to vent aggressive impulses on other people, including their parents, because even the most attentive parents cannot gratify all of their demands immediately. Yet children, also fearing their parents' punishment and the loss of parental love, come to repress most aggressive impulses. The Freudian perspective, in a sense, sees us as "steam engines." By holding in rather than venting "steam," we set the stage for future explosions. Pent-up aggressive impulses demand outlets. They may be expressed toward parents in indirect ways such as destroying furniture, or they may be expressed toward strangers later in life.

According to psychodynamic theory, the best ways to prevent harmful aggression may be to encourage less harmful aggression. In the steam-engine analogy, verbal aggression may vent some of the aggressive steam. So might cheering on one's favorite sports team. Psychoanalysts, therapists adopting a psychodynamic approach, refer to the venting of aggressive impulses as "catharsis."[1] Catharsis is theorized to be a safety valve. But research findings on the usefulness of catharsis are mixed. Some studies suggest that catharsis leads to reductions in tension and a lowered likelihood of future aggression. Other studies, however, suggest that letting some steam escape actually encourages more aggression later on.

The Cognitive Approach. Cognitive psychologists assert that our behavior is influenced by our values, by the ways in which we interpret our situations, and by choice. For example, people who believe that aggression is necessary and justified—as during wartime—are likely to act aggressively, whereas people who believe that a particular war or act of aggression is unjust, or who think that aggression is never justified, are less likely to behave aggressively.

One cognitive theory suggests that aggravating and painful events trigger unpleasant feelings. These feelings, in turn, can lead to aggressive action, but *not* automatically. Cognitive factors intervene. People *decide* whether they will act aggressively or not on the basis of factors such as their experiences with aggression and their interpretation of other people's motives. Supporting evidence comes from research showing that aggressive people often distort other people's motives. For example, they assume that other people mean them harm when they do not.

1. Catharsis: In psychodynamic theory, the purging of strong emotions or the relieving of tensions

Directions: Now answer the questions.

An offshoot of the biological approach called *sociobiology* suggests that aggression is natural and even desirable for people. Sociobiology views much social behavior, including aggressive behavior, as genetically determined. Consider Darwin's theory of evolution. Darwin held that many more individuals are produced than can find food and survive into adulthood. A struggle for survival follows. Those individuals who possess characteristics that provide them with an advantage in the struggle for existence are more likely to survive and contribute their genes to the next generation. In many species, such characteristics include aggressiveness. Because aggressive individuals are more likely to survive and reproduce, whatever genes are linked to aggressive behavior are more likely to be transmitted to subsequent generations.

1. According to Darwin's theory of evolution, members of a species are forced to struggle for survival because

   Ⓐ not all individuals are skilled in finding food
   Ⓑ individuals try to defend their young against attackers
   Ⓒ many more individuals are born than can survive until the age of reproduction
   Ⓓ individuals with certain genes are more likely to reach adulthood

PARAGRAPH 5

The Psychodynamic Approach. Theorists adopting the psychodynamic approach hold that inner conflicts are crucial for understanding human behavior, including aggression. Sigmund Freud, for example, believed that aggressive impulses are inevitable reactions to the frustrations of daily life. Children normally desire to vent aggressive impulses on other people, including their parents, because even the most attentive parents cannot gratify all of their demands immediately. Yet children, also fearing their parents' punishment and the loss of parental love, come to repress most aggressive impulses. The Freudian perspective, in a sense, sees us as "steam engines." By holding in rather than venting "steam," we set the stage for future explosions. Pent-up aggressive impulses demand outlets. They may be expressed toward parents in indirect ways such as destroying furniture, or they may be expressed toward strangers later in life.

2. The word "gratify" in the passage is closest in meaning to

   Ⓐ identify
   Ⓑ modify
   Ⓒ satisfy
   Ⓓ simplify

3. The word "they" in the passage refers to

   Ⓐ future explosions
   Ⓑ pent-up aggressive impulses
   Ⓒ outlets
   Ⓓ indirect ways

4. According to paragraph 5, Freud believed that children experience conflict between a desire to vent aggression on their parents and

   Ⓐ a frustration that their parents do not give them everything they want
   Ⓑ a fear that their parents will punish them and stop loving them
   Ⓒ a desire to take care of their parents
   Ⓓ a desire to vent aggression on other family members

5. Freud describes people as "steam engines" in order to make the point that people

   Ⓐ deliberately build up their aggression to make themselves stronger
   Ⓑ usually release aggression in explosive ways
   Ⓒ must vent their aggression to prevent it from building up
   Ⓓ typically lose their aggression if they do not express it

P A R A G R A P H 7

The Cognitive Approach. Cognitive psychologists assert that our behavior is influenced by our values, by the ways in which we interpret our situations, and by choice. For example, people who believe that aggression is necessary and justified—as during wartime—are likely to act aggressively, whereas people who believe that a particular war or act of aggression is unjust, or who think that aggression is never justified, are less likely to behave aggressively.

P A R A G R A P H 8

One cognitive theory suggests that aggravating and painful events trigger unpleasant feelings. These feelings, in turn, can lead to aggressive action, but *not* automatically. Cognitive factors intervene. People *decide* whether they will act aggressively or not on the basis of factors such as their experiences with aggression and their interpretation of other people's motives. Supporting evidence comes from research showing that aggressive people often distort other people's motives. For example, they assume that other people mean them harm when they do not.

6. Which of the sentences below best expresses the essential information in the highlighted sentence in the passage? Incorrect answer choices change the meaning in important ways or leave out essential information.

   (A) People who believe that they are fighting a just war act aggressively while those who believe that they are fighting an unjust war do not.

   (B) People who believe that aggression is necessary and justified are more likely to act aggressively than those who believe differently.

   (C) People who normally do not believe that aggression is necessary and justified may act aggressively during wartime.

   (D) People who believe that aggression is necessary and justified do not necessarily act aggressively during wartime.

7. According to the cognitive approach described in paragraphs 7 and 8, all of the following may influence the decision whether to act aggressively EXCEPT a person's

   (A) moral values
   (B) previous experiences with aggression
   (C) instinct to avoid aggression
   (D) beliefs about other people's intentions

PARAGRAPH 5

The Psychodynamic Approach. Theorists adopting the psychodynamic approach hold that inner conflicts are crucial for understanding human behavior, including aggression. Sigmund Freud, for example, believed that aggressive impulses are inevitable reactions to the frustrations of daily life. Children normally desire to vent aggressive impulses on other people, including their parents, because even the most attentive parents cannot gratify all of their demands immediately. **(A)** Yet children, also fearing their parents' punishment and the loss of parental love, come to repress most aggressive impulses. **(B)** The Freudian perspective, in a sense, sees us as "steam engines." **(C)** By holding in rather than venting "steam," we set the stage for future explosions. **(D)** Pent-up aggressive impulses demand outlets. They may be expressed toward parents in indirect ways such as destroying furniture, or they may be expressed toward strangers later in life.

8. **Directions:** Look at the part of the passage that is displayed above. The letters **(A)**, **(B)**, **(C)**, and **(D)** indicate where the following sentence could be added.

   According to Freud, however, impulses that have been repressed continue to exist and demand expression.

   Where would the sentence best fit?

   (A) Choice A
   (B) Choice B
   (C) Choice C
   (D) Choice D

9. **Directions:** Complete the table below by matching five of the six answer choices with the approach to aggression that they exemplify. **This question is worth 3 points.**

Approach to Understanding Aggression	Associated Claims
Biological Approach	• _____
Psychodynamic Approach	• _____
	• _____
Cognitive Approach	• _____
	• _____

Answer Choices

A Aggressive impulses toward people are sometimes expressed in indirect ways.
B Aggressiveness is often useful for individuals in the struggle for survival.
C Aggressive behavior may involve a misunderstanding of other people's intentions.
D The need to express aggressive impulses declines with age.
E Acting aggressively is the result of a choice influenced by a person's values and beliefs.
F Repressing aggressive impulses can result in aggressive behavior.

PRACTICE SET 4 ANSWERS AND EXPLANATIONS

1. **C** This is a Factual Information question asking for specific information that can be found in the passage. The correct answer is choice C, "many more individuals are born than can survive until the age of reproduction." This answer choice is essentially a paraphrase of paragraph 3, sentence 4: "Darwin held that many more individuals are produced than can find food and survive into adulthood." Choices A and B are not mentioned at all. Choice D may be true, but it is not stated in the passage as a fact; an inference is needed to support it.

2. **C** This is a Vocabulary question. The word being tested is *gratify*. It is highlighted in the passage. The correct answer is choice C, "satisfy." If a person's desires are gratified, those desires are fulfilled. Thus the person is satisfied.

3. **B** This is a Reference question. The word being tested is *they*. It is highlighted in the passage. The correct answer is choice B, "pent-up aggressive impulses." This is a simple pronoun-referent item. The word *they* here refers to something that "may be expressed toward strangers later in life." This is the "outlet" toward which the "aggressive impulses" mentioned may be directed.

4. **B** This is a Factual Information question asking for specific information that can be found in paragraph 5. The correct answer is choice B, "a fear that their parents will punish them and stop loving them." The question asks what causes the conflict between the desire to vent aggression and children's fears. The answer is found in paragraph 5 in the sentence that reads, "Yet children, also fearing their parents' punishment and the loss of parental love, come to repress most aggressive impulses." Answer choice B is the only choice that correctly identifies the cause of the conflict created by repressing aggression in children.

5. **C** This is a Rhetorical Purpose question. It asks you why the author mentions that Freud described people as "steam engines" in the passage. The phrase being tested is highlighted in the passage. The correct answer is choice C, "must vent their aggression to prevent it from building up." Steam engines will explode if their steam builds up indefinitely. The same is true of people, as choice C indicates. The other choices are not necessarily true of both people and steam engines, so they are incorrect.

6. **B** This is a Sentence Simplification question. As with all of these questions, a single sentence in the passage is highlighted:

> For example, people who believe that aggression is necessary and justified—as during wartime—are likely to act aggressively, whereas people who believe that a particular war or act of aggression is unjust, or who think that aggression is never justified, are less likely to behave aggressively.

The correct answer is choice B. It contains all of the essential information in the highlighted sentence. The highlighted sentence compares people who believe particular acts of aggression are necessary and those who do not, in terms of their relative likelihood to act aggressively under certain conditions. This is precisely what choice B says: "People who believe that aggression is necessary and justified are more likely to act aggressively than those who believe differently." It compares the behavior of one type of person with that of another type of person. Nothing essential has been left out, and the meaning has not been changed.

Choice A changes the meaning of the sentence; it says categorically that "those [people] who believe that they are fighting an unjust war do not [act aggressively]." The highlighted sentence merely says that such people are "less likely" to act aggressively, not that they never will; this changes the meaning.

Choice C says, "People who normally do not believe that aggression is necessary and justified may act aggressively during wartime." This is incorrect because it leaves out critical information: it does not mention people who do believe aggression is necessary. This choice does not make the same comparison as the highlighted sentence.

Choice D, "People who believe that aggression is necessary and justified do not necessarily act aggressively during wartime," also changes the meaning of the sentence by leaving out essential information. In this choice, no mention is made of people who do not believe aggression is necessary. This choice does not make the same comparison as the highlighted sentence.

7. **C** This is a Negative Factual Information question asking for specific information that can be found in paragraphs 7 and 8. Choice C is the correct answer.

Choice A, "moral values," is explicitly mentioned as one of the influences on aggressive behavior, so it is incorrect. Choices B ("previous experiences") and D ("beliefs about other people") are both explicitly mentioned in this context. The sentence in paragraph 8 says, "People decide whether they will act aggressively or not on the basis of factors such as their experiences with aggression and their interpretation of other people's motives." Choice C, the "instinct to avoid aggression," is not mentioned, so it is the correct answer here.

8. **Ⓑ** This is an Insert Text question. You can see the four possible answer choices in paragraph 5.

The Psychodynamic Approach. Theorists adopting the psychodynamic approach hold that inner conflicts are crucial for understanding human behavior, including aggression. Sigmund Freud, for example, believed that aggressive impulses are inevitable reactions to the frustrations of daily life. Children normally desire to vent aggressive impulses on other people, including their parents, because even the most attentive parents cannot gratify all of their demands immediately. **(A)** Yet children, also fearing their parents' punishment and the loss of parental love, come to repress most aggressive impulses. **(B)** The Freudian perspective, in a sense, sees us as "steam engines." **(C)** By holding in rather than venting "steam," we set the stage for future explosions. **(D)** Pent-up aggressive impulses demand outlets. They may be expressed toward parents in indirect ways such as destroying furniture, or they may be expressed toward strangers later in life.

The sentence provided, "According to Freud, however, impulses that have been repressed continue to exist and demand expression," is best inserted at choice **(B)**.

Choice **(B)** is correct because the sentence being inserted is a connective sentence, connecting the idea of childhood repression in the preceding sentence to the "Freudian perspective" in the sentence that follows. The use of the word *however* in this sentence indicates that an idea already introduced (the repression of children's aggressive impulses) is being modified. Here, the inserted sentence tells us that Freud thought that even though these impulses are repressed, they continue to exist. This serves as a connection to the next sentence and the "Freudian perspective." Inserting the sentence at choice **(A)** would place the modification ("however, impulses . . . continue to exist") before the idea that it modifies (repression of impulses). This makes no logical sense. Inserting the sentence at choice **(C)** would move the modifying sentence away from its logical position immediately following the idea that it modifies (repression of impulses). Placing the insert sentence at choice **(D)** moves the sentence farther from its logical antecedent and with no connection to the sentence that follows it.

9. This is a Fill in a Table question. It is completed correctly below. Choice B is the correct answer for the "Biological Approach" row. Choices A and F are the correct answers for the "Psychodynamic Approach" row. Choices C and E are the correct answers for the "Cognitive Approach" row. Choice D should not be used in any row.

Directions: Complete the table below by matching five of the six answer choices with the approach to aggression that they exemplify. **This question is worth 3 points.**

Approach to Understanding Aggression	Associated Claims
Biological Approach	B Aggressiveness is often useful for individuals in the struggle for survival.
Psychodynamic Approach	A Aggressive impulses toward people are sometimes expressed in indirect ways. F Repressing aggressive impulses can result in aggressive behavior.
Cognitive Approach	C Aggressive behavior may involve a misunderstanding of other people's intentions. E Acting aggressively is the result of a choice influenced by a person's values and beliefs.

Answer Choices

A Aggressive impulses toward people are sometimes expressed in indirect ways.

B Aggressiveness is often useful for individuals in the struggle for survival.

C Aggressive behavior may involve a misunderstanding of other people's intentions.

D The need to express aggressive impulses declines with age.

E Acting aggressively is the result of a choice influenced by a person's values and beliefs.

F Repressing aggressive impulses can result in aggressive behavior.

Correct Choices

Choice A: "Aggressive impulses toward people are sometimes expressed in indirect ways" belongs in the "Psychodynamic Approach" row based on paragraph 5. That paragraph, in explaining the psychodynamic approach, states, "Pent-up aggressive impulses demand outlets. They may be expressed toward parents in indirect ways such as destroying furniture . . ."

Choice B: "Aggressiveness is often useful for individuals in the struggle for survival" belongs in the "Biological Approach" row because, as stated in paragraph 3, "An offshoot of the biological approach called *sociobiology* suggests that aggression is natural and even desirable for people." The remainder of that paragraph explains the ways in which aggressive behavior can be useful in the struggle for survival. Neither of the other approaches discusses this idea, so this answer choice belongs here.

Choice C: "Aggressive behavior may involve a misunderstanding of other people's intentions" belongs in the "Cognitive Approach" row based on paragraph 8. The theme of that paragraph is that people decide to be aggressive (or not) largely based upon their interpretations of other people's motives. It goes on to say that these interpretations may be "distorted," or misunderstood. Accordingly, this answer choice belongs in this row.

Choice E: "Acting aggressively is the result of a choice influenced by a person's values and beliefs" belongs in the "Cognitive Approach" row based on paragraph 7, which states, "Cognitive psychologists assert that our behavior is influenced by our values, by the ways in which we interpret our situations, and by choice." Thus this is an important aspect of the cognitive approach.

Choice F: "Repressing aggressive impulses can result in aggressive behavior" belongs in the "Psychodynamic Approach" row based on paragraphs 5 and 6. Both of those paragraphs explicitly make this point in the section of the passage on the psychodynamic approach.

Incorrect Choice

Choice D: "The need to express aggressive impulses declines with age" is not mentioned in connection with any of the approaches to aggression discussed in the passage, so it should not be used.

PRACTICE SET 5

ARTISANS AND INDUSTRIALIZATION

Before 1815 manufacturing in the United States had been done in homes or shops by skilled artisans. As master craftworkers, they imparted the knowledge of their trades to apprentices and journeymen. In addition, women often worked in their homes part-time, making finished articles from raw material supplied by merchant capitalists. After 1815 this older form of manufacturing began to give way to factories with machinery tended by unskilled or semiskilled laborers. Cheap transportation networks, the rise of cities, and the availability of capital and credit all stimulated the shift to factory production.

The creation of a labor force that was accustomed to working in factories did not occur easily. Before the rise of the factory, artisans had worked within the home. Apprentices were considered part of the family, and masters were responsible not only for teaching their apprentices a trade but also for providing them some education and for supervising their moral behavior. Journeymen knew that if they perfected their skill, they could become respected master artisans with their own shops. Also, skilled artisans did not work by the clock, at a steady pace, but rather in bursts of intense labor alternating with more leisurely time.

The factory changed that. Goods produced by factories were not as finished or elegant as those done by hand, and pride in craftsmanship gave way to the pressure to increase rates of productivity. The new methods of doing business involved a new and stricter sense of time. Factory life necessitated a more regimented schedule, where work began at the sound of a bell and workers kept machines going at a constant pace. At the same time, workers were required to discard old habits, for industrialism demanded a worker who was alert, dependable, and self-disciplined. Absenteeism and lateness hurt productivity and, since work was specialized, disrupted the regular factory routine. Industrialization not only produced a fundamental change in the way work was organized; it transformed the very nature of work.

The first generation to experience these changes did not adopt the new attitudes easily. The factory clock became the symbol of the new work rules. One mill worker who finally quit complained revealingly about "obedience to the ding-dong of the bell—just as though we are so many living machines." With the loss of personal freedom also came the loss of standing in the community. Unlike artisan workshops in which apprentices worked closely with the masters supervising them, factories sharply separated workers from management. Few workers rose through the ranks to supervisory positions, and even fewer could achieve the artisan's dream of setting up one's own business. Even well-paid workers sensed their decline in status.

In this newly emerging economic order, workers sometimes organized to protect their rights and traditional ways of life. Craftworkers such as carpenters, printers, and tailors formed unions, and in 1834 individual unions came together in the National Trades' Union. The labor movement gathered some momentum in the decade before the Panic of 1837, but in the depression that followed, labor's strength collapsed. During hard times, few workers were willing to strike[1] or engage in collective action. And skilled craftworkers, who spearheaded the union movement, did not feel a particularly strong bond with semiskilled factory workers and unskilled laborers. More than a decade of agitation did finally bring a workday shortened to 10 hours to most industries by the 1850s, and the courts also recognized workers' right to strike, but these gains had little immediate impact.

Workers were united in resenting the industrial system and their loss of status, but they were divided by ethnic and racial antagonisms, gender, conflicting religious perspectives, occupational differences, political party loyalties, and disagreements over tactics. For them, the factory and industrialism were not agents of opportunity but reminders of their loss of independence and a measure of control over their lives. As United States society became more specialized and differentiated, greater extremes of wealth began to appear. And as the new markets created fortunes for the few, the factory system lowered the wages of workers by dividing labor into smaller, less skilled tasks.

1. Strike: A stopping of work that is organized by workers

Directions: Now answer the questions.

1. Which of the following can be inferred from the passage about articles manufactured before 1815?

   Ⓐ They were primarily produced by women.
   Ⓑ They were generally produced in shops rather than in homes.
   Ⓒ They were produced with more concern for quality than for speed of production.
   Ⓓ They were produced mostly in large cities with extensive transportation networks.

PARAGRAPH 2

The creation of a labor force that was accustomed to working in factories did not occur easily. Before the rise of the factory, artisans had worked within the home. Apprentices were considered part of the family, and masters were responsible not only for teaching their apprentices a trade but also for providing them some education and for supervising their moral behavior. Journeymen knew that if they perfected their skill, they could become respected master artisans with their own shops. Also, skilled artisans did not work by the clock, at a steady pace, but rather in bursts of intense labor alternating with more leisurely time.

2. Which of the sentences below best expresses the essential information in the highlighted sentence in the passage? Incorrect answer choices change the meaning in important ways or leave out essential information.

   Ⓐ Masters demanded moral behavior from apprentices but often treated them irresponsibly.
   Ⓑ The responsibilities of the master to the apprentice went beyond the teaching of a trade.
   Ⓒ Masters preferred to maintain the trade within the family by supervising and educating the younger family members.
   Ⓓ Masters who trained members of their own family as apprentices demanded excellence from them.

PARAGRAPH 3

The factory changed that. Goods produced by factories were not as finished or elegant as those done by hand, and pride in craftsmanship gave way to the pressure to increase rates of productivity. The new methods of doing business involved a new and stricter sense of time. Factory life necessitated a more regimented schedule, where work began at the sound of a bell and workers kept machines going at a constant pace. At the same time, workers were required to discard old habits, for industrialism demanded a worker who was alert, dependable, and self-disciplined. Absenteeism and lateness hurt productivity and, since work was specialized, disrupted the regular factory routine. Industrialization not only produced a fundamental change in the way work was organized; it transformed the very nature of work.

3. The word "disrupted" in the passage is closest in meaning to

(A) prolonged
(B) established
(C) followed
(D) upset

PARAGRAPH 4

The first generation to experience these changes did not adopt the new attitudes easily. The factory clock became the symbol of the new work rules. One mill worker who finally quit complained revealingly about "obedience to the ding-dong of the bell—just as though we are so many living machines." With the loss of personal freedom also came the loss of standing in the community. Unlike artisan workshops in which apprentices worked closely with the masters supervising them, factories sharply separated workers from management. Few workers rose through the ranks to supervisory positions, and even fewer could achieve the artisan's dream of setting up one's own business. Even well-paid workers sensed their decline in status.

4. In paragraph 4, the author includes the quotation from a mill worker in order to

(A) support the idea that it was difficult for workers to adjust to working in factories
(B) show that workers sometimes quit because of the loud noise made by factory machinery
(C) argue that clocks did not have a useful function in factories
(D) emphasize that factories were most successful when workers revealed their complaints

5. All of the following are mentioned in paragraph 4 as consequences of the new system for workers EXCEPT a loss of

(A) freedom
(B) status in the community
(C) opportunities for advancement
(D) contact among workers who were not managers

PARAGRAPH 5

In this newly emerging economic order, workers sometimes organized to protect their rights and traditional ways of life. Craftworkers such as carpenters, printers, and tailors formed unions, and in 1834 individual unions came together in the National Trades' Union. The labor movement gathered some momentum in the decade before the Panic of 1837, but in the depression that followed, labor's strength collapsed. During hard times, few workers were willing to strike or engage in collective action. And skilled craftworkers, who spearheaded the union movement, did not feel a particularly strong bond with semiskilled factory workers and unskilled laborers. More than a decade of agitation did finally bring a workday shortened to 10 hours to most industries by the 1850s, and the courts also recognized workers' right to strike, but these gains had little immediate impact.

6. Which of the following statements about the labor movement of the 1800s is supported by paragraph 5?

(A) It was successful during times of economic crisis.
(B) Its primary purpose was to benefit unskilled laborers
(C) It was slow to improve conditions for workers.
(D) It helped workers of all skill levels form a strong bond with each other.

PARAGRAPH 6

Workers were united in resenting the industrial system and their loss of status, but they were divided by ethnic and racial antagonisms, gender, conflicting religious perspectives, occupational differences, political party loyalties, and disagreements over tactics. For them, the factory and industrialism were not agents of opportunity but reminders of their loss of independence and a measure of control over their lives. As United States society became more specialized and differentiated, greater extremes of wealth began to appear. And as the new markets created fortunes for the few, the factory system lowered the wages of workers by dividing labor into smaller, less skilled tasks.

7. The author identifies "political party loyalties" and "disagreements over tactics" as two of several factors that

(A) encouraged workers to demand higher wages
(B) created divisions among workers
(C) caused work to become more specialized
(D) increased workers' resentment of the industrial system

PARAGRAPH 1

Before 1815 manufacturing in the United States had been done in homes or shops by skilled artisans. **(A)** As master craftworkers, they imparted the knowledge of their trades to apprentices and journeymen. **(B)** In addition, women often worked in their homes part-time, making finished articles from raw material supplied by merchant capitalists. **(C)** After 1815 this older form of manufacturing began to give way to factories with machinery tended by unskilled or semiskilled laborers. **(D)** Cheap transportation networks, the rise of cities, and the availability of capital and credit all stimulated the shift to factory production.

8. **Directions:** Look at the part of the passage that is displayed above. The letters **(A)**, **(B)**, **(C)**, and **(D)** indicate where the following sentence could be added.

   This new form of manufacturing depended on the movement of goods to distant locations and a centralized source of laborers.

   Where would the sentence best fit?

   Ⓐ Choice A
   Ⓑ Choice B
   Ⓒ Choice C
   Ⓓ Choice D

9. **Directions:** Complete the table below by indicating which of the answer choices describe characteristics of the period before 1815 and which describe characteristics of the 1815–1850 period. **This question is worth 3 points.**

Before 1815	1815–1850
•	•
•	•
	•

Answer Choices

A A united, highly successful labor movement took shape.
B Workers took pride in their workmanship.
C The income gap between the rich and the poor increased greatly.
D Transportation networks began to decline.
E Emphasis was placed on following schedules.
F Workers went through an extensive period of training.
G Few workers expected to own their own businesses.

PRACTICE SET 5 ANSWERS AND EXPLANATIONS

1. **C** This is an Inference question asking for an inference that can be supported by the passage. The correct answer is choice C, "They were produced with more concern for quality than for speed of production."

   A number of statements throughout the passage support choice C. Paragraph 1 states, "Before 1815 manufacturing in the United States had been done in homes or shops by skilled artisans . . . After 1815 this older form of manufacturing began to give way to factories with machinery tended by unskilled or semiskilled laborers."

   Paragraph 2 states, "Before the rise of the factory . . . skilled artisans did not work by the clock, at a steady pace, but rather in bursts of intense labor alternating with more leisurely time."

   Paragraph 3 states, "The factory changed that. Goods produced by factories were not as finished or elegant as those done by hand, and pride in craftsmanship gave way to the pressure to increase rates of productivity."

   Taken together, these three statements, about production rates, the rise of factories after 1815, and the decline of craftsmanship after 1815, support the inference that before 1815, the emphasis had been on quality rather than on speed of production. Answer choices A, B, and D are all contradicted by the passage.

2. **B** This is a Sentence Simplification question. As with all of these questions, a single sentence in the passage is highlighted:

   > Apprentices were considered part of the family, and masters were responsible not only for teaching their apprentices a trade but also for providing them some education and for supervising their moral behavior.

   The correct answer is choice B. Choice B contains all of the essential information in the highlighted sentence. The highlighted sentence explains why (part of the family) and how (education, moral behavior) a master's responsibility went beyond teaching a trade. The essential information is the fact that the master's responsibility went beyond teaching a trade. Therefore choice B contains all that is essential without changing the meaning of the highlighted sentence.

   Choice A changes the meaning of the highlighted sentence by stating that masters often treated apprentices irresponsibly.

   Choice C contradicts the essential meaning of the highlighted sentence. The fact that "Apprentices were considered part of the family" suggests that they were not actual family members.

   Choice D, like choice C, changes the meaning of the highlighted sentence by discussing family members as apprentices.

3. **D** This is a Vocabulary question. The word being tested is *disrupted*. It is highlighted in the passage. The correct answer is choice D, "upset." The word *upset* here is used in the context of "hurting productivity." When something is hurt or damaged, it is "upset."

4. **A** This is a Factual Information question asking for specific information that can be found in paragraph 4. The correct answer is choice A, "support the idea that it was difficult for workers to adjust to working in factories." The paragraph begins by stating that workers did not adopt new attitudes toward work easily and that the clock symbolized the new work rules. The author provides the quotation as evidence of that difficulty. There is no indication in the paragraph that workers quit due to loud noise, so choice B is incorrect. Choice C (usefulness of clocks) is contradicted by the paragraph. The factory clock was "useful," but workers hated it. Choice D (workers' complaints as a cause of a factory's success) is not discussed in this paragraph.

5. **D** This is a Negative Factual Information question asking for specific information that can be found in paragraph 4. Choice D, "contact among workers who were not managers," is the correct answer. The paragraph explicitly contradicts this by stating that "factories sharply separated workers from management." The paragraph explicitly states that workers lost choice A (freedom), choice B (status in the community), and choice C (opportunities for advancement) in the new system, so those choices are all incorrect.

6. **C** This is a Factual Information question asking for specific information that can be found in paragraph 5. The correct answer is choice C, "It was slow to improve conditions for workers." The paragraph states, "More than a decade of agitation did finally bring a workday shortened to 10 hours to most industries by the 1850s, and the courts also recognized workers' right to strike, but these gains had little immediate impact." This statement explicitly supports choice C. All three other choices are contradicted by the paragraph.

7. **B** This is a Factual Information question asking for specific information about a particular phrase in the passage. The phrase in question is highlighted in the passage. The correct answer is choice B, "created divisions among workers." The paragraph states, "they (workers) were divided by ethnic and racial antagonisms, gender, conflicting religious perspectives, occupational differences, political party loyalties, and disagreements over tactics." So "political party loyalties" and "disagreements over tactics" are explicitly stated as two causes of division among workers. The other choices are not stated and are incorrect.

8. **D** This is an Insert Text question. You can see the four possible answer choices in paragraph 1.

Before 1815 manufacturing in the United States had been done in homes or shops by skilled artisans. **(A)** As master craftworkers, they imparted the knowledge of their trades to apprentices and journeymen. **(B)** In addition, women often worked in their homes part-time, making finished articles from raw material supplied by merchant capitalists. **(C)** After 1815 this older form of manufacturing began to give way to factories with machinery tended by unskilled or semiskilled laborers. **(D)** Cheap transportation networks, the rise of cities, and the availability of capital and credit all stimulated the shift to factory production.

The sentence provided, "This new form of manufacturing depended on the movement of goods to distant locations and a centralized source of laborers," is best inserted at choice **(D)**. The inserted sentence refers explicitly to a "new form of manufacturing." This "new form of manufacturing" is the one mentioned in the sentence preceding choice **(D)**, "factories with machinery tended by unskilled or semiskilled laborers." The inserted sentence then explains that this new system "depended on the movement of goods to distant locations and a centralized source of laborers." The sentence that follows choice **(D)** goes on to say, "Cheap transportation networks, the rise of cities, and the availability of capital and credit all stimulated the shift to factory production." Thus the inserted sentence contains references to both the sentence before choice **(D)** and the sentence after choice **(D)**. This is not true of any of the other possible insert points, so choice **(D)** is the correct answer.

9.   This is a Fill in a Table question. It is completed correctly below. The correct choices for the "Before 1815" column are B and F. Choices C, E, and G belong in the "1815–1850" column. Choices A and D should not be used in either column.

Directions: Complete the table below by indicating which of the answer choices describe characteristics of the period before 1815 and which describe characteristics of the 1815–1850 period. **This question is worth 3 points.**

Before 1815	1815–1850
B Workers took pride in their workmanship.	C The income gap between the rich and the poor increased greatly.
F Workers went through an extensive period of training.	E Emphasis was placed on following schedules.
	G Few workers expected to own their own businesses.

Answer Choices

A   A united, highly successful labor movement took shape.
B   Workers took pride in their workmanship.
C   The income gap between the rich and the poor increased greatly.
D   Transportation networks began to decline.
E   Emphasis was placed on following schedules.
F   Workers went through an extensive period of training.
G   Few workers expected to own their own businesses.

Correct Choices

Choice B: "Workers took pride in their workmanship" belongs in the "Before 1815" column because it is mentioned in the passage as one of the characteristics of labor before 1815.

Choice C: "The income gap between the rich and the poor increased greatly" belongs in the "1815–1850" column because it is mentioned in the passage as one of the characteristics of society that emerged in the period between 1815 and 1850.

Choice E: "Emphasis was placed on following schedules" belongs in the "1815–1850" column because it is mentioned in the passage as one of the characteristics of labor in the factory system that emerged between 1815 and 1850.

Choice F: "Workers went through an extensive period of training" belongs in the "Before 1815" column because it is mentioned in the passage as one of the characteristics of labor before 1815.

Choice G: "Few workers expected to own their own businesses" belongs in the "1815–1850" column because it is mentioned in the passage as one of the characteristics of society that emerged in the period between 1815 and 1850.

Incorrect Choices

Choice A: "A united, highly successful labor movement took shape" does not belong in the table because it contradicts the passage.

Choice D: "Transportation networks began to decline" does not belong in the table because it is not mentioned in the passage in connection with either the period before 1815 or the period between 1815 and 1850.

PRACTICE SET 6

SWIMMING MACHINES

Tunas, mackerels, and billfishes (marlins, sailfishes, and swordfish) swim continuously. Feeding, courtship, reproduction, and even "rest" are carried out while in constant motion. As a result, practically every aspect of the body form and function of these swimming "machines" is adapted to enhance their ability to swim.

Many of the adaptations of these fishes serve to reduce water resistance (drag). Interestingly enough, several of these hydrodynamic adaptations resemble features designed to improve the aerodynamics of high-speed aircraft. Though human engineers are new to the game, tunas and their relatives evolved their "high-tech" designs long ago.

Tunas, mackerels, and billfishes have made streamlining into an art form. Their bodies are sleek and compact. The body shapes of tunas, in fact, are nearly ideal from an engineering point of view. Most species lack scales over most of the body, making it smooth and slippery. The eyes lie flush with the body and do not protrude at all. They are also covered with a slick, transparent lid that reduces drag. The fins are stiff, smooth, and narrow, qualities that also help cut drag. When not in use, the fins are tucked into special grooves or depressions so that they lie flush with the body and do not break up its smooth contours. Airplanes retract their landing gear while in flight for the same reason.

Tunas, mackerels, and billfishes have even more sophisticated adaptations than these to improve their hydrodynamics. The long bill of marlins, sailfishes, and swordfish probably helps them slip through the water. Many supersonic aircraft have a similar needle at the nose.

Most tunas and billfishes have a series of keels and finlets near the tail. Although most of their scales have been lost, tunas and mackerels retain a patch of coarse scales near the head called the corselet. The keels, finlets, and corselet help direct the flow of water over the body surface in such a way as to reduce resistance (see the figure). Again, supersonic jets have similar features.

Because they are always swimming, tunas simply have to open their mouths and water is forced in and over their gills. Accordingly, they have lost most of the muscles that other fishes use to suck in water and push it past the gills. In fact, tunas must swim to breathe. They must also keep swimming to keep from sinking, since most have largely or completely lost the swim bladder, the gas-filled sac that helps most other fish remain buoyant.

One potential problem is that opening the mouth to breathe detracts from the streamlining of these fishes and tends to slow them down. Some species of tuna have specialized grooves in their tongue. It is thought that these grooves help to channel water through the mouth and out the gill slits, thereby reducing water resistance.

There are adaptations that increase the amount of forward thrust as well as those that reduce drag. Again, these fishes are the envy of engineers. Their high, narrow tails with swept-back tips are almost perfectly adapted to provide propulsion with the least possible effort. Perhaps most important of all to these and other fast swimmers is their ability to sense and make use of swirls and eddies (circular currents) in the water. They can glide past eddies that would slow them down and then gain extra thrust by "pushing off" the eddies. Scientists and engineers are beginning to study this ability of fishes in the hope of designing more efficient propulsion systems for ships.

The muscles of these fishes and the mechanism that maintains a warm body temperature are also highly efficient. A bluefin tuna in water of 7°C (45°F) can maintain a core temperature of over 25°C (77°F). This warm body temperature may help not only the muscles to work better, but also the brain and the eyes. The billfishes have gone one step further. They have evolved special "heaters" of modified muscle tissue that warm the eyes and brain, maintaining peak performance of these critical organs.

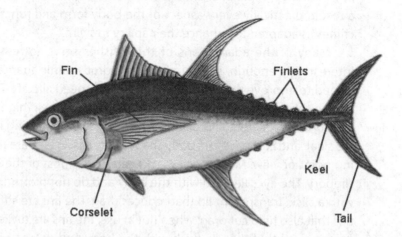

Fin   Finlets

Keel

Corselet   Tail

Directions: Now answer the questions.

PARAGRAPH 1

Tunas, mackerels, and billfishes (marlins, sailfishes, and swordfish) swim continuously. Feeding, courtship, reproduction, and even "rest" are carried out while in constant motion. As a result, practically every aspect of the body form and function of these swimming "machines" is adapted to enhance their ability to swim.

1. The word "enhance" in the passage is closest in meaning to

    (A) use
    (B) improve
    (C) counteract
    (D) balance

PARAGRAPH 3

Tunas, mackerels, and billfishes have made streamlining into an art form. Their bodies are sleek and compact. The body shapes of tunas, in fact, are nearly ideal from an engineering point of view. Most species lack scales over most of the body, making it smooth and slippery. The eyes lie flush with the body and do not protrude at all. They are also covered with a slick, transparent lid that reduces drag. The fins are stiff, smooth, and narrow, qualities that also help cut drag. When not in use, the fins are tucked into special grooves or depressions so that they lie flush with the body and do not break up its smooth contours. Airplanes retract their landing gear while in flight for the same reason.

2. Why does the author mention that "Airplanes retract their landing gear while in flight"?

Ⓐ To show that air resistance and water resistance work differently from each other
Ⓑ To argue that some fishes are better designed than airplanes are
Ⓒ To provide evidence that airplane engineers have studied the design of fish bodies
Ⓓ To demonstrate a similarity in design between certain fishes and airplanes

PARAGRAPH 4

Tunas, mackerels, and billfishes have even more sophisticated adaptations than these to improve their hydrodynamics. The long bill of marlins, sailfishes, and swordfish probably helps them slip through the water. Many supersonic aircraft have a similar needle at the nose.

3. According to paragraph 4, the long bills of marlins, sailfish, and swordfish probably help these fishes by

Ⓐ increasing their ability to defend themselves
Ⓑ allowing them to change direction easily
Ⓒ increasing their ability to detect odors
Ⓓ reducing water resistance as they swim

Because they are always swimming, tunas simply have to open their mouths and water is forced in and over their gills. Accordingly, they have lost most of the muscles that other fishes use to suck in water and push it past the gills. In fact, tunas must swim to breathe. They must also keep swimming to keep from sinking, since most have largely or completely lost the swim bladder, the gas-filled sac that helps most other fish remain buoyant.

4. According to the passage, which of the following is one of the reasons that tunas are in constant motion?

Ⓐ They lack a swim bladder.
Ⓑ They need to suck in more water than other fishes do.
Ⓒ They have large muscles for breathing.
Ⓓ They cannot open their mouths unless they are in motion.

One potential problem is that opening the mouth to breathe detracts from the streamlining of these fishes and tends to slow them down. Some species of tuna have specialized grooves in their tongue. It is thought that these grooves help to channel water through the mouth and out the gill slits, thereby reducing water resistance.

5. Which of the sentences below best expresses the essential information in the highlighted sentence in the passage? Incorrect answer choices change the meaning in important ways or leave out essential information.

Ⓐ These fishes often have a problem opening their mouths while swimming.
Ⓑ The streamlining of these fishes prevents them from slowing down.
Ⓒ The streamlining of these fishes tends to slow down their breathing.
Ⓓ Opening the mouth to breathe can reduce the speed of these fishes.

P
A
R
A
G
R
A
P
H

8
There are adaptations that increase the amount of forward thrust as well as those that reduce drag. Again, these fishes are the envy of engineers. Their high, narrow tails with swept-back tips are almost perfectly adapted to provide propulsion with the least possible effort. Perhaps most important of all to these and other fast swimmers is their ability to sense and make use of swirls and eddies (circular currents) in the water. They can glide past eddies that would slow them down and then gain extra thrust by "pushing off" the eddies. Scientists and engineers are beginning to study this ability of fishes in the hope of designing more efficient propulsion systems for ships.

6. According to the passage, one of the adaptations of fast-swimming fishes that might be used to improve the performance of ships is these fishes' ability to

   (A) swim directly through eddies
   (B) make efficient use of water currents
   (C) cover great distances without stopping
   (D) gain speed by forcing water past their gills

P
A
R
A
G
R
A
P
H

9
The muscles of these fishes and the mechanism that maintains a warm body temperature are also highly efficient. A bluefin tuna in water of 7°C (45°F) can maintain a core temperature of over 25°C (77°F). This warm body temperature may help not only the muscles to work better, but also the brain and the eyes. The billfishes have gone one step further. They have evolved special "heaters" of modified muscle tissue that warm the eyes and brain, maintaining peak performance of these critical organs.

7. According to paragraph 9, which of the following is true of bluefin tunas?

   (A) Their eyes and brain are more efficient than those of any other fish.
   (B) Their body temperature can change greatly depending on the water temperature.
   (C) They can swim in waters that are much colder than their own bodies.
   (D) They have special muscle tissue that warms their eyes and brain.

PARAGRAPHS 5 AND 6

Again, supersonic jets have similar features.

(A) Because they are always swimming, tunas simply have to open their mouths and water is forced in and over their gills. **(B)** Accordingly, they have lost most of the muscles that other fishes use to suck in water and push it past the gills. **(C)** In fact, tunas must swim to breathe. **(D)** They must also keep swimming to keep from sinking, since most have largely or completely lost the swim bladder, the gas-filled sac that helps most other fish remain buoyant.

8. **Directions:** Look at the part of the passage that is displayed above. The letters **(A)**, **(B)**, **(C)**, and **(D)** indicate where the following sentence could be added.

   Consequently, tunas do not need to suck in water.

   Where would the sentence best fit?

   (A) Choice A
   (B) Choice B
   (C) Choice C
   (D) Choice D

9. **Directions:** Complete the table below by indicating which features of fishes are associated in the passage with reducing water resistance and which are associated with increasing thrust. **This question is worth 3 points.**

Reducing Water Resistance	Increasing Thrust
•	•
•	•
•	

Answer Choices

A The absence of scales from most of the body
B The ability to take advantage of eddies
C The ability to feed and reproduce while swimming
D Eyes that do not protrude
E Fins that are stiff, narrow, and smooth
F The habit of swimming with the mouth open
G A high, narrow tail with swept-back tips

PRACTICE SET 6 ANSWERS AND EXPLANATIONS

1. **B** This is a Vocabulary question. The word being tested is *enhance*. It is highlighted in the passage. The correct answer is choice B, "improve." To *enhance* something means to "make it better." If something has been "improved," it has been made better.

2. **D** This is a Rhetorical Purpose question. It asks why the author mentions that "Airplanes retract their landing gear while in flight." The phrase being tested is highlighted in the passage. The correct answer is choice D, "To demonstrate a similarity in design between certain fishes and airplanes." The paragraph in which the highlighted phrase appears describes how certain fish use their fins. The highlighted phrase is used to provide a more familiar example (airplanes) of the principle involved to help the reader visualize how fins work. The paragraph does not discuss airplanes in any other context, so choices B and C are incorrect. Air and water resistance are not mentioned in this paragraph, so choice A is incorrect.

3. **D** This is a Factual Information question asking for specific information that can be found in paragraph 4. The correct answer is choice D, "reducing water resistance as they swim." The overall theme of the passage is how certain fish swim so efficiently. Paragraphs 1 and 2 make the general statement that "practically every aspect of the body form and function of these swimming 'machines' is adapted to enhance their ability to swim. Many of the adaptations of these fishes serve to reduce water resistance (drag)."

   Paragraph 4 explicitly states (emphasis added), "Tunas, mackerels, and billfishes have even more sophisticated *adaptations than these to improve their hydrodynamics. The long bill* of marlins, sailfishes, and swordfish probably helps them slip through the water." This is a specific example of one adaptation that these fish have made to increase their swimming efficiency. None of the other choices is mentioned in the paragraph.

4. **A** This is a Factual Information question asking for specific information that can be found in the passage. The correct answer is choice A, "They lack a swim bladder."

   Paragraph 6 explicitly states, "tunas must swim to breathe. They must also keep swimming to keep from sinking, since most have largely or completely lost the swim bladder." The other choices are not supported by the passage.

5. **D** This is a Sentence Simplification question. As with all of these questions, a single sentence in the passage is highlighted:

   One potential problem is that opening the mouth to breathe detracts from the streamlining of these fishes and tends to slow them down.

   The correct answer is choice D. That choice contains all of the essential ideas in the highlighted sentence. It is also the only choice that does not change the meaning of the sentence. It omits the fact that this is a "problem" and also that it "detracts from the streamlining" because that information is not essential to the meaning.

Choice A says that these fish have trouble opening their mouths while swimming, which is not true. Choice B, that streamlining prevents fish from slowing down, may be true, but it is not mentioned in this sentence. The fish are slowed down when they open their mouths, which reduces streamlining. Choice C, that streamlining slows the fishes' breathing, is also not mentioned.

6. **B** This is a Factual Information question asking for specific information that can be found in the passage. The correct answer is choice B, "make efficient use of water currents." Paragraph 8 explicitly states, "Perhaps most important of all to these and other fast swimmers is their ability to sense and make use of swirls and eddies (circular currents) in the water. They can glide past eddies that would slow them down and then gain extra thrust by 'pushing off' the eddies. Scientists and engineers are beginning to study this ability of fishes in the hope of designing more efficient propulsion systems for ships." The other choices are not mentioned in connection with the performance of ships.

7. **C** This is a Factual Information question asking for specific information that can be found in paragraph 9. The correct answer is choice C, "They can swim in waters that are much colder than their own bodies." That paragraph says, "A bluefin tuna in water of 7°C (45°F) can maintain a core temperature of over 25°C (77°F)." So it is clear that choice C is correct. Choice A is not stated in the paragraph. Choice B is contradicted by the paragraph. Choice D is true of billfish, not bluefin tuna.

8. **B** This is an Insert Text question. You can see the four possible answer choices in paragraph 6.

Again, supersonic jets have similar features.
   (A) Because they are always swimming, tunas simply have to open their mouths and water is forced in and over their gills. **(B)** Accordingly, they have lost most of the muscles that other fishes use to suck in water and push it past the gills. **(C)** In fact, tunas must swim to breathe. **(D)** They must also keep swimming to keep from sinking, since most have largely or completely lost the swim bladder, the gas-filled sac that helps most other fish remain buoyant.

The sentence provided, "Consequently, tunas do not need to suck in water," is best inserted at choice **(B)**. The sentence offers an explanation for the muscle loss described in the sentence that follows choice **(B)** and is a result of the fact described in the preceding sentence, which says that because the fish are always swimming, they only have to open their mouths to suck in water. Thus if the provided sentence is inserted at choice **(B)**, it offers a logical bridge between cause and effect. The sentence makes no logical sense anywhere else.

9. This is a Fill in a Table question. It is completed correctly below. The correct choices for the "Reducing Water Resistance" column are A, D, and E. Choices B and G belong in the "Increasing Thrust" column. Choices C and F should not be used in either column.

Directions: Complete the table below by indicating which features of fishes are associated in the passage with reducing water resistance and which are associated with increasing thrust. **This question is worth 3 points.**

Reducing Water Resistance	Increasing Thrust
A The absence of scales from most of the body	B The ability to take advantage of eddies
D Eyes that do not protrude	G A high, narrow tail with swept-back tips
E Fins that are stiff, narrow, and smooth	

Answer Choices

A The absence of scales from most of the body
B The ability to take advantage of eddies
C The ability to feed and reproduce while swimming
D Eyes that do not protrude
E Fins that are stiff, narrow, and smooth
F The habit of swimming with the mouth open
G A high, narrow tail with swept-back tips

Correct Choices

Choice A: "The absence of scales from most of the body" belongs in the "Reducing Water Resistance" column because it is mentioned in paragraphs 3 and 5 as a factor that reduces water resistance.

Choice B: "The ability to take advantage of eddies" belongs in the "Increasing Thrust" column because it is mentioned in paragraph 8 as a characteristic that helps increase thrust.

Choice D: "Eyes that do not protrude" belongs in the "Reducing Water Resistance" column because it is mentioned in paragraph 3 as a factor that reduces water resistance.

Choice E: "Fins that are stiff, narrow, and smooth" belongs in the "Reducing Water Resistance" column because it is mentioned in paragraph 3 as a factor that reduces water resistance.

Choice G: "A high, narrow tail with swept-back tips" belongs in the "Increasing Thrust" column because it is mentioned in paragraph 8 as a characteristic that helps increase thrust.

Incorrect Choices

Choice C: "The ability to feed and reproduce while swimming" does not belong in the table because it is not mentioned in the passage in connection with either reducing water resistance or increasing thrust.

Choice F: "The habit of swimming with the mouth open" does not belong in the table because it is not mentioned in the passage in connection with either reducing water resistance or increasing thrust.

Listening Section

Read this chapter to learn

- The 8 types of *TOEFL iBT®* test Listening questions
- How to recognize each Listening question type
- Tips for answering each Listening question type
- Strategies for preparing for the Listening section

在托福考试听力部分，考生将会听到3~4个讲座和2~3个对话。每个讲座后会有6个问题，每段对话后将有5个问题。托福考试听力部分的时间为41~57分钟。

Listening Materials

托福听力材料分对话和讲座两类。两者都来源于以英语为交流媒介的大学校园的真实语言。

每个讲座的长度为4~5分钟，每个对话的长度为3分钟，对话和讲座采用真实的学术语言。例如：在讲座中，教授可能会偶尔说些题外话，与学生互动。教授也可能旁征博引，抑或就问题的某一点进行深入挖掘。对话中，可能会出现诸如口误、自我纠正、重复等现实中的口语现象。在听对话和讲座时，考生应该学会做笔记。听力问题并不是在考查考生的记忆能力，而是理解对话和讲座的能力。

Conversations

对话发生的两个场景：

- 办公室
- 学生服务

对话都是发生在以英语为第一语言的大学校园的典型形式。第一个场景发生在学校办公室里。对话可能涉及学术内容或者与课程要求有关，例如：在教授的办公室，一个学生请求推迟交作业（非学术类对话）或者一个学生请求教授解释讲座中提到的内容（学术类对话）。第二个场景是关于学生服务的对话。对话一般发生在大学校园中，通常是非学术性的内容，例如学生询问关于住宿费用方面或课程注册方面的信息。每个对话后会有5个问题。

Lectures

托福听力考试中的讲座一般来源于老师的课堂授课。讲座节选可能只是教授的讲授，或是教授与学生之间的互动交流，如某个学生向教授提问，又如教授请一位学生回答问题。每个讲座时长约为5分钟，其后会有6个相关问题。

讲座内容涉及大学各学科的入门级课程知识。话题涉猎广泛，考生无须对材料所涉及的领域有预先的了解，因为回答问题所需要的信息都在讲座中给出。以下列表为考生提供了在听力部分会出现的话题的类别。

- Arts（艺术）
- Life Science（生命科学）
- Physical Science（自然科学）
- Social Science（社会科学）

艺术类讲座（Arts）包括以下话题：

- Architecture（建筑）
- Industrial design/art（工业设计/艺术）
- City planning（城市规划）
- Crafts (weaving, knitting, fabrics, furniture, carving, mosaics, ceramics, folk and tribal art)（手工艺：纺织、编织、织物、家具、雕刻、镶嵌工艺、陶瓷工艺，以及民间艺术和部落艺术）
- Cave/rock art（岩洞/石壁艺术）
- Music and music history（音乐和音乐史）
- Photography（摄影）
- Literature and authors（文学和作家）
- Books, newspapers, magazines, journals（书籍、报纸、杂志、期刊）

生命科学类讲座（Life Science）包括以下话题：

- Extinction of or conservation efforts for animals and plants（动物的灭绝或保护）
- Fish and other aquatic organisms（鱼类和其他水生生物）
- Bacteria and other one-celled organisms（细菌和其他单细胞生物）
- Viruses（病毒）
- Medical techniques（医疗技术）
- Public health（公共卫生）
- Physiology of sensory organs（感觉器官的生理机能）
- Biochemistry（生物化学）
- Animal behavior (migration, food foraging, defenses)（动物行为：迁徙、觅食、防御行为）
- Habitats and the adaptation of animals and plants to them（动植物的栖息地及动植物对栖息地的适应）
- Nutrition and its impact on the body（营养及其对机体的影响）
- Animal communication（动物交流）

自然科学类讲座（Physical Science）包括以下话题：

- Weather and atmosphere（天气和大气）
- Oceanography（海洋学）
- Glaciers, glacial landforms, ice ages（冰川、冰川地形、冰河纪）
- Deserts and other extreme environments（沙漠和其他极端环境）
- Pollution, alternative energy, environmental policy（污染、替代能源、环境政策）
- Other planets' atmospheres（其他星球的大气层）
- Astronomy and cosmology（天文学和宇宙学）
- Properties of light, optics（光的特性、光学）
- Properties of sound（声的特性）
- Electromagnetic radiation（电磁辐射）
- Particle physics（粒子物理学）
- Technology of TV, radio, radar（电视、广播和雷达技术）
- Chemistry of inorganic things（无机物的化学性质）
- Computer science（计算机科学）
- Seismology (plate structure, earthquakes, tectonics, continental drift, structure of volcanoes)（地震学：板块结构、地震、构造地质学、大陆漂移、火山结构）

社会科学类讲座（Social Science）包括以下话题：

- Anthropology of nonindustrialized civilizations（非工业化文明社会的人类学）
- Early writing systems（早期文字系统）
- Historical linguistics（历史语言学）
- Business, management, marketing, accounting（商业、管理、市场、会计）
- TV/radio as mass communication（作为大众传媒的电视/电台）
- Social behavior of groups, community dynamics, communal behavior（群体的社会行为、群落动态、集群行为）
- Child development（儿童发展）
- Education（教育）
- Modern history (including the history of urbanization and industrialization and their economic and social effects)（现代历史，包括城市化和工业化的历史及其带来的经济和社会影响）

Listening Questions

托福听力的大部分题目，不管是对话还是讲座，都是以传统的四选一的选择题为主。除此以外，还包括其他新增题型：

- 多项选择题（例如从4个选项中选择2个正确答案，或者从5个选项中选择3个正确答案）
- 排序题
- 搭配题（将表格中各项与其所属类别进行搭配）

有些题目会回放讲座或对话的一部分录音，然后考生将根据所听内容回答一道选择题。

在听力部分有8种题型，可分为以下3大类别：

TOEFL® Listening Question Types

Basic Comprehension questions
1. Gist-Content
2. Gist-Purpose
3. Detail

Pragmatic Understanding questions
4. Understanding the Function of What Is Said
5. Understanding the Speaker's Attitude

Connecting Information questions
6. Understanding Organization
7. Connecting Content
8. Making Inferences

以下部分将对这几种题型逐一解释，包括题型识别、例子说明以及每种听力题型的回答技巧等。

Basic Comprehension Questions

托福将采用以下三种方式考查考生对听力材料的基本理解：内容主旨题（Gist-content）、目的主旨题（Gist-purpose）和细节题（Detail）。

Type 1: Gist-Content Questions

内容主旨题要求考生理解讲座或对话的主旨大意。材料有时会明确提出主旨，有时则会很含蓄。内容主旨题会要求考生对所听到的信息进行归纳总结。

How to Recognize Gist-Content Questions

内容主旨题的典型问法如下：

- What problem does the man have?
- What are the speakers mainly discussing?
- What is the main topic of the lecture?
- What is the lecture mainly about?
- What aspect of X does the professor mainly discuss?

Tips for Gist-Content Questions

- 内容主旨题考查的是讲座或对话的总体内容。排除那些只涉及局部听力材料的选项。

- 试着用一个短语或一句话概括讲座或对话的主题。

Example Excerpt from a lecture:

Professor

. . . So the Earth's surface is made up of these huge segments, these tectonic plates. And these plates move, right? But how can, uh, motion of plates, do you think, influence climate on the Earth? Again, all of you probably read this section in the book, I hope, but, uh, uh, how—how can just motion of the plates impact the climate?

. . . when a plate moves, if there's landmass on the plate, then the landmass moves too, okay? That's why continents shift their positions, because the plates they're on move. So as a landmass moves away from the equator, its climate would get colder. So, right now we have a continent—the landmass Antarctica—that's on a pole.

So that's dramatically influencing the climate in Antarctica. Um, there was a time when most of the landmasses were closer to a pole; they weren't so close to the equator. Uh, maybe 200 million years ago Antarctica was attached to the South American continent; oh, and Africa was attached, too, and the three of them began moving away from the equator together.

. . . in the Himalayas. That was where two continental plates collided. Two continents on separate plates. Um, when this, uh, Indian, uh, uh, plate collided with the Asian plate, it wasn't until then that we created the Himalayas. When we did that, then we started creating the type of cold climate that we see there now. Wasn't there until this area was uplifted.

So again, that's something else that plate tectonics plays a critical role in. Now, these processes are relatively slow; the, uh, Himalayas are still rising, but on the order of millimeters per year. So they're not dramatically influencing climate on your—the time scale of your lifetime. But over the last few thousands of—tens of thousands of years, uh—hundreds of thousands of years—yes, they've dramatically influenced it.

Uh, another important thing—number three—on how plate tectonics have influenced climate is how they've influenced—we talked about how changing landmasses can affect atmospheric circulation patterns, but if you alter where the landmasses are connected, it can impact oceanic, uh, uh, uh, circulation patterns.

. . . Um, so, uh, these other processes, if, if we were to disconnect North and South America right through the middle—say, through Panama—that would dramatically influence climate in North and South America—probably the whole globe. So suddenly now as the two continents gradually move apart, you can have different circulation patterns in the ocean between the two. So, uh, that might cause a dramatic change in climate if that were to happen, just as we've had happen here in Antarctica to separate, uh, from South America.

What is the main topic of the lecture?

(A) The differences in climate that occur in different countries
(B) How movement of the Earth's plates can affect climate
(C) Why the ocean has less effect on climate than previously thought
(D) The history of the climate of the region where the university is located

Explanation

Choice B is the answer that best represents the main topic of the lecture. The professor uses Antarctica and the Himalayas as examples to make the general point that climate is affected by plate tectonics, the movement of Earth's plates.

Note that for Gist-Content questions the correct answer and the incorrect choices can sometimes be worded more abstractly than occurs in this example.

The following Gist-Content question refers to the same lecture:

What is the main topic of the lecture?

(A) A climate experiment and its results
(B) A geologic process and its effect
(C) How a theory was disproved
(D) How land movement is measured

Explanation

Once again, the correct answer is choice B. Even though the wording is very different, it basically says the same thing as choice B in the previous example: a geologic process (movement of Earth's plates) has an effect (changes in climate).

Type 2: Gist-Purpose Questions

有些主旨题考查的是对话或讲座的目的而非内容。此类问题较有可能出现在对话中，但偶尔也会出现在讲座中。

How to Recognize Gist-Purpose Questions

目的主旨题的典型问法如下：

- Why does the student visit the professor?
- Why does the student visit the registrar's office?
- Why did the professor ask to see the student?
- Why does the professor explain X?

Tips for Gist-Purpose Questions

- 学生去办公室找教授可以出于各种目的，包括教授邀请学生来办公室讨论其作业的完成情况等。回答目的主旨题时，考生应在自己的笔记中找寻信息以明确学生去找教授的最初目的是什么。

- 对话的目的并不总是跟对话的主要内容相关。例如，学生可能抱着询问评分政策的目的去拜访教授，在回答完学生的问题之后，教授也许会顺便问学生研究项目的进展情况，之后的对话内容就会与这个项目相关了。

- 在学生服务的对话中，通常情况是学生需要解决一个问题。理解学生的问题所在及其解决办法将有助于考生回答目的主旨题。

Example

Narrator

Listen to a conversation between a professor and a student.

Student

I was hoping you could look over my note cards for my presentation . . . just to see what you think of it.

Professor

Okay, so refresh my memory: what's your presentation about?

Student

Two models of decision making . . .

Professor

Oh, yes—the classical and the administrative model.

Student

Yeah, that's it.

Professor

And what's the point of your talk?

Student

I'm gonna talk about the advantages and disadvantages of both models.

Professor

But what's the point of your talk? Are you going to say that one's better than the other?

Student

Well, I think the administrative model's definitely more realistic. But I don't think it's complete. It's kind of a tool . . . a tool to see what can go wrong.

Professor

Okay, so what's the point of your talk? What are you trying to convince me to believe?

Student

Well, uh, the classical model—you shouldn't use it by itself. A lot of companies just try to follow the classical model, but they should really use both models together.

Professor

Okay, good. So let me take a look at your notes here . . . Oh, typed notes, . . . Wow you've got a lot packed in here. Are you sure you're going to be able to follow this during your talk?

Student

Oh, sure; that's why I typed them, because otherwise . . . well, my handwriting's not very clear.

Why does the student visit the professor?

Ⓐ To get some note cards for his presentation
Ⓑ To show her some examples of common errors in research
Ⓒ To review the notes for his presentation with her
Ⓓ To ask for help in finding a topic for his presentation

Explanation

While much of the conversation is concerned with the content of the student's presentation, the correct answer to the question "Why does the student visit the professor?" is choice C: "To review the notes for his presentation with her."

Type 3: Detail Questions

　　细节题要求考生听懂并记住讲座或对话中明晰的细节或事实。通常这些细节通过为文章提供解释、例子或其他支持内容与对话或讲座的主旨联系起来，其联系可能是直接的也可能是间接的。在有些情况下，听力材料中出现了一些与主题不太相关的内容，这类细节可能会考查到。

How to Recognize Detail Questions
　　细节题的典型问法如下：

- According to the professor, what is one way that X can affect Y?
- What is X?
- What resulted from the invention of the X?
- According to the professor, what is the main problem with the X theory?

> *Tips for Detail Questions*
>
> - 回答问题时参看笔记。题目不会考查考生一些小的细节。笔记内容应该包括对话或讲座中的重要细节。
>
> - 不要仅仅因为某个选项中含有讲座或对话中的几个原词就将其认定为正确选项。错误选项经常含有听力材料中的单词或词组。
>
> - 如果无法确定正确选项，就选择一个与讲座或对话的主题最符合的选项。

Examples

Professor

Uh, other things that glaciers can do is, uh, as they retreat, instead of depositing some till, uh, scraped-up soil, in the area, they might leave a big ice block, and it breaks off, and as the ice block melts, it leaves a depression, which can become a lake. These are called kettle lakes. These are very critical ecosystems in this region, um, because, uh, uh, they support some unique biological diversity, these kettle lakes do.

The Great Lakes are kettle lakes; they were left over from the Pleist—from the Pleistocene glaciers. Uh, now, as the glaciers were retreating, the Great Lakes underwent a change. Once the weight of the glacier ice decreased, and the pressure decreased, the land at the bottom of the lakes rose. In some places it rose by as much as one hundred feet.

So I just wanted to tell you a little bit more about glaciers . . .

What are kettle lakes?

(A) Lakes that form in the center of a volcano
(B) Lakes that have been damaged by the greenhouse effect
(C) Lakes formed by unusually large amounts of precipitation
(D) Lakes that form when pieces of glaciers melt

How did the glaciers affect the Great Lakes?

(A) They made the Great Lakes less deep.
(B) They made the Great Lakes larger.
(C) They reduced the biodiversity of the Great Lakes.
(D) They deposited excess soil into the Great Lakes.

Explanation

The answer to the first question is found in the beginning of the lecture when the professor explains what a kettle lake is. Choice D is correct. Remember that new terminology is often tested in Detail questions. The answer to the second question is found later in the lecture where the professor mentions that the lake bottoms rose. Choice A is correct.

Pragmatic Understanding Questions

情景理解题考查考生对英语口语的理解能力，要求考生听出话中隐含的意思。一般来说，这种问题考查考生对某一句话的作用或说话人的立场或态度的理解程度。在大多数情况下，情景理解题所考查的内容是在对话或讲座材料中说话者并没有直接阐明的话语目的或立场。此时，说话人的字面意思与实际意思之间就有了差异。

人们说话时通常希望对方能听出话语的弦外之音。以人们经常引用的一个句子为例——"这里真的很冷。"这句话可以从字面意思上理解，意思是说房间里的温度很低。但是假如说话者是你家里的一位客人，在说这句话的时候，正冻得浑身发抖并望着一扇开着的窗户，此时，说话者的真正目的是希望主人把窗户关上。在这个例子中，说话人真实的意图——让你把窗户关上——隐藏在"这里真的很冷"这句话字面意思的背后。隐藏在字面意思背后的类似的语言功能还有：指示、推荐、抱怨、接受、同意、陈述、质疑等等。

因此，通过上下文理解整个讲座或对话的整体意思对于理解说话人的态度和立场是十分关键的。某一句话究竟是事实还是某人的观点？说话人对其所陈述信息的确定程度究竟有多大？说话人是否在表达其对某个人、某个东西或某件事的某种态度或感觉？在此种情况下，说话人的态度或感觉可能都暗含于文字字面含义之中。所以，以上信息极易被母语为非英语的考生忽略甚至误解。

情景理解题通常会让考生重听听力材料的一小部分内容，其目的在于使考生的注意力能够集中在材料中与此题相关的信息上。情景理解题有两种形式：句子功能题和说话人态度题。

Type 4: Questions Related to Understanding the Function of What Is Said

情景理解题的第一种题型是句子功能题，其主要目的是测试考生是否理解某一句话的功能。考生通常会在重听讲座或对话的一部分后回答此类题目。

How to Recognize Questions Related to Understanding the Function of What Is Said

句子功能题的典型问法如下：

- What does the professor imply when he says this? *(replay)*
- Why does the student say this? *(replay)*
- What does the professor mean when she says this? *(replay)*

Example

Excerpt from a conversation between a male student and a female administrative assistant. They are discussing his dorm fees.

Narrator

Listen again to a part of the conversation. Then answer the question.

Student

Okay. I'll just pay with a credit card. And where do I do that at?

Administrative Assistant

At, um, the housing office.

Student

Housing office, all right.

Administrative Assistant

Do you know where they are?

Narrator

What is the woman trying to find out from the student?

Ⓐ Where the housing office is
Ⓑ Approximately how far away the housing office is
Ⓒ Whether she needs to tell him where the housing office is
Ⓓ Whether he has been to the housing office already

Explanation

The pragmatic function of the woman's question is to ask the student whether or not he needs to be told the location of the housing office. The best answer for this question is choice C.

Type 5: Questions Related to Understanding the Speaker's Attitude

　　情景理解题的第二种题型是说话人态度题，其主要目的是考查考生是否能听出说话人的态度或观点。考生也许会被问及关于说话人的感受、喜恶或者感到焦虑或快乐的原因。同时考生还会被问及关于说话人的把握性的问题：说话人是在引用事实还是在表述观点？材料中所陈述的事实是被广为接受的还是仍有争议的？有时，题目会考查考生发现并理解反语的能力。当说话人要表达的意思跟其实际所说的内容相反时，那么他/她就是在说反语。例如，用某种语气说出 "That's just great" 这句话就可以表达出 "That's not good at all" 的意思。说话人使用反语会出于各种目的，包括强调已提出的要点、营造幽默气氛以引起听众共鸣，或者以间接的方式表示不赞成。考生必须从上下文提供的线索和说话人的语气中推断出反语背后的真正含义。

How to Recognize Questions Related to Understanding the Speaker's Attitude

说话人态度题的典型问法如下：

- What can be inferred about the student?
- What is the professor's attitude toward X?
- What is the professor's opinion of X?
- What can be inferred about the student when she says this? *(replay)*
- What does the woman mean when she says this? *(replay)*

Tip for Questions Related to Understanding the Speaker's Attitude

- 学会关注说话人的语气：说话人听起来是愧疚的、困惑的，还是充满热情的？说话人的语气可以帮助考生回答此类问题。

Example

Excerpt from a conversation between a male student and his female advisor. In this part of a longer conversation, they are discussing the student's job.

Advisor

Well, good. So, bookstore isn't working out?

Student

Oh, bookstore's working out fine. I just, I—this pays almost double what the bookstore does.

Advisor

Oh, wow!

Student

Yeah. Plus credit.

Advisor

Plus credit.

Student

And it's more hours, which . . . The bookstore's—I mean it's a decent job 'n' all. Everybody I work with . . . that part's great; it's just . . . I mean I'm shelving books and kind of hanging out and not doing much else . . . if it weren't for the people, it'd be totally boring.

Narrator

What is the student's attitude toward the people he currently works with?

Ⓐ He finds them boring.
Ⓑ He likes them.
Ⓒ He is annoyed by them.
Ⓓ He does not have much in common with them.

Explanation

In this example it may be easy to confuse the student's attitude toward his job with his attitude toward the people he works with. The correct answer is choice B. The student is bored with the job, not the people he works with.

Connecting Information Questions

整合信息题要求考生将讲座或对话中的信息相互联系起来。此题主要考查考生将讲座或对话中的不同部分作出整合、进行推断，以及得出结论、归纳总结、进行预测的能力。为了选出正确的答案，考生需要能够识别并解释材料中观点和细节之间的联系。而材料则或是明确指出或是含蓄地暗示了这种联系。

整合信息题有三种类型。

Type 6: Understanding Organization Questions

组织结构题要求考生把握整个讲座的结构，或者听力材料中两个部分之间的关系。以下是两个例子及其正确答案：

1. How does the professor organize the information that she presents to the class?
   ○ In the order in which the events occurred

2. How does the professor clarify the points he makes about Mexico?
   ○ By comparing Mexico to a neighboring country

第一题主要考查考生是否能够弄清整个讲座的组织方式，测试考生把握整篇材料的能力。第二题考查了材料中的部分内容，主要考查考生理解听力材料中两个不同观点间关系的能力。

有些组织结构题会考查考生对某一句话在上下文中的功能的理解能力。这些功能包括：转换话题、连接主题和分论点、提供引言或结论、举例子、谈论无关内容甚至开玩笑。

Example

Narrator

Listen again to a statement made by the professor. Then answer the question.

Professor

There's this committee I'm on . . . Th-the name of the thing, and it's probably, well, you don't have to take notes about this, um, the name of the thing is academic standards.

Narrator

Why does the professor tell the students that they do not have to take notes?

(A) The information is in their books.

(B) The information may not be accurate.

(C) She is going to tell a personal story.

(D) They already know what she is going to talk about.

Explanation

The statement preceding the replayed statement is about how bureaucracies work. What follows the replayed statement is a personal story about bureaucracies. The key lies in recognizing that the portion of the lecture following the replayed statement is a personal story. The correct answer is choice C. With the replayed statement the professor indicates to the class that what she is about to say does not have the same status as what she was talking about previously.

How to Recognize Understanding Organization Questions

组织结构题的典型问法如下:

- How does the professor organize the information about X?
- How is the discussion organized?
- Why does the professor discuss X?
- Why does the professor mention X?

Tips for Understanding Organization Questions

- 相对于对话而言,更有可能在讲座之后考查整篇文章的组织结构。可参看笔记来回答这些问题。教授不会一开始就采用时间顺序、由易到难的顺序或其他明显的顺序来进行讲座。

- 注意教授所作的比较。在下面的例子中,教授正在讲解植物的结构。他使用了钢和钢结构的大梁来说明这一问题。教授可能会用一些看似离题的内容来解释一个概念。教授也会用学生熟悉的事物来介绍一个新的理念。

Professor

So we have reproductive parts—the seeds, the fruit walls—we have leaf parts, but the great majority of plant fibers come from vasculature within the stem . . . fibers that occur in stem material. And what we do is consider these fibers—basically they're what are called *bast* fibers. Bast fibers. Now, basically bast fibers are parts of the plant that the plant uses to maintain vertical structure.

Think about it this way: what's the first thing you see when you see a building being built . . . uh, what's the first thing they put up? Besides the foundation, of course? The metalwork, right? They put all those steel girders up there, the framework. OK, well, think of—bast fibers basically constitute the structural framework to support the stem of the plant. OK? So as the plant grows, it basically builds a girder system within that plant, like steel, so to speak.

So suppose you cut across the stem of one of these plants . . . take a look at how the bast fibers are arranged, so you're looking at a cross section . . . you'll see that the fibers run vertically side by side. Up and down next to each other, forming a kind of tube, which is significant . . . 'cause, which is physically stronger: a solid rod or a tube? The tube—physics tells you that. What's essentially happening—well, the plant is forming a structural ring of these bast fibers all around the stem, and that shape allows for structural rigidity, but also allows for bending and motion.

Why does the professor talk about steel?

Ⓐ To identify the substance that has replaced fiber products.
Ⓑ To explain a method for separating fibers from a plant.
Ⓒ To compare the chemical structure of fibers to metals.
Ⓓ To illustrate the function of fibers in a plant's stem.

Why does the professor mention a tube?

Ⓐ To explain how some fibers are arranged in a plant.
Ⓑ To show how plants carry water to growing fibers.
Ⓒ To describe an experiment involving plant fibers.
Ⓓ To explain why some plant stems cannot bend.

Explanation

The lecture is about plants and plant fibers, not steel girders. The professor mentions steel girders only to compare them to the structural framework of fibers in a plant. The correct answer to the first question is choice D. Likewise, the second question also concerns the professor's attempts to help the students visualize a plant's structure. The correct answer to the second question is choice A.

Type 7: Connecting Content Questions

连接内容题考查考生对讲座中各观点之间的关系的理解能力。这些关系有可能被明确指出或需要考生根据所听到的材料进行推测。

连接内容题可能会要求考生使用与原文不同的方式来组织信息。可能要求考生认清比较关系、因果关系或反对/赞同关系。另外，也可能要求考生对事物分门别类，弄清事件的顺序或事物发展过程中的步骤，或从某一角度说明事物之间的具体关系。

Example

Narrator

What type of symmetry do these animals have? Place a check mark in the correct box.

	Asymmetry	Radial Symmetry	Bilateral Symmetry
Earthworm			✓
Human			✓
Sponge	✓		
Sea Anemone	✓	✓	

Explanation

In this question you are asked to present information in a different format from that in which it was presented in a lecture.

Other Connecting Content questions will require you to make inferences about the relationships among things mentioned in the lecture. You may have to predict an outcome, draw a logical conclusion, extrapolate some additional information, infer a cause-and-effect relationship, or specify some particular sequence of events.

How to Recognize Connecting Content Questions

连接内容题的典型问法如下：

- What is the likely outcome of doing procedure X before procedure Y?
- What can be inferred about X?
- What does the professor imply about X?

> **Tip for Connecting Content Questions**
>
> - 填表题或排序题可归为此类题型。考生在听本书所附的听力材料时，注意训练自己做笔记的方式。听清术语及其定义，并听清事件发展过程中的各个步骤，这有助于考生回答此类问题。

Example

Professor

OK, Neptune and its moons. Neptune has several moons, but there's only . . . we'll probably only worry about two of them, the two fairly interesting ones. The first one's Triton. So you have this little struggle with the word *Titan*, which is the big moon of Saturn, and the name *Triton*, which is the big moon of *Neptune*. Triton: it's, it's the only *large moon* in the solar system to go backwards, to go around its—what we call its parent planet—in this case Neptune, the wrong way. OK? Every other large moon orbits the *parent planet* in the same counterclockwise direction . . . same as most of the other bodies in the solar system. But this moon . . . the reverse direction, which is perfectly OK as far as the laws of gravity are concerned. But it indicates some sort of peculiar event in the early solar system that gave this moon a motion in contrast to the general spin of the raw material that it was formed from.

The other moon orbiting Neptune that I want to talk about is Nereid. Nereid is, Nereid has the most eccentric orbit, the most lopsided, elliptical-type orbit for a large moon in the solar system. The others tend more like circular orbits.

. . . Does it mean that Pluto and Neptune might have been related somehow in the past and then drifted slowly into their present orbits? If Pluto . . . did Pluto ever belong to the Neptune system? Do Neptune's moons represent Pluto-type bodies that have been captured by Neptune? Was some sort of . . . was Pluto the object that disrupted the Neptune system at some point in the past?

It's really hard to prove any of those things. But now we're starting to appreciate that there's quite a few junior Plutos out there: not big enough to really call a planet, but large enough that they're significant in history of the early solar system. So we'll come back to those when we talk about comets and other small bodies in the fringes of the outer solar system.

What does the professor imply about the orbits of Triton and Nereid?

Ⓐ They used to be closer together.
Ⓑ They might provide evidence of an undiscovered planet.
Ⓒ They might reverse directions in the future.
Ⓓ They might have been changed by some unusual event.

Explanation

In Connecting Content questions you will have to use information from more than one place in the lecture. In this example, the professor describes the orbits of Triton and Nereid. In both cases he refers to events in the early solar system that might have changed or disrupted their orbits. The correct answer for this question is choice D, "They might have been changed by some unusual event."

Type 8: Making Inferences Questions

连接内容题的最后一种题型是推论题。此时考生需要根据已经听到的内容得出结论。

How to Recognize Making Inferences Questions
推论题的典型问法如下：

- What does the professor imply about X?
- What will the student probably do next?
- What can be inferred about X?
- What does the professor imply when he says this? *(replay)*

Tip for Making Inferences Questions

- 在有些情况下，能否正确回答此类问题取决于考生是否能将讲座或对话中出现的细节整合起来得出结论。在另外一些情况下，教授可能会旁敲侧击地提到某些事实，而并不直接说明。在大多数情况下，正确答案往往使用了讲座或对话中未提到的词汇。

Example

Professor

Dada is often considered under the broader category of Fantasy. It's one of the early directions in the Fantasy style. The term "Dada" itself is a nonsense word—it has no meaning . . . and where the word originated isn't known. The "philosophy" behind the "Dada" movement was to create works that conveyed the concept of *absurdity*—the artwork was meant to shock the public by presenting the ridiculous, absurd concepts. Dada artists rejected reason—or rational thought. They did not believe that rational thought would help solve social problems . . .

. . . When he turned to Dada, he quit painting and devoted himself to making a type of sculpture he referred to as a "ready-made" . . . probably because they were constructed of readily available objects . . . At the time, many people reacted to Dadaism by saying that the works were not art at all . . . and in fact, that's exactly how Duchamp and others conceived of it—as a form of "non-art" . . . or anti-art.

Duchamp also took a reproduction of da Vinci's famous painting the *Mona Lisa*, and he drew a mustache and goatee on the subject's face. Treating this masterpiece with such disrespect was another way Duchamp was challenging the established cultural standards of his day.

What does the professor imply about the philosophy of the Dada movement?

(A) It was not taken seriously by most artists.
(B) It varied from one country to another.
(C) It challenged people's concept of what art is.
(D) It was based on a realistic style of art.

Explanation

Note the highlighted portions of the lecture. You can see that Dadaism was meant to challenge the public's conception of what art was meant to be. The correct answer to the question is choice C.

Strategies for Preparing for and Taking the Listening Section

How to Sharpen Your Listening Skills

听力能力无论对托福考试还是今后的学习生活都是至关重要的。托福考试的四部分中有三个部分都考查了听力理解能力。

提高听力的最佳方法是经常听不同领域（自然科学、社会科学、艺术、商业等）的各类材料。当然，看英文电影和电视节目、听英文广播也是练习听力的绝佳途径。听力磁带或CD都可在图书馆或书店找到；如果有听力原文更佳。互联网上也有大量的听力材料。

以下方法可帮助考生强化听力能力，以达到托福听力考查的三大要求。

1. Listening for basic comprehension

- 扩充词汇量——可使用学习卡片。

- 听的时候请专注于材料的内容和大意，不要受说话人讲话风格和方式的干扰。

- 预测说话人将要说的话，借此方法将注意力集中在听力材料上。在听到新信息时及时调整预测。

- 主动向自己提问（例如，教授所要表达的主要观点是什么？）。

- 将"main idea"、"major points"、"important details"字样在纸上分行列出，提醒自己在听听力材料时需注意这几个方面并记笔记。反复听录音材料，直到写下所有重要的观点和细节。

- 先听讲座中的一部分，听完后写出一个主要观点的简短总结；再逐渐增加所听部分的长度，并进行总结。

2. Listening for pragmatic understanding

- 思考一下每位说话人想要达到的目的：如对话或讲座的目的是什么？说话人是在道歉、抱怨还是在提建议？

- 注意每个说话人的说话方式：该材料中的语言是正式的还是随意的？说话人是否很有把握？说话人的声音听上去很平静还是很激动？从说话人的语气中能得出什么结论？

- 注意说话人的确定程度：说话人对某信息究竟有多确定？说话人的语气是否能为他或她的确定性提供一些暗示？

- 看电视或喜剧电影，注意说话人在表达各种意思时所使用的语调和重音。

- 看电视或电影，注意人物在表达不赞同或提建议时采用的间接方式，目的在于避免伤害另一个人物的感情。

3. Listening to connect ideas

- 思考一下讲座稿的谋篇布局。注意听清听力材料中的标志词，它们会标明文中的引言、主要步骤或观点、例子、结论及总结。

- 弄清材料中各观点之间的关系，可能涉及因果、对比、过程中的步骤等关系。

- 注意听那些能表示观点之间关系的词汇。

- 在听录音时，可以经常将录音暂停，预测下文将出现的信息和观点。

- 在听录音时或听完录音后，写出一个所听到内容的提纲。

- 注意听出说话人的话题转换。说话人会在简短地讲了一些题外话之后再次回到正题上。

Tips for the Day of the Test

- 听录音时要记笔记。考试只考查重点，不要意图把所有细节都记录下来。考试完毕，考生在离开考场前，笔记都会被收集起来并销毁。

- 听讲座时，注意教授介绍的新名词或新概念。这些词也许会被书写在黑板上，通常会考查到。

- 听讲座时，注意讲座的内容结构以及意义连接。

- 选择最佳答案。计算机会请你确认你的选择。点击OK键之后，就会进入下一个问题。

- 听力问题必须按顺序解答。一旦考生点击了OK键，就不能再返回前面的题目。

Listening Practice Sets

PRACTICE SET 1

Now listen to Track 1.

Questions

Directions: Mark your answer by filling in the oval next to your choice.

1. Why does the man go to see his professor?
    - Ⓐ To borrow some charts and graphs from her
    - Ⓑ To ask her to explain some statistical procedures
    - Ⓒ To talk about a report he is writing
    - Ⓓ To discuss a grade he got on a paper

2. What information will the man include in his report?

For each phrase below, place a check mark in the "Include" column or the "Not Include" column.

	Include in Report	Not Include in Report
Climate charts		
Interviews with meteorologists		
Journal notes		
Statistical tests		

3. Why does the professor tell the man about the appointment at the doctor's office?

   Ⓐ To demonstrate a way of remembering things
   Ⓑ To explain why she needs to leave soon
   Ⓒ To illustrate a point that appears in his report
   Ⓓ To emphasize the importance of good health

4. What does the professor offer to do for the man?

   Ⓐ Help him collect more data in other areas of the state
   Ⓑ Submit his research findings for publication
   Ⓒ Give him the doctor's telephone number
   Ⓓ Review the first version of his report

5. *Listen again to part of the conversation by playing Track 2. Then answer the question.*

   Why does the professor say this?

   Ⓐ To question the length of the paper
   Ⓑ To offer encouragement
   Ⓒ To dispute the data sources
   Ⓓ To explain a theory

PRACTICE SET 1 SCRIPT AND ANSWERS

Track 1 Listening Script

Narrator

Listen to a conversation between a student and a professor.

Student

Uh, excuse me, Professor Thompson. I know your office hours are tomorrow, but I was wondering if you had a few minutes free now to discuss something.

Professor

Sure, John. What did you wanna talk about?

Student

Well, I have some quick questions about how to write up the research project I did this semester—about climate variations.

Professor

Oh, yes. You were looking at variations in climate in the Grant City area, right? How far along have you gotten?

Student

I've got all my data, so I'm starting to summarize it now, preparing graphs and stuff. But I'm just . . . I'm looking at it and I'm afraid that it's not enough, but I'm not sure what else to put in the report.

Professor

I hear the same thing from every student. You know, you have to remember now that you're the expert on what you've done. So think about what you'd need to include if you were going to explain your research project to someone with general or casual knowledge about the subject, like . . . like your parents. That's usually my rule of thumb: would my parents understand this?

Student

OK. I get it.

Professor

I hope you can recognize by my saying that how much you do know about the subject.

Student

Right. I understand. I was wondering if I should also include the notes from the research journal you suggested I keep?

Professor

Yes, definitely. You should use them to indicate what your evolution in thought was through time. So just set up, you know, what was the purpose of what you were doing—to try to understand the climate variability of this area—and what you did, and what your approach was.

Student

OK. So, for example, I studied meteorological records; I looked at climate charts; I used different methods for analyzing the data, like certain statistical tests; and then I discuss the results. Is that what you mean?

Professor

Yes, that's right. You should include all of that. The statistical tests are especially important. And also be sure you include a good reference section where all your published and unpublished data came from, 'cause you have a lot of unpublished climate data.

Student

Hmm . . . something just came into my mind and went out the other side.

Professor

That happens to me a lot, so I've come up with a pretty good memory management tool. I carry a little pad with me all the time and jot down questions or ideas that I don't wanna forget. For example, I went to the doctor with my daughter and her baby son last week, and we knew we wouldn't remember everything we wanted to ask the doctor, so we actually made a list of five things we wanted answers to.

Student

A notepad is a good idea. Since I'm so busy now at the end of the semester, I'm getting pretty forgetful these days. OK. I just remembered what I was trying to say before.

Professor

Good. I was hoping you'd come up with it.

Student

Yes. It ends up that I have data on more than just the immediate Grant City area, so I also included some regional data in the report. With everything else it should be a pretty good indicator of the climate in this part of the state.

Professor

Sounds good. I'd be happy to look over a draft version before you hand in the final copy, if you wish.

Student

Great. I'll plan to get you a draft of the paper by next Friday. Thanks very much. Well, see ya.

Professor

OK.

Answers and Explanations

1. **C** This is a Gist-Purpose question. The man says, "I have some quick questions about how to write up the research project I did this semester." He is going to write a report about his project and is unsure of what to include. Choice C is the correct answer.

2. This question is easy to recognize as a Connecting Content question. The student and the professor discuss several sources of information that the student used to investigate climate variation. They do not discuss interviewing meteorologists, even though they mention other kinds of conversations, like the professor's discussion with her child's doctor. The chart correctly filled out looks like this:

For each phrase below, place a check mark in the "Include" column or the "Not Include" column.

	Include in Report	Not Include in Report
Climate charts	✓	
Interviews with meteorologists		✓
Journal notes	✓	
Statistical tests	✓	

3. **A** This is an Understanding Organization question. The correct answer is choice A. The professor's purpose in mentioning the doctor's office is to show the man how writing down questions as they occur can be useful. The man has forgotten a question he wanted to ask the professor. The professor, when she spoke to the doctor, wrote down her questions beforehand, so she would not forget. She mentions the doctor's office in order to give an example of a strategy for remembering.

4. **D** This is a Detail question. The discussion ends with the professor offering to "look over a draft version" of the man's paper.

5. **B** This question requires you to Understand the Function of What Is Said. The question asks you to listen again to this part of the conversation:

Professor

You know, you have to remember now that you're the expert on what you've done. So think about what you'd need to include if you were going to explain your research project to someone with general or casual knowledge about the subject, like ... like your parents. That's usually my rule of thumb: would my parents understand this?

Student

OK. I get it.

Professor

I hope you can recognize by my saying that how much you do know about the subject.

Then you are asked specifically about this sentence:

Narrator

Why does the professor say this:

Professor

I hope you can recognize by my saying that how much you do know about the subject.

The student is unsure of how to present the information in his report. The professor is trying to give the student confidence in his own judgment. Therefore the correct answer is choice B, "To offer encouragement."

PRACTICE SET 2

Now listen to Track 3.

Philosophy
Ethics

extrinsic value
intrinsic value

Questions

Directions: Mark your answer by filling in the oval next to your choice.

1. What is the main purpose of the lecture?

   Ⓐ To illustrate the importance of extrinsic values
   Ⓑ To explain Aristotle's views about the importance of teaching
   Ⓒ To explain why people change what they value
   Ⓓ To discuss Aristotle's views about human happiness

2. The professor gives examples of things that have value for her. Indicate for each example what type of value it has for her.
   Place a check mark in the correct box. **This question is worth 2 points.**

	Only Extrinsic Value	Only Intrinsic Value	Both Extrinsic and Intrinsic Value
Teaching			
Exercise			
Health			
Playing a musical instrument			

3. Why is happiness central to Aristotle's theory?

   Ⓐ Because it is so difficult for people to attain
   Ⓑ Because it is valued for its own sake by all people
   Ⓒ Because it is a means to a productive life
   Ⓓ Because most people agree about what happiness is

4. According to the professor, why does Aristotle think that fame cannot provide true happiness?

   Ⓐ Fame cannot be obtained without help from other people.
   Ⓑ Fame cannot be obtained by all people.
   Ⓒ Fame does not last forever.
   Ⓓ People cannot share their fame with other people.

5. *Listen again to part of the lecture by playing Track 4.*
   Then answer the question.

   What does the professor mean when she says this?

   Ⓐ Teaching is not a highly valued profession in society.
   Ⓑ She may change professions in order to earn more money.
   Ⓒ The reason she is a teacher has little to do with her salary.
   Ⓓ More people would become teachers if the salary were higher.

PRACTICE SET 2 SCRIPT AND ANSWERS

Track 3 Listening Script

Narrator

Listen to part of a lecture in a philosophy class.

Professor

OK. Another ancient Greek philosopher we need to discuss is Aristotle—Aristotle's ethical theory. What Aristotle's ethical theory is all about is this: he's trying to show you how to be happy—what true happiness is.

Now, why is he interested in human happiness? It's not just because it's something that all people want or aim for. It's more than that. But to get there, we need to first make a very important distinction. Let me introduce a couple of technical terms: extrinsic value and intrinsic value.

To understand Aristotle's interest in happiness, you need to understand this distinction.

Some things we aim for and value, not for themselves, but for what they bring about in addition to themselves. If I value something as a means to something else, then it has what we will call "extrinsic value." Other things we desire and hold to be valuable for themselves alone. If we value something not as a means to something else, but for its own sake, let us say that it has "intrinsic value."

Exercise. There may be some people who value exercise for itself, but I don't. I value exercise because if I exercise, I tend to stay healthier than I would if I didn't. So I desire to engage in exercise, and I value exercise extrinsically . . . not for its own sake, but as a means to something beyond it. It brings me good health.

Health. Why do I value good health? Well, here it gets a little more complicated for me. Um, health is important for me because I can't . . . do other things I wanna do—play music, teach philosophy—if I'm ill. So health is important to me—has value to me—as a means to a productive life. But health is also important to me because I just kind of like to be healthy—it feels good. It's pleasant to be healthy, unpleasant not to be. So to some degree I value health both for itself and as a means to something else: productivity. It's got extrinsic and intrinsic value for me.

Then there's some things that are just valued for themselves. I'm a musician, not a professional musician; I just play a musical instrument for fun. Why do I value playing music? Well, like most amateur musicians, I only play because, well, I just enjoy it. It's something that's an end in itself.

Now, something else I value is teaching. Why? Well, it brings in a modest income, but I could make more money doing other things. I'd do it even if they didn't pay me. I just enjoy teaching. In that sense it's an end to itself.

But teaching's not something that has intrinsic value for all people—and that's true generally. Most things that are enjoyed in and of themselves vary from person to person. Some people value teaching intrinsically, but others don't.

So how does all this relate to human happiness? Well, Aristotle asks: is there something that all human beings value . . . and value only intrinsically, for its own sake and only for its own sake? If you could find such a thing, that would be the universal final good, or truly the ultimate purpose or goal for all human beings. Aristotle thought the answer was yes. What is it? Happiness. Everyone will agree, he argues, that happiness is the ultimate end to be valued for itself and really only for itself. For what other purpose is there in being happy? What does it yield? The attainment of happiness becomes the ultimate or highest good for Aristotle.

The next question that Aristotle raises is: what is happiness? We all want it; we all desire it; we all seek it. It's the goal we have in life. But what is it? How do we find it? Here he notes, with some frustration, people disagree.

But he does give us a couple of criteria, or features, to keep in mind as we look for what true human happiness is. True human happiness should be, as he puts it, complete. Complete in that it's all we require. Well, true human happiness . . . if you had that, what else do you need? Nothing.

And, second, true happiness should be something that I can obtain on my own. I shouldn't have to rely on other people for it. Many people value fame and seek fame. Fame for them becomes the goal. But, according to Aristotle, this won't work either, because fame depends altogether too much on other people. I can't get it on my own, without help from other people.

In the end, Aristotle says that true happiness is the exercise of reason—a life of intellectual contemplation . . . of thinking. So let's see how he comes to that.

Answers and Explanations

1. **D** This is a Gist-Purpose question. The professor discusses the difference between extrinsic and intrinsic value, but what is her purpose in doing this? "To understand Aristotle's interest in happiness, you need to understand this distinction [extrinsic and intrinsic]." The professor's purpose is choice D: "To discuss Aristotle's views about human happiness."

2. This question is easy to recognize as a Connecting Content question. The professor gives examples of some activities and discusses whether they have intrinsic value, extrinsic value, or both. Her explanations of why she values exercise, health, and playing a musical instrument are fairly clear and explicit. For teaching, it is clear that for her it has intrinsic value, but she admits this may be different for others. The question is about "what type of value it has for her." The chart correctly filled out looks like this:

	Only Extrinsic Value	Only Intrinsic Value	Both Extrinsic and Intrinsic Value
Teaching		✓	
Exercise	✓		
Health			✓
Playing a musical instrument		✓	

3. **B** This is a Detail question. The question is answered by the professor when she says, "Everyone will agree, he [Aristotle] argues, that happiness is the ultimate end to be valued for itself and really only for itself." The correct answer for this question is choice B. Note that this Detail question is directly related to the main idea or gist of the passage.

4. **A** This is another Detail question. It is not as closely related to the gist as the previous question. At the end of the passage the professor compares happiness and fame. She says, "according to Aristotle, this won't work either, because fame depends altogether too much on other people. I can't get it on my own." The correct answer is choice A.

5. **C** This question requires you to Understand the Function of What Is Said. The professor discusses teaching to stress its intrinsic value for her. Therefore the correct answer is choice C. The reason she is a teacher has little to do with money. Salary would be an extrinsic value, but she does not value teaching because of the salary.

PRACTICE SET 3

Now listen to Track 5.

Psychology
Behavorism

Laryngeal Habits

Questions

Directions: Mark your answer by filling in the oval next to your choice.

1. What is the professor mainly discussing?

   (A) The development of motor skills in children
   (B) How psychologists measure muscle activity in the throat
   (C) A theory about the relationship between muscle activity and thinking
   (D) A study on the problem-solving techniques of people who are deaf

2. What does the professor say about people who use sign language?

   (A) It is not possible to study their thinking habits.
   (B) They exhibit laryngeal habits.
   (C) The muscles in their hands move when they solve problems.
   (D) They do not exhibit ideomotor action.

3. What point does the professor make when he refers to the university library?

   (A) A study on problem solving took place there.
   (B) Students should go there to read more about behaviorism.
   (C) Students' eyes will turn toward it if they think about it.
   (D) He learned about William James's concept of thinking there.

4. The professor describes a magic trick to the class. What does the magic trick demonstrate?

   (A) An action people make that they are not aware of
   (B) That behaviorists are not really scientists
   (C) How psychologists study children
   (D) A method for remembering locations

5. What is the professor's opinion of the motor theory of thinking?

   (A) Most of the evidence he has collected contradicts it.
   (B) It explains adult behavior better than it explains child behavior.
   (C) It is the most valid theory of thinking at the present time.
   (D) It cannot be completely proved or disproved.

6. *Listen again to part of the lecture by playing Track 6. Then answer the question.*

   Why does the professor say this?

   (A) To give an example of a laryngeal habit
   (B) To explain the meaning of a term
   (C) To explain why he is discussing laryngeal habits
   (D) To remind students of a point he had discussed previously

PRACTICE SET 3 SCRIPT AND ANSWERS

Track 5 Listening Script

Narrator

Listen to part of a psychology lecture. The professor is discussing behaviorism.

Professor

Now, many people consider John Watson to be the founder of behaviorism. And like other behaviorists, he believed that psychologists should study only the behaviors they can observe and measure. They're not interested in mental processes. While a person could describe his thoughts, no one else can see or hear them to verify the accuracy of his report. But one thing you can observe is muscular habits. What Watson did was to observe muscular habits because he viewed them as a manifestation of thinking. One kind of habit that he studied are laryngeal habits.

Watson thought laryngeal habits—you know, from *larynx*; in other words, related to the voice box—he thought those habits were an expression of thinking. He argued that for very young children, thinking is really talking out loud to oneself because they talk out loud even if they're not trying to communicate with someone in particular. As the individual matures, that overt talking to oneself becomes covert talking to oneself, but thinking still shows up as a laryngeal habit. One of the bits of evidence that supports this is that when people are trying to solve a problem, they, um, typically have increased muscular activity in the throat region. That is, if you put electrodes on the throat and measure muscle potential—muscle activity—you discover that when people are thinking, like if they're diligently trying to solve a problem, that there is muscular activity in the throat region.

So Watson made the argument that problem solving, or thinking, can be defined as a set of behaviors—a set of responses—and in this case the response he observed was the throat activity. That's what he means when he calls it a laryngeal habit. Now, as I am thinking about what I am going to be saying, my muscles in my throat are responding. So thinking can be measured as muscle activity. Now, the motor theory . . . yes?

Student

Professor Blake, um, did he happen to look at people who sign? I mean deaf people?

Professor

Uh, he did indeed, um, and to jump ahead, what one finds in deaf individuals who use sign language when they're given problems of various kinds, they have muscular changes in their hands when they are trying to solve a problem . . . muscle changes in the hand, just like the muscular changes going on in the throat region for speaking individuals.

So, for Watson, thinking is identical with the activity of muscles. A related concept of thinking was developed by William James. It's called ideomotor action.

Ideomotor action is an activity that occurs without our noticing it, without our being aware of it. I'll give you one simple example. If you think of locations, there tends to be eye movement that occurs with your thinking about that location. In particular, from where we're sitting, imagine that you're asked to think of our university library. Well, if you close your eyes and think of the library, and if you're sitting directly facing me, then according to this notion, your eyeballs will move slightly to the left, to your left, 'cause the library's in that general direction.

James and others said that this is an idea leading to a motor action, and that's why it's called "ideomotor action"—an idea leads to motor activity. If you wish to impress your friends and relatives, you can change this simple process into a magic trick. Ask people to do something such as I've just described: think of something on their left; think of something on their right. You get them to think about two things on either side with their eyes closed, and you watch their eyes very carefully. And if you do that, you'll discover that you can see rather clearly the eye movement—that is, you can see the movement of the eyeballs. Now, then you say, "Think of either one and I'll tell which you're thinking of."

OK. Well, Watson makes the assumption that muscular activity is equivalent to thinking. But given everything we've been talking about here, one has to ask: are there alternatives to this motor theory—this claim that muscular activities are equivalent to thinking? Is there anything else that might account for this change in muscular activity, other than saying that it is thinking? And the answer is clearly yes. Is there any way to answer the question definitively? I think the answer is no.

Answers and Explanations

1. Ⓒ This is a Gist-Content question. The professor discusses two types of muscular activities: laryngeal habits and ideomotor activity, and how they are related to thinking. The correct answer is choice C, "A theory about the relationship between muscle activity and thinking." The other choices are mentioned by the professor, but they are not the main topic of the discussion.

2. Ⓒ This is a Detail question. The professor responds to a student who asks a question about people who use sign language. He says that "they have muscular changes in their hands . . . just like the muscular changes going on in the throat region for speaking individuals." The correct answer is choice C. This Detail question is related to the main idea of the passage, as both are concerned with the relationship between muscular changes and thinking.

3. Ⓒ This is an Understanding Organization question. The professor talks about muscular activity in the eyes that will occur if the students think about the location of the library. The question asks for the conclusion of that example. The correct answer is choice C, "Students' eyes will turn toward it if they think about it."

4. Ⓐ This is a Connecting Content question. Answering the question correctly requires you to understand that the magic trick the professor is describing is an "ideomotor activity" and that this type of activity "occurs without our noticing it, without our being aware of it." The correct answer to this question is choice A.

5. Ⓓ Questions like this one that ask for the professor's opinion require you to Understand the Speaker's Attitude. The professor's opinion can be found at the end of the lecture. He says that there may be alternative theories, but there is no way to answer the question definitively. The correct answer to this question is choice D, "It cannot be completely proved or disproved."

6. Ⓑ This question requires you to Understand the Function of What Is Said. The professor introduces an unusual term, "laryngeal habits." He then says, "you know, from *larynx*; in other words, related to the voice box." His brief explanation is meant to help the students understand the term "laryngeal habits." Choice B is the correct answer to this question.

PRACTICE SET 4

Now listen to Track 7.

Astronomy

0   3   6   12   24

0   3   6   12   24   48   96
↓   ↓   ↓   ↓   ↓   ↓   ↓
4   7   10   16   28   52   100

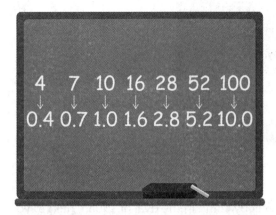

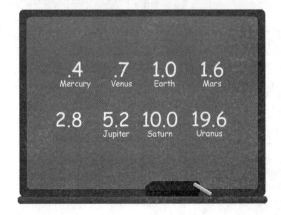

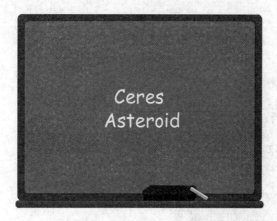

Questions

Directions: Mark your answer by filling in the oval or square next to your choice.

1. What is Bode's Law?

    Ⓐ A law of gravitation
    Ⓑ An estimate of the distance between Mars and Jupiter
    Ⓒ A prediction of how many asteroids there are
    Ⓓ A pattern in the spacing of planets

2. Why does the professor explain Bode's Law to the class?

    Ⓐ To describe the size of the asteroids
    Ⓑ To explain how the asteroid belt was discovered
    Ⓒ To explain how gravitational forces influence the planets
    Ⓓ To describe the impact of telescopes on astronomy

3. How does the professor introduce Bode's Law?

    Ⓐ By demonstrating how it is derived mathematically
    Ⓑ By describing the discovery of Uranus
    Ⓒ By drawing attention to the inaccuracy of a certain pattern
    Ⓓ By telling the names of several of the asteroids

4. According to the professor, what two factors contributed to the discovery of the asteroid Ceres?
    Choose 2 answers.

    ☐ A Improved telescopes
    ☐ B Advances in mathematics
    ☐ C The discovery of a new star
    ☐ D The position of Uranus in a pattern

5. What does the professor imply about the asteroid belt?

   (A) It is farther from the Sun than Uranus.
   (B) Bode believed it was made up of small stars.
   (C) It is located where people expected to find a planet.
   (D) Ceres is the only one of the asteroids that can be seen without a telescope.

6. *Listen again to part of the lecture by playing Track 8.*
   Then answer the question.

   Why does the professor say this?

   (A) To introduce an alternative application of Bode's Law
   (B) To give an example of what Bode's Law cannot explain
   (C) To describe the limitations of gravitational theory
   (D) To contrast Bode's Law with a real scientific law

PRACTICE SET 4 SCRIPT AND ANSWERS

Track 7 Listening Script

Narrator

Listen to part of a lecture in an astronomy class. You will not need to remember the numbers the professor mentions.

Professor

OK. Let's get going. Today I'm going to talk about how the asteroid belt was discovered. And . . . I'm going to start by writing some numbers on the board. Here they are: we'll start with zero, then 3, . . . 6, . . . 12. Uh, tell me what I'm doing.

Female Student

Multiplying by 2?

Professor

Right. I'm doubling the numbers, so 2 times 12 is 24, and the next one I'm going to write after 24 would be . . .

Female Student

48.

Professor

48. Then 96. We'll stop there for now. Uh, now I'll write another row of numbers under that. Tell me what I'm doing: 4, 7, 10 . . . How am I getting this second row?

Male Student

Adding 4 to the numbers in the first row.

Professor

I'm adding 4 to each number in the first row to give you a second row. So the last two will be 52, 100, and now tell me what I'm doing.

Female Student

Putting in a decimal?

Professor

Yes, I divided all those numbers by 10 by putting in a decimal point. Now I'm going to write the names of the planets under the numbers. Mercury . . . Venus . . . Earth . . . Mars.

So, what do the numbers mean? Do you remember from the reading?

Male Student

Is it the distance of the planets from the Sun?

Professor

Right. In astronomical units—not perfect, but tantalizingly close. The value for Mars is off by . . . 6 or 7 percent or so. It's . . . but it's within 10 percent of the average distance to Mars from the Sun. But I kind of have to skip the one after Mars for now. Then Jupiter's right there at 5-point something, and then Saturn is about 10 astronomical units from the Sun. Um, well, this pattern is known as Bode's Law.

Um, it isn't really a scientific law, not in the sense of predicting gravitation mathematically or something, but it's attempting a pattern in the spacing of the planets, and it was noticed by Bode hundreds of years ago. Well, you can imagine that there was some interest in why the 2.8 spot in the pattern was skipped, and um . . . but there wasn't anything obvious there, in the early telescopes. Then what happened in the late 1700s? The discovery of . . . ?

Female Student

Another planet?

Professor

The next planet out, Uranus—after Saturn.

And look, Uranus fits in the next spot in the pattern pretty nicely, um, not perfectly, but close. And so then people got really excited about the validity of this thing and finding the missing object between Mars and Jupiter. And telescopes, remember, were getting better. So people went to work on finding objects that would be at that missing distance from the Sun, and then in 1801, the object Ceres was discovered.

And Ceres was in the right place—the missing spot. Uh, but it was way too faint to be a planet. It looked like a little star. Uh, and because of its starlike appearance, um, it was called an "asteroid." OK? *Aster* is Greek for "star," as in *astronomy*. Um, and so, Ceres was the first and is the largest of what became many objects discovered at that same distance. Not just one thing, but all the objects found at that distance form the asteroid belt. So the asteroid belt is the most famous success of this Bode's Law. That's how the asteroid belt was discovered.

Answers and Explanations

1. **D** This is a Detail question. Although the entire passage is concerned with answering "What is Bode's Law?" the professor specifically answers the question when he says, "it's attempting a pattern in the spacing of the planets." The correct answer to this question is choice D.

2. **B** This is a Gist-Purpose question. Gist questions are not usually answered very explicitly in the passage, but in this case the professor addresses the purpose of the discussion twice. At one point he says, "Today I'm going to talk about how the asteroid belt was discovered," and later he states, "That's how the asteroid belt was discovered." The correct answer to this question is choice B.

3. **A** This is an Understanding Organization question. The professor first demonstrates the pattern of numbers before explaining Bode's Law and what the pattern means. The correct answer to this question is choice A.

4. **A** **D** This is a Detail question. Note that for this question there are two correct answers. The professor explains that "Uranus fits in the next spot in the pattern pretty nicely" and telescopes "were getting better . . . and then in 1801, the object Ceres was discovered." Choices A and D are the correct answers. Advances in mathematics and the discovery of a new star are not mentioned by the professor.

5. **C** This is a Making Inferences question. Starting at the point in the passage where the professor says, "there was some interest in why the 2.8 spot in the pattern was skipped . . . there wasn't anything obvious there," it's clear that what the astronomers were looking for was a planet. He later says, "Ceres was in the right place . . . but it was way too faint to be a planet." The clear implication is that astronomers were expecting to find a planet. The correct answer to the question is choice C.

6. **D** This replay question requires you to Understand the Function of What Is Said. The pattern the professor describes is called Bode's Law. The professor is pointing out how Bode's Law differs from other scientific laws. The correct answer to this question is choice D.

PRACTICE SET 5

Now listen to Track 9.

Questions

Directions: Mark your answer by filling in the oval or square next to your choice.

1. What aspect of Manila hemp fibers does the professor mainly describe in the lecture?

    Ⓐ Similarities between cotton fibers and Manila hemp fibers
    Ⓑ Various types of Manila hemp fibers
    Ⓒ The economic importance of Manila hemp fibers
    Ⓓ A use of Manila hemp fibers

2. What does the professor imply about the name "Manila hemp"?

    Ⓐ It is a commercial brand name.
    Ⓑ Part of the name is inappropriate.
    Ⓒ The name has recently changed.
    Ⓓ The name was first used in the 1940s.

3. Why does the professor mention the Golden Gate Bridge?

    Ⓐ To demonstrate a disadvantage of steel cables
    Ⓑ To give an example of the creative use of color
    Ⓒ To show that steel cables are able to resist salt water
    Ⓓ To give an example of a use of Manila hemp

4. According to the professor, what was the main reason that many ships used Manila hemp ropes instead of steel cables?

    Ⓐ Manila hemp was cheaper.
    Ⓑ Manila hemp was easier to produce.
    Ⓒ Manila hemp is more resistant to salt water.
    Ⓓ Manila hemp is lighter in weight.

5. According to the lecture, what are two ways to increase the strength of rope made from Manila hemp fibers?
    Choose 2 answers.

    ☐A Coat the fibers with zinc-based paint
    ☐B Combine the fibers into bundles
    ☐C Soak bundles of fibers in salt water
    ☐D Twist bundles of fibers

6. *Listen again to part of the lecture by playing Track 10.*
    Then answer the question.

    Why does the professor mention going away for the weekend?

    Ⓐ To tell the class a joke
    Ⓑ To apologize for not completing some work
    Ⓒ To introduce the topic of the lecture
    Ⓓ To encourage students to ask about her trip

PRACTICE SET 5 SCRIPT AND ANSWERS

Track 9 Listening Script

Narrator

Listen to part of a lecture from a botany class.

Professor

Hi, everyone. Good to see you all today. Actually, I expected the population to be a lot lower today. It typically runs between 50 and 60 percent on the day the research paper is due. Um, I was hoping to have your exams back today, but, uh, the situation was that I went away for the weekend, and I was supposed to get in yesterday at five, and I expected to fully complete all the exams by midnight or so, which is the time that I usually go to bed, but my flight was delayed, and I ended up not getting in until one o'clock in the morning. Anyway, I'll do my best to have them finished by the next time we meet.

OK. In the last class, we started talking about useful plant fibers. In particular, we talked about cotton fibers, which we said were very useful, not only in the textile industry, but also in the chemical industry, and in the production of many products, such as plastics, paper, explosives, and so on. Today we'll continue talking about useful fibers, and we'll begin with a fiber that's commonly known as "Manila hemp."

Now, for some strange reason, many people believe that Manila hemp is a hemp plant. But Manila hemp is not really hemp. It's actually a member of the banana family—it even bears little banana-shaped fruits. The "Manila" part of the name makes sense, because Manila hemp is produced chiefly in the Philippine Islands, and, of course, the capital city of the Philippines is Manila.

Now, as fibers go, Manila hemp fibers are very long. They can easily be several feet in length, and they're also very strong, very flexible. They have one more characteristic that's very important, and that is that they are exceptionally resistant to salt water. And this combination of characteristics—long, strong, flexible, resistant to salt water—makes Manila hemp a great material for ropes, especially for ropes that are gonna be used on oceangoing ships. In fact, by the early 1940s, even though steel cables were available, most ships in the United States Navy were not moored with steel cables; they were moored with Manila hemp ropes.

Now, why was that? Well, the main reason was that steel cables degrade very, very quickly in contact with salt water. If you've ever been to San Francisco, you know that the Golden Gate Bridge is red. And it's red because of the zinc paint that goes on those stainless steel cables. That, if they start at one end of the bridge and they work to the other end, by the time they finish, it's already time to go back and start painting the beginning of the bridge again, because the bridge was built with steel cables, and steel cables can't take the salt air unless they're treated repeatedly with a zinc-based paint.

On the other hand, plant products like Manila hemp, you can drag through the ocean for weeks on end. If you wanna tie your anchor to it and drop it right into the ocean, that's no problem, because plant fibers can stand up for months, even years, in direct contact with salt water. OK. So how do you take plant fibers that individually you could break with your hands and turn them into a rope that's strong enough to moor a ship that weighs thousands of tons? Well, what you do is extract these long fibers from the Manila hemp plant, and then you take several of these fibers, and you group them into a bundle, because by grouping the fibers, you greatly increase their breaking strength—that bundle of fibers is much stronger than any of the individual fibers that compose it. And then you take that bundle of fibers and you twist it a little bit, because by twisting it, you increase its breaking strength even more. And then you take several of these little bundles, and you group and twist them into bigger bundles, which you then group and twist into even bigger bundles, and so on, until eventually, you end up with a very, very strong rope.

Answers and Explanations

1. **D** Questions like this one that ask about what the professor mainly discusses are Gist-Content questions. This question asks what aspect of Manila hemp fibers are mainly discussed, so it has a narrower focus than other Gist-Content questions. The professor mainly discusses characteristics of Manila hemp and how these characteristics make Manila hemp useful to the shipping industry. The correct answer to this question is choice D.

2. **B** This is a Making Inferences question. The professor explains that Manila hemp is produced chiefly in the area near Manila, so the word *Manila* in the name is appropriate. However, Manila hemp is not a type of hemp plant, so the word *hemp* in the name is not appropriate. The correct answer to this question is choice B.

3. **A** This is an Understanding Organization question. The professor mentions the Golden Gate Bridge in order to make a comparison between the steel cables of the bridge and Manila hemp ropes. The fact that the steel cables must be constantly repainted is a disadvantage. The correct answer to the question is choice A.

4. **C** This is a Detail question. It is related to the professor's main point about Manila hemp. The professor says that Manila hemp is "exceptionally resistant to salt water." Much of the lecture deals with the professor's reinforcing and exemplifying this point. The correct answer to this question is choice C.

5. **B** **D** Near the end of the lecture, the professor describes how Manila hemp ropes are made. The answer to this Detail question can be found there. The professor talks about grouping fibers into bundles and then twisting the bundles to make them stronger. Note that this question requires two answers. The correct answers to this question are choices B and D.

6. **B** This replay question requires you to Understand the Function of What Is Said. The professor mentions that she went away for the weekend and because a flight was delayed, she was late returning. She tells this story in order to apologize for not completing marking exams. The correct answer to this question is choice B.

4

Speaking Section

The Speaking Section

托福口语考试的目的在于测试那些母语为非英语、想在英语国家或地区攻读本科或研究生学位的学生英语口语表达的熟练程度。与托福考试其他部分一样，口语部分同样在互联网上进行。

在口语部分，考生需要就基于个人经历、校园环境和学术性材料提出的各种话题用英语表达自己的观点。口语部分共有四道题。第一道题是独立口语任务，考生需要完全依据自己的观点、见解或经历来回答问题。另外三道题是综合口语任务，考生需要听一则对话或节选的讲座片段，或先读一篇文章然后听一个简短的讨论或讲座的节选，最后答题。这部分之所以被称为"综合任务"是因为它将各种英语能力结合起来——听、说兼顾，或者听、读和说结合。在回答此类问题的时候，考生需要根据所听到的讨论或讲座中的信息答题，或结合听力材料和阅读材料一起答题。

TIP

对于口语部分的所有题目，考生有45~60秒的答题时间。所以备考中注意做相应的计时练习。

口语部分历时17分钟，每道题有45~60秒的答题时间。在涉及听力的口语部分中，考生会在耳机中听到一段简短的文章或对话。在涉及阅读的口语部分中，考生会在屏幕上读到一段短文章。在整个口语考试中，考生可以记笔记，并在回答时作参考。在四道口语题目中，考生会有简短的准备时间。考生通过麦克风回答问题，回答会被记录下来并传送到评分中心。专业的评分人和自动评分系统SpeechRater®会对考生的回答打分。

TIP

熟悉评分标准，这会帮助考生了解评分的过程。

评分人将对考生的回答进行综合评分，即评分人会综合考虑考生回答的各方面的特点，然后根据考生在答题过程中展现出来的综合能力给出分数。尽管各个题目的评分标准有所差异，但是总体上评分人会综合以下因素：

- 总体陈述印象：考生是否能做到清晰表达。好的表达应该流畅清晰、发音正确、语速适中、语音语调自然。

- 语言运用：考生是否能有效地使用英文语法和词汇来表达自己的思想。评分人会考查考生能否熟练运用简单和复杂的语言结构和恰当的词汇。

- 话题发展：考生是否能完成命题所要求的所有任务，表达是否连贯一致。好的表达应该能在规定时间内完成，并且能够让评分人很容易听出各个观点之间的关系和思想之间的衔接。

另外重要的一点就是评分人并没有指望考生的回答完美无缺，高分的回答也可能会在以上三个方面有一些小错误。

本书第180~183页有详细的评分标准说明，供考生参考。

Speaking Tasks

The Independent Task

Question 1: Paired Choice

在这个独立口语任务题中，考生将会在屏幕上看到两种有可能发生的行为、情景或观点。题目要求考生谈论更喜欢哪一种行为或情景，或是认为哪种观点更合理，作出选择后详细解释作出这种选择的原因。考生有45秒钟时间作答。

这道题目涉及的话题都是与学生的日常生活和兴趣爱好息息相关的，例如：在家学习好还是在图书馆学习好；学生在选择课程时应该广泛涉猎还是应该集中在某一个特定领域。或者，考生也可能看到对于一个熟悉的话题的两种截然不同的观点，例如：电视对人类而言到底是利大于弊还是弊大于利。另外，题目还有可能要求考生选择同意其中的一个观点，例如：一年级的大学生应该住在学校宿舍还是住在校外自己的公寓。

在这道题目中，考生要说明自己的选择、喜好或者观点是什么，并解释原因，即：用理由、解释、细节或事例来支持自己的回答。一定要对问题的各个部分作出全面的回答，对自己的观点应十分清楚，并且一定要给出作出某个选择的理由。考生选择哪种行为、场景或观点都没关系，与第一题一样，回答是没有"对"与"错"之分的。考生的选择不会影响评分，而考生对所作的选择是如何给出理由和细节进行支持的才是评分人的关注点所在。

> **TIP**
>
> 一个非常好的训练方法就是自己陈述一个观点或一个偏好，然后给出清晰的理由和细节进行支持。

本题的题目将会呈现在电脑屏幕上，与此同时会由人声朗读问题，考生将会有15秒钟时间进行准备。在准备过程中，应该想想自己该说些什么，组织一下思路，并简单记下认为对自己作答有帮助的内容。但是切记不要试图写下所有的回答，只记下几个能够在作答过程中给予提醒和线索的单词或短语就可以了。

> **TIP**
>
> 学习并练习一些常用的表达观点的单词和短语，如：
> *In my opinion . . .*
> *I believe . . .*

Example The following example shows how a question of this type will appear on your computer screen.

Some students study for classes individually. Others study in groups. Which method of studying do you think is better for students and why?

| Preparation Time: 15 Seconds |
| Response Time: 45 Seconds |

After you hear the question, you will be told when to begin to prepare your response and when to begin speaking. A "Preparation Time" clock will appear below the question and begin to count down from 15 seconds (00:00:15). At the end of 15 seconds you will hear a short beep. After the beep, the clock will change to read "Response Time" and will begin to count down from 45 seconds (00:00:45). When the response time has ended, recording will stop and a new screen will appear alerting you that the response time has ended.

In answering a question like this one, it is important that you begin by clearly stating what your opinion is: do you think it is better for students to study for classes individually, or do you think it is better for them to study in groups? If you do not begin by stating your opinion, it may be difficult for someone listening to your response to understand your reasons for holding that opinion. As for the reasons you give in support of your opinion, they can vary widely and may be based on your own experience and observations. For example, if the position you take is that it is better for students to study alone, you might say that when students meet to study in groups, they often waste time discussing matters that have nothing to do with their class work. You might continue this explanation by contrasting the inefficiency of studying in a group with the kind of productivity a student can achieve when studying alone. If you have personal experiences that help illustrate your point, you might want to include them in your explanation. If so, you should be clear about how they illustrate your point. Or perhaps you want to take the opposite position, that it is better for students to study in groups. In that case, you would explain the advantages of group study and the disadvantages of studying alone. Perhaps you think that the more capable students can help the less capable students when students study together. Or perhaps you have found that students who study in groups often share each other's lecture notes, and this way they can make sure everyone understands all the material that has been covered in a course. There are many good reasons for either choice. In fact, it may be your opinion that in some cases it is better to study in groups and in other cases it is better to study alone. If that is the opinion you would like to express, you should explain—with reasons, examples, and/or specific details—why group study is better in some cases and individual study is better in others. Here again, there is no "right" or "wrong" answer to a question like this. The important thing is to clearly communicate to the person who will be listening to your response what your opinion is and explain the reasons you have for holding it.

TIP

不要在考试前背答案，尤其是那些你从网上或者辅导老师那里获取的答案。提前背答案不是备考的好方法，这会降低你的分数。评分者可以识别出提前背好的回答，因为这样的答案在节奏、语调、甚至内容上都不同于即兴回答。提前背好的回答很容易被识别出来。

The Integrated Tasks

Question 2: Fit and Explain

这道题是口语考试三道综合任务题中的第一道。在这道题中，考生会在电脑屏幕中读到一篇与校园生活话题相关的短文。考生会听到两个人谈论该话题，并且就短文中所提到的话题表达自己的观点。接着，考生要依据所读到的和所听到的内容回答一个问题。考生有60秒的时间作口头回答。这些话题涉及的领域一般包括大学里的政策、规定或办事程序，大学的计划，校园设施，以及校园内的生活质量等。话题适合所有的应试者，考生不必事先具备在北美校园生活的经验。

阅读材料的形式多种多样。例如：有可能是大学行政管理部门有关新的停车规则的布告；或是一封致校报编辑的信，写信者表达对学校限制在宿舍收听无线电广播这个新规定的看法；又或是一篇校报的文章，讨论修建新的足球场的提案。除了对提案进行描述以外，阅读材料中通常还会列举两条要么支持要么反对该提案的理由。阅读文章很简短，一般包含80~110个单词，考生会有足够的时间阅读文章。

在阅读材料之后的对话中，考生会听到一个或是两个说话者——通常是学生——谈论刚才读到的文章（或信件、布告）中的话题。如果对话中有两个说话者，其中之一通常会对相关话题持鲜明观点——要么赞成，要么反对——并且还会给出理由支持自己的观点。两人的讨论也十分简短，通常在60~80秒之间。

在读完材料并听完讨论后，考生将被问到一个与所读和所听内容有关的问题。例如：阅读材料是有关设立新的大学规章制度的，还有一段对话是一位教授和一名学生对这项新的规章制度的讨论。如果在这段对话中，学生认为该制度是不合理的，题目就会要求考生依据阅读和听力材料中的信息说明这名学生的观点是什么，以及他/她给出了什么理由来支持自己的观点。

这项任务考查考生从两个信息源——阅读和听力——中综合信息，并对其中某方面进行总结的能力。阅读材料提供上下文以便考生理解听力材料中对话者所谈论的话题，而对话者通常只会间接地涉及阅读材料中的内容。因此，在阅读的过程中，考生必须对以下事情加以注意：提案的描述（即提出了什么，计划了什么，或改变了什么），以及支持或是反对该提案的理由。这将有助于考生在听对话时理解两个说话者到底在讨论些什么。

在有些情况下，说话者会反对阅读材料中的某个立场，并且提供信息对材料中支持该立场的理由进行质疑。在其他一些情况下，说话者会赞成阅读材料中的立场，并提供信息予以支持。因此，在听对话的过程中，考生必须要明确说话者对于提案的观点，并且弄清楚说话者所说的话和从阅读材料中所获取的信息之间的关系。

回答这道题时，考生不但要明白题目要求做什么，也要明白题目不要求做什么。这类综合任务题并不需要考生说明自己的观点，而是要求考生陈述其中一个说话者的观点，并且总结说话者持该观点的理由。

考生将会有40~45秒钟的时间来阅读短文，阅读时间的长短取决于文章的长短，之后会听到一段讨论。然后，考生将会有30秒的时间进行准备和60秒钟的时间作答。和其他所有题目一样，考生可以在阅读和听材料的过程中做笔记，并且可在答题时进行参照。

TIP

记住，考生可以在托福考试的综合口语任务中就阅读和听力材料做笔记。但不要把完整的答案都写出来，因为准备的时间并不长，并且评分人希望听到你回答这个问题，而不是念笔记。

Example
The following sample question consists of an announcement of a university's decision to increase tuition and a discussion between students about whether the increase is justified. This example shows how a question of this type will be presented to you on your computer.

You will hear:

Narrator

In this question, you will read a short passage about a campus situation and then listen to a talk on the same topic. You will then answer a question using information from both the reading passage and the talk. After you hear the question, you will have 30 seconds to prepare your response and 60 seconds to speak.

Then you will hear this:

Narrator

City University is planning to increase tuition and fees. Read the announcement about the increase from the president of City University.

You will have 45 seconds to read the announcement. Begin reading now.

Announcement from the President

The university has decided to increase tuition and fees for all students by approximately 8% next semester. For the past 5 years, the tuition and fees have remained the same, but it is necessary to increase them now for several reasons. The university has many more students than we had 5 years ago, and we must hire additional professors to teach these students. We have also made a new commitment to research and technology and will be renovating and upgrading our laboratory facilities to better meet our students' needs.

The reading passage will appear on the screen.

When the passage appears, a clock at the top of your computer screen will begin counting down the time you have to read. When reading time has ended, the passage will disappear from the screen and will be replaced by a picture of two students engaged in conversation.

You will then hear:

Narrator

Now listen to two students as they discuss the announcement.

Then the dialogue will begin.

Man

Oh, great, now we have to come up with more money for next semester.

Woman

Yeah, I know, but I can see why. When I first started here, classes were so much smaller than they are now. With this many students, it's hard to get the personal attention you need . . .

Man

Yeah, I guess you're right. You know, in some classes I can't even get a seat. And I couldn't take the math course I wanted to because it was already full when I signed up.

Woman

And the other thing is, well, I am kind of worried about not being able to get a job after I graduate.

Man

Why? I mean you're doing really well in your classes, aren't you?

Woman

I'm doing OK, but the facilities here are so limited. There are some great new experiments in microbiology that we can't even do here . . . there isn't enough equipment in the laboratories, and the equipment they have is out of date. How am I going to compete for jobs with people who have practical research experience? I think the extra tuition will be a good investment.

When the dialogue has ended, the picture of the students will be replaced by the following:

Now get ready to answer the question.

The question will then appear on your computer screen and will also be read aloud by the narrator.

> The woman expresses her opinion of the announcement by the university president. State her opinion and explain the reasons she gives for holding that opinion.
>
> **Preparation Time: 30 Seconds**
> **Response Time: 60 Seconds**

After you hear the question, you will be told when to begin to prepare your response and when to begin speaking. A "Preparation Time" clock will appear below the question and begin to count down from 30 seconds (00:00:30). At the end of 30 seconds you will hear a short beep. After the beep, the clock will change to read "Response Time" and will begin counting down from 60 seconds (00:01:00). When the response time has ended, recording will stop and a new screen will appear alerting you that the response time has ended.

TIP

尽量通过说话人的语调、重读和选词听出说话人的态度。这有助于理解他/她的观点并有助于考生规划自己的回答。

在回答这个问题的时候，考生应该先陈述女士对于增加学费的观点，然后解释她持该观点的原因。考生在听材料的时候可能已经注意到她的理由与校方的理由非常相似，只不过她是从学生的角度来谈的。所以在回答时，考生可以将听力材料和阅读材料中的信息联系起来。开始可以说："The woman agrees with the announcement and thinks that the university is right to increase its fees." 在描述她的理由的时候，可以说："She thinks the tuition increase is necessary because the university can then hire more teachers. She feels that classes are getting too crowded and more teachers are needed." 你还可以提一下："She has found it hard to get personal attention from her professors." 并指出："She agrees that the money should be spent to improve laboratory facilities because they are out of date, and this has made it hard for her to get the practical laboratory experience she feels she needs to get a good job." 回答应该尽可能完整，以使没有看过这则通知或没有听过对话的人在听了你的表达后，也能了解新的政策、女士的观点以及她的理由。在阅读文章和对话中有很多信息，考生无须在回答中一一总结所有信息。

Question 3: General/Specific

本题是综合口语任务的第二道题。在这道题中，考生需要先读一篇学术类短文，然后听一个教授有关此话题的讲座的节选。之后，考生需要根据听力和阅读材料答题，答题时间是60秒。

TIP

找一些自己感兴趣的听力和阅读材料。听力材料和阅读材料的观点可以相似也可以相反。在听和读的时候可以自己记笔记并且列出纲要。根据笔记和纲要对听力和阅读材料中的信息进行口头总结。尽量使用不同的单词和语法结构对所听到和读到的信息进行转述。

本题中的话题涉及很多领域：生命科学、社会科学、自然科学和人文科学。尽管本题中的材料带有学术色彩，但是考生无须事先对材料涉及的领域有任何了解。不管考生的学术背景如何，一般都能理解材料中的语言和概念。

短文长度通常为80~110词。它会提供一些背景知识使考生能够理解接下来教授的讲座。短文对材料的处理一般比较笼统和抽象，而讲座通过扩展事例、举反例或运用短文中的概念，通常会更具体、更详细。回答这道题时，考生需要依据短文和讲座中的信息并且对其中的关键信息进行整合和表达。

例如，有些题目中的短文对一个总的规则或过程下了定义，讲座中谈到与此相关的一个具体例子或反例。这样的题目会要求考生用讲座中的具体例子解释短文中的规则或过程。另一种情况是短文描述了一个问题，而听力材料描述了针对该问题的一些或成功或失败，甚至会带来意想不到的结果的解决方案。题目要求考生解释问题的解决方案并说明其结果。

下面的题目是一个很典型的例子。开始是一篇短文，描写了一个总的概念——动物的驯养，主要描述了适宜驯养的动物的两个特点。在这篇文章之后的讲座中，教授谈到了两类动物的行为——一种是大家所熟知的、具有以上两个特征的动物，另一种是普通的、不具有以上两个特征的、未经驯养的动物。问题要求考生将短文中的一般规则运用在讲座提到的例子中，并解释两种动物的行为是如何决定它们是否适合被驯养的。

Example

The following example shows how a question of this type will be presented to you on your computer. Question 3 will be presented visually in the same way as question 2.

First you will hear the narrator say this:

Narrator

In this question, you will read a short passage on an academic subject and then listen to a talk on the same topic. You will then answer a question using information from both the reading passage and the talk. After you hear the question, you will have 30 seconds to prepare your response and 60 seconds to speak.

Then you will hear this:

Narrator

Now read the passage about animal domestication. You have 45 seconds to read the passage. Begin reading now.

The reading passage will then appear on the screen.

Animal Domestication

For thousands of years, humans have been able to domesticate, or tame, many large mammals that in the wild live together in herds. Once tamed, these mammals are used for agricultural work and transportation. Yet some herd mammals are not easily domesticated.

A good indicator of an animal's suitability for domestication is how protective the animal is of its territory. Nonterritorial animals are more easily domesticated than territorial animals because they can live close together with animals from other herds. A second indicator is that animals with a hierarchical social structure, in which herd members follow a leader, are easy to domesticate, since a human can function as the "leader."

A clock at the top of your computer screen will count down the time you have to read. When reading time has ended, a picture of a professor in front of a class will appear on the screen:

And you will hear this:

Narrator

Now listen to a lecture on this topic in an ecology class.

Then you will hear the lecture.

Professor

So we've been discussing the suitability of animals for domestication . . . particularly animals that live together in herds. Now, if we take horses, for example . . . in the wild, horses live in herds that consist of one male and several females and their young. When a herd moves, the dominant male leads, with the dominant female and her young immediately behind him. The dominant female and her young are then followed immediately by the second most important female and her young, and so on. This is why domesticated horses can be harnessed one after the other in a row. They're "programmed" to follow the lead of another horse. On top of that, you often find different herds of horses in the wild occupying overlapping areas—they don't fight off other herds that enter the same territory.

But it's exactly the opposite with an animal like the, uh, the antelope . . . which . . . well, antelopes are herd animals too. But unlike horses, a male antelope will fight fiercely to prevent another male from entering its territory during the breeding season; OK—very different from the behavior of horses. Try keeping a couple of male antelopes together in a small space and see what happens. Also, antelopes don't have a social hierarchy—they don't instinctively follow any leader. That makes it harder for humans to control their behavior.

When the lecture has ended, the picture of the professor will be replaced by a screen instructing you to get ready to answer the question. Then the question will appear on the screen and will be read aloud by a narrator as well.

The professor describes the behavior of horses and antelope in herds. Explain how their behavior is related to their suitability for domestication.

Preparation Time: 30 Seconds
Response Time: 60 Seconds

After you hear the question, you will be told when to begin to prepare your response and when to begin speaking. A "Preparation Time" clock will appear below the question and begin to count down from 30 seconds (00:00:30). At the end of 30 seconds you will hear a short beep. After the beep, the clock will change to read "Response Time" and will begin to count down from 60 seconds (00:01:00). When the response time has ended, recording will stop and a new screen will appear alerting you that the response time has ended.

TIP

阅读一篇短文，把文中的主要观点列成提纲。使用提纲对短文进行口头总结。然后，在提纲中加入细节，并再次口头总结。

回答这个问题时，考生需要使用来自于听力和阅读材料中的信息，并把教授在讲座中提到的具体例子和阅读短文中较笼统的概念相联系。例如，考生开始可以说："Herd animals can be easily domesticated if they have a hierarchical social structure and are not territorial, and this is why it is easier to domesticate horses than antelopes." 考生还可以提供一些关于马的行为的细节信息，并指出："Their hierarchical social structure makes them willing to follow one another and thus allows a human being to act as their leader." 你还可以说："Because horses are not territorial, they can be harnessed together without fighting." 如果想把马和羚羊的占地行为作对比，那么可以说："Unlike horses, male antelopes fight if they are together, and because antelopes do not have a social hierarchy, humans cannot control them by acting as their leader." 请注意：考生无须一一总结阅读材料和讲座中的所有信息，但是考生需要提供足够的细节信息，以使即便没有看过短文或没听过讲座的人也能理解你的表达。注意，在所有学术类的口语表达任务中，答题所需的所有信息都在材料中，考生无须具备额外的知识。

Question 4: Summary

综合任务的最后一题是学术类题目。在这个问题中，考生首先要听教授就某一个学术问题所作讲座的节选，然后考生需要就此节选的内容答题。答题时间为60秒。

与其他综合任务（以及其他关于学术类内容的口语题）一样，话题内容涉及生命科学、社会科学、自然科学和人文科学。同样，考生无须对材料所涉及的领域有任何了解即可听懂讲座并且答题。

讲座时间大约为60~90秒，重点集中于某一个学术话题。通常教授开始会解释一个概念、强调一个问题或介绍一种现象，然后讨论它的几个重要方面或与其相关的观点。讲座中会有一些说明性的例子来解释或阐明主要的概念或问题。题目主要是要求考生使用讲座中的观点和例子来说明其中的主要概念和问题。

讲座关于程序、方法、理论、观点或任何现象——自然、社会、心理现象，或者其他。如果讲座是关于一个程序，教授可能通过描述它的一些功能来解释这个程序。如果讲座是关于一个理论，教授可能通过描述它的运用来解释这个理论。如果该讲座是关于一个现象，教授可能通过解释它的原因和影响来描述这个现象。

TIP

找一本每章之后都附有相关问题的课本，练习口头回答每个题目。

在下面的样题中，讲座是关于美国20世纪早期出现国家文化这一社会现象。教授通过描述促成它的两个因素——电台和汽车——来说明这个现象。听完讲座后，考生需要根据讲座的内容说明这两个因素是如何促进美国文化的形成的。

Example

The following example shows how a question of this type will be presented to you on your computer.

First you will hear the narrator say this:

Narrator

In this question, you will listen to a short lecture. You will then be asked to summarize important information from the lecture. After you hear the question, you will have 20 seconds to prepare your response and 60 seconds to speak.

Then a picture of a professor standing in front of a class will appear on your screen.

You will hear:

Narrator

Now listen to part of a talk in a United States history class.

The professor will then begin the lecture.

Professor

Because the United States is such a large country, it took time for a common national culture to emerge. One hundred years ago there was very little communication among the different regions of the United States. One result of this lack of communication was that people around the United States had very little in common with one another. People in different parts of the country spoke differently, dressed differently, and behaved differently. But connections among Americans began to increase thanks to two technological innovations: the automobile and the radio.

Automobiles began to be mass-produced in the 1920s, which meant they became less expensive and more widely available. Americans in small towns and rural communities now had the ability to travel with ease to nearby cities. They could even take vacations to other parts of the country. The increased mobility provided by automobiles changed people's attitudes and created links that had not existed before. For example, people in small towns began to adopt behaviors, clothes, and speech that were popular in big cities or in other parts of the country.

As more Americans were purchasing cars, radio ownership was also increasing dramatically. Americans in different regions of the country began to listen to the same popular radio programs and musical artists. People repeated things they heard on the radio—some phrases and speech patterns heard in songs and radio programs began to be used by people all over the United States. People also listened to news reports on the radio. They heard the same news throughout the country, whereas in newspapers much news tended to be local. Radio brought Americans together by offering them shared experiences and information about events around the country.

When the lecture has ended, the picture of the professor will be replaced by a screen instructing you to get ready to answer the question. Then the question will appear on the screen and be read aloud at the same time by the narrator.

Using points and examples from the talk, explain how the automobile and the radio contributed to a common culture in the United States.

Preparation Time: 20 Seconds
Response Time: 60 Seconds

After you hear the question, you will be told when to begin preparing your response and when to begin speaking. A "Preparation Time" clock will appear below the question and begin to count down from 20 seconds (00:00:20). At the end of 20 seconds you will hear a short beep. After the beep, the clock will change to read "Response Time" and will begin to count down from 60 seconds (00:01:00). When the response time has ended, recording will stop and a new screen will appear alerting you that the response time has ended.

回答这个问题时，考生可以介绍一些背景知识："The United States did not have a common culture 100 years ago because people in different regions of the country did not communicate much with each other." 然后可以说："The automobile and the radio changed this situation." 接下来对讲座中关于该现象起因的信息进行总结，例如："When automobiles became inexpensive, people from small towns could travel easily to cities or to other parts of the country, and when they began to do this, they started acting like people from those other regions and started to dress and speak in the same way." 至于电台起的作用，考生可以指出："When radio became popular, people from different parts of the country began listening to the same programs and the same news reports and began to speak alike and have similar experiences and ideas." 如果还有时间，可以下个结论："These similar ways of speaking and dressing and thinking became the national culture of the United States." 记住：考生无须重复讲座中的所有信息。讲座中的信息太多，无法一一罗列。但考生需要提供足够的信息使没有听过讲座的人也能很好地了解教授的授课。

总结题中的讲座的内容还可能包括人类是如何学习的，其中心概念是当两个事件在人的大脑中发生联系的时候，学习过程就开始了。教授通过描写事件在大脑中联系的两种方法来说明这个问题。题目会要求考生使用讲座中的观点和例子来说明事件联系的这些方式是怎样促成学习过程的。抑或是一个关于货币的讲座，教授会提出货币的两种不同定义并用例子来说明。考生需要使用讲座中的例子来解释这些定义。讲座后的题目通常会要求考生使用讲座中的观点和例子来说明人类学习的方式或货币的定义。

Speaking Scoring Rubric

Independent Task: Question 1

Score	General Description	Delivery	Language Use	Topic Development
4	The response fulfills the demands of the task, with at most minor lapses in completeness. It is highly intelligible and exhibits sustained, coherent discourse. A response at this level is characterized by all of the following:	Generally well-paced flow (fluid expression). Speech is clear. It may include minor lapses, or minor difficulties with pronunciation or intonation patterns, which do not affect intelligibility.	The response demonstrates effective use of grammar and vocabulary. It exhibits a fairly high degree of automaticity with good control of basic and complex structures (as appropriate). Some minor (or systematic) errors are noticeable but do not obscure meaning.	Response is sustained and sufficient to the task. It is generally well developed and coherent; relationships between ideas are clear (or there is a clear progression of ideas).
3	The response addresses the task appropriately, but may fall short of being fully developed. It is generally intelligible and coherent, with some fluidity of expression, though it exhibits some noticeable lapses in the expression of ideas. A response at this level is characterized by at least two of the following:	Speech is generally clear, with some fluidity of expression, though minor difficulties with pronunciation, intonation, or pacing are noticeable and may require listener effort at times (though overall intelligibility is not significantly affected).	The response demonstrates fairly automatic and effective use of grammar and vocabulary and fairly coherent expression of relevant ideas. Response may exhibit some imprecise or inaccurate use of vocabulary or grammatical structures. This may affect overall fluency, but it does not seriously interfere with the communication of the message.	Response is mostly coherent and sustained and conveys relevant ideas/information. Overall development is somewhat limited, usually lacking elaboration or specificity. Relationships between ideas may at times not be immediately clear.

Speaking Scoring Rubric

Independent Task: Question 1

Score	General Description	Delivery	Language Use	Topic Development
2	The response addresses the task, but development of the topic is limited. It contains intelligible speech, although problems with delivery and/or overall coherence occur; meaning may be obscured in places. A response at this level is characterized by at least two of the following:	Speech is basically intelligible, though listener effort is needed because of unclear articulation, awkward intonation, or choppy rhythm/pace; meaning may be obscured in places.	The response demonstrates limited range and control of grammar and vocabulary. These limitations often prevent full expression of ideas. For the most part, only basic sentence structures are used successfully and spoken with fluidity. Structures and vocabulary may express mainly simple (short) and/or general propositions, with simple or unclear connections made among them (serial listing, conjunction, juxtaposition).	The response is connected to the task, though the number of ideas presented or the development of ideas is limited. Mostly basic ideas are expressed, with limited elaboration (details and support). At times relevant substance may be vaguely expressed or repetitious. Connections of ideas may be unclear.
1	The response is very limited in content and/or coherence or is only minimally connected to the task, or speech is largely unintelligible. A response at this level is characterized by at least two of the following:	Consistent pronunciation, stress, and intonation difficulties cause considerable listener effort; delivery is choppy, fragmented, or telegraphic; frequent pauses and hesitations.	Range and control of grammar and vocabulary severely limit (or prevent) expression of ideas and connections among ideas. Some low-level responses may rely heavily on practiced or formulaic expressions.	Limited relevant content expressed. The response generally lacks substance beyond expression of very basic ideas. Speaker may be unable to sustain speech to complete the task and may rely heavily on repetition of the prompt.
0	Speaker makes no attempt to respond OR response is unrelated to the topic.			

Speaking Scoring Rubric

Integrated Tasks: Questions 2, 3, and 4

Score	General Description	Delivery	Language Use	Topic Development
4	The response fulfills the demands of the task, with at most minor lapses in completeness. It is highly intelligible and exhibits sustained, coherent discourse. A response at this level is characterized by all of the following:	Speech is generally clear, fluid, and sustained. It may include minor lapses or minor difficulties with pronunciation or intonation. Pace may vary at times as speaker attempts to recall information. Overall intelligibility remains high.	The response demonstrates good control of basic and complex grammatical structures that allow for coherent, efficient (automatic) expression of relevant ideas. Contains generally effective word choice. Though some minor (or systematic) errors or imprecise use may be noticeable, they do not require listener effort (or obscure meaning).	The response presents a clear progression of ideas and conveys the relevant information required by the task. It includes appropriate detail, though it may have minor errors or minor omissions.
3	The response addresses the task appropriately, but may fall short of being fully developed. It is generally intelligible and coherent, with some fluidity of expression, though it exhibits some noticeable lapses in the expression of ideas. A response at this level is characterized by at least two of the following:	Speech is generally clear, with some fluidity of expression, but it exhibits minor difficulties with pronunciation, intonation, or pacing and may require some listener effort at times. Overall intelligibility remains good, however.	The response demonstrates fairly automatic and effective use of grammar and vocabulary and fairly coherent expression of relevant ideas. Response may exhibit some imprecise or inaccurate use of vocabulary or grammatical structures or be somewhat limited in the range of structures used. Such limitations do not seriously interfere with the communication of the message.	The response is sustained and conveys relevant information required by the task. However, it exhibits some incompleteness, inaccuracy, lack of specificity with respect to content, or choppiness in the progression of ideas.

Speaking Scoring Rubric

Integrated Tasks: Questions 2, 3, and 4

Score	General Description	Delivery	Language Use	Topic Development
2	The response is connected to the task, though it may be missing some relevant information or contain inaccuracies. It contains some intelligible speech, but at times problems with intelligibility and/or overall coherence may obscure meaning. A response at this level is characterized by at least two of the following:	Speech is clear at times, though it exhibits problems with pronunciation, intonation, or pacing and so may require significant listener effort. Speech may not be sustained at a consistent level throughout. Problems with intelligibility may obscure meaning in places (but not throughout).	The response is limited in the range and control of vocabulary and grammar demonstrated (some complex structures may be used, but typically contain errors). This results in limited or inaccurate connections. Automaticity of expression may be evident only at the phrasal level.	The response conveys some relevant information but is clearly incomplete or inaccurate. It is incomplete if it omits key ideas, makes vague reference to key ideas, or demonstrates limited development of important information. An inaccurate response demonstrates misunderstanding of key ideas from the stimulus. Typically, ideas expressed may not be well connected or cohesive, so that familiarity with the stimulus is necessary in order to follow what is being discussed.
1	The response is very limited in content or coherence or is only minimally connected to the task. Speech may be largely unintelligible. A response at this level is characterized by at least two of the following:	Consistent pronunciation and intonation problems cause considerable listener effort and frequently obscure meaning. Delivery is choppy, fragmented, or telegraphic. Speech contains frequent pauses and hesitations.	Range and control of grammar and vocabulary severely limit (or prevent) expression of ideas and connections among ideas. Some very low-level responses may rely on isolated words or short utterances to communicate ideas.	The response fails to provide much relevant content. Ideas that are expressed are often inaccurate, or limited to vague utterances or repetitions (including repetition of prompt).
0	Speaker makes no attempt to respond OR response is unrelated to the topic.			

Strategies for Preparing for and Taking the Speaking Section

Preparing for the Speaking Section

- 考生在做本书的托福考试测试题的口语部分时，要仔细听自己的每一个回答录音。用一套指导性问题来评估自己的回答。可参考以下问题：

  ○ Did I complete the task?
  ○ Did I speak clearly?
  ○ Did I avoid grammatical errors?
  ○ Did I use words correctly?
  ○ Did I organize my ideas clearly and appropriately?
  ○ Did I provide a complete response?
  ○ Did I use the time effectively?

  一旦评估结束，想一想自己的回答可以作哪些改进。然后再录一遍。比较两次的回答，看是否还需要进一步改进。

- 经常分析自己口语表达中的优缺点。试着去了解自己的优势、劣势及其原因。

- 当评估自己的口语表达时，注意语速。在每次练习后问自己以下问题：

  ○ Did I speak too fast?
  ○ Did I speak too slowly?
  ○ Did I pause too often?

- 为了记录自己进步的轨迹，考生可以制作一个"口语日志"，用来存放自己的回答。也可以把它拿给朋友或老师听，并询问他们的建议。

Tips for the Day of the Test

- 记住：托福口语综合任务的听力和阅读材料都是允许做笔记的。

- 仔细听每部分的答题说明，明确题目到底要求做什么。

- 尽可能有效地使用准备时间。用一种简单有序的方式来组织自己想要表达的重要观点。

- 不要在规定时间开始之前答题。

- 在规定时间内尽可能完整地回答问题。

- 务必调整麦克风的位置并调节音量。

- 以适中的音量对准麦克风说话。不要让嘴巴直接碰到麦克风，不然，评分人会听不清你的回答。

- 不要低声说话。如果这样，评分人会听不清回答。

Frequently Asked Questions About the *TOEFL®* Speaking Section

1. Why does the TOEFL iBT® test include a Speaking section?

The focus of the test is on communicative competence and encompasses your ability to use English to communicate effectively in an academic setting. Speaking is a key communication skill, along with listening, reading, and writing.

2. Why are some of the questions in the Speaking section based on reading passages and/or dialogues or lectures?

Speaking tasks that combine reading passages and/or dialogues or lectures with speaking are called integrated tasks. They are included in the *TOEFL iBT®* test in recognition of the fact that to succeed academically in English-speaking colleges and universities, students need to be able to combine all their English language skills—in reading, listening, and speaking, as well as writing—inside and outside the classroom.

3. How much reading and listening will I have to do for the Speaking section?

The reading and listening materials that are associated with the integrated tasks vary in length but are all quite brief. Reading passages range from approximately 80 to 110 words, and the dialogues or lectures are generally between 60 and 90 seconds long. In addition to being short, the reading passages, dialogues, and lectures are not intended to be difficult. They are designed to provide you with clear and accessible information to use in answering the questions.

4. May I take notes at all times during the Speaking section?

Yes. You may take notes at any time during the Speaking section—while reading the written passages, listening to the spoken dialogues or lectures, and preparing your responses. While you listen to the dialogues or lectures and take notes, you should *not* try to write down word for word everything you hear. If you try to do this, you will probably miss hearing important information. Similarly, while preparing your spoken response, do not try to write out an answer that you will then try to speak. You will not have enough time to write out a full response, and raters will be rating you on your ability to speak, not on your ability to read aloud from a text that you have written. Instead, you should use your preparation time to review whatever notes you have taken and to organize your ideas.

5. How will my responses be rated?

Each Speaking response is scored by both human raters and the ETS automated scoring engine, *SpeechRater®*. The human raters evaluate your response for topic development, delivery, and language use, using the *TOEFL iBT®* Speaking rubrics. *SpeechRater®* primarily measures features described in the Speaking rubrics under Language Use and Delivery.

6. How will the total Speaking section score be determined?

Human scores are combined with the *SpeechRater®* machine scores, then optimally weighted to produce raw scores. The raw scores are then converted to scaled scores of 0 to 30, which is the Speaking section score that will be reported to the institutions that you request.

7. How will mistakes affect my score?

Raters will not focus on the number of errors you make. They will score the response based on the overall performance. A response that contains minor or occasional errors may still be scored at the highest level.

8. What happens if I do not have time to finish my answer?

You may find that for some tasks, you are not able to include in your answer all the information you would like to. The time allotted for each speaking response is considered sufficient for you to give a complete answer, and you should try to give as thorough an answer as possible. However, the raters who evaluate your responses recognize that it may not always be possible for you to anticipate precisely how much of what you want to say will fit into the amount of time provided. Keep in mind that how clearly and coherently you convey information is as important as how much information you convey. Therefore you should avoid speaking at an unnaturally rapid pace if you see that time is going to run out before you say everything you have planned to say. You may find it useful to time yourself when practicing the speaking tasks. This will help you get an idea of how much can be said in the allotted time.

9. What happens if I finish my response before time runs out?

If you finish your answer before time runs out, you may want to consider what additional information you could add that would make your answer more complete. If you have extra time, it may not be a good idea for you to merely repeat what you have already said. Rather, ask yourself what else you could say to clarify, elaborate on, or otherwise develop your response more fully. Timing yourself when practicing the speaking tasks should help you get accustomed to the time allowances.

10. May I go back and change an answer?

No. Each of your spoken responses is recorded, and it is not possible to go back and rerecord what you have said. For each question, you will be given some time to prepare your answer, and this should help you plan ahead of time what you want to say. You should also remember that your speaking responses are not expected to be perfect. If in the course of giving your spoken response, you realize that you should have said something differently, you should feel free to correct your mistake if you wish, just as you would if you had made a mistake while speaking in your native language and wanted to correct it. Otherwise you may want to simply ignore an error and continue with your response, making sure that the remainder of what you say is as intelligible, coherent, and accurate as possible.

11. How will my accent and pronunciation affect my score?

All *TOEFL iBT®* test takers speak with an accent to some degree or another, and your score will not be affected by your accent, unless your accent interferes with the intelligibility of your response. Minor and/or occasional pronunciation mistakes are also expected, even among the most proficient test takers, and, here again, as long as pronunciation mistakes do not interfere with the intelligibility of your response, they will not count against your score.

5 Writing Section

Read this chapter to learn	▶ The format of *TOEFL iBT*® test Writing tasks
	▶ How your written responses are evaluated
	▶ Tips for answering each Writing task type
	▶ Strategies for preparing for the Writing section

The Writing Section

托福考试写作部分包括两道题目：一道为综合写作，另一道为独立写作。

由于综合写作涉及部分听力内容，因此先于独立写作进行。考生在考试正式开始时，应使用头戴式耳机。在20分钟的综合写作考试结束后，考生可将耳机取下，继续进行写作考试的另一项：独立写作。独立写作的考试时间为30分钟。

本章将详细介绍两道写作题目及考生可以用来评估自己作文的评分标准；具体内容包含两项写作测试的样题、每道题的参考范文，以及如何写好作文的具体指导。

对于写作部分的两道题目，评分人一般会认为考生的作文是考生第一手写出的文章，他们并没有期望考生写出经过深思熟虑、深入研究、高度专业化的内容。即便作文中有某些错误，仍可得高分。

The Integrated Writing Task

考生需要在3分钟内阅读完一篇学术性文章，接着听一段与该话题相关的讲座录音，随后就讲座的要点写一篇概述。在概述中，考生需要阐明讲座的主要论点是如何与阅读文章中的观点相互联系的。

综合写作题目考查考生以写作的形式交流所读和所听到的学术信息的能力。

Example A reading passage like the following will appear on your computer screen. You will have three minutes to read the passage.

> In many organizations, perhaps the best way to approach certain new projects is to assemble a group of people into a team. Having a team of people attack a project offers several advantages. First of all, a group of people has a wider range of knowledge, expertise, and skills than any single individual is likely to possess. Also, because of the number of people involved and the greater resources they possess, a group can work more quickly in response to the task assigned to it and can come up with highly creative solutions to problems and issues. Sometimes these creative solutions come about because a group is more likely to make risky decisions that an individual might not undertake. This is because the group spreads responsibility for a decision to all the members and thus no single individual can be held accountable if the decision turns out to be wrong.
>
> Taking part in a group process can be very rewarding for members of the team. Team members who have a voice in making a decision will no doubt feel better about carrying out the work that is entailed by that decision than they might doing work that is imposed on them by others. Also, the individual team member has a much better chance to "shine," to get his or her contributions and ideas not only recognized but recognized as highly significant, because a team's overall results can be more far-reaching and have greater impact than what might have otherwise been possible for the person to accomplish or contribute working alone.

Then you will hear:

Narrator

Now listen to part of a lecture on the topic you just read about.

Professor

Now I want to tell you about what one company found when it decided that it would turn over some of its new projects to teams of people and make the team responsible for planning the projects and getting the work done. After about six months, the company took a look at how well the teams performed.

On virtually every team, some members got almost a "free ride" . . . they didn't contribute much at all, but if their team did a good job, they nevertheless benefited from the recognition the team got. And what about group members who worked especially well and who provided a lot of insight on problems and issues? Well . . . the recognition for a job well done went to the group as a whole; no names were named. So it won't surprise you to learn that when the real contributors were asked how they felt about the group process, their attitude was just the opposite of what the reading predicts.

Another finding was that some projects just didn't move very quickly. Why? Because it took so long to reach consensus; it took many, many meetings to build the agreement among group members about how they would move the project along. On the other hand, there were other instances where one or two people managed to become very influential over what their group did. Sometimes when those influencers said, "That will never work" about an idea the group was developing, the idea was quickly dropped instead of being further discussed. And then there was another occasion when a couple influencers convinced the group that a plan of theirs was "highly creative." And even though some members tried to warn the rest of the group that the project was moving in directions that might not work, they were basically ignored by other group members. Can you guess the ending to this story? When the project failed, the blame was placed on all the members of the group.

The reading passage will then reappear on your computer screen, along with the following directions and writing task:

You have **20 minutes** to plan and write your response. Your response will be judged on the basis of the quality of your writing and on how well your response presents the points in the lecture and their relationship to the reading passage. Typically, an effective response will be 150 to 225 words.

Summarize the points made in the lecture you just heard, explaining how they cast doubt on the points made in the reading passage.

The writing clock will then start a countdown for 20 minutes of writing time.

How the Task Is Phrased

如果讲座中的论点与阅读文章中的观点相抵触，考生可以通过下列其中一种方法进行分析说明：

- 总结概括讲座中的要点，解释这些要点如何对阅读文章中的某些具体观点产生怀疑。
- 总结概括讲座中的要点，解释这些要点如何对阅读文章中的某些具体陈述和论点提出质疑。
- 总结概括讲座中的要点，确切地解释这些要点如何回答阅读文章中所提出的问题。

如果讲座中的论点支持并强化阅读文章中的内容，考生可以通过下列其中一种方法进行分析说明：

- 总结概括讲座中的要点，准确说明这些要点如何支持阅读文章中的解释性论述。
- 总结概括讲座中的要点，准确说明这些要点如何加强阅读文章中的某些具体观点。

Strategies for Taking the Integrated Writing Task

在阅读文章时：

- 在草稿纸上做笔记。

- 找出阅读文章的中心思想。中心思想通常是与某一问题的政策、实践活动，或与某一问题的立场有关，也可能是对某些行为过程或某些自然现象的产生作出的一些概括性假设。

- 了解作者是如何评价并展开中心思想的。展开中心思想通常有以下两种方式：

  1. 用议论性或说明性语言支持中心思想。例如：说明为什么有理由相信某些政策或实践行为是有益的；或证实这些政策、实践行为是有用的、明智的；或者说明为什么某些政策或实践行为在过去是好的。

  2. 用议论、说明或者提出问题的方式引出人们关心的问题——为什么某种政策、实践行为、某个审视问题的立场或某种假设行不通、无法实施、毫无用处或者不明智。

- 不用记住阅读文章中的内容。在开始写作时，阅读文章会在屏幕上再次出现。

- 既要注意文章中那些支持中心思想的论点，也要关注那些对中心思想提出质疑的论点。通常，中心思想会通过三点展开。

在听听力短文时：

- 在草稿纸上做笔记。

- 努力听出那些使阅读文章中的观点看起来错误、不具有说服力甚至不真实的信息、事例或者解释。例如，在刚才所给的范例中，短文说在团队中工作是件好事，因为它能为成员提供突显个人能力的机会，但是讲座录音却说即使团队中有的人什么工作都不做，也同样会得到与他人同样的荣誉；短文说一个团队的工作往往进展很快，因为每个人都把自己的专长施展出来，但是讲座录音却持完全相反的观点，认为一个团队要花很长的时间使大家达成一致意见，还认为当团队中少数几个成员犯了错误时，整个团队都将受到批评。这样，讲座的观点就对短文的观点——团队能够集体面对风险，具有创造力——提出了质疑。

在写作过程中：

- 考生可以摘下头戴式耳机。托福考试的以下剩余部分不需要戴耳机。

- 开始写作前，再读一遍短文，参考笔记，列一个写作提纲。可以将提纲列在草稿纸上，也可以在阅读文章和讲座的笔记上画出重点，还可以直接将提纲和笔记键入屏幕上的答案区域，然后将这些内容写成句子和段落，写进自己的作文。

- 记住，综合写作不要求考生发表个人观点，而是让考生解释说明讲座中的观点是如何与阅读文章的观点联系在一起的。

- 写出完整的英语句子。作文中要列出阅读文章与讲座中相对立的观点，可以写成一个长段落，也可以写成几个短段落。偶尔出现一些语言错误，只要不至于使表述阅读文章与讲座的观点时出现误解，就不会对作文成绩产生影响。

- 牢记自己的任务是从讲座中挑出与阅读文章相关的重要信息，并将这些信息连贯、准确地在作文中表述出来。作文应符合下列要求：

  1. 包含讲座中的一些确切观点、解释说明和议论。这些内容恰好对阅读文章中的观点提出质疑或与其相反。

  2. 陈述各观点时要连贯、准确。用语要恰当，能够准确地表达讲座和阅读文章的观点。

  3. 条理清晰、结构连贯。这样的作文能够使读者理解讲座中的观点与阅读文章中的观点是如何相互联系的。

- 作文长度为150~225词。只要作文回答了试题的问题，字数多一些也不会扣分。

- 注意：如果作文全部是照阅读短文抄下来的，得0分；如果只写了有关阅读文章的观点，得1分。要写出高分作文，考生必须尽可能写清楚讲座的观点是如何与阅读文章的一些具体观点相联系的。

Integrated Writing Scoring Rubric

下面列出了综合写作题目的官方评分指导。

Score	Task Description
5	A response at this level successfully selects the important information from the lecture and coherently and accurately presents this information in relation to the relevant information presented in the reading. The response is well organized, and occasional language errors that are present do not result in inaccurate or imprecise presentation of content or connections.
4	A response at this level is generally good in selecting the important information from the lecture and in coherently and accurately presenting this information in relation to the relevant information in the reading, but it may have minor omission, inaccuracy, vagueness, or imprecision of some content from the lecture or in connection to points made in the reading. A response is also scored at this level if it has more frequent or noticeable minor language errors, as long as such usage and grammatical structures do not result in anything more than an occasional lapse of clarity or in the connection of ideas.
3	A response at this level contains some important information from the lecture and conveys some relevant connection to the reading, but it is marked by one or more of the following:

- Although the overall response is definitely oriented to the task, it conveys only vague, global, unclear, or somewhat imprecise connection of the points made in the lecture to points made in the reading.

- The response may omit one major key point made in the lecture.

- Some key points made in the lecture or the reading, or connections between the two, may be incomplete, inaccurate, or imprecise.

- Errors of usage and/or grammar may be more frequent or may result in noticeably vague expressions or obscured meanings in conveying ideas and connections.

Score	Task Description

2   A response at this level contains some relevant information from the lecture, but is marked by significant language difficulties or by significant omission or inaccuracy of important ideas from the lecture or in the connections between the lecture and the reading; a response at this level is marked by one or more of the following:

- The response significantly misrepresents or completely omits the overall connection between the lecture and the reading.

- The response significantly omits or significantly misrepresents important points made in the lecture.

- The response contains language errors or expressions that largely obscure connections or meaning at key junctures, or that would likely obscure under-standing of key ideas for a reader not already familiar with the reading and the lecture.

1   A response at this level is marked by one or more of the following:

- The response provides little or no meaningful or relevant coherent content from the lecture.

- The language level of the response is so low that it is difficult to derive meaning.

0   A response at this level merely copies sentences from the reading, rejects the topic or is otherwise not connected to the topic, is written in a foreign language, consists of keystroke characters, or is blank.

Sample Scored Responses for the Integrated Writing Task

下面列出的是第188~189页样题"在团队中工作"的参考范文。

Score 5 Response

The lecturer talks about research conducted by a firm that used the group system to handle their work. He says that the theory stated in the passage was very different and somewhat inaccurate when compared to what happened for real.

First, some members got free rides. That is, some didn't work hard but gotrecognition for the success nontheless. This also indicates that people who worked hard was not given recognition they should have got. In other words, they weren't given the oppotunity to "shine." This derectly contradicts what the passage indicates.

Second, groups were slow in progress. The passage says that groups are nore responsive than individuals because of the number of people involved and their aggregated resources. However, the speaker talks about how the firm found out that groups were slower than individuals in dicision making. Groups needed more time for meetings, which are neccesary procceedures in decision making. This was another part where experience contradicted theory.

Third, influetial people might emerge, and lead the group towards glory or failure. If the influent people are going in the right direction there would be no problem. But in cases where they go in the wrong direction, there is nobody that has enough influence to counter the decision made. In other words, the group might turn into a dictatorship, with the influential party as the leader, and might be less flexible in thinking. They might become one-sided, and thus fail to succeed.

Rater Comments

There are several errors of spelling, word formation, and subject-verb agreement in this response; however, most of these errors seem to be the result of typing errors common to first drafts. This writer does an excellent job of presenting the lecturer's points that contradict the arguments made in the reading passage. The writer is very specific and has organized his or her points so that they are parallel with one another: in each of the supporting paragraphs, the lecturer's observation of what really happened is given first, then explicitly connected to a theoretical point from the reading. The final paragraph contains one noticeable error ("influent"), which is then used correctly two sentences later ("influential"). Overall, this is a successful response and earns a score of 5.

Score 4 Response

> The lecture that followed the paragraph on the team work in organizations, gave some negative views of the team work itself. Firstly, though it was said in the paragraph that the whole team idea would probably be faster than the individual work, it was said in the lecture just the opposite: it could actually be a lot slower. That is because team members would sometimes take more time than needed just to reach the same conclussions, or just even to simply decide where to go from certain point to the next on.
>
> Secondly, paragraph suggests that by doing work as a team might give you an "edge," the lecture suggests that that might also be a negative thing as well. The people who made themselves leaders in the group may just be wrong in certain decisions, or just simple thing something is so creative, when in reality it is not and it would not work, but the rest of the people would nevertheless still follow them, and end up not doing well at all.
>
> And lastly, paragraph says that everyone feels responsible for their own part, and all together they are all more effective as a team. The lecture suggests quite the opposite in this case as well. It suggests that some team members are there only for the "free ride," and they don't do much of anything to contribute, but still get the credit as a whole.

Rater Comments

The writer of this response is clearly attempting to interweave the points from the passage and lecture and does a good job of discussing what the lecturer says about group decision making and the issue of some group members failing to contribute. The writer's second point, however, is not as clearly stated as the first and third points. The key sentence in this paragraph ("The people who made themselves leaders in the group may just be wrong in certain decisions, or just simple thing something is so creative, when in reality it is not and it would not work, but the rest of the people would nevertheless still follow them, and end up not doing well at all.") is difficult to follow. This is what the Scoring Guide calls "an occasional lapse of clarity" in a response that earns a score of 4. Overall, this is still a very strong response that directly addresses the task and generally presents the relevant information from the lecture.

Score 3 Response

The lecturer provide the opposite opinion concerning what the article offered. The team work often bring negative effet. As we all know superficially, team work and team spirits are quite popular in today's business world and also the fashionable terms.

However, the lecturer find deeper and hiding results.

Firstly, the working results of team members can't be fully valued. For example, if a team member does nothing in the process of team discussion, decision making and final pratice, his or her work deliquency will not be recognized because we only emphasize team work. Also, the real excellent and creative member's work might be obliterated for the same reason.

Secondly, the team work might lose its value when team members are leading by several influential people in the group. One of the essential merits of team is to avoid the individule wrong. But one or two influential or persuasive people will make the team useless.

Thirdly, team work oftem become the excuse of taking responsibillity. All in charge, nobody care.

All in all, what we should do is the fully distinguish the advantages and disadvantages of a concept or widely used method. That is to keep the common sense.

Rater Comments

This response frames the issue well. The first point is clearly stated and accurately conveys the lecturer's comments about team members who contribute very little and team members who contribute a great deal. However, the writer discusses the second point about influencers in somewhat error-prone or vague and non-idiomatic language ("hiding results," "working results," and "when team members are leading by . . . influential people"). The point about influencers drops off at making the team "useless" and does not fully explain the reason these influencers create problems. The final point, beginning with the word "Thirdly," is not fully related to the passage and lecture, and the meaning of it is unclear. This response illustrates many of the typical features that can cause a response to receive a score of 3.

Score 2 Response

In a company's experement, some new projects were planed and acomplished by different teams. Some teams got very good results while some teams didn't. That is to say it's not nessesary for teams to achieve more than individuals do because some team members may only contribute a little in a team for they may relying on the others to do the majority.

Another thing is the recognition for the achievement by the team is for the whole team, for everyone in the team. It's not only the dicision makers in the team feel good after successfully finishing the project, but also every member in the team.

It is also showed in the lecture that in a team with one or two leaders, sometimes good ideas from some team member are dropped and ignored while sometimes they may be highly creative. In some teams decisions were made without collecting ideas from all team members. Then it would be hard to achieve creative solutions.

For those failed projects, blames are always given to the whole team even though it's the leader or someone in the team who caught the unexpected result.

Rater Comments

Although it has the appearance of a stronger response, on close reading, this example suffers from significant problems with connecting ideas and misrepresenting points. For instance, the third sentence of paragraph 1 seems to be getting at a point from the lecture ("some team members may only contribute a little . . ."). However, it is couched in a way that makes it very unclear how it relates to the point of the task ("That is to say it's not necessary for teams to achieve more than individuals do because some team members may only contribute . . ."). In addition, it is not clear where the information in paragraph 2 is coming from and what point the writer is trying to make. In paragraph 3 the writer tries to make a point about influencers, but again, it is not clear what information relates to what. For all these reasons, this response earns a score of 2.

Score 1 Response

In this lecture, the example shows only one of the group succeed the project. Why the group will succeed on this project it is because of few factor.

First of all,a group of people has a wider range of knowledge,expertise,and skills than any single individual is like to prossess, and easier to gather the information and resources to make the work effectively and the group will willingly to trey sometihing is risky decision to make the project for interesting and suceessful it is because all the member of the group carries the differnt responsibility for a decision, so once the decision turn wrong, no a any individual one will be blame for the whole responsiblity.

On the other way, the groups which are fail the project is because they are lay on some more influence people in the group,so even the idea is come out. Once the inflenced people say that is no good, then the process of the idea will be drop down immediately instead taking more further discussion! So the idea will not be easy to settle down for a group.

The form of the group is very important, and each of the member should be respect another and try out all the idea others had suggested, then it will develop a huge idea and the cooperate work environment for each other for effectively work!

Rater Comments

The level of language used in this response is fairly low, and it is lowest in the second paragraph, which is the only reference to the lecture. Because the reader has difficulty gleaning meaning from that paragraph, the response contributes little coherent information and therefore earns a score of 1.

The Independent Writing Task

托福考试写作试题的第二部分是独立写作，要求考生针对某个问题提出自己的观点，并在30分钟的时间内写出一篇短文。考生需要在作文中就某个问题阐述自己的看法。下面是这类问题的典型表达：

Do you agree or disagree with the following statement?

[A sentence or sentences presenting an issue will appear here.]

Use specific reasons and examples to support your answer. Be sure to use your own words. Do **not** use memorized examples.

通常，一篇作文大约需要写300词。少于300词的作文也可能获得高分，但是经验表明，较短的作文无法对一些论点展开讨论，而要获得5分的成绩，讨论这些论点是十分必要的。作文字数没有上限。在限定的时间内，考生可以想写多少就写多少，但是不要为写作而写作，应当针对所给话题有的放矢地写。作文中观点的数目固然重要，但是评分人更看重观点的质量和陈述观点的有效性。

Example Do you agree or disagree with the following statement?

Always telling the truth is the most important consideration in any relationship.

Use specific reasons and examples to support your answer. Be sure to use your own words. Do **not** use memorized examples.

Essay-Writing Tips

- 动笔前要思考。在草稿纸上列提纲或者记笔记，以帮助组织思路。也可以直接将提纲和笔记键入屏幕中答案区域，然后将这些内容写成句子和段落，写进自己的作文。

- 掌握时间。尽可能在倒计时还剩4到5分钟时结束写作，用剩余的时间检查所写内容，并作最后的修改。在30分钟结束时，计算机将会自动保存作文。

- 写作时，不要用死记硬背下来的例子或论证。评分人不会将这种完全是背诵的语言看作考生自己的写作，考生也会因此获得低分。

How Essays Are Scored

评分人会评估考生作文的质量，即评估考生如何展开论点、组织文章结构，并运用语言表达自己的观点。

展开论点就是用各种支持内容（包括事例、细节、理由等）来支持文章的观点。要得高分，就要按照评分指导的原则写作文——"很好地展开论点、运用恰当清晰的解释、例证和细节"。评分人会评估考生的作文是否切题，文章中的细节、事例、理由在多大程度上支持了论点。

不要仅仅为了增加文章字数而死记硬背一些冗长的首、末段，评分人不会看好类似下列的累赘的首、末段：

The importance of the issue raised by the posed statement, namely creating a new holiday for people, cannot be underestimated, as it concerns the very fabric of society. As it stands, the issue of creating a new holiday raises profound implications for the future. However, although the subject matter in general cannot be dismissed lightheartedly, the perspective of the issue as presented by the statement raises certain qualms regarding practical application.

In conclusion, although I have to accept that it is imperative that something be done about creating a new holiday for people and find the underlying thrust of the implied proposal utterly convincing, I cannot help but feel wary of taking such irrevocable steps and personally feel that a more measured approach would be more rewarding.

同样，不要在主体段落使用死记硬背的句子和例证。死记硬背的文字并不代表考生的真实学术写作能力。包括提前背好的例子、论点或写作模板的文章会获得比考生用自己话写的文章更低的分数。下面是一个过多使用死记硬背的文本的例子：

Question: *Is honesty an important quality for a leader?*

By taking in mind the honesty, we can learn proper social behavior. in addition to my personal experience, there is a research that confirms my opinion. A poll, conducted by the New York times, stated an overwheming 72% who did not think the honesty lack the code of conduct in society. however, people who did regularly comtemplate the importance of not lying were better regulating themselves in the societies. the major characteristic were that they do not lie in their daily life and seve honesty is the most important value in the societies because there is a order for people's lives. therefore it helps one abiltiy to be successful either in business or in academia. it helps people to strive and achieve their goal and making them successful in life.

上面的例子中的所有文字都是提前背好的，并在在文章中重复使用，包括在《纽约时报》中发表过的投票。这段并不是对题目的真正展开，也不会得到评分者的认可。这样的作文通常会得到低分。上面这篇文章的得分是1分。

同样，评分人也不会看好下列段落，这些段落堆砌了大量词语，但却没有针对论点展开论述：

At the heart of any discussion regarding an issue pertaining to creating a new holiday, it has to be borne in mind that a delicate line has to be trod when dealing with such matters. The human resources involved in such matters cannot be guaranteed regardless of all the good intentions that may be lavished. While it is true that creating a new holiday might be a viable and laudable remedy, it is transparently clear that applied wrongly such a course of action could be calamitous and compound the problem rather than provide a solution.

在作文中，一定要针对所给话题对一些具体的论点展开讨论。不要仅用大量单词叙述某个问题确实存在。即使把作文写到300甚至400词，如果写得像上面列出的段落那样空洞，没有实质内容，也只能得1~2分。

当考生的文章没有用很好的结构时，评分人会立刻注意到这一点。如果一篇作文结构严谨，读者就能毫无障碍地从头读到尾。分段写作并在两个观点之间运用过渡可以帮助读者跟上作者的思路。但要知道，仅仅使用"first"、"second"这样的连接词并不能保证作文结构的严谨，还要注意让所有的观点与文章的主题相关，紧扣中心思想。换句话说，作文要有统一性。评分原则中提到了"统一性"、"渐进性"和"连贯性"——这些都是评估作文结构是否严谨、读者能否比较容易跟上作者思路的标准。要得高分，需要避免累赘（某些观点的重复）、离题（一些与主要论点没有关联的观点，会使论述丧失"统一性"），以及条理不清晰的衔接（让读者难以理解文章的两个观点或两个部分是如何连接在一起的）。

语言运用是第三个评分标准。要想得高分，作文必须要体现"语言运用的和谐流畅"，作文的句子应结构多样，措辞应贴切得体。作文中出现一些小的词汇和语法错误仍然能得高分。但是，如果出现了大量语法错误，使得作文意思令人费解，得分会低一些。评分人还会评估句子结构的复杂程度以及考生所使用词汇的数量和复杂程度。使用非常简单的句子结构和非常基本的词汇，就不可能表达比较复杂的观点。因此如果考生写出的作文语言难懂、句子简单、词汇量有限，那么无论观点多么令人印象深刻，得分也不会超过3分。

Independent Writing Scoring Rubric

下面列出了独立写作题目的官方评分指导

Score	Task Description

5   An essay at this level largely accomplishes all of the following:

- Effectively addresses the topic and task

- Is well organized and well developed, using clearly appropriate explanations, exemplifications, and/or details

- Displays unity, progression, and coherence

- Displays consistent facility in the use of language, demonstrating syntactic variety, appropriate word choice, and idiomaticity, though it may have minor lexical or grammatical errors

4   An essay at this level largely accomplishes all of the following:

- Addresses the topic and task well, though some points may not be fully elaborated

- Is generally well organized and well developed, using appropriate and sufficient explanations, exemplifications, and/or details

- Displays unity, progression, and coherence, though it may contain occasional redundancy, digression, or unclear connections

- Displays facility in the use of language, demonstrating syntactic variety and range of vocabulary, though it will probably have occasional noticeable minor errors in structure, word form, or use of idiomatic language that do not interfere with meaning

3   An essay at this level is marked by one or more of the following:

- Addresses the topic and task using somewhat developed explanations, exemplifications, and/or details

- Displays unity, progression, and coherence, though connection of ideas may be occasionally obscured

- May demonstrate inconsistent facility in sentence formation and word choice that may result in lack of clarity and occasionally obscure meaning

- May display accurate but limited range of syntactic structures and vocabulary

Score	Task Description

2 An essay at this level may reveal one or more of the following weaknesses:

- Limited development in response to the topic and task

- Inadequate organization or connection of ideas

- Inappropriate or insufficient exemplifications, explanations, or details to support or illustrate generalizations in response to the task

- A noticeably inappropriate choice of words or word forms

- An accumulation of errors in sentence structure and/or usage

1 An essay at this level is seriously flawed by one or more of the following weaknesses:

- Serious disorganization or underdevelopment

- Little or no detail, or irrelevant specifics, or questionable responsiveness to the task

- Serious and frequent errors in sentence structure or usage

0 An essay at this level merely copies words from the topic, rejects the topic or is otherwise not connected to the topic, is written in a foreign language, consists of keystroke characters, or is blank.

Sample Scored Responses for the Independent Writing Task

下列范文是针对以下独立写作题目的一些回答：

Do you agree or disagree with the following statement?

Always telling the truth is the most important consideration in any relationship.

Use specific reasons and examples to support your answer. Be sure to use your own words. Do **not** use memorized examples.

这个话题可以引出几种处理问题的不同态度。一部分人不同意上述论点，并举例说明有些情况下说谎也可以接受，典型的例子就是那些善意的谎言，即为了避免伤害他人而说的谎话，以及在商务环境中的谎言（这样做是为了保护公司或业主的商业或个人信息而纯粹撒谎）；也有人选择另一个角度，认为谎言会导致更多的谎言，最终破坏相互的信任，并举例证实自己所说的；还有人从问题的两个方面着眼，描绘或归纳出他们认为说谎可接受的情况，以及说谎不妥、甚至可能引起严重后果的情况。在写作中，讲故事——真实的或虚构的——是可以接受的，在本题中，用事例说明自己对这一话题的看法就非常合理。

Score 5 Essay

DISHONESTY KILLS RELIABILITY

There are certain considerations or factors that everyone takes into account in a relationship. People may look for honesty, altruism, understanding, loyalty, being thoughtful etc! Everyone would more or less wish that the person s/he is dealing with, has some of these virtues above. Putting them in an order according to their importance, however can be very subjective and relative.

When someone asks him/herself the question "What do I consider to be the most important thing in my relationship?" the answer depends on a lot of factors such as how his/her earlier relationships were.

After stating that everyone's opinion can be different about this, for me honesty, in other words, always telling the truth is the most important consideration in a relationship. Opposite of this is inarguably lying and if someone needs to lie, either s/he is hiding something or is afraid of telling me something.

In any relationship of mine, I would wish that first of all, the person I'm dealing with is honest. Even though s/he thinks that s/he did something wrong that I wouldn't like, s/he'd better tell me the truth and not lie about it. Later on if I find out about a lie or hear the truth from someone else, that'd be much more unpleasant. In that case how can I ever believe or trust that person again? How can I ever believe that this person has enough confidence in me to forgive him/her and carry on with the relationship from there. So if I cannot trust a person anymore, if the person doesn't think I can handle the truth, there's no point to continuing that relationship.

> Although I would like to see altruistic, understanding, thoughtful and loyal behavior from people, an instance of the opposite of these behaviors would not upset me as much as dishonesty would. Among all the possible behaviors, dishonesty is the only one for me that terminates how I feel about a person's reliability. Therefore honesty would be my first concern and the most important consideration in a relationship.

Rater Comments

In this response the writer first approaches the topic by underscoring that a number of character traits are important to a relationship. The writer then effectively develops an argument that, unlike other negative behaviors, dishonesty or unwillingness to fully disclose some bad action cannot be forgiven and can be the most important factor in destroying a relationship. The writer's language is fluent, accurate, and varied enough to effectively support the progression and connection of ideas. There is a variety of sentence structures, including rhetorical questions. The essay is not mechanically perfect, but as long as such errors are occasional, are minor, and do not interfere with the reader's understanding, an essay like this one can still earn a top score.

Score 4 Essay

> Always telling the truth in any relationship is really the most important consideration for many reasons. I could say that when you lie to someone, this person will not trust you anymore and what is a relationship based on? Trust, confidence, so the sense of relationship is being lost. Another point is that if the true is ommited once, it will surely appear sometime, somewhere and probably in the most unexpected way, causing lots of problems for the ones involved. So, the truth is the basis for everything.
>
> First, confidence is the most important aspect of a friendship or a marriage, or anything like that, so, once it is lost, the whole thing goes down in a way that no one can bear it. To avoid losing confidence, there is only one way, telling the truth, lying will just help throwing it away. For example, a couple decided to go out on the weekend, but the man has a party to go with his friends to where he can not take his girlfriend and then he lies to her saying that he is sick and can not go to the date. She undertands him and they do not see each other in that weekend, but he goes to the party and has much fun. Suppose on monday, the girl talks to a friend that saw him at the party and asked why did not she go with him. She found out the true and all confidence was lost, the basis for their relation is now gone and what happens next is that they break up or if they do not, he will persist on lyes and someday it will end.
>
> What happened to this couple is very common around here and many relationships, even friends and marriages end because of something like that. Some may argue that lying once or another will not interfere anything and it is part of a relation, but I strongly disagree, the most important thing is the true, even if it is to determine the end of a relation, it must be told. There are more chances to end something lying than saying what really happened

Rater Comments

This essay earned a score of 4. It clearly develops reasons why lying is a bad thing, with a first paragraph that introduces the writer's position ("truth is the basis for everything"), a hypothetical story in paragraph 2, and a final paragraph that entertains and quickly dismisses a possible counterargument. All this amounts to solid development of the idea. The response displays facility in language use through a variety of sentence structures and the use of clear transitions between sentences. However, sometimes the writer's sentences include noticeable errors in word form ("if the true is ommited," "lying will just help throwing it away," "persist on lyes," "lying once or another"), and in some places the writer extends, or "runs on," a sentence to include many steps in the argument when using two or more sentences would make the relationships between ideas clearer. For example, "Some may argue that lying once or another will not interfere anything and it is part of a relation, but I strongly disagree, the most important thing is the true, even if it is to determine the end of a relation, it must be told."

Score 3 Essay

Some people believe that it is one of the most important value in many relationships to tell the truth all the time. However, it cannot be always the best choice to tell the truth in many situatioins. Sometimes white lies are indispensible to keep relationships more lively and dilightly. There are some examples to support this idea.

Firstly, in the relationships between lovers, it is often essential to compliment their lovers on their appearance and their behavior. Even though they do not think that their boyfriend or girlfriend looks good on their new shoes and new clothes, it will probably diss them by telling the truth. On the other hand, little compliments will make them confident and happy making their relationship more tight.

Secondly, parents need to encourage their children by telling lies. Even if they are doing bad work on studying or exercising, telling the truth will hurt their hearts. What they need is a little encouraging words instead of truthful words.

Thirdly, for some patients telling them their current state of their desease will probably desperate them. It is accepted publically not to let the patients know the truth. They may be able to have hope to overcome their desease without knowing the truth.

In conclusion, it is not always better to tell the truth than lies. Some lies are acceptable in terms of making people's life more profusely. Not everybody has to know the truth, and it will lead them more happier not knowing it. In these cases, white lies are worth to be regarded as a virtue of people's relationships

Rater Comments

This essay focuses on explaining why "white lies" are sometimes appropriate. The explanations here are somewhat developed. Each example does support the main point; however, at critical junctures in the writer's attempt to explain why the positive effect of the white lie outweighs any negative effect, inconsistent facility with language hinders the writer's effort. So, with errors in both structure and vocabulary that obscure meaning ("keep relationships . . . dilightly," "will probably desperate them," "making people's life more profusely," "it will lead them more happier not knowing it"), this essay earns a score of 3.

Score 2 Essay

Recently, there is a big debate on the issue that telling the truth or not is the most important consideration in the relationship between people. For my experience, I think telling a truth is the most important consideration in people's relationship. In the following, I will illustrate my opinion by two reasons.

First of all, honest make the trust stronger between friends or colleages. As we know, if people tell a lie to others he will not be trusted. When he tell a truth, others will believe that he tells a lie. For example, a person who is honest to others, can get real help and get trust of others.

Secondly, telling a lie always makes things worse not only in work but also in family life. When somebody do something wrong in his job he should annouce his mistake to his manager. If he don't do that others may continue their jobs base on the mistake. Consequently, the work will be worse and worse.

On the contrary, sometimes it is better to tell a lie to others, such as telling a lie to a patient. As we know, the sick become worse when a cancer patient know his illness. A good way to protect their life is to tell a lie. So that many doctors will not tell the truth to a dying patient.

To sum up, people should tell the truth to maintain their relationship with other people, although sometimes people have to tell a lie. People can get trust when they are honest to others.

Rater Comments

This essay is quite long, but even though it uses several examples, each idea is only partly developed, and the connections among ideas are weak or contradictory. For instance, in paragraph 2 the first sentence says, "honest make the trust stronger." The next two sentences present a contrast: "if people tell a lie to others he will not be trusted"; then "when he tell a truth, others will believe that he tells a lie." Then the last sentence in the paragraph says, "For example, a person who is honest to others, can get real help and get trust of others." But that is not an example of the previous sentence and only confuses the reader. This last sentence does not advance the progression of ideas much beyond the first sentence and certainly is not an example of the point made by the second and third sentences. Thus connections throughout this paragraph are tenuous. Paragraph 3 begins by saying that telling a lie makes things worse at work and at home, but it does not follow through at all on the latter. The "On the contrary" paragraph comes as a surprise to the reader, since paragraph 1 said that the writer was going to give two reasons why telling the truth was the most important consideration in human relationships. Because of all these weaknesses, this essay earns a score of 2.

Score 1 Essay

Nowadays, many people think that the people who always telling the true is the most important consideration in any relationship between human. but another think that is necessary to tell some lies. It is seldom to reach the same issue.I agree with the first thinking because of the following reasons.

First fo all, we all live in the realized world , people can respect you unless you want to use correct method to communicate with other people. It is very important, especially in business , if you want to recieve the good resulit ,you must tell the ture about your own so that gain the considement.

Secondly, if you are honest man/woman, many people may be want to make friend with you. You can have more chance to communate with other people . you may be gain more information from them.

However,sometimes we must speak some lie.for examlpe, when our relatives have heavy illness such as cancer,we couldn't telling them the ture. because that not good for their health,and may be affect their life.

In conclusion,tellingthe ture is the people good behavire .we must require most of people to tell the ture.thus,we can see the better world in our life unless we always tell the ture.

Rater Comments

This essay contains serious and frequent errors in sentence structure and usage. Paragraph 2, beginning "First fo all," is nearly incomprehensible and contains vocabulary that is either vague at best or nonstandard English ("realized world," "considement"). Paragraph 3 is completely vague, and paragraph 4 (actually one sentence), though it mentions a familiar example, is poorly expressed and certainly underdeveloped. For all these reasons, this essay earns a score of 1.

Independent Writing Topics

下面列出了老托福考试中独立写作的一些题目，以及备考新托福考试的模拟题。可以看出，这些话题与托福网考中独立写作的话题非常相似。不论话题是什么，都要求考生提出自己的论点，并用具体的理由和事例支持自己的论点。

在作文中，考生是否赞同某一论点并不重要，经过培训的评分人能够接受所有不同类型的观点。重要的是上文提到的考生在论述过程中需具备的各种能力：直接切中问题的能力，明确提出主张的能力，以及写出结构严谨、例证恰当、句子多样且用词正确的文章的能力。请注意，对于死记硬背下来的例子或论证，评分人不会看作考生自己的写作。

考试中没有一个话题需要很强的专业知识，大部分话题都基于普通人，特别是学生的日常经历。

如何使用下列独立写作的题目呢？为了备考托福考试，考生应当从下列题目中选出几个进行写作练习。一定要给自己设定时间限制，用30分钟读题、列提纲并完成写作。写完之后通读一遍，根据评分指导原则为自己的作文评分。如果有条件，最好找一位朋友或老师根据评分标准给你的作文评分，然后给出反馈意见。

Topic List

- The expression "Never, never give up" means to keep trying and never stop working for your goals. Do you agree or disagree with this statement? Use specific reasons and examples to support your answer.

- Why do you think some people are attracted to dangerous sports or other dangerous activities? Use specific reasons and examples to support your answer.

- What are the important qualities of a good son or daughter? Have these qualities changed or remained the same over time in your culture? Use specific reasons and examples to support your answer.

- People work because they need money to live. What are some **other** reasons that people work? Discuss one or more of these reasons. Use specific examples and details to support your answer.

- Some people like to do only what they already do well. Other people prefer to try new things and take risks. Which do you prefer? Use specific reasons and examples to support your choice.

- If you could study a subject that you have never had the opportunity to study, what would you choose? Explain your choice, using specific reasons and details.

- Do you agree or disagree with the following statement? Grades (marks) encourage students to learn. Use specific reasons and examples to support your opinion.

- Some people say that computers have made life easier and more convenient. Other people say that computers have made life more complex and stressful. What is your opinion? Use specific reasons and examples to support your answer.

- Your city has decided to build a statue or monument to honor a famous person in your country. Whom would you choose? Use reasons and specific examples to support your choice.

- Describe a custom from your country that you would like people from other countries to adopt. Explain your choice, using specific reasons and examples.

- Do you agree or disagree with the following statement? Technology has made the world a better place to live. Use specific reasons and examples to support your opinion.

- Do you agree or disagree with the following statement? The content of advertisements in a particular country can tell you a lot about that country. Use specific reasons and examples to support your answer.

- Do you agree or disagree with the following statement? Modern technology is creating a single world culture. Use specific reasons and examples to support your opinion.

- A foreign visitor has only one day to spend in your country. Where should this visitor go on that day? Why? Use specific reasons and details to support your choice.

- If you could go back to some time and place in the past, when and where would you go? Why? Use specific reasons and details to support your choice.

- What discovery in the last 100 years has been most beneficial for people in your country? Use specific reasons and examples to support your choice.

- Do you agree or disagree with the following statement? Dancing plays an important role in a culture. Use specific reasons and examples to support your answer.

- If you could meet a famous entertainer or athlete, who would that be, and why? Use specific reasons and examples to support your choice.

- If you could ask a famous person one question, what would you ask? Why? Use specific reasons and details to support your choice.

- Your teacher has given you a large assignment that must be completed in one month. You can complete the assignment gradually by working on it a little bit each day, or you can complete the work quickly by working on it intensively for three or four days. Which method do you prefer? Use specific reasons and examples to support your choice.

- You have a choice of movies to see. What influences you the most in choosing which movie to see?

  - Whether your favorite actors are in it
  - What kind of movie it is (action, romance, comedy, etc.)
  - What other people are saying about it

  Use specific reasons and examples to support your choice.

- Many people believe that greed, or the desire to have more wealth than other people have, is a bad characteristic; people who are greedy are often considered selfish or unkind. However, some people argue that greed is actually a good characteristic for a person to have because greedy people will work harder than others to become successful. Do you believe that greed can be a good characteristic? Why or why not? Use specific reasons and examples to support your answer.

- Which is more important for a leader: the ability to win an argument about an issue or the ability to help others come to an agreement about an issue? Use specific reasons and examples to support your answer.

- Your city or province has received a large donation of money to improve the education of children. It must choose between spending the money on improvement of early childhood education (for children ages 4 to 7) and spending the money on the improvement of education for older children (ages 11 to 14). Which do you think is the better option? Use specific reasons and details to support your answer.

- Do you agree or disagree with the following statement? For students who are planning to work in business, learning about psychology is more important than learning about technology. Use specific reasons and examples to support your answer.

- Do you agree or disagree with the following statement? Practice and hard work are more important to an athlete's success than natural ability and talent. Use specific reasons and examples to support your answer.

- Do you agree or disagree with the following statement? Today's media (TV and online news sites, for example) offer a lot of information on many topics, but people do not use this information to really learn something thoroughly and in depth. Use specific reasons and examples to support your answer.

- Do you agree or disagree with the following statement? People who have had difficulty learning a skill go on to become better teachers of that skill than people who learned it easily. Use specific reasons and examples to support your answer.

- Do you agree or disagree with the following statement? Children today would be happier if they had fewer possessions. Use specific reasons and examples to support your answer.

- Do you agree or disagree with the following statement? Traditional ways of celebrating holidays are much less important today than they were in the past. Use specific reasons and examples to support your answer.

- Do you agree or disagree with the following statement? Improving transportation is the best way for governments to promote economic growth. Use specific reasons and examples to support your answer.

- Do you agree or disagree with the following statement? As long as they meet deadlines and attend meetings, company employees should be allowed to work any hours they choose. Use specific reasons and examples to support your answer.

- Do you agree or disagree with the following statement? Although technology has made communication easier, there are still as many misunderstandings among people as there were in the past. Use specific reasons and examples to support your answer.

- Do you agree or disagree with the following statement? People today are much better informed about international news than they were in the past. Use specific reasons and examples to support your answer.

- Do you agree or disagree with the following statement? For students, the ability to listen well is just as important as the ability to read well. Use specific reasons and examples to support your answer.

- Do you agree or disagree with the following statement? For most jobs or areas of work, understanding the limits of your knowledge is more important than the knowledge you have. Use specific reasons and examples to support your answer.

- Do you agree or disagree with the following statement? Television does not give people an accurate view of human nature. Use specific reasons and examples to support your answer.

- Do you agree or disagree with the following statement? It is more interesting to read a good book or see a good movie the second time than the first. Use specific reasons and examples to support your answer.

- Do you agree or disagree with the following statement? All jobs should provide some opportunity for physical exercise. Use specific reasons and examples to support your answer.

Authentic *TOEFL iBT*® Practice Test 1

　　本章是托福考试四套真题练习中的第一套。考生可以通过两种不同的方式进行测试：

- 通过本书：在接下来的书页中，考生可以看到所有的测试题目，请将答案写在规定的空白处。关于本测试中的听力部分，考生可以按照序号提示，播放对应音频。

- 在电脑上：为了更真实地体验托福考试的实考环境，考生可以下载电脑版软件在电脑上进行模考。电脑版软件中的试题与书中的完全一样。阅读文章和相关问题将显示在屏幕上，考生可以点击给出的空白处输入答案。听力部分的测试则根据提示进行。

　　测试题目之后是答案和评分信息，以及听力部分的文字材料。除此以外，考生还可以看到答案的详细解释、口语回答样本和写作范文。

TOEFL iBT® **Practice Test 1**
READING

This section measures your ability to understand academic passages in English. You will have **54 minutes** to read and answer questions about **3 passages**. A clock at the top of the screen will display the starting time as **00 : 54 : 00** and show you how much time is remaining.

Most questions are worth 1 point, but the last question for each passage is worth more than 1 point. The directions for the last question indicate how many points you may receive.

Some passages in the computer-based test include a word or phrase that is underlined in blue. When you click on the word or phrase underlined in blue, you will see a verbal or visual definition of the word or term. In this book, those definitions are provided as endnotes below the reading passage.

Within this section, you can move to the next question by clicking on **Next**. You can skip questions and go back to them later as long as there is time remaining. If you want to return to previous questions, click on **Back**. You can click on **Review** at any time and the review screen will show you which questions you have answered and which you have not answered. From this review screen, you may go directly to any question you have already seen in the Reading section.

During this practice test, you may click the **Pause** icon at any time. This will stop the test until you decide to continue. You may continue the test in a few minutes or at any time during the period that your test is activated.

You will now begin the Reading section. Again, in an actual test you will have **54 minutes** to read the 3 passages and answer the questions. NOTE: In an actual test, some test takers might receive 4 passages; those test takers will have 72 minutes (1 hour and 12 minutes) to answer the questions.

Turn the page to begin the Reading section.

NINETEENTH-CENTURY POLITICS IN THE UNITED STATES

The development of the modern presidency in the United States began with Andrew Jackson, who swept to power in 1829 at the head of the Democratic Party and served until 1837. During his administration he immeasurably enlarged the power of the presidency. "The president is the direct representative of the American people," he lectured the Senate when it opposed him. "He was elected by the people, and is responsible to them." With this declaration, Jackson redefined the character of the presidential office and its relationship to the people.

During Jackson's second term, his opponents had gradually come together to form the Whig Party. Whigs and Democrats held different attitudes toward the changes brought about by the market, banks, and commerce. The Democrats tended to view society as a continuing conflict between "the people"—farmers, planters, and workers—and a set of greedy aristocrats. This "paper money aristocracy" of bankers and investors manipulated the banking system for their own profit, Democrats claimed, and sapped the nation's virtue by encouraging speculation and the desire for sudden, unearned wealth. The Democrats wanted the rewards of the market without sacrificing the features of a simple agrarian republic. They wanted the wealth that the market offered without the competitive, changing society; the complex dealing; the dominance of urban centers; and the loss of independence that came with it.

Whigs, on the other hand, were more comfortable with the market. For them, commerce and economic development were agents of civilization. Nor did the Whigs envision any conflict in society between farmers and workers on the one hand and businesspeople and bankers on the other. Economic growth would benefit everyone by raising national income and expanding opportunity. The government's responsibility was to provide a well-regulated economy that guaranteed opportunity for citizens of ability.

Whigs and Democrats differed not only in their attitudes toward the market but also about how active the central government should be in people's lives. Despite Andrew Jackson's inclination to be a strong president, Democrats as a rule believed in limited government. Government's role in the economy was to promote competition by destroying monopolies[1] and special privileges. In keeping with this philosophy of limited government, Democrats also rejected the idea that moral beliefs were the proper sphere of government action. Religion and politics, they believed, should be kept clearly separate, and they generally opposed humanitarian legislation.

The Whigs, in contrast, viewed government power positively. They believed that it should be used to protect individual rights and public liberty, and that it had a special role where individual effort was ineffective. By regulating the economy and competition, the government could ensure equal opportunity. Indeed, for Whigs the concept of government promoting the general welfare went beyond the economy. In particular, Whigs in the northern sections of the United States also believed that government power should be used to foster the moral welfare of the country. They were much more likely to favor social-reform legislation and aid to education.

In some ways the social makeup of the two parties was similar. To be competitive in winning votes, Whigs and Democrats both had to have significant support among farmers, the largest group in society, and workers. Neither party could win an election by appealing exclusively to the rich or the poor. The Whigs, however, enjoyed disproportionate strength among the business and commercial classes. Whigs appealed to planters who needed credit to finance their cotton and rice trade in the world market, to farmers who were eager to sell their surpluses, and to workers who wished to improve themselves. Democrats attracted farmers isolated from the market or uncomfortable with it, workers alienated from the emerging industrial system, and rising entrepreneurs who wanted to break monopolies and open the economy to newcomers like themselves. The Whigs were strongest in the towns, cities, and those rural areas that were fully integrated into the market economy, whereas Democrats dominated areas of semisubsistence farming that were more isolated and languishing economically.

1. **monopolies:** Companies or individuals that exclusively own or control commercial enterprises with no competitors

Directions: Now answer the questions.

PARAGRAPH 1

The development of the modern presidency in the United States began with Andrew Jackson, who swept to power in 1829 at the head of the Democratic Party and served until 1837. During his administration he immeasurably enlarged the power of the presidency. "The president is the direct representative of the American people," he lectured the Senate when it opposed him. "He was elected by the people, and is responsible to them." With this declaration, Jackson redefined the character of the presidential office and its relationship to the people.

1. According to paragraph 1, the presidency of Andrew Jackson was especially significant for which of the following reasons?

    (A) The president granted a portion of his power to the Senate.
    (B) The president began to address the Senate on a regular basis.
    (C) It was the beginning of the modern presidency in the United States.
    (D) It was the first time that the Senate had been known to oppose the president.

GO ON TO THE NEXT PAGE

PARAGRAPH 2

During Jackson's second term, his opponents had gradually come together to form the Whig Party. Whigs and Democrats held different attitudes toward the changes brought about by the market, banks, and commerce. The Democrats tended to view society as a continuing conflict between "the people"—farmers, planters, and workers—and a set of greedy aristocrats. This "paper money aristocracy" of bankers and investors manipulated the banking system for their own profit, Democrats claimed, and sapped the nation's virtue by encouraging speculation and the desire for sudden, unearned wealth. The Democrats wanted the rewards of the market without sacrificing the features of a simple agrarian republic. They wanted the wealth that the market offered without the competitive, changing society; the complex dealing; the dominance of urban centers; and the loss of independence that came with it.

2. The author mentions "bankers and investors" in the passage as an example of which of the following?

Ⓐ The Democratic Party's main source of support
Ⓑ The people that Democrats claimed were unfairly becoming rich
Ⓒ The people most interested in a return to a simple agrarian republic
Ⓓ One of the groups in favor of Andrew Jackson's presidency

PARAGRAPH 3

Whigs, on the other hand, were more comfortable with the market. For them, commerce and economic development were agents of civilization. Nor did the Whigs envision any conflict in society between farmers and workers on the one hand and businesspeople and bankers on the other. Economic growth would benefit everyone by raising national income and expanding opportunity. The government's responsibility was to provide a well-regulated economy that guaranteed opportunity for citizens of ability.

3. According to paragraph 3, Whigs believed that commerce and economic development would have which of the following effects on society?

Ⓐ They would promote the advancement of society as a whole.
Ⓑ They would cause disagreements between Whigs and Democrats.
Ⓒ They would supply new positions for Whig Party members.
Ⓓ They would prevent conflict between farmers and workers.

4. According to paragraph 3, which of the following describes the Whig Party's view of the role of government?

Ⓐ To regulate the continuing conflict between farmers and businesspeople
Ⓑ To restrict the changes brought about by the market
Ⓒ To maintain an economy that allowed all capable citizens to benefit
Ⓓ To reduce the emphasis on economic development

PARAGRAPH 4

Whigs and Democrats differed not only in their attitudes toward the market but also about how active the central government should be in people's lives. Despite Andrew Jackson's inclination to be a strong president, Democrats as a rule believed in limited government. Government's role in the economy was to promote competition by destroying monopolies[1] and special privileges. In keeping with this philosophy of limited government, Democrats also rejected the idea that moral beliefs were the proper sphere of government action. Religion and politics, they believed, should be kept clearly separate, and they generally opposed humanitarian legislation.

1. **monopolies:** Companies or individuals that exclusively own or control commercial enterprises with no competitors

5. According to paragraph 4, a Democrat would be most likely to support government action in which of the following areas?

   (A) Creating a state religion
   (B) Supporting humanitarian legislation
   (C) Destroying monopolies
   (D) Recommending particular moral beliefs

PARAGRAPH 5

The Whigs, in contrast, viewed government power positively. They believed that it should be used to protect individual rights and public liberty, and that it had a special role where individual effort was ineffective. By regulating the economy and competition, the government could ensure equal opportunity. Indeed, for Whigs the concept of government promoting the general welfare went beyond the economy. In particular, Whigs in the northern sections of the United States also believed that government power should be used to foster the moral welfare of the country. They were much more likely to favor social-reform legislation and aid to education.

6. The word "concept" in the passage is closest in meaning to

   (A) power
   (B) reality
   (C) difficulty
   (D) idea

7. Which of the following can be inferred from paragraph 5 about variations in political beliefs within the Whig Party?

   (A) They were focused on issues of public liberty.
   (B) They caused some members to leave the Whig Party.
   (C) They were unimportant to most Whigs.
   (D) They reflected regional interests.

GO ON TO THE NEXT PAGE

PARAGRAPH 6

In some ways the social makeup of the two parties was similar. To be competitive in winning votes, Whigs and Democrats both had to have significant support among farmers, the largest group in society, and workers. Neither party could win an election by appealing exclusively to the rich or the poor. The Whigs, however, enjoyed disproportionate strength among the business and commercial classes. Whigs appealed to planters who needed credit to finance their cotton and rice trade in the world market, to farmers who were eager to sell their surpluses, and to workers who wished to improve themselves. Democrats attracted farmers isolated from the market or uncomfortable with it, workers alienated from the emerging industrial system, and rising entrepreneurs who wanted to break monopolies and open the economy to newcomers like themselves. The Whigs were strongest in the towns, cities, and those rural areas that were fully integrated into the market economy, whereas Democrats dominated areas of semisubsistence farming that were more isolated and languishing economically.

8. Which of the sentences below best expresses the essential information in the highlighted sentence in the passage? Incorrect choices change the meaning in important ways or leave out essential information.

   (A) Whigs were able to attract support only in the wealthiest parts of the economy because Democrats dominated in other areas.

   (B) Whig and Democratic areas of influence were naturally split between urban and rural areas, respectively.

   (C) The semisubsistence farming areas dominated by Democrats became increasingly isolated by the Whigs' control of the market economy.

   (D) The Democrats' power was greatest in poorer areas, while the Whigs were strongest in those areas where the market was already fully operating.

During Jackson's second term, his opponents had gradually come together to form the Whig Party. **(A)** Whigs and Democrats held different attitudes toward the changes brought about by the market, banks, and commerce. **(B)** The Democrats tended to view society as a continuing conflict between "the people"—farmers, planters, and workers—and a set of greedy aristocrats. **(C)** This "paper money aristocracy" of bankers and investors manipulated the banking system for their own profit, Democrats claimed, and sapped the nation's virtue by encouraging speculation and the desire for sudden, unearned wealth. **(D)** The Democrats wanted the rewards of the market without sacrificing the features of a simple agrarian republic. They wanted the wealth that the market offered without the competitive, changing society; the complex dealing; the dominance of urban centers; and the loss of independence that came with it.

9. **Directions:** Look at the part of the passage that is displayed above. The letters **(A)**, **(B)**, **(C)**, and **(D)** indicate where the following sentence could be added.

This new party argued against the policies of Jackson and his party in a number of important areas, beginning with the economy.

Where would the sentence best fit?

Ⓐ Choice A
Ⓑ Choice B
Ⓒ Choice C
Ⓓ Choice D

GO ON TO THE NEXT PAGE

10. **Directions:** An introductory sentence for a brief summary of the passage is provided below. Complete the summary by selecting the THREE answer choices that express the most important ideas in the passage. Some answer choices do not belong in the summary because they express ideas that are not presented in the passage or are minor ideas in the passage. **This question is worth 2 points.**

The political system of the United States in the mid-nineteenth century was strongly influenced by the social and economic circumstances of the time.

-
-
-

Answer Choices

A The Democratic and Whig Parties developed in response to the needs of competing economic and political constituencies.

B During Andrew Jackson's two terms as president, he served as leader of both the Democratic and Whig Parties.

C The Democratic Party primarily represented the interests of the market, banks, and commerce.

D In contrast to the Democrats, the Whigs favored government aid for education.

E A fundamental difference between Whigs and Democrats involved the importance of the market in society.

F The role of government in the lives of the people was an important political distinction between the two parties.

THE EXPRESSION OF EMOTIONS

Joy and sadness are experienced by people in all cultures around the world, but how can we tell when other people are happy or despondent? It turns out that the expression of many emotions may be universal. Smiling is apparently a universal sign of friendliness and approval. Baring the teeth in a hostile way, as noted by Charles Darwin in the nineteenth century, may be a universal sign of anger. As the originator of the theory of evolution, Darwin believed that the universal recognition of facial expressions would have survival value. For example, facial expressions could signal the approach of enemies (or friends) in the absence of language.

Most investigators concur that certain facial expressions suggest the same emotions in all people. Moreover, people in diverse cultures recognize the emotions manifested by the facial expressions. In classic research Paul Ekman took photographs of people exhibiting the emotions of anger, disgust, fear, happiness, and sadness. He then asked people around the world to indicate what emotions were being depicted in them. Those queried ranged from European college students to members of the Fore, a tribe that dwells in the New Guinea highlands. All groups, including the Fore, who had almost no contact with Western culture, agreed on the portrayed emotions. The Fore also displayed familiar facial expressions when asked how they would respond if they were the characters in stories that called for basic emotional responses. Ekman and his colleagues more recently obtained similar results in a study of ten cultures in which participants were permitted to report that multiple emotions were shown by facial expressions. The participants generally agreed on which two emotions were being shown and which emotion was more intense.

Psychological researchers generally recognize that facial expressions reflect emotional states. In fact, various emotional states give rise to certain patterns of electrical activity in the facial muscles and in the brain. The facial-feedback hypothesis argues, however, that the causal relationship between emotions and facial expressions can also work in the opposite direction. According to this hypothesis, signals from the facial muscles ("feedback") are sent back to emotion centers of the brain, and so a person's facial expression can influence that person's emotional state. Consider Darwin's words: "The free expression by outward signs of an emotion intensifies it. On the other hand, the repression, as far as possible, of all outward signs softens our emotions." Can smiling give rise to feelings of goodwill, for example, and frowning to anger?

Psychological research has given rise to some interesting findings concerning the facial-feedback hypothesis. Causing participants in experiments to smile, for example, leads them to report more positive feelings and to rate cartoons (humorous drawings of people or situations) as being more humorous. When they are caused to frown, they rate cartoons as being more aggressive.

What are the possible links between facial expressions and emotion? One link is arousal, which is the level of activity or preparedness for activity in an organism. Intense contraction of facial muscles, such as those used in signifying fear, heightens arousal. Self-perception of heightened arousal then leads to heightened emotional activity. Other links may involve changes in brain temperature and the release of neurotransmitters (substances that transmit nerve impulses). The contraction of facial muscles both influences

GO ON TO THE NEXT PAGE

the internal emotional state and reflects it. Ekman has found that the so-called Duchenne smile, which is characterized by "crow's-feet" wrinkles around the eyes and a subtle drop in the eye cover fold so that the skin above the eye moves down slightly toward the eyeball, can lead to pleasant feelings.

Ekman's observation may be relevant to the British expression "keep a stiff upper lip"[1] as a recommendation for handling stress. It might be that a "stiff" lip suppresses emotional response—as long as the lip is not quivering with fear or tension. But when the emotion that leads to stiffening the lip is more intense, and involves strong muscle tension, facial feedback may heighten emotional response.

1. **"keep a stiff upper lip":** Avoid showing emotions in difficult situations

Directions: Now answer the questions.

PARAGRAPH 1

Joy and sadness are experienced by people in all cultures around the world, but how can we tell when other people are happy or despondent? It turns out that the expression of many emotions may be universal. Smiling is apparently a universal sign of friendliness and approval. Baring the teeth in a hostile way, as noted by Charles Darwin in the nineteenth century, may be a universal sign of anger. As the originator of the theory of evolution, Darwin believed that the universal recognition of facial expressions would have survival value. For example, facial expressions could signal the approach of enemies (or friends) in the absence of language.

1. The author mentions "Baring the teeth in a hostile way" in order to

   Ⓐ differentiate one possible meaning of a particular facial expression from other meanings of it

   Ⓑ support Darwin's theory of evolution

   Ⓒ provide an example of a facial expression whose meaning is widely understood

   Ⓓ contrast a facial expression that is easily understood with other facial expressions

P
A
R
A
G
R
A
P
H

2

Most investigators concur that certain facial expressions suggest the same emotions in all people. Moreover, people in diverse cultures recognize the emotions manifested by the facial expressions. In classic research Paul Ekman took photographs of people exhibiting the emotions of anger, disgust, fear, happiness, and sadness. He then asked people around the world to indicate what emotions were being depicted in them. Those queried ranged from European college students to members of the Fore, a tribe that dwells in the New Guinea highlands. All groups, including the Fore, who had almost no contact with Western culture, agreed on the portrayed emotions. The Fore also displayed familiar facial expressions when asked how they would respond if they were the characters in stories that called for basic emotional responses. Ekman and his colleagues more recently obtained similar results in a study of ten cultures in which participants were permitted to report that multiple emotions were shown by facial expressions. The participants generally agreed on which two emotions were being shown and which emotion was more intense.

2. The word "concur" in the passage is closest in meaning to

   Ⓐ estimate
   Ⓑ agree
   Ⓒ expect
   Ⓓ understand

3. According to paragraph 2, which of the following was true of the Fore people of New Guinea?

   Ⓐ They did not want to be shown photographs.
   Ⓑ They were famous for their storytelling skills.
   Ⓒ They knew very little about Western culture.
   Ⓓ They did not encourage the expression of emotions.

GO ON TO THE NEXT PAGE ▶

PARAGRAPH 3

Psychological researchers generally recognize that facial expressions reflect emotional states. In fact, various emotional states give rise to certain patterns of electrical activity in the facial muscles and in the brain. The facial-feedback hypothesis argues, however, that the causal relationship between emotions and facial expressions can also work in the opposite direction. According to this hypothesis, signals from the facial muscles ("feedback") are sent back to emotion centers of the brain, and so a person's facial expression can influence that person's emotional state. Consider Darwin's words: "The free expression by outward signs of an emotion intensifies it. On the other hand, the repression, as far as possible, of all outward signs softens our emotions." Can smiling give rise to feelings of goodwill, for example, and frowning to anger?

4. According to the passage, what did Darwin believe would happen to human emotions that were not expressed?

   Ⓐ They would become less intense.
   Ⓑ They would last longer than usual.
   Ⓒ They would cause problems later.
   Ⓓ They would become more negative.

PARAGRAPH 4

Psychological research has given rise to some interesting findings concerning the facial-feedback hypothesis. Causing participants in experiments to smile, for example, leads them to report more positive feelings and to rate cartoons (humorous drawings of people or situations) as being more humorous. When they are caused to frown, they rate cartoons as being more aggressive.

5. According to the passage, research involving which of the following supported the "facial-feedback hypothesis"?

   Ⓐ The reactions of people in experiments to cartoons
   Ⓑ The tendency of people in experiments to cooperate
   Ⓒ The release of neurotransmitters by people during experiments
   Ⓓ The long-term effects of repressing emotions

6. The word "rate" in the passage is closest in meaning to

   Ⓐ judge
   Ⓑ reject
   Ⓒ draw
   Ⓓ want

PARAGRAPH 6

Ekman's observation may be relevant to the British expression "keep a stiff upper lip" as a recommendation for handling stress. It might be that a "stiff" lip suppresses emotional response—as long as the lip is not quivering with fear or tension. But when the emotion that leads to stiffening the lip is more intense, and involves strong muscle tension, facial feedback may heighten emotional response.

7. The word "relevant" in the passage is closest in meaning to

   Ⓐ contradictory
   Ⓑ confusing
   Ⓒ dependent
   Ⓓ applicable

8. According to the passage, stiffening the upper lip may have which of the following effects?

   Ⓐ It first suppresses stress, then intensifies it.
   Ⓑ It may cause fear and tension in those who see it.
   Ⓒ It can damage the lip muscles.
   Ⓓ It may either heighten or reduce emotional response.

PARAGRAPHS 1 AND 2

For example, facial expressions could signal the approach of enemies (or friends) in the absence of language.

(A) Most investigators concur that certain facial expressions suggest the same emotions in all people. **(B)** Moreover, people in diverse cultures recognize the emotions manifested by the facial expressions. **(C)** In classic research Paul Ekman took photographs of people exhibiting the emotions of anger, disgust, fear, happiness, and sadness. **(D)** He then asked people around the world to indicate what emotions were being depicted in them. Those queried ranged from European college students to members of the Fore, a tribe that dwells in the New Guinea highlands. All groups, including the Fore, who had almost no contact with Western culture, agreed on the portrayed emotions. The Fore also displayed familiar facial expressions when asked how they would respond if they were the characters in stories that called for basic emotional responses. Ekman and his colleagues more recently obtained similar results in a study of ten cultures in which participants were permitted to report that multiple emotions were shown by facial expressions. The participants generally agreed on which two emotions were being shown and which emotion was more intense.

9. **Directions:** Look at the part of the passage that is displayed above. The letters **(A)**, **(B)**, **(C)**, and **(D)** indicate where the following sentence could be added.

   This universality in the recognition of emotions was demonstrated by using rather simple methods.

   Where would the sentence best fit?

   Ⓐ Choice A
   Ⓑ Choice B
   Ⓒ Choice C
   Ⓓ Choice D

GO ON TO THE NEXT PAGE ↘

10. **Directions:** An introductory sentence for a brief summary of the passage is provided below. Complete the summary by selecting the THREE answer choices that express the most important ideas in the passage. Some sentences do not belong in the summary because they express ideas that are not presented in the passage or are minor ideas in the passage. **This question is worth 2 points.**

Psychological research seems to confirm that people associate particular facial expressions with the same emotions across cultures.

-
-
-

Answer Choices

- A Artificially producing the Duchenne smile can cause a person to have pleasant feelings.
- B Facial expressions and emotional states interact with each other through a variety of feedback mechanisms.
- C People commonly believe that they can control their facial expressions so that their true emotions remain hidden.
- D A person's facial expression may reflect the person's emotional state.
- E Ekman argued that the ability to accurately recognize the emotional content of facial expressions was valuable for human beings.
- F Facial expressions that occur as a result of an individual's emotional state may themselves feed back information that influences the person's emotions.

GEOLOGY AND LANDSCAPE

Most people consider the landscape to be unchanging, but Earth is a dynamic body, and its surface is continually altering—slowly on the human time scale, but relatively rapidly when compared to the great age of Earth (about 4.5 billion years). There are two principal influences that shape the terrain: constructive processes such as uplift, which create new landscape features, and destructive forces such as erosion, which gradually wear away exposed landforms.

Hills and mountains are often regarded as the epitome of permanence, successfully resisting the destructive forces of nature, but in fact they tend to be relatively short-lived in geological terms. As a general rule, the higher a mountain is, the more recently it was formed; for example, the high mountains of the Himalayas are only about 50 million years old. Lower mountains tend to be older, and are often the eroded relics of much higher mountain chains. About 400 million years ago, when the present-day continents of North America and Europe were joined, the Caledonian mountain chain was the same size as the modern Himalayas. Today, however, the relics of the Caledonian orogeny (mountain-building period) exist as the comparatively low mountains of Greenland, the northern Appalachians in the United States, the Scottish Highlands, and the Norwegian coastal plateau.

The Earth's crust is thought to be divided into huge, movable segments, called plates, which float on a soft plastic layer of rock. Some mountains were formed as a result of these plates crashing into each other and forcing up the rock at the plate margins. In this process, sedimentary rocks that originally formed on the seabed may be folded upwards to altitudes of more than 26,000 feet. Other mountains may be raised by earthquakes, which fracture the Earth's crust and can displace enough rock to produce block mountains. A third type of mountain may be formed as a result of volcanic activity which occurs in regions of active fold mountain belts, such as in the Cascade Range of western North America. The Cascades are made up of lavas and volcanic materials. Many of the peaks are extinct volcanoes.

Whatever the reason for mountain formation, as soon as land rises above sea level it is subjected to destructive forces. The exposed rocks are attacked by the various weather processes and gradually broken down into fragments, which are then carried away and later deposited as sediments. Thus, any landscape represents only a temporary stage in the continuous battle between the forces of uplift and those of erosion.

The weather, in its many forms, is the main agent of erosion. Rain washes away loose soil and penetrates cracks in the rocks. Carbon dioxide in the air reacts with the rainwater, forming a weak acid (carbonic acid) that may chemically attack the rocks. The rain seeps underground and the water may reappear later as springs. These springs are the sources of streams and rivers, which cut through the rocks and carry away debris from the mountains to the lowlands.

Under very cold conditions, rocks can be shattered by ice and frost. Glaciers may form in permanently cold areas, and these slowly moving masses of ice cut out valleys, carrying with them huge quantities of eroded rock debris. In dry areas the wind is the principal agent of erosion. It carries fine particles of sand, which bombard exposed rock surfaces, thereby wearing them into yet more sand. Even living things contribute to the formation

GO ON TO THE NEXT PAGE

of landscapes. Tree roots force their way into cracks in rocks and, in so doing, speed their splitting. In contrast, the roots of grasses and other small plants may help to hold loose soil fragments together, thereby helping to prevent erosion by the wind.

Directions: Now answer the questions.

**P
A
R
A
G
R
A
P
H

1**

Most people consider the landscape to be unchanging, but Earth is a dynamic body, and its surface is continually altering—slowly on the human time scale, but relatively rapidly when compared to the great age of Earth (about 4.5 billion years). There are two principal influences that shape the terrain: constructive processes such as uplift, which create new landscape features, and destructive forces such as erosion, which gradually wear away exposed landforms.

1. According to paragraph 1, which of the following statements is true of changes in Earth's landscape?

    Ⓐ They occur more often by uplift than by erosion.
    Ⓑ They occur only at special times.
    Ⓒ They occur less frequently now than they once did.
    Ⓓ They occur quickly in geological terms.

2. The word "relatively" in the passage is closest in meaning to

    Ⓐ unusually
    Ⓑ comparatively
    Ⓒ occasionally
    Ⓓ naturally

PARAGRAPH 2

Hills and mountains are often regarded as the epitome of permanence, successfully resisting the destructive forces of nature, but in fact they tend to be relatively short-lived in geological terms. As a general rule, the higher a mountain is, the more recently it was formed; for example, the high mountains of the Himalayas are only about 50 million years old. Lower mountains tend to be older, and are often the eroded relics of much higher mountain chains. About 400 million years ago, when the present-day continents of North America and Europe were joined, the Caledonian mountain chain was the same size as the modern Himalayas. Today, however, the relics of the Caledonian orogeny (mountain-building period) exist as the comparatively low mountains of Greenland, the northern Appalachians in the United States, the Scottish Highlands, and the Norwegian coastal plateau.

3. Which of the sentences below best expresses the essential information in the high-lighted sentence in the passage? Incorrect choices change the meaning in important ways or leave out essential information.

   Ⓐ When they are relatively young, hills and mountains successfully resist the destructive forces of nature.

   Ⓑ Although they seem permanent, hills and mountains exist for a relatively short period of geological time.

   Ⓒ Hills and mountains successfully resist the destructive forces of nature, but only for a short time.

   Ⓓ Hills and mountains resist the destructive forces of nature better than other types of landforms.

4. Which of the following can be inferred from paragraph 2 about the mountains of the Himalayas?

   Ⓐ Their current height is not an indication of their age.

   Ⓑ At present, they are much higher than the mountains of the Caledonian range.

   Ⓒ They were a uniform height about 400 million years ago.

   Ⓓ They are not as high as the Caledonian mountains were 400 million years ago.

GO ON TO THE NEXT PAGE ➤

PARAGRAPH 3

The Earth's crust is thought to be divided into huge, movable segments, called plates, which float on a soft plastic layer of rock. Some mountains were formed as a result of these plates crashing into each other and forcing up the rock at the plate margins. In this process, sedimentary rocks that originally formed on the seabed may be folded upwards to altitudes of more than 26,000 feet. Other mountains may be raised by earthquakes, which fracture the Earth's crust and can displace enough rock to produce block mountains. A third type of mountain may be formed as a result of volcanic activity which occurs in regions of active fold mountain belts, such as in the Cascade Range of western North America. The Cascades are made up of lavas and volcanic materials. Many of the peaks are extinct volcanoes.

5. According to paragraph 3, one cause of mountain formation is the

(A) effect of climatic change on sea level
(B) slowing down of volcanic activity
(C) force of Earth's crustal plates hitting each other
(D) replacement of sedimentary rock with volcanic rock

PARAGRAPH 5

The weather, in its many forms, is the main agent of erosion. Rain washes away loose soil and penetrates cracks in the rocks. Carbon dioxide in the air reacts with the rainwater, forming a weak acid (carbonic acid) that may chemically attack the rocks. The rain seeps underground and the water may reappear later as springs. These springs are the sources of streams and rivers, which cut through the rocks and carry away debris from the mountains to the lowlands.

6. Why does the author mention "Carbon dioxide" in the passage?

(A) To explain the origin of a chemical that can erode rocks
(B) To contrast carbon dioxide with carbonic acid
(C) To give an example of how rainwater penetrates soil
(D) To argue for the desirability of preventing erosion

PARAGRAPH 6

Under very cold conditions, rocks can be shattered by ice and frost. Glaciers may form in permanently cold areas, and these slowly moving masses of ice cut out valleys, carrying with them huge quantities of eroded rock debris. In dry areas the wind is the principal agent of erosion. It carries fine particles of sand, which bombard exposed rock surfaces, thereby wearing them into yet more sand. Even living things contribute to the formation of landscapes. Tree roots force their way into cracks in rocks and, in so doing, speed their splitting. In contrast, the roots of grasses and other small plants may help to hold loose soil fragments together, thereby helping to prevent erosion by the wind.

7. According to paragraph 6, which of the following is both a cause and result of erosion?

Ⓐ Glacial activity
Ⓑ Rock debris
Ⓒ Tree roots
Ⓓ Sand

PARAGRAPH 6

Under very cold conditions, rocks can be shattered by ice and frost. Glaciers may form in permanently cold areas, and these slowly moving masses of ice cut out valleys, carrying with them huge quantities of eroded rock debris. **(A)** In dry areas the wind is the principal agent of erosion. **(B)** It carries fine particles of sand, which bombard exposed rock surfaces, thereby wearing them into yet more sand. **(C)** Even living things contribute to the formation of landscapes. **(D)** Tree roots force their way into cracks in rocks and, in so doing, speed their splitting. In contrast, the roots of grasses and other small plants may help to hold loose soil fragments together, thereby helping to prevent erosion by the wind.

8. **Directions:** Look at the part of the passage that is displayed above. The letters **(A)**, **(B)**, **(C)**, and **(D)** indicate where the following sentence could be added.

Under different climatic conditions, another type of destructive force contributes to erosion.

Where would the sentence best fit?

Ⓐ Choice A
Ⓑ Choice B
Ⓒ Choice C
Ⓓ Choice D

GO ON TO THE NEXT PAGE ⬖

9. **Directions:** Three of the answer choices below are used in the passage to illustrate constructive processes, and two are used to illustrate destructive processes. Complete the table by matching appropriate answer choices to the processes they are used to illustrate. **This question is worth 3 points.**

Constructive Processes	Destructive Processes
•	•
•	•
•	

Answer Choices

A Collision of Earth's crustal plates
B Separation of continents
C Wind-driven sand
D Formation of grass roots in soil
E Earthquakes
F Volcanic activity
G Weather processes

STOP. This is the end of the Reading section of *TOEFL iBT* ® Practice Test 1.

LISTENING

Directions: This section measures your ability to understand conversations and lectures in English.

You should listen to each conversation and lecture only **once**.

After each conversation or lecture, you will answer some questions about it. The questions typically ask about the main idea and supporting details. Some questions ask about the purpose of a speaker's statement or a speaker's attitude. Answer the questions based on what is stated or implied by the speakers.

You may take notes while you listen. You may use your notes to help you answer the questions. Your notes will **not** be scored.

In some questions, you will see this icon: This means that you will hear, but not see, part of the question.

Most questions are worth 1 point. If a question is worth more than 1 point, it will have special directions that indicate how many points you can receive.

It will take about **41 minutes** to listen to the conversations and lectures and to answer the questions. You should answer each question, even if you must guess the answer. Answer each question before moving on. Do not return to previous questions.

At the end of this Practice Test you will find an answer key, information to help you determine your score, scripts for the audio tracks, and explanations of the answers.

Turn the page to begin the Listening section.

Listen to Track 11.

Questions

Directions: Mark your answer by filling in the oval or square next to your choice.

1. Why does the student go to see the professor?

   Ⓐ To prepare for her graduate school interview
   Ⓑ To get advice about her graduate school application
   Ⓒ To give the professor her graduate school application
   Ⓓ To find out if she was accepted into graduate school

2. According to the professor, what information should the student include in her statement of purpose?
   Choose 2 answers.

   Ⓐ Her academic motivation
   Ⓑ Her background in medicine
   Ⓒ Some personal information
   Ⓓ The ways her teachers have influenced her

3. What does the professor consider unusual about the student's background?

   Ⓐ Her work experience
   Ⓑ Her creative writing experience
   Ⓒ Her athletic achievements
   Ⓓ Her music training

4. Why does the professor tell a story about his friend who went to medical school?

   Ⓐ To warn the student about how difficult graduate school can be
   Ⓑ To illustrate a point he is making
   Ⓒ To help the student relax
   Ⓓ To change the subject

5. What does the professor imply about the people who admit students to graduate school?

   Ⓐ They often lack expertise in the fields of the applicants.
   Ⓑ They do not usually read the statement of purpose.
   Ⓒ They are influenced by the appearance of an application.
   Ⓓ They remember most of the applications they receive.

GO ON TO THE NEXT PAGE ➘

Listen to Track 12.

Environmental Science

Questions

6. What is the talk mainly about?

    Ⓐ A common method of managing water supplies
    Ⓑ The formation of underground water systems
    Ⓒ Natural processes that renew water supplies
    Ⓓ Maintaining the purity of underground water systems

7. What is the professor's point of view concerning the method of "safe yield"?

    Ⓐ It has helped to preserve the environment.
    Ⓑ It should be researched in states other than Arizona.
    Ⓒ It is not an effective resource policy.
    Ⓓ It ignores the different ways people use water.

8. According to the professor, what are two problems associated with removing water from an underground system?

   Choose 2 answers.

   A Pollutants can enter the water more quickly.
   B The surface area can dry and crack.
   C The amount of water stored in the system can drop.
   D Dependent streams and springs can dry up.

9. What is a key feature of a sustainable water system?

   Ⓐ It is able to satisfy short-term and long-term needs.
   Ⓑ It is not affected by changing environmental conditions.
   Ⓒ It usually originates in lakes, springs, or streams.
   Ⓓ It is not used to supply human needs.

10. What does the professor imply about water systems managed by the "safe-yield" method?

   Ⓐ They recharge at a rapid rate.
   Ⓑ They are not sustainable.
   Ⓒ They must have large storage areas.
   Ⓓ They provide a poor quality of water.

11. *Listen to Track 13 to answer the question.*

   Why does the professor say this?

   Ⓐ To find out whether the students are familiar with the issue
   Ⓑ To introduce a new problem for discussion
   Ⓒ To respond to a student's question
   Ⓓ To encourage the students to care about the topic

GO ON TO THE NEXT PAGE

Listen to Track 14.

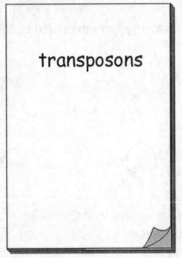

transposons

Questions

12. What are the students mainly discussing?

    (A) Drugs that are harmful to the human body
    (B) Bacteria that produce antibiotics
    (C) DNA that is related to athletic performance
    (D) Genes that protect bacteria from antibiotics

13. According to the conversation, why are transposons sometimes called "jumping genes"?

    (A) They are able to move from one bacteria cell to another.
    (B) They are found in people with exceptional jumping ability.
    (C) They occur in every other generation of bacteria.
    (D) Their movements are rapid and unpredictable.

14. According to the conversation, what are two ways in which bacteria cells get resistance genes?
Choose 2 answers.

    A The resistance genes are carried from nearby cells.
    B The resistance genes are carried by white blood cells.
    C The resistance genes are inherited from the parent cell.
    D The resistance genes are carried by antibiotics.

15. What can be inferred about the resistance genes discussed in the conversation?

    (A) They are found in all bacteria cells.
    (B) They are not able to resist antibiotics.
    (C) They make the treatment of bacterial diseases more difficult.
    (D) They are essential to the body's defenses against bacteria.

16. *Listen to Track 15 to answer the question.*
    Why does the woman say this?

    (A) To find out if the man has done his assignment
    (B) To ask the man to find out if the library is open
    (C) To let the man know that she cannot study much longer
    (D) To ask if the man has ever met her roommate

GO ON TO THE NEXT PAGE

Listen to Track 16.

Botany

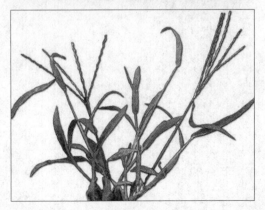

Questions

17. What is the main topic of the lecture?

   Ⓐ The size of root systems
   Ⓑ Various types of root systems
   Ⓒ The nutrients required by rye plants
   Ⓓ Improving two types of plant species

18. According to the professor, why did one scientist grow a rye plant in water?

   Ⓐ To expose the roots to sunlight
   Ⓑ To be able to fertilize it with gas
   Ⓒ To be able to see its entire root system
   Ⓓ To see how minerals penetrate its roots

19. The professor mentions houseplants that receive too much water. Why does she mention them?

   Ⓐ To show that many different types of plants can grow in water
   Ⓑ To explain why plants grown in water should have a gas bubbled through them
   Ⓒ To remind the students of the importance of their next experiment
   Ⓓ To make a point about the length of houseplants' roots

20. According to the professor, what similarity is there between crabgrass and rye plants?

   Ⓐ Both start growing in the month of May.
   Ⓑ Both have root systems that require a lot of water.
   Ⓒ Both have more shoot surface than root surface.
   Ⓓ Both produce many shoots from a single seed.

GO ON TO THE NEXT PAGE ↘

21. *Listen again to part of the lecture by playing Track 17.*
    Then answer the question.

    Why did the professor say this?

    (A) She wanted to correct the wording of a previous statement.
    (B) She wishes she did not have to bubble gas through it.
    (C) She realized the odor of gas could be unpleasant.
    (D) She forgot to tell the students about a step in the experiment.

22. *Listen again to part of the lecture by playing Track 18.*
    Then answer the question.

    What does the professor intend to explain?

    (A) Why a mistake made in textbooks was never corrected
    (B) Why she does not believe that the roots of rye plants extend to 1,000 kilometers
    (C) How the roots of rye plants develop to such a great length
    (D) How plants grown in water make use of fertilizer

Listen to Track 19.

Business Management

Questions

23. What is the lecture mainly about?

  (A) Technological innovations in the automobile industry
  (B) The organizational structure of companies
  (C) Ways to improve efficiency in an engineering department
  (D) Methods of resolving conflicts in organizations

24. Why does the professor talk about a construction company that has work in different cities?

  (A) To give an example of functional organization
  (B) To give an example of organization around projects
  (C) To illustrate problems with functional organization
  (D) To illustrate the types of conflict that can arise in companies

GO ON TO THE NEXT PAGE

25. What is an example of a violation of the "unity of command" principle?

   (A) More than one person supervises the same employee.
   (B) A company decides not to standardize its products.
   (C) Several project managers are responsible for designing a new product.
   (D) An employee does not follow a supervisor's instructions.

26. According to the professor, where might there be a conflict in an organizational structure based on both projects and function?

   (A) Between architects and finance experts
   (B) Between the need to specialize and the need to standardize
   (C) Between two engineers who work on the same project
   (D) Between the needs of projects in different cities

27. Indicate whether each sentence below describes functional organization or project organization. Place a check mark in the correct box.

	Functional Organization	Project Organization
It encourages people with similar expertise to work closely together.		
It helps the company to adapt quickly and meet changing needs.		
It helps to achieve uniformity in projects.		

28. *Listen again to part of the lecture by playing Track 20. Then answer the question.*

   Why does the professor say this?

   (A) He does not understand why the student is talking about engineers.
   (B) He wants to know how the engineers will communicate with their coworkers.
   (C) The student has not provided a complete answer to his question.
   (D) He wants the student to do more research on the topic.

STOP. This is the end of the Listening section of *TOEFL iBT*® Practice Test 1.

SPEAKING

Directions: The following Speaking section of the test will last approximately **17 minutes**. To complete it, you will need a recording device that you can play back to listen to your responses.

During the test, you will answer four speaking questions. One of the questions asks about a familiar topic. Three questions ask about short conversations, lectures, and reading passages. You may take notes as you listen to the conversations and lectures. The questions and the reading passages are printed here. The time you will have to prepare your response and to speak is printed below each question. You should answer all of the questions as completely as possible in the time allowed.

Play the audio tracks listed in the test instructions. Record each of your responses.

At the end of this Practice Test you will find scripts for the audio tracks, important points for each question, directions for listening to sample spoken responses, and comments on those responses by official raters.

Questions

1. *You will now be asked to give your opinion about a familiar topic. After you hear the question, you will have 15 seconds to prepare your response and 45 seconds to speak.*

Now play Track 21 to hear Question 1.

> Some people who unexpectedly receive a large amount of money spend it on practical things, while others spend it for pleasure only. Which do you think is better and why?
>
> | **Preparation Time: 15 Seconds** |
> | **Response Time: 45 Seconds** |

2. *You will now read a short passage and then listen to a conversation on the same topic. You will then be asked a question about them. After you hear the question, you will have 30 seconds to prepare your response and 60 seconds to speak.*

Now play Track 22 to hear Question 2.

| **Reading Time: 50 Seconds** |

Student Health Services Need Improvement

The situation at the health center is unacceptable: you sit in a crowded waiting room for hours waiting to get treatment for minor ailments. Then when it's your turn, you get about three minutes with an overworked doctor. I have two suggestions: first, the health center needs to hire more doctors so that each patient receives quality treatment. And as far as the wait time issue is concerned, the health center is currently open only Monday through Fridays, which means that people who get sick over the weekend wait until the following week to get treatment. So, opening the health center on weekends should solve that problem too.

Sincerely,

Megan Finch

The man expresses his opinion about the student's suggestions that are made in the letter. State the man's opinion and explain the reasons he gives for holding that opinion.

Preparation Time: 30 Seconds
Response Time: 60 Seconds

3. You will now read a short passage and then listen to a talk on the same academic topic. You will then be asked a question about them. After you hear the question, you will have 30 seconds to prepare your response and 60 seconds to speak.

Now play Track 23 to hear Question 3.

Reading Time: 45 Seconds

Social Loafing

When people work in groups to perform a task, individual group members may feel less motivated to contribute, since no one person is held directly responsible for completing the task. The result is that people may not work as hard, or accomplish as much, as they would if they were working alone and their individual output were being measured. This decrease in personal effort, especially on a simple group task, is known as social loafing. While it is not a deliberate behavior, the consequence of social loafing is less personal efficiency when working in groups than when working on one's own.

GO ON TO THE NEXT PAGE

Using the example from the lecture, explain what social loafing is and how it affects people's behavior.

Preparation Time: 30 Seconds
Response Time: 60 Seconds

4. You will now listen to part of a lecture. You will then be asked a question about it. After you hear the question, you will have 20 seconds to prepare your response and 60 seconds to speak.

Now play Track 24 to hear Question 4.

Using points and examples from the talk, explain internal and external locus of control.

Preparation Time: 20 Seconds
Response Time: 60 Seconds

STOP. This is the end of the Speaking section of *TOEFL iBT*® Practice Test 1.

WRITING

Directions: This section measures your ability to use writing to communicate in an academic environment. There will be two writing tasks.

For the first writing task, you will read a passage and listen to a lecture and then answer a question based on what you have read and heard. For the second task, you will answer a question based on your own knowledge and experience.

At the end of this Practice Test you will find a script for the audio track, topic notes, sample test taker essays, and comments on those essays by official raters.

Turn the page to see the directions for the first writing task.

Writing Based on Reading and Listening

Directions: For this task, you will read a passage about an academic topic and you will listen to a lecture about the same topic. You may take notes while you read and listen.

Then you will write a response to a question that asks you about the relationship between the lecture you heard and the reading passage. Try to answer the question as completely as possible using information from the reading passage and the lecture. The question does not ask you to express your personal opinion. You may refer to the reading passage again when you write. You may use your notes to help you answer the question.

Typically, an effective response will be 150 to 225 words. Your response will be judged on the quality of your writing and on the completeness and accuracy of the content.

Give yourself **3 minutes** to read the passage.

Reading Time: 3 minutes

Altruism is a type of behavior in which an animal sacrifices its own interest for that of another animal or group of animals. Altruism is the opposite of selfishness; individuals performing altruistic acts gain nothing for themselves.

Examples of altruism abound, both among humans and among other mammals. Unselfish acts among humans range from the sharing of food with strangers to the donation of body organs to family members, and even to strangers. Such acts are altruistic in that they benefit another, yet provide little reward to the one performing the act.

In fact, many species of animals appear willing to sacrifice food, or even their life, to assist other members of their group. The meerkat, which is a mammal that dwells in burrows in grassland areas of Africa, is often cited as an example. In groups of meerkats, an individual acts as a sentinel, standing guard and looking out for predators while the others hunt for food or eat food they have obtained. If the sentinel meerkat sees a predator such as a hawk approaching the group, it gives an alarm cry alerting the other meerkats to run and seek shelter. By standing guard, the sentinel meerkat gains nothing—it goes without food while the others eat, and it places itself in grave danger. After it issues an alarm, it has to flee alone, which might make it more at risk to a predator, since animals in groups are often able to work together to fend off a predator. So the altruistic sentinel behavior helps ensure the survival of other members of the meerkat's group.

Now play Track 25.

Question

Summarize the points made in the lecture, being sure to explain how they oppose specific points made in the reading passage.

You have 20 minutes to plan and write your response.

Response Time: 20 minutes

_____

_____

_____

_____

_____

_____

_____

_____

_____

_____

_____

GO ON TO THE NEXT PAGE ➤

Writing Based on Knowledge and Experience

Directions: For this task, you will write an essay in response to a question that asks you to state, explain, and support your opinion on an issue.

Typically, an effective essay will contain a minimum of 300 words. Your essay will be judged on the quality of your writing. This includes the development of your ideas, the organization of your essay, and the quality and accuracy of the language you use to express your ideas.

You have **30 minutes** to plan and complete your essay.

Write your essay in the space provided.

Question

Some young adults want independence from their parents as soon as possible. Other young adults prefer to live with their families for a longer time. Which of these situations do you think is better?

Use specific reasons and examples to support your answer. Be sure to use your own words. Do not use memorized examples.

Response Time: 30 minutes

GO ON TO THE NEXT PAGE

_____

_____

_____

_____

_____

_____

_____

_____

_____

_____

_____

_____

_____

_____

_____

_____

_____

_____

_____

_____

_____

_____

_____

_____

_____

_____

STOP. This is the end of the Writing section of *TOEFL iBT*® Practice Test 1.

TOEFL iBT® Practice Test 1
Answers, Explanations, and Listening Scripts

Reading

Answer Key and Self-Scoring Chart

Directions: Check your answers against the answer key below. Write the number 1 on the line to the right of each question if you picked the correct answer. For questions worth more than one point, follow the directions given. Total your points at the bottom of the chart.

Question Number	Correct Answer	Your Raw Points
Nineteenth-Century Politics in the United States		
1.	C	
2.	B	
3.	A	
4.	C	
5.	C	
6.	D	
7.	D	
8.	D	
9.	A	

For question 10, write 2 if you picked all three correct answers. Write 1 if you picked two correct answers.

10.	A, E, F	

Question Number	Correct Answer	Your Raw Points
The Expression of Emotions		
1.	C	
2.	B	
3.	C	
4.	A	
5.	A	
6.	A	
7.	D	
8.	D	
9.	C	

For question 10, write 2 if you picked all three correct answers. Write 1 if you picked two correct answers.

10.	B, D, F	

Question Number	Correct Answer	Your Raw Points
Geology and Landscape		
1.	D	
2.	B	
3.	B	
4.	B	
5.	C	
6.	A	
7.	D	
8.	A	

For question 9, write 3 if you placed five answer choices correctly. Write 2 if you placed four choices correctly. Write 1 if you placed three choices correctly.

9. Constructive:	A, E, F	
Destructive:	C, G	
	TOTAL:	

On the next page is a table that converts your Reading practice section answers into a *TOEFL iBT®* Reading scaled score. Take the total of raw points from your answer key and find that number in the left-hand column of the table. The right-hand column of the table gives a range of TOEFL iBT Reading scores for each number of raw points. For example, if the total points from your answer key is 20, the table shows a scaled score of 17 to 22. Your scaled score is given as a range instead of a single number for the following reasons:

- The estimates of scores are based on the performance of students who participated in a field study for these Reading Comprehension questions. Those students took the test on computer; you used a book. Although the two experiences are comparable, the differences make exact comparisons impossible.

- The students who participated in the field study were volunteers and may have differed in average ability from the actual *TOEFL*® test-taking population.

- The conversion of scores from the field study in which these questions were administered to the current TOEFL iBT scale involved two scale conversions. Converting from one scale to another always involves some statistical error.

You should use your score estimate as a general guide only. Your actual score on the TOEFL iBT test may be higher or lower than your score on the practice version.

Reading

Raw Point Total	Scaled Score
32–33	30
31	29–30
30	28–30
29	27–28
28	26–29
27	25–28
26	24–27
25	23–26
24	21–25
23	20–25
22	19–24
21	18–23
20	17–22
19	15–21
18	14–20
17	13–19
16	11–18
15	10–17
14	8–16
13	7–15
12	5–13
11	4–12
10	2–10
9	1–9
8	1–7
7	0–5
6	0–4
5	0–2
4	0–1
3 or below	0

Answer Explanations

Nineteenth-Century Politics in the United States

1. **C** This is a Factual Information question asking for specific information that can be found in paragraph 1. The correct answer is choice C because the first sentence of the paragraph explicitly states that this was when the development of the modern presidency began. The remainder of the paragraph is devoted to explaining the significant changes in government that this development involved. The result, as stated in sentence 5, was that the nature of the presidency itself was redefined. Choice A is contradicted by the paragraph; Jackson did not give presidential power away, but rather he increased it. Choice B is not mentioned in the paragraph: it says Jackson addressed the Senate, but not that this was the beginning of regular addresses. Choice D, which says that this was the first time the Senate opposed the president, is not stated in the passage.

2. **B** This is a Rhetorical Purpose question. It is asking you why the author mentions "bankers and investors" in the passage. The phrase being tested is highlighted in the passage. The correct answer is choice B. The author is using bankers and investors as examples of people that the Democrats claimed "manipulated" the banking system for their own profit. That means that they were unfairly becoming rich. Choices A, C, and D are all incorrect because, based upon the passage, they seem unlikely to be true. Therefore the author would not use them as examples.

3. **A** This is a Factual Information question asking for specific information that can be found in paragraph 3. Choice A is the correct answer. The paragraph says that Whigs believed commerce and economic development "would benefit everyone." That means essentially the same thing as choice A, which says that Whigs believed economic growth "would promote the advancement of society as a whole." "Society as a whole" is another way of saying "everyone." Choices B and C are not mentioned in the paragraph. Choice D, about conflict between groups, is mentioned but in a different context, so it is not a belief held by Whigs.

4. **C** This is a Factual Information question asking for specific information that can be found in paragraph 3. The correct answer is choice C: the Whigs viewed government as responsible for maintaining an economy that allowed all capable citizens to benefit. This is a restatement of paragraph 3, sentence 5. The paragraph states that Whigs did not envision continuing conflict between farmers and businesspeople, so choice A is wrong. Whigs favored changes brought about by the market, so choice B is wrong. Whigs were in favor of increased emphasis on economic development, so choice D is incorrect.

5. **C** This is a Factual Information question asking for specific information that can be found in paragraph 4. The correct answer is choice C, which is explicitly stated in sentence 3 of the paragraph. Sentences 4 and 5 explicitly refute the other choices.

6. **D** This is a Vocabulary question. The word being tested is *concept*. It is highlighted in the passage. The passage says, "for Whigs the concept of government . . ." In other words, "the way Whigs thought about government . . ." That process of thinking represents ideas, so choice D is the correct answer here.

7. **D** This is an Inference question asking for an inference that can be supported by paragraph 5. The correct answer is choice D: variations in Whigs' political beliefs reflected regional differences. This is supported by sentence 5 of the paragraph, which says that certain beliefs "In particular" reflected the views of northern Whigs. That suggests that Whigs in other regions of the country had beliefs that varied from this view and implies that such differences were regional. The other three choices are not mentioned in the passage in connection with "variations" in Whig beliefs, so there is no basis for inferring any of them.

8. **D** This is a Sentence Simplification question. As with all of these questions, a single sentence in the passage is highlighted:

> The Whigs were strongest in the towns, cities, and those rural areas that were fully integrated into the market economy, whereas Democrats dominated areas of semisubsistence farming that were more isolated and languishing economically.

The correct answer is choice D. Choice D contains all of the essential information in the tested sentence, but the order in which it is presented is reversed. The highlighted sentence describes areas of Whig strength first, and then the areas where Democrats were strong. The correct answer, choice D, describes Democrat strongholds first, and then Whig areas. No meaning has been changed, and no information has been left out.

Choice A is incorrect because it states that Whigs were able to attract support only in the wealthiest areas. The highlighted sentence does not say that; it says their support came from places integrated into the market, which can include areas of all economic levels.

Choice B is incorrect because it says that the two parties were split between rural and urban areas. However, the highlighted sentence says that Whigs were strong in rural areas that were integrated into the market economy. In other words, the split between the parties was based on the degree to which an area was integrated into the market, not whether it was urban or rural.

Choice C is incorrect because the highlighted sentence makes no mention of how (or if) the Whigs' control of the market economy affected the areas dominated by the Democrats.

9. **Ⓐ** This is an Insert Text question. You can see the four possible answer choices in paragraph 2.

During Jackson's second term, his opponents had gradually come together to form the Whig Party. **(A)** Whigs and Democrats held different attitudes toward the changes brought about by the market, banks, and commerce. **(B)** The Democrats tended to view society as a continuing conflict between "the people"—farmers, planters, and workers—and a set of greedy aristocrats. **(C)** This "paper money aristocracy" of bankers and investors manipulated the banking system for their own profit, Democrats claimed, and sapped the nation's virtue by encouraging speculation and the desire for sudden, unearned wealth. **(D)** The Democrats wanted the rewards of the market without sacrificing the features of a simple agrarian republic. They wanted the wealth that the market offered without the competitive, changing society; the complex dealing; the dominance of urban centers; and the loss of independence that came with it.

The sentence provided, "This new party argued against the policies of Jackson and his party in a number of important areas, beginning with the economy," is best inserted at choice **(A)**.

Choice **(A)** is correct because the phrase "This new party" refers directly and only to the Whigs, who are first mentioned (as a recently formed party) in sentence 1 of this paragraph.

Choice **(B)** is incorrect because the sentence before is not limited to the new Whig Party. It discusses both Whigs and Democrats.

Choices **(C)** and **(D)** are both incorrect because the sentences preceding them refer to the Democrats (the old party), not the Whigs.

10. **Ⓐ Ⓔ Ⓕ** This is a Prose Summary question. It is completed correctly below. The correct choices are A, E, and F. Choices B, C, and D are therefore incorrect.

Directions: An introductory sentence for a brief summary of the passage is provided below. Complete the summary by selecting the THREE answer choices that express the most important ideas in the passage. Some answer choices do not belong in the summary because they express ideas that are not presented in the passage or are minor ideas in the passage. **This question is worth 2 points.**

> **The political system of the United States in the mid-nineteenth century was strongly influenced by the social and economic circumstances of the time.**

> A The Democratic and Whig Parties developed in response to the needs of competing economic and political constituencies.
> E A fundamental difference between Whigs and Democrats involved the importance of the market in society.
> F The role of government in the lives of the people was an important political distinction between the two parties.

Answer Choices

A The Democratic and Whig Parties developed in response to the needs of competing economic and political constituencies.

B During Andrew Jackson's two terms as president, he served as leader of both the Democratic and Whig Parties.

C The Democratic Party primarily represented the interests of the market, banks, and commerce.

D In contrast to the Democrats, the Whigs favored government aid for education.

E A fundamental difference between Whigs and Democrats involved the importance of the market in society.

F The role of government in the lives of the people was an important political distinction between the two parties.

Correct Choices

Choice A, "The Democratic and Whig Parties developed in response to the needs of competing economic and political constituencies," is correct because it is a recurring theme throughout the entire passage. It is a general statement about the development of the Whigs and Democrats. Paragraphs 2, 3, 4, 5, and 6 all provide support for this statement with examples of the nature of the competing constituencies in the United States at that time and the ways in which these two parties responded to them.

Choice E, "A fundamental difference between Whigs and Democrats involved the importance of the market in society," is correct because it is a general statement about the differences between the Whigs and Democrats. Paragraphs 2, 3, 4, and 6 all provide support for this statement with examples of the differences in the ways that the two parties viewed the market and society.

Choice F, "The role of government in the lives of the people was an important political distinction between the two parties," is correct because it is another general statement about the differences between the Whigs and Democrats. Paragraphs 2, 3, 4, and 5 all explicitly explore this distinction between Whigs and Democrats.

Incorrect Choices

Choice B, "During Andrew Jackson's two terms as president, he served as leader of both the Democratic and Whig Parties," is incorrect because it contradicts the passage. Jackson was head of the Democratic Party.

Choice C, "The Democratic Party primarily represented the interests of the market, banks, and commerce," is incorrect because it is not true. The Whigs primarily represented these groups, as stated in paragraphs 3 and 6.

Choice D, "In contrast to the Democrats, the Whigs favored government aid for education," is incorrect because the passage states only that Whigs in the North were likely to favor aid to education. It is not clearly stated how other Whigs or Democrats felt on this issue.

The Expression of Emotions

1. **C** This is a Rhetorical Purpose question. It is asking you why the author mentions "Baring the teeth in a hostile way" in the passage. This phrase is highlighted in the passage. The correct answer is choice C; baring the teeth is "an example of a facial expression whose meaning is widely understood." The central theme of paragraph 1 of the passage is facial expressions that are universal. The author provides various examples of such expressions, and baring the teeth is mentioned as a universal sign of anger. The other choices are all mentioned in the passage, but not in conjunction with baring the teeth, so they are all incorrect.

2. **B** This is a Vocabulary question. The word being tested is *concur*. It is highlighted in the passage. The correct answer is choice B, "agree." *Concur* means "agree," so if investigators concur about the meaning of certain facial expressions, they agree on their meaning.

3. **C** This is a Factual Information question asking for specific information that can be found in paragraph 2. The correct answer is choice C, which states that the Fore people of New Guinea "knew very little about Western culture." The paragraph explicitly says that the Fore had almost no contact with Western culture. None of the other three choices is mentioned in connection with the Fore, so none of them is correct.

4. **A** This is a Factual Information question asking for specific information that can be found in the passage. The correct answer is choice A: emotions that are not expressed become less intense. This is correct based on the direct quotation of Darwin in paragraph 3. In that quotation, Darwin says that emotions that are freely expressed become more intense, while "On the other hand" those that are not freely expressed are softened, meaning that they become less intense. Choices B, C, and D are all incorrect because there is nothing in the passage that indicates Darwin ever believed these things about expressing emotions. Some or all of them may actually be true, but there is nothing in this passage that supports them.

5. **A** This is a Factual Information question asking for specific information that can be found in the passage. You can see that the phrase "facial-feedback hypothesis" is highlighted where it first appears in the passage in paragraph 3. The correct answer is choice A: research supporting this hypothesis came from studying experiments of the reactions of people to cartoons. This idea is found in paragraph 4, which uses these experiments as an example of how facial feedback works.

   Choice C, the release of neurotransmitters, is mentioned in paragraph 5, but not in connection with the facial-feedback hypothesis, so it is incorrect.

   Choices B and D are not explicitly mentioned at all in the passage.

6. **A** This is a Vocabulary question. The word being tested is *rate,* and it is highlighted in the passage. The correct answer is choice A, "judge." *Rate* in this context means "judge."

7. **D** This is a Vocabulary question. The word being tested is *relevant,* and it is highlighted in the passage. The correct answer is choice D, "applicable." *Relevant* means that Ekman's observation applies ("is applicable") to an expression.

8. **D** This is a Factual Information question asking for specific information that can be found in the passage. The correct answer is choice D: stiffening the upper lip "may either heighten or reduce emotional response." This is stated explicitly in paragraph 6 of the passage as a possible paradox in the relationship between facial expressions and emotions.

   Choice A is incorrect because paragraph 6 contradicts it.

   Choice B is incorrect because the passage mentions only the fear and tension of a person trying to keep a stiff upper lip, not any fear or tension that the expression may cause in others.

   Choice C is incorrect because there is no suggestion anywhere in the passage that stiffening the upper lip may damage lip muscles.

9. **C** This is an Insert Text question. You can see the four possible answer choices in paragraph 2.

> For example, facial expressions could signal the approach of enemies (or friends) in the absence of language.
>
> **(A)** Most investigators concur that certain facial expressions suggest the same emotions in all people. **(B)** Moreover, people in diverse cultures recognize the emotions manifested by the facial expressions. **(C)** In classic research Paul Ekman took photographs of people exhibiting the emotions of anger, disgust, fear, happiness, and sadness. **(D)** He then asked people around the world to indicate what emotions were being depicted in them. Those queried ranged from European college students to members of the Fore, a tribe that dwells in the New Guinea highlands. All groups, including the Fore, who had almost no contact with Western culture, agreed on the portrayed emotions. The Fore also displayed familiar facial expressions when asked how they would respond if they were the characters in stories that called for basic emotional responses. Ekman and his colleagues more recently obtained similar results in a study of ten cultures in which participants were permitted to report that multiple emotions were shown by facial expressions. The participants generally agreed on which two emotions were being shown and which emotion was more intense.

The sentence provided, "This universality in the recognition of emotions was demonstrated by using rather simple methods," is best inserted at choice **(C)**.

Choice **(C)** is correct because the inserted sentence begins with the phrase "This universality." The universality being referred to is the fact, stated in the second sentence, that "people in diverse cultures recognize the emotions manifested by the facial expressions."

None of the other answer choices follows a sentence that contains a universal statement. Sentence 1 mentions that "Most investigators concur," which means that some do not. Therefore this is not a universal statement, and choice B is incorrect.

Choices **(A)** and **(D)** are incorrect because there is nothing in either of the preceding sentences to which "This universality" could refer.

10. **B** **D** **F** This is a Prose Summary question. It is completed correctly below. The correct choices are B, D, and F. Choices A, C, and E are therefore incorrect.

Directions: An introductory sentence for a brief summary of the passage is provided below. Complete the summary by selecting the THREE answer choices that express the most important ideas in the passage. Some answer choices do not belong in the summary because they express ideas that are not presented in the passage or are minor ideas in the passage. **This question is worth 2 points.**

Psychological research seems to confirm that people associate particular facial expressions with the same emotions across cultures.

> B Facial expressions and emotional states interact with each other through a variety of feedback mechanisms.
> D A person's facial expression may reflect the person's emotional state.
> F Facial expressions that occur as a result of an individual's emotional state may themselves feed back information that influences the person's emotions.

Answer Choices

A Artificially producing the Duchenne smile can cause a person to have pleasant feelings.

B Facial expressions and emotional states interact with each other through a variety of feedback mechanisms.

C People commonly believe that they can control their facial expressions so that their true emotions remain hidden.

D A person's facial expression may reflect the person's emotional state.

E Ekman argued that the ability to accurately recognize the emotional content of facial expressions was valuable for human beings.

F Facial expressions that occur as a result of an individual's emotional state may themselves feed back information that influences the person's emotions.

Correct Choices

Choice B, "Facial expressions and emotional states interact with each other through a variety of feedback mechanisms," is correct because it is a general statement that is developed throughout the passage. Questions about the nature of this interaction and details of research on this issue are discussed in every paragraph, so it is clearly a "main idea."

Choice D, "A person's facial expression may reflect the person's emotional state," is correct because, like choice B, it is a major idea that the passage explores in detail. Paragraphs 3, 4, 5, and 6 are devoted to discussing attempts to understand whether and how facial expressions may reflect a person's emotional state.

Choice F, "Facial expressions that occur as a result of an individual's emotional state may themselves feed back information that influences the person's emotions," is correct because it is the main tenet of the "facial-feedback hypothesis" that is extensively discussed in paragraphs 3, 4, 5, and 6.

Incorrect Choices

Choice A, "Artificially producing the Duchenne smile can cause a person to have pleasant feelings," is incorrect because it is a minor, supporting detail mentioned in paragraph 5 as an example of a more general, and important, statement about the links between facial expressions and emotion (see choice F, above).

Choice C, "People commonly believe that they can control their facial expressions so that their true emotions remain hidden," is incorrect because while it may be true, the passage does not make this claim.

Choice E, "Ekman argued that the ability to accurately recognize the emotional content of facial expressions was valuable for human beings," is incorrect because according to the passage, Ekman did not make this argument; Charles Darwin did. Ekman's research was directed toward determining the universality of certain facial expressions, not the "value" of people's ability to recognize those expressions.

Geology and Landscape

1. **D** This is a Factual Information question asking for specific information that can be found in paragraph 1. The correct answer is choice D. Sentence 1 of the paragraph explicitly states that Earth's landscape changes relatively rapidly compared with Earth's overall age. Choice A, on the frequency of landscape changes, is contradicted by the paragraph. Choice B, that landscape changes occur only at special times, is also contradicted by the paragraph. Choice C, the frequency of landscape changes, is not mentioned.

2. **B** This is a Vocabulary question. The word being tested is *relatively,* and it is highlighted in the passage. The correct answer is choice B. The sentence in which *relatively* appears is comparing Earth's time scale with the human time scale, so "comparatively" is the correct answer.

3. **B** This is a Sentence Simplification question. As with all of these questions, a single sentence in the passage is highlighted:

> Hills and mountains are often regarded as the epitome of permanence, successfully resisting the destructive forces of nature, but in fact they tend to be relatively short-lived in geological terms.

The correct answer is choice B. That choice contains all of the essential information in the highlighted sentence. It omits the information in the second clause of the highlighted sentence ("successfully resisting the destructive forces of nature") because that information is not essential to the meaning.

Choices A, C, and D are all incorrect because they change the meaning of the highlighted sentence. Choice A adds information on the age of a mountain that is not mentioned in the highlighted sentence.

Choice C introduces information about how long mountains resist forces of nature in absolute terms; the highlighted sentence says that the resistance is relatively short in geological terms, which is an entirely different meaning.

Choice D compares mountains with other landforms. The highlighted sentence does not make any such comparison.

4. **B** This is an Inference question asking for an inference that can be supported by paragraph 2. The correct answer is choice B: the Himalayas are higher than the Caledonian mountains. The paragraph states that younger mountains are generally higher than older mountains. It also states that the Himalayas are much younger than the Caledonians. Since the Himalayas are the younger range and younger mountain ranges are higher than older ranges, we can infer that the younger Himalayas are higher than the older Caledonians.

Choices A and D are incorrect because they explicitly contradict the passage. The height of the Himalayas is an indication of their age, and the Himalayas are about the same height that the Caledonians were 400 million years ago.

Choice C is incorrect because there is nothing in the paragraph about "uniform height."

5. **C** This is a Factual Information question asking for specific information that can be found in paragraph 3. The correct answer is choice C: mountains are formed by crustal plates hitting each other. The paragraph states that mountains are formed in three ways: by crustal plates hitting each other, by earthquakes, and by volcanoes. Choices A, B, and D are not among these causes of mountain formation; they are therefore incorrect.

6. **A** This is a Rhetorical Purpose question. It asks why the author mentions "Carbon dioxide" in the passage. This term is highlighted in the passage. The correct answer is choice A: carbon dioxide is mentioned to explain the origin of a chemical that can erode rocks. The author is describing a particular cause of erosion, and the starting point of that process is carbon dioxide.

7. **D** This is a Factual Information question asking for specific information that can be found in paragraph 6. The correct answer is choice D, "Sand." Sentences 3 and 4 of that paragraph describe erosion in dry areas. Sand is carried by wind and bombards rock; this bombardment breaks down the rock, and, as a result, more sand is created. Thus sand is both the cause and the result of erosion, so choice D is correct. Glacial activity (choice A) and tree roots (choice C) are both mentioned only as causes of erosion. Rock debris (choice B) is mentioned only as a result of erosion.

8. **A** This is an Insert Text question. You can see the four possible answer choices in paragraph 6.

Under very cold conditions, rocks can be shattered by ice and frost. Glaciers may form in permanently cold areas, and these slowly moving masses of ice cut out valleys, carrying with them huge quantities of eroded rock debris. **(A)** In dry areas the wind is the principal agent of erosion. **(B)** It carries fine particles of sand, which bombard exposed rock surfaces, thereby wearing them into yet more sand. **(C)** Even living things contribute to the formation of landscapes. **(D)** Tree roots force their way into cracks in rocks and, in so doing, speed their splitting. In contrast, the roots of grasses and other small plants may help to hold loose soil fragments together, thereby helping to prevent erosion by the wind.

The sentence provided, "Under different climatic conditions, another type of destructive force contributes to erosion," is best inserted at choice **(A)**.

Choice **(A)** is correct because the inserted sentence is a transitional sentence, moving the discussion away from one set of climatic conditions (cold) to another set of climatic conditions (dryness). It is at choice **(A)** that the transition between topics takes place.

Choices **(B)**, **(C)**, and **(D)** all precede sentences that provide details of dry climatic conditions. No transition is taking place at any of those places, so the inserted sentence is not needed.

9. (A) (C) (E) (F) (G) This is a Fill in a Table question. It is completed correctly below. The correct choices for the "Constructive Processes" column are A, E, and F. Choices C and G are the correct choices for the "Destructive Processes" column. Choices B and D should not be used in either column.

Directions: Three of the answer choices below are used in the passage to illustrate constructive processes, and two are used to illustrate destructive processes. Complete the table by matching appropriate answer choices to the processes they are used to illustrate. **This question is worth 3 points.**

Constructive Processes	Destructive Processes
A Collision of Earth's crustal plates	C Wind-driven sand
E Earthquakes	G Weather processes
F Volcanic activity	

Answer Choices

A Collision of Earth's crustal plates
B Separation of continents
C Wind-driven sand
D Formation of grass roots in soil
E Earthquakes
F Volcanic activity
G Weather processes

Correct Choices

Choice A: "Collision of Earth's crustal plates" (Constructive Process) belongs in this column because it is mentioned in the passage as one of the constructive processes by which mountains are formed.

Choice C: "Wind-driven sand" (Destructive Process) belongs in this column because it is mentioned in the passage as one of the destructive forces that wear away the land.

Choice E: "Earthquakes" (Constructive Process) belongs in this column because it is mentioned in the passage as one of the constructive forces by which mountains are formed.

Choice F: "Volcanic activity" (Constructive Process) belongs in this column because it is mentioned in the passage as one of the constructive forces by which mountains are formed.

Choice G: "Weather processes" (Destructive Process) belongs in this column because it is mentioned in the passage as one of the destructive forces that wear away the land.

Incorrect Choices

Choice B: "Separation of continents" does not belong in the table because it is not mentioned in the passage as either a constructive or destructive process.

Choice D: "Formation of grass roots in soil" does not belong in the table because it is not mentioned in the passage as either a constructive or destructive process.

Listening

Answer Key and Self-Scoring Chart

Directions: Check your answers against the answer key below. Write the number 1 on the line to the right of each question if you picked the correct answer. For questions worth more than one point, follow the directions given. Total your points at the bottom of the chart.

Question Number	Correct Answer	Your Raw Points
1.	B	
2.	A, C	
3.	D	
4.	B	
5.	C	
6.	A	
7.	C	
8.	C, D	
9.	A	
10.	B	
11.	D	
12.	D	
13.	A	
14.	A, C	
15.	C	
16.	C	
17.	A	
18.	C	
19.	B	
20.	D	
21.	A	
22.	C	
23.	B	
24.	B	
25.	A	
26.	B	

For question 27, write 1 if you placed three answer choices correctly. Write 0 if you placed fewer than three choices correctly.

27. Functional:	A, C	
Project:	B	
28.	C	
Total:		

On the next page is a table that converts your Listening section answers into a *TOEFL iBT®* scaled score. Take the total of raw points from your answer key and find that number in the left-hand column of the table. On the right-hand side of the table is a range of TOEFL iBT Listening scores for that number of raw points. Your scaled score is given as a range instead of a single number for the following reasons:

- The estimates of scores are based on the performance of students who participated in a field study for these listening comprehension questions. Those students took the test on computer. You took your practice test by listening to audio tracks and answering questions in a book. Although the two experiences are comparable, the differences make it impossible to give an exact prediction of your score.

- The students who participated in the field study were volunteers and may have differed in average ability from the actual *TOEFL®* test-taking population.

- The conversion of scores from the field study in which these questions were administered to the current TOEFL iBT test score scale involved two scale conversions. Converting from one scale to another always involves some statistical error.

- You should use your score estimate as a general guide only. Your actual score on the TOEFL iBT test may be higher or lower than your score on the practice section.

Listening

Raw Point Total	Scale Score
28	30
27	29–30
26	27–30
25	25–30
24	24–29
23	23–27
22	22–26
21	21–25
20	19–24
19	18–23
18	17–21
17	16–20
16	14–19
15	13–18
14	12–17
13	10–15
12	9–14
11	7–13
10	6–12
9	5–10
8	3–9
7	2–7
6	1–6
5	1–4
4	0–2
3	0–1
2	0
1	0
0	0

Listening Scripts and Answer Explanations

Questions 1–5

Track 11 Listening Script

Narrator

Listen to a conversation between a student and a professor.

Professor

Hey, Ellen. How are you doing?

Student

Oh, pretty good, thanks. How are you?

Professor

OK.

Student

Did you, um, have a chance to look at my grad school application . . . you know, the statement of purpose I wrote?

Professor

Well, yeah. In fact, here it is. I just read it.

Student

Oh, great! What did you think?

Professor

Basically, it's good. What you might actually do is take some of these different points here, and actually break them out into separate paragraphs. So, um, one: your purpose for applying for graduate study—uh, why do you want to go to graduate school—and an area of specialty; and, uh, why you want to do the area you're specifying; um, and what you want to do with your degree once you get it.

Student

OK.

Professor

So those are . . . they're pretty clear on those four points they want.

Student

Right.

Professor

So you might just break them out into, uh . . . you know, separate paragraphs and expand on each point some. But really what's critical with these is that, um, you've gotta let yourself come through. See, you gotta let them see you in these statements. Expand some more on what's happened in your own life and what shows your . . . your motivation and interest in this area—in geology. Let 'em see what really, what . . . what captures your imagination about this field.

Student

OK. So make it a little more . . . personal? That's OK?

Professor

That's fine. They look for that stuff. You don't wanna go overboard . . .

Student

Right.

Professor

. . . but it's critical that . . . that somebody sees what your passion is—your personal motivation for doing this.

Student

OK.

Professor

And that's gotta come out in here. Um, and let's see, uh, you might also give a little, uh—since this is your only chance to do it, you might give a little more explanation about your unique undergraduate background. So, you know, how you went through, you know, the music program; what you got from that; why you decided to change. I mean it's kind of unusual to go from music to geology, right?

Student

Yeah. I was . . . I was afraid that, you know, maybe the personal-type stuff wouldn't be what they wanted, but . . .

Professor

No, in fact it's . . . um, give an example: I . . . I had a friend, when I was an undergrad, um, went to medical school. And he put on his med school application—and he could actually tell if somebody actually read it 'cause, um, he had asthma and the reason that he wanted to go to med school was he said he wanted to do sports medicine because he, you know, he had this real interest. He was an athlete too, and . . . and wanted to help athletes who had this physical problem. And he could always tell if somebody actually read his letter, because they would always ask him about that.

Student

. . . Mmm . . . so something unique.

Professor

Yeah. So see, you know, that's what's good and, and, I think for you probably, you know, your music background's the most unique thing that you've got in your record.

Student

Right.

Professor

. . . Mmm . . . so you see, you gotta make yourself stand out from a coupla hundred applications. Does that help any?

Student

Yeah, it does. It gives me some good ideas.

Professor

And . . . what you might also do too is, you know, uh, you might get a friend to proof it or something at some point.

Student

Oh, sure . . . sure.

Professor

Also, think about presentation—how the application looks. In a way, you're actually showing some other skills here, like organization. A lot of stuff that's . . . that they're not . . . they're not formally asking for, they're looking at. So your presentation format, your grammar, all that stuff, they're looking at in your materials at the same time.

Student

Right. OK.

Answer Explanations

1. **B** For Listening conversations that take place during a professor's office hours, it is very likely that the first question will be a Gist-Purpose question. That is the case here. This discussion is about how the woman should write her graduate school application, not about an interview or whether she had been admitted. The professor already has her application and has reviewed it, so the purpose cannot be for her to give him the application. Thus choice B is the correct answer: she wants advice about the application.

2. **A C** When you are taking the *TOEFL iBT*® test on computer, whenever you see squares in front of the question choices instead of ovals, you should recognize that the question calls for you to select two or more answers from among the choices. In this case, the professor stresses the following two items that the woman needs to include in her application letter:

1. How her college career has made her interested in graduate school
2. How she stands out as an individual

   Thus the correct answers are choices A and C. She does not have a background in medicine (choice B), and the professor does not mention her teachers (choice D).

3. **D** This is a Detail question. The professor mentions twice that the woman's decision to go from studying music to geology is unusual.

4. **B** This is an Understanding Organization question. Clearly the professor is illustrating his point that a good application should individualize the writer. His friend who went to medical school is an example.

5. **C** This is a Making Inferences question. The last thing the professor mentions to the student is that she should think about the format of her application and the statement of purpose. He says that the format of the application can demonstrate her organizational skills and strongly implies that avoiding any writing errors shows thoroughness. By making these points, he is implying that the readers of the application will be influenced by its appearance, even if the influence is unconscious. He says nothing about the readers' expertise (choice A); he implies that sometimes they may not read the application carefully, but he does not imply that this is what usually happens (choice B); and he says the opposite of choice D. The correct answer is choice C.

Questions 6–11

Track 12 Listening Script

Narrator

Listen to part of a talk in an environmental science class.

Environmental Science

Professor

So I wanted to discuss a few other terms here . . . actually, some, uh, some ideas about how we manage our resources.

Let's talk about what that . . . what that means. If we take a resource like water . . . well, maybe we should get a little bit more specific here—back up from the more general case—and talk about underground water in particular.

So hydrogeologists have tried to figure out . . . how much water can you take out from underground sources? This has been an important question. Let me ask you guys: how much water, based on what you know so far, could you take out of, say, an aquifer . . . under the city?

Male Student

As . . . as much as would get recharged?

Professor

OK. So we wouldn't want to take out any more than naturally comes into it. The implication is that, uh, well, if you only take as much out as comes in, you're not gonna deplete the amount of water that's stored in there, right?

Wrong, but that's the principle. That's the idea behind how we manage our water supplies. It's called "safe yield." Basically what this method says is that you can pump as much water out of a system as naturally recharges . . . as naturally flows back in.

So this principle of safe yield—it's based on balancing what we take out with what gets recharged. But what it does is, it ignores how much water naturally comes out of the system.

In a natural system, a certain amount of recharge comes in and a certain amount of water naturally flows out through springs, streams, and lakes. And over the long term the amount that's stored in the aquifer doesn't really change much. It's balanced. Now humans come in . . . and start taking water out of the system. How have we changed the equation?

Female Student

It's not balanced anymore?

Professor

Right. We take water out, but water also naturally flows out. And the recharge rate doesn't change, so the result is we've reduced the amount of water that's stored in the underground system.

If you keep doing that long enough—if you pump as much water out as naturally comes in—gradually the underground water levels drop. And when that happens, that can affect surface water. How? Well, in underground systems there are natural discharge points—places where the water flows out of the underground systems, out to lakes and streams. Well, a drop in the water level can mean those discharge points will eventually dry up. That means water's not getting to lakes and streams that depend on it. So we've ended up reducing the surface water supply, too.

You know, in the state of Arizona we're managing some major water supplies with this principle of safe yield, under a method that will eventually dry up the natural discharge points of those aquifer systems.

Now, why is this an issue? Well, aren't some of you going to want to live in this state for a while? Want your kids to grow up here, and your kids' kids? You might be concerned with . . . does Arizona have a water supply which is sustainable—key word here? What that means . . . the general definition of *sustainable* is will there be enough to meet the needs of the present without compromising the ability of the future to have the availability . . . to have the same resources?

Now, I hope you see that these two ideas are incompatible: sustainability and safe yield. Because what sustainability means is that it's sustainable for all systems dependent on the water—for the people that use it and for . . . uh, for supplying water to the dependent lakes and streams.

So I'm gonna repeat this: so if we're using a safe-yield method, if we're only balancing what we take out with what gets recharged, but—don't forget, water's also flowing out naturally—then the amount stored underground is gonna gradually get reduced and that's gonna lead to another problem. These discharge points—where the water flows out to the lakes and streams—they're gonna dry up. OK.

Answer Explanations

6. **(A)** The first question in this set is a Gist-Content question, as is usually the case in a lecture set. It is important to remember that you are hearing only part of the lecture.

   The beginning of this excerpt shows that the professor is talking about different ways to manage natural resources. He chooses underground water as an example of a natural resource, and then goes on to discuss one particular way of managing the underground water supply called "safe yield." His focus is on the "safe-yield" approach to managing underground water supplies. Thus the correct answer is choice A. The other choices are aspects of underground water that an environmental scientist might discuss, but they are not the focus of this excerpt.

7. **(C)** The lecture makes clear that the professor does not think the "safe-yield" approach is appropriate. He communicates this indirectly in several ways, particularly when he says, "we're managing some major water supplies with this principle of safe yield, under a method that will eventually dry up the natural discharge points of those aquifer systems." Although the term "safe yield" indicates that it is safe, the professor is saying that it is, in reality, not safe, because it does not take into account the other ways that water can leave the system besides pumping water out for people's use. The correct answer is choice C.

8. **C D** This is a Detail question. All four choices are possible results of removing water from an underground system, but the professor discusses only C and D.

9. **A** This is a Detail question. The professor defines *sustainability* as the ability to meet present and future needs. Since his main criticism of "safe-yield" management is that it is not sustainable, knowing the meaning of *sustainable* is key to understanding the lecture. "Short-term and long-term needs" are the same as "present and future needs," so choice A is the correct answer.

10. **B** Because the question uses the word *imply*, we expect this to be a Making Inferences question. It is, however, a very easy inference. The professor says, "these two ideas are incompatible: sustainability and safe yield." If the "safe-yield" method is incompatible with sustainability, then water supplies managed by "safe yield" are not sustainable. The correct answer is choice B.

11. **D** This question requires that you Understand the Function of What Is Said. The professor asks these questions:

    Now, why is this an issue? Well, aren't some of you going to want to live in this state for a while? Want your kids to grow up here, and your kids' kids?

    The purpose is to point out to the students that, over time, there will be serious consequences to depleting the underground water supply. He thinks the students should consider the future of the state of Arizona. Therefore the correct answer is choice D.

Questions 12–16

Track 14 Listening Script

Narrator

Listen to part of a conversation between two students. The woman is helping the man review for a biology examination.

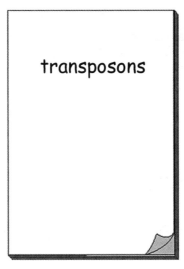

transposons

Male Student

OK, so . . . what do you think we should go over next?

Female Student

How about if we go over this stuff about how bacteria become resistant to antibiotics.

Male Student

OK.

Female Student

Um, but first of all, though, how many pages do we have left? I told my roommate I'd meet her at the library at seven o'clock.

Male Student

Ummm . . . There's only a few pages left. We should be finished in a few minutes.

Female Student

OK. So, ummm . . .

Male Student

About how bacteria become resistant to antibiotics.

Female Student

Oh yeah, OK. So you know that some bacteria cells are able to resist the drugs we use against them, and that's because they have these special genes that, like, protect them from the drugs.

Male Student

Right. If I remember correctly, I think the genes, like . . . weaken the antibiotics, or, like . . . stop the antibiotics from getting into the bacteria cell, something like that?

Female Student

Exactly. So when bacteria have these genes, it's very difficult for the antibiotics to kill the bacteria.

Male Student

Right.

Female Student

So do you remember what those genes are called?

Male Student

Umm . . .

Female Student

Resistance genes.

Male Student

Resistance genes. Right. Resistance genes. OK.

Female Student

And that makes sense, right? Because they help the bacteria resist the antibiotics.

Male Student

Yeah, that makes sense. OK.

Female Student

OK. But the question is: how do bacteria get the resistance genes?

Male Student

How do they get the resistance genes? They just inherit them from the parent cell, right?

Female Student

OK, yeah, that's true. They can inherit them from the parent cell, but that's not what I'm talking about.

Male Student

OK.

Female Student

I'm talking about how they get resistance genes from other cells in their environment, you know, from the other cells around them.

Male Student

Oh, I see what you mean. Umm, is that that stuff about "hopping genes," or something like that?

Female Student

Right. Although actually they're called "jumping genes," not "hopping genes."

Male Student

Oh, OK. Jumping genes.

Female Student

Yeah, but they have another name, too, that I can't think of. Umm . . . lemme see if I can find it here in the book . . .

Male Student

I think it's probably on . . .

Female Student

Oh, OK. Here it is. Transposons. That's what they're called.

Male Student

Lemme see. OK. Trans . . . po . . . sons . . . trans . . . posons. So "transposon" is another name for a jumping gene?

Female Student

Right. And these transposons are, you know, like, little bits of DNA that are able to move from one cell to another. That's why they're called "jumping genes." They kind of, you know, "jump" from one cell to another.

Male Student

OK.

Female Student

And these transposons are how resistance genes are able to get from one bacteria cell to another bacteria cell. What happens is that a resistance gene from one cell attaches itself to a transposon and then, when the transposon jumps to another cell . . .

Male Student

The other cell gets the resistance gene and . . .

Female Student

Right.

Male Student

That's how it becomes resistant to antibiotics.

Female Student

Right.

Male Student

Wow. That's really cool. So that's how it happens.

Female Student

That's how it happens.

Answer Explanations

12. **D** This conversation is about academic content in the area of Life Science. The man is trying to learn something for his biology test. It makes sense, then, that the first question is a Gist-Content question: "What are the students mainly discussing?" The students discuss drugs, but they are drugs that fight bacteria, so choice A is eliminated. They are not discussing how antibiotics are produced, but how they are resisted, so choice B is eliminated. If all you understood was "jumping" and "hopping," you might think they were discussing athletics, but that is not how those words are being used, so choice C is eliminated. Choice D is the correct answer: the man is learning how some bacteria acquire genes that make them resistant to antibiotics.

13. **A** This is a Detail question. When you hear a new term defined, in either a lecture or a conversation, you should note it. Here the students spend a large part of the conversation discussing why the "transposons" are called "jumping genes." The woman says twice that the reason is that the genes can migrate, or "jump," from one cell to another. The correct answer is choice A.

14. **A C** This is another Detail question. It asks you to identify two ways that bacteria acquire the resistance gene. Both students mention that the gene can be inherited from a parent cell. They then have a longer discussion about the "jumping gene" and how a "jumping gene" can carry the resistance gene to a new cell. Nothing is mentioned about "white blood cells," and resistance genes being "carried by antibiotics" is directly contradicted by the discussion. The correct answers are choices A and C.

15. **C** The question uses the verb *inferred*, so you know this is a Making Inferences question. The students say that some bacteria "resist the drugs we use against them." From this you can infer that an antibiotic is a medicine used against some bacteria. The students say the resistance genes "weaken the antibiotics" and "stop the antibiotics." From these clues you should infer that choice C, the resistance genes "make the treatment of bacterial diseases more difficult," is the correct answer.

16. **C** This replay question requires you to Understand the Function of What Is Said. You are asked why the woman says the following:

Um, but first of all, though, how many pages do we have left? I told my roommate I'd meet her at the library at seven o'clock.

Her statement about meeting her roommate is part of the context in which the main discussion takes place. The man is trying to learn about bacteria, but she is saying they have only a limited amount of time to spend on the discussion. The function of her statement is to tell the man that she must keep her appointment with her roommate and therefore they must finish soon.

Questions 17–22

Track 16 Listening Script

Narrator

Listen to part of a talk in a botany class.

Professor

OK. So we've talked about some different types of root systems of plants, and I've shown you some pretty cool slides, but now I want to talk about the extent of the root system—the overall size of the root system . . . the depth. I want to tell you about one particular experiment. I think you're going to find this pretty amazing. OK. So there was this scientist . . . this very meticulous scientist decided that the best place to see a whole root system—to actually see how big the entire system got—the best place would be to grow it . . . where?

Female Student

Um, water?

Professor

In water. So he took rye plants—it was rye plants—and he started growing them in water. Now, you've all heard of growing stuff in water before, right?

Male Student

It's done commercially, right? Uh, like to grow vegetables and flowers?

Professor

Right. They grow all kinds of commercial crops in water. So if you're growing things in water, you can add the fertilizer. What do you need to do to that water besides put fertilizer in it? Anyone ever actually tried to grow plants in water? You must bubble water through it. Bubble gas through it. I'm sorry, you must bubble gas through it. So, gas, you have to bubble through. Think about the soil we talked about last week, about growing plants in soil. Think about some of you who have killed your favorite houseplants, 'cause you loved them too much. If you overwater, why do your favorite houseplants die?

Female Student

Oh, no oxygen.

Professor

Not enough oxygen for the roots . . . which do what twenty-four hours a day in all seasons?

Female Student

Respiration?

Professor

Respire . . . respiration . . . they breathe. So if you just stick rye plants in water, it doesn't make a difference how much fertilizer you add, you also need to bubble gas through the water, so they have access to that oxygen. If they don't have that, they're in big trouble. OK. So this guy—this scientist—grew a rye plant in water so he could see the root system, how big it got—its surface area. I read about this and the book said one thousand kilometers of roots. I kept thinking: this has to be a mistake. It just doesn't make any sense to me that . . . that . . . that could be right. But that's what all the books have, and no one's ever corrected it. So let me explain to you about this rye plant. If you take a little seed of many grasses—and remember rye is a grass; if you take a tiny little seed and you germinate it—actually, take one of my least favorite grasses that starts growing about May. What's my least favorite grass that starts growing about May?

Male Student

Crabgrass.

Professor

Crabgrass.

Remember how I showed you in the lab, one little seed starts out producing one little shoot. Then at a week or so later you've got about six shoots, and then, three weeks later you've got about fifteen shoots coming out all directions like this—all those little shoots up there? Well, that's what they did with the rye. And the little seedling started and pretty soon there were several shoots, and then more shoots. In the end, that one single seed produced eighty shoots, with an average of fifty centi-meters of height . . . from one seed. Eighty shoots coming out, average fifty centimeters high. When they looked at the shoot versus the root surface, they found that the shoot surface, with all of its leaves, had a total surface area of about five square meters. Now, here's the biggie: when they looked at the root surface area, you would expect that the root and the shoot would be in balance, right? So they should be pretty close in terms of surface area, right?

Male Student

Uh-un.

Professor

What's that? Did somebody say "no"? Well, you're absolutely correct. Instead of five square meters, the root system was found to have more than two hundred square meters of surface area. Where did all of that extra surface area come from? Who did it? Who was responsible for all those extra square meters of surface area? What did roots do to increase their surface area?

Female Student

Root hairs.

Professor

Root hairs, that's exactly it. So those root hairs were responsible for an incredible chunk of surface area. They constantly have to be spread out in the water so they can absorb miner-als from the fertilizer, and of course they need oxygen access as well.

Answer Explanations

17. **Ⓐ** This is a Gist-Content question. This lecture is not highly organized and includes interaction from the students. However, despite the short digres-sions, the lecturer at the beginning and at the end repeats that the point of the talk is to explain how big root systems can be compared with the other parts of the plant. She mentions nutrients and different kinds of grasses, but they are subordinate to her main point. The correct answer is choice A.

18. **Ⓒ** This is a Detail question. The professor says that the scientist in the exper-iment wanted "to actually see how big the entire system got." That "entire system" refers to the root system, so the correct answer is choice C.

19. **B** This is an Understanding Organization question. Although this might seem to be a digression, the professor is using an example to explain why plants that are grown in water must have gas bubbled through the water. When people give houseplants too much water, they are, in effect, "growing the plants in water" unintentionally. The plants die because the roots are deprived of oxygen. The purpose of the discussion of houseplants is to explain why, in the experiment, gas was bubbled through the water. The correct answer is choice B.

20. **D** This is a Detail question. The professor mentions crabgrass because it is more familiar to her students than rye. She is making the point that many different kinds of grasses produce many roots from a single seed. She mentions that crabgrass begins growing in May, but that is not her point (choice A). She does not say anything about how much water it requires (choice B). Choice C is the opposite of what she says. Choice D is the correct answer.

21. **A** This question requires that you Understand the Function of What Is Said. You are asked to listen to this part of the lecture again:

    What do you need to do to that water besides put fertilizer in it? Anyone ever actually tried to grow plants in water? You must bubble water through it. Bubble gas through it. I'm sorry, you must bubble gas through it. So, gas, you have to bubble through.

    Then you are asked specifically why the professor says, "I'm sorry, you must bubble gas through it."

    In real speech, people sometimes misspeak; that is, they say a word that is different from the one they intended. This happens more often in informal speech, and this discussion is informal. As you can see from the script, in the previous sentence the professor said, "You must bubble water through it." *It* refers to water. So she has said, in effect, "You must bubble water through water," which does not make sense. The professor immediately corrects herself and repeats the correction twice, so the students know she meant to say "gas." Her purpose is to correct her previous words, so choice A is the correct answer.

22. **C** You are asked to listen again to this part of the lecture:

    I read about this and the book said one thousand kilometers of roots. I kept thinking: this has to be a mistake. It just doesn't make any sense to me that . . . that . . . that could be right. But that's what all the books have, and no one's ever corrected it. So let me explain to you about this rye plant.

    Like most replay questions, this question requires that you Understand the Function of What Is Said. The lecturer says that "one thousand kilometers of roots" did not make any sense to her. She seems to be expressing doubt. But her next sentence makes clear that the "one thousand kilometers" figure is accurate. She intends to explain why such a surprising, or unbelievable, statement is true. The correct answer is choice C.

Questions 23–28

Track 19 Listening Script

Narrator

Listen to part of a lecture in a business management class.

Professor

OK. Uh, let's talk about organization and structure in a company. How are companies typically structured?

Female Student

Functionally.

Professor

And ... ?

Female Student

By projects.

Professor

Right. By function ... and by projects. Twenty years ago companies were organized in function groups, where people with a certain expertise worked together as a unit—the, uh, architects in one unit, the finance people in another unit. Well, nowadays a lot of companies are organized around projects—like a construction company could be building an office building in one city and an apartment house somewhere else, and each project has its own architects and engineers.

Now, the good thing about project organization is that it's easier to change to adapt to the needs of the project—it's a small group, a dedicated team, not the whole company.

Now, with that in mind, here's a question for you: why do we continue to organize ourselves by function, even now, when in fact we admit that projects are the lifeblood of a lot of organizations? Why do some companies maintain a functional organization instead of organizing around projects? Yes?

Female Student

Because, um, if you don't have that functional structure within your organization, chances are you'd have a harder time meeting the goals of the projects.

Professor

Why?

Female Student

Why?

Professor

Listen, let's say we got four new cars we want to design. Why do we need a functional organization? Why not just organize the company around the four projects—these people make car number one, these other people make car number two . . .

Female Student

Yeah, but who's gonna be responsible for what? You know, the way you tell who's . . .

Professor

Well . . . well, we'll appoint a manager: new car number one manager, car number two manager—they're completely responsible. Why should we have a single engineering department that has all four cars passing through it?

Female Student

When you design a car, you need the expertise of all the engineers in the company. Each engineer needs to be in touch with the entire engineering department.

Professor

Yeah, but I keep . . . I keep asking why. I wanna know why. Yes.

Male Student

Well, to eliminate redundancy's probably one of the biggest factors in an organization. So that, uh. . . so that there's, there's . . . standards of . . . for uniformity and efficiency in the organization.

Professor

OK. And . . . and that's probably the primary reason for functional organization right there—is that we want some engineering consistency. We want the same kind of technology used in all four cars. If we disperse those four engineers into four parts of the organization and they work by themselves, there's a lot less chance that the technology's gonna be the same from car to car. So instead we maintain the functional organization—that means the engineers work together in one part of the building. And their offices are next to each other because we want them to talk to each other. When an engineer works on a project, they bring the expertise of their whole functional group with them.

But there's a downside of that, though, isn't there? I mean organizing a company into functional groups is not all positive. Where's the allegiance of those engineers? It's to their coordinator, right? It's to that chief engineer. But we really want our one engineer, the engineer that's working on car number one, we want that person's loyalty to be to that project as well as to the head of the engineering group. We . . . we really want both, don't we? We want to maintain the functional organization, so we can maintain uniformity and technology transfer, and expertise. We want the cutting-edge expertise in every group. But at the same time we also want the engineer to be totally dedicated to the needs of the project. Ideally, we have a . . . a hybrid, a combination of both functional and project organization.

But there's a problem with this kind of hybrid structure. When you have both functional and project organization, well, what does that violate in terms of basic management principles?

Female Student

Unity of command.

Professor

Unity of command. That's exactly right. So this . . . this is a vicious violation of unity of command, isn't it? It says that this engineer working on a project seems to have two bosses. We . . . we got the engineering boss, and we got the project manager boss. But the project manager is responsible for the project, and is not the official manager of the engineer who works on the project. And we try to maintain peace in the organizations, and sometimes it's disrupted and we have conflicts, don't we? The project manager for car one wants a car part to fit in a particular way, for a specific situation, a specialized case. Well, the, uh, engineering director says no, we gotta have standardization. We gotta have all the cars done this way. We can't make a special mold for that particular part for that particular car. We're not gonna do that. So we got a conflict.

Answer Explanations

23. **B** This is a Gist-Content question. Although the lecture includes exchanges between the professor and the students, it is clearly organized around a comparison of the strengths and weaknesses of two different organizational principles. It is not about the automobile industry; that is just an example (choice A). It is not even about engineering; that is a function that is used as an example (choice C). It does not offer a resolution of the conflict it describes (choice D). The correct choice is B: it is about two alternative organizational structures.

24. **B** This is an Understanding Organization question. The professor discusses the construction company as an example of the kind of company that could be organized around project teams. Choice B is correct. The other choices are about functional organization, the opposite organizing principle.

25. Ⓐ This is a Detail question. In this lecture, the professor does not explicitly define "unity of command." But in the last part of the talk, he gives an example of the absence of unity of command: "this engineer working on a project seems to have two bosses." Choice A is the correct answer.

26. Ⓑ To answer this question, you need to recognize the difference between the examples the professor uses in the lecture and the principle that the lecture is actually about. The question asks about a "conflict" discussed in the lecture. Choices A, C, and D are about specific conflicts that might occur in one of the organizations the professor uses as examples. Only choice B is about the general principle of a conflict between two equally important goals. Choice B is the correct answer.

27. This question is easy to recognize as a Connecting Content question. Based on information in the lecture, you must indicate whether certain statements describe functional organization or project organization. The chart correctly filled out looks like this:

	Functional Organization	Project Organization
It encourages people with similar expertise to work closely together.	✓	
It helps the company to adapt quickly and meet changing needs.		✓
It helps to achieve uniformity in projects.	✓	

28. Ⓒ In this replay question, you listen again to a question from the professor, an answer by a student, and another question by the professor. It requires that you Understand the Function of What Is Said. In order to understand the professor's second question, you must recognize that it is a repetition of the previous question. By repeating his question after the student's answer, the professor is signaling that it has not been satisfactorily answered. He is also signaling that the answer to his question is an important point. The correct answer is choice C: the student's answer does not include a point the professor wants to make.

Speaking

Listening Scripts, Important Points, and Sample Responses with Rater Comments

Use the sample Independent and Integrated Speaking rubrics on pages 180–183 to see how responses are scored. The raters who listen to your responses will analyze them in three general categories. These categories are Delivery, Language Use, and Topic Development. All three categories have equal importance.

This section includes important points that should be covered when answering each question. All of these points must be present in a response in order for it to receive the highest score in the Topic Development category. These important points are guides to the kind of information raters expect to hear in a high-level response.

This section also refers to example responses on the accompanying audio tracks. Some responses were scored at the highest level, while others were not. The responses are followed by comments by certified ETS raters.

Question 1: Paired Choice

Track 21 Listening Script

Narrator

Some people who unexpectedly receive a large amount of money spend it on practical things, while others spend it for pleasure only. Which do you think is better and why?

Preparation Time: 15 Seconds
Response Time: 45 Seconds

Important Points

In this question you need to choose the action you think is better and explain why. In order to give an effective response, you should provide a clear reason for your opinion. You will not be scored on which action you prefer, but rather on how effectively you are able to present and support your opinion. You may choose to speak about this topic more generally by describing what people in this situation would do, or you may choose to respond from a personal standpoint by talking about what you would do if you were given this money unexpectedly.

Whichever option you choose—spending money on practical things or spending it for pleasure—you should include specific details and examples. For example, if you choose to spend money on practical things, you could mention what type of practical objects or experiences you mean (such as a new washing machine or car to make your family's life easier or something to further your career, such as paying for college tuition). If you choose to spend the money for pleasure, be specific about what kinds of things would give you pleasure and why (taking a trip to a favorite vacation spot, donating to a charity, giving a gift for your mother, and so on). It is also acceptable to support your choice of one option by explaining what is wrong with the other option.

Sample Responses

Play Track 26 to hear a high-level response for Question 1.

Rater Comments

In this high-level response, the speaker chooses to develop the idea of using money for practical items and explains why she thinks this is better than spending money on things for pleasure. To explain her opinion, she uses very specific detailed language with almost no errors or awkward phrasing: *"there's been a lot of cases with people who win the lottery and they spent almost all the money for their own pleasure."* She goes on further to explain that this leads to a *"luxurious lifestyle,"* which she claims is unsustainable. However, this response is not perfect. It lacks some specificity: she does not describe what she would consider "practical things" that people should spend money on, so while the listeners know what the speaker **disapproves of**, they do not know what she would **approve of** when spending money. Lastly, her pronunciation is clear throughout, and her words are easily followed. Her intonation and pausing are natural and appropriate and do not distract the listener. Overall, this is a mostly well-developed response that is easy to follow.

Play Track 27 to hear a mid-level response for Question 1.

Rater Comments

This speaker is able to express an opinion—that the money should be used for pleasure—and provides a general reason for her choice. However, she does not develop her reason at all. The content is vague and lacks details. She states that spending money on things for pleasure is better: *"First, because now the life is so stressful, if you can buy something or do something to relax is so important."* This is an interesting idea, but it would be better to include more specific information such as **what** to buy with the money and **how** or why that would give someone pleasure. While she has good, basic vocabulary and grammar, she does make some errors such as using *"so"* instead of *"very"* or she says, *"the life"* instead of *"life."* She has mostly clear pronunciation; it is usually easy to understand her words. However, she speaks very slowly, enunciating each word separately, and as a result, her use of intonation is limited and her speech lacks fluidity.

Question 2: Fit and Explain

Track 22 Listening Script

Narrator

A student has written a letter to the editor of City University's newspaper concerning the campus health center. You have 50 seconds to read the letter. Begin reading now.

Reading Time: 50 Seconds

Student Health Services Need Improvement

The situation at the health center is unacceptable: you sit in a crowded waiting room for hours waiting to get treatment for minor ailments. Then when it's your turn, you get about three minutes with an overworked doctor. I have two suggestions: first, the health center needs to hire more doctors so that each patient receives quality treatment. And as far as the wait time issue is concerned, the health center is currently open only Monday through Fridays, which means that people who get sick over the weekend wait until the following week to get treatment. So, opening the health center on weekends should solve that problem too.

Sincerely,

Megan Finch

Narrator

Now listen to two students discussing the letter.

Woman

Did you read that letter in the paper?

Man

Sure. And though she's right about the problems, I don't think what she proposes will do much good.

Woman

Really?

Man

Yeah, take her first suggestion—I mean, have you seen the health center?

Woman

Of course. Why?

Man

Well, it's tiny, right? The center suffers from lack of space. So unless they build more treatment rooms or offices or something. . . .

Woman

I see.

Man

And also, her second suggestion . . .

Woman

Seems like that'll help things out.

Man

Well, not necessarily. I mean think about it. A lot of students aren't even here on the weekends.

Woman

That's true.

Man

They leave town and get away. There's not a lot of people here . . .

Woman

Yeah, like me . . . I go home probably at least twice a month.

Man

Right. And a lot of us leave campus for the weekend even more often than that. So there's just not a lot of demand for treatment then. See what I mean?

Narrator

The man expresses his opinion about the student's suggestions that are made in the letter. State the man's opinion and explain the reasons he gives for holding that opinion.

> **Preparation Time: 30 Seconds**
> **Response Time: 60 Seconds**

Important Points

To respond to this question, you could explain that the man does not think that the student's suggestions will improve treatment quality or wait times at the health center. To explain the reasons he gives, you should say that he does not think hiring more doctors will help, since there is not enough space at the health center for additional staff. Optionally, you could add that he mentions the health center would need more treatment rooms. You should also explain that he does not think opening the center on weekends will be helpful because many students go away for the weekend.

Sample Responses

Play Track 28 to hear a high-level response for Question 2.

Rater Comments

This speaker effectively combines the important points from the reading and the listening in his response, though he could have included more detail about the points made in the reading (for instance, he could have mentioned the problem with wait times at the health center). He demonstrates good control of grammar with only minor errors and uses varied vocabulary (*"take into consideration," "viable"*) to express the ideas. While his pronunciation is obviously influenced by his native language, the response is mostly clear and is easy to follow.

Play Track 29 to hear a mid-level response for Question 2.

Rater Comments

This speaker demonstrates a basic understanding of the information from the conversation. However, because of some limitations with language use, the response does not effectively convey the points from the listening or link them to points from the reading. Limited vocabulary and grammar are evident in the repetition of simple phrases such as *"he think that"* and vague expression of ideas (*"The man's opinion is he think that a student's opinion is not so good"*). The response also contains many grammatical errors. Despite some pronunciation difficulties, the speaker is generally clear enough to be understandable, with no major problems in pacing.

Question 3: General/Specific

Track 23 Listening Script

Narrator

Now read the passage about the nature of social interaction. You will have 45 seconds to read the passage. Begin reading now.

Reading Time: 45 Seconds

Social Loafing

When people work in groups to perform a task, individual group members may feel less motivated to contribute, since no one person is held directly responsible for completing the task. The result is that people may not work as hard, or accomplish as much, as they would if they were working alone and their individual output were being measured. This decrease in personal effort, especially on a simple group task, is known as *social loafing*. While it is not a deliberate behavior, the consequence of social loafing is less personal efficiency when working in groups than when working on one's own.

Narrator

Listen to part of a lecture in a psychology class.

Professor

Now, a study was done that illustrated this phenomenon. In the study people were given an ordinary task that everyone has probably done before—they were simply asked to peel potatoes. And to peel as many potatoes as possible in a given amount of time. OK, so some people worked alone—and they were told that the number of potatoes they each peeled would be recorded. Others peeled potatoes together, as part of a group, and they were told that only the total number of potatoes peeled would be recorded. So it would be impossible to tell how many any one person had done.

   Then researchers compared the results of the people who worked alone and those that worked together to see if there was any difference. That is, they took the average score of the people working alone and compared it to the average score of the people working together in a group. And they **did** discover a difference. It turns out that people working as a group peeled significantly **fewer** potatoes than people who worked alone.

Narrator

Using the example from the lecture, explain what social loafing is and how it affects people's behavior.

Preparation Time: 30 Seconds
Response Time: 60 Seconds

Important Points

In this item, you need to explain the concept of social loafing and explain how the professor's example relates to this idea. Social loafing is a term that describes what happens when people work in groups. Members of a group may not be as motivated and may not do as much as they would if they were working by themselves. The reading states that this happens because one person does not feel responsible for the task. The professor's example then describes people's behavior in a study in which people were asked to peel potatoes. Some people worked alone, and others worked in groups. The people working in the group did not peel as many potatoes as the people working alone. This study is a good example of social loafing because it illustrates that people working in a group do not do as much as people working by themselves.

Sample Responses

Play Track 30 to hear a high-level response for Question 3.

Rater Comments

This speaker provides a complete and clear response to the task. She first explains what social loafing is and why it might happen ("It means that people who work in a group do not feel responsible for the result"). She then describes the example of people peeling potatoes and again explains why the people in the group may not be peeling as many potatoes ("They know they're not going to be held responsible for the number of potatoes that are peeled in a group"). This effectively explains how the example relates to the reading. The speaker's pronunciation is clear, and her pace of speech is also good. She does hesitate at times and makes a few minor language errors, but these do not prevent her from communicating her ideas.

Play Track 31 to hear a mid-level response for Question 3.

Rater Comments

This speaker does provide important information from the reading and the lecture, but she is not able to show their relationship very clearly. She starts with a definition and struggles to find language for that but is able to communicate her idea somewhat ("Social loafing is decreasing an individual's efficiency in a work when they're working in a group"). She then describes the example but is slowed down by trying to provide information that is not really necessary ("they were not sure how to count how many potatoes they did each when they worked in a group"). The response has this lack of precise language and wording throughout, as well as language difficulties and a slower pace when the speaker is searching for language. On the positive side, she does include some important and accurate information about the study, and her pronunciation is clear for the most part. She has difficulty, however, connecting the material from the reading with the example. She gets across the idea that people work less efficiently in a group, but she leaves out the very important point about people in a group having less motivation or not feeling as responsible for their work.

Question 4: Summary

Track 24 Listening Script

Narrator

Now listen to part of a talk in a psychology class.

Professor

OK. Ever thought about the things that happen to you, and what's responsible for them? We psychologists have a term—*locus of control*. Locus of control refers to *[hesitates]* where people think control over their lives comes from: whether it comes from themselves, or from somewhere else. People who think that control is in *themselves* are "internals." And people who think it comes from somewhere else are "externals."

Let's say there're two people going for job interviews. One of them is an "internal"—she has an *internal* locus of control. Since she thinks that control comes from *within* herself, she'll believe that her success and her preparation are really her responsibility. So, she's likely to really work on her interview skills ahead of time. Then, if she gets the job, she'll believe that it's because she's worked so hard, and if she doesn't get it, well . . . she'll probably be disappointed with herself and try to figure out how she can improve for the next time.

OK, and another job candidate is an "external." He perceives other things—say, his *interviewers*—to have more influence. After all, it's their decision. It depends on what mood they're in, and you know . . . luck! Now, with his external locus of control, he's not as hard on himself, so he's more likely to take risks. He might interview for a job that he's not completely qualified for. If he gets it, he'll think he's really lucky and, because he believes external forces are in control, he might think it's because the interviewers were having a good day. If he doesn't get it, he'll probably *blame* the interviewers . . . or bad luck . . . rather than look at himself and try to figure out what he could've done better.

Narrator

Using points and examples from the talk, explain internal and external locus of control.

> **Preparation Time: 20 Seconds**
> **Response Time: 60 Seconds**

Important Points

In your response to this prompt, you need to explain that locus of control refers to where people believe control over their lives comes from, internal (from within the person) or external (from somewhere else). You should explain the example the professor discusses about job candidates. A job candidate who has an internal locus of control sees herself as responsible for her own success. She feels that whether she gets a job is the result of the effort she puts into preparing. A job candidate who has an external locus of control perceives other forces to be in control. He feels that whether he gets a job is the result of other factors such as luck or the mood of the interviewers.

Sample Responses

Play Track 32 to hear a high-level response for Question 4.

Rater Comments

This speaker conveys his understanding of the concept through a discussion of the example about the people interviewing for the job. He uses intonation very effectively ("it's **her** responsibility to get the job . . .") to convey the ideas, and his pronunciation is clear. Use of vocabulary and grammar is varied and precise. While there is some occasional natural hesitation while the speaker gathers his thoughts, overall the response flows and is easy to follow.

Play Track 33 to hear a mid-level response for Question 4.

Rater Comments

This speaker is able to convey the ideas from the lecture fairly well; however, issues with word choice and grammar prevent the response from being fully and clearly developed. For example, the speaker's definition of the two types of locus of control is somewhat vague ("internal locus of control means one believe that she can control her life and she will response for her . . . behaviors, and the external control means the opposite"). Inaccurate word choice causes some confusion for the listener ("if she lost it she would disappear," and "the external person will do the interview just for risk"). Some difficulties with pronunciation also cause listener effort at times.

Writing

Listening Script, Topic Notes, and Sample Responses with Rater Comments

Use the Integrated Writing and Independent Writing scoring rubrics on pages 193–194 and 203–204 to see how responses are scored.

Writing Based on Reading and Listening

Track 25 Listening Script

Narrator
Now listen to part of a lecture on the topic you just read about.

Professor
You know, often in science, new findings force us to re-examine earlier beliefs and assumptions. And a recent study of meerkats is having exactly this effect. The study examined the meerkat's behavior quite closely, much more closely than had ever been done before. And some interesting things were found . . . like about eating habits . . . it showed that typically meerkats eat before they stand guard—so the ones standing guard had a full stomach! And the study also found that since the sentinel is the first to see a predator coming, it's the most likely to escape . . . because it often stands guard near a burrow, so it can run immediately into the burrow after giving the alarm. The other meerkats, the ones scattered about looking for food, are actually in greater danger.

And in fact, other studies have suggested that when an animal creates an alarm, the alarm call might cause the other group members either to gather together or else to move about very quickly, behaviors that might actually draw the predator's attention away from the caller, increasing that animal's own chances of survival.

And what about people—what about some human acts that might be considered altruistic? Let's take an extreme case: uh, suppose a person donates a kidney to a relative, or even to a complete stranger. A selfless act, right? But . . . doesn't the donor receive appreciation and approval from the stranger and from society? Doesn't the donor gain an increased sense of self-worth? Couldn't such nonmaterial rewards be considered very valuable to some people?

Narrator
Summarize the points made in the lecture, being sure to explain how they oppose specific points made in the reading passage.

Topic Notes

You should understand the meaning of *altruism* and *altruistic acts*. The definitions are given in the reading passage: *altruism* describes behavior that is the opposite of selfishness; it is behavior that benefits another individual or the group with no reward. The lecturer questions whether the examples meet the definition.

A high-scoring response will include the following points made by the lecturer:

Point Made in the Reading Passage	Contrasting Point from the Lecture
Human organ donors gain nothing from their action.	The donors receive appreciation and approval from the rest of society.
Sentinel meerkats go without food to stand guard.	Sentinels actually eat before the other meerkats.
Sentinel meerkats place themselves in danger from predators.	Sentinels are actually the first to escape the predators.

Responses scoring 4 and 5 discuss altruistic/nonaltruistic aspects of the three points in the table: human organ donation, meerkat sentinel eating behavior, and meerkat sentinel ability to escape.

Sample Responses with Rater Comments

High-Level Response

> The lecture completely refutes the passage. It is said in the lecture that, the perceived acts of altruism are nothing more than sneaky methods of gaining advantage for one's self.Contrary to the belief in the passage that sentinels risk their lives for the cause of the whole group, the professor says that the meerkat sentinels are in fact less prone to outside threats. The alarm sentinels give off causes to group to move rashly which draws the predators attention towards them, thus drawing away the attention from the sentinels. The lecture refutes the fact that these meerkats are altruistic in the sense that they gain nothing in exchange of their services. In fact, researches have shown that they have a full stomach as they perform this "altruistic" duty and have a better chance of escaping from danger because they witness it ifrst Proffesor also offers a different underlying motivation that causes people to believe that acts such as donating an organ or sharing food with someone in need are altruistic. She says that people gain appreciation as a result of such acts, which may be deemed by some much more important than materialistic gains.

Rater Comments

This answer meets the criteria for a high-level response to an integrated task. The writer does a good job of selecting, framing, and interweaving points from the lecture and reading, explicitly and fluently presenting accurate connections between the relevant points. All three points made by the lecturer are included. Language is used accurately and effectively, and the overall piece is well organized.

Mid-Level Response

> According to the lecture, examinig closely to the eating habits of meerkats, these animals are not altruistic. The fact is that the sentinel, being the first that sees the predator, is able to be the first in escape. Also the other meerkats that are hunting and looking for food are the ones in danger. Considering the altruistic human acts, the donation of body organs shouldn't be considered like that, mainly because when a person donates an organ he or she receives appreciation and recognition of society.
>
> Because of this points the lecture might make the reader doubt, mainly because the eating habits of the meerkats have been studied closely, giving arguments in order to justify that meerkats aren't doing altruistic acts.
>
> The other argument about human and their altruistic actions sounds logical and a situiation in which a person would donate organs just to get appreciation of society couls be probable.
>
> Because of this both, reading and lecture, are completely opposite, might make the user doubt and reflect more about altruism.

Rater Comments

The response includes some of the important information about sentinel meerkats and organ donation from the lecture. However, it is very vague in how it relates the points in the lecture to the points in the reading. There is no clear reference to any explanation of the other meerkats being in danger. The statement commenting on organ donation, "The other argument about human and their altruistic actions sounds logical and a situation in which a person would donate organs just to get appreciation of society couls be probable," is not very clear. The response also completely omits the point about meerkat sentinels and food.

Writing Based on Knowledge and Experience

Question

Some young adults want independence from their parents as soon as possible. Other young adults prefer to live with their families for a longer time. Which of these situations do you think is better? Use specific reasons and examples to support your opinion. Be sure to use your own words. Do **not** use memorized examples.

Topic Notes

This topic, in effect, equates independence with living apart from one's family. Both broader and narrower definitions of independence and "nonindependence" are acceptable as possible responses to the given topic, even though a majority of writers will write to the dichotomy presented by the question. Some writers take a general overview, and their choices and examples are general and "philo-sophical." Others use specific personal examples or personal narratives in their approach to the topic. Some writers take a specific side of the issue, and others approach the topic by discussing conditions under which it is better to move away and conditions under which a young adult might do better to stay longer with the family. All these approaches are valid, on-topic responses and are judged by the raters on their merits according to the scoring guidelines for this task type.

Sample Responses with Rater Comments

High-Level Essay

Every young adults will grow and live apart from their parents to form their own families. The ages for those young adults to be independent depends on each person. Some people may have to live longer with their parents and some others may not. This essay will discuss the issue of independent life and living with their families for a longer time.

Most young adults prefer to have a seperate or independent life from their parents or families as soon as possible. This is because they have a strong urge for freedom in doing what they desire. But in fact many of them fail. This should not be surprising since often they are actually not ready mentally although they are physically ready. It is widely understood that to live independently requires a lot of energy and is not easy at all. In this twenty first century, people may need more and more preparation because competition is increasing rapidly. An observation shows that many University graduated students are unemployed. Therefore, they will not be able to support and fulfill their necessities.

So living independently at an early age is not suitable for all young adults, some young adults may need to take more time to prepare themselves before going out to struggle. Young adults need to be ready to support themselves. Taking time to get more education and living with their families for a longer time may lead them to a better independent life because they will be well prepared for the hard-life outside. Still, living with their families for *too* long will not be a good idea because they could get to used to it and tend to be less independent.

The time to live independently depends on the person himself. He or she must decide whether they are ready to leave their parents to have an independent life or not. The decision will vary from one person to another. A person should judge that he is capable of fulfilling his needs without being dependent on his parents; this indicates that he is ready for his independent life. Otherwise he might need to stay longer with his parents.

Rater Comments

This well-developed essay meets all the criteria for earning a high score. The writer develops the topic through a detailed discussion of independence and of the suitability of living independently. The essay is unified and coherent. Sentence structure is varied, especially in paragraphs 2 and 3. The writer does not use high-level vocabulary, but word choice is correct throughout. There are minor errors ("University graduated students," "fulfill their necessities"), but these in no way interrupt the flow or meaning of the essay.

Mid-Level Essay

Right now adults have different points of view about live. Independent from their parents as soon as possible or continue to to live with their parents. Live with your parents have many differents advantage. First, some people dont want to have resposabilities, they want their parents still take the desicion. For example, house's responsabilities or pays. Secound, When peoples live with their parents they dont expend a lot money for haouse or food. Third, they belief that their family is a great company. But in the other hand, when people live along have important advantage. For example, They live independient, they dont heve limitation in their own house. They dont need to negociate with other persons or family. Morover, they have a graet oportunity to learn about how administarte a house, amd what is the real value of the money. They can understand everytuhing about responsability in their house. Finally They have more freedom.

   Both live independient and live with your parents have many different disadvantage. On the first points of view, live independient, the most important problem is money and expensive. For example, right now young adults need to find a good job for live in a good place because rents are expensive. It is the same with food and services. They need to have a excellent imcome to live in good conditions. Also, they need to work in the house along because dont have company. They need to clean, do the laundry, buy the food, and cook along. Although pepole think live independient have a huge sacrifies, also live with their parents it is difficult and have a lot of disadvantage. For example, when people live with thier parents have many different limitation with activities in the house, every time need to negociate with your family. In addition,

Rater Comments

This essay is somewhat developed and is longer than the average mid-level essay. It has a coherent organization based on describing the pros and cons of living apart from one's parents and living with them, with supporting points. In some cases, however, this approach leads to redundancy, especially toward the end of the essay. Additionally, even discounting typographical mistakes, the various errors clearly reveal weakness in command of language ("Live with your parents have many differents advantage," "the most important problem is . . . expensive"). Meaning is also sometimes obscured ("house's responsabilities or pays," "they need to work in the house along because dont have company").

7 Authentic *TOEFL iBT*® Practice Test 2

本章是托福考试四套真题练习中的第二套。考生可以通过两种不同的方式进行测试：

- 通过本书：在接下来的书页中，考生可以看到所有的测试题目，请将答案写在规定的空白处。关于本测试中的听力部分，考生可以按照序号提示，播放对应音频。

- 在电脑上：为了更真实地体验托福考试的实考环境，考生可以下载电脑版软件在电脑上进行模考。电脑版软件中的试题与书中的完全一样。阅读文章和相关问题将显示在屏幕上，考生可以点击给出的空白处输入答案。听力部分的测试则根据提示进行。

测试题目之后是答案和评分信息，以及听力部分的文字材料。除此以外，考生还可以看到答案的详细解释、口语回答样本和写作范文。

TOEFL iBT® Practice Test 2
READING

This section measures your ability to understand academic passages in English. You will have **54 minutes** to read and answer questions about **3 passages**. A clock at the top of the screen will display the starting time as **00 : 54 : 00** and show you how much time is remaining.

Most questions are worth 1 point, but the last question for each passage is worth more than 1 point. The directions for the last question indicate how many points you may receive.

Some passages in the computer-based test include a word or phrase that is underlined in blue. When you click on the word or phrase underlined in blue, you will see a verbal or visual definition of the word or term. In this book, those definitions are provided as endnotes below the reading passage.

Within this section, you can move to the next question by clicking on **Next**. You can skip questions and go back to them later as long as there is time remaining. If you want to return to previous questions, click on **Back**. You can click on **Review** at any time and the review screen will show you which questions you have answered and which you have not answered. From this review screen, you may go directly to any question you have already seen in the Reading section.

During this practice test, you may click the **Pause** icon at any time. This will stop the test until you decide to continue. You may continue the test in a few minutes or at any time during the period that your test is activated.

You will now begin the Reading section. Again, in an actual test you will have **54 minutes** to read the 3 passages and answer the questions. NOTE: In an actual test, some test takers might receive 4 passages; those test takers will have 72 minutes (1 hour and 12 minutes) to answer the questions.

Turn the page to begin the Reading section.

FEEDING HABITS OF EAST AFRICAN HERBIVORES

Buffalo, zebras, wildebeests, topi, and Thomson's gazelles live in huge groups that together make up some 90 percent of the total weight of mammals living on the Serengeti Plain of East Africa. They are all herbivores (plant-eating animals), and they all appear to be living on the same diet of grasses, herbs, and small bushes. This appearance, however, is illusory. When biologist Richard Bell and his colleagues analyzed the stomach contents of four of the five species (they did not study buffalo), they found that each species was living on a different part of the vegetation. The different vegetational parts differ in their food qualities: lower down, there are succulent, nutritious leaves; higher up are the harder stems. There are also sparsely distributed, highly nutritious fruits, and Bell found that only the Thomson's gazelles eat much of these. The other three species differ in the proportion of lower leaves and higher stems that they eat: zebras eat the most stem matter, wildebeests eat the most leaves, and topi are intermediate.

How are we to understand their different feeding preferences? The answer lies in two associated differences among the species, in their digestive systems and body sizes. According to their digestive systems, these herbivores can be divided into two categories: the nonruminants (such as the zebra, which has a digestive system like a horse) and the ruminants (such as the wildebeest, topi, and gazelle, which are like the cow). Nonruminants cannot extract much energy from the hard parts of a plant; however, this is more than made up for by the fast speed at which food passes through their guts. Thus, when there is only a short supply of poor-quality food, the wildebeest, topi, and gazelle enjoy an advantage. They are ruminants and have a special structure (the rumen) in their stomachs, which contains microorganisms that can break down the hard parts of plants. Food passes only slowly through the ruminant's gut because ruminating—digesting the hard parts—takes time. The ruminant continually regurgitates food from its stomach back to its mouth to chew it up further (that is what a cow is doing when "chewing cud"). Only when it has been chewed up and digested almost to a liquid can the food pass through the rumen and on through the gut. Larger particles cannot pass through until they have been chewed down to size. Therefore, when food is in short supply, a ruminant can last longer than a nonruminant because it can derive more energy out of the same food. The difference can partially explain the eating habits of the Serengeti herbivores. The zebra chooses areas where there is more low-quality food. It migrates first to unexploited areas and chomps the abundant low-quality stems before moving on. It is a fast-in/fast-out feeder, relying on a high output of incompletely digested food. By the time the wildebeests (and other ruminants) arrive, the grazing and trampling of the zebras will have worn the vegetation down. As the ruminants then set to work, they eat down to the lower, leafier parts of the vegetation. All of this fits in with the differences in stomach contents with which we began.

The other part of the explanation is body size. Larger animals require more food than smaller animals, but smaller animals have a higher metabolic rate. Smaller animals can therefore live where there is less food, provided that such food is of high energy content. That is why the smallest of the herbivores, Thomson's gazelle, lives on fruit that is very nutritious but too thin on the ground to support a larger animal. By contrast, the large zebra lives on the masses of low-quality stem material.

The differences in feeding preferences lead, in turn, to differences in migratory habits. The wildebeests follow, in their migration, the pattern of local rainfall. The other species do likewise. But when a new area is fueled by rain, the mammals migrate toward it in a set order to exploit it. The larger, less fastidious feeders, the zebras, move in first; the choosier, smaller wildebeests come later; and the smallest species of all, Thomson's gazelle, arrives last. The later species all depend on the preparations of the earlier one, for the actions of the zebra alter the vegetation to suit the stomachs of the wildebeest, topi, and gazelle.

Directions: Now answer the questions.

PARAGRAPH 1

Buffalo, zebras, wildebeests, topi, and Thomson's gazelles live in huge groups that together make up some 90 percent of the total weight of mammals living on the Serengeti Plain of East Africa. They are all herbivores (plant-eating animals), and they all appear to be living on the same diet of grasses, herbs, and small bushes. This appearance, however, is illusory. When biologist Richard Bell and his colleagues analyzed the stomach contents of four of the five species (they did not study buffalo), they found that each species was living on a different part of the vegetation. The different vegetational parts differ in their food qualities: lower down, there are succulent, nutritious leaves; higher up are the harder stems. There are also sparsely distributed, highly nutritious fruits, and Bell found that only the Thomson's gazelles eat much of these. The other three species differ in the proportion of lower leaves and higher stems that they eat: zebras eat the most stem matter, wildebeests eat the most leaves, and topi are intermediate.

1. The word "illusory" in the passage is closest in meaning to
    (A) definite
    (B) illuminating
    (C) misleading
    (D) exceptional

2. Which of the following questions about Richard Bell's research is NOT answered in paragraph 1?
    (A) Which of the herbivores studied is the only one to eat much fruit?
    (B) Which part of the plants do wildebeests prefer to eat?
    (C) Where did the study of herbivores' eating habits take place?
    (D) Why were buffalo excluded from the research study?

GO ON TO THE NEXT PAGE

PARAGRAPH 2

How are we to understand their different feeding preferences? The answer lies in two associated differences among the species, in their digestive systems and body sizes. According to their digestive systems, these herbivores can be divided into two categories: the nonruminants (such as the zebra, which has a digestive system like a horse) and the ruminants (such as the wildebeest, topi, and gazelle, which are like the cow). Nonruminants cannot extract much energy from the hard parts of a plant; however, this is more than made up for by the fast speed at which food passes through their guts. Thus, when there is only a short supply of poor-quality food, the wildebeest, topi, and gazelle enjoy an advantage. They are ruminants and have a special structure (the rumen) in their stomachs, which contains microorganisms that can break down the hard parts of plants. Food passes only slowly through the ruminant's gut because ruminating—digesting the hard parts—takes time. The ruminant continually regurgitates food from its stomach back to its mouth to chew it up further (that is what a cow is doing when "chewing cud"). Only when it has been chewed up and digested almost to a liquid can the food pass through the rumen and on through the gut. Larger particles cannot pass through until they have been chewed down to size. Therefore, when food is in short supply, a ruminant can last longer than a non-ruminant because it can derive more energy out of the same food. The difference can partially explain the eating habits of the Serengeti herbivores. The zebra chooses areas where there is more low-quality food. It migrates first to unexploited areas and chomps the abundant low-quality stems before moving on. It is a fast-in/fast-out feeder, relying on a high output of incompletely digested food. By the time the wildebeests (and other ruminants) arrive, the grazing and trampling of the zebras will have worn the vegetation down. As the ruminants then set to work, they eat down to the lower, leafier parts of the vegetation. All of this fits in with the differences in stomach contents with which we began.

3. The word "associated" in the passage is closest in meaning to

   Ⓐ obvious
   Ⓑ significant
   Ⓒ expected
   Ⓓ connected

4. The author mentions the cow and the horse in paragraph 2 in order to

   Ⓐ distinguish the functioning of their digestive systems from those of East African mammals
   Ⓑ emphasize that their relatively large body size leads them to have feeding practices similar to those of East African mammals
   Ⓒ illustrate differences between ruminants and nonruminants through the use of animals likely to be familiar to most readers
   Ⓓ emphasize similarities between the diets of cows and horses and the diets of East African mammals

5. Paragraph 2 suggests that which of the following is one of the most important factors in determining differences in feeding preferences of East African herbivores?

   Ⓐ The availability of certain foods
   Ⓑ The differences in stomach structure
   Ⓒ The physical nature of vegetation in the environment
   Ⓓ The ability to migrate when food supplies are low

6. According to paragraph 2, all of the following are true of East African gazelles EXCEPT:

   Ⓐ They digest their food very quickly.
   Ⓑ Microorganisms help them digest their food.
   Ⓒ They are unable to digest large food particles unless these are chewed down considerably.
   Ⓓ They survive well even if food supplies are not abundant.

PARAGRAPH 3

The other part of the explanation is body size. Larger animals require more food than smaller animals, but smaller animals have a higher metabolic rate. Smaller animals can therefore live where there is less food, provided that such food is of high energy content. That is why the smallest of the herbivores, Thomson's gazelle, lives on fruit that is very nutritious but too thin on the ground to support a larger animal. By contrast, the large zebra lives on the masses of low-quality stem material.

7. The phrase "provided that" in the passage is closest in meaning to

   Ⓐ as long as
   Ⓑ unless
   Ⓒ as if
   Ⓓ even though

GO ON TO THE NEXT PAGE

P A R A G R A P H 4

The differences in feeding preferences lead, in turn, to differences in migratory habits. The wildebeests follow, in their migration, the pattern of local rainfall. The other species do likewise. But when a new area is fueled by rain, the mammals migrate toward it in a set order to exploit it. The larger, less fastidious feeders, the zebras, move in first; the choosier, smaller wildebeests come later; and the smallest species of all, Thomson's gazelle, arrives last. The later species all depend on the preparations of the earlier one, for the actions of the zebra alter the vegetation to suit the stomachs of the wildebeest, topi, and gazelle.

8. According to the passage, which of the following is true of wildebeests?

   (A) They eat more stem matter than zebras do.
   (B) They are able to digest large food particles if the food is of a high quality.
   (C) They tend to choose feeding areas in which the vegetation has been worn down.
   (D) They are likely to choose low-quality food to eat in periods when the quantity of rainfall is low.

P A R A G R A P H 4

The differences in feeding preferences lead, in turn, to differences in migratory habits. **(A)** The wildebeests follow, in their migration, the pattern of local rainfall. **(B)** The other species do likewise. **(C)** But when a new area is fueled by rain, the mammals migrate toward it in a set order to exploit it. **(D)** The larger, less fastidious feeders, the zebras, move in first; the choosier, smaller wildebeests come later; and the smallest species of all, Thomson's gazelle, arrives last. The later species all depend on the preparations of the earlier one, for the actions of the zebra alter the vegetation to suit the stomachs of the wildebeest, topi, and gazelle.

9. **Directions:** Look at the part of the passage that is displayed above. The letters **(A)**, **(B)**, **(C)**, and **(D)** indicate where the following sentence could be added.

   The sequence in which they migrate correlates with their body size.

   Where would the sentence best fit?

   (A) Choice A
   (B) Choice B
   (C) Choice C
   (D) Choice D

10. **Directions**: An introductory sentence for a brief summary of the passage is provided below. Complete the summary by selecting the THREE answer choices that express the most important ideas in the passage. Some sentences do not belong in the summary because they express ideas that are not presented in the passage or are minor ideas in the passage. **This question is worth 2 points**.

East African herbivores, though they all live in the same environment, have a range of feeding preferences.

-
-
-

Answer Choices

A The survival of East African mammals depends more than anything else on the quantity of highly nutritious fruits that they are able to find.

B An herbivore's size and metabolic rate affect the kinds of food and the quantities of food it needs to eat.

C Zebras and wildebeests rarely compete for the same food resources in the same locations.

D The different digestive systems of herbivores explain their feeding preferences.

E Migratory habits are influenced by feeding preferences.

F Patterns in the migratory habits of East African herbivores are hard to establish.

GO ON TO THE NEXT PAGE ⬎

LOIE FULLER

The United States dancer Loie Fuller (1862–1928) found theatrical dance in the late nineteenth century artistically unfulfilling. She considered herself an artist rather than a mere entertainer, and she, in turn, attracted the notice of other artists.

Fuller devised a type of dance that focused on the shifting play of lights and colors on the voluminous skirts or draperies she wore, which she kept in constant motion principally through movements of her arms, sometimes extended with wands concealed under her costumes. She rejected the technical virtuosity of movement in ballet, the most prestigious form of theatrical dance at that time, perhaps because her formal dance training was minimal. Although her early theatrical career had included stints as an actress, she was not primarily interested in storytelling or expressing emotions through dance; the drama of her dancing emanated from her visual effects.

Although she discovered and introduced her art in the United States, she achieved her greatest glory in Paris, where she was engaged by the Folies Bergère in 1892 and soon became "La Loie," the darling of Parisian audiences. Many of her dances represented elements or natural objects—Fire, the Lily, the Butterfly, and so on—and thus accorded well with the fashionable Art Nouveau style, which emphasized nature imagery and fluid, sinuous lines. Her dancing also attracted the attention of French poets and painters of the period, for it appealed to their liking for mystery, their belief in art for art's sake, a nineteenth-century idea that art is valuable in itself rather than because it may have some moral or educational benefit, and their efforts to synthesize form and content.

Fuller had scientific leanings and constantly experimented with electrical lighting (which was then in its infancy), colored gels, slide projections, and other aspects of stage technology. She invented and patented special arrangements of mirrors and concocted chemical dyes for her draperies. Her interest in color and light paralleled the research of several artists of the period, notably the painter Seurat, famed for his Pointillist technique of creating a sense of shapes and light on canvas by applying extremely small dots of color rather than by painting lines. One of Fuller's major inventions was underlighting, in which she stood on a pane of frosted glass illuminated from underneath. This was particularly effective in her *Fire Dance* (1895), performed to the music of Richard Wagner's "Ride of the Valkyries." The dance caught the eye of artist Henri de Toulouse-Lautrec, who depicted it in a lithograph.

As her technological expertise grew more sophisticated, so did the other aspects of her dances. Although she gave little thought to music in her earliest dances, she later used scores by Gluck, Beethoven, Schubert, Chopin, and Wagner, eventually graduating to Stravinsky, Fauré, Debussy, and Mussorgsky, composers who were then considered progressive. She began to address more ambitious themes in her dances such as *The Sea,* in which her dancers invisibly agitated a huge expanse of silk, played upon by colored lights. Always open to scientific and technological innovations, she befriended the scientists Marie and Pierre Curie upon their discovery of radium and created a *Radium Dance,* which simulated the phosphorescence of that element. She both appeared in films—then in an early stage of development—and made them herself; the hero of her fairy-tale film *Le Lys de la Vie* (1919) was played by René Clair, later a leading French film director.

At the Paris Exposition in 1900, she had her own theater, where, in addition to her own dances, she presented pantomimes by the Japanese actress Sada Yocco. She assembled an all-female company at this time and established a school around 1908, but neither survived her. Although she is remembered today chiefly for her innovations in stage lighting, her activities also touched Isadora Duncan and Ruth St. Denis, two other United States dancers who were experimenting with new types of dance. She sponsored Duncan's first appearance in Europe. Her theater at the Paris Exposition was visited by St. Denis, who found new ideas about stagecraft in Fuller's work and fresh sources for her art in Sada Yocco's plays. In 1924 St. Denis paid tribute to Fuller with the duet *Valse à la Loie.*

Directions: Now answer the questions.

PARAGRAPH 1

The United States dancer Loie Fuller (1862–1928) found theatrical dance in the late nineteenth century artistically unfulfilling. She considered herself an artist rather than a mere entertainer, and she, in turn, attracted the notice of other artists.

1. What can be inferred from paragraph 1 about theatrical dance in the late nineteenth century?

    (A) It influenced many artists outside of the field of dance.
    (B) It was very similar to theatrical dance of the early nineteenth century.
    (C) It was more a form of entertainment than a form of serious art.
    (D) It was a relatively new art form in the United States.

PARAGRAPH 2

Fuller devised a type of dance that focused on the shifting play of lights and colors on the voluminous skirts or draperies she wore, which she kept in constant motion principally through movements of her arms, sometimes extended with wands concealed under her costumes. She rejected the technical virtuosity of movement in ballet, the most prestigious form of theatrical dance at that time, perhaps because her formal dance training was minimal. Although her early theatrical career had included stints as an actress, she was not primarily interested in storytelling or expressing emotions through dance; the drama of her dancing emanated from her visual effects.

2. According to paragraph 2, all of the following are characteristic of Fuller's type of dance EXCEPT

    (A) experimentation using color
    (B) large and full costumes
    (C) continuous movement of her costumes
    (D) technical virtuosity of movement

GO ON TO THE NEXT PAGE ▶

3. Which of the sentences below best expresses the essential information in the high-lighted sentence in the passage? Incorrect choices change the meaning in important ways or leave out essential information.

Ⓐ Fuller was more interested in dance's visual impact than in its narrative or emotional possibilities.

Ⓑ Fuller used visual effects to dramatize the stories and emotions expressed in her work.

Ⓒ Fuller believed that the drama of her dancing sprang from her emotional style of storytelling.

Ⓓ Fuller's focus on the visual effects of dance resulted from her early theatrical training as an actress.

PARAGRAPH 3

Although she discovered and introduced her art in the United States, she achieved her greatest glory in Paris, where she was engaged by the Folies Bergère in 1892 and soon became "La Loie," the darling of Parisian audiences. Many of her dances represented elements or natural objects—Fire, the Lily, the Butterfly, and so on—and thus accorded well with the fashionable Art Nouveau style, which emphasized nature imagery and fluid, sinuous lines. Her dancing also attracted the attention of French poets and painters of the period, for it appealed to their liking for mystery, their belief in art for art's sake, a nineteenth-century idea that art is valuable in itself rather than because it may have some moral or educational benefit, and their efforts to synthesize form and content.

4. The word "synthesize" in the passage is closest in meaning to

Ⓐ improve
Ⓑ define
Ⓒ simplify
Ⓓ integrate

5. According to paragraph 3, why was Fuller's work well received in Paris?

Ⓐ Parisian audiences were particularly interested in artists and artistic movements from the United States.

Ⓑ Influential poets tried to interest dancers in Fuller's work when she arrived in Paris.

Ⓒ Fuller's work at this time borrowed directly from French artists working in other media.

Ⓓ Fuller's dances were in harmony with the artistic values already present in Paris.

PARAGRAPH 4

Fuller had scientific leanings and constantly experimented with electrical lighting (which was then in its infancy), colored gels, slide projections, and other aspects of stage technology. She invented and patented special arrangements of mirrors and concocted chemical dyes for her draperies. Her interest in color and light paralleled the research of several artists of the period, notably the painter Seurat, famed for his Pointillist technique of creating a sense of shapes and light on canvas by applying extremely small dots of color rather than by painting lines. One of Fuller's major inventions was underlighting, in which she stood on a pane of frosted glass illuminated from underneath. This was particularly effective in her *Fire Dance* (1895), performed to the music of Richard Wagner's "Ride of the Valkyries." The dance caught the eye of artist Henri de Toulouse-Lautrec, who depicted it in a lithograph.

6. According to paragraph 4, Fuller's *Fire Dance* was notable in part for its

   (A) use of colored gels to illuminate glass
   (B) use of dyes and paints to create an image of fire
   (C) technique of lighting the dancer from beneath
   (D) draperies with small dots resembling the Pointillist technique of Seurat

PARAGRAPH 5

As her technological expertise grew more sophisticated, so did the other aspects of her dances. Although she gave little thought to music in her earliest dances, she later used scores by Gluck, Beethoven, Schubert, Chopin, and Wagner, eventually graduating to Stravinsky, Fauré, Debussy, and Mussorgsky, composers who were then considered progressive. She began to address more ambitious themes in her dances such as *The Sea,* in which her dancers invisibly agitated a huge expanse of silk, played upon by colored lights. Always open to scientific and technological innovations, she befriended the scientists Marie and Pierre Curie upon their discovery of radium and created a *Radium Dance,* which simulated the phosphorescence of that element. She both appeared in films—then in an early stage of development—and made them herself; the hero of her fairy-tale film *Le Lys de la Vie* (1919) was played by René Clair, later a leading French film director.

7. Why does the author mention Fuller's "*The Sea*"?

   (A) To point out a dance of Fuller's in which music did not play an important role
   (B) To explain why Fuller sometimes used music by progressive composers
   (C) To illustrate a particular way in which Fuller developed as an artist
   (D) To illustrate how Fuller's interest in science was reflected in her work

GO ON TO THE NEXT PAGE

P
A
R
A
G
R
A
P
H

6
At the Paris Exposition in 1900, she had her own theater, where, in addition to her own dances, she presented pantomimes by the Japanese actress Sada Yocco. She assembled an all-female company at this time and established a school around 1908, but neither survived her. Although she is remembered today chiefly for her innovations in stage lighting, her activities also touched Isadora Duncan and Ruth St. Denis, two other United States dancers who were experimenting with new types of dance. She sponsored Duncan's first appearance in Europe. Her theater at the Paris Exposition was visited by St. Denis, who found new ideas about stagecraft in Fuller's work and fresh sources for her art in Sada Yocco's plays. In 1924 St. Denis paid tribute to Fuller with the duet *Valse à la Loie*.

8. According to paragraph 6, what was true of Fuller's theater at the Paris Exposition?

    (A) It presented some works that were not by Fuller.
    (B) It featured performances by prominent male as well as female dancers.
    (C) It became a famous school that is still named in honor of Fuller.
    (D) It continued to operate as a theater after Fuller died.

P
A
R
A
G
R
A
P
H

5
As her technological expertise grew more sophisticated, so did the other aspects of her dances. **(A)** Although she gave little thought to music in her earliest dances, she later used scores by Gluck, Beethoven, Schubert, Chopin, and Wagner, eventually graduating to Stravinsky, Fauré, Debussy, and Mussorgsky, composers who were then considered progressive. **(B)** She began to address more ambitious themes in her dances such as *The Sea*, in which her dancers invisibly agitated a huge expanse of silk, played upon by colored lights. **(C)** Always open to scientific and technological innovations, she befriended the scientists Marie and Pierre Curie upon their discovery of radium and created a *Radium Dance*, which simulated the phosphorescence of that element. **(D)** She both appeared in films—then in an early stage of development—and made them herself; the hero of her fairy-tale film *Le Lys de la Vie* (1919) was played by René Clair, later a leading French film director.

9. **Directions:** Look at the part of the passage that is displayed above. The letters **(A)**, **(B)**, **(C)**, and **(D)** indicate where the following sentence could be added.

For all her originality in dance, her interests expanded beyond it into newly emerging artistic media.

Where would the sentence best fit?
    (A) Choice A
    (B) Choice B
    (C) Choice C
    (D) Choice D

10. **Directions:** An introductory sentence for a brief summary of the passage is provided below. Complete the summary by selecting the THREE answer choices that express the most important ideas in the passage. Some sentences do not belong in the summary because they express ideas that are not presented in the passage or are minor ideas in the passage. **This question is worth 2 points.**

Loie Fuller was an important and innovative dancer.

-
-
-

Answer Choices

A Fuller believed that audiences in the late nineteenth century had lost interest in most theatrical dance.

B Fuller transformed dance in part by creating dance interpretations of works by poets and painters.

C Fuller's work influenced a number of other dancers who were interested in experimental dance.

D Fuller introduced many technical innovations to the staging of theatrical dance.

E Fuller continued to develop throughout her career, creating more complex works and exploring new artistic media.

F By the 1920s, Fuller's theater at the Paris Exposition had become the world center for innovative dance.

GO ON TO THE NEXT PAGE

GREEN ICEBERGS

Icebergs are massive blocks of ice, irregular in shape; they float with only about 12 percent of their mass above the sea surface. They are formed by glaciers—large rivers of ice that begin inland in the snows of Greenland, Antarctica, and Alaska—and move slowly toward the sea. The forward movement, the melting at the base of the glacier where it meets the ocean, and waves and tidal action cause blocks of ice to break off and float out to sea.

Icebergs are ordinarily blue to white, although they sometimes appear dark or opaque because they carry gravel and bits of rock. They may change color with changing light conditions and cloud cover, glowing pink or gold in the morning or evening light, but this color change is generally related to the low angle of the Sun above the horizon. However, travelers to Antarctica have repeatedly reported seeing green icebergs in the Weddell Sea and, more commonly, close to the Amery Ice Shelf in East Antarctica.

One explanation for green icebergs attributes their color to an optical illusion when blue ice is illuminated by a near-horizon red Sun, but green icebergs stand out among white and blue icebergs under a great variety of light conditions. Another suggestion is that the color might be related to ice with high levels of metallic compounds, including copper and iron. Recent expeditions have taken ice samples from green icebergs and ice cores—vertical, cylindrical ice samples reaching down to great depths—from the glacial ice shelves along the Antarctic continent. Analyses of these cores and samples provide a different solution to the problem.

The ice shelf cores, with a total length of 215 meters (705 feet), were long enough to penetrate through glacial ice—which is formed from the compaction of snow and contains air bubbles—and to continue into the clear, bubble-free ice formed from seawater that freezes onto the bottom of the glacial ice. The properties of this clear sea ice were very similar to the ice from the green iceberg. The scientists concluded that green icebergs form when a two-layer block of shelf ice breaks away and capsizes (turns upside down), exposing the bubble-free shelf ice that was formed from seawater.

A green iceberg that stranded just west of the Amery Ice Shelf showed two distinct layers: bubbly blue-white ice and bubble-free green ice separated by a one-meter-long ice layer containing sediments. The green ice portion was textured by seawater erosion. Where cracks were present, the color was light green because of light scattering; where no cracks were present, the color was dark green. No air bubbles were present in the green ice, suggesting that the ice was not formed from the compression of snow but instead from the freezing of seawater. Large concentrations of single-celled organisms with green pigments (coloring substances) occur along the edges of the ice shelves in this region, and the seawater is rich in their decomposing organic material. The green iceberg did not contain large amounts of particles from these organisms, but the ice had accumulated dissolved organic matter from the seawater. It appears that unlike salt, dissolved organic substances are not excluded from the ice in the freezing process. Analysis shows that the dissolved organic material absorbs enough blue wavelengths from solar light to make the ice appear green.

Chemical evidence shows that platelets (minute flat portions) of ice form in the water and then accrete and stick to the bottom of the ice shelf to form a slush (partially melted snow). The slush is compacted by an unknown mechanism, and solid, bubble-free ice is formed from water high in soluble organic substances. When an iceberg separates from the ice shelf and capsizes, the green ice is exposed.

The Amery Ice Shelf appears to be uniquely suited to the production of green icebergs. Once detached from the ice shelf, these bergs drift in the currents and wind systems surrounding Antarctica and can be found scattered among Antarctica's less colorful icebergs.

Directions: Now answer the questions.

PARAGRAPH 1

Icebergs are massive blocks of ice, irregular in shape; they float with only about 12 percent of their mass above the sea surface. They are formed by glaciers—large rivers of ice that begin inland in the snows of Greenland, Antarctica, and Alaska—and move slowly toward the sea. The forward movement, the melting at the base of the glacier where it meets the ocean, and waves and tidal action cause blocks of ice to break off and float out to sea.

1. According to paragraph 1, all of the following are true of icebergs EXCEPT:

    (A) They do not have a regular shape.
    (B) They are formed where glaciers meet the ocean.
    (C) Most of their mass is above the sea surface.
    (D) Waves and tides cause them to break off glaciers.

PARAGRAPH 2

Icebergs are ordinarily blue to white, although they sometimes appear dark or opaque because they carry gravel and bits of rock. They may change color with changing light conditions and cloud cover, glowing pink or gold in the morning or evening light, but this color change is generally related to the low angle of the Sun above the horizon. However, travelers to Antarctica have repeatedly reported seeing green icebergs in the Weddell Sea and, more commonly, close to the Amery Ice Shelf in East Antarctica.

2. According to paragraph 2, what causes icebergs to sometimes appear dark or opaque?

    (A) A heavy cloud cover
    (B) The presence of gravel or bits of rock
    (C) The low angle of the Sun above the horizon
    (D) The presence of large cracks in their surface

GO ON TO THE NEXT PAGE

PARAGRAPH 4

The ice shelf cores, with a total length of 215 meters (705 feet), were long enough to penetrate through glacial ice—which is formed from the compaction of snow and contains air bubbles—and to continue into the clear, bubble-free ice formed from seawater that freezes onto the bottom of the glacial ice. The properties of this clear sea ice were very similar to the ice from the green iceberg. The scientists concluded that green icebergs form when a two-layer block of shelf ice breaks away and capsizes (turns upside down), exposing the bubble-free shelf ice that was formed from seawater.

3. The word "penetrate" in the passage is closest in meaning to

   (A) collect
   (B) pierce
   (C) melt
   (D) endure

4. According to paragraph 4, how is glacial ice formed?
   (A) By the compaction of snow
   (B) By the freezing of seawater on the bottom of ice shelves
   (C) By breaking away from the ice shelf
   (D) By the capsizing of a two-layer block of shelf ice

5. According to paragraph 4, ice shelf cores helped scientists explain the formation of green icebergs by showing that

   (A) the ice at the bottom of green icebergs is bubble-free ice formed from frozen seawater
   (B) bubble-free ice is found at the top of the ice shelf
   (C) glacial ice is lighter and floats better than sea ice
   (D) the clear sea ice at the bottom of the ice shelf is similar to ice from a green iceberg

PARAGRAPH 5

A green iceberg that stranded just west of the Amery Ice Shelf showed two distinct layers: bubbly blue-white ice and bubble-free green ice separated by a one-meter-long ice layer containing sediments. The green ice portion was textured by seawater erosion. Where cracks were present, the color was light green because of light scattering; where no cracks were present, the color was dark green. No air bubbles were present in the green ice, suggesting that the ice was not formed from the compression of snow but instead from the freezing of seawater. Large concentrations of single-celled organisms with green pigments (coloring substances) occur along the edges of the ice shelves in this region, and the seawater is rich in their decomposing organic material. The green iceberg did not contain large amounts of particles from these organisms, but the ice had accumulated dissolved organic matter from the seawater. It appears that unlike salt, dissolved organic substances are not excluded from the ice in the freezing process. Analysis shows that the dissolved organic material absorbs enough blue wavelengths from solar light to make the ice appear green.

6. Why does the author mention that "The green ice portion was textured by seawater erosion"?

    Ⓐ To explain why cracks in the iceberg appeared light green instead of dark green
    Ⓑ To suggest that green ice is more easily eroded by seawater than white ice is
    Ⓒ To support the idea that the green ice had been the bottom layer before capsizing
    Ⓓ To explain how the air bubbles had been removed from the green ice

7. The word "excluded" in the passage is closest in meaning to

    Ⓐ kept out
    Ⓑ compressed
    Ⓒ damaged
    Ⓓ gathered together

PARAGRAPH 6

Chemical evidence shows that platelets (minute flat portions) of ice form in the water and then accrete and stick to the bottom of the ice shelf to form a slush (partially melted snow). The slush is compacted by an unknown mechanism, and solid, bubble-free ice is formed from water high in soluble organic substances. When an iceberg separates from the ice shelf and capsizes, the green ice is exposed.

8. The passage supports which of the following statements about the Amery Ice Shelf?

    Ⓐ The Amery Ice Shelf produces only green icebergs.
    Ⓑ The Amery Ice Shelf produces green icebergs because its ice contains high levels of metallic compounds such as copper and iron.
    Ⓒ The Amery Ice Shelf produces green icebergs because the seawater is rich in a particular kind of soluble organic material.
    Ⓓ No green icebergs are found far from the Amery Ice Shelf.

GO ON TO THE NEXT PAGE ➘

Icebergs are ordinarily blue to white, although they sometimes appear dark or opaque because they carry gravel and bits of rock. They may change color with changing light conditions and cloud cover, glowing pink or gold in the morning or evening light, but this color change is generally related to the low angle of the Sun above the horizon. **(A)** However, travelers to Antarctica have repeatedly reported seeing green icebergs in the Weddell Sea and, more commonly, close to the Amery Ice Shelf in East Antarctica.

(B) One explanation for green icebergs attributes their color to an optical illusion when blue ice is illuminated by a near-horizon red Sun, but green icebergs stand out among white and blue icebergs under a great variety of light conditions. **(C)** Another suggestion is that the color might be related to ice with high levels of metallic compounds, including copper and iron. **(D)** Recent expeditions have taken ice samples from green icebergs and ice cores—vertical, cylindrical ice samples reaching down to great depths—from the glacial ice shelves along the Antarctic continent. Analyses of these cores and samples provide a different solution to the problem.

9. **Directions:** Look at the part of the passage that is displayed above. The letters **(A)**, **(B)**, **(C)**, and **(D)** indicate where the following sentence could be added.

   Scientists have differed as to whether icebergs appear green as a result of light conditions or because of something in the ice itself.

   Where would the sentence best fit?

   Ⓐ Choice A
   Ⓑ Choice B
   Ⓒ Choice C
   Ⓓ Choice D

10. **Directions:** An introductory sentence for a brief summary of the passage is provided below. Complete the summary by selecting the THREE answer choices that express the most important ideas in the passage. Some sentences do not belong in the summary because they express ideas that are not presented in the passage or are minor ideas in the passage. **This question is worth 2 points.**

Several suggestions, ranging from light conditions to the presence of metallic compounds, have been offered to explain why some icebergs appear green.

-
-
-

Answer Choices

A Ice cores were used to determine that green icebergs were formed from the compaction of metallic compounds, including copper and iron.

B All ice shelves can produce green icebergs, but the Amery Ice Shelf is especially well suited to do so.

C Green icebergs form when a two-layer block of ice breaks away from a glacier and capsizes, exposing the bottom sea ice to view.

D Ice cores and samples revealed that both ice shelves and green icebergs contain a layer of bubbly glacial ice and a layer of bubble-free sea ice.

E Green icebergs are white until they come into contact with seawater containing platelets and soluble organic green pigments.

F In a green iceberg, the sea ice contains large concentrations of organic matter from the seawater.

STOP. This is the end of the Reading section of *TOEFL iBT*® Practice Test 2.

GO ON TO THE NEXT PAGE

LISTENING

Directions: This section measures your ability to understand conversations and lectures in English.

You should listen to each conversation and lecture only **once**.

After each conversation or lecture, you will answer some questions about it. The questions typically ask about the main idea and supporting details. Some questions ask about the purpose of a speaker's statement or a speaker's attitude. Answer the questions based on what is stated or implied by the speakers.

You may take notes while you listen. You may use your notes to help you answer the questions. Your notes will **not** be scored.

In some questions, you will see this icon: This means that you will hear, but not see, part of the question.

Most questions are worth 1 point. If a question is worth more than 1 point, it will have special directions that indicate how many points you can receive.

It will take about **41 minutes** to listen to the conversations and lectures and to answer the questions. You should answer each question, even if you must guess the answer. Answer each question before moving on. Do not return to previous questions.

At the end of this Practice Test you will find an answer key, information to help you determine your score, scripts for the audio tracks, and explanations of the answers.

Listen to Track 34.

Questions

Directions: Mark your answer by filling in the oval or square next to your choice.

1. Why does the student go to see the professor?

   (A) For suggestions on how to write interview questions
   (B) For assistance in finding a person to interview
   (C) To ask for advice on starting a business
   (D) To schedule an interview with him

2. Why does the student mention her high school newspaper?

   (A) To inform the professor that she plans to print the interview there
   (B) To explain why the assignment is difficult for her
   (C) To show that she enjoys writing for school newspapers
   (D) To indicate that she has experience with conducting interviews

3. How does the professor help the student?

   (A) He gives her a list of local business owners.
   (B) He allows her to interview business owners in her hometown.
   (C) He suggests that she read the business section of the newspaper.
   (D) He gives her more time to complete the assignment.

4. What does the professor want the students to learn from the assignment?

    Ⓐ That starting a business is risky

    Ⓑ Why writing articles on local businesses is important

    Ⓒ How to develop a detailed business plan

    Ⓓ What personality traits are typical of business owners

5. *Listen again to part of the conversation by playing Track 35.*
Then answer the question.

    What does the student imply?

    Ⓐ She is surprised by the professor's reaction.

    Ⓑ The professor has not quite identified her concern.

    Ⓒ The professor has guessed correctly what her problem is.

    Ⓓ She does not want to finish the assignment.

GO ON TO THE NEXT PAGE ➤

Listen to Track 36.

Anthropology

Questions

6. What does the professor mainly discuss?

   Ⓐ Various errors in early calendars
   Ⓑ Why people came to believe that Earth moves around the Sun
   Ⓒ Examples of various types of calendars used in different cultures
   Ⓓ The belief that the position of planets and stars can predict future events

7. The professor discusses various theories on how Stonehenge was used.
   What can be inferred about the professor's opinion?

   Ⓐ She is sure Stonehenge was used as a calendar.
   Ⓑ She believes the main use for Stonehenge was probably as a temple or a tomb.
   Ⓒ She thinks that the stones were mainly used as a record of historical events.
   Ⓓ She admits that the purpose for which Stonehenge was constructed may never be known.

8. According to the professor, how was the Mayan calendar mainly used?

   (A) To keep track of long historical cycles
   (B) To keep track of the lunar months
   (C) To predict the outcome of royal decisions
   (D) To allow priests to compare the orbits of Earth and Venus

9. According to the professor, what was the basis of the ancient Chinese astrological cycle?

   (A) The cycle of night and day
   (B) The orbit of the Moon
   (C) The cycle of the seasons
   (D) The orbit of the planet Jupiter

10. How did the Romans succeed in making their calendar more precise?

   (A) By changing the number of weeks in a year
   (B) By adding an extra day every four years
   (C) By carefully observing the motion of the planet Jupiter
   (D) By adopting elements of the Chinese calendar

11. How does the professor organize the lecture?

   (A) By mentioning the problem of creating a calendar, then describing various attempts to deal with it
   (B) By speaking of the modern calendar first, then comparing it with earlier ones
   (C) By discussing how a prehistoric calendar was adapted by several different cultures
   (D) By emphasizing the advantages and disadvantages of using various time cycles

GO ON TO THE NEXT PAGE ◥

Listen to Track 37.

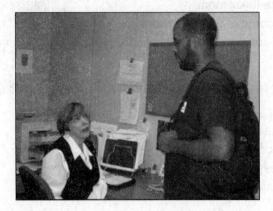

Questions

12. Why does the student go to Professor Kirk's office?

     Ⓐ To find out if he needs to take a certain class to graduate

     Ⓑ To respond to Professor Kirk's invitation

     Ⓒ To ask Professor Kirk to be his advisor

     Ⓓ To ask Professor Kirk to sign a form

13. Why is the woman surprised at the man's request?

     Ⓐ He has not tried to sign up for Introduction to Biology at the registrar's office.

     Ⓑ He has waited until his senior year to take Introduction to Biology.

     Ⓒ A journalism student should not need a biology class.

     Ⓓ Professor Kirk no longer teaches Introduction to Biology.

14. What does the man say about his advisor?

     Ⓐ She encouraged the man to take a science class.

     Ⓑ She encouraged the man to major in journalism.

     Ⓒ She is not aware of the man's problem.

     Ⓓ She thinks very highly of Professor Kirk.

15. How will the man probably try to communicate his problem to Professor Kirk?

    Ⓐ By calling her

    Ⓑ By sending an e-mail to her

    Ⓒ By leaving her a note

    Ⓓ By visiting her during office hours

16. *Listen to Track 38 to answer the question.*

    Why does the man say this to the woman?

    Ⓐ To thank the woman for solving his problem

    Ⓑ To politely refuse the woman's suggestion

    Ⓒ To explain why he needs the woman's help

    Ⓓ To show that he understands that the woman is busy

GO ON TO THE NEXT PAGE ➹

Listen to Track 39. 🎧

Astronomy

Questions

17. What is the lecture mainly about?

    Ⓐ Various theories explaining why Mars cannot sustain life
    Ⓑ Various causes of geological changes on Mars
    Ⓒ The development of views about the nature of Mars
    Ⓓ Why it has been difficult to obtain information about Mars

18. According to the professor, what was concluded about Mars after the first spacecraft flew by it in 1965?

    Ⓐ It had few geological features of interest.
    Ⓑ It was similar to Earth but colder.
    Ⓒ It had at one time supported life.
    Ⓓ It had water under its surface.

19. What does the professor imply about conditions on Mars billions of years ago?
    Choose 2 answers.

    A Mars was probably even drier than it is today.
    B The atmospheric pressure and the temperature may have been higher than they are today.
    C Mars was inhabited by organisms that have since become fossilized.
    D Large floods were shaping the planet's surface.

20. What is the possible significance of the gullies found on Mars in recent years?

    A They may indicate current volcanic activity on Mars.
    B They may indicate that the surface of Mars is becoming increasingly drier.
    C They may indicate the current existence of water on Mars.
    D They may hold fossils of organisms that once existed on Mars.

21. *Listen to Track 40 to answer the question.*

    Why does the professor say this?

    A To stress that Mars is no longer interesting to explore
    B To describe items that the spacecraft brought back from Mars
    C To share his interest in the study of fossils
    D To show how much the view of Mars changed based on new evidence

22. *Listen again to part of the lecture by playing Track 41.*
    Then answer the question.

    Why does the student say this?

    A To ask for clarification of a previous statement
    B To convey his opinion
    C To rephrase an earlier question
    D To express his approval

GO ON TO THE NEXT PAGE

Listen to Track 42.

Art History
Colossal Statues

Questions

23. What does the professor mainly discuss?

    Ⓐ The design and creation of the Statue of Liberty
    Ⓑ The creators of two colossal statues in the United States
    Ⓒ The purpose and symbolism of colossal statues
    Ⓓ The cost of colossal statues in ancient versus modern times

24. What evidence does the professor give that supports the idea that modern-day colossal statues are valued social and political symbols?

    Ⓐ They are very costly to build.
    Ⓑ They are studied in classrooms around the world.
    Ⓒ They are designed to last for thousands of years.
    Ⓓ They are inspired by great poetry.

25. According to the professor, what was one result of the Great Depression of the 1930s?

    Ⓐ International alliances eroded.
    Ⓑ Immigration to the United States increased.
    Ⓒ The public experienced a loss of confidence.
    Ⓓ The government could no longer provide funds for the arts.

26. According to the professor, why did the state of South Dakota originally want to create a colossal monument?

    Ⓐ To generate income from tourism
    Ⓑ To symbolize the unity of society
    Ⓒ To commemorate the Great Depression
    Ⓓ To honor United States presidents

27. Why does the professor discuss the poem by Emma Lazarus?

    Ⓐ To emphasize the close relationship between literature and sculpture
    Ⓑ To illustrate how the meaning associated with a monument can change
    Ⓒ To stress the importance of the friendship between France and the United States
    Ⓓ To point out a difference between Mount Rushmore and the Statue of Liberty

GO ON TO THE NEXT PAGE ➤

28. *Listen again to part of the lecture by playing Track 43.* 🎧
    Then answer the question.

    What does the professor imply about the poem by Emma Lazarus?

    (A) It is one of his favorite poems.
    (B) Few people have read the entire poem.
    (C) He does not need to recite the full text of the poem.
    (D) Lazarus was not able to complete the poem.

STOP. This is the end of the Listening section of *TOEFL iBT*® Practice Test 2.

SPEAKING

Directions: The following Speaking section of the test will last approximately **17 minutes**. To complete it, you will need a recording device that you can play back to listen to your responses.

During the test, you will answer four speaking questions. One question asks about a familiar topic. Three questions ask about short conversations, lectures, and reading passages. You may take notes as you listen to the conversations and lectures. The questions and the reading passages are printed here. The time you will have to prepare your response and to speak is printed below each question. You should answer all of the questions as completely as possible in the time allowed.

Play the audio tracks listed in the test instructions. Record each of your responses.

At the end of this Practice Test you will find scripts for the audio tracks, important points for each question, directions for listening to sample spoken responses, and comments on those responses by official raters.

Questions

1. You will now be asked to give your opinion about a familiar topic. After you hear the question, you will have 15 seconds to prepare your response and 45 seconds to speak.

Now play Track 44 to hear Question 1.

Some students would prefer to live with roommates. Others would prefer to live alone. Which option would you prefer and why?

Preparation Time: 15 Seconds
Response Time: 45 Seconds

2. You will now read a short passage and then listen to a conversation on the same topic. You will then be asked a question about them. After you hear the question, you will have 30 seconds to prepare your response and 60 seconds to speak.

Now play Track 45 to hear Question 2.

Reading Time: 50 Seconds

University May Build New Student Apartments Off Campus

The Department of Student Housing is considering whether to build new student housing off campus in a residential area of town. Two of the major factors influencing the decision will be parking and space. Those who support building off campus argue that building new housing on campus would further increase the number of cars on and around campus and consume space that could be better used for future projects that the entire university community could benefit from. Supporters also say that students might even have a richer college experience by being connected to the local community and patronizing stores and other businesses in town.

The woman expresses her opinion of the university's plan. State her opinion and explain the reasons she gives for holding that opinion.

Preparation Time: 30 Seconds
Response Time: 60 Seconds

3. You will now read a short passage and then listen to a talk on the same academic topic. You will then be asked a question about them. After you hear the question, you will have 30 seconds to prepare your response and 60 seconds to speak.

Now play Track 46 to hear Question 3.

Reading Time: 45 Seconds

Actor-Observer

People account for their own behavior differently from how they account for the behavior of others. When observing the behavior of others, we tend to attribute their actions to their character or their personality rather than to external factors. In contrast, we tend to explain our own behavior in terms of situational factors beyond our own control rather than attributing it to our own character. One explanation for this difference is that people are aware of the situational forces affecting them but not of situational forces affecting other people. Thus, when evaluating someone else's behavior, we focus on the person rather than the situation.

GO ON TO THE NEXT PAGE

Explain how the two examples discussed by the professor illustrate differences in the ways people explain behavior.

Preparation Time: 30 Seconds
Response Time: 60 Seconds

4. You will now listen to part of a lecture. You will then be asked a question about it. After you hear the question, you will have 20 seconds to prepare your response and 60 seconds to speak.

Now play Track 47 to hear Question 4.

Using points and examples from the talk, explain how learning art can impact a child's development.

Preparation Time: 20 Seconds
Response Time: 60 Seconds

STOP. This is the end of the Speaking section of *TOEFL iBT*® Practice Test 2.

WRITING

Directions: This section measures your ability to use writing to communicate in an academic environment. There will be two writing tasks.

For the first writing task, you will read a passage and listen to a lecture and then answer a question based on what you have read and heard. For the second task, you will answer a question based on your own knowledge and experience.

At the end of this Practice Test you will find a script for the audio track, topic notes, sample test taker essays, and comments on those essays by official raters.

Turn the page to see the directions for the first writing task.

Writing Based on Reading and Listening

Directions: For this task, you will read a passage about an academic topic and you will listen to a lecture about the same topic. You may take notes while you read and listen.

Then you will write a response to a question that asks you about the relationship between the lecture you heard and the reading passage. Try to answer the question as completely as possible using information from the reading passage and the lecture. The question does not ask you to express your personal opinion. You may refer to the reading passage again when you write. You may use your notes to help you answer the question.

Typically, an effective response will be 150 to 225 words. Your response will be judged on the quality of your writing and on the completeness and accuracy of the content.

Give yourself **3 minutes** to read the passage.

Reading Time: 3 minutes

Professors are normally found in university classrooms, offices, and libraries doing research and lecturing to their students. More and more, however, they also appear as guests on television news programs, giving expert commentary on the latest events in the world. These television appearances are of great benefit to the professors themselves as well as to their universities and the general public.

Professors benefit from appearing on television because by doing so they acquire reputations as authorities in their academic fields among a much wider audience than they have on campus. If a professor publishes views in an academic journal, only other scholars will learn about and appreciate those views. But when a professor appears on TV, thousands of people outside the narrow academic community become aware of the professor's ideas. So when professors share their ideas with a television audience, the professors' importance as scholars is enhanced.

Universities also benefit from such appearances. The universities receive positive publicity when their professors appear on TV. When people see a knowledgeable faculty member of a university on television, they think more highly of that university. That then leads to an improved reputation for the university. And that improved reputation in turn leads to more donations for the university and more applications from potential students.

Finally, the public gains from professors' appearing on television. Most television viewers normally have no contact with university professors. When professors appear on television, viewers have a chance to learn from experts and to be exposed to views they might otherwise never hear about. Television is generally a medium for commentary that tends to be superficial, not deep or thoughtful. From professors on television, by contrast, viewers get a taste of real expertise and insight.

Now play Track 48.

Question

Summarize the points made in the lecture, being sure to explain how they oppose specific points made in the reading passage.

You have 20 minutes to plan and write your response.

Response Time: 20 minutes

_____

_____

_____

_____

_____

_____

_____

_____

_____

_____

_____

_____

GO ON TO THE NEXT PAGE

Writing Based on Knowledge and Experience

Directions: For this task, you will write an essay in response to a question that asks you to state, explain, and support your opinion on an issue.

Typically, an effective essay will contain a minimum of 300 words. Your essay will be judged on the quality of your writing. This includes the development of your ideas, the organization of your essay, and the quality and accuracy of the language you use to express your ideas.

You have **30 minutes** to plan and complete your essay.

Write your essay in the space provided.

Question

Do you agree or disagree with the following statement?

Young people enjoy life more than older people do.

Use specific reasons and examples to support your answer. Be sure to use your own words. Do **not** use memorized examples.

Response Time: 30 minutes

GO ON TO THE NEXT PAGE

_____

_____

_____

_____

_____

_____

_____

_____

_____

_____

_____

_____

_____

_____

_____

_____

_____

_____

_____

_____

_____

_____

STOP. This is the end of the Writing section of *TOEFL iBT*® Practice Test 2.

Answers, Explanations, and Listening Scripts

Reading

Answer Key and Self-Scoring Chart

Directions: Check your answers against the answer key below. Write the number 1 on the line to the right of each question if you picked the correct answer. (For questions worth more than one point, follow the directions given.) Total your points at the bottom of the chart.

Question Number	Correct Answer	Your Raw Points
Feeding Habits of East African Herbivores		
1.	C	
2.	D	
3.	D	
4.	C	
5.	B	
6.	A	
7.	A	
8.	C	
9.	D	

For question 10, write 2 if you picked all three correct answers. Write 1 if you picked two correct answers.

10.	B, D, E	

Question Number	Correct Answer	Your Raw Points
Loie Fuller		
1.	C	
2.	D	
3.	A	
4.	D	
5.	D	
6.	C	
7.	C	
8.	A	
9.	D	

For question 10, write 2 if you picked all three correct answers. Write 1 if you picked two correct answers.

10.	C, D, E	

Question Number	Correct Answer	Your Raw Points
Green Icebergs		
1.	C	
2.	B	
3.	B	
4.	A	
5.	D	
6.	C	
7.	A	
8.	C	
9.	B	

For question 10, write 2 if you picked all three correct answers. Write 1 if you picked two correct answers.

10.	C, D, F	
	TOTAL:	

Below is a table that converts your Reading section answers into a *TOEFL iBT*® Reading scaled score. Take the total of raw points from your answer key and find that number in the left-hand column of the table. The right-hand column of the table gives a TOEFL iBT Reading scaled score for each number of raw points. For example, if the total points from your answer key is 17, the table shows a scaled score of 13 to 19.

You should use your score estimate as a general guide only. Your actual score on the TOEFL iBT test may be higher or lower than your score on the practice version.

Reading Comprehension

Raw Point Total	Scaled Score
32–33	30
31	29–30
30	28–30
29	27–28
28	26–29
27	25–28
26	24–27
25	23–26
24	21–25
23	20–25
22	19–24
21	18–23
20	17–22
19	15–21
18	14–20
17	13–19
16	11–18
15	10–17
14	8–16
13	7–15
12	5–13
11	4–12
10	2–10
9	1–9
8	1–7
7	0–5
6	0–4
5	0–2
4	0–1
3 or below	0

Answer Explanations

Feeding Habits of East African Herbivores

1. **C** This is a Vocabulary question. The word being tested is *illusory*. It is high-lighted in paragraph 1. The correct answer is choice C, "misleading." In other words, the idea that all East African herbivores have the same diet is false, or misleading.

2. **D** This is a Negative Factual Information question asking for specific information that can be found in paragraph 1. The correct answer is choice D. While the text states clearly that buffalo were not studied, it never states *why* they were not studied. The text provides the answer to the question in choice A by stating that Thomson's gazelles eat a large amount of fruit. The text provides the answer to the question in choice B by stating that wildebeests prefer to eat leaves. The text provides the answer to the question in choice C by indicating that the study took place on the Serengeti Plain in East Africa.

3. **D** This is a Vocabulary question. The word being tested is *associated*. It is highlighted in paragraph 2. The correct answer is choice D, "connected." In other words, the differences between the species are related, or connected.

4. **C** This is a Rhetorical Purpose question. It is asking you why the author mentions the cow and the horse in paragraph 2. The correct answer is choice C. Cows and horses are animals that are familiar to most people, so they are a useful reference point for the reader to understand the types of animals that are ruminants and nonruminants. Choice A is incorrect because the author is actually trying to show that the digestive systems of cows and horses are similar to those of some East African mammals. Choice B is incorrect because there is no comparison made between the body size of cows and horses and that of East African mammals. The effect of body size on the feeding habits of East African mammals is discussed in paragraph 3. Choice D is incorrect because the diets of cows and horses are not discussed at all in the passage. Therefore a comparison to the diets of East African mammals cannot be emphasized or even made.

5. **B** This is an Inference question asking for an inference that can be supported by paragraph 2. The correct answer is choice B, "The differences in stomach structure." Paragraph 2 is devoted to discussing the differences in feeding preferences that result from the different digestive systems, and therefore different stomach structures, of ruminants and nonruminants. The factors given in choices A, C, and D are all mentioned in paragraph 2, but they are more indirectly and occasionally related to feeding preferences, whereas the differences in stomach structures are shown in the paragraph to always be the primary factor in feeding preferences.

6. **A** This is a Negative Factual Information question asking for specific information that can be found in paragraph 2. The correct answer is choice A. The paragraph states that gazelles are ruminants and that it "takes time" for ruminants to digest their food. Therefore it is incorrect to say that gazelles digest their food quickly. The information given in choices B, C, and D is stated in the paragraph as facts about ruminants.

7. **A** This is a Vocabulary question. The phrase being tested is *provided that*. It is highlighted in the paragraph. The correct answer is choice A, "as long as." In other words, small animals can live with less food as long as, or if, that food has enough energy.

8. **C** This is a Factual Information question asking for specific information that can be found in the passage. The correct answer is choice C. Paragraph 2 states that zebras wear down the vegetation in a given habitat, and then ruminants, such as wildebeests, arrive to feed on the remaining, lower, leafier vegetation. Paragraph 1 supports this idea by stating that wildebeests prefer to eat lower leaves. Choice A is contradicted in several places: paragraphs 1 and 2 each state that zebras eat stems, and wildebeests eat leaves. Choice B is contradicted in paragraph 2, which states that large food particles simply cannot pass through the digestive system of ruminants such as wildebeests. Choice D is contradicted in paragraph 2, which states that ruminants such as wildebeests do not have to resort to eating low-quality food because they can derive energy from the same quantity of food for a long time.

9. **D** This is an Insert Text question. You can see the four possible answer choices in paragraph 4.

The differences in feeding preferences lead, in turn, to differences in migratory habits. **(A)** The wildebeests follow, in their migration, the pattern of local rainfall. **(B)** The other species do likewise. **(C)** But when a new area is fueled by rain, the mammals migrate toward it in a set order to exploit it. **(D)** The larger, less fastidious feeders, the zebras, move in first; the choosier, smaller wildebeests come later; and the smallest species of all, Thomson's gazelle, arrives last. The later species all depend on the preparations of the earlier one, for the actions of the zebra alter the vegetation to suit the demands of the wildebeest, topi, and gazelle.

The sentence provided, "The sequence in which they migrate correlates with their body size," is best inserted at choice **(D)**.

Choice **(D)** is correct because the phrase "The sequence" refers to the set order in which mammals migrate, which is mentioned in the sentence preceding choice **(D)**. Furthermore, the phrase "correlates with their body size" prepares the reader for the discussion of the larger, smaller, and smallest animals mentioned in the sentence following choice **(D)**.

Choices **(A)**, **(B)**, and **(C)** are incorrect because none of the preceding or following sentences makes a clear reference to a sequence or to body size.

10. **B** **D** **E** This is a Prose Summary question. It is completed correctly below. The correct choices are B, D, and E. Choices A, C, and F are therefore incorrect.

Directions: An introductory sentence for a brief summary of the passage is provided below. Complete the summary by selecting the THREE answer choices that express the most important ideas in the passage. Some answer choices do not belong in the summary because they express ideas that are not presented in the passage or are minor ideas in the passage. **This question is worth 2 points.**

East African herbivores, though they all live in the same environment, have a range of feeding preferences.

B   An herbivore's size and metabolic rate affect the kinds of food and the quantities of food it needs to eat.
D   The different digestive systems of herbivores explain their feeding preferences.
E   Migratory habits are influenced by feeding preferences.

Answer Choices

A   The survival of East African mammals depends more than anything else on the quantity of highly nutritious fruits that they are able to find.
B   An herbivore's size and metabolic rate affect the kinds of food and the quantities of food it needs to eat.
C   Zebras and wildebeests rarely compete for the same food resources in the same locations.
D   The different digestive systems of herbivores explain their feeding preferences.
E   Migratory habits are influenced by feeding preferences.
F   Patterns in the migratory habits of East African herbivores are hard to establish.

Correct Choices

Choice B, "An herbivore's size and metabolic rate affect the kinds of food and the quantities of food it needs to eat," is correct because it is a main idea introduced in paragraph 2 and elaborated on in paragraph 3. Sentence 2 in paragraph 2 states that body size is one of two main factors that explain feeding preferences. Paragraph 3 then explains in detail why body size is a main factor.

Choice D, "The different digestive systems of herbivores explain their feeding preferences," is correct because it is a major idea that is elaborated on at length in paragraph 2. This paragraph details the different digestive systems of ruminants and nonruminants and then describes the resulting feeding habits of those two types of mammals.

Choice E, "Migratory habits are influenced by feeding preferences," is correct because this is a major idea that is introduced in paragraph 2 and elaborated on in paragraph 4. It is a logical follow-up to the discussion in paragraphs 1 and 2 of the reasons for different feeding preferences.

Incorrect Choices

Choice A, "The survival of East African mammals depends more than anything else on the quantity of highly nutritious fruits that they are able to find," is incorrect according to the passage. Paragraph 1 states that only Thomson's gazelles eat fruit. Other East African mammals discussed in the passage eat only stems and leaves.

Choice C, "Zebras and wildebeests rarely compete for the same food resources in the same locations," is incorrect because it is a minor idea in the passage. The feeding habits of zebras and wildebeests are discussed in the passage as specific examples of the larger ideas given in choices B, D, and E.

Choice F, "Patterns in the migratory habits of East African herbivores are hard to establish," is contradicted by the passage. Paragraph 4 states that species follow the pattern of local rainfall in their migrations.

Loie Fuller

1. **C** This is an Inference question asking about an inference that can be supported by paragraph 1. The correct answer is choice C. The phrase "mere entertainer" in sentence 2 suggests that entertainment is less serious than art. Choice A is incorrect because we know only that other artists were attracted to Loie Fuller as an artist; there is no information about what fields these artists were in or if their work was actually influenced by Loie Fuller. Choice B is incorrect because there is no information about theatrical dance in the early nineteenth century. Choice D is incorrect because there is no indication in the paragraph about the length of time theatrical dance had been practiced.

2. **D** This is a Negative Factual Information question asking for specific information that can be found in paragraph 2. Choice D is the correct answer. Sentence 2 in the paragraph states that Loie Fuller rejected technical virtuosity, so it cannot be a characteristic of her type of dance. The information in choices A, B, and C is stated in sentence 1 as part of her type of dance.

3. **A** This is a Sentence Simplification question. As with all of these questions, a single sentence in the passage is highlighted:

> Although her early theatrical career had included stints as an actress, she was not primarily interested in storytelling or expressing emotions through dance; the drama of her dancing emanated from her visual effects.

The correct answer is choice A. Choice A contains all of the essential information in the tested sentence. It omits the information in the first clause ("Although her early theatrical career had included stints as an actress") because this information is secondary to Loie Fuller's main interest in dance.

Choices B, C, and D are all incorrect because they change the meaning of the highlighted sentence. Choices B and C are incorrect because the highlighted sentence states that Fuller was not interested in storytelling, so to say that she dramatized stories or had a particular style of storytelling is incorrect.

Choice D is incorrect because the highlighted sentence indicates the opposite idea: it indicates that Fuller's early career had little effect on her style of dance.

4. **D** This is a Vocabulary question. The word being tested is *synthesize*. It is highlighted in the passage. The correct answer is choice D, "integrate." According to the passage, French poets and painters wanted to blend, or integrate, form and content.

5. **D** This is a Factual Information question asking for specific information that can be found in paragraph 3. The correct answer is choice D. Sentence 2 in this paragraph states that Fuller's dances were in accord, or agreed, with the Art Nouveau style that was fashionable in Paris at the time. Choice A is incorrect because the paragraph says only that Parisian audiences liked Fuller's work; artists and artistic movements from the United States, in general, are not mentioned in this paragraph. Choice B is incorrect because the paragraph states that poets themselves were interested in Fuller's work. It does not state that poets tried to make other people interested in her work. Choice C is incorrect because the paragraph states in the first sentence that Fuller discovered and introduced her ideas herself; she did not borrow or take them from other artists.

6. **C** This is a Factual Information question asking for specific information that can be found in paragraph 4. The correct answer is choice C. Sentence 4 in the paragraph states that Fuller invented the technique of underlighting, or lighting the dancer from beneath. Choices A, B, and D are incorrect because they inaccurately describe how certain techniques were used by Fuller. Furthermore, none of these techniques is mentioned in connection with Fuller's *Fire Dance*.

7. **C** This is a Rhetorical Purpose question asking why the author mentions Fuller's dance titled *The Sea*. The correct answer is choice C. The paragraph begins by stating that aspects of Fuller's expertise with dance grew along with her technical expertise. *The Sea* is mentioned as an example of one way that Fuller's expertise grew, or one way that she developed as an artist, which, in this case, is in the scope of her themes. Choices A and B are incorrect because *The Sea* is not mentioned in connection with the use of music. Choice D is incorrect because *The Sea* is not mentioned in connection with science. The paragraph states that science is the theme of a different dance by Fuller, the *Radium Dance*.

8. **A** This is a Factual Information question asking for specific information that can be found in paragraph 6. The correct answer is choice A. Sentence 1 in this paragraph states that Fuller presented works by another artist, Sada Yocco. Choice B is incorrect because the paragraph states that Fuller created an all-female dance company at the time of the Paris Exposition, but we do not know if that company, or any particular company, performed in Fuller's theater. Choice C is incorrect because the paragraph states only that she established a school in 1908; we do not know that the school directly resulted from the Paris Exposition. Furthermore, we do not know from the paragraph that a school exists today that is named after Fuller. Choice D is incorrect because the paragraph does not state that Fuller's theater continued to operate after the Paris Exposition ended.

9. **D** This is an Insert Text question. You can see the four possible answer choices in paragraph 5.

As her technological expertise grew more sophisticated, so did other aspects of her dances. **(A)** Although she gave little thought to music in her earliest dances, she later used scores by Gluck, Beethoven, Schubert, Chopin, and Wagner, eventually graduating to Stravinsky, Fauré, Debussy, and Mussorgsky, composers who were then considered progressive. **(B)** She began to address more ambitious themes in her dances such as *The Sea*, in which her dancers invisibly agitated a huge expanse of silk, played upon by colored lights. **(C)** Always open to scientific and technological innovations, she befriended the scientists Marie and Pierre Curie upon their discovery of radium and created *Radium Dance*, which simulated the phosphorescence of that element. **(D)** She both appeared in films—then in an early stage of development—and made them herself; the hero of her fairy-tale film *Le Lys de la Vie* (1919) was played by René Clair, later a leading French film director.

The sentence provided, "For all of her originality in dance, her interests expanded beyond it into newly emerging artistic media," is best inserted at choice **(D)**.

The "newly emerging artistic media" are elaborated on with the information about films in the sentence following choice **(D)**.

Choices **(A)**, **(B)**, and **(C)** are incorrect because the information provided in the sentences before and after each of these squares is focused on Fuller's dance work, whereas the given sentence directs the reader away from Fuller's dance work and toward other forms of art.

10. **C** **D** **E** This is a Prose Summary question. It is completed correctly below. The correct choices are C, D, and E. Choices A, B, and F are therefore incorrect.

Directions: An introductory sentence for a brief summary of the passage is provided below. Complete the summary by selecting the THREE answer choices that express the most important ideas in the passage. Some answer choices do not belong in the summary because they express ideas that are not presented in the passage or are minor ideas in the passage. **This question is worth 2 points.**

Loie Fuller was an important and innovative dancer.

> C Fuller's work influenced a number of other dancers who were interested in experimental dance.
> D Fuller introduced many technical innovations to the staging of theatrical dance.
> E Fuller continued to develop throughout her career, creating more complex works and exploring new artistic media.

Answer Choices

A Fuller believed that audiences in the late nineteenth century had lost interest in most theatrical dance.

B Fuller transformed dance in part by creating dance interpretations of works by poets and painters.

C Fuller's work influenced a number of other dancers who were interested in experimental dance.

D Fuller introduced many technical innovations to the staging of theatrical dance.

E Fuller continued to develop throughout her career, creating more complex works and exploring new artistic media.

F By the 1920s, Fuller's theater at the Paris Exposition had become the world center for innovative dance.

Correct Choices

Choice C: "Fuller's work influenced a number of other dancers who were interested in experimental dance." This is a main idea, presented in paragraph 6. Fuller's influence on dancers who later became famous for their own work is discussed.

Choice D: "Fuller introduced many technical innovations to the staging of theatrical dance." This is a main theme of the passage that is repeated in several paragraphs. Her technical innovations are detailed at length in paragraph 4 but are also mentioned in paragraphs 5 and 6.

Choice E: "Fuller continued to develop throughout her career, creating more complex works and exploring new artistic media." This main idea is the focus of paragraph 5, which discusses her use of music, the more complex themes that she addressed in her dances, and also the films that she appeared in and directed.

Choice A, "Fuller believed that audiences in the late nineteenth century had lost interest in most theatrical dance," is incorrect because, while it could be true, the passage never makes this claim. The passage suggests only that Fuller lost interest in theatrical dance.

Choice B, "Fuller transformed dance in part by creating dance interpretations of works by poets and painters," is incorrect because the passage does not state that Fuller based her dances on the works of other artists. The passage states several times that Fuller's work was entirely original: she developed her own work and, in fact, invented many techniques.

Choice F, "By the 1920s, Fuller's theater at the Paris Exposition had become the world center for innovative dance," is incorrect because Fuller's theater existed for only one year, the year of the Paris Exposition (1900). Furthermore, the passage makes no claim about any particular place as being the "center for innovative dance."

Green Icebergs

1. **C** This is a Negative Factual Information question testing specific information in paragraph 1. The correct answer is choice C. The information in choice C is contradicted in sentence 1, which states that icebergs "float with only about 12 percent of their mass above the sea surface." The information given in the other choices is stated in the paragraph.

2. **B** This is a Factual Information question testing specific information in paragraph 2. The correct answer is choice B. The information in choice B is taken directly from sentence 1 in the paragraph, which states that icebergs "sometimes appear dark or opaque because they carry gravel and bits of rock." Choice A is incorrect because, as sentence 2 states, cloud cover may result in "pink or gold" colors, not dark colors. Choice C is incorrect because "the low angle of the Sun above the horizon" is discussed as a possible cause of pink or gold colors. Choice D is incorrect because the issue of large cracks in icebergs is not discussed in paragraph 2.

3. **B** This is a Vocabulary question. The word being tested is *penetrate*. It is highlighted in the passage. The correct answer is choice B, "pierce." In other words, ice shelf cores were long enough to pierce through glacial ice.

4. **A** This is a Factual Information question testing specific information in paragraph 4. The correct answer is choice A. Sentence 1 in the paragraph discusses "glacial ice—which is formed from the compaction of snow." Choice B is incorrect because the information given describes sea ice, a different type of ice. Choice C is incorrect because the information given describes the first step in the formation of green icebergs. Choice D is incorrect because the information given describes the second step in the formation of green icebergs.

5. **D** This is a Factual Information question testing specific information in paragraph 4. The correct answer is choice D. Sentence 2 in the paragraph states that clear sea ice is "very similar" to the ice from green icebergs. Choices A, B, and C do not answer the question asked. Choice A is also incorrect because it mistakenly identifies green icebergs as having frozen seawater at the bottom, whereas sentence 1 in the paragraph says that frozen seawater is found on the bottom of glacial ice. Choice B is incorrect because the information given is the opposite of what is stated in the passage, which is that bubble-free ice is formed and found on the bottom of shelf ice. Choice C is incorrect because the information given is not discussed in the passage at all.

6. **C** This is a Rhetorical Purpose question. It tests why the author mentions that "The green ice portion was textured by seawater erosion." This sentence is highlighted in the passage. The correct answer is choice C. The highlighted sentence is evidence that the green ice part of the iceberg was once under water. The fact that this green ice is no longer under water but is now exposed to air is evidence that the green icebergs are formed from pieces of the ice shelf that have broken off and turned upside down. Choice A is incorrect because the information given, while factual according to the passage, does not explain why the author includes the information that the green ice portion was textured by seawater. Choice B is incorrect because there is no comparison made between the erosion of green ice and white ice in the paragraph. Choice D is incorrect because, while sentences 1 and 4 in the paragraph state that green ice has no bubbles, there is no information in the paragraph indicating that green ice initially has bubbles and that they are removed.

7. **A** This is a Vocabulary question. The word being tested is *excluded*. It is highlighted in the passage. The correct answer is choice A, "kept out." In other words, dissolved organic substances are not kept out of the ice in the freezing process.

8. **C** This is an Inference question asking for an inference that can be supported by the passage. The correct answer is choice C. Sentences 5, 6, and 7 in paragraph 5 support this information by indicating that the seawater around these icebergs contains the decomposing material of green-pigmented organisms. This decomposing material dissolves in seawater, which then freezes as part of the iceberg. The information in choice A is incorrect because paragraph 7 says that the Amery Ice Shelf is well suited to the production of green icebergs. This does not mean that the Amery Ice Shelf produces *only* green icebergs. The information in choice B is incorrect because copper and iron are mentioned in paragraph 3 only as *possible* color sources in green icebergs. The last sentence in paragraph 3 states that a source other than copper and iron was found. The information in choice D is incorrect because the passage gives no indication of where all green icebergs are located. Paragraph 2 mentions the Weddell Sea in Antarctica, and paragraph 7 states that green icebergs "drift" around Antarctica. Therefore green icebergs can be found far from the Amery Ice Shelf.

9. **Ⓑ** This is an Insert Text question. You can see the four possible answer choices in paragraphs 2 and 3.

Icebergs are ordinarily blue to white, although they sometimes appear dark or opaque because they carry gravel and bits of rock. They may change color with changing light conditions or cloud cover, glowing pink or gold in the morning or evening light, but this color change is generally related to the low angle of the Sun above the horizon. **(A)** However, travelers to Antarctica have repeatedly reported seeing green icebergs in the Weddell Sea and, more commonly, close to the Amery Ice Shelf in East Antarctica.

(B) One explanation for green icebergs attributes their color to an optical illusion when blue ice is illuminated by a near-horizon red Sun, but green icebergs stand out among white and blue icebergs under a great variety of light conditions. **(C)** Another suggestion is that color might be related to ice with high levels of metallic compounds, including copper and iron. **(D)** Recent expeditions have taken ice samples from green icebergs and ice cores—vertical, cylindrical ice samples reaching down to great depths—from the glacial ice shelves along the Antarctic continent. Analyses of these cores and samples provide a different solution to the problem.

The sentence provided, "Scientists have differed as to whether icebergs appear green as a result of light conditions or because of something in the ice itself," is best inserted at choice **(B)**.

Choice **(B)** is correct because the sentence provided introduces two possible explanations for the color of green icebergs. Paragraph 3 is the first place in the passage where explanations are offered for the color of green icebergs. The beginning of paragraph 3 is the only appropriate place to introduce these possible explanations.

Choice **(A)** is incorrect because green icebergs are mentioned for the first time in the last sentence in paragraph 2. It does not make sense to insert the given sentence, which introduces explanations for the color of green icebergs, before the first mention of green icebergs.

Choice **(C)** is incorrect because its position is *between* the detailed discussions of the two explanations introduced in the given sentence. The given sentence introduces the two explanations; therefore it must come *before* the discussions.

Choice **(D)** is incorrect because its position is *after* the detailed discussions of the two explanations introduced in the given sentence. The given sentence introduces the two explanations; therefore it must come *before* the discussions.

10. **C D F** This is a Prose Summary question. It is completed correctly below. The correct choices are C, D, and F. Choices A, B, and E are therefore incorrect.

Directions: An introductory sentence for a brief summary of the passage is provided below. Complete the summary by selecting the THREE answer choices that express the most important ideas in the passage. Some answer choices do not belong in the summary because they express ideas that are not presented in the passage or are minor ideas in the passage. **This question is worth 2 points.**

Several suggestions, ranging from light conditions to the presence of metallic compounds, have been offered to explain why some icebergs appear green.

> C Green icebergs form when a two-layer block of ice breaks away from a glacier and capsizes, exposing the bottom sea ice to view.
>
> D Ice cores and samples revealed that both ice shelves and green icebergs contain a layer of bubbly glacial ice and a layer of bubble-free sea ice.
>
> F In a green iceberg, the sea ice contains large concentrations of organic matter from the seawater.

Answer Choices

A Ice cores were used to determine that green icebergs were formed from the compaction of metallic compounds, including copper and iron.

B All ice shelves can produce green icebergs, but the Amery Ice Shelf is especially well suited to do so.

C Green icebergs form when a two-layer block of ice breaks away from a glacier and capsizes, exposing the bottom sea ice to view.

D Ice cores and samples revealed that both ice shelves and green icebergs contain a layer of bubbly glacial ice and a layer of bubble-free sea ice.

E Green icebergs are white until they come into contact with seawater containing platelets and soluble organic green pigments.

F In a green iceberg, the sea ice contains large concentrations of organic matter from the seawater.

Correct Choices

Choice C, "Green icebergs form when a two-layer block of ice breaks away from a glacier and capsizes, exposing the bottom sea ice to view," is correct because it summarizes important parts of paragraphs 4 and 5. These explain that green icebergs are capsized pieces of ice that have broken off of an ice shelf.

Choice D, "Ice cores and samples revealed that both ice shelves and green icebergs contain a layer of bubbly glacial ice and a layer of bubble-free sea ice," is correct because it summarizes the key information in paragraphs 3 and 4 that explains how scientists were able to determine how green icebergs are formed. The scientists compared ice from green icebergs to ice from ice shelves by drilling ice core samples out of ice shelves.

Choice F, "In a green iceberg, the sea ice contains large concentrations of organic matter from the seawater," is correct because it summarizes the key information from paragraph 5 about the source of the green pigments in green icebergs.

Incorrect Choices

Choice A, "Ice cores were used to determine that green icebergs were formed from the compaction of metallic compounds, including copper and iron," is incorrect because it is factually incorrect according to the passage. The last sentence in paragraph 3 contradicts this idea.

Choice B, "All ice shelves can produce green icebergs, but the Amery Ice Shelf is especially well suited to do so," is incorrect because the passage does not state at any point that ice shelves other than the Amery Ice Shelf can produce green icebergs.

Choice E, "Green icebergs are white until they come into contact with seawater containing platelets and soluble organic green pigments," is incorrect because the passage never discusses whether green icebergs are originally white, or any particular color.

Listening

Answer Key and Self-Scoring Chart

Directions: Check your answers against the answer key below. Write the number 1 on the line to the right of each question if you picked the correct answer. Total your points at the bottom of the chart.

Question Number	Correct Answer	Your Raw Points
1.	B	
2.	D	
3.	C	
4.	D	
5.	B	
6.	C	
7.	A	
8.	A	
9.	D	
10.	B	
11.	A	
12.	D	
13.	B	
14.	A	
15.	C	
16.	B	
17.	C	
18.	A	

For question 19, write 1 if you picked both correct answers. Write 0 if you picked only one correct answer or no correct answers.

19.	B, D	
20.	C	
21.	D	
22.	B	
23.	C	
24.	A	
25.	C	
26.	A	
27.	B	
28.	C	
TOTAL:		

Below is a table that converts your Listening section answers into a *TOEFL iBT®* Listening scaled score. Take the total of raw points from your answer key and find that number in the left-hand column of the table. The right-hand column of the table gives a TOEFL iBT Listening scaled score for each total of raw points. For example, if the total points from your answer key is 27, the table shows a scaled score of 29 to 30.

You should use your score estimate as a general guide only. Your actual score on the TOEFL iBT test may be higher or lower than your score on the practice version.

Listening

Raw Point Total	Scaled Score
28	30
27	29–30
26	27–30
25	25–30
24	24–29
23	23–27
22	22–26
21	21–25
20	19–24
19	18–23
18	17–21
17	16–20
16	14–19
15	13–18
14	12–17
13	10–15
12	9–14
11	7–13
10	6–12
9	5–10
8	3–9
7	2–7
6	1–6
5	1–4
4	0–2
3	0–1
2	0
1	0
0	0

Listening Scripts and Answer Explanations

Questions 1–5

Track 34 Listening Script

Narrator

Listen to a conversation between a student and a professor.

Professor

Sandy, how's class been going for you this semester?

Female Student

Oh, it's great. I really like your business psychology class, but I have one major concern about the last assignment: you know—the one where we have to interview a local business owner, uh, I mean entrepreneur?

Professor

Are you having trouble coming up with interview questions?

Female Student

Well, that's just it. I mean I worked on my high school newspaper for years, so I actually have great questions to ask. The thing is . . . I'm new to the area, and I don't know people off campus . . . So I was wondering if . . . well, could you possibly give me the name of someone I could interview . . . ?

Professor

You don't know anyone who owns a business?

Female Student

Well, yeah, back home . . . my next-door neighbors—they own a shoe store, and they're really successful—but they're not local.

Professor

Well, it wouldn't be fair to the other students if I gave you the name of a contact—but I could help you figure out a way to find someone on your own. Let's see . . . Do you read the local newspaper?

Female Student

Sure, whenever I have the time.

Professor

Well, the business section in the paper often has stories about local business people who've been successful. If you find an article, you could call the person who is profiled.

Female Student

You mean, just call them up . . . out of the blue . . . and ask them if they'll talk to me?

Professor

Sure, why not?

Female Student

Well, aren't people like that awfully busy? Too busy to talk to a random college student.

Professor

Many people enjoy telling the story of how they got started. Remember, this is a business psychology class, and for this assignment, I want you to get some real insight about business owners, their personality, what drives them to become an entrepreneur.

Female Student

Like, how they think?

Professor

And what motivates them. Why did they start their business? I'm sure they'd talk to you, especially if you tell them you might start a business someday.

Female Student

I'm not sure I'd have the guts to do that. Opening a business seems so risky, so scary.

Professor

Well, you can ask them if they felt that way too. Now you just need to find someone to interview to see if your instincts are correct.

Track 35 Listening Script (Question 5)

Narrator

Listen again to part of the conversation.

Professor

Are you having trouble coming up with interview questions?

Student

Well, that's just it. I mean I worked on my high school newspaper for years, so I actually have great questions to ask.

Narrator

What does the student imply?

Answer Explanations

1. **B** This is a Gist-Purpose question. This type of question is typically asked first in listening conversations that take place in a professor's office. At the beginning of the conversation, the student explains that she does not know anyone off campus to interview for her business class assignment and asks the professor if he could recommend someone. This is why she came to his office, so choice B is correct. The student mentions that she has already written her questions; therefore she does not need suggestions on how to write them (choice A). She does not ask for advice on how she might start a business (choice C). She does not say anything about scheduling an interview or any further meetings with the professor (choice D).

2. **D** This is an Understand Organization question. You need to understand why the student talks about having worked on her high school newspaper. Choice A is incorrect because the interview is for a class assignment, not for publication in a newspaper. The student suggests that working on her high school newspaper has made part of the assignment—coming up with questions—easy for her, not difficult (choice B). And while it may be true that she enjoys newspaper work (choice C), that is not why she mentions her high school paper. She mentions it to show she is an experienced interviewer; thus the correct choice is D.

3. **C** This is a Detail question. To help the student solve her problem, the professor does not offer a list of business owners (choice A), nor does he offer to change the due date of the student's assignment (choice D). The student mentions people who own a shoe store in her hometown, but she does not ask the professor to allow her to interview them (choice B) because she realizes that the assignment is to interview owners of a *local* business. The professor helps the student by referring her to the business section of the local newspaper, which often prints stories about successful businesspeople in the local area; thus choice C is correct.

4. **D** This is another Detail question. It is the student, not the professor, who says that opening a business seems risky (choice A); the assignment does not involve writing an article (choice B) or developing a detailed business plan (choice C). The professor says explicitly that he wants the class to learn about the personalities of business owners and what motivates them. Therefore choice D is the correct answer.

5. **B** This question requires that you Make an Inference. The conversation begins with the student telling the professor that she has a concern about the assignment, but she does not say at first exactly what her concern is. When the professor asks if she is having trouble coming up with interview questions, he is trying to find out what her specific concern is. When she says that she has written some great questions already, she is telling him indirectly that interview questions are not the problem. He has not quite identified her

concern, so choice B is the correct answer, and choice C, which states the opposite, is incorrect. Nothing in the student's words or tone of voice suggests that she does not want to finish the assignment (choice D) or that she is surprised by what the professor has said to her (choice A).

Questions 6–11

Track 36 Listening Script

Narrator

Listen to part of a lecture in an anthropology class.

Anthropology

Professor

OK, I, I want to begin today by talking about calendars. I know, some of you are thinking it's not all that fascinating, right? But listen, the next time you look at a calendar, I want you to keep something in mind. There are at least three natural ways of measuring the . . . the passage of time—by day, by month, and by year. And these are all pretty easy to see, right? I mean a day is based on one rotation of Earth. A month is how long the Moon takes to move around the Earth. And a year is the time it takes for Earth to move around the Sun, right? So they're all based on natural events. But the natural clocks of Earth, the Moon, and the Sun run on different times, and you can't divide any one of these time periods by another one without having some messy fraction left over. I mean one lunar month—that's the time it takes for the Moon to go around Earth—one month is about 29 and a half days . . . not really a nice round number. And one year is a little more than 365 days. So these are obviously numbers that don't divide into each other very neatly. And this makes it pretty difficult to create some sort of tidy calendar that really works.

Not that different cultures haven't tried. Have any of you ever been to Stonehenge? No . . . you know, that amazing circle of giant stones in England? Well, if you ever go, and find yourself wondering why this culture way back in prehistoric England would go to so much work to construct this monumental ring of enormous stones, . . . well, keep in mind that a lot of us think it was designed, at least partially, as a calendar—to mark when the seasons of the year begin, according to the exact day when the Sun comes up from a particular direction. I have colleagues who insist it's a temple, maybe, or a tomb . . . but they can't deny that it was also used as a calendar . . . probably to help figure out, for example, when farmers should begin their planting each year.

The Mayans, in Central America, also invented a calendar, but for a different purpose. The Mayans, especially the royalty and priests, wanted to look at long cycles of history—so the calendar they used had to be able to count far into the future as well as far into the past. And not only were the Mayans keeping track of the natural timekeepers we mentioned before—Earth, the Moon, and the Sun—but another natural timekeeper: the planet Venus.

Venus rises in the sky as the morning star every 584 days, and the Venus cycle was incorporated in the Mayan calendar. So the Mayans kept track of long periods of time, and they did it so accurately, in fact, that their calendar is considered about as complicated and sophisticated as any in the world.

Now, the ancient Chinese believed very strongly in astrology—the idea that you can predict future events based on the positions of the stars and planets like, say, Jupiter. Incidentally, the whole Chinese system of astrology was based on the fact that the planet Jupiter goes around the Sun once every 12 years, so one orbit of Jupiter lasts 12 of our Earth years. Apparently, that's why the Chinese calendar has a cycle of 12 years. You know, like, "The Year of the Dragon," "The Year of the Tiger," and so on . . . all parts of a 12-year astrological cycle, that we get from the orbit of Jupiter.

Calendars based on the orbits of other planets, though, are a lot less common than those based on the cycle of the Moon—the lunar month. I could mention any number of important cultures around the world that have depended on lunar calendars, but there really isn't time.

So let's go right to the calendar that's now used throughout most of the world—a solar calendar—based on the number of days in a year. This calendar's mainly derived from the one the ancient Romans devised a couple thousand years ago. I mean the Romans—with more than a little help from the Greeks—realized that a year actually lasts about 365 and one-quarter days. And so they decided to round off most years to 365 days but make every fourth year into a leap year. I mean, somehow, you have to account for that extra one-fourth of a day each year, so every four years, they made the calendar one day longer. By adding the leap year, the Romans were able to make a calendar that worked so well—that, with a few minor adjustments, this calendar is still widely used today.

Answer Explanations

6. **C** This is a Gist-Content question. Choice C is correct because the professor spends almost the entire lecture discussing four types of calendars used historically in England, Central America, China, and ancient Rome, as well as the modern calendar used throughout the world today. Errors in early calendars (choice A) are not discussed; in fact, the professor emphasizes how surprisingly accurate and sophisticated these early calendars were. Choice D is incorrect because astrology—the belief that the position of stars and planets can predict events—is mentioned only in the context of the Chinese calendar. Why people came to believe that Earth moves around the Sun (choice B) is not discussed at all.

7. **A** This question requires you to Understand the Speaker's Attitude. The professor indirectly expresses her certainty that Stonehenge served as a calendar by stating, "a lot of us think it was designed, at least partially, as a calendar." Her use of the pronoun *us* indicates that she includes herself in that group. When mentioning colleagues who think Stonehenge served another purpose, she adds that "they can't deny that it was also used as a calendar." Thus the correct answer is choice A.

8. **A** This is a Detail question. Choice A is correct because the professor states that the Mayans were interested in tracking long cycles of history. There is no mention of lunar months in the discussion of the Mayan calendar (choice B). It was the ancient Chinese, not the Mayans, who wanted a calendar system to predict events (choice C). The Mayan calendar was *based on* the appearance of Venus in the morning sky and on the movements of other natural time-keepers like Earth, but comparing the orbits of Earth and Venus (choice D) was not the calendar's *purpose*.

9. **D** This is another Detail question. Choice D is correct because the professor states that the ancient Chinese calendar was based on Jupiter's 12-year-long orbit around the Sun, not on night-day cycles (choice A), the Moon (choice B), or the seasons (choice C).

10. **B** This is also a Detail question. Choice B is correct because the professor says that the ancient Romans put an extra day into the calendar every 4 years to account for the actual length of a single Earth orbit, which is 365¼ days. According to the professor, this addition, which improved the calendar's precision, is what made the calendar work so well that it is still widely used.

11. **A** This is an Understanding Organization question. Before discussing any specific calendars, the professor identifies a problem: that all calendars are based on natural astronomical cycles, which are not coordinated with one another mathematically. The professor then describes various historical calendars and the natural cycles on which they were based, ending with a description of the modern calendar and its solution to the coordination problem. Thus choice A is correct.

Questions 12–16

Track 37 Listening Script

Narrator

Listen to part of a conversation between a student and a university employee.

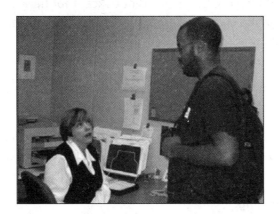

Employee

Oh, hello . . . can I help you?

Student

Um . . . yeah . . . I'm looking for Professor Kirk; is she here? I mean is this her office?

Employee

Yes, you're in the right place—Professor Kirk's office is right behind me—but no . . . she's not here right now.

Student

Um, do you know when she'll be back?

Employee

Well, she's teaching all morning. She won't be back until . . . let me check . . . hmm, she won't be back until . . . after lunch. That's when she has her office hours. Perhaps you could come back then?

Student

Oh, unfortunately no. I have class this afternoon. And I was really hoping to talk to her today. Hey, um, do you know if . . . she's accepting any more students into her Introduction to Biology class?

Employee

You wanna know if you can take the class?

Student

Yes, if she's letting any more students sign up, I'd like, I'd like to join the class.

Employee

Introduction to Biology is a very popular class, especially when she teaches it. A lot of students take it.

Student

Yeah, that's why the registrar said it was full. I've got the form the registrar gave me, um, to get her permission to take the class. It's all filled out except for her signature. I'm hoping she'll let me in even though the class is full. You, see, I'm a senior this year, and, uh . . . this'll be my last semester, so it's my last chance . . .

Employee

Oh, wow, really. I mean most students fulfill their science requirement the first year.

Student

Well, I mean, um . . . to be honest, I kept putting it off. I'm not really a big fan of science classes in general, and with the labs and everything, I've never quite found the time.

Employee

Your advisor didn't say anything?

Student

Well, to tell you the truth, she's been after me to take a class like this for a while, but I'm double-majoring in art and journalism and so my schedule's been really tight with all the classes I gotta take, so somehow I never . . .

Employee

Well, perhaps you could leave the form with me and I'll see if she'll sign it for you.

Student

You know, I appreciate that, but maybe I should explain the problem to her in person . . . I didn't want to do it, but I guess I'll have to send her an e-mail.

Employee

Hmm. You know, not all professors check their e-mails regularly—I . . . I'm not sure if Professor Kirk does it or not. Here's an idea . . . why don't you stick a note explaining your situation under her door and ask her to call you if she needs more information?

Student

Hey, that's a good idea, and then I can leave the form with you—if you still don't mind.

Track 38 Listening Script (Question 16)

Narrator

Why does the man say this to the woman:

Student

You know, I appreciate that, but maybe I should explain the problem to her in person . . .

Answer Explanations

12. **D** This is a Gist-Purpose question. The student wants Professor Kirk to give him permission to enroll in a course that is already full. In order to do this, the professor must sign a form that the student has brought with him. That is why he is there; thus choice D is correct. The student already knows that he must take a science course in order to graduate (choice A). There is no indication that Professor Kirk has invited the student to her office (choice B), and the student already has an advisor (choice C).

13. **B** This is a Detail question. When the man says he will graduate soon, the woman says, "Oh, wow" and points out that most students fulfill their science requirement their first year. This indicates that she is surprised that the man has waited so long, making choice B the correct answer. None of the other choices is factually true, according to the information in the conversation.

14. **A** This is another Detail question. Choice A is correct because it paraphrases the man's statement that his advisor has "been after me to take a class like this for a while." She wants him to take the class because she is aware of the man's situation and knows he cannot graduate without the science class. Therefore choice C, which states that she is unaware of his problem, is incorrect. There is nothing in the conversation indicating that the advisor encouraged the man to major in journalism (choice B). And although Professor Kirk's popularity among students is mentioned in the conversation, no reference is made to the advisor's opinion of Professor Kirk (choice D).

15. **C** This is a Connecting Content question. After the woman suggests that the man stick a note under Professor Kirk's door, the man says, "that's a good idea," indicating that he will follow her advice. Thus choice C is correct. There is some discussion about sending an e-mail (choice B), but that idea is rejected. There is no discussion of calling Professor Kirk (choice A), and the man explains early in the conversation that his schedule conflicts with the professor's office hours (choice D).

16. **B** This question requires you to Understand the Function of What Is Said. In the replayed audio, the man rejects the woman's offer to give the form to Professor Kirk. Instead of simply saying, "No," the man says he does "appreciate" her offer but thinks it would be better for him to speak with Professor Kirk directly. Choice B captures both the man's politeness and his intention. The man's problem is not yet solved (choice A), and he has already explained what he needs (choice C). Choice D is incorrect because the woman implied earlier that it is Professor Kirk, not she, who is busy.

Questions 17–22

Track 39 Listening Script

Narrator

Listen to part of a lecture in an astronomy class.

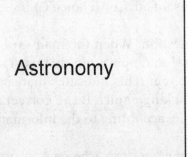

Professor

I'm sure y'all have been following the news about Mars. A lot of spacecraft have been visiting the planet recently—some have gone into orbit around it, while others have landed on it. And, they've sent back a . . . an abundance of data that's reshaping our knowledge . . . our vision of the planet in a lot of ways. Is there anything that you've been particularly struck by in all the news reports?

Female Student

Well, they seem to mention water a lot, which kinda surprised me, as I have this picture in my head that Mars is dry . . . sorta dry and dead.

Professor

You're not the only one. You know, for centuries, most of our knowledge of the planet came from what we saw through telescopes, so, obviously, it was pretty limited—and our views of the planet were formed as much by writers . . . as they were by serious scientists. When the first science-fiction stories came out, Mars was described as being a lot like Earth except . . .

Male Student

I know: the planet was red and, uh, the people were green. I've seen some of those old movies. What were they thinking? I mean really . . . they . . .

Professor

Well, it seems silly to us now, but those ideas were quite imaginative and, occasionally, scary in their time. Anyway, we began to rethink our image of Mars when the first spacecraft flew by the planet in 1965 and sent pictures back to Earth. Those pictures showed a planet that looked a lot more like our Moon than Earth—lots of craters and not much else. It was bitterly cold, it had a very thin atmosphere, and that atmosphere was mostly carbon dioxide. So the view of Mars after this first flyby mission was that dry, dead planet that Lisa mentioned.

But, then there were more visits to the planet in the 1970s—and this time the spacecraft didn't just fly by; they orbited . . . or landed. This allowed us to receive much more detailed images of the planet, and it turned out to be a pretty interesting place. Mars had . . . has a lot more than craters—it has giant volcanoes and deep canyons. It also showed signs of dried-up riverbeds and plains that had been formed by massive floods. So we concluded that there must have been water on the planet at one time—billions of years ago. Now, what does it take for water to exist?

Male Student

You need to have a warm-enough temperature so that it doesn't freeze.

Professor

That's one thing—and the other is that you need enough atmospheric pressure, thick-enough air so that the water doesn't instantly vaporize. The Mars we see today doesn't have either of those conditions—it is too cold and the air is too thin—but a long time ago, there may have been a thicker atmosphere that created a greenhouse effect that raised temperatures—and maybe that combination produced water on the surface of the planet. So maybe Mars wasn't just a dead, boring rock; maybe, it was, uh, a fascinating fossil that was once alive and dynamic—worthy of exploration. Now let's jump forward a few decades to the beginning of this century, and a new generation of orbiters and landers that have been sent to Mars. Of course, the scientific instruments now surveying Mars are far more sophisticated than the instruments of the '70s, so we're getting all kinds of new data for analysis. And, not surprisingly, that data is challenging our notions of what Mars is like. Lisa, you mentioned that a lot of the news reports talked about water—do you remember any of the details?

Female Student

Well, they were showing these pictures of these long, uh, cuts in the ground, which would be gullies here; I mean on Earth. They say that since, uh, gullies are usually formed by water, it seems like they might be evidence that water still exists on Mars, but I didn't get how that worked.

Professor

I'm not surprised. There're a lot of theories . . . a lot of speculation . . . and some argue the formations aren't caused by water at all. But there're some ingenious theories that assume that there's a lot of water right under the planet's surface that somehow is causing the gullies to form. If we could only get a lander there . . . but the gullies aren't in places where we can send landers yet. Anyway, if there is some kind of water activity, it may change our view of the planet once again . . . to something that's not dead, not even a fossil, but rather a planet like Earth that undergoes cycles—think of our ice ages—over long periods of time. Maybe Mars could sustain water again at some distant date.

Track 40 Listening Script (Question 21)

Narrator

Why does the professor say this:

Professor

So maybe Mars wasn't just a dead, boring rock; maybe, it was, uh, a fascinating fossil that was once alive and dynamic—worthy of exploration.

Track 41 Listening Script (Question 22)

Male Student

I know: the planet was red and, uh, the people were green. I've seen some of those old movies. What were they thinking? I mean really . . .

Narrator

Why does the student say this:

Male Student

What were they thinking?

Answer Explanations

17. **C** This is a Gist-Content question. The professor begins by saying that an abundance of data is reshaping "our vision of the planet in a lot of ways." He goes on to discuss how Mars was imagined before it was visited by spacecraft, and then how, in recent years, successive spacecraft have sent back detailed images that are providing an increasingly realistic view of the planet. Thus choice C is correct.

18. **A** This is a Detail question. Choice A is correct because the professor says that the images obtained in 1965 made Mars appear as dry and dead as the Moon, with "lots of craters and not much else." He mentions the 1965 view that Mars was very cold, but he does not say that the images showed it to be similar to Earth (choice B)—quite the opposite. The existence of life on Mars in the distant past is presented not as a conclusion (choice C) but as a matter of theory and speculation coming after the 1970s orbits and the even more recent Mars landings. The theory that water exists under Mars's surface (choice D) is also a recent development.

19. **B** **D** This is a Making Inferences question. Note that the square boxes in front of the answer choices indicate that you must select two correct answers. In the lecture, the professor contrasts the dry conditions of Mars today with the possibility that Mars had water on its surface billions of years ago. Choice B, which says that the atmospheric pressure and the temperature may have been higher on Mars in the past than they are today, forms part of his explanation of how Mars could once have had water. Choice D is also correct because part of the evidence for the existence of water on Mars is the plains and the dried-up riverbeds currently visible on Mars's surface; according to the professor, they could have been created by flooding.

20. **C** This is a Detail question. One of the students mentions that she has seen news reports that showed gullies on Mars, and she says that they seem to be evidence of water. The professor confirms that gullies may indeed be evidence of water on Mars and says that there are theories that water under the surface caused the gullies to form. Thus choice C is correct. The professor mentions volcanoes on Mars (choice A) and Mars's dry climate (choice B), but he does not associate either with gullies. References are made to fossils but not to any actual fossils (choice D); the professor uses the word *fossil* metaphorically when he likens the entire planet to an object that may be dead but that is nevertheless worth investigating because it was once alive.

21. **D** This is an Understanding Organization question. In this replayed statement, the professor uses imagery to describe the early conception of Mars— "a dead, boring rock"—and the modern conception formed by additional evidence—"a fascinating fossil that was once alive and dynamic." By making this contrast, the professor both sums up the lecture and emphasizes that the change in our view of Mars was a very significant one. Thus the correct answer is choice D.

22. **B** This question requires you to Understand the Function of What Is Said. The student's comment is an indirect criticism of early filmmakers for their unrealistic portrayals of Mars. Thus choice B is correct. His opinion is a negative one, so he is not expressing approval (choice D). The student is not seeking clarification or rephrasing a previous question, so choices A and C do not accurately reflect the intention of his statement.

Questions 23–28

Track 42 Listening Script

Narrator

Listen to part of a lecture in an art history class. The professor has been talking about colossal statues.

Art History
Colossal Statues

Professor

We've been looking at colossal statues—works of exceptionally huge size—and their essentially public role, in commemorating a political or religious figure. We've seen how some of these statues date back thousands of years . . . like the statues of the pharaohs of ancient Egypt—which you can still visit today—and how others, though surviving only in legend, have fired the imagination of writers and artists right up to our own time, such as the Colossus of Rhodes, that 110-foot statue of the Greek god Helios. Remember, this same word, *colossus*—which means a giant or larger-than-life-size statue—is what today's term *colossal* derives from.

Now, it was one thing to build such statues, at an equally colossal cost, when the funds were being allocated by ancient kings and pharaohs. But if we're going to think about modern-day colossal statues, we need to reexamine more closely their role as social and political symbols, in order to understand why a society today—a society of free, taxpaying citizens—would agree to allocate so much of its resources to erecting them. A good example to start out with would be Mount Rushmore.

Now, many of you have probably seen pictures of Mount Rushmore; perhaps you've actually visited the place. Mount Rushmore, in South Dakota, is a colossal representation of the faces of four U.S. presidents: George Washington, Thomas Jefferson, Theodore Roosevelt, and Abraham Lincoln, carved directly into a mountain. Imagine: each of those faces in the rock is over 60 feet high! Now, carving their faces took over six and a half years, and cost almost a million dollars. And this was in the 1930s, during the worst economic depression in U.S. history! Does that strike any of you as odd?

Well, I personally think that the Great Depression of the 1930s actually makes this more understandable, not less so. Often it's the case that, precisely at times of hardship—when the very fabric of society seems to be unraveling and confidence is eroding—uh, that people clamor for some public expression of strength and optimism, perhaps as a way of symbolizing its endurance in the face of difficulty.

So with that in mind, let's go back to Mount Rushmore. Actually, the original motivation for a colossal monument in South Dakota had very little to do with all this symbolism . . . and everything to do with money: you see, it was first conceived of basically as a tourist attraction, and it was supposed to feature the images of legendary figures of the American West, like the explorers Lewis and Clark. The government of South Dakota thought it would bring lots of money into the state.

It was only later on that the sculptor—the artist who designed and oversaw the project, a man named Gutzon Borglum—decided the project should be a monument honoring four of the most-respected presidents in U.S. history; much more than a tourist attraction . . . its very prominence and permanence became perceived as a symbol of the endurance of U.S. ideals and the greatness of the country's early leaders. So, you see, what began as a tourist attraction became something far loftier.

Let's look at another example of this phenomenon.

The Statue of Liberty is another colossal statue—one that I assume a number of you are familiar with. But, umm, I would guess that—like many people today—you don't realize that, when it was designed, over a century ago—by a French sculptor—it was intended to symbolize the long friendship between the people of France and the people of the United States—one which dated back to France's support of the American colonies' war for independence from the British.

But the shift in the statue's meaning started soon after it was built. Back in 1883, Emma Lazarus wrote that famous poem—you know, the one that goes: "Give me your tired, your poor . . ." and so on and so forth. That poem describes the Statue of Liberty as a beacon of welcome for the entire world. Well, in the early 1900s, it was put on a plaque on the pedestal that the Statue of Liberty stands on.

From that point on, the Statue of Liberty was no longer perceived as just a gift between friendly republics. It now became a tribute to the United States' history of immigration and openness.

This association was strengthened in the imagination of the general public just a few decades after the statue's completion, with the immigration waves of the early twentieth century . . . especially since the statue happened to be the first sign of America seen by those immigrants sailing into the port of New York. So, as with Mount Rushmore, the original motivation for this colossal statue was forgotten, and the statue is now valued for more important reasons.

Track 43 Listening Script (Question 28)

Professor

Back in 1883, Emma Lazarus wrote that famous poem—you know, the one that goes: "Give me your tired, your poor . . ." and so on and so forth.

Narrator

What does the professor imply about the poem by Emma Lazarus?

Answer Explanations

23. **C** This is a Gist-Content question. The lecture is part of a larger art history lecture on the general topic of colossal statues. Having completed his discussion of ancient colossal statues, the professor now focuses on modern times and begins by raising this question: why would elected officials be willing to invest enormous sums of public money to create colossal statues? To understand why, he says, one needs to "reexamine more closely their role as social and political symbols." Choice C best expresses that idea. Choices A, B, and D are mentioned but are not the main focus of this excerpt.

24. **A** This is a Making Inferences question. In examining the role of modern colossal statues as social and political symbols, the professor explains that these very expensive statues are built only when free, taxpaying citizens agree to fund their construction. If these symbols are so costly to build, then the people who agree to fund their construction must place a high value on them. Therefore choice A is correct. While it is probably true that important colossal statues are discussed in many classrooms (choice B), this fact is not mentioned by the professor. The fact that the statues last thousands of years is discussed with regard to ancient, not modern, statues (choice C). A famous poem is discussed in the lecture, but this poem was inspired by the Statue of Liberty, not the other way around (choice D).

25. **C** This is a Detail question. In his discussion of the Great Depression, the professor says that people's confidence gets eroded in times of financial hardship, making choice C correct. While the other events may have resulted from the Great Depression, they are not mentioned by the professor in this regard.

26. **A** This is a Detail question. At the opening and again at the closing of his discussion of Mount Rushmore, the professor says that the monument was originally intended as a tourist attraction to bring money to the state of South Dakota. Choice A is correct because it paraphrases these statements. The unity of society (choice B) is addressed in the lecture in connection with colossal statues, and symbolizing this ideal might have been one of the sculptor's goals. Nevertheless, the professor emphasizes that neither unifying society nor the Great Depression (choice C) was the original motivation for the state of South Dakota. Choice D is incorrect for the same reason: honoring United States presidents was not the original purpose of the statue; in fact, the monument started out as a depiction of legendary figures of the American West, not U.S. presidents.

27. **B** This is an Understanding Organization question. Choice B is correct because the professor talks about Emma Lazarus's poem as a second example of how the meaning associated with a monument can change. Before mentioning the poem, the professor points out that the Statue of Liberty was given to the United States by France as a gift symbolizing the long friendship between the two countries. But then Lazarus wrote the poem describing the

statue as a beacon of welcome for the entire world. The professor says that the poem gave a new meaning to the statue and that this meaning strengthened after the poem was placed on the statue's pedestal. The professor is not making a general observation about literature and sculpture (choice A). He mentions the friendship between the United States and France only to set up a contrast with the newer meaning of the statue (choice C). And he discusses the poem to show a similarity, not a difference, between Mount Rushmore and the Statue of Liberty, that similarity being the fact that the symbolism of both monuments has shifted over time.

28. **C** You are asked to listen again to part of the lecture and to decide what the professor is implying about the poem.

Back in 1883, Emma Lazarus wrote that famous poem—you know, the one that goes: "Give me your tired, your poor . . . " and so on and so forth.

This is a Making Inferences question. To arrive at the correct answer (choice C), you must understand that the expression "so on and so forth" is typically used when a listener does not need any further information to understand what the speaker is referring to. In this case, the professor assumes that the students are very familiar with the poem, so he does not need to recite more than the first few words of it.

Speaking

Listening Scripts, Important Points, and Sample Responses with Rater Comments

Use the sample Independent and Integrated Speaking rubrics on pages 180–183 to see how responses are scored. The raters who listen to your responses will analyze them in three general categories. These categories are Delivery, Language Use, and Topic Development. All three categories have equal importance.

This section includes important points that should be covered when answering each question. All of these points must be present in a response in order for it to receive the highest score in the Topic Development category. These important points are guides to the kind of information raters expect to hear in a high-level response.

This section also refers to example responses on the accompanying audio tracks. Some responses were scored at the highest level, while others were not. The responses are followed by comments from certified ETS raters.

Question 1: Paired Choice

Track 44 Listening Script

Narrator

Some students would prefer to live with roommates. Others would prefer to live alone. Which option would you prefer and why?

> **Preparation Time: 15 Seconds**
> **Response Time: 45 Seconds**

Important Points

In this question, you need to state whether you, as a student, would prefer to live with roommates or live alone, and then you need to explain your preference. You should explain your reason or reasons fully and clearly, using details and examples where you can. For instance, you could say you prefer to live with a roommate and then explain one or two reasons, such as having someone to discuss problems with, being able to share the cooking and cleaning, or avoiding loneliness. If you want to talk about the advantages or disadvantages of *both* options and say they are equally good, that is permissible. However, it might be more difficult for you to finish discussing both options in the time allowed.

Sample Responses

Play Track 49 to hear a high-level response for Question 1.

Rater Comments

This speaker's response presents a clear progression of ideas. He chooses to discuss an advantage of living with a roommate before he describes the disadvantages, which, to him, are stronger than the advantage. He gives an example of how a roommate might be a problem, then states his preference—living alone—and relates it to his personal experience. His pronunciation is easy to understand, and he speaks very fluently. A few of his word choices are not precise, but this would not prevent a listener from understanding his ideas.

Play Track 50 to hear a low-level response for Question 1.

Rater Comments

For the first part of his response, the speaker is only reading the question aloud and not actually answering it. His pronunciation is strongly affected by his first language, so the listener must make a great effort to try to understand what he is saying. His response is marked by long pauses as he tries to think of the next word to say, indicating that he possesses a very limited English vocabulary. The lowest level of the rubric describes the characteristics of this response.

Question 2: Fit and Explain

Track 45 Listening Script

Narrator

Read the article from the university newspaper about the plan to build new student housing. You will have 50 seconds to read the article. Begin reading now.

> **Reading Time: 50 Seconds**

University May Build New Student Apartments Off Campus

The Department of Student Housing is considering whether to build new student housing off campus in a residential area of town. Two of the major factors influencing the decision will be parking and space. Those who support building off campus argue that building new housing on campus would further increase the number of cars on and around campus and consume space that could be better used for future projects that the entire university community could benefit from. Supporters also say that students might even have a richer college experience by being connected to the local community and patronizing stores and other businesses in town.

Narrator

Now listen to two students discussing the article.

Woman

I can't believe these plans. It just doesn't make sense to me.

Man

Really? Seemed OK to me, especially the argument about the cars.

Woman

Yeah, I know. But the thing is, it doesn't matter where students live 'cause they still have to get to class somehow, right? At least if they built new dorms on campus, students would use campus transportation . . .

Man

. . . instead of their cars. I see what you're getting at. If they live off campus, they're *still* going to have to drive and park on campus. Might even create more traffic.

Woman

Exactly.

Man

OK. Still, though . . . the point about students interacting more with people in the community: that doesn't seem to be a bad thing, does it?

Woman

But the more time spent off campus, in town, the less time spent on campus. What about all the clubs, shows, discussions, a—all the campus happenings that just kind of . . . happen? It's important to be *on* campus to really take advantage of these things. Having a different living experience shouldn't be given up at the expense of not being as much a part of the *university* community.

Narrator

The woman expresses her opinion of the university's plan. State her opinion and explain the reasons she gives for holding that opinion.

Preparation Time: 30 Seconds
Response Time: 60 Seconds

Important Points

The woman disagrees with the housing department's plan to build new student housing off campus. She thinks students will still have to drive to campus to get to class, so there will not be any decrease in the number of cars around campus. She also thinks students will miss opportunities to be involved in on-campus activities, which are just as important as the experience of living in town.

Sample Responses

Play Track 51 to hear a high-level response for Question 2.

Rater Comments

The speaker gives a sustained, coherent response that accurately and efficiently explains the woman's opinion of the main points of the newspaper article. He did not waste time by including unimportant details from the conversation or reading. His pacing is fluid, and he demonstrates good control of a variety of grammatical structures and vocabulary. His pronunciation is exceptionally clear.

Play Track 52 to hear a mid-level response for Question 2.

Rater Comments

This speaker covers all the important points of the woman's opinion. However, the speaker never states what the university plan is, so she does not make it entirely clear what, in general, the woman in the conversation is disagreeing with. Her response contains some minor errors in word choice, such as *assist* rather than *attend*, but overall she demonstrates good control of both vocabulary and grammar. Her pacing is usually steady, though with a number of hesitations that require listener effort at times.

Question 3: General/Specific

Track 46 Listening Script

Narrator

Now read the passage about a topic in psychology. You will have 45 seconds to read the passage. Begin reading now.

Reading Time: 45 Seconds

Actor-Observer

People account for their own behavior differently from how they account for the behavior of others. When observing the behavior of others, we tend to attribute their actions to their character or their personality rather than to external factors. In contrast, we tend to explain our own behavior in terms of situational factors beyond our own control rather than attributing it to our own character. One explanation for this difference is that people are aware of the situational forces affecting them but not of situational forces affecting other people. Thus, when evaluating someone else's behavior, we focus on the person rather than the situation.

Narrator

Now listen to part of a lecture in a psychology class.

Professor

So we encounter this in life all the time, but many of us are unaware that we do this . . . even psychologists who study it . . . like me. For example, the other day I was at the store and I was getting in line to buy something. But just before I was actually in line, some guy comes out of nowhere and cuts right in front of me. Well, I was really annoyed and thought, "That was rude!" I assumed he was just a selfish, inconsiderate person when, in fact, I had no idea why he cut in line in front of me or whether he even realized he was doing it. Maybe he didn't think I was actually in line yet . . . But my immediate reaction was to assume he was a selfish or rude person.

OK, so a few days after that, I was at the store again. Only this time I was in a real hurry—I was late for an important meeting—and I was frustrated that everything was taking so long. And what's worse, all the checkout lines were long, and it seemed like everyone was moving so slowly. But then I saw a slightly shorter line! But some woman with a lot of stuff to buy was walking toward it, so I basically ran to get there first, before her, and, well, I did. Now, I didn't think of myself as a bad or rude person for doing this. I had an important meeting to get to—I was in a hurry, so, you know, I had done nothing wrong.

Narrator

Explain how the two examples discussed by the professor illustrate differences in the ways people explain behavior.

> **Preparation Time: 30 Seconds**
> **Response Time: 60 Seconds**

Important Points

We explain others' behavior differently from how we explain our own behavior. The professor describes how he thought that the man who cut ahead of him in line was a rude person. This example shows that we tend to explain the behavior of others by attributing it to their character or personality. Then the professor describes how he similarly cut into line but did not think of himself as rude, because he was late for a meeting. This illustrates how we explain our own behavior not in terms of our character, but by attributing it to situational factors.

Sample Responses

Play Track 53 to hear a high-level response for Question 3.

Rater Comments

This speaker clearly shows how the professor's examples illustrate the idea that we explain other people's behavior one way and our own behavior in a different way. He covers the main points efficiently in the time allotted. His response is sustained and fluid, and his pronunciation is easy to understand, with only occasional, minor difficulties. There are several minor grammatical errors that do not hinder understanding, and overall he demonstrates good control of grammatical structures.

Play Track 54 to hear a mid-level response for Question 3.

Rater Comments

The speaker is able to cover both of the professor's examples in a basic way, but he never clearly connects the second example to the concept from the reading (that people explain their own behavior based on situational factors, not character). His pronunciation is easy to understand, but his response is still difficult to follow at times because of his frequent hesitations.

Question 4: Summary

Track 47 Listening Script

Narrator

Now listen to part of a lecture in a child development class.

Professor

OK. Young children and art. Research suggests that learning art skills can benefit a young child's development. Umm . . . two of the ways it can do this is by providing a platform to express complex emotions and by encouraging persistence.

Now, what do I mean when I say "a platform to express complex emotions"? Young children have limited vocabulary. So how would they communicate the feeling of pride, for example? A drawing, though, making a drawing of feeling proud . . . this is something a young child could do. So a little girl might draw herself jumping up in the air next to her bike. In the drawing, her arms are raised up in the air and she's smiling. Children can communicate their emotions, whether positive or negative, through the drawing—mm—better than they could with words.

And encouraging persistence? Art skills can help children to develop patience and concentration to persist in an activity . . . the willingness to keep trying to reach a goal. So suppose there's a little boy who wants to mold a lump of clay into the shape of a car. The first attempt doesn't look too much like a car. He's disappointed but wants to try again. The second, third, fourth try still don't look quite right, but there's improvement with every attempt. So, after some time, he gets to the point where he's satisfied with his creation. The newly shaped clay car is an instant reminder of an accomplishment—a success resulting from his persistence. The boy may be able to transfer this lesson toward other situations and activities because, well, he's had the experience of successfully accomplishing a goal through hard work.

Narrator

Using points and examples from the talk, explain how learning art can impact a child's development.

| Preparation Time: 20 Seconds |
| Response Time: 60 Seconds |

Important Points

Learning art skills can have an important impact on the emotional development of young children in two ways. One is by helping them to express complex emotions. Drawing can, for example, help children express emotions that they cannot express in words. The little girl expressed pride when she drew a picture of herself looking proud of learning to ride a bike.

The second way art can help young children is by teaching them persistence. After spending time perfecting an art piece—such as the little boy sculpting a car out of clay—they can see their success.

Sample Responses

Play Track 55 to hear a high-level response for Question 4.

Rater Comments

This speaker efficiently summarizes the key points from the lecture in order to explain how learning art skills can influence a child's development. His speech is highly intelligible and fluid, though there are a few minor lapses in flow. His response also demonstrates good control of both basic and more complex grammatical structures as used in spoken language.

Play Track 56 to hear a mid-level response for Question 4.

Rater Comments

The speaker makes major errors in content as he attempts to summarize the lecture. He does not mention the second point—that learning the value of persistence is one of the ways that art can help children's emotional development. Also, his summary of the first point is inaccurate; he confuses the example for the second point with the example for the first point (helping children express emotions). His pronunciation is generally clear, but his response lacks full coherence; it is not always easy to see how one idea connects to the next.

Writing

Listening Script, Topic Notes, and Sample Responses with Rater Comments

Use the Integrated Writing and Independent Writing scoring rubrics on pages 193–194 and 203–204 to see how responses are scored.

Writing Based on Reading and Listening

Track 48 Listening Script

Narrator

Now listen to part of a lecture on the topic you just read about.

Professor

Lately, we've been seeing some professors on television. Though it's sometimes claimed to be a good thing, we should question whether anybody really benefits from it. First of all, it's not good for the professors themselves—not from a professional standpoint. Rightly or wrongly, a professor who appears on TV tends to get the reputation among fellow professors of being someone who is not a serious scholar—someone who chooses to entertain rather than to educate. And for that reason, TV professors may not be invited to important conferences—important meetings to discuss their academic work. They may even have difficulty getting money to do research. So for professors, being a TV celebrity has important disadvantages.

A second point is that being on TV can take a lot of a professor's time—not just the time on TV but also time figuring out what to present and time spent rehearsing, travel time, even time getting made up to look good for the cameras. And all this time comes out of the time the professor can spend doing research, meeting with students, and attending to university business. So you can certainly see there are problems for the university and its students when professors are in the TV studio and not on campus.

So who does benefit? The public? Umm . . . that's not so clear either. Look, professors do have a lot of knowledge to offer, but TV networks don't want really serious, in-depth academic lectures for after-dinner viewing. What the networks want is the academic title, not the intellectual substance. The material that professors usually present on TV—such as background on current events, or some brief historical introduction to a new movie version of a great literary work—this material is not much different from what viewers would get from a TV reporter who had done a little homework.

Narrator

Summarize the points made in the lecture, being sure to explain how they oppose specific points made in the reading passage.

Topic Notes

You should understand the reasons presented in the lecture for why it is not necessarily good that professors appear on television. The lecturer questions each of the benefits mentioned in the reading passage: about the professor's reputation, about the professor's time, and about educating the public.

A high-scoring response will include the following points made by the lecturer that address the points made in the reading passage:

Point Made in the Reading Passage	Contrasting Point from the Lecture
TV appearances improve the professor's reputation.	1. Their reputation suffers, because they are considered entertainers by their peers and not serious scholars. 2. As a result, they may get fewer invitations to academic conferences or lose research funding.
TV appearances benefit the university and lead to more student applications and more donations.	Professors spend a lot of time preparing for the TV appearances, which takes away from their true academic work, such as teaching and doing research.
TV appearances benefit the public because the public is exposed to more in-depth knowledge about a subject.	Professors generally do not give in-depth academic lectures on TV.

Responses with scores of 4 and 5 generally clearly discuss all three of the main points in the table.

Sample Responses with Rater Comments

High-Level Response

> The passage introduced three reasons why professors should appear on TV: gaining reputation for the professor, for the college, and to educate the general public. However, the lecture disagrees.
>
> Professors who appear frequently on TV are not generally viewed as a serious scholar. As a result, those professors will receive less invitation to attend academic conferences or less likely to receive research grant. This seriously hinders the professor's opportunity to further grow as a researcher
>
> Professors who frequently appear on TV also has negative effect on students and the university. Appearing on TV takes a lot of time to prepare, including preperation for the material, transportation time, and even time to dress up. This precious time can also be

used to teach class, help students, or even do further research. As a result, professors who appear on TV waste a lot of time that they can contribute to teaching and research.

Professors appearing on TV doesn't usually help educating the general public. The TV network is not interested in having the professor explaining the intellectual substances of their researches. Rather, they are interested in having them explain some basic background information or history. This type of information can be easily presented by a serious reporter who has done his work properly.

Because of the above reasons, it is highly questionable whether professors appearing on TV has any advantage. In fact, it could bring negative consequence both to the professors themselves and the universities they teach.

Rater Comments

This response successfully conveys all three of the main points from the lecture. The response is well organized and developed. Explicit connection between the reading passage and the lecture is explained in the first and final paragraphs. In each body paragraph, the writer opens with a topic sentence that captures how the lecture point opposes the point made in the reading passage in general, and the writer proceeds to develop the lecturer's point using relevant details and examples. The language used by the writer is not perfect; there are minor grammatical errors in subject-verb agreement and preposition use ("Professors . . . has negative effect," "preperation for the material," "the universities they teach"). However, note that the Scoring Guide for the integrated task allows even level 5 responses to contain occasional minor errors that do not result in inaccurate or imprecise presentation of content or connections. The errors in this response do not interfere with meaning or disrupt the flow of the response.

Mid-Level Response

The question which is asked is to know if the apparition of a professor on television is a good or a bad think? On this point, the text and the lecture completely disagree.

First, we can think that it is a good thing for the professors themselves. It seems to be something logical because today a lot of people want to be known and the television is perhaps the best thing to be known. But what the lecture say is that such a professor don't have a good reputation. People think they are not very serious when they pass on television. The effect is that they are no more invited to important conferences.

In what concerned the students and the university, the text shows the facts that some of these apparitions can bring some donation to the university, what is very good. But in the other hand according to the lecture, this professor spend a lot of time travelling and during that time, he isn't available for the students or for the researches and the university lose therefore some money.

Finally for the public himself, they could learn some interesting things and it could be a very big chance because a lot of these persons haven't had the chance going in the university. But it is true that such intervention isn't often best as something that a journalist could prepare.

Rater Comments

The writer organizes the response fairly well. After a brief introduction, each reading passage point is briefly summarized and then followed by ideas from the related point in the lecture. However, the response earns a mid-level score because the writer's summaries of the lecture suffer from several problems. There is imprecision (the idea that "people" rather than fellow academics think the professor appearing on television is not serious); there is omission (the idea that television networks are not interested in in-depth lectures is missing); and there is poor connection of ideas (the idea that a university loses "some money" is not connected to the idea that television appearances take away from professors' time at the university). Most importantly, there are lapses of clarity due to the writer's poor language control. Errors in word choice ("pass on television," "intervention isn't often best as something") obscure meaning to such an extent that the lecturer's response to the first point is conveyed only vaguely, and the response to the last point is completely unclear. Although the writer of this response may have had a good grasp of many ideas he or she wanted to write about, he or she failed to communicate those ideas clearly to the reader.

Writing Based on Knowledge and Experience

Question

Do you agree or disagree with the following statement?

Young people enjoy life more than older people do.

Use specific reasons and examples to support your answer. Be sure to use your own words. Do **not** use memorized examples.

Topic Notes

This topic requires you to write about whether young people enjoy life more than older people do. If you agree with this statement, you should present examples and reasons. For example, young people may tend to go out more and participate in fun activities while older people may tend to stay at home more. Another reason that older people may enjoy life less is because they have more responsibilities and pressure from work, family, and money than young people. A third reason might be that young people are more physically fit and able to enjoy more activities than older people.

If you disagree with this statement in your response, you should present examples and reasons that older people enjoy life more. For example, older people may better know what satisfies them and makes them happy than young people do.

Some good responses explain that the group that enjoys life more depends on where they live. All of these approaches can be developed into a good response.

Sample Responses with Rater Comments

High-Level Essay

People often complain about seing themselves becoming older too quickly. But does that mean that they are enjoying their lives less than they did before? Personally, I rather disagree with this statement. It would probably be more accurate to say that every time of a person's life is worth being lived and enjoyed.

There is no denying that young people have far less responsibilities with, for instance, family and work. Thus, they can spend more time on their hobbies than people who are working all day long and who have to care about their children at night when they come home. But one cannot overlook that having a family to care about can be considered as a satisfying pleasure in itself. Besides, many people find fullfillment in their work and enjoy spending most of their time on it.

Moreover, it is customary to say that older people tend to have more health problems than teenagers or students do. However, it is well worth noticing that this assertion cannot be taken as a general rule, as also many young people develop painfull illnesses. A striking example of a disease which tends to affect more and more teenagers is back ache, because they are sitting for too long periods of time and doing too little sport to compensate. Consequently, the argument supporting that good health makes life more enjoyable when you are young may be called into question.

In addition to that, one should not forget that today's teenagers are expected to take important decisions about their future at an early age, and that they have to cope with heavy responsibilities even before getting their first school degree. As it becomes more and more difficult to find a job these days, young people have to worry about what to study and they even often have to fix priorities according to what the job market offers, and not according to their personal preferences.

Last but not least, one cannot forget that after working hard for long years, people retire and are then given the chance to concentrate on their centers of interest and hobbies again. Up to a certain point, when taking into account the arguments of the previous paragraph concerning the early responsibilities teenagers have to assume, pensioners are even more free to enjoy their lives without thinking of potential problems of the future.

To put it in a nutshell, that all amounts to saying that there is no period of time in a person's life which is more prone to hapiness than the others. People only have to learn to make the best of every situation and of what they have . . . even if it is easier said than done!

Rater Comments

This well-structured essay meets all the criteria needed to earn a high score. It takes issue with the statement presented. It first develops its points somewhat inductively. In paragraph 2, it presents reasons why younger people may enjoy life more (fewer responsibilities) but ends by explaining why these same responsibilities can be fulfilling for older people. Paragraph 3 advances the claim that older people have more health problems and goes on to explain that young people can have health issues as well. The last point developed in paragraphs 4 and 5 discusses how younger people have to worry about their studies and their future, while older people who are retired are free to enjoy their lives—their hobbies and interests. Sentence structures are varied and complex, and the response displays good vocabulary choice; these allow the writer to convey meaning accurately. There is a minor organizational issue: the writer makes the statement in the introductory paragraph, "It would probably be more accurate to say that every time of a person's life is worth being lived and enjoyed," and also concludes with this same notion. This is a bit misleading because the focus of the body paragraphs is not on enjoyment at all stages of life—much is discussed about things that are not so pleasant at particular times of life. However, this misleading statement is not a major issue, and the bulk of the essay is a well-organized, coherent discussion of why it cannot be said that younger people enjoy life more than older people do.

Mid-Level Essay

Nowadays, young people have a lot of opportunities to enjoy life, more than older people have known when they were young. Thought, values especially in the way to bring up children have changed. I think that young people enjoy life more than older people do for that reason and for several others. Young people are usually in good health, so they have more envy to live their life, more than older people who may have health problems or do not want to have too much activities. It is obvious that young people have time to enjoy their life, they are still on studies so they can have several activities, they have the possibility to do a lot of new experiences. Older people usually have a job and a family to look after, thet cannot do what they want, they have to give stability to them and their family. Nomad people are often single, it is difficult to enjoy your life free when you have assignements.

Moreover, when you are young you are very curious, interested by all you may learn. It is the exemple of the young child who wants to discover his environment. Generally, older people have already done a lot of things in their life such as sports, travels . . .

Young people want to learn others things, they like to meet with friends to go to cinema or to museum. The best way to discover other cultures is obviously to travel to foreign countries and meet locals to understand their culturs without judgments. I think the best way to discover other countries is to travel to them or to study during a year in them. Study abroad is a very exciting experience during which you can learn a lot, especially on yourself. I think it makes you grow up. You have to be adaptive, to ask you questions . . .

Finally, young people are incitated to move, to enjoy their lives through media, who help them to wide their mind to discovers and to other cultures. It is fundamental to young to discover all the world and open them to others, it should be a way to give them the possibility to continue to enjoy their life when they will be older.

Rater Comments

This essay earns a mid-level score because it lacks development of its key points. The writer lists a number of reasons to support the idea that younger people enjoy life more than older people do. Some of these reasons are fairly clear, but they are not substantiated by concrete examples that can be readily understood as supporting the overall idea the writer presents in the first two sentences. It is not clear how the example of nomadic people relates to the idea that older people have more responsibilities. The most developed paragraph, about meeting friends and traveling abroad, has a number of ideas relevant to the question asked, but it is fairly difficult to understand how the ideas within the paragraph are connected. It is also difficult to see how all of the information is related to the topic or the writer's opinion overall. For example, the writer does not explain how the statements that older people may have missed opportunities when they were young ties into the writer's point. While much of the essay's meaning is clear, this response is marked by some errors in grammar and word choice ("incitated to move," "wide their mind"), and some of these are very difficult to understand ("more envy to live").

Authentic *TOEFL iBT*®
Practice Test 3

本章是托福考试四套真题练习中的第三套。考生可以通过两种不同的方式进行测试：

- 通过本书：在接下来的书页中，考生可以看到所有的测试题目，请将答案写在规定的空白处。关于本测试中的听力部分，考生可以按照序号提示，播放对应音频。

- 在电脑上：为了更真实地体验托福考试的实考环境，考生可以下载电脑版软件在电脑上进行模考。电脑版软件中的试题与书中的完全一样。阅读文章和相关问题将显示在屏幕上，考生可以点击给出的空白处输入答案。听力部分的测试则根据提示进行。

测试题目之后是答案和评分信息，以及听力部分的文字材料。除此以外，考生还可以看到答案的详细解释、口语回答样本和写作范文。

TOEFL iBT® Practice Test 3
READING

This section measures your ability to understand academic passages in English. You will have **54 minutes** to read and answer questions about **3 passages**. A clock at the top of the screen will display the starting time as **00 : 54 : 00** and show you how much time is remaining.

Most questions are worth 1 point, but the last question for each passage is worth more than 1 point. The directions for the last question indicate how many points you may receive.

Some passages in the computer-based test include a word or phrase that is underlined in blue. When you click on the word or phrase underlined in blue, you will see a verbal or visual definition of the word or term. In this book, those definitions are provided as endnotes below the reading passage.

Within this section, you can move to the next question by clicking on **Next**. You can skip questions and go back to them later as long as there is time remaining. If you want to return to previous questions, click on **Back**. You can click on **Review** at any time and the review screen will show you which questions you have answered and which you have not answered. From this review screen, you may go directly to any question you have already seen in the Reading section.

During this practice test, you may click the **Pause** icon at any time. This will stop the test until you decide to continue. You may continue the test in a few minutes or at any time during the period that your test is activated.

You will now begin the Reading section. Again, in an actual test you will have **54 minutes** to read the 3 passages and answer the questions. NOTE: In an actual test, some test takers might receive 4 passages; those test takers will have 72 minutes (1 hour and 12 minutes) to answer the questions.

Turn the page to begin the Reading section.

ARCHITECTURE

Architecture is the art and science of designing structures that organize and enclose space for practical and symbolic purposes. Because architecture grows out of human needs and aspirations, it clearly communicates cultural values. Of all the visual arts, architecture affects our lives most directly for it determines the character of the human environment in major ways.

Architecture is a three-dimensional form. It utilizes space, mass, texture, line, light, and color. To be architecture, a building must achieve a working harmony with a variety of elements. Humans instinctively seek structures that will shelter and enhance their way of life. It is the work of architects to create buildings that are not simply constructions but also offer inspiration and delight. Buildings contribute to human life when they provide shelter, enrich space, complement their site, suit the climate, and are economically feasible. The client who pays for the building and defines its function is an important member of the architectural team. The mediocre design of many contemporary buildings can be traced to both clients and architects.

In order for the structure to achieve the size and strength necessary to meet its purpose, architecture employs methods of support that, because they are based on physical laws, have changed little since people first discovered them—even while building materials have changed dramatically. The world's architectural structures have also been devised in relation to the objective limitations of materials. Structures can be analyzed in terms of how they deal with downward forces created by gravity. They are designed to withstand the forces of *compression* (pushing together), *tension* (pulling apart), *bending*, or a combination of these in different parts of the structure.

Every development in architecture has been the result of major technological changes. Materials and methods of construction are integral parts of the design of architectural structures. In earlier times it was necessary to design structural systems suitable for the materials that were available, such as wood, stone, or brick. Today technology has progressed to the point where it is possible to invent new building materials to suit the type of structure desired. Enormous changes in materials and techniques of construction within the last few generations have made it possible to enclose space with much greater ease and speed and with a minimum of material. Progress in this area can be measured by the difference in weight between buildings built now and those of comparable size built one hundred years ago.

Modern architectural forms generally have three separate components comparable to elements of the human body: a supporting *skeleton* or frame, an outer *skin* enclosing the interior spaces, and *equipment*, similar to the body's vital organs and systems. The equipment includes plumbing, electrical wiring, hot water, and air-conditioning. Of course in early architecture—such as igloos and adobe structures—there was no such equipment, and the skeleton and skin were often one.

Much of the world's great architecture has been constructed of stone because of its beauty, permanence, and availability. In the past, whole cities grew from the arduous task of cutting and piling stone upon stone. Some of the world's finest stone architecture can be seen in the ruins of the ancient Inca city of Machu Picchu high in the eastern Andes Mountains of Peru. The doorways and windows are made possible by placing over the open spaces thick stone beams that support the weight from above. A structural invention had to be made before the physical limitations of stone could be overcome and new architectural forms could be created. That invention was the *arch*, a curved structure originally made of separate stone or brick segments. The arch was used by the early cultures of the Mediterranean area chiefly for underground drains, but it was the Romans who first developed and used the arch extensively in aboveground structures. Roman builders perfected the semicircular arch made of separate blocks of stone. As a method of spanning space, the arch can support greater weight than a horizontal beam. It works in compression to divert the weight above it out to the sides, where the weight is borne by the vertical elements on either side of the arch. The arch is among the many important structural breakthroughs that have characterized architecture throughout the centuries.

Directions: Now answer the questions.

PARAGRAPH 1

Architecture is the art and science of designing structures that organize and enclose space for practical and symbolic purposes. Because architecture grows out of human needs and aspirations, it clearly communicates cultural values. Of all the visual arts, architecture affects our lives most directly for it determines the character of the human environment in major ways.

1. According to paragraph 1, all of the following statements about architecture are true EXCEPT:

   (A) Architecture is a visual art.
   (B) Architecture reflects the cultural values of its creators.
   (C) Architecture has both artistic and scientific dimensions.
   (D) Architecture has an indirect effect on life.

PARAGRAPH 2

Architecture is a three-dimensional form. It utilizes space, mass, texture, line, light, and color. To be architecture, a building must achieve a working harmony with a variety of elements. Humans instinctively seek structures that will shelter and enhance their way of life. It is the work of architects to create buildings that are not simply constructions but also offer inspiration and delight. Buildings contribute to human life when they provide shelter, enrich space, complement their site, suit the climate, and are economically feasible. The client who pays for the building and defines its function is an important member of the architectural team. The mediocre design of many contemporary buildings can be traced to both clients and architects.

2. The word "enhance" in the passage is closest in meaning to

   (A) protect
   (B) improve
   (C) organize
   (D) match

GO ON TO THE NEXT PAGE

P A R A G R A P H 3

In order for the structure to achieve the size and strength necessary to meet its purpose, architecture employs methods of support that, because they are based on physical laws, have changed little since people first discovered them—even while building materials have changed dramatically. The world's architectural structures have also been devised in relation to the objective limitations of materials. Structures can be analyzed in terms of how they deal with downward forces created by gravity. They are designed to withstand the forces of *compression* (pushing together), *tension* (pulling apart), *bending*, or a combination of these in different parts of the structure.

3. Which of the sentences below best expresses the essential information in the highlighted sentence in the passage? Incorrect choices change the meaning in important ways or leave out essential information.

Ⓐ Unchanging physical laws have limited the size and strength of buildings that can be made with materials discovered long ago.

Ⓑ Building materials have changed in order to increase architectural size and strength, but physical laws of structure have not changed.

Ⓒ When people first started to build, the structural methods used to provide strength and size were inadequate because they were not based on physical laws.

Ⓓ Unlike building materials, the methods of support used in architecture have not changed over time because they are based on physical laws.

P A R A G R A P H 4

Every development in architecture has been the result of major technological changes. Materials and methods of construction are integral parts of the design of architectural structures. In earlier times it was necessary to design structural systems suitable for the materials that were available, such as wood, stone, or brick. Today technology has progressed to the point where it is possible to invent new building materials to suit the type of structure desired. Enormous changes in materials and techniques of construction within the last few generations have made it possible to enclose space with much greater ease and speed and with a minimum of material. Progress in this area can be measured by the difference in weight between buildings built now and those of comparable size built one hundred years ago.

4. The word "integral" is closest in meaning to

Ⓐ essential
Ⓑ variable
Ⓒ practical
Ⓓ independent

5. According to paragraph 4, which of the following is true about materials used in the construction of buildings?

    (A) Because new building materials are hard to find, construction techniques have changed very little from past generations.

    (B) The availability of suitable building materials no longer limits the types of structures that may be built.

    (C) The primary building materials that are available today are wood, stone, and brick.

    (D) Architects in earlier times did not have enough building materials to enclose large spaces.

6. In paragraph 4, what does the author imply about modern buildings?

    (A) They occupy much less space than buildings constructed one hundred years ago.

    (B) They are not very different from the buildings of a few generations ago.

    (C) They weigh less in relation to their size than buildings constructed one hundred years ago.

    (D) They take a long time to build as a result of their complex construction methods.

PARAGRAPH 6

Much of the world's great architecture has been constructed of stone because of its beauty, permanence, and availability. In the past, whole cities grew from the arduous task of cutting and piling stone upon stone. Some of the world's finest stone architecture can be seen in the ruins of the ancient Inca city of Machu Picchu high in the eastern Andes Mountains of Peru. The doorways and windows are made possible by placing over the open spaces thick stone beams that support the weight from above. A structural invention had to be made before the physical limitations of stone could be overcome and new architectural forms could be created. That invention was the *arch*, a curved structure originally made of separate stone or brick segments. The arch was used by the early cultures of the Mediterranean area chiefly for underground drains, but it was the Romans who first developed and used the arch extensively in aboveground structures. Roman builders perfected the semicircular arch made of separate blocks of stone. As a method of spanning space, the arch can support greater weight than a horizontal beam. It works in compression to divert the weight above it out to the sides, where the weight is borne by the vertical elements on either side of the arch. The arch is among the many important structural breakthroughs that have characterized architecture throughout the centuries.

7. Why does the author include a description of how the "doorways and windows" of Machu Picchu were constructed?

    (A) To indicate that the combined skeletons and skins of the stone buildings of Machu Picchu were similar to igloos and adobe structures

    (B) To indicate the different kinds of stones that had to be cut to build Machu Picchu

    (C) To provide an illustration of the kind of construction that was required before arches were invented

    (D) To explain how ancient builders reduced the amount of time necessary to construct buildings from stone

GO ON TO THE NEXT PAGE

8. According to paragraph 6, which of the following statements is true of the arch?

   (A) The Romans were the first people to use the stone arch.
   (B) The invention of the arch allowed new architectural forms to be developed.
   (C) The arch worked by distributing the structural load of a building toward the center of the arch.
   (D) The Romans followed earlier practices in their use of arches.

PARAGRAPHS 4, 5 AND 6

Progress in this area can be measured by the difference in weight between buildings built now and those of comparable size built one hundred years ago. **(A)** Modern architectural forms generally have three separate components comparable to elements of the human body: a supporting *skeleton* or frame, an outer *skin* enclosing the interior spaces, and *equipment*, similar to the body's vital organs and systems. **(B)** The equipment includes plumbing, electrical wiring, hot water, and air-conditioning. **(C)** Of course in early architecture—such as igloos and adobe structures—there was no such equipment, and the skeleton and skin were often one. **(D)**

Much of the world's great architecture has been constructed of stone because of its beauty, permanence, and availability.

9. **Directions:** Look at the part of the passage that is displayed above. The letters **(A)**, **(B)**, **(C)**, and **(D)** indicate where the following sentence could be added.

   However, some modern architectural designs, such as those using folded plates of concrete or air-inflated structures, are again unifying skeleton and skin.

   Where would the sentence best fit?
   (A) Choice A
   (B) Choice B
   (C) Choice C
   (D) Choice D

10. **Directions:** An introductory sentence for a brief summary of the passage is provided below. Complete the summary by selecting the THREE answer choices that express the most important ideas in the passage. Some answer choices do not belong in the summary because they express ideas that are not presented in the passage or are minor ideas in the passage. **This question is worth 2 points.**

Architecture uses forms and space to express cultural values.

-
-
-

Answer Choices

A Architects seek to create buildings that are both visually appealing and well suited for human use.

B Both clients and architects are responsible for the mediocre designs of some modern buildings.

C Over the course of the history of building, innovations in materials and methods of construction have given architects ever greater freedom to express themselves.

D Modern buildings tend to lack the beauty of ancient stone buildings such as those of Machu Picchu.

E Throughout history buildings have been constructed like human bodies, needing distinct "organ" systems in order to function.

F The discovery and use of the arch typifies the way in which architecture advances by developing more efficient types of structures.

GO ON TO THE NEXT PAGE

THE LONG-TERM STABILITY OF ECOSYSTEMS

Plant communities assemble themselves flexibly, and their particular structure depends on the specific history of the area. Ecologists use the term "succession" to refer to the changes that happen in plant communities and ecosystems over time. The first community in a succession is called a pioneer community, while the long-lived community at the end of succession is called a climax community. Pioneer and successional plant communities are said to change over periods from 1 to 500 years. These changes—in plant numbers and the mix of species—are cumulative. Climax communities themselves change but over periods of time greater than about 500 years.

An ecologist who studies a pond today may well find it relatively unchanged in a year's time. Individual fish may be replaced, but the number of fish will tend to be the same from one year to the next. We can say that the properties of an ecosystem are more stable than the individual organisms that compose the ecosystem.

At one time, ecologists believed that species diversity made ecosystems stable. They believed that the greater the diversity the more stable the ecosystem. Support for this idea came from the observation that long-lasting climax communities usually have more complex food webs and more species diversity than pioneer communities. Ecologists concluded that the apparent stability of climax ecosystems depended on their complexity. To take an extreme example, farmlands dominated by a single crop are so unstable that one year of bad weather or the invasion of a single pest can destroy the entire crop. In contrast, a complex climax community, such as a temperate forest, will tolerate considerable damage from weather or pests.

The question of ecosystem stability is complicated, however. The first problem is that ecologists do not all agree what "stability" means. Stability can be defined as simply lack of change. In that case, the climax community would be considered the most stable, since, by definition, it changes the least over time. Alternatively, stability can be defined as the speed with which an ecosystem returns to a particular form following a major disturbance, such as a fire. This kind of stability is also called *resilience*. In that case, climax communities would be the most fragile and the *least* stable, since they can require hundreds of years to return to the climax state.

Even the kind of stability defined as simple lack of change is not always associated with maximum diversity. At least in temperate zones, maximum diversity is often found in mid-successional stages, not in the climax community. Once a redwood forest matures, for example, the kinds of species and the number of individuals growing on the forest floor are reduced. In general, diversity, by itself, does not ensure stability. Mathematical models of ecosystems likewise suggest that diversity does not guarantee ecosystem stability—just the opposite, in fact. A more complicated system is, in general, more likely than a simple system to break down. (A fifteen-speed racing bicycle is more likely to break down than a child's tricycle.)

Ecologists are especially interested in knowing what factors contribute to the resilience of communities because climax communities all over the world are being severely damaged or destroyed by human activities. The destruction caused by the volcanic explosion of Mount St. Helens, in the northwestern United States, for example, pales in comparison to the destruction caused by humans. We need to know what aspects of a community are most important to the community's resistance to destruction, as well as its recovery.

Many ecologists now think that the relative long-term stability of climax communities comes not from diversity but from the "patchiness" of the environment; an environment that varies from place to place supports more kinds of organisms than an environment that is uniform. A local population that goes extinct is quickly replaced by immigrants from an adjacent community. Even if the new population is of a different species, it can approximately fill the niche vacated by the extinct population and keep the food web intact.

Directions: Now answer the questions.

PARAGRAPH 1

Plant communities assemble themselves flexibly, and their particular structure depends on the specific history of the area. Ecologists use the term "succession" to refer to the changes that happen in plant communities and ecosystems over time. The first community in a succession is called a pioneer community, while the long-lived community at the end of succession is called a climax community. Pioneer and successional plant communities are said to change over periods from 1 to 500 years. These changes—in plant numbers and the mix of species—are cumulative. Climax communities themselves change but over periods of time greater than about 500 years.

1. The word "particular" in the passage is closest in meaning to
    (A) natural
    (B) final
    (C) specific
    (D) complex

PARAGRAPH 2

An ecologist who studies a pond today may well find it relatively unchanged in a year's time. Individual fish may be replaced, but the number of fish will tend to be the same from one year to the next. We can say that the properties of an ecosystem are more stable than the individual organisms that compose the ecosystem.

2. According to paragraph 2, which of the following principles of ecosystems can be learned by studying a pond?
    (A) Ecosystem properties change more slowly than individuals in the system.
    (B) The stability of an ecosystem tends to change as individuals are replaced.
    (C) Individual organisms are stable from one year to the next.
    (D) A change in the numbers of an organism does not affect an ecosystem's properties.

GO ON TO THE NEXT PAGE

P
A
R
A
G
R
A
P
H

4

The question of ecosystem stability is complicated, however. The first problem is that ecologists do not all agree what "stability" means. Stability can be defined as simply lack of change. In that case, the climax community would be considered the most stable, since, by definition, it changes the least over time. Alternatively, stability can be defined as the speed with which an ecosystem returns to a particular form following a major disturbance, such as a fire. This kind of stability is also called *resilience*. In that case, climax communities would be the most fragile and the *least* stable, since they can require hundreds of years to return to the climax state.

3. According to paragraph 4, why is the question of ecosystem stability complicated?

 Ⓐ The reasons for ecosystem change are not always clear.
 Ⓑ Ecologists often confuse the word "stability" with the word "resilience."
 Ⓒ The exact meaning of the word "stability" is debated by ecologists.
 Ⓓ There are many different answers to ecological questions.

4. According to paragraph 4, which of the following is true of climax communities?

 Ⓐ They are more resilient than pioneer communities.
 Ⓑ They can be considered both the most and the least stable communities.
 Ⓒ They are stable because they recover quickly after major disturbances.
 Ⓓ They are the most resilient communities because they change the least over time.

P
A
R
A
G
R
A
P
H

5

Even the kind of stability defined as simple lack of change is not always associated with maximum diversity. At least in temperate zones, maximum diversity is often found in mid-successional stages, not in the climax community. Once a redwood forest matures, for example, the kinds of species and the number of individuals growing on the forest floor are reduced. In general, diversity, by itself, does not ensure stability. Mathematical models of ecosystems likewise suggest that diversity does not guarantee ecosystem stability—just the opposite, in fact. A more complicated system is, in general, more likely than a simple system to break down. (A fifteen-speed racing bicycle is more likely to break down than a child's tricycle.)

5. Which of the following can be inferred from paragraph 5 about redwood forests?

 Ⓐ They become less stable as they mature.
 Ⓑ They support many species when they reach climax.
 Ⓒ They are found in temperate zones.
 Ⓓ They have reduced diversity during mid-successional stages.

6. In paragraph 5, why does the author provide the information that "A fifteen-speed racing bicycle is more likely to break down than a child's tricycle"?

   (A) To illustrate a general principle about the stability of systems by using an everyday example
   (B) To demonstrate that an understanding of stability in ecosystems can be applied to help understand stability in other situations
   (C) To make a comparison that supports the claim that, in general, stability increases with diversity
   (D) To provide an example that contradicts mathematical models of ecosystems

PARAGRAPH 7

Many ecologists now think that the relative long-term stability of climax communities comes not from diversity but from the "patchiness" of the environment; an environment that varies from place to place supports more kinds of organisms than an environment that is uniform. A local population that goes extinct is quickly replaced by immigrants from an adjacent community. Even if the new population is of a different species, it can approximately fill the niche vacated by the extinct population and keep the food web intact.

7. Which of the sentences below best expresses the essential information in the highlighted sentence in the passage? Incorrect choices change the meaning in important ways or leave out essential information.

   (A) Ecologists now think that the stability of an environment is a result of diversity rather than patchiness.
   (B) Patchy environments that vary from place to place do not often have high species diversity.
   (C) Uniform environments cannot be climax communities because they do not support as many types of organisms as patchy environments.
   (D) A patchy environment is thought to increase stability because it is able to support a wide variety of organisms.

8. The word "adjacent" in the passage is closest in meaning to

   (A) foreign
   (B) stable
   (C) fluid
   (D) neighboring

GO ON TO THE NEXT PAGE

P
A
R
A
G
R
A
P
H
S

5

6

A
N
D

7

A more complicated system is, in general, more likely than a simple system to break down. (A fifteen-speed racing bicycle is more likely to break down than a child's tricycle.) **(A)** Ecologists are especially interested in knowing what factors contribute to the resilience of communities because climax communities all over the world are being severely damaged or destroyed by human activities. **(B)** The destruction caused by the volcanic explosion of Mount St. Helens, in the northwestern United States, for example, pales in comparison to the destruction caused by humans. **(C)** We need to know what aspects of a community are most important to the community's resistance to destruction, as well as its recovery. **(D)**

Many ecologists now think that the relative long-term stability of climax communities comes not from diversity but from the "patchiness" of the environment; an environment that varies from place to place supports more kinds of organisms than an environment that is uniform.

9. **Directions:** Look at the part of the passage that is displayed above. The letters **(A)**, **(B)**, **(C)**, and **(D)** indicate where the following sentence could be added.

In fact, damage to the environment by humans is often much more severe than by natural events and processes.

Where would the sentence best fit?

- Ⓐ Choice A
- Ⓑ Choice B
- Ⓒ Choice C
- Ⓓ Choice D

10. **Directions:** An introductory sentence for a brief summary of the passage is provided below. Complete the summary by selecting the THREE answer choices that express the most important ideas in the passage. Some answer choices do not belong in the summary because they express ideas that are not presented in the passage or are minor ideas in the passage. **This question is worth 2 points.**

The process of succession and the stability of a climax community can change over time.

-
-
-

Answer Choices

A The changes that occur in an ecosystem from the pioneer to the climax community can be seen in one human generation.

B Ecologists agree that climax communities are the most stable types of ecosystems.

C A high degree of species diversity does not always result in a stable ecosystem.

D Disagreements over the meaning of the term "stability" make it difficult to identify the most stable ecosystems.

E The level of resilience in a plant community contributes to its long-term stability.

F The resilience of climax communities makes them resistant to destruction caused by humans.

GO ON TO THE NEXT PAGE ➤

DEPLETION OF THE OGALLALA AQUIFER

The vast grasslands of the High Plains in the central United States were settled by farmers and ranchers in the 1880s. This region has a semiarid climate, and for 50 years after its settlement, it supported a low-intensity agricultural economy of cattle ranching and wheat farming. In the early twentieth century, however, it was discovered that much of the High Plains was underlain by a huge aquifer (a rock layer containing large quantities of groundwater). This aquifer was named the Ogallala aquifer after the Ogallala Sioux Indians, who once inhabited the region.

The Ogallala aquifer is a sandstone formation that underlies some 583,000 square kilometers of land extending from northwestern Texas to southern South Dakota. Water from rains and melting snows has been accumulating in the Ogallala for the past 30,000 years. Estimates indicate that the aquifer contains enough water to fill Lake Huron, but unfortunately, under the semiarid climatic conditions that presently exist in the region, rates of addition to the aquifer are minimal, amounting to about half a centimeter a year.

The first wells were drilled into the Ogallala during the drought years of the early 1930s. The ensuing rapid expansion of irrigation agriculture, especially from the 1950s onward, transformed the economy of the region. More than 100,000 wells now tap the Ogallala. Modern irrigation devices, each capable of spraying 4.5 million liters of water a day, have produced a landscape dominated by geometric patterns of circular green islands of crops. Ogallala water has enabled the High Plains region to supply significant amounts of the cotton, sorghum, wheat, and corn grown in the United States. In addition, 40 percent of American grain-fed beef cattle are fattened here.

This unprecedented development of a finite groundwater resource with an almost negligible natural recharge rate—that is, virtually no natural water source to replenish the water supply—has caused water tables in the region to fall drastically. In the 1930s, wells encountered plentiful water at a depth of about 15 meters; currently, they must be dug to depths of 45 to 60 meters or more. In places, the water table is declining at a rate of a meter a year, necessitating the periodic deepening of wells and the use of ever-more-powerful pumps. It is estimated that at current withdrawal rates, much of the aquifer will run dry within 40 years. The situation is most critical in Texas, where the climate is driest, the greatest amount of water is being pumped, and the aquifer contains the least water. It is projected that the remaining Ogallala water will, by the year 2030, support only 35 to 40 percent of the irrigated acreage in Texas that it supported in 1980.

The reaction of farmers to the inevitable depletion of the Ogallala varies. Many have been attempting to conserve water by irrigating less frequently or by switching to crops that require less water. Others, however, have adopted the philosophy that it is best to use the water while it is still economically profitable to do so and to concentrate on high-value crops such as cotton. The incentive of the farmers who wish to conserve water is reduced by their knowledge that many of their neighbors are profiting by using great amounts of water, and in the process are drawing down the entire region's water supplies.

In the face of the upcoming water supply crisis, a number of grandiose schemes have been developed to transport vast quantities of water by canal or pipeline from the Mississippi, the Missouri, or the Arkansas rivers. Unfortunately, the cost of water obtained through any of these schemes would increase pumping costs at least tenfold, making the cost of irrigated agricultural products from the region uncompetitive on the national and international markets. Somewhat more promising have been recent experiments for releasing capillary water (water in the soil) above the water table by injecting compressed air into the ground. Even if this process proves successful, however, it would almost triple water costs. Genetic engineering also may provide a partial solution, as new strains of drought-resistant crops continue to be developed. Whatever the final answer to the water crisis may be, it is evident that within the High Plains, irrigation water will never again be the abundant, inexpensive resource it was during the agricultural boom years of the mid-twentieth century.

Directions: Now answer the questions.

PARAGRAPH 2

The Ogallala aquifer is a sandstone formation that underlies some 583,000 square kilometers of land extending from northwestern Texas to southern South Dakota. Water from rains and melting snows has been accumulating in the Ogallala for the past 30,000 years. Estimates indicate that the aquifer contains enough water to fill Lake Huron, but unfortunately, under the semiarid climatic conditions that presently exist in the region, rates of addition to the aquifer are minimal, amounting to about half a centimeter a year.

1. According to paragraph 2, all of the following statements about the Ogallala aquifer are true EXCEPT:

   (A) The aquifer stretches from South Dakota to Texas.
   (B) The aquifer's water comes from underground springs.
   (C) Water has been gathering in the aquifer for 30,000 years.
   (D) The aquifer's water is stored in a layer of sandstone.

2. Which of the sentences below best expresses the essential information in the highlighted sentence in the passage? Incorrect choices change the meaning in important ways or leave out essential information.

   (A) Despite the current impressive size of the Ogallala aquifer, the region's climate keeps the rates of water addition very small.
   (B) Although the aquifer has been adding water at the rate of only half a centimeter a year, it will eventually accumulate enough water to fill Lake Huron.
   (C) Because of the region's present climatic conditions, water is being added each year to the aquifer.
   (D) Even when the region experiences unfortunate climatic conditions, the rates of addition of water continue to increase.

GO ON TO THE NEXT PAGE ↘

P A R A G R A P H 3

The first wells were drilled into the Ogallala during the drought years of the early 1930s. The ensuing rapid expansion of irrigation agriculture, especially from the 1950s onward, transformed the economy of the region. More than 100,000 wells now tap the Ogallala. Modern irrigation devices, each capable of spraying 4.5 million liters of water a day, have produced a landscape dominated by geometric patterns of circular green islands of crops. Ogallala water has enabled the High Plains region to supply significant amounts of the cotton, sorghum, wheat, and corn grown in the United States. In addition, 40 percent of American grain-fed beef cattle are fattened here.

3. In paragraph 3, why does the author provide the information that 40 percent of American cattle are fattened in the High Plains?

   Ⓐ To suggest that crop cultivation is not the most important part of the economy of the High Plains

   Ⓑ To indicate that not all economic activity in the High Plains is dependent on irrigation

   Ⓒ To provide another example of how water from the Ogallala has transformed the economy of the High Plains

   Ⓓ To contrast cattle-fattening practices in the High Plains with those used in other regions of the United States

P A R A G R A P H 4

This unprecedented development of a finite groundwater resource with an almost negligible natural recharge rate—that is, virtually no natural water source to replenish the water supply—has caused water tables in the region to fall drastically. In the 1930s, wells encountered plentiful water at a depth of about 15 meters; currently, they must be dug to depths of 45 to 60 meters or more. In places, the water table is declining at a rate of a meter a year, necessitating the periodic deepening of wells and the use of ever-more-powerful pumps. It is estimated that at current withdrawal rates, much of the aquifer will run dry within 40 years. The situation is most critical in Texas, where the climate is driest, the greatest amount of water is being pumped, and the aquifer contains the least water. It is projected that the remaining Ogallala water will, by the year 2030, support only 35 to 40 percent of the irrigated acreage in Texas that it supported in 1980.

4. The word "unprecedented" in the passage is closest in meaning to

   Ⓐ difficult to control
   Ⓑ without any restriction
   Ⓒ unlike anything in the past
   Ⓓ rapidly expanding

5. According to paragraph 4, all of the following are consequences of the heavy use of the Ogallala aquifer for irrigation EXCEPT:

   Ⓐ The recharge rate of the aquifer is decreasing.
   Ⓑ Water tables in the region are becoming increasingly lower.
   Ⓒ Wells now have to be dug to much greater depths than before.
   Ⓓ Increasingly powerful pumps are needed to draw water from the aquifer.

6. According to paragraph 4, compared with all other states that use Ogallala water for irrigation, Texas

   (A) has the greatest amount of farmland being irrigated with Ogallala water
   (B) contains the largest amount of Ogallala water underneath the soil
   (C) is expected to face the worst water supply crisis as the Ogallala runs dry
   (D) uses the least amount of Ogallala water for its irrigation needs

PARAGRAPH 5

The reaction of farmers to the inevitable depletion of the Ogallala varies. Many have been attempting to conserve water by irrigating less frequently or by switching to crops that require less water. Others, however, have adopted the philosophy that it is best to use the water while it is still economically profitable to do so and to concentrate on high-value crops such as cotton. The incentive of the farmers who wish to conserve water is reduced by their knowledge that many of their neighbors are profiting by using great amounts of water, and in the process are drawing down the entire region's water supplies.

7. Paragraph 5 mentions which of the following as a source of difficulty for some farmers who try to conserve water?

   (A) Crops that do not need much water are difficult to grow in the High Plains.
   (B) Farmers who grow crops that need a lot of water make higher profits.
   (C) Irrigating less frequently often leads to crop failure.
   (D) Few farmers are convinced that the aquifer will eventually run dry.

PARAGRAPH 6

In the face of the upcoming water supply crisis, a number of grandiose schemes have been developed to transport vast quantities of water by canal or pipeline from the Mississippi, the Missouri, or the Arkansas rivers. Unfortunately, the cost of water obtained through any of these schemes would increase pumping costs at least tenfold, making the cost of irrigated agricultural products from the region uncompetitive on the national and international markets. Somewhat more promising have been recent experiments for releasing capillary water (water in the soil) above the water table by injecting compressed air into the ground. Even if this process proves successful, however, it would almost triple water costs. Genetic engineering also may provide a partial solution, as new strains of drought-resistant crops continue to be developed. Whatever the final answer to the water crisis may be, it is evident that within the High Plains, irrigation water will never again be the abundant, inexpensive resource it was during the agricultural boom years of the mid-twentieth century.

8. According to paragraph 6, what is the main disadvantage of the proposed plans to transport river water to the High Plains?

   (A) The rivers cannot supply sufficient water for the farmers' needs.
   (B) Increased irrigation costs would make the products too expensive.
   (C) The costs of using capillary water for irrigation will increase.
   (D) Farmers will be forced to switch to genetically engineered crops.

GO ON TO THE NEXT PAGE ▶

P A R A G R A P H S

5

A N D

6

The reaction of farmers to the inevitable depletion of the Ogallala varies. Many have been attempting to conserve water by irrigating less frequently or by switching to crops that require less water. **(A)** Others, however, have adopted the philosophy that it is best to use the water while it is still economically profitable to do so and to concentrate on high-value crops such as cotton. **(B)** The incentive of the farmers who wish to conserve water is reduced by their knowledge that many of their neighbors are profiting by using great amounts of water, and in the process are drawing down the entire region's water supplies. **(C)**

In the face of the upcoming water supply crisis, a number of grandiose schemes have been developed to transport vast quantities of water by canal or pipeline from the Mississippi, the Missouri, or the Arkansas rivers. **(D)** Unfortunately, the cost of water obtained through any of these schemes would increase pumping costs at least tenfold, making the cost of irrigated agricultural products from the region uncompetitive on the national and international markets.

9. **Directions:** Look at the part of the passage that is displayed above. The letters **(A)**, **(B)**, **(C)**, and **(D)** indicate where the following sentence could be added.

    But even if uncooperative farmers were to join in the conservation efforts, this would only delay the depletion of the aquifer.

    Where would the sentence best fit?

    Ⓐ Choice A
    Ⓑ Choice B
    Ⓒ Choice C
    Ⓓ Choice D

10. **Directions:** An introductory sentence for a brief summary of the passage is provided below. Complete the summary by selecting the THREE answer choices that express the most important ideas in the passage. Some answer choices do not belong in the summary because they express ideas that are not presented in the passage or are minor ideas in the passage. **This question is worth 2 points.**

The Ogallala aquifer is a large underground source of water in the High Plains region of the United States.

-

-

-

Answer Choices

A The use of the Ogallala for irrigation has allowed the High Plains to become one of the most productive agricultural regions in the United States.

B The periodic deepening of wells and the use of more-powerful pumps would help increase the natural recharge rate of the Ogallala.

C Given the aquifer's low recharge rate, its use for irrigation is causing water tables to drop and will eventually lead to its depletion.

D In Texas, a great deal of attention is being paid to genetic engineering because it is there that the most critical situation exists.

E Releasing capillary water and introducing drought-resistant crops are less promising solutions to the water supply crisis than bringing in river water.

F Several solutions to the upcoming water supply crisis have been proposed, but none of them promises to keep the costs of irrigation low.

STOP. This is the end of the Reading section of *TOEFL iBT* ® Practice Test 3.

LISTENING

Directions: This section measures your ability to understand conversations and lectures in English.

You should listen to each conversation and lecture only **once**.

After each conversation or lecture, you will answer some questions about it. The questions typically ask about the main idea and supporting details. Some questions ask about the purpose of a speaker's statements or a speaker's attitude. Answer the questions based on what is stated or implied by the speakers.

You may take notes while you listen. You may use your notes to help you answer the questions. Your notes will **not** be scored.

In some questions, you will see this icon: This means that you will hear, but not see, part of the question.

Most questions are worth 1 point. If a question is worth more than 1 point, it will have special directions that indicate how many points you can receive.

It will take about **41 minutes** to listen to the conversations and lectures and to answer the questions. You should answer each question, even if you must guess the answer. Answer each question before moving on. Do not return to previous questions.

At the end of this Practice Test you will find an answer key, information to help you determine your score, scripts for the audio tracks, and explanations of the answers.

Turn the page to begin the Listening section.

Listen to Track 57.

Questions

Directions: Mark your answer by filling in the oval or square next to your choice.

1. Why does the woman come to the office?

   Ⓐ To notify the university of her change of address

   Ⓑ To find out where her physics class is being held

   Ⓒ To get directions to the science building

   Ⓓ To complain about her physics class being canceled

2. What happened to the letter the university sent to the woman?

   Ⓐ She threw it away by mistake.

   Ⓑ Her roommate forgot to give it to her.

   Ⓒ It was sent to her old mailing address.

   Ⓓ It was sent to another student by mistake.

3. Why was the woman's physics class canceled?

   Ⓐ Not enough students signed up to take the class.

   Ⓑ No professors were available to teach the class.

   Ⓒ The university changed its requirements for physics students.

   Ⓓ There were no classrooms available in the science building at that hour.

4. What does the man suggest the woman do before the beginning of next semester?

    (A) Consult with her advisor about her class schedule
    (B) Check with the registrar's office about the location of the class
    (C) Register for her classes early
    (D) Call the physics department

5. *Listen again to part of the conversation by playing Track 58.*
    Then answer the question.

    What does the man imply when he says this?

    (A) He knows the physics class has been canceled.
    (B) He is not sure where the science building is.
    (C) Many of the room assignments have been changed.
    (D) The woman can check for herself where her class is.

Listen to Track 59.

Environmental Science

Questions

6. What does the professor mainly discuss?

   (A) Major changes in the migratory patterns of hummingbirds
   (B) The adaptation of hummingbirds to urban environments
   (C) Concern about the reduction of hummingbird habitat
   (D) The impact of ecotourism on hummingbird populations

7. What does the professor imply might cause a decrease in the hummingbird population?

   (A) An increase in the ecotourism industry
   (B) An increase in the use of land to raise crops and cattle
   (C) A decrease in banding studies
   (D) A decrease in the distance traveled during migration

8. What does the professor say people have done to help hummingbirds survive?

    Ⓐ They have built a series of hummingbird feeding stations.
    Ⓑ They have supported new laws that punish polluters of wildlife habitats.
    Ⓒ They have replanted native flowers in once-polluted areas.
    Ⓓ They have learned to identify various hummingbird species.

9. What way of collecting information about migrating hummingbirds does the professor mention?

    Ⓐ Receiving radio signals from electronic tracking devices
    Ⓑ Being contacted by people who recapture banded birds
    Ⓒ Counting the birds that return to the same region every year
    Ⓓ Comparing old and young birds' migration routes

10. What does the professor imply researchers have learned while studying hummingbird migration?

    Ⓐ Hummingbirds have totally disappeared from some countries due to recent habitat destruction.
    Ⓑ Programs to replant flowers native to hummingbird habitats are not succeeding.
    Ⓒ Some groups of hummingbirds have changed their migration patterns.
    Ⓓ Some plant species pollinated by hummingbirds have become extinct.

11. *Listen again to part of the lecture by playing Track 60.*
    Then answer the question.

    What does the professor imply when she says this?

    Ⓐ There is disagreement about the idea she has presented.
    Ⓑ She does not plan to discuss all the details.
    Ⓒ Her next point may seem to contradict what she has just said.
    Ⓓ The point she will make next should be obvious to the students.

GO ON TO THE NEXT PAGE ⬎

Listen to Track 61.

Film History

Jean Painlevé

Jacques Cousteau

Questions

12. What is the main purpose of the lecture?

Ⓐ To discuss the style of an early filmmaker
Ⓑ To describe different types of filmmaking in the 1930s
Ⓒ To discuss the emergence of the documentary film
Ⓓ To describe Painlevé's influence on today's science-fiction films

13. Why are Painlevé's films typical of the films of the 1920s and 1930s?

Ⓐ They do not have sound.
Ⓑ They are filmed underwater.
Ⓒ They are easy to understand.
Ⓓ They are difficult to categorize.

14. According to the professor, how did Painlevé's films confuse the audience?

Ⓐ They showed animals out of their natural habitat.
Ⓑ They depicted animals as having both human and animal characteristics.
Ⓒ The narration was scientific and difficult to understand.
Ⓓ The audiences of the 1920s and 1930s were not used to films shot underwater.

GO ON TO THE NEXT PAGE

15. Why does the professor mention sea horses?

   Ⓐ To explain that they were difficult to film in the 1930s
   Ⓑ To point out that Cousteau made documentaries about them
   Ⓒ To illustrate Painlevé's fascination with unusual animals
   Ⓓ To explain why Painlevé's underwater films were not successful

16. Why does the professor compare the film styles of Jacques Cousteau and Jean Painlevé?

   Ⓐ To explain how Painlevé influenced Cousteau
   Ⓑ To emphasize the uniqueness of Painlevé's filming style
   Ⓒ To emphasize the artistic value of Cousteau's documentary films
   Ⓓ To demonstrate the superiority of Painlevé's filmmaking equipment

17. *Listen to Track 62 to answer the question.*

What does the student imply when he says this?

   Ⓐ He does not like Jean Painlevé's films.
   Ⓑ He thinks that the professor should spend more time discussing Jacques Cousteau's films.
   Ⓒ He believes that high-quality filmmakers are usually well known.
   Ⓓ He believes that Jean Painlevé's films have been unfairly overlooked.

Listen to Track 63.

Questions

18. Why does the student go to see the professor?

   Ⓐ To ask about a class assignment
   Ⓑ To find out about a mid-semester project
   Ⓒ To get information about summer jobs
   Ⓓ To discuss ways to improve his grade

19. What was originally located on the site of the lecture hall?

   Ⓐ A farmhouse
   Ⓑ A pottery factory
   Ⓒ A clothing store
   Ⓓ A bottle-manufacturing plant

20. What is mentioned as an advantage of working on this project?

   Ⓐ Off-campus travel is paid for.
   Ⓑ Students can leave class early.
   Ⓒ The location is convenient.
   Ⓓ It fulfills a graduation requirement.

GO ON TO THE NEXT PAGE ⬭

21. What is the professor considering doing to get more volunteers?

    Ⓐ Offering extra class credit
    Ⓑ Paying the students for their time
    Ⓒ Asking for student volunteers from outside her class
    Ⓓ Providing flexible work schedules

22. What information does the student still need to get from the professor?

    Ⓐ The name of the senior researcher
    Ⓑ What book he needs to read before the next lecture
    Ⓒ When the training session will be scheduled
    Ⓓ Where the project is located

Listen to Track 64.

Art History

Chauvet

Altamira
Lascaux

GO ON TO THE NEXT PAGE

Questions

23. What does the professor mainly discuss?

    Ⓐ The oldest known cave art
    Ⓑ How ancient cave art is dated
    Ⓒ The homes of Paleolithic humans
    Ⓓ How Paleolithic humans thought about animals

24. Why does the professor mention his daughter?

    Ⓐ To describe her reaction to seeing the paintings
    Ⓑ To explain the universal appeal of the Chauvet paintings
    Ⓒ To demonstrate the size of most Paleolithic cave art
    Ⓓ To emphasize his point about the age of the Chauvet paintings

25. What is the professor's opinion about the art at the Chauvet cave?

    Ⓐ It is extremely well done.
    Ⓑ It probably reflected the artists' religious beliefs.
    Ⓒ It is less sophisticated than the art at Lascaux and Altamira.
    Ⓓ It is probably not much older than the art at Lascaux and Altamira.

26. According to the professor, what is the significance of charcoal marks on the walls of the Chauvet cave?

    Ⓐ They suggest that Paleolithic people cooked their food in the cave.
    Ⓑ They prove that people came to the cave long after the paintings were made.
    Ⓒ They show how much light the Paleolithic artists needed for their work.
    Ⓓ They were used in recent times to date the paintings.

27. Compared with other Paleolithic art, what is unusual about the animals painted at Chauvet?

Ⓐ Most of them are horses.
Ⓑ Many of them are dangerous.
Ⓒ Many of them are shown alongside humans.
Ⓓ All of them are species that are still found in France.

28. What are two questions about the Chauvet cave artists that the professor raises but cannot answer?
Choose 2 answers.

A How they lighted their work area
B How they obtained pigments for their paints
C Why they chose to paint certain animals and not others
D Why they placed their art in dark, uninhabited places

STOP. This is the end of the Listening section of *TOEFL iBT*® Practice Test 3.

SPEAKING

Directions: The following Speaking section of the test will last approximately **17 minutes**. To complete it, you will need a recording device that you can play back to listen to your responses.

During the test, you will answer four speaking questions. One question asks about a familiar topic. Three questions ask about short conversations, lectures, and reading passages. You may take notes as you listen to the conversations and lectures. The questions and the reading passages are printed here. The time you will have to prepare your response and to speak is printed below each question. You should answer all of the questions as completely as possible in the time allowed.

Play the audio tracks listed in the test instructions. Record each of your responses.

At the end of this Practice Test you will find scripts for the audio tracks, important points for each question, directions for listening to sample spoken responses, and comments on those responses by official raters.

Questions

1. You will now be asked to give your opinion about a familiar topic. After you hear the question, you will have 15 seconds to prepare your response and 45 seconds to speak.

Now play Track 65 to hear Question 1.

Some students prefer to work on class assignments by themselves. Others believe it is better to work in a group. Which do you prefer? Explain why.

Preparation Time: 15 Seconds
Response Time: 45 Seconds

2. You will now read a short passage and then listen to a conversation on the same topic. You will then be asked a question about them. After you hear the question, you will have 30 seconds to prepare your response and 60 seconds to speak.

Now play Track 66 to hear Question 2.

Reading Time: 45 Seconds

Hot Breakfasts Eliminated

Beginning next month, Dining Services will no longer serve hot breakfast foods at university dining halls. Instead, students will be offered a wide assortment of cold breakfast items in the morning. These cold breakfast foods, such as breads, fruit, and yogurt, are healthier than many of the hot breakfast items that we will stop serving, so health-conscious students should welcome this change. Students will benefit in another way as well, because limiting the breakfast selection to cold food items will save money and allow us to keep our meal plans affordable.

The woman expresses her opinion of the change that has been announced. State her opinion and explain her reasons for holding that opinion.

Preparation Time: 30 Seconds
Response Time: 60 Seconds

3. You will now read a short passage and then listen to a talk on the same academic topic. You will then be asked a question about them. After you hear the question, you will have 30 seconds to prepare your response and 60 seconds to speak.

Now play Track 67 to hear Question 3.

Reading Time: 50 Seconds

Cognitive Dissonance

Individuals sometimes experience a contradiction between their actions and their beliefs—between what they are doing and what they believe they should be doing. These contradictions can cause a kind of mental discomfort known as *cognitive dissonance*. People experiencing cognitive dissonance often do not want to change the way they are acting, so they resolve the contradictory situation in another way: they change their interpretation of the situation in a way that minimizes the contradiction between what they are doing and what they believe they should be doing.

GO ON TO THE NEXT PAGE

Using the example discussed by the professor, explain what cognitive dissonance is and how people often deal with it.

Preparation Time: 30 Seconds
Response Time: 60 Seconds

4. You will now listen to part of a lecture. You will then be asked a question about it. After you hear the question, you will have 20 seconds to prepare your response and 60 seconds to speak.

Now play Track 68 to hear Question 4.

Using the examples from the talk, explain how persuasive strategies are used in advertising.

Preparation Time: 20 Seconds
Response Time: 60 Seconds

STOP. This is the end of the Speaking section of *TOEFL iBT*® Practice Test 3.

WRITING

Directions: This section measures your ability to use writing to communicate in an academic environment. There will be two writing tasks.

For the first writing task, you will read a passage and listen to a lecture and then answer a question based on what you have read and heard. For the second task, you will answer a question based on your own knowledge and experience.

At the end of this Practice Test you will find a script for the audio track, topic notes, sample test taker essays, and comments on those essays by official raters.

Turn the page to see the directions for the first writing task.

Writing Based on Reading and Listening

Directions: For this task, you will read a passage about an academic topic and you will listen to a lecture about the same topic. You may take notes while you read and listen.

Then you will write a response to a question that asks you about the relationship between the lecture you heard and the reading passage. Try to answer the question as completely as possible using information from the reading passage and the lecture. The question does not ask you to express your personal opinion. You may refer to the reading passage when you write. You may use your notes to help you answer the question.

Typically, an effective response will be 150 to 225 words. Your response will be judged on the quality of your writing and on the completeness and accuracy of the content.

Give yourself **3 minutes** to read the passage.

> **Reading Time: 3 minutes**

Rembrandt is the most famous of the seventeenth-century Dutch painters. However, there are doubts whether some paintings attributed to Rembrandt were actually painted by him. One such painting is known as *Portrait of an Elderly Woman in a White Bonnet*. The painting was attributed to Rembrandt because of its style, and indeed the representation of the woman's face is very much like that of portraits known to be by Rembrandt. But there are problems with the painting that suggest it could not be a work by Rembrandt.

First, there is something inconsistent about the way the woman in the portrait is dressed. She is wearing a white linen cap of a kind that only servants would wear—yet the coat she is wearing has a luxurious fur collar that no servant could afford. Rembrandt, who was known for his attention to the details of his subjects' clothing, would not have been guilty of such an inconsistency.

Second, Rembrandt was a master of painting light and shadow, but in this painting these elements do not fit together. The face appears to be illuminated by light reflected onto it from below. But below the face is the dark fur collar, which would absorb light rather than reflect it. So the face should appear partially in shadow—which is not how it appears. Rembrandt would never have made such an error.

Finally, examination of the back of the painting reveals that it was painted on a panel made of several pieces of wood glued together. Although Rembrandt often painted on wood panels, no painting known to be by Rembrandt uses a panel glued together in this way from several pieces of wood.

For these reasons the painting was removed from the official catalog of Rembrandt's paintings in the 1930s.

Now play Track 69.

Question

Summarize the points made in the lecture, being sure to explain how they answer the specific problems presented in the reading passage.

You have 20 minutes to plan and write your response.

Response Time: 20 minutes

_____

_____

_____

_____

_____

_____

_____

_____

_____

_____

_____

_____

GO ON TO THE NEXT PAGE ➥

Writing Based on Knowledge and Experience

Directions: For this task, you will write an essay in response to a question that asks you to state, explain, and support your opinion on an issue.

Typically, an effective essay will contain a minimum of 300 words. Your essay will be judged on the quality of your writing. This includes the development of your ideas, the organization of your essay, and the quality and accuracy of the language you use to express your ideas.

You have **30 minutes** to plan and complete your essay.

Write your essay in the space provided.

Question

Do you agree or disagree with the following statement?

It is more important to keep your old friends than it is to make new friends.

Use specific reasons and examples to support your answer. Be sure to use your own words. Do **not** use memorized examples.

Response Time: 30 minutes

_____

_____

_____

_____

_____

_____

_____

_____

_____

_____

_____

_____

_____

GO ON TO THE NEXT PAGE

_____

_____

_____

_____

_____

_____

_____

_____

_____

_____

_____

_____

_____

_____

_____

_____

_____

_____

_____

_____

_____

_____

_____

_____

_____

STOP. This is the end of the Writing section of *TOEFL iBT*® Practice Test 3.

Answers, Explanations, and Listening Scripts

Reading

Answer Key and Self-Scoring Chart

Directions: Check your answers against the answer key below. Write the number 1 on the line to the right of each question if you picked the correct answer. For questions worth more than one point, follow the directions given. Total your points at the bottom of the chart.

Question Number	Correct Answer	Your Raw Points
Architecture		
1.	D	
2.	B	
3.	D	
4.	A	
5.	B	
6.	C	
7.	C	
8.	B	
9.	D	

For question 10, write 2 if you picked all three correct answers. Write 1 if you picked two correct answers.

10.	A, C, F	

Question Number	Correct Answer	Your Raw Points
The Long-Term Stability of Ecosystems		
1.	C	
2.	A	
3.	C	
4.	B	
5.	C	
6.	A	
7.	D	
8.	D	
9.	B	

For question 10, write 2 if you picked all three correct answers. Write 1 if you picked two correct answers.

10.	C, D, E	

Question Number	Correct Answer	Your Raw Points
Depletion of the Ogallala Aquifer		
1.	B	
2.	A	
3.	C	
4.	C	
5.	A	
6.	C	
7.	B	
8.	B	
9.	C	

For question 10, write 2 if you picked all three correct answers. Write 1 if you picked two correct answers.

10.	A, C, F	
Total:		

Below is a table that converts your Reading section answers into a *TOEFL iBT®* Reading scaled score. Take the total of raw points from your answer key and find that number in the left-hand column of the table. The right-hand column of the table gives a TOEFL iBT Reading scaled score for each number of raw points. For example, if the total points from your answer key is 26, the table shows a scaled score of 24–27.

You should use your score estimate as a general guide only. Your actual score on the TOEFL iBT test may be higher or lower than your score on the practice version.

Reading Comprehension

Raw Point Total	Scaled Score
32–33	30
31	29–30
30	28–30
29	27–28
28	26–29
27	25–28
26	24–27
25	23–26
24	21–25
23	20–25
22	19–24
21	18–23
20	17–22
19	15–21
18	14–20
17	13–19
16	11–18
15	10–17
14	8–16
13	7–15
12	5–13
11	4–12
10	2–10
9	1–9
8	1–7
7	0–5
6	0–4
5	0–2
4	0–1
3 or below	0

Answer Explanations

Architecture

1. **D** This is a Negative Factual Information question asking for specific information that can be found in paragraph 1. The correct answer is choice D. Sentence 3 in the paragraph states that "architecture affects our lives most directly," which makes the information in choice D incorrect. The information in choices A to C is stated in sentences 1 and 2 in the paragraph.

2. **B** This is a Vocabulary question. The word being tested is *enhance*. It is highlighted in the passage. The correct answer is choice B, "improve." In other words, humans seek structures that will improve, or better, their lives.

3. **D** This is a Sentence Simplification question. As with all of these questions, a single sentence in the passage is highlighted:

> In order for the structure to achieve the size and strength necessary to meet its purpose, architecture employs methods of support that, because they are based on physical laws, have changed little since people first discovered them—even while building materials have changed dramatically.

The correct answer is choice D. Choice D contains all of the essential information in the highlighted sentence. It omits the information from the introductory phrase about the size and strength of a structure because the information is not essential to the meaning of the sentence.

Choices A, B, and C are all incorrect because they change the meaning of the highlighted sentence. Choice A is incorrect because it inaccurately states that physical laws have limited the size and strength of buildings, whereas the highlighted sentence does not indicate this.

Choice B is incorrect because it wrongly makes a connection between building materials and building strength and size, whereas the highlighted sentence does not make such a connection.

Choice C is incorrect because it wrongly states that the structural methods initially used by people were not based on physical laws, whereas the highlighted sentence states that structural methods that are based on physical laws have been in use since their discovery.

4. **A** This is a Vocabulary question. The word being tested is *integral*. It is highlighted in the passage. The correct answer is choice A, "essential." In other words, materials and methods of construction are essential, or vital, parts of the design of architectural structures.

5.   **B** This is a Factual Information question asking for specific information that can be found in paragraph 4. The correct answer is choice B. Sentence 3 in the paragraph indicates that in the past, structures were built using the available materials. However, sentence 4 in the paragraph indicates that today new materials can be created as needed depending on the design of the structure. Choice A is incorrect because sentence 5 in the paragraph indicates that there have been substantial changes in materials and designs in the recent past. Choice C is incorrect because sentence 4 in the paragraph indicates that there are many types of materials available today. Choice D is incorrect because sentence 5 in the paragraph indicates that it is possible to enclose space more quickly and easily than in the past. It does not indicate that architects were not able to enclose space.

6.   **C** This is an Inference question asking for an inference that can be supported by paragraph 4. The correct answer is choice C. Sentence 5 in the paragraph states that structures are now created with a minimum of material, and sentence 6 indicates that there is a difference in weight between buildings being built now and those that were built one hundred years ago. The combined information from these two sentences suggests that modern buildings weigh less than buildings constructed one hundred years ago. Choice A is incorrect because there is no discussion of the amount of space that buildings constructed in the past or those built now occupy. Choice B is incorrect because sentence 5 in the paragraph states that substantial changes have been made to modern buildings compared with buildings constructed one hundred years ago. Choice D is incorrect because sentence 5 in the paragraph indicates that modern buildings can be built more quickly than those built one hundred years ago.

7.   **C** This is a Rhetorical Purpose question. It is asking why the author includes the description of how the "doorways and windows" of Machu Picchu were constructed. The phrase being tested is highlighted in the passage. The correct answer is choice C. The author discusses the stone structures used to support doorways and windows in order to provide an example of how the physical limitations of stone were overcome before the invention of the arch. Choice A is incorrect because there is no comparison made in the passage between the buildings of Machu Picchu and igloos and adobe structures. Choice B is incorrect because, while the passage does state that stone was used in the buildings of Machu Picchu, it never discusses the kind of stone used. Choice D is incorrect because there is no discussion of the time needed to construct buildings from stone.

8.   **B** This is a Factual Information question asking for specific information that can be found in paragraph 6. The correct answer is choice B. Sentences 5 and 6 in the paragraph indicate that the arch allowed new architectural forms to be created. The remainder of the paragraph elaborates on structures created as a result of the arch. Choice A is incorrect because sentence 7 in the paragraph indicates that early Mediterranean cultures were the first to use

the arch, not the Romans. Choice C is incorrect because sentence 10 in the paragraph indicates that the weight of a structure is distributed to the sides of the arch. Choice D is incorrect because sentence 7 indicates that the Romans created new uses for the arch, namely in aboveground structures.

9. **ⓓ** This is an Insert Text question. You can see the four possible answer choices in paragraph 5.

Progress in this area can be measured by the difference in weight between buildings built now and those of comparable size built one hundred years ago. **(A)** Modern architectural forms generally have three separate components comparable to elements of the human body: a supporting *skeleton* or frame, an outer *skin* enclosing the interior spaces, and *equipment*, similar to the body's vital organs and systems. **(B)** The equipment includes plumbing, electrical wiring, hot water, and air-conditioning. **(C)** Of course in early architecture—such as igloos and adobe structures—there was no such equipment, and the skeleton and skin were often one. **(D)** Much of the world's great architecture has been constructed of stone because of its beauty, permanence, and availability.

The sentence provided, "However, some modern architectural designs, such as those using folded plates of concrete or air-inflated structures, are again unifying skeleton and skin," is best inserted at choice **(D)**.

Choice **(D)** is correct because it is the only place that supports both a contrasting idea and a repeated reference to the unification of skeleton and skin. The inserted sentence represents a contrast to the main idea of the paragraph. The inserted sentence also contains the phrase "again unifying skeleton and skin," indicating that there must be a previous discussion related to unifying the skeleton and skin of a structure. Choice **(D)** is the only place in this paragraph that follows such a discussion.

None of the other answer choices follow a discussion of the unifying of a structure's skeleton and skin, nor do the other answer choices provide a suitable point of contrast for the insert sentence.

10. Ⓐ Ⓒ Ⓕ This is a Prose Summary question. It is completed correctly below. The correct choices are A, C, and F. Choices B, D, and E are therefore incorrect.

Directions: An introductory sentence for a brief summary of the passage is provided below. Complete the summary by selecting the THREE answer choices that express the most important ideas in the passage. Some answer choices do not belong in the summary because they express ideas that are not presented in the passage or are minor ideas in the passage. **This question is worth 2 points.**

Architecture uses forms and space to express cultural values.

> A Architects seek to create buildings that are both visually appealing and well suited for human use.
>
> C Over the course of the history of building, innovations in materials and methods of construction have given architects ever greater freedom to express themselves.
>
> F The discovery and use of the arch typifies the way in which architecture advances by developing more efficient types of structures.

Answer Choices

A Architects seek to create buildings that are both visually appealing and well suited for human use.

B Both clients and architects are responsible for the mediocre designs of some modern buildings.

C Over the course of the history of building, innovations in materials and methods of construction have given architects ever greater freedom to express themselves.

D Modern buildings tend to lack the beauty of ancient stone buildings such as those of Machu Picchu.

E Throughout history buildings have been constructed like human bodies, needing distinct "organ" systems in order to function.

F The discovery and use of the arch typifies the way in which architecture advances by developing more efficient types of structures.

Correct Choices

Choice A, "Architects seek to create buildings that are both visually appealing and well suited for human use," is correct because it is a broad statement that is developed in the first two paragraphs. The first two paragraphs discuss in detail how architecture can affect and possibly improve people's lives.

Choice C, "Over the course of the history of building, innovations in materials and methods of construction have given architects ever greater freedom to express themselves," is correct because it is a general statement that is developed in paragraphs 3 and 4. These paragraphs discuss in detail how materials and methods have changed and improved over the history of building, continually providing architects the chance to create new designs.

Choice F, "The discovery and use of the arch typifies the way in which architecture advances by developing more efficient types of structures," is correct because it captures the main idea of paragraph 6, which provides a lengthy discussion of the ways that the arch has allowed new architectural forms to be created.

Incorrect Choices

Choice B, "Both clients and architects are responsible for the mediocre designs of some modern buildings," is incorrect because it is only a minor, supporting detail, which is mentioned in the last sentence of paragraph 2. It supports the larger idea in the paragraph that the quality of an architectural design depends on a variety of factors.

Choice D, "Modern buildings tend to lack the beauty of ancient stone buildings such as those of Machu Picchu," is incorrect because there is no discussion in the passage of the level of attractiveness of modern buildings.

Choice E, "Throughout history buildings have been constructed like human bodies, needing distinct 'organ' systems in order to function," is incorrect because paragraph 5 states that early architecture did not have equipment, such as plumbing and wiring, that is comparable to vital organs in the human body.

The Long-Term Stability of Ecosystems

1. **C** This is a Vocabulary question. The word being tested is *particular*. It is highlighted in the passage. The correct answer is choice C, "specific." In other words, the specific structure of plant communities depends on the history of the area.

2. **A** This is a Factual Information question asking for specific information that can be found in paragraph 2. The correct answer is choice A. Sentence 3 in the paragraph states that "the properties of an ecosystem are more stable," or change more slowly, than individuals within the system. Choice B is contradicted by sentences 1 and 3 in the paragraph, which indicate that ecosystems remain unchanged as individuals are replaced. Choice C is contradicted by sentence 2 in the paragraph, which indicates that individual organisms

change from year to year. Choice D is incorrect because there is no information in the paragraph about a change in the number of an organism and how that will affect an ecosystem. Furthermore, sentence 2 in the paragraph states that the number of fish, for example, will usually stay the same.

3. **C** This is a Factual Information question asking for specific information that can be found in paragraph 4. The correct answer is choice C. The first two sentences of the paragraph indicate that ecosystem stability is complicated because ecologists do not agree on the meaning of the word *stability*. Choice A is incorrect because it is not discussed in the paragraph. Furthermore, the idea stated in choice A is contradicted in sentence 5 of the paragraph, which states that disturbances such as fires can change an ecosystem. Choice B is incorrect because there is no discussion of confusion on the part of ecologists about the concept of resilience. Resilience is simply defined in the paragraph. Choice D is incorrect because the main idea of the paragraph is to show that the questions of different ecologists are the cause of complications. Furthermore, sentences 4 and 7 in the paragraph provide clear answers to the questions posed by ecologists.

4. **B** This is a Factual Information question asking for specific information provided in paragraph 4. The correct answer is choice B. Sentences 4 and 7 in the paragraph indicate different perspectives on climax communities: they can be viewed as the most or least stable communities. Choice A is incorrect because, according to the resilience theory of ecosystem stability, it is contradicted by sentence 7, which indicates that climax communities are the least resilient. Choice C is also contradicted by sentence 7, which indicates that climax communities take a long time to recover after a major disturbance. Choice D is incorrect because it is a misunderstanding of the concept of resilience. According to sentence 5 in the paragraph, a resilient community will revert back to a particular form after a major disturbance.

5. **C** This is an Inference question asking for an inference that can be supported by paragraph 5. The correct answer is choice C. Sentence 2 introduces the discussion of diversity in successional communities in temperate zones, and sentence 3 presents redwood forests as an example of such a community. Choice A is incorrect because we can infer the opposite, according to the paragraph. Sentence 3 indicates that the diversity in a redwood forest decreases as the forest matures, and sentence 5 indicates that increased diversity can lead to instability. Choice B is incorrect because sentences 2 and 3 indicate that the number of species declines in a redwood forest at the climax stage. Choice D is incorrect because sentences 2 and 3 indicate the opposite, namely that redwood forests have maximum diversity in successional stages.

6. **Ⓐ** This is a Rhetorical Purpose question. It is testing why the author provides the information that "A fifteen-speed racing bicycle is more likely to break down than a child's tricycle." The sentence being tested is highlighted in the passage. The correct answer is choice A. Sentence 6 in the paragraph asserts the general principle that a complicated system is more likely to break down than a simple one. Sentence 7, the highlighted sentence, provides an example about bicycles that the average reader can relate to. Choice B is incorrect because it emphasizes stability, whereas the highlighted information provides an example of the issues related to the complexity of a particular system. Choice C is incorrect because sentence 5 in the paragraph indicates the opposite, specifically that stability does not necessarily increase with diversity. Therefore the highlighted sentence cannot be compared to the incorrect information given in choice C. Choice D is incorrect because the example provided in the highlighted sentence actually supports the mathematical models mentioned in sentence 5.

7. **Ⓓ** This is a Sentence Simplification question. As with all of these questions, a single sentence in the passage is highlighted:

> Many ecologists now think that the relative long-term stability of climax communities comes not from diversity but from the "patchiness" of the environment; an environment that varies from place to place supports more kinds of organisms than an environment that is uniform.

The correct answer is choice D. That choice takes all of the essential information in the two clauses of the highlighted sentence and simplifies it into one concise sentence. It omits information from the second clause that is repetitive and therefore not essential to the meaning.

Choice A is incorrect because its meaning is the opposite of that of the highlighted sentence. Choice A states that diversity is the key to stability, whereas the highlighted sentence indicates that stability does not come from diversity but rather comes from patchiness.

Choice B incorrectly indicates a causal relationship between patchy environments and diversity.

Choice C is incorrect because there is no indication in the highlighted sentence that uniform environments cannot be climax communities.

8. **Ⓓ** This is a Vocabulary question. The word being tested is *adjacent*. It is highlighted in the passage. The correct answer is choice D, "neighboring." In other words, a local population that goes extinct is quickly replaced by organisms from a neighboring, or nearby, community.

9. **B** This is an Insert Text question. You can see the four possible answer choices in paragraph 6.

A more complicated system is, in general, more likely than a simple system to break down. (A fifteen-speed racing bicycle is more likely to break down than a child's tricycle.)

(A) Ecologists are especially interested in knowing what factors contribute to the resilience of communities because climax conditions all over the world are being severely damaged or destroyed by human activities. **(B)** The destruction caused by the volcanic explosion of Mount St. Helens, in the northwestern United States, for example, pales in comparison to the destruction caused by humans. **(C)** We need to know what aspects of a community are most important to the community's resistance to destruction, as well as its recovery. **(D)**

Many ecologists now think that the relative long-term stability of climax communities comes not from diversity but from the "patchiness" of the environment; an environment that varies from place to place supports more kinds of organisms than an environment that is uniform.

The sentence provided, "In fact, damage to the environment by humans is often much more severe than by natural events and processes," is best inserted at choice **(B)**.

Choice **(B)** is correct because it is the best place in the paragraph to elaborate on the idea, introduced in sentence 1, that humans contribute to damage done to the environment. The phrase "In fact" is used to indicate elaboration. Also, the phrase "natural events and processes" in the given sentence provides a logical connection to the example in sentence 2 about the volcanic explosion of Mount St. Helens.

Choice **(A)** is incorrect because it does not make sense to begin the paragraph with a sentence that elaborates on the idea of human damage to the environment before the idea has been introduced.

Choice **(C)** is incorrect because it does not make sense to follow the specific example about the damage caused by the explosion of Mount St. Helens in sentence 2 with a more general statement about damage done by "natural events and processes."

Choice **(D)** is incorrect because the sentence preceding this choice discusses a community's resistance to destruction. This is not a logical place to insert a sentence that specifically elaborates on a different idea.

10. **C** **D** **E** This is a Prose Summary question. It is completed correctly below. The correct choices are C, D, and E. Choices A, B, and F are therefore incorrect.

Directions: An introductory sentence for a brief summary of the passage is provided below. Complete the summary by selecting the THREE answer choices that express the most important ideas in the passage. Some answer choices do not belong in the summary because they express ideas that are not presented in the passage or are minor ideas in the passage. **This question is worth 2 points.**

The process of succession and the stability of a climax community can change over time.

C   A high degree of species diversity does not always result in a stable ecosystem.

D   Disagreements over the meaning of the term "stability" make it difficult to identify the most stable ecosystems.

E   The level of resilience in a plant community contributes to its long-term stability.

Answer Choices

A   The changes that occur in an ecosystem from the pioneer to the climax community can be seen in one human generation.

B   Ecologists agree that climax communities are the most stable types of ecosystems.

C   A high degree of species diversity does not always result in a stable ecosystem.

D   Disagreements over the meaning of the term "stability" make it difficult to identify the most stable ecosystems.

E   The level of resilience in a plant community contributes to its long-term stability.

F   The resilience of climax communities makes them resistant to destruction caused by humans.

Correct Choices

Choice C, "A high degree of species diversity does not always result in a stable ecosystem," is correct because it is a main idea that is developed throughout most of the passage. The first three paragraphs introduce and develop the idea that diversity may result in a stable ecosystem. But paragraphs 4, 5, and 7 introduce arguments to support the idea that diversity does not always result in a stable ecosystem.

Choice D, "Disagreements over the meaning of the term "stability" make it difficult to identify the most stable ecosystems," is correct because the key idea that ecosystem stability is difficult to quantify is introduced in paragraph 4 and developed throughout the rest of the passage.

Choice E, "The level of resilience in a plant community contributes to its long-term stability," is correct because it mentions one important form of stability that is introduced in paragraph 4 and further developed in paragraph 6 in the discussion of environmental damage caused by humans.

Incorrect Choices

Choice A, "The changes that occur in an ecosystem from the pioneer to the climax community can be seen in one human generation," is incorrect because paragraph 1 states that a pioneer community alone can change over a period as long as 500 years. Furthermore, a climax community typically changes over a period longer than 500 years.

Choice B, "Ecologists agree that climax communities are the most stable types of ecosystems," is incorrect because climax communities are described as unstable at several points in the passage, beginning in paragraph 3. The last sentence of paragraph 4 states that climax communities could be the least stable communities, while sentence 2 in paragraph 5 suggests that successional communities may be more stable than climax communities.

Choice F, "The resilience of climax communities makes them resistant to destruction caused by humans," is incorrect because it is a misreading of sentence 1 in paragraph 6. The sentence indicates that ecologists would like to know if resilience could make climax communities resistant to destruction. Climax communities are currently being damaged or destroyed by humans and are not therefore resistant to such destruction.

Depletion of the Ogallala Aquifer

1. **B** This is a Negative Factual Information question asking for specific information that can be found in paragraph 2. The correct answer is choice B. The information in choice B is incorrect according to the paragraph, which states that the water comes "from rains and melting snows." There is no mention of underground springs in the paragraph. The information in choice A about location is stated in sentence 1 of the paragraph. The information in choice C about time is stated in sentence 2 of the paragraph. The information in choice D about sandstone is stated in sentence 1 of the paragraph.

2. **A** This is a Sentence Simplification question. As with all of these questions, a single sentence in the passage is highlighted:

> Estimates indicate that the aquifer contains enough water to fill Lake Huron, but unfortunately, under the semiarid climatic conditions that presently exist in the region, rates of addition to the aquifer are minimal, amounting to about half a centimeter a year.

The correct answer is choice A. The essential information about the size of the aquifer and the rate of addition is expressed in simplified, concise language, but the extra details used to help the reader visualize the information have been removed.

Choice B incorrectly indicates that the aquifer does not currently have the large amount of water that could fill Lake Huron, whereas the highlighted sentence states that the aquifer does have this large amount of water.

Choice C incorrectly implies that the region's present climatic conditions positively affect the aquifer by adding water. However, the highlighted sentence states that the region's dry weather negatively affects the aquifer because it prevents substantial amounts of water from being added.

Choice D incorrectly states that the rates of addition of water are increasing; the highlighted sentence indicates that the rate is steady at half a centimeter a year.

3. **C** This is a Rhetorical Purpose question. It is testing why the author provides the information that 40 percent of American cattle are fattened in the High Plains. The correct answer is choice C. Sentence 2 of the paragraph provides the general statement that irrigation agriculture "transformed the economy of the region," and the remainder of the paragraph provides 3 examples of this transformation. The information about cattle is the last of these examples in the paragraph. Choice A incorrectly implies that crop cultivation was less important than other factors in the economy of the region. However, the paragraph only provides examples of factors that contributed to the transformation of the region's economy; it does not indicate whether one factor was more or less important than another. Choice B incorrectly indicates that economic activity was not dependent on irrigation. However, sentence 2 in the paragraph states explicitly that the economic transformation was a

result of irrigation agriculture. Choice D is incorrect because there is no comparison in the paragraph between cattle-fattening practices in the High Plains and those in other places. The last sentence in the paragraph states only that 40 percent of certain cattle are fattened in this region; there is no discussion of the practices themselves.

4. **C** This is a Vocabulary question. The word being tested is *unprecedented*. The word is highlighted in the passage. The correct answer is choice C, "unlike anything in the past." In other words, a finite groundwater resource with a low natural recharge rate is unlike anything that existed in the past.

5. **A** This is a Negative Factual Information question asking for specific information that can be found in paragraph 4. The correct answer is choice A. Sentence 1 in the paragraph indicates that the aquifer has a low recharge rate, but there is no indication that this recharge rate is a result of irrigation. Furthermore, sentence 1 implies that the recharge rate is steady, not decreasing. The information in choice B about water tables is provided in sentence 1 in the paragraph. The information in choice C about the depth of wells is provided in sentence 2 in the paragraph. The information in choice D about water pumps is provided in sentence 3 in the paragraph.

6. **C** This is a Factual Information question asking for specific information that can be found in paragraph 4. The correct answer is choice C. Sentences 4 and 5 in the paragraph indicate that much of the aquifer will dry out and specify "The situation is most critical in Texas." Choice A is incorrect because there is no indication in the paragraph as to which area has the greatest amount of farmland being irrigated. Choice B is incorrect because there is no indication in the paragraph as to which area has the largest amount of Ogallala water beneath its soil. Choice D incorrectly states that Texas uses the least amount of Ogallala water, whereas sentence 5 states that in Texas "the greatest amount of water is being pumped."

7. **B** This is a Factual Information question asking for specific information that can be found in paragraph 5. The correct answer is choice B. Sentence 4 in the paragraph indicates that some farmers are less motivated to conserve water because other farmers make money by using large amounts of water. Choice A is incorrect because it attributes some farmers' difficulties to the difficulty of growing certain crops. However, sentence 2 in the paragraph states only that some farmers have switched to crops that use less water; this is not presented as a difficulty. Choice C incorrectly states that irrigating less frequently leads to crop failure, whereas sentence 2 in the paragraph mentions less frequent irrigation only as a method of conserving water. Choice D incorrectly implies that there are many farmers who do not believe that the aquifer will run dry. However, the paragraph does not explicitly state what farmers believe or do not believe. Only the reactions of farmers to the depletion of the aquifer are discussed. We can infer from these reactions that many farmers do believe the aquifer will run dry.

8. **B** This is a Factual Information question asking for specific information that can be found in paragraph 6. The correct answer is choice B. Sentence 2 in the paragraph states that the cost of agricultural products irrigated with transported river water would become too high and therefore uncompetitive. Choice A is incorrect because it states that there is not sufficient river water to meet farmers' needs, but sentence 1 in the paragraph implies that there are "vast quantities" of river water that could be used for irrigation purposes. Choice C is incorrect because the paragraph does not indicate that the cost of using capillary water will increase, but instead, sentence 4 in the paragraph indicates that using capillary water will cause the cost of water to increase. Choice D incorrectly states that farmers will be forced to switch to genetically engineered crops; the paragraph indicates that there are multiple possible solutions to the water supply crisis that farmers may choose from.

9. **C** This is an Insert Text question. You can see the four possible answer choices in paragraphs 5 and 6.

The reaction of farmers to the inevitable depletion of the Ogallala varies. Many have been attempting to conserve water by irrigating less frequently or by switching to crops that require less water. **(A)** Others, however, have adopted the philosophy that it is best to use the water while it is still economically profitable to do so and to concentrate on high-value crops such as cotton. **(B)** The incentive of the farmers who wish to conserve water is reduced by their knowledge that many of their neighbors are profiting by using great amounts of water, and in the process are drawing down the entire region's water supplies. **(C)**

In the face of the upcoming water supply crisis, a number of grandiose schemes have been developed to transport vast quantities of water by canal or pipeline from the Mississippi, the Missouri, or the Arkansas rivers. **(D)** Unfortunately, the cost of water obtained through any of these schemes would increase pumping costs at least tenfold, making the cost of irrigated agricultural products from the region uncompetitive on the national and international markets.

The sentence provided, "But even if uncooperative farmers were to join in the conservation efforts, this would only delay the depletion of the aquifer," is best inserted at choice **(C)**. The preceding sentence refers to farmers who use great amounts of water, or uncooperative farmers, and the following sentence at the beginning of the next paragraph refers to the water supply crisis, or the depletion of the aquifer. Choice **(C)** is the only place that provides logical connections to both the preceding and following sentences.

Choice **(A)** is incorrect because the preceding sentence refers to cooperative farmers who have attempted to conserve water, and the following sentence already provides a contrast to these cooperative farmers with the words "Others, however." Therefore the sentence provided would be repetitive.

Choice **(B)** is incorrect because the following sentence continues to discuss farmers, whereas the sentence provided leads the reader to expect a further discussion of the depletion of the aquifer.

Choice **(D)** is incorrect because the topic of the preceding and following sentences is potential solutions to the water crisis. There is no connection to be made with the actions of uncooperative farmers.

10. **Ⓐ Ⓒ Ⓕ** This is a Prose Summary question. It is completed correctly below. The correct choices are A, C, and F. Choices B, D, and E are therefore incorrect.

Directions: An introductory sentence for a brief summary of the passage is provided below. Complete the summary by selecting the THREE answer choices that express the most important ideas in the passage. Some answer choices do not belong in the summary because they express ideas that are not presented in the passage or are minor ideas in the passage. **This question is worth 2 points.**

The Ogallala aquifer is a large underground source of water in the High Plains region of the United States.

> Ⓐ The use of the Ogallala for irrigation has allowed the High Plains to become one of the most productive agricultural regions in the United States.
> Ⓒ Given the aquifer's low recharge rate, its use for irrigation is causing water tables to drop and will eventually lead to its depletion.
> Ⓕ Several solutions to the upcoming water supply crisis have been proposed, but none of them promises to keep the costs of irrigation low.

Answer Choices

Ⓐ The use of the Ogallala for irrigation has allowed the High Plains to become one of the most productive agricultural regions in the United States.

Ⓑ The periodic deepening of wells and the use of more-powerful pumps would help increase the natural recharge rate of the Ogallala.

Ⓒ Given the aquifer's low recharge rate, its use for irrigation is causing water tables to drop and will eventually lead to its depletion.

Ⓓ In Texas, a great deal of attention is being paid to genetic engineering because it is there that the most critical situation exists.

Ⓔ Releasing capillary water and introducing drought-resistant crops are less promising solutions to the water supply crisis than bringing in river water.

Ⓕ Several solutions to the upcoming water supply crisis have been proposed, but none of them promises to keep the costs of irrigation low.

Correct Choices

Choice A, "The use of the Ogallala for irrigation has allowed the High Plains to become one of the most productive agricultural regions in the United States," is correct because it is the main idea of paragraph 3. This choice summarizes the background information needed to understand the later discussion of the depletion of the aquifer.

Choice C, "Given the aquifer's low recharge rate, its use for irrigation is causing water tables to drop and will eventually lead to its depletion," is correct because it is a main idea that is developed throughout paragraphs 3 to 5. The information in this choice concisely captures the cause of the aquifer's depletion.

Choice F, "Several solutions to the upcoming water supply crisis have been proposed, but none of them promises to keep the costs of irrigation low," is correct because this is the main idea of the final paragraph of the passage. The information in this choice concisely captures the likely results of the aquifer's depletion.

Incorrect Choices

Choice B, "The periodic deepening of wells and the use of more-powerful pumps would help increase the natural recharge rate of the Ogallala," is incorrect because it is a misreading of the information given in paragraph 4 about wells and pumps. Paragraph 4 states different information, which is that the low recharge rate of the aquifer has resulted in the need to deepen wells and use more-powerful pumps.

Choice D, "In Texas, a great deal of attention is being paid to genetic engineering because it is there that the most critical situation exists," is incorrect because paragraph 6 states that genetic engineering is being considered as one of several solutions to the water supply crisis, but it is never stated who, exactly, is considering this solution. Furthermore, while it is true according to paragraph 4 that Texas has the most critical situation, there is no mention in the passage of what solutions Texas, in particular, is considering.

Choice E, "Releasing capillary water and introducing drought-resistant crops are less promising solutions to the water supply crisis than bringing in river water," is incorrect because the passage never indicates that one of these solutions is more or less promising than the others. The passage indicates in the last sentence only that all potential solutions will lead to more expensive irrigation water.

Listening

Answer Key and Self-Scoring Chart

Directions: Check your answers against the answer key below. Write the number 1 on the line to the right of each question if you picked the correct answer. Total your points at the bottom of the chart.

Question Number	Correct Answer	Your Raw Points
1.	B	
2.	C	
3.	A	
4.	D	
5.	D	
6.	C	
7.	B	
8.	C	
9.	B	
10.	C	
11.	D	
12.	A	
13.	D	
14.	B	
15.	C	
16.	B	
17.	C	
18.	B	
19.	A	
20.	C	
21.	A	
22.	C	
23.	A	
24.	D	
25.	A	
26.	B	
27.	B	

For question 28, write 1 if you picked both correct answers. Write 0 if you picked only one correct answer or no correct answers.

28.	C, D	
	TOTAL:	

Below is a table that converts your Listening section answers into a *TOEFL iBT®* Listening scaled score. Take the total of raw points from your answer key and find that number in the left-hand column of the table. The right-hand column of the table gives a TOEFL iBT Listening scaled score for each number of raw points. For example, if the total points from your answer key is 27, the table shows a scaled score of 29 to 30.

You should use your score estimate as a general guide only. Your actual score on the TOEFL iBT test may be higher or lower than your score on the practice version.

Listening

Raw Point Total	Scaled Score
28	30
27	29–30
26	27–30
25	25–30
24	24–29
23	23–27
22	22–26
21	21–25
20	19–24
19	18–23
18	17–21
17	16–20
16	14–19
15	13–18
14	12–17
13	10–15
12	9–14
11	7–13
10	6–12
9	5–10
8	3–9
7	2–7
6	1–6
5	1–4
4	0–2
3	0–1
2	0
1	0
0	0

Listening Scripts and Answer Explanations

Questions 1–5

Track 57 Listening Script

Narrator

Listen to a conversation between a student and a receptionist at the registrar's office on the first day of the semester.

Female Student

Excuse me, uh, I'm supposed to be having my physics class in the science building, but no one's in the classroom . . . Could you tell me where the class is? Physics 403? Has it been moved?

Receptionist

Well, there's a room assignment sheet on the bulletin board outside this office . . .

Female Student

Yeah, I know, but my class isn't listed there. There must be some kinda mistake or something. Could you look it up, please?

Receptionist

Mm, okay, let me check on the computer. It's physics, right? Wait, did you say Physics 403?

Female Student

Yeah.

Receptionist

Well, I'm sorry, but . . . it says here that it was canceled . . . You should've gotten a letter from the registrar's office about this . . .

Female Student

What? I never got it.

Receptionist

Are you sure? 'Cause it says on the computer that the letter was sent out to students a week ago.

Female Student

Really? I shoulda gotten it by now . . . I wonder if I threw it away with all the junk mail by mistake . . .

Receptionist

Well, it does happen . . . Um, let me check something. What's your name?

Female Student

Woodhouse. Laura Woodhouse.

Receptionist

OK, ummm, Woodhouse . . . let me see . . . ah, it says here we sent it to your apartment on . . . uh . . . Center Street.

Female Student

Oh, that's my old apartment . . . I moved out of there a little while ago . . .

Receptionist

Well . . . and I suppose you haven't changed your mailing address at the administration office. Well, that would explain it.

Female Student

Yeah, I guess that's it. But, how can they cancel a class after offering it? If I'd known this was gonna happen, I'd've taken it last semester.

Receptionist

I know, it's really inconvenient for you; I understand that, but, um . . . if we don't have enough students signed up for the course, the college can't offer it. You know, it's, um, a practical issue, like, we can't have an instructor when there're only a few students in the class. You see what I mean?

Female Student

I guess, but now I don't know what course I should take instead.

Receptionist

Okay, let's see . . . do you have any courses you were gonna take next semester? If you do, you might wanna take 'em now and sign up for Physics 403 next semester.

Female Student

Yeah, I guess I could do that. I just hope it won't be canceled again. Do you know how many people have to be enrolled in order to keep a class from being canceled?

Receptionist

Well, it depends on the class, but for that class, you have to have . . . um . . . let's see . . . usually it'd be at least 10 people, but since it was canceled this semester, they might even do it with less. But you know what you should do? Give the physics department a call a coupla weeks before the semester starts. They'll be able to tell you if they're planning to go through with it . . . It's their decision, actually.

Female Student

Oh, OK, I'll do that. Thanks for the info.

Receptionist

No problem. Sorry about the class . . . Oh, why don't you go change your mailing address now; it'll only take a minute.

Female Student

Oh, oh, sure, I'll do that right away.

Answer Explanations

1. **B** This is a Gist-Purpose question. Before coming to the registrar's office, the woman had gone to where her physics class was supposed to meet. Finding the room empty, she assumed that the class must be meeting elsewhere and went to the registrar's office to find out the new location. Choice B therefore is the correct answer. She and the man discuss her change of address (choice A) only after she learns that the class had been canceled. She does not need to know where the science building is (choice C) because she has already been there. She does complain about the course's being canceled (choice D), but only after the man informs her about it.

2. **C** This is a Connecting Content question. Identifying the correct answer, choice C, requires integrating information that the man and the woman exchange—his telling her that the college sent the cancellation notice to the woman's apartment on Center Street, and her replying that she had moved away from that address. The woman initially speculates that she might have thrown away the letter (choice A), but she did not. Nothing about a room-mate (choice B) or about the notice's having been sent to the wrong student (choice D) is mentioned or implied by either speaker.

3. **A** This is a Detail question. The correct answer, choice A, paraphrases the man's explanation that the college cannot offer a course if too few students sign up to take it. This point is reinforced later when the man says that, generally, at least 10 students must sign up for a course or it will be canceled.

4. **D** This is also a Detail question. Toward the end of the conversation, the man advises the woman to call the physics department before the next semester begins to find out if enough people had signed up for Physics 403. Thus choice D is correct.

5. **D** You are asked to listen again to this part of the conversation:

Female Student

Excuse me, uh, I'm supposed to be having my physics class in the science building, but no one's in the classroom . . . Could you tell me where the class is? Physics 403? Has it been moved?

Receptionist

Well, there's a room assignment sheet on the bulletin board outside this office . . .

Then you are asked what the man implies when he says this:

Well, there's a room assignment sheet on the bulletin board outside this office . . .

Like most replay questions, this question requires you to Understand the Function of What Is Said. In responding to the woman's question by pointing out that class locations are on display nearby, the receptionist implies that the woman can get that information without his help. Thus choice D is correct. At this point in the conversation, the receptionist has not yet checked the computer, which is how he discovers the cancellation (choice A). It is possible that the receptionist does not know where the science building is (choice B) and that many room assignments have been changed (choice C), but the conversation does not touch on either of these possibilities.

Questions 6–11

Track 59 Listening Script

Narrator
Listen to part of a lecture in an environmental science class.

Environmental Science

Professor

Now, we've been talking about the loss of animal habitat from housing developments, um, growing cities . . . small habitat losses. But today I want to begin talking about what happens when habitat is reduced across a large area. There are, of course, animal species that require large areas of habitat . . . and, um, some migrate over very long distances. So what's the impact of habitat loss on those animals? Animals that need large areas of habitat?

Well, I'll use the hummingbirds as an example. Now, you know a hummingbird is amazingly small. But even though it's really tiny, it migrates over very long distances . . . travels up and down the Western Hemisphere . . . the Americas . . . back and forth between where it breeds in the summer and the warmer climates where it spends the winter. So we would say that this whole area over which it migrates is its habitat, because on this long-distance journey, it needs to come down to feed and sleep every so often, right?

Well, the hummingbird beats its wings—get this—about 3,000 times per minute. So you think, wow, it must need a lot of energy, a lot of food, right? Well, it does—it drinks a lot of nectar from flowers and feeds on some insects—but it's energy-efficient, too. You can't say it isn't. I mean as it flies all the way across the Gulf of Mexico, it uses up almost none of its body fat. But that doesn't mean it doesn't need to eat! So hummingbirds have to rely on plants in their natural habitat. And it goes without saying, but . . . well, the opposite is true as well. Plants depend on hummingbirds too. There are some flowers that can only be pollinated by the hummingbird. Without it stopping to feed and spreading pollen from flower to flower, these plants would cease to exist!

But the problem, well . . . as natural habitat along these migration routes is developed by humans for housing or agriculture, or, um, cleared for raising cattle, for instance . . . there's less food available for migrating hummingbirds. Their nesting sites are affected, too . . . the same . . . by the same sorts of human activities. And all of these activities pose a real threat to the hummingbird population.

So, to help them survive, we need to preserve their habitats . . . And one of the concrete ways people have been doing this is by cleaning up polluted habitat areas . . . and then replanting flowers, uh, replanting native flowers that hummingbirds feed on. Promoting ecological tourism is another way to help save their habitat. As the number of visitors—ecotourists who come to hummingbird habitats to watch the birds—the more the number of visitors grows, the more local businesses profit. So ecological tourism can bring financial rewards. All the more reason to value these beautiful little creatures and their habitat, right?

But to understand more about how to protect and support hummingbirds the best we can, we've gotta learn more about their breeding . . . nesting . . . sites and, uh, migration routes—and also about the natural habitats we find there. That should help us determine how to prevent further decline in the population.

A good research method . . . a good way to learn more . . . is by, um, running a banding study. Banding the birds allows us to track them over their lifetime. It's a practice that's been used by researchers for years. In fact, most of what we know about hummingbirds comes from banding studies . . . where we, uh, capture a hummingbird and make sure all the information about it—like . . . its weight and, um, age and length—are all recorded . . . put into international . . . an international information database. And, then we place an extremely lightweight band around one of its legs . . . well, what looks like a leg—although, technically it's considered part of the bird's foot. Anyway, these bands are perfectly safe. And some hummingbirds have worn them for years with no evidence of any problems. The band is labeled with a tracking number . . . oh, and there's a phone number on the band for people to call, for free, to report a banded bird they've found or recaptured.

So when a banded bird is recaptured and reported, we learn about its migration route, its growth . . . and how long it's been alive . . . its life span. One recaptured bird had been banded almost 12 years earlier! She's one of the oldest hummingbirds on record.

Another interesting thing we've learned is . . . that some hummingbirds, uh, they no longer use a certain route; they travel by a different route to reach their destination. And findings like these have been of interest to biologists and environmental scientists in a number of countries, who are trying to understand the complexities of how changes in a habitat . . . affect the species in it—species like the hummingbirds.

Answer Explanations

6. **C** This is a Gist-Content question. After the professor establishes loss of wildlife habitat as the general topic, she turns to the hummingbird's migratory routes as an extended example of the potential impact of losing large habitats and efforts being made to reverse this trend. Thus choice C is the correct answer. Changes in the migratory patterns of hummingbirds (choice A) are discussed only briefly at the end of the lecture as an interesting finding. The adaptation of hummingbirds to urban environments (choice B) is not mentioned at all. Ecotourism (choice D) is mentioned only in passing, as one of a number of ways to preserve habitats.

7. **B** This is a Making Inferences question. Choice B is the correct answer. The professor explains how land along hummingbird migration routes is being used in farming and cattle raising, among other things. She points out that these activities reduce food availability for hummingbirds and affect their nesting sites. In saying that these human activities all "pose a real threat to the hummingbird population," she implies a potential decrease in the population if more land is used this way.

8. **C** This is a Detail question. The professor explicitly states that people have been trying to preserve hummingbird habitats by cleaning up polluted areas and then planting native flowers for the birds to feed on. Thus choice C is the correct answer. Building feeding stations (choice A), punishing polluters (choice B), and identifying various species (choice D) are also things that people could conceivably do to help hummingbirds survive, but the professor does not mention any of them.

9. **B** This is another Detail question. Choice B is correct. The professor describes a research study designed to collect information about humming-bird migration. This research involves placing lightweight bands on hummingbirds. Information is collected when people who find or recapture the hummingbirds use the phone number on the band to contact the researchers. The study does not involve radio tracking devices (choice A), counting yearly returns by birds to the same region (choice C), or comparing the migration routes of old and young birds (choice D).

10. **C** This is a Connecting Content question. A research finding mentioned at the end of the lecture is that some hummingbirds have stopped using certain routes "to reach their destination." Since the destinations the professor is referring to are migration destinations, she is implying that for some hummingbirds, a change in migration patterns has occurred. Choice C is therefore the correct answer. The other answer choices consist of specific statements concerning habitats (choice A), preservation efforts (choice B), and food sources (choice D); nothing the professor says in the lecture supports these specific statements.

11. **D** You are asked to listen again to this part of the lecture:

So hummingbirds have to rely on plants in their natural habitat. And it goes without saying, but . . . well, the opposite is true as well. Plants depend on hummingbirds too.

You are then asked what the professor implies when she says this:

And it goes without saying . . .

This question requires you to Understand the Function of What Is Said. Choice D is the correct answer. "It goes without saying" is a common phrase used by speakers to signal that they are about to say (or have just said) something that probably does not need to be said because it is very obvious. The other answer choices are all potential misunderstandings of this phrase.

Questions 12–17

Track 61 Listening Script

Narrator
Listen to part of a lecture in a film history class.

Professor
Okay, we've been discussing film in the 1920s and '30s, and, ah, how back then, film categories as we know them today had not yet been established. We, ah, said that, by today's standards, many of the films of the '20s and '30s would be considered "hybrids"; that is, a mixture of styles that wouldn't exactly fit into any of today's categories. And in that context, today we're going to talk about a, a filmmaker who began making very unique films in the late 1920s. He was French, and his name was Jean Painlevé.

Jean Painlevé was born in 1902. He made his first film in 1928. Now, in a way, Painlevé's films conform to norms of the '20s and '30s; that is, they don't fit very neatly into the categories we use to classify films today. That said, even by the standards of the '20s and '30s, Painlevé's films were a unique hybrid of styles. He had a special way of fusing—or, or some people might say confusing—science and fiction; his films begin with facts, but then they become more and more fictional—they gradually add more and more fictional elements. In fact, Painlevé was known for saying that "science is fiction."

Painlevé was a, a pioneer in underwater filmmaking, and a lot of his short films focus on the aquatic animal world. He liked to show small underwater creatures displaying what seemed like familiar human characteristics—what we think of as unique to humans. He might take a, a clip of a mollusk going up and down in the water and set it to music—you know, to make it look as if the mollusk were dancing to the music like a human being. That sort of thing. But then he'd suddenly change the image or narration to remind us how different the animals are, how unlike humans. He confused his audience in the way he portrayed the animals he filmed, mixing up our notions of the categories "human" and "animal." The films make us a little uncomfortable at times because we're uncertain about what we're seeing. It gives his films an uncanny feature . . . the familiar made unfamiliar, the normal made suspicious. He liked twists; he liked the unusual. In fact, one of his favorite sea animals was the sea horse because with sea horses, it's the male that gets pregnant, it's the male that carries the babies. And he thought that was great. His first and most celebrated underwater film is about the sea horse.

Susan? You have a question?

Female Student

But underwater filmmaking wasn't that unusual, was it? I mean weren't there other people making movies underwater?

Professor

Well, actually it was pretty rare at that time. I mean we're talking the early 1930s here.

Female Student

But what about Jacques Cousteau? Wasn't he, like, an innovator, you know, with underwater photography, too?

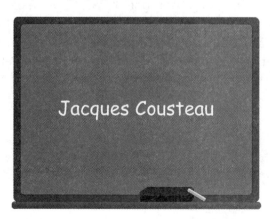

Professor

Ah, Jacques Cousteau. Well, Painlevé and Cousteau did both film underwater, and they were both innovators, so you're right in that sense, but that's pretty much where the similarities end. First of all, Painlevé was about 20 years ahead of Cousteau . . . Um, and Cousteau's adventures were high-tech, with lots of fancy equipment, whereas Painlevé kind of patched equipment together as he needed it . . . Uh, Cousteau usually filmed large animals, usually in the open sea, whereas Painlevé generally filmed smaller animals, and, and he liked to film in shallow water . . . Uh, what else? Well, the main difference was that Cousteau simply investigated and presented the facts; he, he didn't mix in fiction. He was a strict documentarist; he set the standard, really, for the nature documentary. Painlevé, on the other hand, as we said before, mixed in elements of fiction, and his films are much more artistic, incorporating music as an important element.

John, you have a question?

Male Student

Well, maybe I shouldn't be asking this . . . Uh, but if Painlevé's films are so special, so good, why haven't we ever heard of them? I mean everyone's heard of Jacques Cousteau . . .

Professor

Well, that's a fair question. Uh, the short answer is that Painlevé's style just never caught on with the general public. I mean it probably goes back, at least in part, to what we mentioned earlier, that, that people didn't know what to make of his films, that they were confused by them. Whereas Cousteau's documentaries were very straightforward, uh, met people's expectations more than Painlevé's films did. But your true film-history buffs know about him, and Painlevé's still highly respected in many circles.

Answer Explanations

12. **A** This is a Gist-Purpose question. The correct answer is choice A. The professor begins the lecture by briefly reviewing a previous discussion about films of the 1920s and 1930s and their hybrid style. Then he turns to a discussion of the style of one particular filmmaker, Jean Painlevé, and spends the rest of the lecture talking about him and his films.

13. **D** This is a Connecting Content question. Choice D is the correct answer. Identifying it requires integrating two important pieces of information. The first is the professor's statement at the beginning of the lecture that films from the 1920s and '30s do not fit neatly into today's film categories. The second piece of information comes right afterward, when the professor says that "Painlevé's films conform to norms of the '20s and '30s," meaning that his films, too, are difficult to categorize.

14. **B** This is a Detail question. The professor discusses the confusing aspects of Painlevé's films at considerable length and focuses, in particular, on the way Painlevé mixes up the audience's notions of human and animal characteristics. Thus the correct answer is choice B.

15. **C** This is an Understanding Organization question. The reason that the professor discusses sea horses is to illustrate the unusualness of Painlevé's subject matter. Painlevé's first film was about sea horses, which are unusual because the males carry the babies. Choice C is therefore the correct answer.

16. **B** This is another Connecting Content question. The professor compares the film styles of Jacques Cousteau and Painlevé in response to an objection raised by the female student. She questions the professor's characterization of Painlevé's films as special and points out that other filmmakers, like Cousteau, also made underwater films. The professor emphasizes the uniqueness of Painlevé's films by explaining that Cousteau's films were straightforward, fact-based documentaries that met people's expectations, unlike Painlevé's films, which mixed fact with fiction in a way that was both unique and confusing. Thus choice B is the correct answer.

17. **C** You are asked to decide what the student is implying when he says this:

Well, maybe I shouldn't be asking this . . . Uh, but if Painlevé's films are so special, so good, why haven't we ever heard of them? I mean everyone's heard of Jacques Cousteau . . .

This question requires you to Understand the Function of What Is Said. After listening to what the professor has been saying about Painlevé's films, the student cannot understand why they are not more popular or better known. The student's replayed statement suggests that he believes that Painlevé's films deserve the same level of recognition that Cousteau's films have received. Thus choice C is the correct answer.

Questions 18–22

Track 63 Listening Script

Narrator

Listen to a conversation between a student and a professor.

Male Student

Hi, Professor Archer. You know how in class last week you said that you were looking for students who were interested in volunteering for your archaeology project?

Professor

Of course. Are you volunteering?

Male Student

Yes, I am. It sounds really interesting. But, ummm, do I need to have any experience with these kinds of projects?

Professor

No, not really. I assume that most students taking the introductory-level class will have little or no experience with archaeological research, but that's OK.

Male Student

Oh, good—that's a relief. Actually, that's why I'm volunteering for the project—to get experience. What kind of work is it?

Professor

Well, as you know, we're studying the history of the campus this semester. This used to be an agricultural area, and we already know that where the main lecture hall now stands there once were a farmhouse and barn that were erected in the late 1700s. We're excavating near the lecture hall to see what types of artifacts we find—you know, things people used in the past that got buried when the campus was constructed. We've already begun to find some very interesting items like, um, old bottles, buttons, pieces of clay pottery . . .

Male Student

Buttons and clay pottery? Did the old owners leave in such a hurry that they left their clothes and dishes behind?

Professor

That's just one of the questions we hope to answer with this project.

Male Student

Wow—and it's all right here on campus . . .

Professor

That's right, no traveling involved. I wouldn't expect volunteers to travel to a site, especially in the middle of the semester. We expect to find many more things, but we do need more people to help.

Male Student

So . . . how many student volunteers are you looking for?

Professor

I'm hoping to get five or six. I've asked for volunteers in all the classes I teach, but no one's responded. You're the first person to express interest.

Male Student

Uh . . . sounds like it could be a lot of work. Is there . . . umm . . . is there any way I can use the experience to get some extra credit in class? I mean can I write a paper about it?

Professor

I think it'll depend on what type of work you do in the excavation, but I imagine we can arrange something. Well, actually, I've been considering offering extra credit for class because I've been having a tough time getting volunteers . . . Extra credit is always a good incentive for students.

Male Student

And . . . how often would you want the volunteers to work?

Professor

We're asking for three or four hours per week, depending on your schedule. A senior researcher—I think you know John Franklin, my assistant—is on-site every day.

Male Student

Sure, I know John. By the way, will there be some sort of training?

Professor

Yes, uh, I wanna wait till Friday to see how many students volunteer. And then I'll schedule a training class next week at a time that's convenient for everyone.

Male Student

OK, I'll wait to hear from you. Thanks a lot for accepting me!

Answer Explanations

18. **B** This is a Gist-Purpose question. The correct answer is choice B. The student opens the conversation by asking the professor about her request for volunteers for an archaeology project. The project's timing—the middle of the semester—is mentioned later, when the professor says that she would not expect students to travel to a site in the middle of the semester. Choosing the correct answer thus requires the integration of these two pieces of information from different parts of the conversation. Choice A is incorrect because the project is voluntary, not an assignment. It takes place during the semester, not during the summer (choice C). Although the student asks about extra credit, presumably to improve his grade (choice D), he brings this up as an afterthought, when he hears how much work is involved.

19. **A** This is a Detail question. The professor states that the lecture hall was built where a farmhouse and barn from the 1700s once stood. Thus choice A is correct. Pottery (choice B), clothes (choice C), and bottles (choice D) are mentioned in the context of artifacts—items that may have belonged to the farm's owners.

20. **C** This is a Detail question. The on-campus location of the project is mentioned several times during the conversation, and both speakers cite this as an advantage: volunteers will not need to travel. Thus choice C is correct.

21. **A** This is another Detail question. Choice A is correct. When the student asks if he could earn extra credit for volunteering, the professor responds by pointing out that she is considering offering extra credit as an incentive for more students to volunteer. The other three choices could be plausible incentives as well, but the professor does not mention any of them as a way to get more volunteers.

22. **C** This is a Connecting Content question. When the student asks about training, the professor notes that she has not scheduled a specific time for it, and he responds that he will wait to hear from her. Choice C is therefore the correct answer. The professor already provided the name of the senior researcher (choice A), so this is not information the student still needs. Books (choice B) are not mentioned at all in the conversation. As for the project's location (choice D), this is information the student was given early on.

Questions 23–28

Track 64 Listening Script

Narrator

Listen to part of a lecture in an art history class. The professor has been discussing the origins of art.

Professor

Some of the world's oldest preserved art is the cave art of Europe, most of it in Spain and France. And, uh, the earliest cave paintings found to date are those of the Chauvet cave in France, discovered in 1994.

And, you know, I remember when I heard about the results of the dating of the Chauvet paintings. I said to my wife, "Can you believe these paintings are over 30,000 years old?" and my three-year-old daughter piped up and said, "Is that older than my great-grandmother?" That was the oldest age she knew. And, you know, come to think of it, it's pretty hard for me to really understand how long 30,000 years is too. I mean, we tend to think the people who lived at that time must have been pretty primitive . . . but I'm gonna show you some slides in a few minutes, and I think you'll agree with me that this art is anything but primitive—they're masterpieces. And they look so real, so alive, that it's very hard to imagine that they're so very old.

Now, not everyone agrees on exactly how old. A number of the Chauvet paintings have been dated—by a lab—to 30,000 or more years ago. That would make them not just older than any other cave art, but about twice as old as the art in the caves at Altamira or Lascaux, which you may have heard of.

Some people find it hard to believe Chauvet is so much older than Altamira and Lascaux, and they noted that only one lab did the dating for Chauvet, without independent confirmation from any other lab.

But be that as it may, whatever the exact date, whether it's 15,000, 20,000, or 30,000 years ago, the Chauvet paintings are from the dawn of art, so they're a good place to start our discussion of cave painting.

Now, one thing you've gotta remember is the context of these paintings. Paleolithic humans—that's the period we're talking about here, the Paleolithic, the early Stone Age, not too long after humans first arrived in Europe. The climate was significantly colder then, and so rock shelters—shallow caves—were valued as homes protected from the wind and rain. And in some cases at least, artists drew on the walls of their homes. But many of the truly great cave art sites—like Chauvet—were never inhabited. These paintings were made deep inside a dark cave, where no natural light can penetrate. There's no evidence of people ever living here—cave bears, yes, but not humans.

You would have had to make a special trip into the cave to make the paintings, and a special trip to go see it, and each time you'd have to bring along torches to light your way. And people did go see the art—there's charcoal marks from their torches on the cave walls, clearly dating from thousands of years after the paintings were made—so we can tell people went there. They came, but they didn't stay. Deep inside a cave like that is not really a place you'd want to stay, so, uh, why? What inspired the Paleolithic artists to make such beautiful art in such inaccessible places? We'll never really know, of course, though it's interesting to speculate.

But, uh . . . getting to the paintings themselves. Virtually all Paleolithic cave art represents animals, and Chauvet is no exception. The artists were highly skilled at using—or even enhancing—the natural shape of the cave walls to give depth and perspective to their drawings. The sense of motion and vitality in these animals—well, wait till I show you the slides. Anyway, most Paleolithic cave art depicts large herbivores. Horses are most common overall, with deer and bison pretty common too. Probably animals they hunted. But earlier, at Chauvet, there's a significant interest in large, dangerous animals. Lots of rhinoceroses, lions, mammoths, bears . . . remember that the ranges of many animal species were different back then, so all these animals actually lived in the region at that time—but, uh, the Chauvet artists didn't paint people. There's a half-man, half-bison creature, and there's outlines of human hands, but no depiction of a full human.

So why these precise animals? Why not birds . . . fish . . . snakes? Was it for their religion? Magic? Or sheer beauty? We don't know, but whatever it was, it was worth it to them to spend hours deep inside a cave, with just a torch between them and utter darkness. So, on that note, let's dim the lights so we can see these slides and actually look at the techniques they used.

Answer Explanations

23. **Ⓐ** This is a Gist-Content question. The professor begins by pointing out that Europe is the home of the oldest examples of preserved cave art. He then identifies the Chauvet cave in France as the site of the earliest cave paintings, dating from "the dawn of art." The rest of the lecture focuses on various aspects of the paintings in the Chauvet cave. Thus choice A is the correct answer. The other choices contain words or ideas that the professor refers to, but they are not the main topic of the lecture.

24. **Ⓓ** This is an Understanding Organization question. The professor mentions his young daughter's effort to grasp a very long time line through her most familiar frame of reference: her great-grandmother. He mentions his daughter to reinforce the difficulty that he personally has grasping the notion of 30,000 years—the age of the cave drawings he is talking about. Choice D is therefore the correct answer.

25. **Ⓐ** This question requires you to Understand the Speaker's Attitude. You are asked to identify an opinion that is expressed by the professor. Choice A is correct because it paraphrases the professor's description of the Chauvet drawings as "masterpieces." The professor only speculates about the *possible* religious significance of the drawings, which is different from saying that the drawings *probably* reflected the artists' religious beliefs (choice B). He mentions Lascaux and Altamira not to compare the sophistication of drawings in those caves with the Chauvet drawings (choice C), but to compare them in terms of age. Choice D misstates the age comparison: the professor believes that the Chauvet drawings are considerably older.

26. **Ⓑ** This is a Making Inferences question. The professor says that the charcoal marks on the walls of the Chauvet cave came from torches of people who went to see the paintings. He also says that the marks date from thousands of years after the paintings were made. Since the date of the marks can be established relative to when the paintings were made, the relative date of the visits can be established as well—thousands of years after the paintings were made. Thus choice B is the correct answer.

27. **Ⓑ** This is a Detail question. Choice B is correct. The professor first notes that the animals represented in most Paleolithic art were large herbivores—plant-eating animals that were probably hunted. He then contrasts these animals with the large, dangerous animals depicted at Chauvet, including rhinoceroses, lions, mammoths, and bears.

28. **Ⓒ Ⓓ** This is another Detail question. The two correct answers come from different parts of the lecture. In the middle of the lecture, the professor discusses a curious aspect of the Chauvet paintings—their location deep inside an inaccessible cave where sunlight cannot reach. He says, "We'll never really know" what led artists to create beautiful art in such a remote place (choice D). Later in the lecture, he wonders aloud why the cave artists drew rhinoceroses, lions, mammoths, and bears instead of other animals, like birds, fish, or snakes. Here, too, he says, we do not know the reason. Thus choice C is also correct.

Speaking

Listening Scripts, Important Points, and Sample Responses with Rater Comments

Use the sample Independent and Integrated Speaking rubrics on pages 180–183 to see how responses are scored. The raters who listen to your responses will analyze them in three general categories. These categories are Delivery, Language Use, and Topic Development. All three categories have equal importance.

This section includes important points that should be covered when answering each question. All of these points must be present in a response in order for it to receive the highest score in the Topic Development category. These important points are guides to the kind of information raters expect to hear in a high-level response.

This section also refers to example responses on the accompanying audio tracks. Some responses were scored at the highest level, while others were not. The responses are followed by explanations of their scores.

Question 1: Paired Choice

Track 65 Listening Script

Narrator

Some students prefer to work on class assignments by themselves. Others believe it is better to work in a group. Which do you prefer? Explain why.

> **Preparation Time: 15 Seconds**
> **Response Time: 45 Seconds**

Important Points

In this question, you need to say whether you prefer to work alone or in groups to complete class assignments, and then explain the reason for your preference. You should not simply give a list of reasons, such as *"I prefer to work in groups because it is more interesting plus many people help and also you can learn from other people . . ."* It is better if you develop one or two reasons fully. For example, if you prefer to work in groups, you could say, *"I prefer working in groups because usually in group work, different people know different things about the topic, and because of that, you get a deeper understanding of the assignment. For example, there was a student from Venezuela in a group assignment I had, and we were supposed to describe how crude oil prices are set. She helped us understand problems in oil production in a much deeper way because her parents worked in oil production . . ."*

Sample Responses

Play Track 70 to hear a high-level response for Question 1.

Rater Comments

This is a fully developed response to the question. She gives two reasons for preferring to work by herself—having strong opinions and managing time well—and gives a clear explanation of why each is more suitable for working alone. Her speech is fluent, and she uses appropriate intonation and stress on certain words (such as "*I*" in *the way **I** see them*) to convey meaning. She uses advanced-level vocabulary, such as *a structured approach,* and high-level grammatical constructions with ease.

Play Track 71 to hear a low-level response for Question 1.

Rater Comments

While her pronunciation is clear, this speaker struggles and often fails to come up with words to express her meaning, such as using *good things* rather than the more appropriate and specific *advantages* or *benefits*. Since she spends time trying to describe benefits of both group work and working alone, she runs out of time before she can support her true preference for working alone, other than saying it allows more independence. Her answer is very choppy and vague. She does not demonstrate that she has command of grammar beyond a very basic level.

Question 2: Fit and Explain

Track 66 Listening Script

Narrator

The university's Dining Services Department has announced a change. Read an announcement about this change. You will have 45 seconds to read the announcement. Begin reading now.

> **Reading Time: 45 Seconds**

Hot Breakfasts Eliminated

Beginning next month, Dining Services will no longer serve hot breakfast foods at university dining halls. Instead, students will be offered a wide assortment of cold breakfast items in the morning. These cold breakfast foods, such as breads, fruit, and yogurt, are healthier than many of the hot breakfast items that we will stop serving, so health-conscious students should welcome this change. Students will benefit in another way as well, because limiting the breakfast selection to cold food items will save money and allow us to keep our meal plans affordable.

Narrator

Now listen to two students discussing the announcement.

Woman

Do you believe any of this? It's ridiculous.

Man

What do you mean? It is important to eat healthy foods . . .

Woman

Sure it is, but they're saying yogurt's better for you than an omelet . . . or than hot cereal? I mean whether something's hot or cold, that shouldn't be the issue. Except maybe on a really cold morning, but in that case, which is going to be better for you—a bowl of cold cereal or a nice warm omelet? It's obvious; there's no question.

Man

I'm not going to argue with you there.

Woman

And this whole thing about saving money . . .

Man

What about it?

Woman

Well, they're actually going to make things worse for us, not better. 'Cause if they start cutting back and we can't get what we want right here, on campus, well, we're going to be going off campus and pay off-campus prices, and you know what? That will be expensive. Even if it's only two or three mornings a week, it can add up.

Narrator

The woman expresses her opinion of the change that has been announced. State her opinion and explain her reasons for holding that opinion.

> **Preparation Time: 30 Seconds**
> **Response Time: 60 Seconds**

Important Points

The woman does not think that Dining Services should stop providing hot breakfast foods. She says that for health, the temperature of the food is not the issue (except on cold days, when warm food is better). She also says that the change will not make breakfasts more affordable, but rather will make them more expensive, since students will have to go off campus (where the prices are higher) to buy the food they want.

Sample Responses

Play Track 72 to hear a high-level response for Question 2.

Rater Comments

This response covers all the key points of the article and conversation with great clarity and supporting details. The speaker's pronunciation is very clear, and he uses good rhythm and intonation. He uses a good variety of vocabulary and idiomatic expressions that help him express his meaning clearly.

Play Track 73 to hear a mid-level response for Question 2.

Rater Comments

This speaker does a fairly good job of explaining the woman's disagreement with the proposal in the article, but her speech is very choppy (not fluent). She has to pause often to think of the correct word or phrase to say. Sometimes her limited vocabulary prevents her from clearly expressing what she means (for example, the meaning of *the offer is their last offer for choosing* is unclear). Her pronunciation is generally easy to understand but occasionally requires listener effort.

Question 3: General/Specific

Track 67 Listening Script

Narrator

Read the passage from a sociology textbook. You have 50 seconds to read the passage. Begin reading now.

Reading Time: 50 Seconds

Cognitive Dissonance

Individuals sometimes experience a contradiction between their actions and their beliefs—between what they are doing and what they believe they should be doing. These contradictions can cause a kind of mental discomfort known as *cognitive dissonance*. People experiencing cognitive dissonance often do not want to change the way they are acting, so they resolve the contradictory situation in another way: they change their interpretation of the situation in a way that minimizes the contradiction between what they are doing and what they believe they should be doing.

Narrator

Now listen to part of a lecture about this topic in a sociology class.

Professor

This is a true story—from my own life. In my first year in high school, I was addicted to video games. I played them all the time, and I wasn't studying enough—I was failing chemistry; that was my hardest class. So this was a conflict for me because I wanted a good job when I grew up, and I believed—I knew—that if you want a good career, you gotta do well in school. But . . . I just couldn't give up video games.

I was completely torn. And my solution was to . . . to change my perspective. See, the only class I was doing really badly in was chemistry. In the others I was, I was okay. So I asked myself if I wanted to be a chemist when I grew up, and the fact is I didn't. I was pretty sure I wanted to be a sociologist. So . . . I told myself my chemistry class didn't matter because sociologists don't really need to know chemistry. In other words, I changed my understanding of what it meant to do well in school. I reinterpreted my situation: I used to think that doing well in school meant doing well in all my classes, but now I decided that succeeding in school meant only doing well in the classes that related directly to my future career.

I eliminated the conflict, at least in my mind.

Narrator

Using the example discussed by the professor, explain what cognitive dissonance is and how people often deal with it.

> **Preparation Time: 30 Seconds**
> **Response Time: 60 Seconds**

Important Points

Cognitive dissonance occurs when people's beliefs and actions are in conflict with each other. People deal with cognitive dissonance by changing their interpretation of the situation. For example, the professor could not stop playing video games even though he believed it was causing him to fail chemistry. He then told himself that since he wanted to be a sociologist, he did not need to do well in chemistry.

Sample Responses

Play Track 74 to hear a high-level response for Question 3.

Rater Comments

This speaker efficiently and accurately explains the concept of cognitive dissonance and how people deal with it, as in the professor's example. Her speech is fluid, and she uses intonation and stress effectively to convey emphasis and meaning—for example, by stressing the words *actions* and *interpretation* as a contrast to demonstrate how people deal with cognitive dissonance (by changing their interpretation of a situation rather than their actions). She uses advanced-level vocabulary with accuracy and ease.

Play Track 75 to hear a mid-level response for Question 3.

Rater Comments

In this response, the speaker conveys the relevant information in the task, but not always with precision. For instance, when describing the professor's example, instead of saying the professor changed his *interpretation* of the situation, she says he began to *make up his own opinion*. Her pronunciation is clear, but her speech is marked by many pauses and hesitations.

Question 4: Summary

Track 68 Listening Script

Narrator

Now listen to part of a lecture in a psychology class. The professor is discussing advertising strategies.

Professor

In advertising, various strategies are used to persuade people to buy products. In order to sell more products, advertisers will often try to make us believe that a product will meet our needs or desires perfectly . . . even if it's not true. The strategies they use can be subtle, uh, "friendly" forms of persuasion that are sometimes hard to recognize.

In a lot of ads, repetition is a key strategy. Research shows that repeated exposure to a message, even something meaningless or untrue, is enough to make people accept it or see it in a positive light. You've all seen the car commercials on TV . . . like . . . uh, the one that refers to its "roomy" cars . . . over and over again. You know which one I mean . . . this guy is driving around and he keeps stopping to pick up different people—he picks up 3 or 4 people. And each time, the narrator says, "Plenty of room for friends, plenty of room for family, plenty of room for everybody." The same message is repeated several times in the course of the commercial. Now, the car, uh, the car actually looks kind of small . . . it's not a very big car at all, but you get the sense that it's pretty spacious. You'd think that the viewer would reach the logical conclusion that the slogan, uh, misrepresents the product. Instead, what usually happens is that when the statement "plenty of room" is repeated often enough, people are actually convinced it's true.

Um, another strategy they use is to get a celebrity to advertise a product. It turns out that we're more likely to accept an advertising claim made by somebody famous—a person we admire and find appealing. We tend to think they're trustworthy. So . . . um, you might have a car commercial that features a well-known race car driver. Now, it may not be a very fast car—uh, it could even be an inexpensive vehicle with a low performance rating. But if a popular race car driver is shown driving it, and saying, "I like my cars fast!" then people will believe the car is impressive for its speed.

Narrator

Using the examples from the talk, explain how persuasive strategies are used in advertising.

Preparation Time: 20 Seconds
Response Time: 60 Seconds

Important Points

Advertisers persuade people to buy their products by using persuasive strategies. One strategy is repetition of information (which may not be true information), such as when an advertisement for a small car keeps repeating that it has plenty of room. Another strategy is to use celebrities, because people trust them. For example, a famous race car driver might be used in an advertisement for a car (to give the impression the car is fast, even if it is not).

Sample Responses

Play Track 76 to hear a high-level response for Question 4.

Rater Comments

The speaker conveys all of the main and supporting points from the lecture. His speech is clear and fluid, and although he does not pronounce *subtle* correctly, this is a minor error that does not interfere with overall understanding of his speech. His pacing slows down at times as he attempts to recall information, but it is still easy to follow what he is saying. He also uses a variety of advanced-level vocabulary and grammatical constructions with good control.

Play Track 77 to hear a mid-level response for Question 4.

Rater Comments

This speaker discusses both advertising strategies described in the lecture, but in a vague way that is sometimes difficult to understand. For instance, he never mentions that the first example refers to a car advertisement, so it is unclear what he means when he says the message that *lots of your friends have space in it* is repeated. His pronunciation is easy to understand, but he pauses frequently throughout his response and demonstrates only a limited vocabulary range and control of grammar.

Writing

Listening Script, Topic Notes, and Sample Responses with Rater Comments

Use the Integrated Writing and Independent Writing scoring rubrics on pages 193–194 and 203–204 to see how responses are scored.

Writing Based on Reading and Listening

Track 69 Listening Script

Narrator

Now listen to part of a lecture on the topic you just read about.

Professor

Everything you just read about *Portrait of an Elderly Woman in a White Bonnet* is true, and yet, after a thorough reexamination of the painting, a panel of experts has recently concluded that it's indeed a work by Rembrandt. And here's why.

First, the fur collar. X-rays and analysis of the pigments in the paint have shown that the fur collar wasn't part of the original painting. The fur collar was painted over the top of the original painting about a hundred years after the painting was made. Why? Someone probably wanted to increase the value of the painting by making it look like a formal portrait of an aristocratic lady.

Second, the supposed error with light and shadow. Once the paint of the added fur collar was removed, the original painting could be seen. In the original painting the woman is wearing a simple collar of light-colored cloth. The light-colored cloth of this collar reflects light that illuminates part of the woman's face. That's why the face is not in partial shadow. So in the original painting, light and shadow are very realistic and just what we would expect from Rembrandt.

Finally, the wood panel. It turns out that when the fur collar was added, the wood panel was also enlarged with extra wood pieces glued to the sides and the top to make the painting more grand—and more valuable. So the original painting is actually painted on a single piece of wood—as would be expected from a Rembrandt painting. And in fact, researchers have found that the piece of wood in the original form of *Portrait of an Elderly Woman in a White Bonnet* is from the very same tree as the wood panel used for another painting by Rembrandt, his *Self-Portrait with a Hat*.

Narrator

Summarize the points made in the lecture, being sure to explain how they answer the specific problems presented in the reading passage.

Topic Notes

You should understand the reasons presented in the lecture that address the concerns in the reading passage. While the reading passage explains why people do not think the painting *Portrait of an Elderly Woman* was created by Rembrandt, the lecture presents new evidence showing that the painting was indeed created by Rembrandt.

A high-scoring essay will include the following points made by the lecturer and will explain how they address the points made in the reading passage:

Point Made in the Reading Passage	Contrasting Point from the Lecture
The fur collar in the painting does not match clothing typical of a servant woman, a detail that Rembrandt would not have overlooked.	The fur collar was added later in an attempt to increase the painting's value.
The light and shadow appear incorrectly in the painting, but Rembrandt was a master of painting light and shadow.	The light and shadow appeared incorrectly because of the fur collar that was added later. Once the fur collar was removed, revealing the original white collar, the light and shadow appeared correctly.
The portrait was painted on multiple wood panels, which was not typical of Rembrandt's works.	The original was painted on a single wood panel. Additional wood panels were added to the painting later in an attempt to increase its value.

Responses with scores of 4 and 5 generally clearly discuss all three main points in the table.

Sample Responses with Rater Comments

High-Level Response

Both texts deal with the question wheather or not the painting "Portrait of an Elderly Woman in a White Bonnet" was painted by the most famous Dutch painter Rembrandt. The text clearly states, that many facts prove that it wasn't painted by Rembrandt himself, but just attributed to him because of its style. In the lecture however the professor gives proof why it is in fact a work of the famous Dutch painter.

The first contradicting fact are the clothes of the woman in the portrait. She is wearing a white linen cap which gives her the appearance of a simple servant, whereas the luxurious fur collar she also wears doesn't fit. In the lecture is said, that after a thorough research people found out that the fur collar was added to the painting about 100 years later in order to increase the value of the workpiece, because now it illustrated an aristocratic lady instead of a servant.

Another problem with the painting was the display of light and shadow. Rembandt was known as a master of painting light and shadow, yet contradictionally the elements in the work don't fit together. But this problem could also be explained by now. By removing the additional fur collar one could see that the lady is wearing a simple light colored cloth, which reflects light into her face.

The third aspect which let people wonder about the origins of the painting was the fact, that the panel was made of several pieces of wood glued together instead of just one panel which was usual for works of Rembrandt. But the additional panels were also added later to enlarge the paiting. by doing this the painting seemed to be more valuable.

Another interesting fact is, that the main panel is made from the same tree like another painting of Rembrandt, 'Selfportrait with a hat'.

In the end it is clear that this painting is indeed a work of the Dutch painter and it should be reintegrated in the catalog of Rembrandt's paintings.

Rater Comments

This essay earns a high score because it successfully explains the opposing relationship between the reading and the lecture and goes on to identify all the important points and details. The response is appropriately organized, with the topic stated in the first and final paragraphs and each main point discussed in separate body paragraphs. Each main point is discussed clearly and with a good amount of detail. The writer, for example, correctly represents in the second paragraph the idea that the fur collar was added to the painting at a later date to make it appear more valuable. In the third paragraph, the light-and-shadow inconsistency is not described in concrete terms, but the writer does indicate it in general terms and explains its cause. Connectors and connecting phrases ("Another problem," "By removing the additional fur collar," "In the end") help make the writing cohesive and easy to read. The language is generally accurate, and minor errors ("In the lecture is said," "after a thorough research," "contradictionally") do not interfere with meaning.

Mid-Level Response

There are doubts whether Rembramdt painted Portrait of an Elderly Woman in a White Bonnet. The reading says that the painting wasn't paint by Rembrandt because of the leck of consistency observed. On the other hand the lecture says that Rembrandt is the real painter. The opinion expressed in the lecture is based on a third examination of the painting when the experts decided that Rembrandt is the real painter because of the examination of the fur colar, the light and shadow that were realistic and finally the elements of the wood panel.

Examining the fur colar from the painting, the experts noticed that the actual colar was painted over the top of the original painting over 100 years later. The reason of doing this was to increase the value of the painting.

Further on the light and color were very realistic, says the lecture. This opinion is formulated in opossition to the one from the reading that says that in this painting this elements do not fit together.

Finally the last reason why the lecture affirms that the painting belongs to Rebmrandt is based on the examination of the wood panel. Even though the wood panel was enlarged it was used the same tree that Rembrandt used in Self Portrait with a Hat.

In conclusion it seems that the argument given by the lecture overpower the reading part.

Rater Comments

Although this response clearly describes the relationship between the reading and the lecture in the first paragraph, it earns a mid-level score because it lacks some important details related to the three main points that follow. In the second paragraph, the writer does explain that the fur collar was added to the painting 100 years after it was created to increase its value, but the writer does not explain the initial problem mentioned in the reading (that the fur collar was not consistent with a servant woman's apparel). This makes it difficult for a reader who is not familiar with the passage and the lecture to see how the information about the collar is relevant to the topic. The third paragraph, in contrast, does indicate that the information from the reading and the information from the lecture regarding light and shadow differ, but this section lacks most of the important details. The third point, in paragraph 4, is not expressed precisely. The writer indicates that the fact that the wood came from the same tree as the wood for another Rembrandt painting is proof of its authenticity, yet it is not clear whether the writer is referring to the original panel or to the added panels. The writer also does not explain why the original panel was enlarged. Overall, the essay responds to the task and touches on all three main ideas, but these ideas are either vaguely or imprecisely conveyed. The language is generally clear, with only a few minor errors ("the painting wasn't paint by Rembrandt," "this elements do not fit together") that do not interfere with meaning.

Writing Based on Knowledge and Experience

Question

Do you agree or disagree with the following statement?

It is more important to keep your old friends than it is to make new friends.

Use specific reasons and examples to support your answer. Be sure to use your own words. Do **not** use memorized examples.

Topic Notes

This topic asks you to write about whether keeping old friends is more important than making new friends. Successful responses can agree with the statement, disagree with the statement, or discuss why old and new friends are equally important. No matter which position you take, it is important to support your opinion with details and examples.

If you agree with the statement, you should present and develop reasons that old friends are better than new friends. Some reasons for preferring old friends may include their ability to understand you, their willingness to help you in difficult situations, and interests and experiences they share with you. As part of supporting this approach, you could also mention that new friends do not have these attributes.

If you disagree with the statement, you should present and develop reasons that new friends are better than old friends. Some reasons for preferring new friends may include the opportunity to learn about different opinions and cultures, the chance to have new experiences, and the benefit of being around friends who understand changes in your life.

If you believe that old and new friends are equally important, you should present a balanced argument that explains the benefits of both types of friends. This can include points mentioned above, but many reasons not mentioned here can also be used in an effective essay.

Sample Responses with Rater Comments

High-Level Essay

In a lifetime, we are bound to meet many people, we get on well with some of them and they become our friends. As we grow up we meet new people and make new friends but it does not imply that they will replace our old ones. That is why I disagree with people who think that keeping old friends is more important than making new friends.

I think that there is no matter of more importance. Since old friends and new friends do not bring us the same things, we can not compare them. Indeed old friends are the ones we can count on; we trust them, they know us well, we have complicity and real friendship is just wondrful. When I feel sad or when I need to talk to someone about a serious problem, I go to see my old friends because they are reliable and I know that they will understand me more than anyone else. My old friends are very important to me and I agree with the fact that it is important to keep them and make efforts to keep contact.

However, I must admit that we are bound to lose some of our old friends sometimes. For example, I had a very good friend a few years ago but we do not see each other anymore since I moved in an other town. I guess that we also grew up and took a different way and there is no use to keep old friends when you realize that you have nothing left in common.

Therefore, it is also very important to make new friends. That is a way to learn, to change and they bring us different things. Making new friends makes us more open-minded, and in this way we can discover new personalities. For my part I enjoy making new friends, at school, at work, on holidays. I am conscious not to have close relationships with them at first but I need to be with other people and have fun. Sometimes they just remain acquaintances but they can also become good friends who could become old friends one day. For instance, I met a german girl on holiday two years ago and we got on very well, so we kept in touch and I went to visit her in Germany twice. She belongs to this kind of people who you know that they will be important in your life, and who you know you can have a long and strong friendship with.

As a conclusion I would say that everybody need to have a at least few real and strong friendship.

Rater Comments

This high-level essay effectively responds to the question by arguing the importance of having both old and new friends. The essay is organized logically, beginning with an introductory paragraph that states a clear thesis and continuing with three body paragraphs that develop distinct reasons that support the thesis. Each of the writer's points is well developed with appropriate details and examples. The first point, that old friends are reliable and understanding, is supported by the idea that old friends can help with serious problems. This is followed in the third paragraph by the idea that it is sometimes possible to lose old friendships. Here, the writer gives the example of losing a friend because of a move and no longer having anything in common. This third paragraph provides a nice connection between the ideas of wanting to keep old friends in the second paragraph and needing to make new friends in the fourth paragraph. This cohesion is also accomplished by using effective transitions ("However, I must admit," "Therefore, it is also very important to make new friends."). The final point, that it is important to make new friends, is also well supported by details about learning new things. The essay is rounded out by a personal example that shows that new friends can become old friends. Overall, this essay has nice progression and displays consistently strong language. The few language errors ("moved in an other town," "She belongs to this kind of people who you know") that do exist do not interfere with meaning and are not prevalent enough to lower the essay's score.

Mid-Level Essay

One of the most important thing in life is to spend time with the person you consider to be your best friend, in my opinion.

Firstable, nobody cannot know you better than an old friend does.

Your old friend can really guess you before you begin to speak. You do not have to explain all of your feelings he knows you too much for that. This feeling of understanding is incredibly good. It is like you are not alone anymore.

Secondly, keeping your old friends is the best way to have a link between your past and your life. It is a excellent pattern to know if you have changed well or not. It helps to keep your personnality and your personnal interests throught your life.

In addition, Old friends continue to be friends because they helps each other with the life difficulties.

The kind of helps creates a really deep love and friendship and it is why we say friends forever. It is too deep to give up. Consequently, friends become part of the family after many years. For example, I have had the same best friend since 1990. I know her and she knows me perfectly. I am closer to her than my own sister. We have share everything and we could be separate more than one month. I like her advices and our complementarity.

To clarify my opinion, I would say that for me it is also good to make new friends and to change your routine. Everybody needs that to progress and to fell good. But when I am thinking about the most importamt thing my choice is clear I really need more my old friend that the new I have met.

To conclude, Keep your old friends cloth to you and enj

Rater Comments

While this essay generally addresses the topic clearly, it earns a mid-level score because it features flaws in the development of some of its ideas and in overall structure. The writer lists three points to support the idea that old friends are important. The first two points, that old friends understand each other's feelings and that they provide a link to a person's past, are clearly expressed but only somewhat developed with vague explanations. The third point, that old friends can help each other through difficult times, is entirely unsupported. In addition, some elements in the response interrupt the progression of the essay. It is not clear how the sixth paragraph, which discusses the writer's best friend, supports any of the three points mentioned earlier in the essay. The first sentence in the seventh paragraph ("To clarify my opinion, I would say that for me it is also good to make new friends and to change your routine.") is also out of place and suggests that a new topic will be discussed, although the focus of the essay remains on the importance of old friends. These flaws, along with minor language errors ("they helps each other with the life difficulties," "I really need more my old friends that the new I have met."), earn this essay a mid-level score.

Authentic *TOEFL iBT*® Practice Test 4

本章是托福考试四套真题练习中的第四套。考生可以通过两种不同的方式进行测试：

- 通过本书：在接下来的书页中，考生可以看到所有的测试题目，请将答案写在规定的空白处。关于本测试中的听力部分，考生可以按照序号提示，播放对应音频。

- 电脑上：为了更真实地体验托福考试的实考环境，考生可以下载电脑版软件在电脑上进行模考。电脑版软件中的试题与书中的完全一样。阅读文章和相关问题将显示在屏幕上，考生可以点击给出的空白处输入答案。听力部分的测试则根据提示进行。

测试题目之后是答案和评分信息，以及听力部分的文字材料。除此以外，考生还可以看到答案的详细解释、口语回答样本和写作范文。

TOEFL iBT® **Practice Test 4**
READING

This section measures your ability to understand academic passages in English. You will have **54 minutes** to read and answer questions about **3 passages**. A clock at the top of the screen will display the starting time as **00 : 54 : 00** and show you how much time is remaining.

Most questions are worth 1 point, but the last question for each passage is worth more than 1 point. The directions for the last question indicate how many points you may receive.

Some passages in the computer-based test include a word or phrase that is underlined in blue. When you click on the word or phrase underlined in blue, you will see a verbal or visual definition of the word or term. In this book, those definitions are provided as endnotes below the reading passage.

Within this section, you can move to the next question by clicking on **Next**. You can skip questions and go back to them later as long as there is time remaining. If you want to return to previous questions, click on **Back**. You can click on **Review** at any time and the review screen will show you which questions you have answered and which you have not answered. From this review screen, you may go directly to any question you have already seen in the Reading section.

During this practice test, you may click the **Pause** icon at any time. This will stop the test until you decide to continue. You may continue the test in a few minutes or at any time during the period that your test is activated.

You will now begin the Reading section. Again, in an actual test you will have **54 minutes** to read the 3 passages and answer the questions. NOTE: In an actual test, some test takers might receive 4 passages; those test takers will have 72 minutes (1 hour and 12 minutes) to answer the questions.

Turn the page to begin the Reading section.

INDUSTRIALIZATION IN THE NETHERLANDS AND SCANDINAVIA

While some European countries, such as England and Germany, began to industrialize in the eighteenth century, the Netherlands and the Scandinavian countries of Denmark, Norway, and Sweden developed later. All four of these countries lagged considerably behind in the early nineteenth century. However, they industrialized rapidly in the second half of the century, especially in the last two or three decades. In view of their later start and their lack of coal—undoubtedly the main reason they were not among the early industrializers—it is important to understand the sources of their success.

All had small populations. At the beginning of the nineteenth century, Denmark and Norway had fewer than 1 million people, while Sweden and the Netherlands had fewer than 2.5 million inhabitants. All exhibited moderate growth rates in the course of the century (Denmark the highest and Sweden the lowest), but all more than doubled in population by 1900. Density varied greatly. The Netherlands had one of the highest population densities in Europe, whereas Norway and Sweden had the lowest. Denmark was in between but closer to the Netherlands.

Considering human capital as a characteristic of the population, however, all four countries were advantaged by the large percentages of their populations who could read and write. In both 1850 and 1914, the Scandinavian countries had the highest literacy rates in Europe, or in the world, and the Netherlands was well above the European average. This fact was of enormous value in helping the national economies find their niches in the evolving currents of the international economy.

Location was an important factor for all four countries. All had immediate access to the sea, and this had important implications for a significant international resource, fish, as well as for cheap transport, merchant marines, and the shipbuilding industry. Each took advantage of these opportunities in its own way. The people of the Netherlands, with a long tradition of fisheries and mercantile shipping, had difficulty in developing good harbors suitable for steamships; eventually they did so at Rotterdam and Amsterdam, with exceptional results for transit trade with Germany and central Europe and for the processing of overseas foodstuffs and raw materials (sugar, tobacco, chocolate, grain, and eventually oil). Denmark also had an admirable commercial history, particularly with respect to traffic through the Sound (the strait separating Denmark and Sweden). In 1857, in return for a payment of 63 million kronor from other commercial nations, Denmark abolished the Sound toll dues, the fees it had collected since 1497 for the use of the Sound. This, along with other policy shifts toward free trade, resulted in a significant increase in traffic through the Sound and in the port of Copenhagen.

The political institutions of the four countries posed no significant barriers to industrialization or economic growth. The nineteenth century passed relatively peacefully for these countries, with progressive democratization taking place in all of them. They were reasonably well governed, without notable corruption or grandiose state projects, although in all of them the government gave some aid to railways, and in Sweden the state built the main lines. As small countries dependent on foreign markets, they had few or low barriers to foreign trade in the main, though a protectionist movement developed in Sweden. In Denmark and Sweden agricultural reforms took place gradually from the late eighteenth century through the first half of the nineteenth, resulting in a new class of peasant landowners with a definite market orientation.

The key factor in the success of these countries (along with high literacy, which contributed to it) was their ability to adapt to the international division of labor determined by the early industrializers and to stake out areas of specialization in international markets for which they were especially well suited. This meant a great dependence on international commerce, which had notorious fluctuations; however, it also meant high returns to those aspects of production that were fortunate enough to be well placed in times of prosperity. In Sweden exports accounted for 18 percent of the national income in 1870, and in 1913, 22 percent of a much larger national income. In the early twentieth century, Denmark exported 63 percent of its agricultural production: butter, pork products, and eggs. It exported 80 percent of its butter, almost all to Great Britain, where it accounted for 40 percent of British butter imports.

Directions: Now answer the questions.

PARAGRAPH 1

While some European countries, such as England and Germany, began to industrialize in the eighteenth century, the Netherlands and the Scandinavian countries of Denmark, Norway, and Sweden developed later. All four of these countries lagged considerably behind in the early nineteenth century. However, they industrialized rapidly in the second half of the century, especially in the last two or three decades. In view of their later start and their lack of coal—undoubtedly the main reason they were not among the early industrializers—it is important to understand the sources of their success.

1. Paragraph 1 supports which of the following ideas about England and Germany?
   - (A) They were completely industrialized by the start of the nineteenth century.
   - (B) They possessed plentiful supplies of coal.
   - (C) They were overtaken economically by the Netherlands and Scandinavia during the early nineteenth century.
   - (D) They succeeded for the same reasons that the Netherlands and Scandinavia did.

GO ON TO THE NEXT PAGE

P A R A G R A P H S 2 A N D 3

All had small populations. At the beginning of the nineteenth century, Denmark and Norway had fewer than 1 million people, while Sweden and the Netherlands had fewer than 2.5 million inhabitants. All exhibited moderate growth rates in the course of the century (Denmark the highest and Sweden the lowest), but all more than doubled in population by 1900. Density varied greatly. The Netherlands had one of the highest population densities in Europe, whereas Norway and Sweden had the lowest. Denmark was in between but closer to the Netherlands.

Considering human capital as a characteristic of the population, however, all four countries were advantaged by the large percentages of their populations who could read and write. In both 1850 and 1914, the Scandinavian countries had the highest literacy rates in Europe, or in the world, and the Netherlands was well above the European average. This fact was of enormous value in helping the national economies find their niches in the evolving currents of the international economy.

2. According to paragraphs 2 and 3, which of the following contributed significantly to the successful economic development of the Netherlands and of Scandinavia?

   (A) The relatively small size of their populations
   (B) The rapid rate at which their populations were growing
   (C) The large amount of capital they had available for investment
   (D) The high proportion of their citizens who were educated

P A R A G R A P H 4

Location was an important factor for all four countries. All had immediate access to the sea, and this had important implications for a significant international resource, fish, as well as for cheap transport, merchant marines, and the shipbuilding industry. Each took advantage of these opportunities in its own way. The people of the Netherlands, with a long tradition of fisheries and mercantile shipping, had difficulty in developing good harbors suitable for steamships; eventually they did so at Rotterdam and Amsterdam, with exceptional results for transit trade with Germany and central Europe and for the processing of overseas foodstuffs and raw materials (sugar, tobacco, chocolate, grain, and eventually oil). Denmark also had an admirable commercial history, particularly with respect to traffic through the Sound (the strait separating Denmark and Sweden). In 1857, in return for a payment of 63 million kronor from other commercial nations, Denmark abolished the Sound toll dues, the fees it had collected since 1497 for the use of the Sound. This, along with other policy shifts toward free trade, resulted in a significant increase in traffic through the Sound and in the port of Copenhagen.

3. The word "abolished" in the passage is closest in meaning to

   (A) ended
   (B) raised
   (C) returned
   (D) lowered

4. According to paragraph 4, because of their location, the Netherlands and the Scandinavian countries had all of the following advantages when they began to industrialize EXCEPT

   Ⓐ low-cost transportation of goods
   Ⓑ access to fish
   Ⓒ shipbuilding industries
   Ⓓ military control of the seas

P A R A G R A P H 5

The political institutions of the four countries posed no significant barriers to industrialization or economic growth. The nineteenth century passed relatively peacefully for these countries, with progressive democratization taking place in all of them. They were reasonably well governed, without notable corruption or grandiose state projects, although in all of them the government gave some aid to railways, and in Sweden the state built the main lines. As small countries dependent on foreign markets, they had few or low barriers to foreign trade in the main, though a protectionist movement developed in Sweden. In Denmark and Sweden agricultural reforms took place gradually from the late eighteenth century through the first half of the nineteenth, resulting in a new class of peasant landowners with a definite market orientation.

5. The author includes the information that "a protectionist movement developed in Sweden" in order to

   Ⓐ support the claim that the political institutions of the four countries posed no significant barriers to industrialization or economic growth
   Ⓑ identify an exception to the general trend favoring few or low barriers to trade
   Ⓒ explain why Sweden industrialized less quickly than the other Scandinavian countries and the Netherlands
   Ⓓ provide evidence that agriculture reforms take place more quickly in countries that have few or low barriers to trade than in those that do not

6. According to paragraph 5, each of the following contributed positively to the industrialization of the Netherlands and Scandinavia EXCEPT

   Ⓐ a lack of obstacles to foreign trade
   Ⓑ huge projects undertaken by the state
   Ⓒ relatively uncorrupt government
   Ⓓ relatively little social or political disruption

GO ON TO THE NEXT PAGE ▶

PARAGRAPH 6

The key factor in the success of these countries (along with high literacy, which contributed to it) was their ability to adapt to the international division of labor determined by the early industrializers and to stake out areas of specialization in international markets for which they were especially well suited. This meant a great dependence on international commerce, which had notorious fluctuations; but it also meant high returns to those factors of production that were fortunate enough to be well placed in times of prosperity. In Sweden exports accounted for 18 percent of the national income in 1870, and in 1913, 22 percent of a much larger national income. In the early twentieth century, Denmark exported 63 percent of its agricultural production: butter, pork products, and eggs. It exported 80 percent of its butter, almost all to Great Britain, where it accounted for 40 percent of British butter imports.

7. Which of the sentences below best expresses the essential information in the high-lighted sentence in the passage? Incorrect choices change the meaning in important ways or leave out essential information.

   Ⓐ The early industrializers controlled most of the international economy, leaving these countries to stake out new areas of specialization along the margins.

   Ⓑ Aided by their high literacy rates, these countries were able to claim areas of specialization within established international markets.

   Ⓒ High literacy rates enabled these countries to take over international markets and adapt the international division of labor to suit their strengths.

   Ⓓ The international division of labor established by the early industrializers was well suited to these countries, a key factor in their success.

8. According to paragraph 6, a major problem with depending heavily on international markets was that they

   Ⓐ lacked stability

   Ⓑ were not well suited to agricultural products

   Ⓒ were largely controlled by the early industrializers

   Ⓓ led to slower growth of local industries

PARAGRAPHS 1 AND 2

While some European countries, such as England and Germany, began to industrialize in the eighteenth century, the Netherlands and the Scandinavian countries of Denmark, Norway, and Sweden developed later. **(A)** All four of these countries lagged considerably behind in the early nineteenth century. **(B)** However, they industrialized rapidly in the second half of the century, especially in the last two or three decades. **(C)** In view of their later start and their lack of coal—undoubtedly the main reason they were not among the early industrializers—it is important to understand the sources of their success. **(D)**

All had small populations.

9.   **Directions:** Look at the part of the passage that is displayed above. The letters **(A)**, **(B)**, **(C)**, and **(D)** indicate where the following sentence could be added.

During this period, Sweden had the highest rate of growth of output per capita of any country in Europe, and Denmark was second.

Where would the sentence best fit?

(A) Choice A
(B) Choice B
(C) Choice C
(D) Choice D

GO ON TO THE NEXT PAGE

10. **Directions:** An introductory sentence for a brief summary of the passage is provided below. Complete the summary by selecting the THREE answer choices that express the most important ideas in the passage. Some sentences do not belong in the summary because they express ideas that are not presented in the passage or are minor ideas in the passage. **This question is worth 2 points.**

Write your answer choices in the spaces where they belong. You can either write the number of your answer choice or you can copy the sentence.

Although the Netherlands and Scandinavia began to industrialize relatively late, they did so very successfully.

-
-
-

Answer Choices

A Although these countries all started with small, uneducated populations, industrialization led to significant population growth and higher literacy rates.

B Thanks to their ready access to the sea, these countries enjoyed advantages in mercantile shipping, fishing, and shipbuilding.

C Because they all had good harbors for steamships, these countries started with an important advantage in the competition for transit trade.

D These countries were helped by the fact that their governments were relatively stable and honest and had polices that generally encouraged rather than blocked trade.

E These countries were successful primarily because their high literacy rates helped them fill specialized market niches.

F Because they were never fully dependent on international commerce, these countries were able to survive notorious fluctuations in international markets.

THE MYSTERY OF YAWNING

According to conventional theory, yawning takes place when people are bored or sleepy and serves the function of increasing alertness by reversing, through deeper breathing, the drop in blood oxygen levels that are caused by the shallow breathing that accompanies lack of sleep or boredom. Unfortunately, the few scientific investigations of yawning have failed to find any connection between how often someone yawns and how much sleep they have had or how tired they are. About the closest any research has come to supporting the tiredness theory is to confirm that adults yawn more often on weekdays than at weekends, and that school children yawn more frequently in their first year at primary school than they do in kindergarten.

Another flaw of the tiredness theory is that yawning does not raise alertness or physiological activity, as the theory would predict. When researchers measured the heart rate, muscle tension, and skin conductance of people before, during, and after yawning, they did detect some changes in skin conductance following yawning, indicating a slight increase in physiological activity. However, similar changes occurred when the subjects were asked simply to open their mouths or to breathe deeply. Yawning did nothing special to their state of physiological activity. Experiments have also cast serious doubt on the belief that yawning is triggered by a drop in blood oxygen or a rise in blood carbon dioxide. Volunteers were told to think about yawning while they breathed either normal air, pure oxygen, or an air mixture with an above-normal level of carbon dioxide. If the theory was correct, breathing air with extra carbon dioxide should have triggered yawning, while breathing pure oxygen should have suppressed yawning. In fact, neither condition made any difference to the frequency of yawning, which remained constant at about 24 yawns per hour. Another experiment demonstrated that physical exercise, which was sufficiently vigorous to double the rate of breathing, had no effect on the frequency of yawning. Again, the implication is that yawning has little or nothing to do with oxygen.

A completely different theory holds that yawning assists in the physical development of the lungs early in life, but has no remaining biological function in adults. It has been suggested that yawning and hiccupping might serve to clear out the fetus's airways. The lungs of a fetus secrete a liquid that then mixes with its mother's amniotic fluid. Babies with congenital blockages that prevent this fluid from escaping from their lungs are sometimes born with deformed lungs. It might be that yawning helps to clear out the lungs by periodically lowering the pressure in them. According to this theory, yawning in adults is just a developmental fossil with no biological function. But, while accepting that not everything in life can be explained by Darwinian evolution, there are sound reasons for being skeptical of theories like this one, which avoid the issue of what yawning does for adults. Yawning is distracting, consumes energy, and takes time. It is almost certainly doing something significant in adults as well as in fetuses. What could it be?

The empirical evidence, such as it is, suggests an altogether different function for yawning—namely, that yawning prepares us for a change in activity level. Support for this theory came from a study of yawning behavior in everyday life. Volunteers wore wrist-mounted devices that automatically recorded their physical activity for up to two weeks; the volunteers also recorded their yawns by pressing a button on the device each time they yawned. The data showed that yawning tended to occur about 15 minutes before a period

GO ON TO THE NEXT PAGE ↘

of increased behavioral activity. Yawning bore no relationship to sleep patterns, however. This accords with anecdotal evidence that people often yawn in situations where they are neither tired nor bored, but are preparing for impending mental and physical activity. Such yawning is often referred to as "incongruous" because it seems out of place, at least in the tiredness view: soldiers yawning before combat, musicians yawning before performing, and athletes yawning before competing. Their yawning seems to have nothing to do with sleepiness or boredom—quite the reverse—but it does precede a change in activity level.

Directions: Now answer the questions.

PARAGRAPH 1

According to conventional theory, yawning takes place when people are bored or sleepy and serves the function of increasing alertness by reversing, through deeper breathing, the drop in blood oxygen levels that are caused by the shallow breathing that accompanies lack of sleep or boredom. Unfortunately, the few scientific investigations of yawning have failed to find any connection between how often someone yawns and how much sleep they have had or how tired they are. About the closest any research has come to supporting the tiredness theory is to confirm that adults yawn more often on weekdays than at weekends, and that school children yawn more frequently in their first year at primary school than they do in kindergarten.

1. Which of the sentences below best expresses the essential information in the highlighted sentence in the passage? Incorrect choices change the meaning in important ways or leave out essential information.

   A It is the conventional theory that when people are bored or sleepy, they often experience a drop in blood oxygen levels due to their shallow breathing.

   B The conventional theory is that people yawn when bored or sleepy because yawning raises blood oxygen levels, which in turn raises alertness.

   C According to conventional theory, yawning is more likely to occur when people are bored or sleepy than when they are alert and breathing deeply.

   D Yawning, according to the conventional theory, is caused by boredom or lack of sleep and can be avoided through deeper breathing.

2. In paragraph 1, what point does the author make about the evidence for the tiredness theory of yawning?

   A There is no scientific evidence linking yawning with tiredness.

   B The evidence is wide-ranging because it covers multiple age-groups.

   C The evidence is reliable because it was collected over a long period of time.

   D The evidence is questionable because the yawning patterns of children and adults should be different.

P
A
R
A
G
R
A
P
H

2

Another flaw of the tiredness theory is that yawning does not raise alertness or physiological activity, as the theory would predict. When researchers measured the heart rate, muscle tension and skin conductance of people before, during and after yawning, they did detect some changes in skin conductance following yawning, indicating a slight increase in physiological activity. However, similar changes occurred when the subjects were asked simply to open their mouths or to breathe deeply. Yawning did nothing special to their state of physiological activity. Experiments have also cast serious doubt on the belief that yawning is triggered by a drop in blood oxygen or a rise in blood carbon dioxide. Volunteers were told to think about yawning while they breathed either normal air, pure oxygen, or an air mixture with an above-normal level of carbon dioxide. If the theory was correct, breathing air with extra carbon dioxide should have triggered yawning, while breathing pure oxygen should have suppressed yawning. In fact, neither condition made any difference to the frequency of yawning, which remained constant at about 24 yawns per hour. Another experiment demonstrated that physical exercise, which was sufficiently vigorous to double the rate of breathing, had no effect on the frequency of yawning. Again, the implication is that yawning has little or nothing to do with oxygen.

3. The word "flaw" in the passage is closest in meaning to

   (A) fault
   (B) aspect
   (C) confusion
   (D) mystery

4. In paragraph 2, why does the author compare the physiological changes that occur when subjects simply opened their mouths or breathed deeply with those that occur when people yawned?

   (A) To present an argument in support of the tiredness theory
   (B) To cast doubt on the reliability of the tests that measured heart rate, muscle tension, and skin conductance
   (C) To argue against the hypothesis that yawning provides a special way to improve alertness or raise physiological activity
   (D) To support the idea that opening the mouth or breathing deeply can affect blood oxygen levels

5. Paragraph 2 answers all of the following questions about yawning EXCEPT:

   (A) Does yawning increase alertness or physiological activity?
   (B) Does thinking about yawning increase yawning over not thinking about yawning?
   (C) Does the amount of carbon dioxide and oxygen in the air affect the rate at which people yawn?
   (D) Does the rate of breathing affect the rate at which people yawn?

GO ON TO THE NEXT PAGE ➦

PARAGRAPH 3

A completely different theory holds that yawning assists in the physical development of the lungs early in life, but has no remaining biological function in adults. It has been suggested that yawning and hiccupping might serve to clear out the fetus's airways. The lungs of a fetus secrete a liquid that then mixes with its mother's amniotic fluid. Babies with congenital blockages that prevent this fluid from escaping from their lungs are sometimes born with deformed lungs. It might be that yawning helps to clear out the lungs by periodically lowering the pressure in them. According to this theory, yawning in adults is just a developmental fossil with no biological function. But, while accepting that not everything in life can be explained by Darwinian evolution, there are sound reasons for being skeptical of theories like this one, which avoid the issue of what yawning does for adults. Yawning is distracting, consumes energy and takes time. It is almost certainly doing something significant in adults as well as in fetuses.

6. According to the development theory of yawning presented in paragraph 3, what is the role of yawning?

   Ⓐ It causes hiccups, which aid in the development of the lungs.
   Ⓑ It controls the amount of pressure the lungs place on other developing organs.
   Ⓒ It prevents amniotic fluid from entering the lungs.
   Ⓓ It removes a potentially harmful fluid from the lungs.

PARAGRAPH 4

The empirical evidence, such as it is, suggests an altogether different function for yawning—namely, that yawning prepares us for a change in activity level. Support for this theory came from a study of yawning behavior in everyday life. Volunteers wore wrist-mounted devices that automatically recorded their physical activity for up to two weeks; the volunteers also recorded their yawns by pressing a button on the device each time they yawned. The data showed that yawning tended to occur about 15 minutes before a period of increased behavioral activity. Yawning bore no relationship to sleep patterns, however. This accords with anecdotal evidence that people often yawn in situations where they are neither tired nor bored, but are preparing for impending mental and physical activity. Such yawning is often referred to as "incongruous" because it seems out of place, at least on the tiredness view: soldiers yawning before combat, musicians yawning before performing, and athletes yawning before competing. Their yawning seems to have nothing to do with sleepiness or boredom—quite the reverse—but it does precede a change in activity level.

7. The word "empirical" in the passage is closest in meaning to

   Ⓐ reliable
   Ⓑ based on common sense
   Ⓒ relevant
   Ⓓ based on observation

8. The study of yawning behavior discussed in paragraph 4 supports which of the following conclusions?

   Ⓐ Yawning is associated with an expectation of increased physical activity.
   Ⓑ Yawning occurs more frequently when people are asked to record their yawning.
   Ⓒ People tend to yawn about fifteen minutes before they become tired or bored.
   Ⓓ Mental or physical stress tends to make people yawn.

PARAGRAPH 2

Another flaw of the tiredness theory is that yawning does not raise alertness or physiological activity, as the theory would predict. When researchers measured the heart rate, muscle tension and skin conductance of people before, during and after yawning, they did detect some changes in skin conductance following yawning, indicating a slight increase in physiological activity. However, similar changes occurred when the subjects were asked simply to open their mouths or to breathe deeply. Yawning did nothing special to their state of physiological activity. Experiments have also cast serious doubt on the belief that yawning is triggered by a drop in blood oxygen or a rise in blood carbon dioxide. **(A)** Volunteers were told to think about yawning while they breathed either normal air, pure oxygen, or an air mixture with an above-normal level of carbon dioxide. **(B)** If the theory was correct, breathing air with extra carbon dioxide should have triggered yawning, while breathing pure oxygen should have suppressed yawning. **(C)** In fact, neither condition made any difference to the frequency of yawning, which remained constant at about 24 yawns per hour. **(D)** Another experiment demonstrated that physical exercise, which was sufficiently vigorous to double the rate of breathing, had no effect on the frequency of yawning. Again, the implication is that yawning has little or nothing to do with oxygen.

9. **Directions:** Look at the part of the passage that is displayed above. The letters **(A)**, **(B)**, **(C)**, and **(D)** indicate where the following sentence could be added.

   This, however, was not the case.

   Where would the sentence best fit?
   Ⓐ Choice A
   Ⓑ Choice B
   Ⓒ Choice C
   Ⓓ Choice D

GO ON TO THE NEXT PAGE ↘

10. **Directions:** An introductory sentence for a brief summary of the passage is provided below. Complete the summary by selecting the THREE answer choices that express the most important ideas in the passage. Some sentences do not belong in the summary because they express ideas that are not presented in the passage or are minor ideas in the passage. **This question is worth 2 points.**

Write your answer choices in the spaces where they belong. You can either write the number of your answer choice or you can copy the sentence.

The tiredness theory of yawning does not seem to explain why yawning occurs.

-
-
-

Answer Choices

A Although earlier scientific studies strongly supported the tiredness theory, new evidence has cast doubt on these findings.

B Evidence has shown that yawning is almost completely unrelated to the amount of oxygen in the blood and is unrelated to sleep behavior.

C Some have proposed that yawning plays a role in the development of the lungs before birth, but it seems unlikely that yawning serves no purpose in adults.

D Fluids in the lungs of the fetus prevent yawning from occurring, which disproves the development theory of yawning.

E New studies, along with anecdotal evidence, have shown that the frequency of yawning increases during extended periods of inactivity.

F There is some evidence that suggests that yawning prepares the body and mind for a change in activity level.

LIGHTNING

Lightning is a brilliant flash of light produced by an electrical discharge from a storm cloud. The electrical discharge takes place when the attractive tension between a region of negatively charged particles and a region of positively charged particles becomes so great that the charged particles suddenly rush together. The coming together of the oppositely charged particles neutralizes the electrical tension and releases a tremendous amount of energy, which we see as lightning. The separation of positively and negatively charged particles takes place during the development of the storm cloud.

The separation of charged particles that forms in a storm cloud has a sandwich-like structure. Concentrations of positively charged particles develop at the top and bottom of the cloud, but the middle region becomes negatively charged. Recent measurements made in the field together with laboratory simulations (imitations of the process done in a laboratory) offer a promising explanation of how this structure of charged particles forms. What happens is that small (millimeter- to centimeter-size) pellets of ice form in the cold upper regions of the cloud. When these ice pellets fall, some of them strike much smaller ice crystals in the center of the cloud. The temperature at the center of the cloud is about $-15°C$ or lower. At such temperatures, the collision between the ice pellets and the ice crystals causes electrical charges to shift so that the ice pellets acquire a negative charge and the ice crystals become positively charged. Then updraft wind currents carry the light, positively charged ice crystals up to the top of the cloud. The heavier, negatively charged ice pellets are left to concentrate in the center. This process explains why the top of the cloud becomes positively charged, while the center becomes negatively charged. The negatively charged region is large: several hundred meters thick and several kilometers in diameter. Below this large, cold, negatively charged region, the cloud is warmer than $-15°C$, and at these temperatures, collisions between ice crystals and falling ice pellets produce positively charged ice pellets that then populate a small region at the base of the cloud.

Most lightning takes place within a cloud when the charge separation within the cloud collapses. However, as the storm cloud develops, the ground beneath the cloud becomes positively charged and lightning can take place in the form of an electrical discharge between the negative charge of the cloud and the positively charged ground. Lightning that strikes the ground is the most likely to be destructive, so even though it represents only 20 percent of all lightning, it has received a lot of scientific attention.

Using high-speed photography, scientists have determined that there are two steps to the occurrence of lightning from a cloud to the ground. First, a channel, or path, is formed that connects the cloud and the ground. Then a strong current of electrons follows that path from the cloud to the ground, and it is that current that illuminates the channel as the lightning we see.

The formation of the channel is initiated when electrons surge from the cloud base toward the ground. When a stream of these negatively charged electrons comes within 100 meters of the ground, it is met by a stream of positively charged particles that comes up from the ground. When the negatively and positively charged streams meet, a complete channel connecting the cloud and the ground is formed. The channel is only a few centimeters in diameter, but that is wide enough for electrons to follow the channel to the ground in the visible form of a flash of lightning. The stream of positive particles that meets the

GO ON TO THE NEXT PAGE

surge of electrons from the cloud often arises from a tall, pointed structure such as a metal flagpole or a tower. That is why the subsequent lightning that follows the completed channel often strikes a tall structure.

Once a channel has been formed, it is usually used by several lightning discharges, each of them consisting of a stream of electrons from the cloud meeting a stream of positive particles along the established path. Sometimes, however, a stream of electrons following an established channel is met by a positive stream making a new path up from the ground. The result is a forked lightning that strikes the ground in two places.

Directions: Now answer the questions.

PARAGRAPH 1

Lightning is a brilliant flash of light produced by an electrical discharge from a storm cloud. The electrical discharge takes place when the attractive tension between a region of negatively charged particles and a region of positively charged particles becomes so great that the charged particles suddenly rush together. The coming together of the oppositely charged particles neutralizes the electrical tension and releases a tremendous amount of energy, which we see as lightning. The separation of positively and negatively charged particles takes place during the development of the storm cloud.

1. According to paragraph 1, all of the following take place in the development of a flash of lightning EXCEPT

   Ⓐ great tension between two oppositely charged regions
   Ⓑ an increase in negatively charged particles over positively charged particles
   Ⓒ oppositely charged particles coming together
   Ⓓ the release of electrical energy in the form of visible light

PARAGRAPH 2

The separation of charged particles that forms in a storm cloud has a sandwich-like structure. Concentrations of positively charged particles develop at the top and bottom of the cloud, but the middle region becomes negatively charged. Recent measurements made in the field together with laboratory simulations (imitations of the process done in a laboratory) offer a promising explanation of how this structure of charged particles forms. What happens is that small (millimeter- to centimeter-size) pellets of ice form in the cold upper regions of the cloud. When these ice pellets fall, some of them strike much smaller ice crystals in the center of the cloud. The temperature at the center of the cloud is about –15°C or lower. At such temperatures, the collision between the ice pellets and the ice crystals causes electrical charges to shift so that the ice pellets acquire a negative charge and the ice crystals become positively charged. Then updraft wind currents carry the light, positively charged ice crystals up to the top of the cloud. The heavier, negatively charged ice pellets are left to concentrate in the center. This process explains why the top of the cloud becomes positively charged, while the center becomes negatively charged. The negatively charged region is large: several hundred meters thick and several kilometers in diameter. Below this large, cold, negatively charged region, the cloud is warmer than –15°C, and at these temperatures, collisions between ice crystals and falling ice pellets produce positively charged ice pellets that then populate a small region at the base of the cloud.

2. According to paragraph 2, what causes ice crystals to become positively charged?
   (A) Collisions with ice pellets
   (B) Collisions with negatively charged ice crystals at the base of the cloud
   (C) Becoming concentrated in the central region of the cloud
   (D) Forming at a temperature greater than –15°C

3. According to paragraph 2, why are positively charged ice pellets produced in the lower part of the cloud?
   (A) Collisions between ice crystals and ice pellets increase in number in the lower part of the cloud.
   (B) The lower part of the cloud is smaller than the region above it.
   (C) More ice pellets than ice crystals reach the lower part of the cloud.
   (D) Temperatures in the lower part of the cloud are warmer than –15°C.

4. According to paragraph 2, the middle region of a cloud becomes negatively charged due to all of the following EXCEPT
   (A) a shift of electrical charges between ice pellets and ice crystals
   (B) negatively charged ice pellets that remain in the middle
   (C) a temperature of –15°C or less
   (D) the development of a positive charge at the base of the cloud

GO ON TO THE NEXT PAGE

5. It can be inferred from paragraph 2 that part of the reason that the top of a storm cloud becomes positively charged is that

   (A) the top of the cloud is warmer than the middle of the cloud
   (B) the middle of the cloud is already occupied by positively charged particles
   (C) the negatively charged ice pellets are too heavy to be carried by the updrafts that move ice crystals
   (D) collisions between ice pellets in the top of the cloud produce mainly positively charged particles

PARAGRAPH 3

Most lightning takes place within a cloud when the charge separation within the cloud collapses. However, as the storm cloud develops, the ground beneath the cloud becomes positively charged and lightning can take place in the form of an electrical discharge between the negative charge of the cloud and the positively charged ground. Lightning that strikes the ground is the most likely to be destructive, so even though it represents only 20 percent of all lightning, it has received a lot of scientific attention.

6. The author remarks that "Lightning that strikes the ground is the most likely to be destructive" in order to explain why

   (A) this form of lightning has been investigated so much
   (B) this form of lightning is not as common as lightning within a cloud
   (C) scientific understanding of this form of lightning is important
   (D) the buildup of positive charge on the ground beneath a storm cloud can have serious consequences

PARAGRAPH 5

The formation of the channel is initiated when electrons surge from the cloud base toward the ground. When a stream of these negatively charged electrons comes within 100 meters of the ground, it is met by a stream of positively charged particles that comes up from the ground. When the negatively and positively charged streams meet, a complete channel connecting the cloud and the ground is formed. The channel is only a few centimeters in diameter, but that is wide enough for electrons to follow the channel to the ground in the visible form of a flash of lightning. The stream of positive particles that meets the surge of electrons from the cloud often arises from a tall, pointed structure such as a metal flagpole or a tower. That is why the subsequent lightning that follows the completed channel often strikes a tall structure.

7. The word "initiated" in the passage is closest in meaning to

   (A) started
   (B) intensified
   (C) finished
   (D) expected

8. According to paragraph 5, which of the following is true of the stream of charged particles from the ground?

   Ⓐ It prevents streams of electrons from the cloud from striking the ground.
   Ⓑ It completes a channel that connects the storm cloud with the ground.
   Ⓒ It produces a stream of electrons from the cloud.
   Ⓓ It widens the path made by the initial stream of electrons from the cloud.

PARAGRAPHS 4 AND 5

That is why the subsequent lightning that follows the completed channel often strikes a tall structure. **(A)**

Once a channel has been formed, it is usually used by several lightning discharges, each of them consisting of a stream of electrons from the cloud meeting a stream of positive particles along the established path. **(B)** Sometimes, however, a stream of electrons following an established channel is met by a positive stream making a new path up from the ground. **(C)** The result is a forked lightning that strikes the ground in two places. **(D)**

9. **Directions:** Look at the part of the passage that is displayed above. The letters **(A)**, **(B)**, **(C)**, and **(D)** indicate where the following sentence could be added.

   The descending stream of electrons divides at the point where the new positive-stream channel intersects the established path.

   Where would the sentence best fit?

   Ⓐ Choice A
   Ⓑ Choice B
   Ⓒ Choice C
   Ⓓ Choice D

GO ON TO THE NEXT PAGE ◥

10. **Directions:** An introductory sentence for a brief summary of the passage is provided below. Complete the summary by selecting the THREE answer choices that express the most important ideas in the passage. Some sentences do not belong in the summary because they express ideas that are not presented in the passage or are minor ideas in the passage. **This question is worth 2 points.**

Write your answer choices in the spaces where they belong. You can either write the number of your answer choice or you can copy the sentence.

Lightning takes place when a separation of positive and negative electrical particles that develop in a storm cloud suddenly collapses.

- •
- •
- •

Answer Choices

[A] A storm cloud first develops a positively charged layer at the top, then a negatively charged middle layer, and finally, a positively charged layer at the bottom.

[B] A separation of oppositely charged particles in clouds develops from collisions of falling ice pellets with ice crystals, from updrafts, and from temperature variations.

[C] Lightning from cloud to ground follows a channel that forms when a stream of electrons moving down meets a stream of positive particles coming up from the ground.

[D] Field studies, laboratory stimulations, and high-speed photography have all been used to investigate the way charge separations develop in clouds.

[E] Lightning from a cloud to the ground is more likely to be destructive than is lightning that takes place within a cloud.

[F] Once a channel has been formed, it is usually used by several successive electrical discharges that illuminate the channel as flashes of light.

STOP. This is the end of the Reading section of *TOEFL iBT*® Practice Test 4.

LISTENING

Directions: This section measures your ability to understand conversations and lectures in English.

You should listen to each conversation and lecture only **once**.

After each conversation or lecture, you will answer some questions about it. The questions typically ask about the main idea and supporting details. Some questions ask about the purpose of a speaker's statements or a speaker's attitude. Answer the questions based on what is stated or implied by the speakers.

You may take notes while you listen. You may use your notes to help you answer the questions. Your notes will **not** be scored.

In some questions, you will see this icon: 🎧 This means that you will hear, but not see, part of the question.

Most questions are worth 1 point. If a question is worth more than 1 point, it will have special directions that indicate how many points you can receive.

It will take about **41 minutes** to listen to the conversations and lectures and to answer the questions. You should answer each question, even if you must guess the answer. Answer each question before moving on. Do not return to previous questions.

At the end of this Practice Test you will find an answer key, information to help you determine your score, scripts for the audio tracks, and explanations of the answers.

Turn the page to begin the Listening section.

Listen to Track 78.

Questions

1. Why does the student go to the university office?

   Ⓐ To apply for a position at the university library
   Ⓑ To get information about hosting an exchange student
   Ⓒ To find out if there are any jobs available on campus
   Ⓓ To find out the hours of the computer lab

2. Why did the student transfer to Central University?

   Ⓐ To take advantage of an academic program
   Ⓑ To participate in a student exchange program
   Ⓒ To attend a smaller university than the one he was at before
   Ⓓ To benefit from Central University's international reputation

3. Why does the student mention hosting foreign-exchange students?

   Ⓐ To explain his interest in a particular field of study
   Ⓑ To explain why he is looking for a job so late in the semester
   Ⓒ To explain why he would like to be an exchange student the following year
   Ⓓ To explain how he learned his computer skills

4. What can be inferred about students who apply for the open position at the technology-support helpdesk?

    (A) They must be enrolled in a computer course.
    (B) They will only be able to work on weekends.
    (C) They are willing to work many hours each day they work.
    (D) They are willing to work irregular hours.

5. *Listen again to part of the conversation by playing Track 79.* *Then answer the question.*

    Why does the woman say this?

    (A) To dissuade the student from starting a job right away
    (B) To suggest looking for an off-campus job
    (C) To imply that the student might not like the job that is available
    (D) To encourage the student to apply to a work-study program

GO ON TO THE NEXT PAGE

Listen to Track 80.

Art History

Elaine Gazda

Questions

6. What is the lecture mainly about?

   Ⓐ Different views of a type of sculpture popular in ancient Roman times
   Ⓑ Evidence that Romans had outstanding artistic ability
   Ⓒ The differences between Greek sculpture and Roman sculpture
   Ⓓ The relationship between art and politics in ancient Roman times

7. According to traditional art historians, why did the Romans copy Greek sculpture?

   Ⓐ The Roman public was not interested in original works of art.
   Ⓑ The Roman government did not support other forms of art.
   Ⓒ Roman artists did not have sufficient skill to create original sculpture.
   Ⓓ Romans wanted to imitate the art they admired.

8. What is Gazda's view of the Roman copies of Greek statues?

   Ⓐ The copies represented the idea that Roman society was similar to Greek society.
   Ⓑ The copies introduced the citizens of the Roman Empire to Greek history.
   Ⓒ The copies were inferior to the original statues.
   Ⓓ The copies had both artistic and political functions.

9. Why does the professor mention Roman coins?

   Ⓐ To show the similarity between the likenesses of the emperor in statues and on coins
   Ⓑ To illustrate the Roman policy of distributing the emperor's image throughout the empire
   Ⓒ To imply that the citizens of the Roman Empire became quite wealthy
   Ⓓ To suggest that the Romans also copied Greek art on their coins

GO ON TO THE NEXT PAGE ➤

10. According to the professor, why did the Romans sometimes remove the emperor's head from a statue?

    Choose 2 answers.

    A   The head made the statue too heavy to transport.
    B   The head was placed on the body of a different statue.
    C   The emperor was no longer in power.
    D   The emperor was not satisfied with the quality of the statue.

11. *Listen again to part of the lecture by playing Track 81.*
    Then answer the question.

    What does the professor imply when he says this?

    A Art historians frequently change their views.
    B The contemporary view is not easy to understand.
    C It is not difficult to determine why the Romans copied Greek sculptures.
    D The view of traditional art historians is probably incorrect.

Listen to Track 82.

Questions

12. What is the conversation mainly about?

    Ⓐ The topic of the man's research paper
    Ⓑ Some current research projects in sociology
    Ⓒ Effective ways of conducting sociology research
    Ⓓ The man's possible participation in a research project

13. What does the professor imply about the man's outline?

    Ⓐ It has revealed that he should limit the focus of his paper.
    Ⓑ It does not provide enough information for him to write the paper.
    Ⓒ It will help him write clearly about a complex topic.
    Ⓓ It overstates the connection between sociology and marketing.

14. What is the main goal of the study that the professor's colleague is conducting?

    Ⓐ To find out if some television shows will be popular with people in a certain age range
    Ⓑ To collect information about food products that college students like
    Ⓒ To generate ideas for new television shows
    Ⓓ To determine sociological factors that are related to people's television-viewing preferences

GO ON TO THE NEXT PAGE

15. What does the professor imply about the owners of Fox's Diner?

- (A) They would probably do a favor for her.
- (B) They are unlikely to grant the man's request.
- (C) They would enjoy participating in the research study.
- (D) They often advertise on television.

16. *Listen again to part of the conversation by playing Track 83. Then answer the question.*

What does the professor mean when she says this?

- (A) The student could probably find a marketing professor who has an interest in sociology.
- (B) The student's marketing professor might not be aware of the television study.
- (C) No more students are needed to participate in the television study.
- (D) The marketing department needs students for several research studies.

Listen to Track 84.

European History

Questions

17. What is the main purpose of the lecture?

    Ⓐ To explore the use of spices in cooking in the Middle Ages
    Ⓑ To explain the significance of spices for medieval society
    Ⓒ To describe how the spice trade evolved in medieval Europe
    Ⓓ To examine changes in the role that spices played in the Middle Ages

18. Based on the lecture, indicate whether each of the following is true about spices in medieval Europe.

Mark your answers with an "X" below.

	YES	NO
1. They had to be imported.		
2. They were unaffordable for many people.		
3. They were used to preserve meat during the winter.		
4. They were believed to have medicinal properties.		
5. Their sale in public markets was closely regulated.		

GO ON TO THE NEXT PAGE ▶

19. What two factors explain why medieval Europeans did not use spices to cover the taste of spoiled meat?

    Choose two answers.

    - [A] Fresh meat was less expensive than spices were.
    - [B] Spices were mainly used in incense and perfume.
    - [C] The sale of spoiled food was prohibited.
    - [D] Salt was cheaper than most spices were.

20. Why does the professor mention the collapse of the Roman Empire?

    - (A) To indicate that the spice trade became more direct
    - (B) To explain why the price of pepper suddenly increased
    - (C) To indicate that spices were not available in Europe for centuries
    - (D) To explain why the origins of spices became more mysterious

21. What does the professor say about European explorers during the age of discovery?

    - (A) Their discoveries caused the price of certain spices to increase.
    - (B) They were responding to the demand for spices.
    - (C) They did not expect to find spices during their explorations.
    - (D) Their main goal was to discover unknown lands.

22. *Listen again to part of the lecture by playing Track 85.*
    Then answer the question.

    Why does the professor say this?

    - (A) To indicate that pepper was commonly used as payment
    - (B) To indicate where pepper could be found at the time
    - (C) To emphasize the high value of pepper at the time
    - (D) To suggest that pepper was nearly as plentiful as gold

Listen to Track 86.

GO ON TO THE NEXT PAGE

Questions

23. What is the main purpose of the lecture?

    Ⓐ To explain the biological advantages of a physical change that occurs in North American wood frogs
    Ⓑ To explain why the North American wood frog's habitat range has expanded
    Ⓒ To describe the functioning of the circulatory system of the North American wood frog
    Ⓓ To introduce students to an unusual phenomenon affecting North American wood frogs

24. Why does the professor first mention the arrival of spring?

    Ⓐ To encourage students to look for thawing wood frogs
    Ⓑ To point out the time period when frogs begin mating
    Ⓒ To explain why the class will soon be doing experiments with wood frogs
    Ⓓ To emphasize the speed of the thawing process

25. What happens to a wood frog as it begins to freeze?

    Ⓐ Blood is concentrated in the center of its body.
    Ⓑ Blood stops producing sugar.
    Ⓒ Water moves out of its internal organs.
    Ⓓ Water from just beneath the skin begins to evaporate.

26. What are two points the professor makes about the thawing process of the wood frog?

    Choose 2 answers.

    Ⓐ The thawing process is not fully understood.
    Ⓑ The thawing process takes longer than the freezing process.
    Ⓒ The frog's internal organs thaw before its outer skin thaws.
    Ⓓ Thawing occurs when the frog's heart begins pumping glucose through its body.

27. What impact does freezing have on some thawed wood frogs?

    Ⓐ It increases their reproductive success.

    Ⓑ It decreases their life span.

    Ⓒ It causes them to be more vocal and active.

    Ⓓ It reduces their ability to recognize potential mates.

28. *Listen again to part of the lecture by playing Track 87.*
Then answer the question.

    What does the professor imply when she says this?

    Ⓐ She wants the student to clarify his question.

    Ⓑ She wants the student to draw his own conclusions.

    Ⓒ She thinks the student does not understand how car antifreeze works.

    Ⓓ She thinks the student has misunderstood her point.

STOP. This is the end of the Listening section of *TOEFL iBT*® Practice Test 4.

GO ON TO THE NEXT PAGE ◥

SPEAKING

Directions: The following Speaking section of the test will last approximately **17 minutes**. To complete it, you will need a recording device that you can play back to listen to your responses.

During the test, you will answer four speaking questions. One question asks about a familiar topic. Three questions ask about short conversations, lectures, and reading passages. You may take notes as you listen to the conversations and lectures. The questions and the reading passages are printed here. The time you will have to prepare your response and to speak is printed below each question. You should answer all of the questions as completely as possible in the time allowed.

Play the audio tracks listed in the test instructions. Record each of your responses.

At the end of this Practice Test you will find scripts for the audio tracks, important points for each question, directions for listening to sample spoken responses, and comments on those responses by official raters.

Questions

1. You will now be asked to give your opinion about a familiar topic. After you hear the question, you will have 15 seconds to prepare your response and 45 seconds to speak.

Now play Track 88 to hear Question 1.

Do you agree or disagree with the following statement?

It is important to learn about other cultures.

Use details and examples to explain your opinion.

> **Preparation Time: 15 Seconds**
> **Response Time: 45 Seconds**

---

2. You will now read a short passage and listen to a conversation on the same topic. You will then be asked a question about them. After you hear the question, you will have 30 seconds to prepare your response and 60 seconds to speak.

Now play Track 89 to hear Question 2.

> **Reading Time: 50 Seconds**

University Choir to Enter Off-Campus Singing Competitions

Currently, the university choir gives singing concerts only on campus. Next year, however, the choir will add competitive events at other locations to its schedule. The choir's new director feels that entering singing competitions will make the quality of the choir's performance even better than it is now. "Competitions will motivate students in the choir to pursue a higher standard of excellence in singing," he said. In addition, it is hoped that getting the choir off campus and out in the public will strengthen the reputation of the university's music program. This in turn will help the program grow.

The man expresses his opinion about the change described in the article. Briefly summarize the change. Then state his opinion about the change and explain the reasons he gives for holding that opinion.

Preparation Time: 30 Seconds
Response Time: 60 Seconds

3. You will now read a short passage and listen to a lecture on the same topic. You will then be asked a question about them. After you hear the question, you will have 30 seconds to prepare your response and 60 seconds to speak.

Now play Track 90 to hear Question 3.

Reading Time: 50 Seconds

Relict Behaviors

In general, animals act in ways that help them to survive within their specific habitats. However, sometimes an animal species may display a behavior that no longer serves a clear purpose. The original purpose for the behavior may have disappeared long ago, even thousands of years before. These behaviors, known as *relict behaviors*, were useful to the animal when the species' habitat was different; but now, because of changed conditions, the behavior no longer serves its original purpose. Left over from an earlier time, the behavior remains as a relict, or remnant, long after the environmental circumstance that influenced its evolution has vanished.

GO ON TO THE NEXT PAGE ↘

Using the example of the pronghorn and lion, explain the concept of a relict behavior.

| Preparation Time: 30 Seconds |
| Response Time: 60 Seconds |

4. *You will now listen to part of a lecture. You will then be asked a question about it. After you hear the question, you will have 20 seconds to prepare your response and 60 seconds to speak.*

Now play Track 91 to hear Question 4.

Using points and examples from the lecture, explain how the characteristics of target customers influence marketing strategy for products.

Preparation Time: 20 Seconds
Response Time: 60 Seconds

STOP. This is the end of the Speaking section of *TOEFL iBT* ® Practice Test 4.

WRITING

Directions: This section measures your ability to use writing to communicate in an academic environment. There will be two writing tasks.

For the first writing task, you will read a passage and listen to a lecture and then answer a question based on what you have read and heard. For the second task, you will answer a question based on your own knowledge and experience.

At the end of this Practice Test you will find a script for the audio track, topic notes, sample test taker essays, and comments on those essays by official raters.

Turn the page to see the directions for the first writing task.

Writing Based on Reading and Listening

Directions: For this task, you will read a passage about an academic topic and you will listen to a lecture about the same topic. You may take notes while you read and listen.

Then you will write a response to a question that asks you about the relationship between the lecture you heard and the reading passage. Try to answer the question as completely as possible using information from the reading passage and the lecture. The question does not ask you to express your personal opinion. You may refer to the reading passage when you write. You may use your notes to help you answer the question.

Typically, an effective response will be 150 to 225 words. Your response will be judged on the quality of your writing and on the completeness and accuracy of the content.

Give yourself **3 minutes** to read the passage.

Reading Time: 3 minutes

In the 1950s *Torreya taxifolia*, a type of evergreen tree once very common in the state of Florida, started to die out. No one is sure exactly what caused the decline, but chances are good that if nothing is done, *Torreya* will soon become extinct. Experts are considering three ways to address the decline of *Torreya*.

The first option is to reestablish *Torreya* in the same location in which it thrived for thousands of years. *Torreya* used to be found in abundance in the northern part of Florida, which has a specific microclimate. A microclimate exists when weather conditions inside a relatively small area differ from the region of which that area is a part. Northern Florida's microclimate is very favorable to *Torreya*'s growth. This microclimate is wetter and cooler than the surrounding region's relatively dry, warm climate. Scientists have been working to plant *Torreya* seeds in the coolest, dampest areas of the microclimate.

The second option is to move *Torreya* to an entirely different location, far from its Florida microclimate. *Torreya* seeds and saplings have been successfully planted and grown in forests further north, where the temperature is significantly cooler. Some scientists believe that *Torreya* probably thrived in areas much further north in the distant past, so by relocating it now, in a process known as assisted migration, humans would simply be helping *Torreya* return to an environment that is more suited to its survival.

The third option is to preserve *Torreya* in research centers. Seeds and saplings can be moved from the wild and preserved in a closely monitored environment where it will be easier for scientists both to protect the species and to conduct research on *Torreya*. This research can then be used to ensure the continued survival of the species.

Now play Track 92.

the black locust tree

Question

Summarize the points made in the lecture, being sure to explain how they cast doubt on the specific solutions presented in the reading passage.

You have 20 minutes to plan and write your response.

Response Time: 20 minutes

_____

_____

_____

_____

Writing Based on Knowledge and Experience

Directions: For this task, you will write an essay in response to a question that asks you to state, explain, and support your opinion on an issue. Typically, an effective essay will contain a minimum of 300 words. Your essay will be judged on the quality of your writing. This includes the development of your ideas, the organization of your essay, and the quality and accuracy of the language you use to express your ideas.

You have **30 minutes** to plan and complete your essay.

Write your essay in the space provided.

Question

Do you agree or disagree with the following statement?

Students are more influenced by their teachers than by their friends.

Use specific reasons and examples to support your answer. Be sure to use your own words. Do **not** use memorized examples.

> **Response Time: 30 minutes**

_____

_____

_____

_____

_____

_____

_____

_____

_____

_____

_____

_____

_____

_____

_____

GO ON TO THE NEXT PAGE

_____

_____

_____

_____

_____

_____

_____

_____

_____

_____

_____

_____

_____

_____

_____

_____

_____

_____

_____

_____

_____

_____

STOP. This is the end of the Writing section of *TOEFL iBT*® Practice Test 4.

Answers, Explanations, and Listening Scripts

Reading

Answer Key and Self-Scoring Chart

Directions: Check your answers against the answer key below. Write the number 1 on the line to the right of each question if you picked the correct answer. For questions worth more than one point, follow the directions given. Total your points at the bottom of the chart.

Question Number	Correct Answer	Your Raw Points
Industrialization in the Netherlands and Scandinavia		
1.	B	
2.	D	
3.	A	
4.	D	
5.	B	
6.	B	
7.	B	
8.	A	
9.	C	

For question 10, write 2 if you picked all three correct answers. Write 1 if you picked two correct answers.

10.	B, D, E	

Question Number	Correct Answer	Your Raw Points
The Mystery of Yawning		
1.	B	
2.	A	
3.	A	
4.	C	
5.	B	
6.	D	
7.	D	
8.	A	
9.	C	

For question 10, write 2 if you picked all three correct answers. Write 1 if you picked two correct answers.

10.	B, C, F	

Question Number	Correct Answer	Your Raw Points
Lightning		
1.	B	
2.	A	
3.	D	
4.	D	
5.	C	
6.	A	
7.	A	
8.	B	
9.	C	

For question 10, write 2 if you picked all three correct answers. Write 1 if you picked two correct answers.

10.	B, C, F	
TOTAL:		

Below is a table that converts your Reading section answers into a *TOEFL iBT®* Reading scaled score. Take the total of raw points from your answer key and find that number in the left-hand column of the table. The right-hand column of the table gives a TOEFL iBT Reading scaled score for each number of raw points. For example, if the total points from your answer key is 25, the table shows a scaled score of 23 to 26.

You should use your score estimate as a general guide only. Your actual score on the TOEFL iBT test may be higher or lower than your score on the practice version.

Reading Comprehension

Raw Point Total	Scaled Score
32–33	30
31	29–30
30	28–30
29	27–28
28	26–29
27	25–28
26	24–27
25	23–26
24	21–25
23	20–25
22	19–24
21	18–23
20	17–22
19	15–21
18	14–20
17	13–19
16	11–18
15	10–17
14	8–16
13	7–15
12	5–13
11	4–12
10	2–10
9	1–9
8	1–7
7	0–5
6	0–4
5	0–2
4	0–1
3 or below	0

Answer Explanations

Industrialization in the Netherlands and Scandinavia

1. **B** This is an Inference question asking for information that can be inferred from paragraph 1. The correct answer choice is B. Sentence 1 of the paragraph says that England and Germany industrialized early, while sentence 3 says that the main reason that the Netherlands and the Scandinavian countries did not industrialize early is that they lacked coal. From these two pieces of information, readers can infer that coal was essential for early industrialization and that England and Germany therefore had coal.

   While the paragraph says that England and Germany "began to industrialize in the eighteenth century," there is no support for thinking that the industrial process was complete by the "start of the nineteenth century," so choice A is wrong. Choice C is contradicted in the paragraph by the statement "All four of these countries lagged considerably behind in the early nineteenth century." Although the paragraph indicates that the Netherlands and Scandinavia eventually succeeded in industrializing, it is clear that the reasons for their success were different from those that led to industrialization in England and Germany—England and Germany industrialized because they had coal—making choice D wrong. The reasons for the success of the Netherlands and the Scandinavian countries are explored in the rest of the passage.

2. **D** This is a Factual Information question asking for specific information that can be found in paragraphs 2 and 3. The correct answer choice is D. Sentence 1 of paragraph 3 explains that the Netherlands and the Scandinavian countries were "advantaged" by having "large percentages of their populations who could read and write," making choice D the correct answer.

   Sentence 1 of paragraph 2 indicates that the Netherlands and the Scandinavian countries had small populations, but there is no indication that having a small population contributed to the economic success of these countries, so choice A is wrong. It does not answer the specific question asked. Choice B is factually incorrect: sentence 3 of paragraph 2 indicates that the Netherlands and the Scandinavian countries experienced "moderate" population growth, not "rapid" growth. Sentence 1 of paragraph 2 mentions "human capital," meaning the human population of the Netherlands and Scandinavian countries, but this population was small and, as previously explained, there is no indication that having a small population encouraged economic success. *Capital* in the sense of money available for economic investment is not mentioned in either of the paragraphs. For all of these reasons, choice C is incorrect.

3. **A** This is a Vocabulary question. The word being tested is *abolished*. It is highlighted in the passage. The correct answer choice is A, "ended." To abolish a practice is to stop it, making choice A the best answer.

4. **D** This is a Negative Factual Information question asking for specific information that can be found in paragraph 4. The correct answer choice is D. Paragraph 4 discusses various trade and commercial advantages that the Netherlands and the Scandinavian countries had because of their location. There is no mention of the military or of military activity, making choice D correct.

   Sentence 2 of paragraph 4 says that "transport" was "cheap," making choice A true. The same sentence indicates that the Netherlands and the Scandinavian countries had "immediate access to the sea" and thus to "fish," making choice B true, and that all these countries had a "shipbuilding industry," making choice C true. Thus, the only unsupported choice is D.

5. **B** This is a Rhetorical Purpose question. It asks readers why the author included the information that "a protectionist movement developed in Sweden." The correct answer choice is B. Sentence 4 of the paragraph says that the Netherlands and the Scandinavian countries generally had policies that encouraged trade. However, the rise of a "protectionist movement" is not favorable to trade, a fact signaled by the word "though." Thus choice B is the best answer.

   Choice A is contradicted by the paragraph: the rise of a "protectionist movement" was a barrier to trade, not support for the claim that there were no significant barriers. Choice C is factually incorrect: there is no information indicating that Sweden was slower to industrialize than the other countries discussed. Choice D is wrong for a similar reason: agricultural reforms are mentioned, but there is no discussion of what makes such reforms occur quickly.

6. **B** This is a Negative Factual Information question asking for specific information that can be found in paragraph 5. The correct answer choice is B. Choice B is contradicted in the paragraph. Sentence 3 of the paragraph says that the governments of the Netherlands and the Scandinavian countries did NOT undertake "grandiose state projects," making choice B wrong.

   Sentence 4 says that the Netherlands and the Scandinavian countries "had few or low barriers to trade," indicating that choice A is true; sentence 3 says that these countries lacked "notable corruption," indicating that choice C is true; and sentence 2 says that the "nineteenth century passed peacefully for these countries," indicating that choice D is true.

7. **B** This is a Sentence Simplification question. As with all questions of this type, a single sentence is highlighted in the passage:

   The key factor in the success of these countries (along with high literacy, which contributed to it) was their ability to adapt to the international division of labor determined by the early industrializers and to stake out areas of specialization in international markets for which they were especially well suited.

The correct answer choice is B. Choice B accurately summarizes the essential information in the highlighted sentence. The highlighted sentence explains that the success of the Netherlands and the Scandinavian countries was due to their ability to specialize ("stake out areas of specialization") in the international market that had already been established ("the international division of labor determined by early industrializers"), an adaptation made possible by the "high literacy" rates of these countries.

Choice A changes the meaning of the highlighted sentence by saying that early industrializers, not the Netherlands and Scandinavian countries, staked out new areas of specialization.

Choice C changes the meaning of the highlighted sentence by saying that the Netherlands and the Scandinavian countries controlled international markets and changed the division of labor. They did neither.

Choice D changes the meaning of the highlighted sentence by making the overly broad claim that that the division of labor established by early industrializers was well suited to the Netherlands and Scandinavian countries. The tested sentence leaves out the information that these countries succeeded by developing specializations and that these specializations were in the parts of the established market that were well suited for the Netherlands and Scandinavian countries, implying that some parts were not well suited.

8. **A** This is a Factual Information question asking for specific information that can be found in paragraph 6. The correct answer is A. Choice A means the same as the information in sentence 2 that international commerce "had notorious fluctuations." Choice B, the idea that agricultural products were poorly suited for international markets, is contradicted by the information that Denmark exported 80 percent of its butter. Choice C is incorrect because there is no indication that control of international markets by early industrializers was a "major problem," so the choice does not answer the question asked. Choice D is incorrect because the idea that heavy dependence on international markets led to slower growth is not expressed in the passage.

9. **C** This is an Insert Text question. You can see the four possible answer choices in paragraph 1.

While some European countries, such as England and Germany, began to industrialize in the eighteenth century, the Netherlands and the Scandinavian countries of Denmark, Norway, and Sweden developed later. **(A)** All four of these countries lagged considerably behind in the early nineteenth century. **(B)** However, they industrialized rapidly in the second half of the century, especially in the last two or three decades. **(C)** In view of their later start and their lack of coal—undoubtedly the main reason they were not among the early industrializers—it is important to understand the sources of their success. **(D)**

All had small populations.

The sentence provided, "During this period, Sweden had the highest rate of growth per capita of any country in Europe, and Denmark was second," is best inserted at choice **(C)**. Choice **(C)** is correct because when the sentence is placed at **(C)**, the phrase "During this period" has a clear and logical grammatical referent ("the last two or three decades") and because the information about the impressive growth rates of Sweden and Denmark is a logical elaboration of the comment in the previous sentence that the Netherlands and the Scandinavian countries "industrialized rapidly in the second half of the century."

Choice **(A)** is incorrect because when placed at **(A)**, the phrase "During this period" would refer to "the eighteenth century," which makes no sense. The first sentence says that the Netherlands and the Scandinavian countries developed *after* the eighteenth century. Choice **(B)** is wrong for a similar reason: placed at **(B)**, the phrase "During this period" would refer to "the early nineteenth century." Sentence 2 says that the economies of the Netherlands and the Scandinavian countries "lagged considerably behind in the early nineteenth century," which contradicts the insert sentence about the impressive growth of the Swedish and Danish economies. The insert sentence is illogical at choice **(D)** because **(D)** introduces a new topic—the sources (causes) of the success of the economies of the Netherlands and the Scandinavian countries, and the insert sentence contains no information about sources of success.

14. **B** **D** **E** This is a Prose Summary question. It is completed correctly below. The correct answer choices are B, D, and E. Choices A, C, and F are therefore incorrect.

Although the Netherlands and Scandinavia began to industrialize relatively late, they did so very successfully.

B Thanks to their ready access to the sea, these countries enjoyed advantages in mercantile shipping, fishing, and shipbuilding.

D These countries were helped by the fact that their governments were relatively stable and honest and had polices that generally encouraged rather than blocked trade.

E These countries were successful primarily because their high literacy rates helped them fill specialized market niches.

Answer Choices

A Although these countries all started with small, uneducated populations, industrialization led to significant population growth and higher literacy rates.

B Thanks to their ready access to the sea, these countries enjoyed advantages in mercantile shipping, fishing, and shipbuilding.

C Because they all had good harbors for steamships, these countries started with an important advantage in the competition for transit trade.

D These countries were helped by the fact that their governments were relatively stable and honest and had polices that generally encouraged rather than blocked trade.

E These countries were successful primarily because their high literacy rates helped them fill specialized market niches.

F Because they were never fully dependent on international commerce, these countries were able to survive notorious fluctuations in international markets.

Correct Choices

Choice B: "Thanks to their ready access to the sea, these countries enjoyed advantages in mercantile shipping, fishing, and shipbuilding." This statement summarizes information in paragraph 4 explaining that the location of these countries created economic opportunities for fishing, trade, and shipbuilding. It is the first of the three "sources" discussed in the passage for "success in industrialization."

Choice D: "These countries were helped by the fact that their governments were relatively stable and had policies that generally encouraged rather than blocked trade." This choice summarizes information in paragraph 5 asserting that having a peaceful and relatively uncorrupt government with policies friendly to trade was helpful for industrialization.

Choice E: "These countries were successful primarily because their high literacy rates helped them fill specialized market niches." This choice summarizes information in paragraph 6 explaining that the countries succeeded economically because they were able to specialize in areas of the established international market in part because of their high literary rates.

Incorrect Choices

Choice A: "Although these countries all started with small, uneducated populations, industrialization led to significant population growth and higher literacy rates." It is untrue that the countries started out with "uneducated" populations and that "literacy rates" grew significantly, making this choice incorrect.

Choice C: "Because they all had good harbors for steamships, these countries started with an important advantage in the competition for transit trade." The Netherlands did not initially have good harbors for steamships (paragraph 4, sentence 4), so it is incorrect to say that "all" the countries "started with" this particular advantage. Another reason that this choice is incorrect is that it is too narrowly focused. The passage discusses shipping, but it does so in the larger context of the larger issue of the advantageous location of the countries. This larger point is a main idea, not shipping by itself.

Choice F: "Because they were never fully dependent on international commerce, these countries were able to survive notorious fluctuations in international markets." It is not clear from the passage that this statement is true because there is no discussion in the passage of the reasons why the economies of the countries survived market fluctuations. Therefore, this statement cannot be a main idea.

The Mystery of Yawning

1. **B** This is a Sentence Simplification question. As with all questions of this type, a single sentence is highlighted in the passage:

> According to conventional theory, yawning takes place when people are bored or sleepy and serves the function of increasing alertness by reversing, through deeper breathing, the drop in blood oxygen levels that are caused by the shallow breathing that accompanies lack of sleep or boredom.

The correct answer choice is B. Choice B contains all the essential information in the highlighted sentence and correctly expresses the relationships among the various essential pieces of information: the conventional view is being expressed, the conventional view is that people yawn when they are bored or sleepy, the conventional understanding for why yawning occurs is that it increases alertness, and the conventional understanding of why yawning increases alertness is that it increases blood oxygen levels.

Choice A changes the meaning of the highlighted sentence by incorrectly stating that yawning is followed by a decrease in blood oxygen levels and includes the correct but unnecessary information that low blood oxygen levels are caused by shallow breathing.

Choice C is incorrect because it leaves out the conventional theory's explanations about why people yawn and how yawning increases their alertness.

Choice D also leaves out essential information about why people yawn and instead talks about avoiding yawning, a topic not raised in the highlighted sentence.

2. **A** This is a Factual Information question asking for specific information that can be found in paragraph 1. The correct answer choice is A, "There is no scientific evidence linking yawning with tiredness." Choice A is supported by sentence 2, which indicates that researchers have "failed to find any connection" between yawning and tiredness. Choices B, C, and D are wrong for the same reason. Since there is no evidence linking yawning and tiredness, it makes no sense to talk about evidence for the theory being "wide-ranging" (choice B), "reliable" (choice C), or even "questionable" (choice D). Choice D may seem attractive because it is negative, but it is wrong in two respects. The theory that yawning is caused by tiredness is questionable, not the non-existent evidence for the theory. Moreover, there is no reason to expect the behavior of adults to differ from that of children if yawning in both is caused by the same thing—namely, tiredness.

3. **A** This is a Vocabulary question. The word being tested is *flaw*. It is highlighted in the passage. The correct answer choice is A, "fault." A flaw is an imperfection or weakness, making "fault" the best choice.

4. **C** This is a Rhetorical Purpose question. It asks you why the author compared the physiological changes that occur when people yawn, simply open their mouths, and breathe deeply. The correct answer choice is C, "To argue against the hypothesis that yawning provides a special way to improve alertness or raise physiological activity." The paragraph indicates that three actions—yawning, simply opening the mouth, and breathing deeply—all cause the same physiological changes. This outcome contradicts the expectations of the theory that yawning is caused by tiredness. If that theory were true, yawning should cause different or more intense physiological changes than the other actions do. Thus the comparison of yawning to the other actions has been included to show that the tiredness theory is wrong.

   Choice A says that the comparison supports the tiredness theory, which is incorrect. Choice B is also incorrect. In the argument against the tiredness theory being presented in the paragraph, the reliability of the various measurements taken is assumed. There is no claim in the paragraph that opening the mouth or breathing deeply affects blood oxygen levels, so choice D cannot explain why the author included the comparison in the discussion.

5. **B** This is a Negative Factual Information question asking for specific information that can be found in paragraph 2. The correct answer choice is B, "Does thinking about yawning increase yawning over not thinking about yawning?" In one experiment described in the paragraph, people were told to think about yawning while they breathed different kinds of air ("normal air, pure oxygen, or air with above-normal levels of carbon dioxide"), but this experiment measured whether the different types of air had any effect of the rate of yawning—it did not measure whether just thinking about yawning changes the rate of yawning, so there is no answer to choice B in the paragraph. Choice A is answered in sentence 2: yawning results in a slight increase in physiological activity. Choice C is answered in sentences 7 and 8: the amount of carbon dioxide and oxygen in air breathed have no effect on the rate of yawning. Choice D is answered in sentence 9: "doubling" the rate of breathing had no effect on yawning.

6. **D** This is a Factual Information question asking for specific information that can be found in paragraph 3. The correct answer choice is D, "It removes a potentially harmful fluid from the lungs." Sentences 3 and 4 explain that fetuses have a liquid in their lungs that needs to be secreted (released) and that lung deformities can occur if this liquid is prevented from being released. The development theory is that fetuses yawn and hiccup to remove this harmful liquid from their lungs. Choice A is incorrect because the development theory holds that yawning and hiccupping have the same purpose—removing harmful liquid from the lungs. Although sentence 5 indicates that removing liquid from the lungs is thought to decrease pressure in the lungs, there is no discussion of the lungs placing pressure on other organs, so choice B is wrong. Sentence 4 talks about fluid being prevented from leaving a fetus's lungs because

of "blockages," but there is no discussion of amniotic fluid entering the lungs. Sentence 3 indicates that fluid from a fetus's lungs mixes with its mother's amniotic fluid, but this mixing occurs after the fetus has secreted (released) its lung fluid, not inside the lungs of the fetus. Thus, choice C is incorrect.

7. **D** This is a Vocabulary question. The word being tested is *empirical*. It is highlighted in the passage. The correct answer choice is D, "based on observation." Something is *empirical* when it is based on experimentation or observation rather than on some other foundation, such as theory.

8. **A** This is an Inference question asking for information that can be inferred from paragraph 4. The correct answer choice is A, "Yawning is associated with an expectation of increased physical activity." This answer is supported by sentence 4: "The data showed that yawning tended to occur about 15 minutes before a period of increased behavioral activity." In the experiment that produced this data, volunteers were asked to record when they yawned, but the experiment did not indicate that people yawned more often when they recorded their yawns than when they did not, making choice B wrong. Choice C also misrepresents information in the paragraph. According to sentence 4, people yawned 15 minutes before their activity level increased, not 15 minutes before becoming "tired or bored." Participating in the activities mentioned in sentence 7 may seem physically or mentally stressful—military combat, musical performances, athletic competitions—but there is no suggestion that these activities cause yawning. According to sentence 6, people are known to yawn while they are "preparing" to participate in such activities, meaning that they yawn before beginning such activities. If yawning were caused by participation in such activities, people would yawn during or after them, not before. Thus, choice D is incorrect.

9. **C** This is an Insert Text question. You can see the four possible answer choices in paragraph 2.

Another flaw of the tiredness theory is that yawning does not raise alertness or physiological activity, as the theory would predict. When researchers measured the heart rate, muscle tension and skin conductance of people before, during and after yawning, they did detect some changes in skin conductance following yawning, indicating a slight increase in physiological activity. However, similar changes occurred when the subjects were asked simply to open their mouths or to breathe deeply. Yawning did nothing special to their state of physiological activity. Experiments have also cast serious doubt on the belief that yawning is triggered by a drop in blood oxygen or a rise in blood carbon dioxide. **(A)** Volunteers were told to think about yawning while they breathed either normal air, pure oxygen, or an air mixture with an above-normal level of carbon dioxide. **(B)** If the theory was correct, breathing air with extra carbon dioxide should have triggered yawning, while breathing pure oxygen should have suppressed yawning. **(C)** In fact, neither condition made any difference to the frequency of yawning, which remained constant at about 24 yawns per hour. **(D)** Another experiment demonstrated that physical exercise, which was sufficiently vigorous to double the rate of breathing, had no effect on the frequency of yawning. Again, the implication is that yawning has little or nothing to do with oxygen.

The sentence provided, "This, however, was not the case," is best inserted at choice **(C)**. Choice **(C)** is best because the insert sentence says that something did not occur or was not true. The only thing mentioned in the search area that did not occur was an increase in yawning when extra carbon dioxide was breathed and a suppression of yawning when pure oxygen was breathed. Therefore, only choice **(C)** makes sense.

10. **Ⓑ Ⓒ Ⓕ** This is a Prose Summary question. It is completed correctly below. The correct answer choices are B, C, and F. Choices A, D, and E are therefore incorrect.

Directions: An introductory sentence for a brief summary of the passage is provided below. Complete the summary by selecting the THREE answer choices that express the most important ideas in the passage. Some sentences do not belong in the summary because they express ideas that are not presented in the passage or are minor ideas in the passage. **This question is worth 2 points.**

The tiredness theory of yawning does not seem to explain why yawning occurs.

> B Evidence has shown that yawning is almost completely unrelated to the amount of oxygen in the blood and is unrelated to sleep behavior.
>
> C Some have proposed that yawning plays a role in the development of the lungs before birth, but it seems unlikely that yawning serves no purpose in adults.
>
> F There is some evidence that suggests that yawning prepares the body and mind for a change in activity level.

Answer Choices

A Although earlier scientific studies strongly supported the tiredness theory, new evidence has cast doubt on these findings.

B Evidence has shown that yawning is almost completely unrelated to the amount of oxygen in the blood and is unrelated to sleep behavior.

C Some have proposed that yawning plays a role in the development of the lungs before birth, but it seems unlikely that yawning serves no purpose in adults.

D Fluids in the lungs of the fetus prevent yawning from occurring, which disproves the development theory of yawning.

E New studies, along with anecdotal evidence, have shown that the frequency of yawning increases during extended periods of inactivity.

F There is some evidence that suggests that yawning prepares the body and mind for a change in activity level.

Correct Choices

Choice B, "Evidence has shown that yawning is almost completely unrelated to the amount of oxygen in the blood and is unrelated to sleep behavior," correctly summarizes the reasons presented in paragraphs 1 and 2 for rejecting the tiredness theory. Thus, it is a main idea of the passage and must be included in any summary of it.

Choice C, "Some have proposed that yawning plays a role in the development of the lungs before birth, but it seems unlikely that yawning serves no purpose in adults," correctly summarizes the discussion in paragraph 3 of the development theory of yawning and why it is likely incorrect: it fails to explain why a behavior that takes time and energy continues into adulthood if it serves no purpose in adulthood.

Choice F, "There is some evidence that suggests that yawning prepares the body and mind for a change in activity level," correctly summarizes the last paragraph, which presents experimental and anecdotal evidence that yawning precedes increases in activity levels.

Incorrect Choices

Choice A, "Although earlier scientific studies strongly supported the tiredness theory, new evidence has cast doubt on these findings." This choice is factually incorrect. It can be inferred from the information in paragraph 1 that "the few scientific investigations of yawning have failed to find any connection" between yawning and tiredness that there have never been any scientific studies supporting the tiredness theory. Paragraph 2 discusses in detail evidence against the tiredness theory. This evidence against the tiredness theory is not challenged in the passage. For these reasons, choice A is incorrect.

Choice D, "Fluids in the lungs of the fetus prevent yawning from occurring, which disproves the development theory of yawning." This choice is also factually incorrect. Paragraph 3 explains that fetuses do have fluid in their lungs, but the development theory is that yawning is performed to remove this harmful liquid from the lungs, not that yawning is prevented from occurring by fluids in the lungs.

Choice E, "New studies, along with anecdotal evidence, have shown that the frequency of yawning increases during extended periods of inactivity." This choice is also factually incorrect. Paragraph 4 explains that yawning has been observed to occur *before* an increase in activity as a way of preparing for increased activity. It does not support the idea that yawning increases *during* extended periods of inactivity.

Lightning

1. **B** This is a Negative Factual Information question asking for specific information that can be found in paragraph 1. The correct answer choice is B, "an increase in negatively charged particles over positively charged particles." There is no indication in the paragraph that more negative than positive particles are present when lightning develops, making choice B the only choice not supported by the paragraph and thus the correct answer. Choice A is supported by sentence 2, which indicates that lightning occurs when the "attractive tension" becomes "great" between "a region of negatively charged particles and a region of positively charged particles." Choice C is supported by the information in sentence 2 that that lightning occurs when the negatively and positively "charged particles suddenly rush together." Choice D is supported by sentence 1, which states that lightning is a "flash of light produced by an electrical discharge."

2. **A** This is a Factual Information question asking for specific information that can be found in paragraph 2. The correct answer is A, "Collisions with ice pellets." Sentences 4 through 7 of the paragraph explain how ice crystals become positively charged: ice pellets fall to the cloud center where they collide with ice crystals, with the result that ice crystals become positively charged and the ice pellets become negatively charged. Choice B is incorrect because there is no information in the passage that positively and negatively charged ice crystals collide at the base of the cloud (or anywhere else). According to sentence 8, negatively charged ice pellets—not negatively charged ice crystals—are concentrated at the center of a storm cloud, making choice C wrong. According to the last sentence of the paragraph, temperatures in the bottom of the cloud are greater than –15°C, but these temperatures are unrelated to ice crystals becoming positively charged, a process that occurs in the middle of the cloud, making choice D incorrect.

3. **D** This is a Factual Information question asking for specific information that can be found in paragraph 2. The correct answer is D, "Temperatures in the lower part of the cloud are warmer than –15°C." The last sentence of the paragraph explains why positively charged ice pellets are produced in the lower part of a storm cloud: In this part of the cloud, temperatures are "warmer than –15°C," and at such temperatures, "collisions between ice crystals and ice pellets produce "positively charged ice pellets." There is no indication that the number of collisions between ice crystals and ice pellets increases in the lower part of the cloud, making choice A incorrect. While it is true that the lower region of the cloud is smaller than the middle region, this difference in size is mentioned simply as a fact, not as a reason why ice pellets are positively charged in the lower region. Thus, choice B is incorrect. There is no comparison in the paragraph of the number of ice crystals to the number of ice pellets in the lower part of the cloud, so choice C is also incorrect.

4. ⓓ This is a Negative Factual Information question asking for specific information that can be found in paragraph 2. The correct answer choice is D, "the development of a positive charge at the base of the cloud." It is true that the base of a storm cloud has a positive charge, but this fact does not explain why the middle part of the cloud becomes negatively charged, so choice D is NOT supported, making it the correct choice. Sentences 6 through 9 identify various factors that interact to cause the center of the cloud to become "negatively charged" (sentence 10). Choice A is supported by sentence 7, which indicates that a shift in the electrical charge of ice pellets and ice crystals occurs when they collide in the middle of the cloud. Choice B is supported by sentence 9 that says that "negatively charged ice pellets . . . concentrate in the center" of the cloud. And sentence 6 indicates that temperatures in the center are "about −15°C or lower."

5. ⓒ This is an Inference question asking for information that can be inferred from paragraph 2. The correct answer choice is C, "the negatively charged ice pellets are too heavy to be carried by the updrafts that move ice crystals." Information in sentences 8, 9, and 10 support this choice. Sentence 8 indicates that ice crystals have a positive charge, are lightweight, and are swept by winds into the upper cloud. Sentence 9 says that ice pellets, which are negatively charged, are heavier than ice crystals and so stay in the middle of the cloud. Sentence 10 summarizes the implication of these facts, namely that the middle cloud becomes negatively charged and the upper cloud becomes positively charged. It can be inferred from the combination of statements that the ice pellets are too heavy for winds to sweep them up into the upper cloud, making choice C correct. Sentence 4 says that the "upper regions" of the cloud are "cold." This, combined with the fact that the bottom of the cloud is warmer than the middle, suggests that the top of the cloud is the coldest region of the cloud, making choice A incorrect. Choice B is factually incorrect: the middle of the cloud is occupied mainly by negatively charged particles, not positively charged ones. Sentence 4 indicates that ice pellets form in the upper cloud, but there is no indication that they collide with each other in the upper cloud, making choice D incorrect.

6. ⓐ This is a Rhetorical Purpose question. It asks you why the author includes the information that "Lightning that strikes the ground is the most likely to be destructive." The correct answer choice is A, "this form of lightning has been investigated so much." The word "so" in sentence 3 indicates that there is a cause-effect relationship between the destructiveness of ground lightning and the high amount of "scientific attention" it has received, thus making choice A correct. While it is factually true that ground lightning is less common than lightning that stays in the sky, this is not why the author includes the information that ground lightning is more destructive, making choice B incorrect. While it may be important to have scientific understanding of ground lightning, this is not a point that the author makes in the paragraph, so choice C is also incorrect. Sentence 2 indicates that the ground beneath a

storm cloud can become positively charged, but this is not the reason that the author includes the information that ground lightning is the most destructive form of lightning, so choice D is also incorrect. Remember, the task in Rhetorical Purpose items is to identify the specific role played in the passage by the information asked about in the question. Choices that include factually accurate information but that do not correctly identify the specific role played by the information asked about are incorrect.

7. **(A)** This is a Vocabulary question. The word being tested is *initiated*. It is highlighted in the passage. The correct answer choice is A, "started." To *initiate* something is to begin it, making "started" the best choice.

8. **(B)** This is a Factual Information question asking for specific information that can be found in paragraph 5. The correct answer choice is B, "It completes a channel that connects the storm cloud with the ground." Sentences 2 and 3 indicate that "a complete channel" is formed when "a stream of negatively charged particles from the cloud comes within 100 meters of the ground," at which point it is met by "a stream of positively charged particles," making choice B correct. Choice A is false: sentence 4 indicates that electrons from the cloud "follow the channel to the ground." Choice C is also false: the stream of charged particles from the ground does not "produce" a stream of electrons from the cloud. According to the paragraph, the cloud produces its own stream of electrons. Sentence 4 discusses the width of the channel that charged particles travel along—it is a narrow path—but there is no support for the idea that the stream of charged particles from the ground changes the channel by making it wider, so choice D is wrong.

9. **(C)** This is an Insert Text question. You can see the four possible answer choices in paragraphs 5 and 6.

That is why the subsequent lightning that follows the completed channel often strikes a tall structure. **(A)**

Once a channel has been formed, it is usually used by several lightning discharges, each of them consisting of a stream of electrons from the cloud meeting a stream of positive particles along the established path. **(B)** Sometimes, however, a stream of electrons following an established channel is met by a positive stream making a new path up from the ground. **(C)** The result is a forked lightning that strikes the ground in two places. **(D)**

The sentence provided, "The descending stream of electrons divides at the point where the new positive-stream channel intersects the established path," is best inserted at choice **(C)**.

Choice **(C)** is correct because it continues the discussion begun in sentence 2 of the last paragraph about forked lightning by explaining how the second leg of such lightning is formed. The only logical place to insert this extension of the process is choice **(C)**. When placed in choices **(A)** or **(B)**, there is no referent for the phrase "the new positive-stream channel," making these choices incorrect. Choice **(D)** may seem attractive because it is about forked lightning, but it summarizes the result of the process described previously. It makes no sense to return to describing the process of how forked lightning is formed after already summarizing the result. The discussion of the process should be continuous, not separated by a summary statement.

10. **Ⓑ Ⓒ Ⓕ** This is a Prose Summary question. It is completed correctly below. The correct answer choices are B, C, and F. Choices A, D, and E are therefore incorrect.

Lightning takes place when a separation of positive and negative electrical particles that develop in a storm cloud suddenly collapses.

   B A separation of oppositely charged particles in clouds develops from collisions of falling ice pellets with ice crystals, from updrafts, and from temperature variations.

   C Lightning from cloud to ground follows a channel that forms when a stream of electrons moving down meets a stream of positive particles coming up from the ground.

   F Once a channel has been formed, it is usually used by several successive electrical discharges that illuminate the channel as flashes of lightning.

Answer Choices

[A] A storm cloud first develops a positively charged layer at the top, then a negatively charged middle layer, and finally, a positively charged layer at the bottom.

[B] A separation of oppositely charged particles in clouds develops from collisions of falling ice pellets with ice crystals, from updrafts, and from temperature variations.

[C] Lightning from cloud to ground follows a channel that forms when a stream of electrons moving down meets a stream of positive particles coming up from the ground.

[D] Field studies, laboratory stimulations, and high-speed photography have all been used to investigate the way charge separations develop in clouds.

[E] Lightning from a cloud to the ground is more likely to be destructive than is lightning that takes place within a cloud.

[F] Once a channel has been formed, it is usually used by several successive electrical discharges that illuminate the channel as flashes of light.

Correct Choices

Choice B, "A separation of oppositely charged particles in clouds develops from collisions of falling ice pellets with ice crystals, from updrafts, and from temperature variations," summarizes events and conditions discussed in paragraph 2 that lead to the "sandwich-like structure" of storm clouds. Lightning occurs when the resulting separate layers collapse. This information is essential to understanding how the electrical energy released in lightning is created, so it must be included in any good summary of the passage.

Choice C, "Lightning from cloud to ground follows a channel that forms when a stream of electrons moving down meets a stream of positive particles coming up from the ground," explains how it is possible for lightning to reach the ground. Because ground lightning is an important focus of the passage, information about how lightning reaches the ground must be included in any good summary of the passage.

Choice F, "Once a channel has been formed, it is usually used by several successive electrical discharges that illuminate the channel as flashes of lightning," which comes from paragraph 6, explains what happens once a channel between a storm cloud and the ground has been formed. This is an important consequence of the processes described earlier in the passage, so it too should be included in any good summary of the passage.

Incorrect Choices

Choice A, "A storm cloud first develops a positively charged layer at the top, then a negatively charged middle layer, and finally, a positively charged layer at the bottom," is factually incorrect. The separation of the cloud layers happens more or less at the same time rather than one layer at a time since the layers are formed as a result of the interactions of cloud particles with each other.

Choice D, "Field studies, laboratory stimulations, and high-speed photography have all been used to investigate the way charge separations develop in clouds," is also incorrect. While paragraph 2 indicates that laboratory simulations and field studies ("recent measurements made in the field") have been used to study the charge separation in clouds, there is no indication of high-speed photography being used for this purpose. This choice is also incorrect because the methods used by scientists to study cloud separation are not a main focus of the passage. The main focus is on the processes involved in the formation of lightning, not on how lightning is studied.

Choice E, "Lightning from a cloud to the ground is more likely to be destructive than is lightning that takes place within a cloud," is also incorrect. This choice may seem attractive, but the destructiveness of lightning is not a main topic of discussion in the passage. For this reason, this information does not belong in a summary of the passage.

Listening

Answer Key and Self-Scoring Chart

Directions: Check your answers against the answer key below. Write the number 1 on the line to the right of each question if you picked the correct answer. Total your points at the bottom of the chart.

Question Number	Correct Answer	Your Raw Points
1.	C	
2.	A	
3.	A	
4.	D	
5.	C	
6.	A	
7.	C	
8.	D	
9.	B	

For question 16, write 1 if you picked both correct answers. Write 0 if you picked only one correct answer or no correct answers.

10.	B, C	
11.	D	
12.	D	
13.	C	
14.	A	
15.	A	
16.	B	
17.	B	

For question 18, write 1 if you placed five answer choices correctly. Write 0 if you placed 4 or fewer choices correctly.

18.	Yes: A, B, D	

Question Number	Correct Answer	Your Raw Points

For question 19, write 1 if you picked both correct answers. Write 0 if you picked only one correct answer or no correct answers.

19.	A, C	
20.	D	
21.	B	
22.	C	
23.	D	
24.	A	
25.	C	

For question 26, write 1 if you picked both correct answers. Write 0 if you picked only one correct answer or no correct answers.

26.	A, C	
27.	D	
28.	B	
TOTAL:		

Below is a table that converts your Listening section answers into a *TOEFL iBT*® Listening scaled score. Take the total of raw points from your answer key and find that number in the left-hand column of the table. The right-hand column of the table gives a TOEFL iBT Listening scaled score for each number of raw points. For example, if the total points from your answer key is 27, the table shows a scaled score of 29 to 30.

You should use your score estimate as a general guide only. Your actual score on the TOEFL iBT test may be higher or lower than your score on the practice version.

Listening

Raw Point Total	Scaled Score
28	30
27	29–30
26	27–30
25	25–30
24	24–29
23	23–27
22	22–26
21	21–25
20	19–24
19	18–23
18	17–21
17	16–20
16	14–19
15	13–18
14	12–17
13	10–15
12	9–14
11	7–13
10	6–12
9	5–10
8	3–9
7	2–7
6	1–6
5	1–4
4	0–2
3	0–1
2	0
1	0
0	0

Listening Scripts and Answer Explanations

Questions 1–5

Track 78 Listening Script

Narrator

Listen to a conversation between a student and an administrator in the university employment office.

Male Student

Hi, I hope you can help me. I just transferred from Northeastern State University, near Chicago . . .

Administrator

Well, welcome to Central University. But Chicago's such a great city, why did you leave?

Male Student

Everyone asks that . . . it's my hometown, and it was sure convenient to go to a school nearby. But Northeastern is still fairly small, and it doesn't have the program I'm interested in . . . I want to major in international studies and the only program in the state is here.

Administrator

We do have a great program. How did you get interested in international studies?

Male Student

My family hosted a few foreign-exchange students while I was growing up . . . then I took part in an international summer program after I graduated from high school. I found I really like meeting people from all over, getting to know them . . .

Administrator

Oh, OK. And that led you to our program. Right now, though, I assume you're looking for a job.

Male Student

Yeah, a part-time job on campus . . . I thought I'd save money, being away from the big city . . . but it doesn't seem to be working that way. Anyway, I'm not having much luck.

Administrator

I'm not surprised. Most of our campus jobs are taken in the first week or two of the semester. What work experience have you had?

Male Student

Well, I worked in the university library last year. But I already checked at the library here . . . they said their remaining positions were for work-study students getting financial aid. I've never run into that before.

Administrator

Well, I guess each school has its own policies. We really don't have much right now. You might be better off waiting until next semester . . . if you **really** want something . . . How are your computer skills?

Male Student

About average, I'd say. I helped teach some of the basic computer classes Northeastern offers for new users, if that helps any.

Administrator

OK . . . Uh, the technology support department needs people to work at its helpdesk. It's basically a customer-service job . . . answering questions, helping people solve their computer problems . . . give you a chance to develop your people skills.

Male Student

Something every diplomat needs. But, is there some problem? I mean, why's the job still open?

Administrator

Well, they have extended hours . . . from 6 A.M. to 2 A.M. every day, so they need a large staff. But right now they only need people early mornings, late nights, and weekends. You'd probably end up with a bit of everything rather than a regular spot. On the bright side, you'd probably be able to get some studying done between calls. At least it'd be a start and then you can try for better hours next semester.

Male Student

Hmm, I see where the hours might be a problem. But . . . I guess I can't afford to be too picky if I want a job. Still, maybe we can work something out.

Answer Explanations

1. **C** This is a Gist-Purpose question. After the student and the administrator talk about the student's reasons for transferring to another institution, the administrator says that she assumes the student has come to the employment office in the hope of finding a job. The student confirms that he is indeed

looking for a part-time job; therefore, the correct answer is choice C. Since the student indicates that he already found out that he is not eligible for the library jobs, choice A is incorrect. He does not say anything that would indicate an interest in hosting an exchange student (choice B) and he does not ask the administrator to tell him the computer lab's hours (choice D).

2. **A** This is a Detail question. At the beginning of the conversation, the student explains that he has transferred from Northeastern State University to Central University because Central University offers a program in international studies. Thus, choice A is the correct response. The student says that he took part in an international summer program, but he makes no mention of participating in an exchange program at the university (choice B). He also says that the problem with his previous university is that it is too small to offer the program he wants, so choice C is incorrect. And though Central University has an international studies *program*, it is not described as having an international *reputation* (choice D).

3. **A** This is an Understanding Organization question. When the student talks about the fact that his family hosted foreign-exchange students, he is replying to the administrator's question about how he became interested in international studies, so choice A is the correct answer. There is no connection between his family's hosting experience and his search for a job (choice B). The student does not mention any plans to become an exchange student while at the university (choice C) and he does not say that he learned his computer skills from an exchange student (choice D).

4. **D** To answer this Making Inferences question, you need to recognize that the regular daytime and evening shifts at the helpdesk have already been filled. You can draw this conclusion because the administrator says that workers are needed only during early mornings, late nights, and weekends. She also says that the student's schedule would probably include a bit of each of these unusual work hours. Working irregular hours would have to be acceptable to students applying for the available helpdesk positions, so the correct answer is choice D.

5. **C** In this replay question, you are asked to listen again to a statement made by the administrator (Track 79). You are then asked to listen once more to a particular phrase that is part of the statement and to identify the reason why the administrator uses that particular phrase. This question requires you to Understand the Function of What Is Said. To answer it correctly (choice C), you need to understand that the administrator is trying to warn the student that the only job currently available is one that most students would rather not have. The tone of her voice when she speaks the phrase helps convey her intention. Choice A would make sense if the administrator's statement stopped with the suggestion that it might be better for the student to wait until next semester to look for a job, but the inclusion of the warning

phrase makes choice A incorrect. Choices B and D might initially appear to make sense, but your understanding of the entire conversation tells you that the administrator is preparing to talk about the job at the computer lab, not about an off-campus job or a work-study program.

Questions 6–11

Track 80 Listening Script

Narrator

Listen to part of a lecture in an art history class.

Art History

Professor

Today, we'll continue our examination of ancient Roman sculpture. We've already looked at **portrait** sculpture—which are busts created to commemorate people who had died—and we've looked at **relief** sculpture, or sculpting on walls. And today we look at yet another category of sculpture—copies. Roman sculptors **often** made copies of famous Greek sculptures.

Female Student

Why did they do that?

Professor

Well, no one knows for sure. You see, in the late fourth century B.C., the Romans began a campaign to expand the Roman Empire . . . and in 300 years they had conquered most of the Mediterranean area and parts of Europe. You know the saying, "To the victor belong the spoils?" Well, the Roman army returned to Rome with many works of Greek art. It's probably fair to say that the Romans were impressed by Greek art and culture—and they began making copies of the Greek statues. Now, the dominant view in traditional art history is that Roman artists lacked creativity and skill, especially compared to the Greek artists who came before them. Essentially, the traditional view—a view that's been prevalent for over 250 years—is that the Romans copied Greek sculptures because they couldn't create sculpture of their own.

But, finally, **some** contemporary art historians have challenged this view. One is Elaine Gazda.

Gazda says that there might be other reasons that Romans made copies. She wasn't convinced that it was because of a lack of creativity. Can anyone think of another possible reason?

Male Student

Well . . . maybe they just admired the sculptures, you know, they liked the way they looked.

Professor

Yes! That's one of Gazda's points. Another is that while nowadays reproduction is easy, it was not so easy in Roman times. Copying statues required a lot of skill, time, and effort. So, Gazda hypothesizes that copying didn't indicate a lack of artistic imagination—or skill—on the part of Roman artists, but rather, the Romans made copies because they admired Greek sculpture. Classical Greek statues represented an idealization of the human body and were considered quite beautiful at the time.

Gazda also believes that it's been a mistake to dismiss the Roman copies as, well, copies for copies' sake, and not to consider the **Roman** function and meaning of the statues.

Female Student

What do you mean . . . the Roman function? Weren't they just for decoration?

Professor

Well, not necessarily. Under the emperor Augustus, at the height of the Roman Empire, portrait statues were sent throughout the empire . . . they were supposed to communicate specific ideas about the emperor and the imperial family, and to help inhabitants of the conquered areas become familiar with the Roman way of life. You know, Roman coins were also distributed throughout the empire. Anybody care to guess what was on them?

Male Student

The emperor's face?

Professor

That's right. The coins were easy to distribute, and they allowed people to see the emperor, or at least his likeness, and served as an additional reminder to let them know, well, who was in charge. And the images helped people become familiar with the emperor—**statues** of him in different roles were sent all over the empire. Now, actually **some** Roman sculptures were original, but others were exact copies of Greek statues. And some Roman sculptures were combinations of some sort; some combined more than one Greek statue, and others combined a Greek god or an athlete with a Roman's head. At the time of Julius Caesar, it wasn't uncommon to create statues that had the body of a god and the head of an emperor.

And the Romans were clever . . . what they did was, they made plaster casts from molds of the sculptures. Then, they shipped these plaster casts to workshops all over the empire, where they were replicated in marble or bronze. And on some statues the heads were removable—they could put an emperor's head on different bodies showing him doing different things. And then later, when the time came, they could even use the head of the **next** emperor on the same body!

Answer Explanations

6. **Ⓐ** This is a Gist-Content item. The class has been studying ancient Roman sculpture. The professor states that it was a common practice among Roman sculptors to make copies of Greek sculptures. He discusses an opinion about this practice that was held by most art historians in the past. Then he discusses a different opinion that has been proposed by a contemporary art historian. This contrast of ideas makes choice A the correct response. The

other choices present topics that are *mentioned* in the lecture but are not the *main subject* of the lecture.

7. Ⓒ This is a Detail question. Early in the lecture, the professor describes how the Romans encountered Greek art during their conquest of the Mediterranean region. The traditional view of art historians, cited by the professor, is that the Romans copied Greek art because they were not as creative as the Greeks, so the correct answer is choice C. Choices A and B are not mentioned in the lecture. Choice D is wrong because it expresses the view of Elaine Gazda, the contemporary art historian, not the view of traditional art historians.

8. Ⓓ This is a Connecting Content question. The professor discusses several points made by Gazda. One point is that making copies of statues requires artistic skill. Another point is that the Romans needed to circulate portrait statues of their emperor to all parts of their empire in order to foster a sense of loyalty among the inhabitants. Thus, the statues had a dual artistic and political function, making choice D the correct answer.

9. Ⓑ This is an Understanding Organization question. The professor has just discussed the Romans' need to distribute portraits of the emperor throughout their empire. He mentions coins because they are stamped with the emperor's portrait and are easy to distribute, being small and lightweight. Thus, choice B is the correct answer. Choice A may appear to be the right response, but it is not, because it is not the professor's intention to show the similarity between the portraits on coins and the portraits on statues.

10. Ⓑ Ⓒ In this Detail question, you are asked to choose two correct answers. At the end of the lecture, the professor explains two reasons why the Romans found it useful to make portrait statues with removable heads. First, each head could be attached to a variety of statues, so choice B is correct. Second, the removable head could eventually be replaced with a different emperor's likeness, so choice C is the second correct answer. Neither the weight of the head (choice A) nor the quality of the statue (choice D) is mentioned by the professor.

11. Ⓓ In this replay question, you are asked to listen again to a small part of the lecture in which the professor describes a belief about Roman art that most art historians have held (Track 81). You are then asked to listen once more to the last sentence of the replay and to draw a conclusion about what it means. Like many replay questions, this one requires you to Understand the Function of What Is Said. In that last sentence, the professor indicates that the belief he has just described has been challenged by some members of the current generation of art historians. Choice D is the only choice that relates to the professor's statement as a whole, and you can tell from the way the professor stresses the word "finally" that the professor agrees with this challenge to the traditional belief, so choice D is correct.

Questions 12–16

Track 82 Listening Script

Narrator

Listen to a conversation between a student and his sociology professor.

Professor

Well, I'm glad you redid your outline. Um, I've made a few comments, but nothing you have to act on. It's in good enough shape for you to start writing your paper.

Male Student

Thanks. At first I was afraid all that prep work would be a waste of time.

Professor

Well, especially with a challenging topic like yours—factors leading to the emergence of sociology as an academic discipline. There's just so much history to consider, you could get lost without a solid outline. Uh, so, did you have a question?

Male Student

Yeah, it's about. . . . You mentioned needing volunteers for a research study?

Professor

Yep. It's not my study, it's my colleague's in the marketing department. She needs people to watch various new TV programs that haven't been broadcast yet. Then indicate on a survey whether they liked it, why, if they'd watch another episode. . . . It'd be kinda fun, plus participants get a $50 gift certificate.

Male Student

Oh, well, I like the sound of that! But—so they're trying to predict if these shows are gonna succeed or fail, right? Based on students' opinions? Why would they care what we think?

Professor

Hey, don't sell yourself short—people your age are a very attractive market for advertisers who promote their products on television. The study's sponsored by a TV network. If enough students don't like a show, the network may actually reconsider putting it on the air.

Male Student

OK, well, how do I sign up?

Professor

You just add your name and phone number to this list and check a time slot. Although it looks like the only times left are next Monday morning and Thursday evening.

Male Student

Oh, well. . . . I have marketing and economics Monday mornings, and Thursday.

Professor

Oh, you're taking a marketing class? Who's teaching it?

Male Student

It's, uh, Professor Larkin, intro to marketing. He hasn't mentioned the study, though.

Professor

Oh. Well . . . the marketing department's pretty big. I happen to be friends with the woman who's doing the TV study. OK, well, we don't want you missing class . . . how's Thursday?

Male Student

Oh, I work from five till nine that night.

Professor

Hmm. No flexibility with your schedule? Where do you work?

Male Student

At Fox's Diner. I'm a server.

Professor

Oh, I love Fox's. I eat there every week. Maybe you could switch shifts with someone.

Male Student

I'm still in training, and the only night my trainer works is Thursday.

Professor

Look, I know the owners there really well. Why don't you let me give them a call and explain the situation?

Male Student

OK. It'd be cool to be part of a real research study. And the gift certificate wouldn't hurt, either!

Answer Explanations

12. **D** This is a Gist-Content question. The professor and the student begin by briefly discussing an outline the student has written for an assignment, but the conversation shifts when the professor says, "Uh, so, did you have a question?" The rest of the conversation mainly focuses on a research project in which the student would like to participate, so the correct answer is D.

13. **C** This question involves Making Inferences. The professor acknowledges that the topic of the student's paper is "challenging" and there's "just so much history to consider," but she does not tell the student to narrow the focus of his paper. Therefore, choice A can be eliminated as the answer. It's clear that the professor has a favorable opinion of the outline when she says, "It's (the outline) in good enough shape for you to start writing your paper." She goes on to say that the student needs a solid outline for such a complex topic, and it's implied that he has produced an outline that is sufficient to help him write about a difficult topic. Therefore, the correct answer is C.

14. **A** This is a Detail question. After the student expresses interest in the research study, the professor briefly explains what is expected of the participants. The study is fairly straightforward, with participants watching several new TV shows and giving their opinions about the quality of the shows. The professor does not mention anything about sociological factors that influence participants' opinions of the shows, so choice D can be eliminated. She does mention that TV networks are interested in the opinions of university students because they are an important market, so the correct answer is A.

15. **A** This question requires Making an Inference. After the student explains why it will be difficult to change his work schedule at Fox's Diner, the professor says, "Look, I know the owners there really well. Why don't you let me give them a call and explain the situation?" The clear implication is that the owners of the restaurant would want to help the professor, so the correct answer is A.

16. **B** This question involves Understanding the Function of What Is Said. You are asking to listen again to part of the conversation (Track 83). The student comments that his marketing professor, Professor Larkin, has not said anything about the research study. The professor responds that the marketing department is big, so the correct answer is B. Choice D could be the meaning of this utterance in a different context, but not in this conversation because only one research study is discussed. Likewise, even though choice A could be correct in a different context, the student does not express a desire to find a marketing professor who is interested in sociology. By pointing out the size of the marketing department, the professor is suggesting that Professor Larkin probably does not know about all of the research projects that are being conducted by professors in the department.

Questions 17–22

Track 84 Listening Script

Narrator

Listen to part of a lecture in a European history class.

Professor

In order to really study the social history of the Middle Ages, you have to understand the role of spices. Now, this might sound a little surprising, even a little strange, but what seem like little things now were, back then, actually rather big things. So, first let's define what a spice is. Technically speaking, a spice is part of an aromatic plant that is not a leaf, or herb. Spices can come from tree bark, like, ah, cinnamon, plant roots like ginger, flower buds like cloves. And in the Middle Ages, Europeans were familiar with lots of different spices, the most important being pepper, cloves, ginger, cinnamon, mace, and nutmeg. These spices literally dominated the way Europeans lived for centuries—how they traded and, uh, even how they used their imaginations.

So why this medieval fascination with spices? We can boil it down to three general ideas, briefly. One was cost and rarity, ah, two was exotic taste and fragrance, and third, mysterious origins and a kind of mythical status.

Now, for cost and rarity: Spices aren't native to Europe, and they had to be imported. Spices only grew in the East Indies, and of course transportation costs were astronomical. So spices were incredibly valuable, even from the very beginning. Here's an example, um, in 408 A.D., the Gothic general who'd captured Rome demanded payment. He wanted 5,000 pounds of gold, among other things, but he also wanted 3,000 pounds of pepper. Maybe that'll give you an idea of exactly where pepper stood at the time. By the Middle Ages, spices were regarded as so important and expensive, they were used in diplomacy—as gifts by heads of state and ambassadors.

Now, for the taste, the diet then was relatively bland compared to today's. There wasn't much variety. Uh, especially the aristocracy, who tended to eat a lot of meat, um, they were always looking for new ways to prepare it—new sauces, new tastes, and this is where spices came in. Now this is a good point to mention one of the biggest myths about spices: It's commonly said that medieval Europeans wanted spices to cover up the taste of spoiled meat, but this isn't really true. Anyone who had to worry about spoiled meat couldn't afford spices in the first place. If you could afford spices, you could definitely afford fresh meat. We also have evidence that various medieval markets employed a kind of police, to make sure that people didn't sell spoiled food. And if you were caught doing it, you were subject to various fines, humiliating public punishments. So, what actually was true was this: In order to have meat for the winter, people would preserve it in salt—not a spice. Spices, actually, aren't very effective as preservatives. And, uh, throughout winter they would eat salted meat, but the taste of the stuff could grow really boring and, and depressing after a while. So the cooks started looking for new ways to improve the taste, and spices were the answer.

Which brings us to mysterious origins and mythical status. Now the ancient Romans had a thriving spice trade, and they sent their ships to the east and back. But when Rome collapsed in the fifth century and the Middle Ages began, um, direct trade stopped, and, uh, so did that kind of hands-on knowledge of travel and geography. Spices now came by way of the trade routes, with lots of intermediaries between the producer and the consumer. So these spices took on an air of mystery. Their origins were shrouded in exotic travels; they had the allure of the unknown, of wild places. Myths grew up of fantasy lands, magical faraway places made entirely of food and spices. Add to that, spices themselves had always been considered special, or magical—not just for eating—and this was already true in the ancient world where legends about spices were abundant. Spices inspired the medieval imagination, they were used as medicines to ward off diseases, and mixed into perfumes, incense. They were used in religious rituals for thousands of years. They took on a life of their own, and they inspired the medieval imagination, spurred on the age of discovery in the fifteenth and sixteenth centuries. When famous explorers like Columbus and Da Gama and Magellan left Europe in their ships, they weren't looking for a new world; they were looking for spices. And we know what important historical repercussions some of those voyages had.

Answer Explanations

17. **B** This is a Gist-Purpose question. The professor introduces her purpose in the first sentence when she says, "In order to really study the social history of the Middle Ages, you have to understand the role of spices." For the rest of the lecture, the professor describes three main reasons why spices were important for medieval society. The correct answer is B.

18. **Ⓐ Ⓑ Ⓓ** This is a Connecting Information question. It involves connecting content from different parts of the lecture. The professor discusses many aspects of spices, one of which is that spices "aren't native to Europe." The fact that spices had to be imported is mentioned throughout the lecture. Also, the professor points out the extremely high cost of spices, which made them inaccessible for many people. When the professor describes the mysterious quality that spices held for medieval Europeans, she points out that they were used for medicinal purposes. The chart correctly filled out looks like this:

	YES	NO
1. They had to be imported.	✗	
2. They were unaffordable for many people.	✗	
3. They were used to preserve meat during the winter.		✗
4. They were believed to have medicinal properties.	✗	
5. Their sale in public markets was closely regulated.		✗

The two statements marked as "No" are not true about spices in medieval Europe for the following reasons:

The professor mentions that "In order to have meat for the winter, people would preserve it in salt—**not** a spice." She goes on to say that spices are not useful as preservatives.

The professor does discuss regulations in public markets, but she's referring to rules concerning the sale of meat, not spices.

19. **Ⓐ Ⓒ** This is a Detail question. While discussing the exotic taste of spices, the professor argues against the idea that medieval Europeans used spices to cover up the taste of spoiled meat. She points out that anyone who could afford spices would be able to buy fresh meat. Also, she describes how "medieval markets employed a kind of police, to make sure that people didn't sell spoiled food." The correct answers are A and C.

20. **Ⓓ** This question involves Understanding Organization. The professor mentions the collapse of the Roman Empire and how this led to an interruption in the trade route between Rome and the East. Specifically, she mentions that, "direct trade stopped," so choice A can be eliminated. Even though a direct route was no longer available, Romans were still able to acquire spices ". . . by way of trade routes, with lots of intermediaries between the producer and the consumer." For this reason, choice C can be eliminated. The lack of a direct trade route and intimate knowledge with "travel and geography" allowed spices to be viewed as mysterious and exotic by the Romans. Therefore, the correct answer is D.

21. Ⓑ This is a Detail question. Near the end of the lecture, the professor explains the growing importance of spices, mentioning how they came to be viewed as special or magical. She says, "When famous explorers like Columbus and Da Gama and Magellan left Europe in their ships, they weren't looking for a new world; they were looking for spices." It's clear that European explorers were not motivated to discover new lands, but to find spices, so the correct answer is B.

22. Ⓒ This question involves Understanding the Function of What Is Said. You are asked to listen again to part of the lecture (Track 85). To emphasize the value of spices in the Middle Ages, the professor provides an example of a general who captured Rome. This general demanded payment in the form of gold and pepper. When she says, "Maybe that'll give you an idea of exactly where pepper stood at the time," the professor is illustrating how valuable spices like pepper were in the Middle Ages, so the correct answer is C.

Questions 23–28

Track 86 Listening Script

Narrator
Listen to part of a lecture in a biology class.

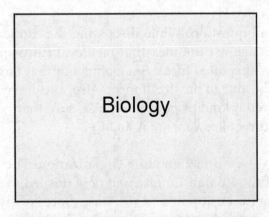

Professor

Well, it's finally looking like spring is arriving—the last of the winter snow will be melting away in a few days. So before we close today, I thought I'd mention, uh, a biological event that's part of the transition from winter to spring . . . something you can go outside and watch, if you have some patience. There's a small creature that lives in this area—you've probably seen it: it's the North American wood frog.

Now the wood frog's not that easy to spot, since it stays pretty close to the ground, under leaves and things, and it blends in really well with its background, as you can see. But they're worth the effort, because they do something very unusual—something you might not have even thought possible.

OK, North American wood frogs live over a very broad territory, or range—they're found all over the northeastern United States, and all through Canada and Alaska—even inside the Arctic Circle. No other frog is able to live that far north. But wherever they live, once the weather starts to turn cold, and the temperatures start to drop below freezing—as soon as the frog even touches an ice crystal or a bit of frozen ground . . . well, it begins to freeze. Yes, Jimmy? You look a bit taken aback.

Male Student

Wait. You mean, it's still alive, but it freezes? Solid?

Professor

Well, almost. Ice forms in all the spaces outside cells, but never within a cell.

Male Student

But . . . then, how does its heart beat?

Professor

It doesn't.

Male Student

But—how can it do. . . .

Professor

How can it do such a thing? Well, that first touch of ice apparently triggers a biological response inside the frog, that first of all starts drawing water away from the center of its body. So the middle part of the frog, its internal organs—its heart, lungs, liver—these start getting drier and drier, while the water that's being pulled away is forming a puddle around the organs, just underneath the skin. And then that puddle of water starts to freeze.

OK, up to now the frog's heart is still beating, right? Slower and slower, but. . . . And in those last few hours before it freezes, it distributes glucose—a blood sugar—throughout its body, its circulatory system. Sort of acts like an antifreeze. . . .

Male Student

A solution of antifreeze, like you put in your car in the winter?

Professor

Well, you tell me. In frogs, the extra glucose makes it harder for the water inside the cells to freeze, so the cells stay just slightly wet—enough so that they can survive the winter. Then after that, the heart stops beating altogether. So, is that the same?

Male Student

I don't really know, but uh . . . how long does it stay that way?

Professor

Well, it could be days or even months—all winter, in fact. But, um, see, the heart really doesn't need to do any pumping now, because the blood is frozen too.

Male Student

I just . . . I guess I just don't see how it isn't—y'know, clinically dead.

Professor

Well, that's the amazing thing. And how it revives is pretty amazing too. After months without a heartbeat, springtime comes around again, the Earth starts to warm up, and suddenly one day—ping! A pulse—followed by another one, then another, until—maybe ten, twelve hours later, the animal is fully recovered.

Male Student

And—does the, uh, thawing process have some kind of trigger as well?

Professor

Well, we're not sure, actually. The peculiar thing is, even though the sun is warming the frog up on the outside, its insides thaw out first—the heart and brain and everything. But somehow, it all just happens that way every spring.

Male Student

And after they thaw? Does it affect them? Like their life span?

Professor

Well, hmm . . . we really don't know a lot about how long a wood frog normally lives—probably just a few years. But there's no evidence that the freezing process affects its longevity. It does have some other impacts, though. In studies we've found that, when it comes to reproduction, freezing diminishes the mating performance of males: after they've been frozen, and thawed of course, they don't seem quite as vocal, they move slower—and they seem to have a harder time recognizing a potential mate. So if a male frog could manage not to go through this freezing cycle, he'd probably have more success at mating.

Answer Explanations

23. **D** This is a Gist-Purpose question. The professor begins by telling her students about an unusual biological process involving North American wood frogs. The majority of the lecture describes this unusual occurrence, explaining in detail the steps involved. During the lecture, the professor does not discuss any biological advantages the wood frog gains from freezing and then thawing. In fact, she points out one negative consequence for some frogs that undergo this process, so choice A can be eliminated. Information about the wood frog's circulatory system is discussed, but this information only serves to describe the larger freezing process. Therefore, choice C can be eliminated. The main purpose of the lecture is to make students aware of an unusual biological process that they can observe in their area, so the correct answer is D.

24. **A** This question involves Understanding Organization. The professor mentions the arrival of spring because this is the time when wood frogs begin to thaw. She says this event is "something you can go outside and watch," and that even though it is not easy to spot the frogs, the effort is worth it. She is encouraging her students to go out and observe these thawing frogs, so the correct answer is A.

25. **C** This is a Detail question. The professor states that after a wood frog first touches ice, there is a response ". . . that first of all starts drawing water away from the center of its body." She goes on to mention that the center of a frog's body contains its internal organs, and that these organs ". . . start getting drier and drier . . ." Therefore, the correct answer is C.

26. **A** **C** This is a Connecting Information question. It requires connecting content from different parts of the lecture. In response to the student's question about whether there is a trigger for the thawing process, the professor states, "Well, we're not sure, actually. The peculiar thing is, even though the sun is warming the frog up on the outside, its insides thaw out first. . . ." The skin is not mentioned in this part of the explanation of the process, but the listener can infer that "first" means before the rest of the frog's body. Therefore, the correct answers are A and C.

27. **D** This is a Detail question. At the end of the lecture, the professor discusses the effects freezing has on these frogs. She says that while it doesn't seem that the freezing process has an impact on how long a frog lives, it does seem to negatively affect the frog's success at reproduction. Specifically, once a frog has thawed, it has trouble identifying potential mates. Therefore, the correct answer is D. Choice A can be eliminated since it is the opposite of the point the professor makes about the effect of freezing on reproduction.

28. **B** This question involves Understanding the Function of What Is Said. You are asked to listen again to part of the lecture (Track 87). After the professor mentions that glucose, a blood sugar, is distributed throughout the frog's body to slow down the freezing process, the student uses a familiar example of antifreeze in a car to see if he has understood the concept. The professor doesn't directly answer his question, but she continues her explanation of how glucose helps reduce the freezing effect. She then asks the student to reconsider his original question, so the correct answer is B.

Speaking

Listening Scripts, Important Points, and Sample Responses with Rater Comments

Use the sample Independent and Integrated Speaking rubrics on pages 180–183 to see how responses are scored. The raters who listen to your responses will analyze them in three general categories. These categories are Delivery, Language Use, and Topic Development. All three categories have equal importance.

This section includes important points that should be covered when answering each question. All of these points must be present in a response in order for it to receive the highest score in the Topic Development category. These important points are guides to the kind of information raters expect to hear in a high-level response.

This section also refers to example responses on the accompanying audio tracks. Some responses were scored at the highest level, while others were not. The responses are followed by explanations of their scores.

Question 1: Paired Choice

Track 88 Listening Script

Narrator

Do you agree or disagree with the following statement?

It is important to learn about other cultures.

Use details and examples to explain your opinion.

| Preparation Time: 15 Seconds |
| Response Time: 45 Seconds |

Important Points

When you answer this question, you should first state whether you believe, or do not believe, it is important to learn about other cultures. You may choose either point of view and will not be evaluated on your choice. The content of your response will be evaluated on how completely and clearly you explain your ideas and support your opinion. If you agree with the statement, you may choose to describe some areas in which it is important (international business, travel and tourism, and so on) and then provide details and specific examples to further explain. If you disagree, you should also provide at least one reason followed by specific details and examples to further explain your idea and to support your opinion.

Sample Responses

Play Track 93 to hear a high-level response for Question 1.

Rater Comments

The speaker is generally very clear and easy to understand. She uses pauses effectively (to separate phrases) and stresses important words within the phrases, which makes it easy for the listener to understand her message. (*"**First of all**, it uh **gives** you the **opportunity** to **understand** your culture **better**."*) Although she makes some minor grammatical errors sometimes, she has a strong ability to create long, accurate phrases and sentences. (*"Then it helps you to understand other people from other countries better [pause] because if you know the back ground of their behavior [pause] then it is easier to understand it and not judge it."*) Her response is full and includes both general reasons for her opinion (*"it helps you understand other people . . ."*) and supports the idea with specific examples and details (since she explains that if you understand others better, then you won't judge them and you won't offend them).

Play Track 94 to hear a mid-level response for Question 1.

Rater Comments

The speaker is mostly clear and easy to understand. However, the message is at times not easily comprehensible because of limitations in grammar and vocabulary. For example, he attempts to express a rather sophisticated idea but the meaning is not clear because of errors in word choice, word form, and agreement in particular. For example, he says *"I'm gonna really expand my **verizon (?) of thoughts (?)** and **philosopher philosophical** uh ideas because I'm gonna inter . . . interact with other back grounds(?) and **that's really give me** the chance to acquire good values from other nations."* A simpler and more effective paraphrase might be, "Interacting with other cultures could help me to expand my horizons/open me up to new experiences and ideas."

Question 2: Fit and Explain

Track 89 Listening Script

Narrator

City University's choir is changing its performance schedule next year. Read an article about it in the student newspaper. You will have 50 seconds to read the article. Begin reading now.

Reading Time: 50 Seconds

> **University Choir to Enter Off-Campus Singing Competitions**
>
> Currently, the university choir gives singing concerts only on campus. Next year, however, the choir will add competitive events at other locations to its schedule. The choir's new director feels that entering singing competitions will make the quality of the choir's performance even better than it is now. "Competitions will motivate students in the choir to pursue a higher standard of excellence in singing," he said. In addition, it is hoped that getting the choir off campus and out in the public will strengthen the reputation of the university's music program. This in turn will help the program grow.

Narrator

Now listen to two students discussing the article.

Female Student

Jim, you're in the choir, right? Whaddaya think about what they're doing next year . . . this article?

Male Student

I really like it.

Female Student

Yeah?

Male Student

Yeah. The new director's right that it will motivate us.

Female Student

How's that?

Male Student

Well, some of the other schools are really good . . . so we'll really have to work hard to go up against them.

Female Student

Yeah . . .

Male Student

I mean, right now we don't rehearse more than once a week, but if we know we'd be competing with other schools, we'd probably rehearse more often and improve our singing a lot.

Female Student

That's true. The more you practice, the better you get. So, um . . . What about what the article said about how this will help the program?

Male Student

I hope it works! Right now, our program is pretty small, but we have some really talented people. And it would be great to attract even more people.

Female Student

So how will this plan help?

Male Student

Well, if we go to these off campus events and other people hear us and think we're really good, we might be able to get some new students interested in coming to this university . . . to be a part of our music program and perform in our choir concerts.

Female Student

You're right. I hadn't really thought about that.

Narrator

The man expresses his opinion about the change described in the article. Briefly summarize the change. Then state his opinion about the change and explain the reasons he gives for holding that opinion.

| Preparation Time: 30 Seconds |
| Response Time: 60 Seconds |

Important Points

For this item, you should be sure to address the information from both the reading and the listening. You could begin by briefly explaining the change described in the article—that the university choir will now be participating in off-campus competitions with other universities (rather than singing only on campus as they do now). You should then explain that the man in the listening agrees with the change. First, he agrees with the director that performing in these competitions would motivate the choir to improve, since they would have to practice or rehearse more often. You should then explain that the man also agrees with the director's idea that the competitions will help the music program grow. He says that if people hear them singing well in the competitions, they may become interested in attending the university (and joining the choir).

Sample Responses

Play Track 95 to hear a high-level response for Question 2.

Rater Comments

This is a full and clear response. Although the speaker stops and starts occasionally while gathering his thoughts, his overall speech is quite fluid, and the response is easy to follow. His vocabulary is accurate and varied. Transition words like *"furthermore"* help the listener follow his response. Some minor grammatical errors, such as *"the director think,"* do not cause problems for the listener. The speaker probably goes into more detail than needed in summarizing the reading; an even more efficient response might have integrated that information into a discussion of the student's reasons for agreeing with the plan. However, the speaker covers all the key information in his response.

Play Track 96 to hear a mid-level response for Question 2.

Rater Comments

While the speaker uses high-level vocabulary (*"pretty happy with the change undertook," "level up their singing proficiency"*), his response is not always easy to follow. Several pronunciation errors and slow pacing require the listener to make some effort in order to understand what he is saying. The content of the response is also occasionally unclear. The speaker never fully explains what the director's plan is for the choir, and he does not cover the final point about how the choir competing off-campus will get new students interested in coming to the university. By improving the fluency and pacing of his speech, this speaker would be able to more efficiently communicate the main ideas asked for in a 60-second response.

Question 3: General/Specific

Track 90 Listening Script

Narrator

Read a passage about relict behaviors from a biology textbook. You will have 50 seconds to read the passage. Begin reading now.

Reading Time: 50 Seconds

Relict Behaviors

In general, animals act in ways that help them to survive within their specific habitats. However, sometimes an animal species may display a behavior that no longer serves a clear purpose. The original purpose for the behavior may have disappeared long ago, even thousands of years before. These behaviors, known as relict behaviors, were useful to the animal when the species' habitat was different; but now, because of changed conditions, the behavior no longer serves its original purpose. Left over from an earlier time, the behavior remains as a relict, or remnant, long after the environmental circumstance that influenced its evolution has vanished.

Narrator

Now listen to part of a lecture in a biology class.

Professor

OK, so a good example of this—found right here in North America—is something an animal called the American **pronghorn** does. Pronghorns, as you may know, are a kinda deer-like animal . . . they live out on the open, grassy plains . . . somewhat in the middle of North America. . . .

And they are super fast. Pronghorns are, in fact, noted for being the **fastest** animal in the Western Hemisphere. Once a pronghorn starts running—zoom!—none of its present-day predators, like the . . . bobcat . . . or coyote, can even **hope** to catch up with it . . . it's off in a flash!

OK, so why then do pronghorns run **so** fast? That's the question.

Well, it turns out that quite a long time ago . . . I'm talking tens of thousands of years . . . things on the grassy plains used to be very different for the pronghorns.

Because back then **lions** used to live on the plains . . . chasing and preying upon the pronghorns. And lions, of course, are a very swift-moving mammal . . . **much** faster than the bobcat or coyote, or other predators that you find on the plains today. . . .

But, **now**, however, lions are all **extinct** in North America. They're no longer a predator of the pronghorn. Tens of thousands of years ago, though, the lions were there, chasing the pronghorns. So, back then, the pronghorn's speed was critical to its survival.

Narrator

Using the example of the pronghorn and lion, explain the concept of a relict behavior.

> **Preparation Time: 30 Seconds**
> **Response Time: 60 Seconds**

Important Points

For this task, the prompt asks you to use the examples from the lecture to explain the concept described in the reading. You should summarize important information from the example presented in the lecture *and* explain how it illustrates the concept, which is generally defined in the reading. The concept here is relict behavior, and one way to begin your response is by *briefly* describing what that is: a relict behavior is a behavior that an animal displays that used to serve a purpose but does not serve the same purpose any more. You should then discuss the example of the pronghorn, connecting this specific example to the general concept. The pronghorn can run very fast, and the great speed of the pronghorn is a relict behavior because the pronghorn no longer needs to run fast. In the past, the pronghorn needed to run fast because the lion was its predator, and lions were also very fast. Now that the lion is extinct in North America, the pronghorn does not need to run as fast because its current predators—the bobcat and the coyote—are not as fast as the lion. Your response should contain information from both the reading and the lecture so that the listener will understand how the pronghorn's speed is a good example of relict behavior.

Sample Responses

Play Track 97 to hear a high-level response for Question 3.

Rater Comments

This is a strong response. Speech is clear overall, and the pace of the response is appropriate, creating no difficulties for the listener. Effective intonation and word stress contributes to meaning, such as when the speaker emphasizes "need" in the last sentence (*"pronghorns don't **need** to run that fast any more"*). She uses a wide range of grammatical structures effectively (*". . . the reasons for having developed that behavior or quality has long disappeared," ". . . the pronghorns had to flee from lions who were preying upon them"*), and her word choice is effective and precise. She also develops her ideas very effectively, starting with a clear definition of relict behavior and providing a clear summary of the example and how it relates to the concept. Her final sentence clearly connects the two, though it might have been more explicit if she had used the term *relict behavior* again.

Play Track 98 to hear a mid-level response for Question 3.

Rater Comments

This speaker provides some accurate content and attempts to connect the concept of relict behavior to the example, but the response is overall incomplete and unclear, primarily because she has difficulty developing her ideas. She does mention relict behavior at the beginning of her response but does not provide a clear description of it, only saying that it *"can be genetically inherit."* The remainder of the response summarizes the lecture, and she does provide key details and demonstrate some understanding of it, but the description is not entirely clear, and the listener is forced to fill in gaps that the speaker does not mention; for example, the pronghorn's speed, the most important point, is not mentioned until the second half of the response, creating confusion. Unclear references create more confusion, such as in *"**This** proves **that** was inherited . . ."* The response also would have been stronger if the speaker specifically said that the pronghorn's speed is a relict behavior, instead of, *"it is not survival for them, they just have it."* Though there are a few awkward pauses, her speech is generally clear and the pace is good in the response. A larger problem is grammar and vocabulary use. There are enough inaccuracies in the response to hinder communication at times, and the ideas do not always progress clearly. Overall, the speaker does not have a wide enough range of vocabulary and grammatical structures to express her ideas clearly.

Question 4: Summary

Track 91 Listening Script

Narrator

Listen to part of a lecture in a business class.

Professor

People who are likely to buy a company's product are called target customers. And these target customers influence a company's marketing strategy. In order to develop a marketing strategy, a company will look at certain characteristics of the target customers to decide when and where to advertise . . . so that they'll reach the target customers most effectively. I'd like to talk to you today about two characteristics of target customers that can influence marketing strategy, specifically age and geographic location of the target customers.

Say a company makes toy cars. Who are its target customers? Kids, right? So, if the company wants to make sure its television advertising reaches its target customers, it'd want to advertise during times when kids are actually watching television, like during children's television shows. That way it can make sure that kids see the advertisements. And that way the company'd get people in that age group to go buy toy cars, or to ask their parents to buy 'em at least.

Now, another important characteristic to consider is geographic location . . . places where the company's target customers live. Think about a company that makes boats. Its target customers are people who own homes near oceans or lakes, places where they can use boats. After all, people who don't live near water don't have much use for boats. So, by placing advertisements on signs along the road or on television in cities and towns that are near oceans or lakes, the company'd be more likely to reach the target customers for its boats . . . and sell more of 'em as a result.

Narrator

Using points and examples from the lecture, explain how the characteristics of target customers influence marketing strategy for products.

> **Preparation Time: 20 Seconds**
> **Response Time: 60 Seconds**

Important Points

This item requires you to listen to a lecture and summarize key points that explain the concept of target customers. In particular, you will concentrate on the characteristics of target customers that the professor discusses—age and geographic location—and how those characteristics influence marketing strategy for products. For age, you should summarize that a company that has children as its target customers should advertise at times when children are watching TV. For the characteristic of geographic location, you should summarize that the target customers for a company that makes boats are people living near water, so the company should advertise in towns near water. You should include both general information from the lecture (in this case, the concept of target customers and the general characteristics of age and location) and the specific examples in your response.

Sample Responses

Play Track 99 to hear a high-level response for Question 4.

Rater Comments

Although the speaker's first sentence is slightly confusing, the response as a whole is clear and complete. The speaker covers all of the important points of the lecture and her response progresses clearly because of her good use of connecting language (*"for example," "so," "also," "in this way"*). Pronunciation and delivery are also good overall, and are a strong point; the few small problems (such as when she is discussing children and TV) do not affect overall intelligibility, and her pauses are mainly to recall information, not due to lack of language. Language use is also strong, and she uses a variety of grammatical structures effectively (for example, *"and this will be the proper time to advertise your toy cars, for example"*). There is some imprecise language (such as, *"how you reach it is . . ."*), but this does not prevent her from getting her point across. Overall, this is an excellent summary of the lecture.

Play Track 100 to hear a mid-level response for Question 4.

Rater Comments

This response does provide much of the key content of the lecture, but it is not as accurate or complete as a high-level response. The pace of the speech is satisfactory and pronunciation in general is acceptable and does not interfere with overall meaning, but there are continual pauses throughout that make the response difficult to follow. The response starts slowly because the speaker uses *"it"* instead of "target customers," which would be clearer. He also has difficulty with the general explanation; his description is not clear because of imprecise grammar and vocabulary (for example, when he says, *"so companies usually seek to put their promotions and advertisement as much as it might be exposed for the targeted customer"* instead of something like, "so companies want to make sure target customers will see their advertisements"). He does better with the specific examples, though he says, *"they are aiming to buy for kids,"* when he means, "sell to kids." Overall, the response should be developed more and should include more details. This speaker did not demonstrate that he has enough language resources to give a full and coherent response.

Writing

Listening Script, Topic Notes, and Sample Responses with Rater Comments

Use the Integrated Writing and Independent Writing scoring rubrics on pages 193–194 and 203–204 to see how responses are scored.

Writing Based on Reading and Listening

Track 92 Listening Script

Narrator

Now listen to part of a lecture on the topic you just read about.

Professor

You've just read about three ways to save *Torreya taxifolia*. Unfortunately, none of these three options provides a satisfactory solution.

About the first solution, reestablishing Torreya in the same location. That's unlikely to be successful because of what's happening to the coolest, dampest areas within Torreya's microclimate. These areas are being strongly affected by changes in the climate of the larger region. This could be because global warming has contributed to an increase in overall temperatures in the region or because wetlands throughout Florida have been drained. Either way, many areas across the region are becoming drier. So it's unlikely that Torreya would have the conditions it needs to survive anywhere within its original Florida microclimate.

Now, about the second solution, relocating Torreya far from where it currently grows. Well, let's look at what happened when humans helped **another** tree, the black locust tree, move north to a new environment.

When they did this, the black locust tree spread so quickly that it killed off many plants and trees in the new environment—and some of these plants and trees were themselves already in danger of becoming extinct. So assisted migration can have unpredicted outcomes for the new environment.

Third, research centers are probably not a solution either. That's because the population of Torreya trees that can be kept in the centers will probably not be able to resist diseases. For a population of trees to survive a disease, it needs to be relatively large and it needs to be genetically diverse. Tree populations in the wild usually satisfy those criteria. But research centers would simply not have enough capacity to keep a large and diverse population of Torreya trees, so trees in such centers will not be capable of surviving diseases in the long term.

Narrator

Summarize the points made in the lecture, being sure to explain how they cast doubt on the specific solutions presented in the reading passage.

Topic Notes

You should understand the reasons presented in the lecture for why the different methods to save the *Torreya* tree might not work. The lecturer questions each of the solutions proposed in the passage: planting *Torreya* in areas where it used to grow, planting it in new areas, and preserving it in research centers.

A high-scoring response will include the following points made by the lecturer that address the points made in the reading passage.

Point Made in the Reading Passage	Contrasting Point from the Lecture
Torreya trees could be planted in areas where they used to grow because those areas have a favorable cool and wet microclimate.	Unfortunately, global warming and human activities have made the locations where *Torreya* used to grow warmer and drier.
Torreya trees could be introduced in other areas whose environmental conditions are suitable for *Torreya* growth.	Introducing a tree in a new area can endanger other plants that already grow there. This has happened previously when the black locust tree was introduced in a new area.
If *Torreya* trees are grown in research centers, they can be both preserved and studied there.	Since research centers are small, the population of *Torreya* trees grown there would not be large and diverse enough to resist diseases.

Responses with scores of 4 and 5 generally clearly discuss all three main points in the table.

Sample Responses with Rater Comments

High-Level Response

Torreya taxifolia is an evergreen tree that was once common in Florida region. From 1950's it is in danger of becoming extinct and scientists are considering different ways to save it.

Plans to reestablish Torreya in Florida has been ruled out by the professor in the lecture because global warming has resulted in a worse climate in that area for the tree to grow and flourish. Wetlands in Florida area have also dried up so these changes in the climate has caused the decreased growth of the tree and it is very hard to reestablish in the same area.

The second option could be very dangerous for the native species of that area. The professor explains by citing another example of black locust tree. When it was taken to a new environment, it grew to such an extent that it killed a large number of local plants and trees and hence they became endangered. So, it's not wise to grow one species by eliminating others. So it is at risk to experi

The third solution is again not appropriate because for a population to be successfull it should be relatively large and genetically diverse so that it is able to resist diseases. Research centres cannot provide a large space for the population to be reestablished.

Rater Comments

This response earns a high score because it successfully conveys most of the important information from the lecture and the reading passage. The subject—saving a tree that is in danger of extinction—is introduced in the first paragraph, and the writer goes on to discuss the weaknesses of each solution that has been proposed. While the writer focuses mainly on discussing what the lecturer said about the weaknesses, it remains quite clear what the solutions described in the reading passage were. The response is generally well organized. The incomplete sentence at the end of the third paragraph does not really take away from the quality of the response. Since we consider responses to be first drafts, minor problems of this kind are not evaluated harshly. There are some minor errors ("plans . . . has been ruled out") and some ideas are not expressed as well as they could be ("it's not wise to grow one species by eliminating others" would be better put as "it's not wise to grow one species at the expense of others"), but the Scoring Guide allows for some minor problems in high-level responses.

Mid-Level Essay

Giving that Torreya started to die out in its naturel location, three solutions were be proposed, but none of them worked.

The first solution is to reestablish the tree in Florida, its naturel home, because historicaly this kind of tree lives thanks to the microclimat of this state. But the plan fall because of the changing of the climat in this area. Benefits of the microclimat, which is specific climat of an area, do not exist yet. So Torreya loose its natural environnement.

The second solution is to establish the tree in a completely different climat, meanning in the north. But as the professor explains, this solution fall in the past with the black locust tree. This historical exemple explains how it is difficult to change the ecosystem, because it is very dangerous to provoc a migration.

Eventuelly, the last solution is to preserve Torreya in reserch centres. One more time this proposition is not good, because all experiences of capted population show that every preserve population lost its capacity to resist to deseas and external atacs. Then even if humans try to recreat a reel diversity, it is not possible, because the recreat area can not be enought to be large and diverse as the nature is.

Rater Comments

This response earns a mid-level score. The writer may have understood most of the passage's points and the lecturer's arguments, but errors of usage and grammar are more than minor and are more frequent throughout the response ("were be"; "fall" for "fail"; incorrect use of tense; "capted"). The errors result in vagueness as well as obscured meanings in conveying ideas and connections. Some important information is also missing. The writer conveys that the microclimate has changed (though no mention is made, specifically, that it is drier or warmer). The sentence "Benefits of the microclimate . . . do not exist yet" is unclear, probably because the writer mistakenly wrote "yet" instead of "anymore." While the black locust is cited as a historical example, the writer is vague and unclear in explaining the rest of the argument: the lecturer did not say that "it is difficult to change the ecosystem," and it is unclear what "provoc a migration" means. If a reader correctly interprets some erroneous expressions ("capted population"), important parts of the third argument become clear; however, it is not the "area" that cannot be large and diverse enough, but the captive tree population.

Writing Based on Knowledge and Experience

Question

Do you agree or disagree with the following statement?

Students are more influenced by their teachers than by their friends.

Use specific reasons and examples to support your answer. Be sure to use your own words. Do **not** use memorized examples.

Topic Notes

This topic requires you to write about whether students are more influenced by their teachers than by their friends.

If you agree with this statement, you should present examples and reasons. For example, you can write that the question of who influences students most depends on students' age or interests: more mature students and those interested in learning are more likely to follow teachers. You can develop the ways that teachers can influence students: for example, teachers can serve as role models or they can inspire and nurture students' creativity and self-confidence.

If you disagree with this statement in your response, you should present examples and reasons for why friends are a more important influence than teachers. For example, you can point out that it is an issue of trust vs. authority. Friends do not judge you but teachers do. The age difference may be an important issue. Also, students spend more time with their friends, share activities outside school, speak the same language, and have the same lifestyle.

Sample Responses with Rater Comments

High-Level Response

> In my opinion, students are more influenced by their friends rather than their teachers. Therefore, I disagree with the statement 'Students are more influenced by their teachers than by their friends'.
>
> I do not disagree with the fact that students get influenced by their teachers, however, I believe that this 'influence' is mostly within the field of academics. In most cases, the only time that students communicate with the teacher is in the school building, in the classroom. Most of the discussions are about topics related to studies. However, with friends, students often tend to discuss a variety of topics, such as studies, friends, relationships and families. Therefore, students are generally influenced more broadly by their friends, while the only influence made by the teachers are mostly academical.
>
> The amount of time spent with the teacher or friend, also effect on how much influence has been made to a person. As mentioned previously, the time that students communicate with the teachers is restricted to school hours. However, students spend or communicate with their friends not only in school but even outside the school campus and school hours. Especially with the emerging technology, and the development of mobile phones and the internet, students are now able to communicate with their friends at any time where ever they are. Since the amount of time spent communicating with their friends are much larger than the time spent with the teachers, there are more chance of the students being influenced by their friends rather than their teachers.
>
> Also, it is normal that the students feel psychologically more attached to the people in their age group, especially with their friends. The teachers are usually from different generations from the students and this may cause the students to feel that there is a distance between how they think/feel and how the teachers think/feel. Since the students are more emotionally and psychologically attached to their friends, they feel more comfortable to discuss their issues with them and accept their responses more openly and easily. This fact relates directly to how much they are influenced by their friends.
>
> For these reasons, I believe that students are more influenced by their friends than by their teachers.

Rater Comments

This essay earns a high score. It does an excellent job in terms of topic development and organization. The first substantive section beginning "I do not disagree" is a nice concession that there is one area where teachers influence students, i.e., "academics," but the writer then goes on to describe other areas where the students are "generally influenced more broadly by their friends." The next substantive section adequately details the fact that students spend more time communicating with and therefore being influenced by their friends, and the final section explains why students are psychologically closer to and therefore more easily influenced by their friends than by their teachers.

There is varied sentence structure (illustrating both coordination and subordination) that effectively moves the reader through the points and relationships among the points that the author is advancing. The combination of mistakes in sentence 1 of paragraph 3 (problems with agreement, punctuation, and collocation) and a couple of other mistakes elsewhere should be considered minor in the context of an otherwise well-written essay; they do not take away from this being a well-written essay.

Mid-Level Essay

When people are young, they like to do the same things as their friends, say the same things as their friends, wear the same things as their friends and much much more.

I think students are influenced by friends more than their teachers, I think this is because of their age, the time spent with each other, and the style of thinking.

Being the same age and going to the same school, the things that become popular are all the same. They would want to buy the same things and would feel that if they did not have the same things I would be left out! Its like being influenced physically than being naturally influenced.

The style of thinking becomes all alike between the students because they have beed living in the same places and going through the same learning curiculum. Also, there are lots of types of students for example. Students that like anime and comics, students that like to do bad things, students that like to play sports. All these students are influencing each other by small pieces.

The biggest reason that friends influence students than teachers, is because of the time spent with each other. The longer students and students be together the stronger the influence would become. I have a friend that I have been with for more than six years. I say the same things, do the same things, play the same things.

Compared to teachers the time spent with each other, age, style of thinking all has a stronger influence. The students would only meet a specific teacher once a day, or if the teacher was his or her homeroom teacher they would only meet him twice or three times a day.

I do not think I have been influenced by a teacher before. I am always spending my time with my friends at school. This is probably the reason why I think friends our more influensive than teachers.

Rater Comments

This response earns a mid-level score. It is characterized by explanations and examples that are quite vague and are only somewhat developed. The connection of some ideas is obscured. In the second paragraph, the writer promises to discuss the influences of age, style of thinking, and "time spent with each other," but in the end all these factors blend together and especially the first two are poorly developed. In the fourth paragraph, it is not completely clear how the idea that many students live in the same places and the idea that there are many different kinds of students are connected. Overall the grammar is mostly accurate but there is a sense of a limited range of structures and vocabulary in this piece of writing that contributes to the lack of specificity and seems to prevent more complex development. For example, when the writer attempts to sum up the main point of paragraph 3 with the sentence "Its like being influenced physically than being naturally influenced," it is difficult to interpret what the writer is trying to convey. The limitations also affect the preceding sentence where the writer does not keep a clear pronoun structure ("If they did not have the same things I would be left out").

10 Writer's Handbook for English Language Learners

Use this Writer's Handbook as a guide to help you write better essays in English. It covers the following topics:

- **Grammar:** explains key grammar rules and gives examples.
- **Usage:** explains important usage rules and gives examples.
- **Mechanics:** describes the basic mechanics rules and gives examples. Mechanics includes spelling and punctuation.
- **Style:** discusses key aspects of effective style.
- **Organization and Development:** gives advice about the writing process and the development of all parts of an essay.
- **Advice to Writers:** discusses different types of essays.
- **Revising, Editing, and Proofreading:** explains what to do in each stage of improving your essay.
- **Glossary:** presents definitions for terms.

Grammar

This section provides information on the following grammatical errors:

- Sentence Errors
- Word Errors
- Other Errors

Sentence Errors

Fragments

A fragment is an incomplete sentence. It does not express a complete thought, even though it starts with a capital letter and ends with a punctuation mark. It is missing either a subject or a verb or both.

Here are three examples of fragments:

Fragment: *Where there were mice and cockroaches.*

Fragment: *A movie that inspires deep emotions.*

Fragment: *Analyzing the characters' motives.*

These three groups of words cannot stand alone as complete sentences. They can be corrected in two ways. One way is to attach the fragment to a complete sentence.

> Corrected sentence: <u>*Peter left the apartment*</u> *where there were mice and cockroaches.*

> Corrected sentence: <u>*I went to see "The Silver Star,"*</u> *a movie that inspires deep emotions.*

Another way to correct fragments is to add a complete subject, a complete verb, or other words that express a complete thought.

> Corrected sentence: *<u>This is</u> where there were mice and cockroaches.*

> Corrected sentence: *A movie that inspires deep emotions <u>is rare</u>.*

> Corrected sentence: *Analyzing the characters' motives <u>is important</u>.*

Summary: Sentence fragments are incomplete sentences. Sometimes readers can figure out the meaning of a fragment by rereading the sentences that come before and after it. However, turning fragments into complete sentences will improve the connections between ideas.

Run-On Sentences

Run-on sentences happen when we join sentences together without a conjunction or the correct punctuation. Run-on sentences can be very confusing to read. Here is an example: *My sister loves to dance she is very good at it.*

There are several ways to correct run-on sentences:

1. Divide the run-on sentence into two separate sentences.

   > Run-on sentence: *My sister loves to dance she is very good at it.*

   > Corrected sentence: *My sister loves to dance. She is very good at it.*

   > Run-on sentence: *Jim showed us his ticket someone gave it to him.*

   > Corrected sentence: *Jim showed us his ticket. Someone gave it to him.*

2. Connect the parts of the run-on sentence with a coordinating conjunction and a comma. These are the most common coordinating conjunctions: *and, but, for, nor, or, so, yet.*

   > Run-on sentence: *My sister loves to dance she is very good at it.*

   > Corrected sentence: *My sister loves to dance, <u>and</u> she is very good at it.*

   > Run-on sentence: *She agreed to chair the meeting she didn't come.*

   > Corrected sentence: *She agreed to chair the meeting, <u>but</u> she didn't come.*

3. Connect the parts of the run-on sentence with a subordinating conjunction. These are the most common subordinating conjunctions: *after, although, as, because, before, if, since, unless, until, when, whereas, while.*

> Run-on sentence: *My sister loves to dance she is very good at it.*
>
> Corrected sentence: *My sister loves to dance because she is very good at it.*

> Run-on sentence: *Maria and John like skiing Karen does not.*
>
> Corrected sentence: *Although Maria and John like skiing, Karen does not.*

4. Separate the parts of the run-on sentence with a semicolon.

> Run-on sentence: *Gordon laughed at Sandy's joke it was funny.*
>
> Corrected sentence: *Gordon laughed at Sandy's joke; it was funny.*

> Run-on sentence: *I thought he was here I was wrong.*
>
> Corrected sentence: *I thought he was here; I was wrong.*

Summary: Run-on sentences are two or more sentences that have been joined together without a conjunction or the correct punctuation. You can usually correct them by using punctuation or conjunctions.

Word Errors

Noun Forms

A noun is usually defined as a *person, place,* or *thing*.

> Person: *man, woman, waiter, John*
>
> Place: *home, office, town, station, Hong Kong*
>
> Thing: *table, car, apple, money, music, love, dog, monkey*

Learning a few basic rules will help you to use nouns effectively:

1. In English, some nouns are countable. That is, they are things that we can count. For example: *house.* We can count *houses.* We can have one, two, three, or more *houses.* Here are more examples of countable nouns:

> *dog, cat, animal, man, person, bottle, box, pound, coin, dollar, bowl, plate, fork, table, chair, suitcase, bag*

Countable nouns can be singular or plural.

> Singular: *I have a friend.*
>
> Plural: *I have two friends.*

2. Usually, to make nouns plural, add -*s*, as in the preceding examples (*friend*, *friends*). However, there are special cases where you do not add -*s*.

    *   When a word ends in -*ch*, -*s*, -*sh*, -*ss*, or –*x*, the plural is formed by adding -*es*. *(benches, gases, dishes, dresses, taxes)*
    *   When a word ends in -*y preceded by a consonant,* the plural form is -*ies*. *(parties, bodies, policies)*
    *   When a word ends in -*y preceded by a vowel,* the plural is formed by adding -*s*. *(trays, joys, keys)*
    *   When a word ends in -*o*, the more common plural ending is -*es* *(tomatoes, potatoes, heroes)*
    *   When the final -*o* is preceded by a vowel, the plural ending is -*s*. *(videos, studios)*
    *   When a word ends in -*f*, the plural is formed in one of two ways:
        *   either by adding -*s (beliefs, puffs)*
        *   or by changing the -*f* to -*v* and adding -*es (wife, wives; leaf, leaves; loaf, loaves)*.
    *   When a word ends in -*ex* or -*ix*, the plural ending is usually -*es*. *(appendixes, indexes)*
    *   In certain cases, the plural form of a word is the same as the singular. *(deer, sheep, fish, series)*

3. Some nouns are uncountable. They represent things that cannot be counted. For example, we cannot count *coffee*. We can count "cups of *coffee*" or "pounds of *coffee*," but we cannot count *coffee* itself. Here are more examples of uncountable nouns:

    > *music, art, love, happiness, advice, information, news, furniture, luggage, rice, sugar, butter, water, electricity, gas, money*

    We usually treat uncountable nouns as singular.

    > Incorrect: *These furnitures are beautiful.*

    > Correct: *This furniture is beautiful.*

4. Some uncountable nouns refer to abstract ideas or emotions. Abstract ideas may refer to qualities that we cannot physically touch. For example: *health, justice.*
    We cannot count abstract nouns, so they are always singular.

    > Incorrect: *Healths are more important than wealths.*

    > Correct: *Health is more important than wealth.*

    > Incorrect: *Have funs at the reunion.*

    > Correct: *Have fun at the reunion.*

5. Some nouns can be countable *and* uncountable, for example: *paper, room, hair, noise, time*. With these nouns, the singular and plural forms often have different meanings.

> Countable: *The Christmas lights make the mall very pretty.*
>
> Uncountable: *This room does not get enough light.*

> Countable: Othello *is one of Shakespeare's most famous works.*
>
> Uncountable: *I have a lot of work to do tonight.*

6. Singular nouns that are countable usually come after an article or other determiner (*a, an, the, this, my, such*).

> Incorrect: *His mother is doctor.*
>
> Incorrect: *Boy standing over there is brother.*
>
> Incorrect: *We saw child in playground.*
>
> Correct: *His mother is a doctor.*
>
> Correct: *The boy standing over there is my brother.*
>
> Correct: *We saw a child in the playground.*

Summary: Nouns are important words in a sentence because they form the subjects or objects. Some nouns can be counted and some cannot. Learning a few rules will help you to use nouns effectively.

Verb Forms

Verbs are parts of speech that express action (*jump, show*) or a state of being (*are, was*). Here are a few tips that may help you to use verbs effectively:

1. Helping verbs (also called *auxiliary verbs*) precede the main verb. All of the following verbs may be helping verbs:

> *be, am, is, are, was, were, being, been, has, have, had, do, does, did, can, will, shall, should, could, would, may, might, must*

Here are examples of sentences with helping verbs:

> *Many people don't know what they are going to do after college.*
>
> *I am going to give you step-by-step instructions.*

2. Words such as *might, must, can, would*, and *should* are also called modals. They express a wide range of meanings (ability, permission, possibility, necessity, etc.).

> The following examples show one use of modals:

> *Tom might have gone to the party if he had been invited.*
>
> *If I had a million dollars, I would buy a house for my parents.*

This use of modals is called the conditional use. One event relies on another or it cannot take place. In the first example, Tom cannot go to the party without being invited. In the second example, I would buy a house for my parents only if I had a million dollars.

3. The infinitive form of the verb is formed by using the word *to* plus the simple form of the verb.

> *He is too tired to go to the barbecue.*
>
> *The manager wants to hire a new secretary.*

The infinitive can also be used as the subject or object of a sentence.

> *To invest now seems risky.*
>
> *The teacher told him to leave.*

In the first example, *To invest* is the subject of the sentence, while in the second example, *to leave* is the object.

We can use the infinitive to show an action that is occurring at the same time as, or later than, the action of the main verb.

> *We like to play video games.*
>
> *My best friend wants to shop at that mall.*

In the first example, the *liking* is happening at the same time as the *playing*. In the second example, the *shopping* is going to happen at a later time than the *wanting*.

4. Do not use *of* after a helping verb. In some verb phrases, there are two or more verbs being used (*should have happened, might be eaten, could have decided*). Here are examples in which the word *of* is used incorrectly:

> Incorrect: *They would of stayed one more month if possible.*
>
> Incorrect: *In that time, he could of finished the project.*
>
> Correct: *They would have stayed one more month if possible.*
>
> Correct: *In that time, he could have finished the project.*

Of is a preposition, not a verb, and in each of these sentences, *of* should be replaced with the helping verb *have*.

Summary: Verbs are very important parts of a sentence. There are a few rules that you can learn to make your use of verbs more effective.

Subject-Verb Agreement

In English, the subject and verb must always agree in number. Here are a few rules that will help you:

1. A singular subject takes a singular verb.

> *The teacher was happy with my answer.*
>
> *My cell phone is not working.*

In the first example, the singular subject *teacher* agrees with the singular verb *was*. In the second example, the singular subject *cell phone* agrees with the singular verb *is*.

2. A plural subject takes a plural verb.

    My parents were happy with my grades.

    Many television stations have reported that story.

    In the first example, the plural subject *parents* matches the plural verb *were*, and in the second example, the plural subject *television stations* matches the plural verb *have*.

    You should never have a plural subject with a singular verb.

    Incorrect: *Many students thinks tomorrow is a holiday.*

    This sentence can be edited to make the subject and verb agree.

    Correct: *Many students think tomorrow is a holiday.*

    Similarly, you should never have a singular subject with a plural verb.

    Incorrect: *The student think tomorrow is a holiday.*

    This sentence can be edited to make the subject and verb agree.

    Correct: *The student thinks tomorrow is a holiday.*

3. Sometimes subjects and verbs are separated by a word or a phrase. When that happens, students sometimes forget to make them agree in number.

    Incorrect: *Your suggestions about the show was excellent.*

    Incorrect: *The use of cell phones during concerts are not allowed.*

    Correct: *Your suggestions about the show were excellent.*

    Correct: *The use of cell phones during concerts is not allowed.*

    In the first example, since the subject of the sentence is *suggestions*, which is plural, the plural verb *were* is used. In the second example, the singular subject *use* needs the singular verb *is*.

4. A compound subject needs a plural verb.

    When you proofread your work, correctly identify the subject in your sentences. For example, the following sentences have more than one subject:

    The camcorder and the tripod were returned yesterday.

    Both Chantel and Rochelle are nice names.

    In the first example, the complete subject is a compound (*camcorder* and *tripod*), and so the verb must be plural (*were*). In the second example, the compound subject is *Chantel and Rochelle* and needs the plural verb *are*.

5. A collective noun must have a verb that agrees with it. Collective nouns are nouns that name a group (*committee, herd, board of directors*). In American English, collective nouns are usually singular.

> Correct: *The committee is made up of twelve people.*

> Correct: *The jury has not arrived at a verdict.*

When you use a collective noun to refer to a group acting as an individual unit, you should make the verb singular. In the first example, the subject (*committee*) is singular, so it takes the singular verb *is*. In the second example, the singular subject (*jury*) takes the singular verb *has*.

However, sometimes you might want to emphasize that the group acted as individuals, each for himself or herself. Then you could write the following:

> Awkward: *The committee were divided in their opinions.*

> Awkward: *The jury have been listening to the tapes for two days.*

In these examples, the individuals in the groups are emphasized, so the plural verbs are used. However, while correct, these sentences sound awkward. You might want to change the word *committee* to *committee members* in the first example, and the word *jury* to *jury members* in the second example.

Summary: A verb should always agree with its subject. A singular subject takes a singular verb, and a plural subject takes a plural verb. Sometimes a phrase separates the subject and the verb, making it hard to find the real subject.

Pronouns

A pronoun is a word that takes the place of one or more nouns. Pronouns are words such as *he, his, she, her, hers, it, they, their, them, these, that, this, those, who, whom, which, what,* and *whose.*

If we did not have pronouns, we would have to repeat a lot of nouns. We would have to say things like:

> *Do you like the new manager? I don't like the new manager. The new manager is too unfriendly.*

With pronouns, we can say the following:

> *Do you like the new manager? I don't like him. He is too unfriendly.*

Learning a few rules will help you to use pronouns correctly and effectively:

1. Pronouns must agree with the nouns they refer to. If your pronoun refers to a girl or woman, you use a feminine pronoun (*she, her, hers*). If your pronoun refers to a boy or man, you use a masculine pronoun (*he, his, him*).

Any pronoun you use must also agree in number with the noun it refers to. If you are using a pronoun to refer to a singular noun, you must use a singular pronoun; if you are using a pronoun to replace a plural noun, you use a plural pronoun.

> *Julia reminded us that <u>she</u> would not stay late.*

> *Bob bought two computers and had <u>them</u> delivered to his office.*

In the first example, the singular pronoun *she* is used to stand for *Julia*, a female person. In the second example, the plural pronoun *them* is used to refer to the plural noun *computers*.

2. Some indefinite pronouns are always singular. Indefinite pronouns such as *each, one, every, everyone, everybody, anyone, anybody, anything, someone, somebody, either, neither, nothing, nobody, none,* and *no one* are always singular, so other pronouns that refer to them must also be singular, as in these examples:

> *<u>Neither</u> of the boys sent in his report.*

> *<u>Everyone</u> must buy her own ticket.*

Note the construction of the second sentence, in which the writer decided to use the pronoun *her*. Some people would prefer the pronoun to be *his or her* to indicate explicitly that each person, regardless of gender, is purchasing a ticket. Some instructors consider *his or her* constructions awkward and allow *everyone* to be treated as plural (*Everyone must buy their own ticket.*). Other instructors consider the plural construction not acceptable in good writing.

3. Some indefinite pronouns are always plural. These include *both* and *many*. Other pronouns that refer to *them* must also be plural.

> *<u>Both</u> of <u>them</u> are here tonight.*

> *<u>Many</u> of the managers have moved into <u>their</u> new offices.*

In the first example, *both* is plural, and so the plural pronoun *them* is used. In the second example, the plural pronoun *their* is used because *many* is plural.

4. Some indefinite pronouns can be singular or plural. Indefinite pronouns such as *all, any, more, most, none,* and *some* can be singular or plural, depending on their meaning in a context.

> *<u>Most</u> of my time <u>is</u> spent reviewing for the test.*

> *<u>Most</u> of the students <u>have</u> turned in <u>their</u> reports.*

In the first example, *most* refers to *time,* a singular noun. It thus takes the singular verb *is.* In the second example, *most* refers to the plural noun *students.* This is why it takes the plural verb *have* and is referred to by the plural pronoun *their.*

5. Overusing pronouns can cause confusion.

> Confusing: *The president informed the vice president that all of <u>his</u> supporters should be meeting with <u>him</u>.*

Whose supporters, the president's or the vice president's? Whom are they meeting with? This sentence needs to be revised to fix the confusion caused by the use of *him* and *his*. This can be accomplished by replacing the pronouns with the appropriate nouns.

> Clear: *The president informed the vice president that all of <u>the president's</u> supporters should be meeting with <u>the president</u>.*

Excessive use of *it* weakens writing, especially when *it* is used to introduce a sentence, as in this example:

> Confusing: *We were visiting the museum. I saw <u>it</u>. <u>It</u> was interesting and unusual. I was amazed by <u>it</u>.*

You can improve *it* by explaining what the first *it* refers to.

> Clear: *We were visiting the museum. I saw <u>the space exhibit</u>. It was interesting and unusual. I was amazed by it.*

In this example, can you figure out what *it* stands for?

> *Although the car hit the tree, <u>it</u> was not damaged.*

Does *it* refer to the car or the tree? You can make the sentence clear by rewriting it.

> *The car was not damaged, although it hit the tree.*

6. When you have nouns joined by a conjunction (*and, or,* or *nor*), do not forget to make a pronoun that refers to them agree in number, as in these examples:

> *If <u>Bob and Rick</u> want to go, <u>they</u> will need to take the bus because I don't have room in my car.*
>
> *Whether I buy a <u>dishwasher</u> or <u>dryer</u>, it will have to go in the kitchen.*

In the first example, there is a compound noun, as *Bob* and *Rick* are joined by the conjunction *and*. So the plural pronoun *they* must be used. In the second example, the noun is singular (*dishwasher* or *dryer*). Thus the singular pronoun *it* is used.

7. You should know when to use *who, whom, which,* or *that. Who* and *whom* refer to people. *Which* refers to things, and *that* can refer to either people or things.

> *The committee interviewed all the candidates <u>who</u> applied.*
>
> *Do you still have the magazine <u>that</u> I lent you last week?*
>
> *<u>Which</u> courses should I take in the fall?*

In the first example, *who* refers to a group of people (*candidates*). In the second example, *that* refers to a thing (*magazine*). In the third example, *which* refers to things (*courses*).

Summary: A pronoun is a word used to take the place of one or more nouns. Singular pronouns must be used to refer to singular nouns, and plural pronouns must be used to refer to plural nouns. Some indefinite pronouns can be singular or plural, according to their meaning in the sentence.

Possessive Pronouns

Possessive pronouns are used to show possession or ownership. Here are a few rules that will help you to use possessive pronouns effectively:

1. When you are using possessive pronouns such as *his, hers, mine, theirs, yours,* or *ours,* make sure that the possessive pronoun agrees in number with the noun to which it refers.

   Incorrect: *I have my car, and my husband has theirs.*
   Incorrect: *This is the children's room. All those toys are hers.*

   Correct: *I have my car, and my husband has his.*
   Correct: *This is the children's room. All those toys are theirs.*

   In the first sentence, the singular pronoun *his* should be used to show that the car belongs to the singular noun *husband*. In the second sentence, *theirs* should be used to show that the toys belong to the plural noun *children*.

2. Possessive pronouns do not take an apostrophe. *His, hers, its, ours, yours, theirs,* and *whose* are pronouns that already convey possession, so do not add an apostrophe to them.

   Incorrect: *Each art room has it's own sink.*
   Incorrect: *His' office is on the third floor.*

   Correct: *Each art room has its own sink.*
   Correct: *His office is on the third floor.*

   In the first sentence, a possessive pronoun is needed (*its*) not *it's*, which means "it is." In the second sentence, the possessive pronoun *his* is needed; *his'* is never used.

Other Ways to Show Possession

Besides possessive pronouns, there are other ways to show possession, such as using an apostrophe and an *-s* (*-'s*).

   My neighbor's house is bigger than mine.
   Henry's cat likes to play with our baby.

Below are some rules for indicating possession:

1. When a noun ends in -*s* and the addition of -*'s* makes the word sound odd, some writers add only an apostrophe, as in these examples:

   I like James' company.

   This is Harris' wife, Anna.

2. Make sure you put the apostrophe in the right place. Put the apostrophe *before* the -*s* if the word is singular.

   The teacher's desk is right in front. (one teacher)

   My sister's haircut cost $70. (one sister)

   You will put the apostrophe *after* the -*s* only if it is a plural word.

   We borrowed our parents' car. (more than one parent)

   I went to a party at my friends' house. (more than one friend)

3. When two or more people share ownership, you use an apostrophe and -*s* on the last noun. When each person has separate ownership, you need to indicate that, as in these examples:

   John and Jack's room is very messy. (John and Jack share one room.)

   Ian's and George's dreams are very different, even though the two boys come from the same family. (Ian and George have different dreams.)

4. Do not use an apostrophe when you want to make a noun plural. An apostrophe shows possession, not the plural of a noun. These sentences are wrong: they should not have apostrophes:

   The new student's look confused.

   There are too many car's on our street's.

Summary: Possessive pronouns are used to show possession, or ownership. There are a few rules that can help you to use them correctly.

Prepositions

A preposition is a word that is used before a noun (or noun phrase) to give more information in a sentence. Prepositions are usually used to show where something is located or when something happened. Examples of prepositions include *in, among, between, across, at, with, beside, behind, in, into, from, during, before,* and *after.*

   Prepositions are used to show place, time, and action or movement.

- Place:

   The main office is in New York.

   I'm meeting my colleagues at the coffee shop.

- Time:

  Let's try to get there by 3:30.

  Please do not talk during the show.

- Action or movement:

  He jumped into the river.

  We flew from Los Angeles to Toronto.

Some verbs and adjectives are usually followed by certain prepositions.

They always argue about money.

I borrowed a book from the library.

Here are more examples of words and prepositions that usually go together:

familiar with, afraid of, far from, close to, believe in, borrow from, lend to, absent from, nice to, argue with, made of, take off, turn on, happy with, sad about, famous for

The following sentences contain *incorrect* uses of prepositions:

Incorrect: *I am afraid at losing my textbooks.*

Incorrect: *The student argued at the teacher.*

Correct: *I am afraid of losing my textbooks.*

Correct: *The student argued with the teacher.*

The first sentence can be corrected by changing *at* to *of*. In the second sentence, the preposition that should go with *argued* is *with*.

Summary: Prepositions are used to show relationships between a noun and other parts of a sentence. There are a few rules that can help you to use prepositions correctly.

Other Errors

Wrong or Missing Word

When writing or typing quickly, people often use the wrong word or omit words. When you begin to revise, edit, and proofread, read carefully for wrong words or words that you have left out.

One of the most frequent problems is the use of *the* instead of *they*.

Incorrect: *The went to the store each Monday.*

The writer most likely intended the following:

Correct: *They went to the store each Monday.*

Another common error is a missing noun after the word *the*.

Incorrect: *The go to the store each Monday.*

Correct: *The brothers go to the store each Monday.*

Summary: Wrong or missing words commonly occur but are easy to correct. Proofread your sentences carefully.

Keyboard Errors or Typos

Sometimes while writing the first drafts of an essay, you might leave out letters or make keyboard errors. They might be grammatical, usage, or mechanics errors, or they could be omitted letters or typos. Proofread carefully to correct these errors when you edit and revise your writing.

Usage

This section provides information on the following usage errors:

- Article or Determiner Errors
- Confused Words
- Wrong Form of Word
- Faulty Comparison
- Nonstandard Verb or Word Form

Article or Determiner Errors

This section features rules and explanations for using articles and includes examples of how articles are used correctly when you are writing in English.

What Are Articles?

A, an, and *the* are called *articles*. These are words that come before a noun or its modifier. (A *modifier* is a word that makes a noun clearer or more specific. Modifiers tell how many or which one.)

a thinker	*an* apple	*the* house
a car	*an* old house	*the* newspapers

There are two types of articles in English. *A* and *an* are called indefinite articles. *The* is called a definite article.

When to Use *a* or *an*

A or *an* is used before a *singular* noun when the noun refers to *any* member of a group.

> James must write *an essay* for his writing class today.
>
> *A newspaper* is a good source of information on current events.

If the noun or the modifier that follows the article begins with a consonant sound, you should use the article *a*.

> *a* basketball   *a* new automobile

On the other hand, if the noun or its modifier begins with a vowel sound—a, e, i, o, u—you should use the article *an*.

> *an* elephant   *an* old truck

A/an is used before a noun if the noun can be counted. For example:

> I received *a letter* from my sister.
>
> Sending *an e-mail* is a fast way to communicate with classmates.

Sometimes a noun or a modifier can begin with a vowel *letter* but not a vowel *sound*. For example, here the vowel *o* in the word *one* sounds like the consonant *w* in *won*:

> This will be *a* one-time charge to your account.

When to Use *the*

The is used before singular and plural nouns when the noun is a particular or specific noun. Use the article *the* if you can answer the question "Which one?" or "What?"

> *The art class* that I want to take is taught by a famous painter.
>
> *The students* in Ms. Jones's class do not want to participate in *the debate*.

In addition, *the* is used in the following ways:

* To refer to things known to everyone (*the* sky, *the* stars)
* To refer to things that are unique (*the* White House)
* To refer to time (*the* past, *the* present, *the* future)

When Not to Use an Article

A/an is not used before a noun if the noun cannot be counted.

> I like to drink milk. (*Milk* is not counted.)

If a quantity of milk is specified, then the article would be used.

> I like to drink *a glass of milk* before I go to bed.

Sometimes nouns used to represent abstract general concepts (such as *anger*, *beauty*, *love*, or *employment*) do not take *a* or *an* before them.

> *Love* is a difficult emotion to describe in words.

> *Money* alone cannot buy happiness.

The is not used when a plural noun is used in a general sense.

> *Computers* are helpful tools for student writers. (*Computers* refers to the general concept of computers, not to specific computers.)

> *The computers* in that classroom are used for writing class. (*The computers* refers to a specific set of computers.)

Other Determiner Errors

The adjectives *this, that, these,* and *those* modify nouns that follow them by telling "which one." These adjectives must agree in number with the nouns they modify. *This* and *that* are used to describe a singular noun. *These* and *those* are used to describe plural nouns.

> Incorrect: *I would buy these house for those reason.*

> Incorrect: *This kinds of technologies will affect people's behavior.*

> Correct: *I would buy this house for that reason.*

> Correct: *These kinds of technologies will affect people's behavior.*

Confused Words

This section explains how to avoid errors involving confused words such as homonyms and words with similar sounds and spellings.

Homonyms

Certain words are known as *homonyms*. These are words that sound the same but differ in meaning, spelling, or usage. Homonyms can be of two types: words that are spelled alike and words that sound alike. Words that are spelled alike but differ in meaning are called *homographs*. An example of a homograph is the word *bear*, which can mean a type of animal or the verb *bear*, which means "to carry." Words that sound alike but differ in meaning and spelling are called *homophones*. The words *whole* and *hole* are homophones. *Whole* is an adjective meaning "complete," and *hole* is a noun meaning "an empty place." What follows are examples of some common homonyms. Always check your writing to make sure you are using the appropriate words.

> **here** *adverb* meaning "in this place"

> *We have been waiting **here** for an hour.*

> **hear** *verb* meaning "to listen"

> *Do you **hear** the birds singing?*

hole *noun* meaning "an empty place"

*The children dug a big **hole** in their sandbox.*

whole *adjective* meaning "with no part removed or left out; complete"

*Our **whole** project will involve cooperation from everyone.*

its *pronoun* possessive form of *it*

*The kitten hurt **its** paw.*

it's contraction of *it is*

***It's** not fair to leave her behind.*

know *verb* meaning "to feel certain, or to recognize"

*Do you **know** how to get to the subway?*

no *adverb* used as a denial or refusal

*The employee said **no** to the job offer.*

knew *verb* past tense of the verb *to know*

*The boy **knew** how to count to ten.*

new *adjective* meaning "not old"

*At the start of the school year, the students bought **new** books.*

desert *noun* meaning "a dry and sandy place"

*It rarely rains in the **desert**.*

desert *verb* meaning "to abandon"

*The officer commanded the troops to not **desert** their posts.*

dessert *noun* meaning "the final course of a meal"

*After a big meal, I enjoy a simple **dessert** of vanilla ice cream.*

to *preposition* meaning "toward"

*The man pointed **to** the sky.*

two *adjective* or *pronoun* meaning "the number 2"

*Five is **two** more than three.*

too *adverb* meaning "also"

*Tom and Eleanor wanted to go with them **too**.*

they're *contraction* meaning "they are"

> **They're** both coming to the party.

their *possessive pronoun* meaning "belonging to them"

> That is **their** blue house on the corner.

there *adverb* meaning "at that place"

> Did you see anyone you knew **there**?

through *adverb* meaning "completed, or finished"

> When she was **through** eating, she put her plate in the sink.

threw *past tense* of the verb *throw*, meaning "tossed"

> The boy **threw** the ball to his sister.

Other Confused Words

Besides homonyms, other words are confused in English because they are similar in spelling, sound, or meaning. Examples of some commonly confused words include *accept/except, advice/advise, affect/effect,* and *loose/lose.* Computer spell-checkers will not catch these words if you have misused them. When you review your work, proofread to see whether you have used the correct word. Even native speakers of English often make mistakes with confused words when they are writing, especially when they are in a hurry. Review the meanings of some commonly confused words.

accept *verb* meaning "to receive; to agree, or to take what is offered"

> I **accept** your kind invitation.

except *preposition* meaning "other than, or leaving out; excluding"

> Everyone **except** Phil can attend the conference.

advice *noun* meaning "an opinion given about what to do or how to behave"

> He has always given me valuable **advice** regarding my future plans.

advise *verb* meaning "to recommend or counsel"

> I **advise** you to stay in school and study hard.

affect *verb* meaning "to influence, or to produce an effect on"

> The weather can **affect** a person's mood.

effect *noun* meaning "result"

> When students study for tests, they see a positive **effect** on their test results.

effect *verb* meaning "to bring about"

> The governor can **effect** change in state education policies.

loose *adjective* meaning "detached, not rigidly fixed; not tight"

*She lost her bracelet because it was too **loose** on her wrist.*

lose *verb* meaning "to be deprived, or to no longer have; to not win"

*If you don't pay attention to the signs, you might **lose** your way.*

quiet *adjective* meaning "not loud or noisy"

*Please be **quiet** when other people are speaking.*

quit *verb* meaning "to give up or abandon; to stop"

*The boys will **quit** their jobs the week before school starts.*

quite *adverb* meaning "to some extent"

*Moving to a new city will be **quite** a change for my family.*

sense *noun* meaning "consciousness, awareness, or rationality; the faculty of perceiving by means of sense organs"

*My brother had the good **sense** to keep out of trouble.*

*The doctor explained that my **sense** of smell is not functioning well.*

since *adverb* meaning "from a definite past time until now"; *conjunction* meaning "later than"

*Ginny has lived in the same house ever **since** she moved to town.*

*Karl has worked as an accountant **since** graduating from college.*

than *conjunction* used when comparing two elements

*Her puppy is smaller **than** mine.*

then *adverb* meaning "at that time, or next"

*First I will stop at the store, and **then** I will go home.*

These are just a few examples of words that are often confused in English. When you are unsure of the proper usage of a word, consult an English dictionary.

Wrong Form of Word

When you write quickly, sometimes you use a word form that is different from the one that you intended to use. One reason why this error occurs is that a word can be used in different ways in a sentence depending on its purpose.

When you revise, read your writing very carefully to find these errors. You can also get someone else to read your work and to help you see where you are not clear. Here are examples of wrong word forms that can occur:

Incorrect: *But certain types of businesses will continue to grow to an extend, he thinks.*

Extend is a verb, and this writer meant to use the noun *extent*.

Correct: *But certain types of businesses will continue to grow to an extent, he thinks.*

Here is another example of a wrong word form in a sentence:

Incorrect: *I want to work with children who are <u>disable</u>.*

This writer should revise *disable* to *disabled*.

Correct: *I want to work with children who are <u>disabled</u>.*

Learning the parts of speech can teach you how each functions in a sentence. Proofreading your own work can help you correct these errors as well.

Faulty Comparison

A faulty comparison error occurs when the word *more* is used within a comparison with a word that ends in *-er,* or when the word *most* is used within a comparison with a word that ends in *-est*.

Incorrect: *The boy with the red hair is <u>more taller</u> than the girl with the black hair.*

Incorrect: *James thinks that Mary is the <u>most prettiest</u> girl in school.*

To avoid making these kinds of errors in your writing, you should review the following rules:
When comparing one thing with another, add the ending *-er* to short words (usually of one syllable).

Correct: *The boy with the red hair is <u>taller</u> than the girl with the black hair.*

Correct: *Today it is hot, but yesterday it was even <u>hotter</u>.*

When comparing three or more things, add the ending *-est* to short words (usually of one syllable).

Correct: *The girl in the back of the room is the <u>tallest</u> girl in her entire class.*

Correct: *Yesterday was the <u>hottest</u> day ever recorded by the National Weather Service.*

In many cases, with words of two or more syllables, you do not add *-er* or *-est* to the word; instead, use the word *more* before the word when comparing two things, and use the word *most* when comparing three or more things.

Correct: *The judges must decide which of the two remaining singers is <u>more talented</u>.*

Correct: *Of the three new students, John is the <u>most intelligent</u>.*

Comparisons that are negative use *less* for comparisons of two things and *least* for comparisons of three or more things.

Correct: *The third-floor apartment is <u>less costly</u> than the first-floor apartment.*

Correct: *Of the three colleges that I've visited, this one is the <u>least expensive</u>.*

Nonstandard Verb or Word Form

The words you use in everyday conversation are often different from the words you use in standard written English. While a reader might understand these informal words—*gotta, gonna, wanna, kinda*—you should not write them in an essay. Here are two examples of nonstandard words used in sentences:

Nonstandard: *I told her I gotta go to school now.*

Correct: *I told her I have got to go to school now.*

Nonstandard: *Do you wanna go to college?*

Correct: *Do you want to go to college?*

Even though you can understand what the writer means, the words *gotta* and *wanna* do not exist in standard written English.

Mechanics

This section provides information on the following types of mechanics errors:

- Capitalization
- Spelling
- Punctuation
- Other Errors

Capitalization

To *capitalize* means to use capital letters. Below are some guidelines for capitalization:

1. Capitalize the first word of every sentence.

   He is the most famous director in Hollywood right now. No doubt about it.

   Give it to me. It looks like mine.

2. Capitalize all proper nouns; for example, names of individuals, titles, and places.

   Francis Lloyd Mantel lives on Moore Street.

   The class is reading Adventures of Huckleberry Finn.

In the first example, "Francis Lloyd Mantel" is the name of an individual, so it is capitalized. "Moore Street" is the name of a place, so it is also a proper noun. The second example contains the title of a book, so it is capitalized.

All names are proper nouns and must be capitalized. Other examples:

- Names of institutions, places, and geographical areas

  She is a new faculty member at Stanford University.

  Their main office is in New Delhi, India.

- Names of historical events, days, months, and holidays

  Martin Luther King Day is a school holiday.

  Classes don't meet until October.

- Names of languages and proper adjectives

  He speaks Spanish and Italian fluently.

  They teach Korean dances at the academy.

3. The first-person pronoun *I* is always capitalized, even when it is in the middle of a sentence.

   It is I who sent you that letter.

   They told me that I should call for an appointment.

4. Capitalize words such as *father, mother, aunt,* and *uncle* when used with proper names or when addressing a particular person.

   Aunt Bessie and Uncle Jesse just bought a country house.

   Yes, Mom, I'm going after dinner.

   However, when these words are used with possessive pronouns, they are not proper names and therefore are not capitalized.

   My father is not at home.

   Their mother is my aunt.

   In the above examples, *father, mother,* and *aunt* are not capitalized because they are used with the possessive pronouns *my* and *their.*

Summary: In English, the first letter of the first word in a sentence is always capitalized. You must also capitalize all proper nouns. Proper nouns include all names and titles. The first-person pronoun *I* is always capitalized too.

Spelling

English spelling rules are complex. Here are a few rules that may help you:

1. Write *i* before *e* (*fiery, friend, dried*), except

   - after *c* (*receive*)
   - with syllables sounding like *a* as in *neighbor* (*weigh, heir*)

Note these examples:

> *All applicants will rec<u>ei</u>ve a response within three weeks.*
>
> *The breakfast special is fr<u>ie</u>d eggs and sausage.*

Adding Endings to Words

2. If a word ends with a silent *-e*, drop the *-e* when adding a suffix that begins with a vowel (for example, the *-ing* suffix). However, do *not* drop the *-e* when the suffix begins with a consonant (for example, the *-ful* suffix).

    > *I like to skate. I enjoy skat<u>ing</u>.*
    >
    > *I could use a dictionary. A dictionary is very use<u>ful</u>.*

    In the first example (*skate–skating*), the *-e* is dropped because the *-ing* suffix begins with the vowel *i*. In the second example, the *-e* is not dropped, because the *-ful* suffix begins with the consonant *f*.

3. When *-y* is the last letter in a word and the letter before *-y* is a consonant, drop *-y* and add *-i* before adding a suffix.

    > *The beaches in Thailand are extremely beaut<u>i</u>ful.*
    >
    > *They hurr<u>ie</u>d to the gate because they were so late.*

    In both examples, the *-y* is replaced with *-i* (*beauty–beautiful*; *hurry–hurried*).

4. When forming the plural of a word that ends with a *-y* preceded by a vowel, just add *-s*. But if the letter before *-y* is a consonant, drop *-y* and add *-ie* before adding the *-s*.

    > *FAO Schwartz is a famous t<u>oy</u> store. It sells all kinds of toy<u>s</u>.*
    >
    > *Lad<u>ie</u>s and gentlemen, please be seated.*

    In the first example, the letter *o* (a vowel) comes before *-y*. So you need to add only *-s* to form the plural noun. But in the second example, in the word *lady*, the letter *d* (a consonant) comes before *-y*. You have to drop *-y* and add *-ies* to make the word plural.

5. When a word ends in a consonant preceded by one vowel, double the final consonant before adding a suffix that begins with a vowel.

    > *The children swi<u>m</u> at the community pool. They love swi<u>mm</u>ing.*
    >
    > *You should begi<u>n</u> at the begi<u>nn</u>ing. Start by writing the title.*

    In the first example, the word *swim* ends with the letter *m*. In the second example, the word *begin* ends with the letter *n*. Both *m* and *n* are consonants. When adding *-ing*, a suffix starting with a vowel, you just need to double the final consonant.

Remember: when the ending begins with a vowel and the word ends in an *-e*, do not double the consonant. Instead, drop the *-e* and add the ending.

Incorrect: *The children go skatting in the winter.*

Correct: *The children go skating in the winter.*

The following examples contain *incorrect* spelling:

Incorrect: *We visited the monkey house at the zoo. There were monkies from all over the world.*

Incorrect: *My neice is a student in your class.*

In the first sentence, the plural form of *monkey* is *monkeys*. This is because when forming the plural of a word that ends with a *-y* preceded by a vowel, you should just add *-s*. In the second sentence, *niece* is the correct spelling. Remember, "*i* before *e* except **after** *c*" is a very useful rule!

Correct: *We visited the monkey house at the zoo. There were monkeys from all over the world.*

Correct: *My niece is a student in your class.*

These are all useful rules for learning English spelling. However, there are also some exceptions that are not covered by these rules, so it is a good idea to learn a few strategies for spelling as well.

For example, there are times when we make mistakes because we type too fast. It is easy to make the following errors on the computer:

Incorrect: *A letter frrom her former neighbor came in the mail today.*

Incorrect: *Becuase I lost my homework, I had to do it again.*

Both sentences contain typos, or mistakes we make when we type. One strategy for dealing with typos is to use the spell-check function on the computer.

However, there are mistakes that will not be caught by the spell-checker. For example:

Incorrect: *Would you know weather he is at work today?*

Incorrect: *Are their any good Indian restaurants in this area?*

In these examples, although the underlined word is a correct spelling (of a homophone), it is not the correct spelling of the word intended in the sentence. The spell-checker will not be able to find such errors, so after spell-checking, you should check for these errors as you read each sentence for meaning.

Another strategy is to keep a list of words that you often misspell. Memorize as many as you can. Check your writing specifically for these words.

You could also use a dictionary while you write to check the spelling of words that you are unsure of.

Summary: English spelling is complex and may sometimes seem strange. There are rules that can be memorized and learned, and there are strategies that can help you to spell better. For example, use a dictionary and the spell-check function on your computer.

Punctuation

Punctuation refers to the use of punctuation marks. Some punctuation marks, such as the *apostrophe,* are used with individual words. Some, such as *commas,* are used either to separate parts of sentences or to separate digits in numbers. Others, such as *periods, question marks,* and *exclamation points,* are used to separate sentences. They help us to make the meaning of our sentences clear.

Apostrophe

Use an apostrophe when you write a contraction. A contraction is the joining of two words by eliminating some letters and adding an apostrophe. It is a kind of short form. For example, *can't* is the contraction of *cannot, shouldn't* is the contraction of *should not,* and *let's* is the contraction of *let us.* Other contractions are *won't, it's, wouldn't,* and *couldn't.*

> *They won't be able to enter without their tickets.*
>
> *We could hear them, but we couldn't see them.*

In the first example, *won't* is the contraction of *will not,* and in the second sentence, *couldn't* is the contraction of *could not.*

Some people write contractions without the apostrophe. They are incorrect. The following sentence shows an incorrect use of a contraction:

> Incorrect: *Lets go to the park tomorrow.*
>
> Correct: *Let's go to the park tomorrow.*

Let's is the contraction of *let us.* Without the apostrophe, the word means "allows," as in this sentence:

> Correct: *She lets us use the computer when she's not using it.*

In order to be used correctly, the apostrophe must be in the proper position. Below are examples of misplaced apostrophes:

> Incorrect: *We could'nt understand the lecture.*
>
> Incorrect: *Students were'nt in school in the summer.*
>
> Correct: *We couldn't understand the lecture.*
>
> Correct: *Students weren't in school in the summer.*

Note that the apostrophe should replace the vowel that is being deleted.

Summary: The apostrophe is used to show contraction and possession. For other uses of the apostrophe, refer to the section "Possessive Pronouns."

Comma

The comma is the most common form of punctuation within a sentence. It is a signal for the reader to pause. In fact, if you read the examples below carefully, you will notice a natural pause where the commas are situated.

Learning a few basic rules will help you to use the comma effectively:

1. Use a comma and conjunction (such as *and* or *but*) to join two clauses in a compound sentence.

    The causes of the civil war were many, and the effects of the war were numerous.

    The experiment was incomplete, but the lessons learned were important.

    In the above examples, because the two clauses are independent clauses (or complete sentences) joined together by a conjunction, they need a comma between them.

2. Use a comma to connect words to the beginning or end of your sentence. We often add information to our sentences by attaching one or more words to the beginning or end. When you do that, you can use a comma to help your reader find your main message.

    Last night, my friend and I celebrated his 58th birthday.

    Many years ago, I studied French and German.

    Each of these sentences begins with a phrase that indicates time. This information is separated from the main sentence by a comma.

3. Use a comma between each item of a list when you are listing three or more items in a sentence.

    The flag was red, white, and blue.

    I bought milk, bread, cheese, and butter.

    The commas in the above examples clearly mark where one item on the list ends and the next one begins.

4. Use a comma between adjectives. If you have two adjectives together before the noun they describe, they must be separated by a comma.

    The cold, wintry wind chilled me to my bones.

    The complex, diverse cultures in the city add to its excitement.

    In the above examples, the adjectives describing *wind* and *cultures* are placed before the noun, separated by commas.

5. Use commas to set off additional information in the middle of a sentence. Some information, often telling details about the subject of the sentence, needs to be distinguished from the rest of the sentence (the verb and object). We place commas before and after these groups of words.

Ms. Johnson, <u>the company president</u>, will announce the winner.

My brother Tom, <u>who loves to read</u>, uses the library every day.

In the above examples, if you take away the parts that are set off by commas, you still have a complete sentence.

6. Use commas to separate quoted matter from the rest of the sentence.

    "Take a break," said the instructor.

    Nancy announces, "I'm getting married tomorrow."

In each example, the quotation is set apart from the rest of the sentence by a comma.

7. Use commas to set off the name of a state or country when it follows a city, county, or equivalent.

    The newspaper is based in Chicago, Illinois.

    Her flight to Beijing, China, took twelve hours.

In the above examples, the comma is used to set off the name of a state or country from a city within it.

8. In written American English, use commas to set off numbers in groups of four or more digits and between the words for the day, month, and year of a date.

    He won $1,000,000 in the lottery.

    The date is March 15, 2003.

In the first example, commas are used because of the numbers (of four or more digits). In the second example, it is used in a date.

The following sentences are missing commas:

Incorrect: *Conrad Redding the father of the bride cried at the wedding.*

Incorrect: *In conclusion I believe that technology will be the main factor affecting life in the twenty-first century.*

In the first sentence, "the father of the bride" should be set off by a pair of commas. In the second sentence, there should be a comma after "In conclusion."

Correct: *Conrad Redding, the father of the bride, cried at the wedding.*

Correct: *In conclusion, I believe that technology will be the main factor affecting life in the twenty-first century.*

Summary: Commas are used to separate parts of sentences and make meaning clearer. There are rules that can help you to use commas more effectively.

Hyphen

The hyphen is the punctuation mark used to join two words together to form a compound word. The most common uses of hyphens are as part of an adjective phrase, in numbers that are spelled out, and as prefixes.

1. Hyphens with compound adjectives. Use a hyphen to join two or more words serving as a single adjective *before* a noun. For example:

    His uncle is a <u>well-known</u> author.

    However, when compound adjectives come *after* a noun, they are not hyphenated. For example:

    The author is <u>well known</u> for his mystery stories.

2. Hyphens with compound numbers. A hyphen should be used in fractions and in the numbers twenty-one and above.

    The cup is <u>three-quarters</u> full.

    Our teacher is <u>sixty-three</u> years old.

    In the above examples, the compound numbers are joined with hyphens.

3. Hyphens with prefixes. A *prefix* is a syllable or word added to the beginning of another word to change its meaning. The prefixes *self-, ex-,* and *great-* always require a hyphen when they are added to words.

    The instructions are <u>self-explanatory</u>.

    The children are with their <u>great-grandparents</u>.

    However, for prefixes such as *dis-, pre-, re-,* and *un-,* a hyphen is normally not used.

    My aunt <u>dislikes</u> loud music.

    The answer to that question is <u>unknown</u>.

Summary: We use hyphens to link some compound words, but not all compound words are hyphenated. In fact, American English is tending toward using fewer and fewer hyphens. Always check a recent dictionary to be sure you are hyphenating correctly.

Final Punctuation

There are a few punctuation marks that help us to end our sentences. These are the question mark, the period, and the exclamation point.

Question Mark

Use a question mark at the end of a direct question.

When did World War II begin<u>?</u>

What were the key stages in the Romantic Art movement<u>?</u>

Period

Periods are used to mark the end of a sentence that is a not a question. A period is also used at the end of an indirect question.

I just completed the project.

Cindy asked me who would be taking notes at the meeting.

Exclamation Point

Use an exclamation point after a sentence that expresses strong feeling or requires emphasis. An exclamation point also serves to make a sentence stand out.

Correct: *That was utter nonsense!*

Correct: *What absolutely gorgeous flowers! Thank you!*

The following examples contain *incorrect* use of final punctuation:

Incorrect: *Have you called Ms. Han yet.*

Incorrect: *Oh, that's an amazing story?*

The first example is a question and needs a question mark. The second example should have either an exclamation point or a period, not a question mark.

Correct: *Have you called Ms. Han yet?*

Correct: *Oh, that's an amazing story!*

Summary: Question marks, periods, and exclamation points are used to end sentences. Use question marks to end direct questions, periods to end other sentences, and exclamation points when you want to express strong emotions or emphasis. Do not use too many exclamation points in your writing, or you may sound as if you are shouting!

Other Errors

Compound Words

A *compound word* is a word that has two or more parts. For example, the word *everywhere* is made up of two distinct words: *every* and *where*. But as a compound word, *everywhere* has a new meaning that is different from the meanings of *every* and *where*. Although there are times when experts cannot agree if a word should be a compound, in most cases there are clear rules. In the following sentences, you can see where student writers make mistakes when using compound words:

Incorrect: *I work to support my self and my family.*

Incorrect: *You can learn from every thing happening today.*

In each of these sentences, compound words have been written incorrectly as two separate words. The underlined words in each sentence should be written as one compound word.

Correct: *I work to support myself and my family.*

Correct: *You can learn from everything happening today.*

Summary: In English, words, especially adjectives and nouns, are sometimes combined into compound words in a variety of ways. Compound words have a meaning that is different from the meanings of the two words that form them. Not all words can be joined this way. When you are not sure whether a word is a compound, check your dictionary.

Fused Words

Sometimes writers fuse two words together to form an incorrect compound word. The sentences below show examples of fused words:

Incorrect: *Some people say that highschool is the best time of your life.*

Incorrect: *I like to play soccer alot.*

Each of the underlined fused words should be two separate words.

Correct: *Some people say that high school is the best time of your life.*

Correct: *I like to play soccer a lot.*

Summary: When you join words together incorrectly, you get fused words. When you are not sure whether two words should be compounded, check your dictionary.

Duplicate Words

When writing a first draft, you might make errors simply because you are thinking faster than you can write or type. As a result, you might write the same word twice. Sometimes you might write two words in a row that, though different, function in the same way. It is very common for writers to type two verbs, pronouns, or articles in a row in early drafts.

Incorrect: *Sally's older sister can may help her pay for college.*

Incorrect: *He was as silly as a the clown.*

In each sentence, one of the underlined words should be deleted.

Correct: *Sally's older sister can help her pay for college.* (meaning that the sister is able to help Sally)

Correct: *Sally's older sister may help her pay for college.* (meaning that the sister might decide to help Sally)

Correct: *He was as silly as a clown.* (meaning that he generally acts clownish)

Correct: *He was as silly as the clown.* (meaning that he acts like a specific clown)

Summary: You "duplicate" when you write the same word twice or when you use two different words that serve the same function. A real duplicate is easy to correct, as the spell-checker will usually identify it. But if you have typed two words that serve the same function and are not sure which to keep, check a dictionary to help you choose the word with the most appropriate meaning.

Style

This section provides information on how you can address the following kinds of problems in writing:

- Word Repetition
- Inappropriate Words or Phrases
- Too Many Passive Sentences
- Too Many Long Sentences
- Too Many Short Sentences
- Sentences Beginning with Coordinating Conjunctions

Word Repetition

Repeating some words to emphasize your key points is a good writing technique. However, repeating the same words or sets of words too often gives your writing an immature style. It can also make your essay seem boring.

To write more effectively, try using a variety of vocabulary. Here are a few ideas that can help you:

1. Use synonyms (words that have similar meanings) to replace repeated words. For example, instead of repeating a common verb such as *make*, where appropriate, use synonyms like these:

   create, produce, perform, do, execute, bring about, cause, form, manufacture, construct, build, put up, set up, put together, compose

   You can find synonyms in a thesaurus.

   In the following paragraph, the noun *student* is repeated too many times:

   Think about this situation. A student interviewed many students about what it is like to be an only child. If the teachers in charge of the school paper did not edit names of students from the paper or facts that would give that particular student away to other students, then serious problems could be caused for the students who gave their information.

   We can improve this paragraph by using a variety of other words to refer to *student*. For example:

Think about this situation. A <u>reporter</u> interviewed many <u>students</u> about what it is like to be an only child. If the teachers in charge of the school paper did not edit the <u>individuals'</u> names from the paper or facts that would give <u>each person</u> away to the <u>readers</u>, then serious problems could be caused for the <u>students</u> who gave their information.

2. Use phrases such as *the former, the latter, the first one,* and *the other* to avoid repeating the same nouns. In the following paragraph, the same names are repeated several times:

    Of the two sisters, <u>Grace</u> is confident and at ease with everyone. <u>Lily</u> is shy and cautious. <u>Grace</u> always gets what she wants. <u>Lily</u> waits patiently for whatever comes her way. <u>Grace</u> never misses a chance to show off her many talents. <u>Lily</u> never says a word unless someone asks her a question.

    This paragraph can be improved by using a variety of phrases:

    Of the two sisters, <u>Grace</u> is confident and at ease with everyone. <u>Lily</u> is shy and cautious. <u>The former</u> always gets what she wants. <u>The latter</u> waits patiently for whatever comes her way. <u>Grace</u> never misses a chance to show off her many talents. <u>Her sister</u> never says a word unless someone asks her a question.

Summary: When you look over your writing, think about how you can replace over-used words and phrases. You can use a thesaurus to help you add variety to your writing.

Inappropriate Words or Phrases

Language that is too informal, such as slang, is not appropriate for academic writing. It is not always easy to tell when an expression is too informal. Some expressions are used so often in spoken English that we may think it is all right to use them in academic writing too.

Too informal: *No way would I ever vote.*

Much better: *There is no way I would vote.*

Too informal: *People just need to get it all together and participate in democracy.*

Much better: *People need to consider their beliefs and opinions and participate in democracy.*

Summary: Written language is usually more formal than spoken language. Try to avoid expressions that are too informal when writing academic essays.

Too Many Passive Sentences

A sentence is active when the subject is the *doer* of the action. It is passive when the subject is the *receiver* of the action.

> Active sentence: *Two hundred million people saw the movie.*
>
> Passive sentence: *The movie was seen by 200 million people.*

In the above examples, the action is *seeing*. In the active sentence, the subject (*two hundred million people*) is the doer of the action. In the passive sentence, the subject (*the movie*) is the receiver of the action.

Because passive sentences are usually longer and harder to read, using too many passive sentences can make your writing slow and uninteresting. Many experts think that passive sentences should make up only about 5 percent of your writing.

Active sentences, on the other hand, generally are clearer, are more direct, and seem stronger. However, this does not mean that you should stop using passive sentences. Appropriate use of passive sentences can make your writing more powerful.

Here are a few suggestions about when to use passive sentences:

1. When the *action* is more important than the doer

   > *The theater was opened last month.*
   >
   > *New students are invited to meet the dean in Room 226.*

   In these sentences, the theater being opened and the new students being invited are more important than the "doers" (the people who opened the theater or invited the new students). In fact, the "doers" are not important enough to mention.

2. When the *receiver* of the action is more important than the doer

   > *Everyone was given a key to the gym.*
   >
   > *The letters were faxed this morning.*

   In the first sentence, we care more about the people who were given a key than the people who were doing the giving. In the second sentence, the letters that were faxed are more important than the person who did the faxing.

3. When the *result* of the action is more important than the doer

   > *Our advice was followed by our clients.*
   >
   > *The new computers were installed by the systems staff.*

   In the first sentence, the advice being followed is more important than the people giving the advice. In the second sentence, the installation of the computers is more important than the people who installed them.

4. When you do not know who did an action, do not care, or do not want your reader to know

   Passive: *A mistake was made, and all the scholarship application files were lost.*

   Passive: *This report was written at the last minute.*

   The active forms of these examples would be as follows:

   Active: *I made a mistake and lost all the scholarship application files.*

   Active: *I wrote this report at the last minute.*

   If you were the person who made the mistake in the first sentence, or the person who wrote the report in the second, would you choose the active or passive voice?

5. When you want to sound objective

   Using passive sentences is a common practice in scientific and technical writing. When you are reporting the results of an experiment or describing a study, it helps to sound objective and fair. Thus reports are filled with sentences like these:

   The pigeons were observed over a period of three weeks.

   The subjects were divided into three groups.

   The use of the passive voice in lab reports also keeps the reader focused on the experiment itself, rather than on the researchers.

Summary: When you look over your writing, think about whether you have used too many passive sentences. Passive sentences are longer and more difficult to read and understand, so use them only when they help you to emphasize something important.

Too Many Long Sentences

Experts believe that the average sentence length should be between 15 and 20 words. This length allows your reader to absorb your ideas more easily. For example, the following sentence may be confusing to read because of its length:

   My favorite place to visit is my grandparents' house near the lake where we love to fish and swim, and we often take the boat out on the lake.

Breaking the sentence into two (or more) can make your writing clearer and more interesting.

   My favorite place to visit is my grandparents' house near the lake. We love to fish and swim there, and we often take the boat out on the lake.

Good writers usually mix longer sentences with shorter ones to make their writing more effective. You may even want to try a short sentence (or a single-word sentence) after a few long ones to help you to emphasize what you are saying.

> *Benjamin Franklin, who was one of America's Founding Fathers helped write the Declaration of Independence. He also invented many things such as bifocals and the Franklin stove, and he discovered electricity. Think about that discovery. Where would we be without electricity?*

In the example above, the paragraph starts with long sentences and ends with short ones. This combination makes the paragraph more lively and effective. Compare it with the paragraph below, which is made up of only long sentences:

> *Benjamin Franklin, who was one of America's Founding Fathers helped write the Declaration of Independence. He also invented many things such as bifocals and the Franklin stove, and he discovered electricity, which became very important to modern life.*

Which paragraph do you prefer?

Summary: It is a good idea to mix long sentences with short ones. A good combination of long and short sentences makes writing lively.

Too Many Short Sentences

You may have too many short sentences in your writing. Good writing usually contains a variety of sentence lengths to make the writing more interesting. Too many short sentences often make the writing sound choppy. You should combine some of your short sentences to make the writing smoother. Here is an example of a paragraph with too many short sentences:

> *I knew my friends would throw me a party. It was for my birthday. There was something in the air. I felt it for a whole week before that. I was nervous. I was also very excited. I got home that night. My friends didn't disappoint me. I walked in my house. All my friends yelled, "Surprise!"*

The paragraph can be improved by joining some of the short sentences using sentence connectors:

> *<u>Because</u> it was my birthday, I knew my friends would throw me a party. There was something in the air <u>for a</u> whole week before that. I was nervous <u>but excited when</u> I got home that night. I wasn't disappointed. <u>When</u> I walked in my house, all my friends yelled, "Surprise!"*

Summary: Good writing usually contains a variety of long and short sentences. A good mix of sentence lengths makes the writing more interesting. Too many short sentences often make the writing sound choppy.

Sentences Beginning with Coordinating Conjunctions

Coordinating conjunctions are words such as *and, but, as, or, yet, for,* and *nor.* They link or join thoughts together in the middle of a sentence. For example:

I love pizza, so I eat it for breakfast.

Mother drove to town to buy groceries, but she came home with a present for me.

Coordinating conjunctions can also be used to begin sentences, as in these examples:

And I didn't like parties.

So I did not do well on that test.

When you have too many sentences beginning with coordinating conjunctions, your writing becomes choppy. To make your writing smoother, use coordinating conjunctions only when joining ideas within sentences.

In the paragraph below, the writer uses a lot of coordinating conjunctions to begin sentences:

Baseball is the great American sport. And, it is thought of as a summer pastime. So as soon as the weather turns warm, all the neighborhood kids find a field to toss a ball around. And soon they form teams and play each other. But all summer, they always find time to listen to pro games on the radio. And they watch them on TV.

The paragraph can be improved by getting rid of beginning coordinating conjunctions:

Baseball, the great American sport, is thought of as a summer pastime. As soon as the weather turns warm, the neighborhood kids find a field to toss a ball around. Soon, they form teams to play each other, but all summer, they always find time to listen to pro games on the radio and to watch them on TV.

Summary: Coordinating conjunctions are very useful for joining thoughts together in the middle of a sentence. However, try to avoid using them to begin sentences in academic writing.

Organization and Development

The purpose of this section is to explain how a strong essay is typically organized and how to develop your ideas in an essay. It will provide answers to the following questions:

Introduction

- What is an introduction?
- How do I write an introduction?

Thesis

- What is a thesis?
- How do I make sure that my reader understands my thesis?
- Do I have enough main ideas to support my thesis?

Main Ideas

- Does each of my main ideas begin with a topic sentence?
- Have I discussed each main idea completely?
- Have I arranged my ideas in an orderly manner?

Supporting Ideas

- What are some ways to develop supporting ideas?
- Have I done my best to support and develop my ideas?
- Does each of my paragraphs support and develop/explain the main idea/topic sentence?

Transitional Words and Phrases

- Do I use transitional words and phrases to take the reader from one idea to the next?

Conclusion

- What is a conclusion?
- How do I write a conclusion?

Introduction

What Is an Introduction?

An introduction is the first paragraph or two of an essay. It tells the reader what the essay is about and provides background for the thesis (main idea).
    A good introductory paragraph does several things:

- It makes the reader want to read the essay.
- It tells the reader the overall topic of the essay.
- It tells the reader the main idea (thesis) of the essay.

How Do I Write an Introduction?

Introductions can be written in many different ways. Here are some ideas you can use to write a good introduction:

- Background about the topic
- Narrative
- Quotation
- Dramatic statistics/facts

- Shocking statement
- Questions that lead to the thesis

The following are examples of these ideas. The essay's thesis sentence is highlighted in bold.

Background About the Topic

Since the beginning of time, there have been teachers. The "classroom" teacher has many important tasks to do. A teacher has to teach information while keeping things interesting. She also sometimes has to be a referee, a coach, and a secretary. At times, a teacher has to be a nurse or just a good listener. **This career demands a lot, but it's a career I most want to have.**

Narrative

My fourth-grade teacher, Ms. Vela, was not a big woman. She was about five feet tall and was no longer young. Even though she did not look very strong, she never had trouble controlling all her students. She could quiet us down with just a stare. We always wanted to make her happy because we knew how much Miss Vela cared about us. She expected us to do the best we could, and we all tried our hardest. **Miss Vela was the kind of teacher who made me know that I wanted to be a teacher.**

Quotation

"Teaching is better than tossing a pebble into a pond of water and watching those ripples move out from the middle. With teaching, you never know where those ripples will end." I remember those words of my fourth-grade teacher. Miss Vela once told me that years after they left her class, her students would come back to tell how much she helped them. Miss Vela's students said that it was because of her that they learned to work hard and to feel proud of what they did. **I would like to teach because I would like to make that kind of difference.**

Dramatic Statistics/Facts

Three out of four people said that they thought it didn't matter how many students were taught in one class. However, our class researched this and found that the opposite is true. Studies completed at a university show that having small class sizes, especially in the primary grades, makes a big difference in how much students learn. **Before we decide how many students to assign to a primary school teacher, we need to think more carefully about how important smaller class size is.**

Shocking Statement

Some teenagers today say that they think that wives should earn money and that husbands should help with child care and other household tasks. Recent studies indicate that 13 percent of teenage boys would prefer a wife to stay at home, while 96 percent of the teenage girls surveyed wanted to work outside of the home. **However, couples who marry today may have grown up in very traditional households and therefore may find it difficult to accept wives of equal, not to mention greater, job status.**

Thesis

What Is a Thesis?

The thesis statement tells the main idea—or most important idea—of the essay. It emphasizes the writer's idea of the topic and often answers the question, "What important or interesting things do I have to say?" Thinking about the thesis statement can help you decide what other information needs to be presented or omitted in the rest of the essay.

A good thesis statement

- gives the reader some hint about what you will say about the topic

- presents your opinion about the topic and is not just a fact or an observation

- is written as a complete statement

- does not formally announce your opinion about the topic

A good thesis statement gives the reader some hint about what you will say about the topic.

Weak thesis: *Mahatma Gandhi was an interesting man.*

Good thesis: *Mahatma Gandhi was a person of contradictions.*

Weak thesis: *Television is a total waste of time.*

Good thesis: *Parents should carefully choose appropriate, educational television shows for their children to watch.*

A good thesis statement presents your opinion about the topic and is not just a fact or an observation.

Weak thesis: *London is the capital of England.*

Good thesis: *For tourists interested in British history, London is an ideal travel destination.*

Weak thesis: *Many movies today are violent.*

Good thesis: *The violence in movies today makes children less sensitive to other people's suffering.*

A good thesis statement is written as a complete statement.

> Weak thesis: *Should something be done about bad drivers?*
>
> Good thesis: *Bad drivers should have to take a driving course before being allowed to drive again.*

> Weak thesis: *There is a problem with the information on the Internet.*
>
> Good thesis: *To make sure information found on the Internet is valid, Internet users must make sure the sources of the information are credible.*

A good thesis statement does not formally announce your opinion about the topic.

> Weak thesis: *In my paper, I will write about whether schools should require uniforms.*
>
> Good thesis: *Public schools should not require uniforms.*

> Weak thesis: *The subject of this essay is drug testing.*
>
> Good thesis: *Drug testing is needed for all professional athletes.*

How Do I Make Sure That My Reader Understands My Thesis?

Sometimes you might use a word in your introduction or thesis that you should define or explain. For example, if you are writing about "Who is a hero?" you should first explain what you think the word *hero* means. Is a hero a person who risks his or her life to save others? Is a hero a person whom you admire for any reason? People might have their own ways of thinking about a certain word. When you define the word, you help your reader better understand what you mean.

Do I Have Enough Main Ideas to Support My Thesis?

A main idea is a point that you feel strongly about. It is important to you, and you want the reader to understand this idea. Some writers like to give the reader three main ideas. However, the number of main ideas will vary among good essays. The important thing to remember is that your main ideas need to support your thesis adequately.

If you do not have enough main ideas, you may want to do some rethinking. Here are five suggestions for how to think of more ideas about your subject.

Ask yourself these questions to get you started again:

- **Who?**

    Who in my life has influenced me to consider becoming a teacher?

- **What?**

    What do teachers do?

- **When?**

    When did I start thinking about becoming a teacher?

- **Where?**

  Where are teachers needed the most?

- **Why?**

  Why would a person want to become a teacher? Why do I want to become a teacher?

- **How? How much?**

  How does a teacher learn how to teach?

  How has my idea of becoming a teacher changed over the years?

  How much does a teacher influence his or her students?

  How much time does a teacher have to work outside of school?

- **What if? Why not?**

  What if teachers do not have all of the materials they need?

  Why teach in the classroom and not just over the Internet?

Talk to others about your topic.

Lots of people are happy to share what they know. Take good notes, because you may want to quote them in your essay.

- Other students in your school probably have opinions.

- A teacher who knows about the issue or subject could give you some opinions.

- Other people who are experts may have valuable information or opinions.

- Research your subject on the Internet or in a library.

- Send an e-mail to someone who may be an expert.

Think about the kind of writing you are doing.

Consider the questions below to help you figure out which ideas you need to add or how you should arrange those ideas.

- Are you explaining how things are alike (comparison) and different (contrast)? You can use this purpose when you are describing some-thing *(such as how to teach primary school students compared with how to teach high school students)* or when you are analyzing different view-points *(such as whether children should go to school year-round).*

- Are you putting your ideas in categories? You might be able to describe something in general and then describe its particular qualities. *For exam-ple, you might want to talk about what it takes to be a good teacher and then talk about the unique qualities of a particular teacher you have had.*

- Are you giving reasons to show how a problem developed and what the effects of the problem are? *For example, if you were discussing how students' attitudes are affected by their environment, you might want first to describe what has caused a particular attitude to develop. Then you might want to discuss the effects of that attitude.*

- Are you trying to persuade someone to think like you or to do something that will improve a situation in the way that you want it to be improved? *For example, if you are trying to persuade a friend to think about an issue the way you think about it, you might want to start by saying what the issue is and why your ideas are the best.*

Start all over and see where you go this time with your writing.

Do not be afraid to start over. Lots of writers get new and better ideas when they write about something more than once.

Reread your draft.

Look at your previous draft and start where the writing is the most interesting or at the point that you think is your best statement.

- Try to write three more sentences to explain your best sentence.

- Review the three new sentences, pick the best one, and write three more sentences that explain the most important idea in that best sentence.

Main Ideas

Does Each of My Main Ideas Begin with a Topic Sentence?

Each main idea needs to be discussed fully. The main idea is part of a sentence that explains the idea. This sentence is called the topic sentence, and its goal is to help the reader think of questions about the topic.

Pretend that you are the reader of this topic sentence:

> *Not passing a test in fourth grade in Miss Vela's class made me think about what a teacher is.*

What questions do you have?

Do you want to know more about what happened to this writer in fourth grade?

Do you think that you will learn what the writer thought or meant by the words "what a teacher is"?

Use your topic sentence to prepare the reader for understanding what is written in the essay.

You can review your sentences to see which words are the influential words. They are the words that seem more important in your sentence.

In this topic sentence, which words or phrases are important?

> *Teachers don't get paid for every hour that they work.*

Would you say that "every hour that they work" are the important words?

Here are the other sentences in this paragraph:

Teachers sometimes do work even when they are not in the classroom. Sometimes my mother grades papers and projects all day on Sunday. Even though she does not get paid, she says that that is the only time she can grade all of her students' work. My neighbor spends three weeks of his summer vacation on a ship that does scientific experiments. He doesn't get paid for any of that work, but he says the things that he learns help him be a better teacher.

Use topic sentences to connect two paragraphs or two main ideas.

Here is a sample paragraph that begins with a topic sentence:

Teachers get many benefits in their careers. My neighbor has children and likes having the summer off when his children are home. Some teachers say their work is very enjoyable. At least that's what my mom says when she mixes up her magic bubble formula for science class. My mom also says that one of the benefits of teaching is that she is using her college education every day. She also gets paid to take refresher courses. But she works hard.

Can you see how the next topic sentence connects to another thought?

In fact, teachers don't get paid for every hour that they work, but the teachers that I know say that they love their work.

What do you expect the writer to tell you about in this paragraph?

Have I Discussed Each Main Idea Completely?

In good writing, you (the writer) and the reader feel as if all of your questions/concerns have been discussed. Remember that your reader needs to understand what you are writing, so discuss each idea completely.

Give each main idea its own paragraph.

Each main idea should be treated as a unit. However, if a main idea is very broad, it will need more than one paragraph, because it is too complicated to be discussed in a single paragraph.

Have I Arranged My Ideas in an Orderly Manner?

You can arrange your ideas in many different ways. You can organize your ideas in chronological order, which means the order in time in which they occurred. You can begin with the oldest point first and then use paragraphs to discuss what happened next or later.

Here are two main ideas that will be developed into paragraphs:

Idea 1

I have wanted to be a teacher ever since I failed a test in Miss Vela's class in fourth grade.

Idea 2

Then in eighth grade I had an assignment to teach a science lesson to a class in my former primary school, and that experience showed me how good I felt when the students didn't want the class to be over.

You can organize your ideas by importance, either most important to least important or the other way around.

> **TIP**
>
> *If your writing assignment has to be completed in a short time, as in an essay test, you probably want to begin with the most important parts or reasons first.*

Here are what two different writers think is their most important idea:

Writer 1

The most important reason to be a science teacher is to help the next generation learn about the Earth.

Writer 2

Getting to do fun activities is the reason why I want to be a science teacher.

Supporting Ideas

What Are Some Ways to Develop Supporting Ideas?

Supporting ideas help to convince your reader that your main idea is a good one. Here are some things that professional writers do:

- Tell a story that clarifies the main idea.
- Give examples of the main idea to explain what the paragraph is about.
- Give reasons that support the thesis. These can be facts, logical arguments, or the opinion of experts.
- Use details that are very specific so the reader can understand how this idea is different from others.
- Tell what can be seen, heard, smelled, touched, felt, or experienced.
- Try to see the idea from many different angles.
- Tell how other events, people, or things might have an influence on the main idea.
- Use metaphors or analogies to help the reader understand an idea by comparing it to something else.

Have I Done My Best to Support and Develop My Ideas?

Think of your reader as a curious person. Assume that your reader wants to know everything that you can say about this subject.

Here are some specific questions that are appropriate for certain types of writing:

- **If you are describing a problem or issue, you might want to consider the following:**

  What type of problem or issue is it?

  What are the signs that a problem or issue exists?

  Who or what is affected by the problem or issue?

  What is the history of the problem or issue—what or who caused it or contributed to it, and what is the state of the problem now?

  Why is the issue or problem significant? What makes this issue or problem important or less important?

- **If you are arguing or trying to persuade your reader to agree with your opinion, consider the following:**

  What facts or statistics could you mention as support?

  What ideas could you discuss to prove your points?

  What comparison could you make that would help the reader understand the issue?

  What expert opinion would make your opinion more valid?

  Could you support your point with some examples?

  Could you describe the views of someone holding a different opinion?

TIP

Strong arguments are often made by discussing what is good in the opponent's view. You can use expressions such as "although that is a point well taken," "granted, while it is true that," *or* "I agree that" *to discuss an opposite view.*

- **If you are analyzing literature or writing a review of a story or movie, consider these questions:**

  Can you summarize the story so that your reader knows what happens?

  Can you give the details about the place or time so that your reader has a context for understanding the story?

  What can you say about the main characters so that the reader can understand what makes them special or interesting?

  Can you describe the point where the main character(s) is (are) in a crisis and must make an interesting choice?

  Can you quote what characters say about each other or about what they are experiencing?

  Does the story have a deeper theme that you could discuss?

  Can you describe the style in which the story is told or the camera angles of the movie?

  Are there interesting images or symbols?

- **If you are describing something or providing a definition, consider the following:**

  Can you tell what the thing looks like or what its parts are?

  Can you say what it does or means?

  If what it does or means has changed over time, can you describe what it used to mean or used to do and what it now means or does?

  If what you are describing has a different name or meaning, can you tell the reader the different name or meaning?

- **If you are telling how to do or make something, consider these points:**

  Have you started at the right place—the first step—and proceeded logically?

  Have you defined any terms that might be unfamiliar to your reader?

  Have you given an example that might help your reader understand what you mean?

  Have you tried to explain your instructions clearly? Have you numbered these instructions so that the reader knows the order in which it is best to do them?

> **TIP**
>
> *You may want to think of a way to arrange your material so that your reader can understand it better. For example, in a recipe the ingredients are listed at the top and the instructions are in short paragraphs or are numbered as steps.*

Does Each of My Paragraphs Support and Develop/Explain the Main Idea/Topic Sentence?

Paragraphs are a group of sentences about a thought or discussion. Each paragraph is about a main topic.

Some paragraphs are long and some are short. Some paragraphs are just one sentence, which can be a very interesting way to present information.

Some contain an interesting story that can take several sentences to tell.

Some paragraphs answer all of the topic issues. Others are more like transitions between two main ideas.

Here are some questions to help you evaluate your paragraphs:

- **Have you said enough so that each paragraph is complete?**

> **TIP**
>
> *Try giving each paragraph a title and see if, read by itself, it could be something meaningful. If the reader asked you a specific question, would this paragraph be the answer? If some of the sentences do not fit as an answer, then you should probably delete them.*

- **Have you used words that need to be explained or defined?** If you are trying to sound important and do not explain what you mean, your reader might feel frustrated. Try using more than one sentence to define or explain something. Three sentences might really explain your idea!

- **Have you provided evidence (proof)? Would an example show what you mean?** Use a good example to show that what you say is true. This is important.

- **Is there a personal experience or quotation from another source that would validate what you are trying to say?**

TIP

Personal experiences are appropriate in some essays but not in others. Make sure you understand the type of information that is expected in each essay you write.

TIP

If you are quoting from another source, make certain that you are quoting (reproducing the words) accurately. Also be sure that you are using quotation marks correctly.

Transitional Words and Phrases

Do I Use Transitional Words and Phrases to Take the Reader from One Idea to the Next?

Transitional words and phrases connect what a reader has already read to what the reader is going to read. They give the reader an idea of the relationships between the various ideas and supporting points. They also help to show the relationship between sentences.

You might think of your paragraph as a train and the sentences as cars (and the topic sentence as an engine). Do all the parts of the paragraph link or fit together? You can guide the reader as he or she reads an essay by using transitional words or phrases in paragraphs and sentences.

These words can help you talk about time and the relationship between events:
today, tomorrow, next week, yesterday, meanwhile, about, before, during, at, after, soon, immediately, afterward, later, finally, then, when, next, simultaneously, as a result

These words can help you show the order of ideas:
first, second, third, finally, lastly, most important, of least importance

These words can help you show location:

above, over, below, beneath, behind, in front of, in back of, on top of, inside, outside, near, between, beside, among, around, against, throughout, off, onto, into, beyond

These words can help you compare or demonstrate similarity:

also, as, similarly, in the same way, likewise, like

These words can help you contrast or demonstrate difference:

in contrast, however, although, still, even though, on the other hand, but

These words can help you add information:

in addition, for instance, for example, moreover, next, likewise, besides, another, additionally, again, also, in fact

These words can help you clarify a point:

in other words, for instance, that is, just to reiterate, in summary

These words can help you add emphasis to a point that you are making:

truly, in fact, for this reason, again, just to reiterate

These words can help you conclude or summarize:

all in all, lastly, as a result, in summary, therefore, finally

Conclusion

What Is a Conclusion?

The concluding paragraph is separate from the other paragraphs and brings closure to the essay.

- It discusses the importance of your ideas.
- It restates the thesis with fresh wording.
- It sums up the main ideas of the paper.
- It can also include an anecdote, a quotation, statistics, or a suggestion.

How Do I Write a Conclusion?

You might consider some of the following approaches to writing concluding paragraphs:

- Summarize main points.
- Provide a summarizing story.
- Include a provocative or memorable quotation.
- Make a prediction or suggestion.
- Leave the reader with something to think about.

Here are two different concluding paragraphs:

Good teaching requires flexibility, compassion, organization, knowledge, energy, and enthusiasm. A good teacher must decide when a student needs to be prodded and when that student needs mercy. Good teaching requires knowing when to listen and reflect and when to advise or correct. It requires a delicate balance of many skills, and often a different mix of approaches for different students and different situations. Is this profession demanding? Yes! Boring? Never! Exciting? Absolutely!

When I become a teacher, I want fourth graders like Ms. Vela's. We adored her and wanted to please her. But more important, I want to be a Miss Vela for my students. I want to challenge my students to become good citizens. When the river in our town flooded its banks and some classmates had to be evacuated, Ms. Vela asked us to think about what we could do. We came up with three decisions. We packed lunches for our classmates, we shared our books and pencils in class, and we gave them clothing. Later when we studied civics, we realized that we were taking care of our classmates the way the local or federal government does in a disaster. Ms. Vela was helping her fourth graders become more civic minded. I'm hoping to help my students think like that when I'm a teacher.

Advice to Writers

This section provides information about the different kinds of essays you may be asked to write.

- Persuasion
- Informative Writing
- Comparison/Contrast
- Description
- Narration
- Cause and Effect
- Problem and Solution
- Description of a Process ("How-to")
- Writing as Part of an Assessment
- Response to Literature
- Writing in the Workplace

Persuasion

When you write a persuasive essay, you are trying to make the reader agree with you. You thus have to offer good reasons to support your opinion, deal with opposing views, and perhaps offer a solution.

Here is how to start:

- List specific arguments for and against your opinion (the pros and cons).

- Decide whether you need to find more information (for example, *statistics* that support your argument, *direct quotes* from experts, *examples* that make your ideas concrete, *personal experience*, *facts*).

- Think of good arguments from someone who holds the opposite view. How could you respond to that person?

In this kind of writing, you might want to keep your best argument for last.

Summary: When you write a persuasive essay, you have to be clear and convincing. Any kind of writing improves with practice. Try to practice writing and revising, and expose yourself to as many good models of persuasive essays as you can.

Informative Writing

This kind of writing presents information that helps your reader understand a subject (for example, climate change, jazz music, pollution). Informative writing can be based on formal research (reading, interviews, Internet browsing). Sometimes you may also be asked to write about a personal experience or observation.

Here is how to start:

- Find a specific focus (for example, not *recycling in general* but *the recycling of paper*).

- Choose several important points to discuss (*how paper is recycled, what recycled paper is used for*).

- Think about the supporting details for each point. These details can be facts, observations, descriptions, and/or examples (*items that use recycled paper are paper towels, greeting cards*).

Comparison/Contrast

Writing a comparison/contrast paper involves comparing and contrasting two subjects. A comparison shows how two things are alike. A contrast shows how two things are different.

You can use comparison and contrast to describe, define, analyze, or make an argument—for, in fact, almost any kind of writing.

Here is how to start:

- Select two subjects that have some basic similarities or differences.

- Look for how these subjects are similar and different.

- Decide how you want to present your information. Choose one way and stick with it throughout your essay.
  - Do you want to discuss a point for one subject and then the same point for the second subject?
  - Do you want to show all the important points of one subject and then all the important points of the second subject?
  - Do you want to discuss how your two subjects are the same and then how they are different from each other?

- Remember to make clear to your reader when you are switching from one point of comparison or contrast to another. Use clear transitions. Some transition words that you may find useful are as follows:

  For similarities: *similarly, likewise, furthermore, besides*

  For differences: *in contrast, in comparison, on the other hand, although, however, nevertheless, on the other hand, whereas, yet*

Description

In descriptive writing, you write about people, places, things, moments, and theories with enough detail to help the reader create a mental picture of what is being described. You can do this by using a wide range of vocabulary, imaginative language, interesting comparisons, and images that appeal to the senses.

Here is how to start:

- Let the reader see, smell, hear, taste, and feel what you are writing about. Use your five senses in the description (for example, *The ancient driver nervously steered the old car down the red mud road, with me bouncing along on the backseat.*).

- Be specific (not *this dessert is good* but *the fudge brownie is moist, chewy, and very tasty*).

- Show the reader where things are located from your perspective (for example, *As I passed through the wooden gates, I heard a cough. A tiny woman came out from behind the trees.*).

- Decide whether you want to give a personal view (subjective) or a neutral viewpoint (objective).

TIP

What seems unusual or contradictory can make your subject more interesting (for example, "Martin Luther King probably contributed more than anyone else to changes in civil rights, but he hardly earned any money for his speeches and work.").

Narration

This kind of essay offers you a chance to think and write a story about yourself, an incident, memories, and experiences. Narratives or stories usually include a plot, a setting (where something happened), characters, a climax, and an ending. Narratives are generally written in the first person, using *I*. However, as the storyteller, you can choose to "speak" like different people to make the story more interesting.

Here is how to start:

- If you are writing about a quarrel with a friend:
  - Think of what caused the quarrel.
  - Think of who is involved and how.
  - Think of how the quarrel developed, how it was settled, or whether you and your friend are talking now.
- Remember the details that make the event real to you (for example, what your friend said to you and the tone of voice your friend used).
- Try to answer the question, "What did this event mean to me?"
- Choose a way to begin; for example:
  - Build your story in scenes (the way you see in movies).
  - Summarize what happened and describe only the most important scene.
  - Begin at the ending and tell why this was such an important event.

Cause and Effect

Cause-and-effect essays are concerned with why things happen (causes) and what happens as a result (effects). In the cause-and-effect essay, it is very important that your tone be reasonable and that your presentation look factual and believable.

Here is how to start:

- Think about the event or issue you want to write about.
- Brainstorm ideas.
- Introduce your main idea.
- Find relevant and appropriate supporting details to back up your main idea. You can organize these details in the following ways:
  - *Chronological,* the order in which things/events happen
  - *Order of importance,* from least to most important or vice versa
  - *Categorical,* by dividing the topic into parts or categories

- Use appropriate transition words and phrases, such as the following:

  because, thus, therefore, due to, one cause is, another is, since, for, first, second, consequently, as a result, resulted in, one result is, another is

Problem and Solution

A problem-solution essay starts by identifying a problem (or problems) and then proposes one or more solutions. It is usually based on topics that both the writer and the reader care about (such as the quality of cafeteria food).

Here is how to start:

- Think of all the reasons that the problem exists.
  - Why did it happen?
  - How did it begin?
  - Why does it exist now?
- List possible solutions to the problem.
- Evaluate your solutions—which ones will most likely work?
- Write the pros and cons of one or more good solutions, but give the most space in your essay to the best solution.
- Explain why the best solution is the one to choose.

Description of a Process ("How-to")

This kind of essay explains how to do something (for example, *how to bake your favorite cake*) or how something occurs (for example, *how movies are made*).

For how to do something, here is how to start, along with the pertinent questions:

- Think about all the equipment, skills, or materials needed.
- How many steps are there in the process? Put the steps in the right order. Why is each step important?
- What difficulties are involved in each step?
- How long does the process take?

TIP

Give any signs or any advice that can help the reader accomplish the step with success.

For how something occurs, here is how to start:

- Give any background that can help your reader understand the process.
- Tell what happens in the order that it happens.

TIP

Be sure to explain any terms that your reader might not understand.

Process essays are usually organized according to time: they begin with the first step in the process and continue until the last step. To indicate that one step has been completed and a new one will begin, we use transitions. Some common transition words and phrases used in process essays are as follows:

first of all, first, second, third, next, soon after, after a few hours, afterward, initially, at the same time, in the meantime, before, before this, immediately before, in the meanwhile, currently, during, meanwhile, later, then, previously, at last, eventually, finally, last, last but not least, lastly

Writing as Part of an Assessment

This kind of writing may be more difficult because you are trying to write your best in a certain place and a limited amount of time. There are a few strategies, however.

Here is how to start:

- Take a few moments to understand the question and to note down some ideas that come to mind.
- Before beginning to write, take a few moments to plan. How are you going to organize your main ideas and supporting details? Some students find making an outline to be a helpful strategy.
- During your writing, if other ideas come to mind and they feel right, use them.
- Keep track of your time, but do not panic.
- Revise. Look at the paper from the reader's point of view; reorganize and add explanations if necessary.
- Proofread if you have time.

TIP

As with any other kind of writing, writing on a test improves with practice. You can practice this skill by writing and revising essays while working within a set time limit.

Response to Literature

When you write about literature, you are telling why that work of literature (story, movie, poem, or play) is interesting and what makes it effective (for example, why it makes you laugh, why you care about the characters).

You can write about why the literary work seems true, you can analyze the characters or actions, or you can analyze how the literary work accomplishes its effect.

There are many ways to respond to literature, but here are a few ways to start, along with pertinent questions:

- Write for a while about your personal feelings about the literature. Are you most interested in the setting, the situation, the characters, or the atmosphere that the work creates? These are clues to what you can write about.

- What is the situation or the mood?

- What clues does the author give you about the true meaning of this story, poem, or movie? (For example, the many "Cinderella" stories in the world have the same meaning: kindness is rewarded no matter how poor you are.)

- Organize your thoughts and support them with examples from the literary work. Do not assume that your reader knows the story or movie that you are writing about!

Writing in the Workplace

Letters, memos, and reports are the kinds of writing that are most often done when we do business with each other. In this kind of writing, you want to make your points as quickly and clearly as possible. So try to be brief and direct.

Here is how to start:

- Organize your thoughts. Most business letters should take one page.

- Think about whether there is a special format you should follow.

- Decide if you want the reader to take action (persuasive), to understand a problem (informative), or to fix something (problem-solution). (*Refer to the relevant sections under this "Advice to Writers" heading.*)

- Write clearly and courteously.

- Include relevant quotations.

- Leave the reader with something to think about (for example, make a prediction or suggestion).

Revising, Editing, and Proofreading

The Writing Process

The writing process has several stages: planning, drafting, writing, revising, editing, and proofreading. Many writers and instructors maintain that improving your essay has three distinct stages: revising, editing, and proofreading. Review each column of the following chart to understand each stage completely.

As you write, you may wish to revise and edit your essay several times as you clarify and develop your ideas. The Writer's Handbook sections on Style, Organization and Development, and Advice to Writers can be very helpful as you revise and edit your essay. When you have a final version of your essay, be sure to proofread it carefully.

	Revising	Editing	Proofreading
Purpose	See the complete concept. Decide if your essay says what you want it to say. Add ideas.	Correct grammar and usage. Make changes in word choice, style, and the way you explain your ideas.	Correct typos as well as spelling, punctuation, and formatting errors.
When	After you have written your first draft, do not do anything with it; then begin revising.	Begin when you have a complete draft of your essay.	Make this the final stage before you submit your essay.
What	Read your entire essay from beginning to end.	As you read each sentence, revise that sentence before you do the next sentence.	Read word by word and line by line to make corrections.
Strategies	Identify each part of the essay: introduction, thesis, main ideas, supporting ideas, and conclusion. Review carefully how the ideas are connected and the order of paragraphs. Do not be afraid to cut and paste, delete, or add new ideas. Ask a peer reviewer to say what is good and what could be better in your essay.	Ask your teacher, a peer editor, or a friend to give you ideas and advice. List the kinds of grammar and usage errors you make and look at those errors first. If a sentence seems right, do not revise it. Think about just the parts that seem to have problems. Use a handbook to help you correct errors and rewrite sentences.	Print a copy of your essay and make the changes on the paper copy. Read your essay aloud to your teacher or to someone who is more English proficient than you and circle identified errors. Have a peer reviewer who is more proficient in English read your essay backward. Start with the last sentence, then the second to the last, and so on. Use a dictionary, handbook, and spell-checker to help you correct errors.

Step 1: Organization and Development

Think about your topic and, if necessary, change the way your essay is organized and developed.

Step 2: Style

Read each sentence to see if your ideas are easy to understand.

Step 3: Grammar, Usage, Mechanics

Check each word and sentence for errors.

Step 4: Proofreading

Check for spelling and typing mistakes as you read your final draft.

Using a Computer to Write

Computers make the writing process much easier than handwriting. Computers let you do all of the following:

- Write faster than you can with a pen
- Save or delete ideas and drafts
- Move words, paragraphs, and sentences
- Try out new ways of expressing yourself
- Locate and correct mistakes

Always remember that the computer is a tool that lets you think about how to write. You will still have to make decisions about how to draft and revise your essays and other writing.

Glossary

active voice—English sentences can be written in either the active or passive voice. In the active voice, the subject is the doer of an action. For example, in *Sam kicked the ball*, the action is *kicked*, and the doer is *Sam*. An active sentence emphasizes the doer of an action.

adjective—Adjectives give more information about nouns. In English, they usually come before nouns. For example: *a red umbrella, a rainy day, a beautiful woman*.

adverb—Adverbs are words such as *quickly, happily*, or *carefully*. They can tell more about an adjective (for example, *very big*), another adverb (for example, *very quietly*), or a verb (for example, *walk slowly*).

antecedent—A noun to which a pronoun refers is the antecedent. In the following sentence, *John* is the antecedent of the pronoun *he*: *John was late for school because he missed the bus*.

apostrophe—This punctuation mark (') shows the omission of letters in contractions (*cannot–can't*), or possession (the *girl's* dress, the *animals'* cages).

article—Articles are *a, an*, and *the*, the little words in English that come before nouns. English has two types of articles. The definite article (*the*) is used to refer to one or more specific things, animals, or people (for example, *the house on the hill*). The indefinite articles (*a, an*) are used to refer to a thing, animal, or person in a nonspecific or general way (for example, *a house, an elephant*).

clause—A clause is a group of related words that contains a subject and a verb. There are two kinds of clauses: independent and dependent. An independent clause expresses a complete thought and can be seen as a sentence (for example, *She saw Jim.*). A dependent clause is a part of a sentence and cannot stand on its own. (*When she saw Jim* is a dependent clause.) To make a complete sentence, you need to add an independent clause (for example, *When she saw Jim, she smiled.*).

collective noun—A collective noun refers to a *group* of people or animals: *population, family, troop, committee*.

comma—This punctuation mark (,) is used to separate words (*She bought apples, oranges, and grapes.*) or parts of a sentence (*He was here, but he left.*).

compound subject—This is a plural subject, a subject that consists of more than one part: *Lions, tigers, and bears are kept in the zoo*.

compound verb—This type of verb consists of more than one part: *The baby started crying*.

compound words—These are words that are made up of two words: *everywhere, boyfriend, himself, weekend*.

conclusion—This is the last paragraph of an essay, the paragraph that closes the essay. In a conclusion, you can restate the thesis or sum up the main ideas of the essay.

conjunction—A conjunction is a word that connects words, phrases, or sentences. It also shows relationships between words or clauses. There are two kinds of conjunctions: coordinating and subordinating. Coordinating conjunctions such as *and, but, or, nor,* and *for* connect parts that are equal: In the sentence *She bought a desk and a chair,* both *desk* and *chair* are nouns. Subordinating conjunctions such as *although, because, if, since,* and *when* connect parts that are not equal: In the sentence *Because he missed the train, he was late for work,* the clause *Because he missed the train* is a dependent clause, and *he was late for work* is an independent clause.

contraction—Contractions are short forms. You make a contraction when you combine two words, shorten one of them, and add an apostrophe: *cannot–can't; does not–doesn't; should not–shouldn't; it is–it's.*

dependent clause—A dependent clause is a part of a sentence and cannot stand on its own. For example, *When she saw Jim* is a dependent clause. To make a complete sentence, you need to add an independent clause: *When she saw Jim, she smiled.*

exclamation point—This mark of punctuation (!) at the end of a sentence is used to show surprise or strong emotion.

fragment—A fragment is a group of words that is not a complete sentence, even though it sometimes starts with a capital letter or ends with a punctuation mark and often contains a subject and verb.

helping verb—This type of verb is also called an auxiliary verb. Helping verbs are used with main verbs in a verb phrase: *is going; were singing; can talk; may leave; must tell; will see.*

hyphen—This mark (-) is used to separate the different parts of a compound word: *mother-in-law, self-motivated student.*

independent clause—An independent clause has a subject and a verb, expresses a complete thought, and can be seen as a sentence (for example, *She saw him.*). It can also be combined with another independent clause to make a compound sentence (*She saw him, so she called him over.*). It can also take a dependent clause to make a complex sentence (*She saw him, even though it was dark.*).

infinitive verb—An infinitive consists of the word *to* plus a *verb* (for example, *to go, to swim, to wish*). It can function as a noun, adjective, or adverb. For example: *To swim the English Channel is my friend's strongest dream.* Here, the infinitive *to swim* acts as a noun. It is the subject of the sentence.

intransitive verb—This type of verb does not need an object to complete its meaning. For example: *John ran. Bob left. Jane slept.*

introduction—An introduction is the first paragraph of an essay. Effective introductions do two basic things: grab the reader's interest and let the reader know what the whole essay is about. This is why most introductions include a thesis statement that clearly states the writer's topic and main argument.

main idea—Main ideas are the important points of an essay. They state what will be discussed in each paragraph (or set of paragraphs for longer essays). Main ideas develop the thesis statement of an essay and are in turn developed by supporting details.

modal verb—A modal verb is a kind of helping verb. Modal verbs help to express meanings such as permission (*may*), obligation (*must*), prediction (*will*, *shall*), or ability (*can*).

noun phrase—This type of phrase consists of several words that together function as the noun of a sentence. For example: *Talking to my mother made me feel better*. Here, *Talking to my mother* is a noun phrase that is acting as the subject of this sentence.

paragraph—An essay is made up of smaller sections called paragraphs. Each paragraph should focus on one main idea; you tell your reader what this idea is by using a topic sentence. A good paragraph is one in which every sentence supports the topic sentence.

passive voice—English sentences can be written in either the active or passive voice. In a passive sentence, the verb *to be* is combined with the past participle form of a verb (for example, *John was kicked*.). A passive sentence emphasizes the receiver or the results of an action.

period—In English grammar, this punctuation mark (.) is used to signal the end of a declarative sentence. (A declarative sentence is one that is not a question or an exclamation.) It is also used to indicate abbreviations (for example, *Mr., St., Ave.*).

phrase—A phrase is a group of related words with a single grammatical function (for example, a noun phrase or a verb phrase). The noun phrase acts as a noun or subject in this sentence: *The girl in the corner is Mary*.

plural—*Plural* means "more than one." In English grammar, nouns, pronouns, and verbs can take plural forms. For example, *cars* is a plural noun, *they* is a plural pronoun, and *climb* is a plural verb.

possessive pronoun—These are pronouns that show possession or ownership (for example, *my, our, his, her, their, whose*). Some possessive pronouns can function as nouns: *Is this yours? That book is mine*.

prefix—A prefix is a word part, such as *co-* in *costar*, attached to the front of a word to make a new word. For another example, the prefix *re-* can be added to the word *sell* to make the word *resell*, which means "to sell again."

preposition—Prepositions are words such as *in, of, by*, and *from*. They describe the relationship between words in a sentence. In the sentence *The professor sat on the desk*, the preposition *on* shows the location of the professor in relation to the desk.

pronoun—A pronoun can replace a noun or another pronoun. You can use pronouns such as *she, it, which*, and *they* to make your writing less repetitive.

question mark—This is the punctuation mark (?) used at the end of a direct question. For example: *Is David coming to the party?*

sentence combining—Sometimes writers combine two or more short sentences to make a longer one. The reason for doing this is that too many short sentences often make the writing sound choppy. Using sentence-combining techniques in the revising process can improve the style of your essay.

singular—*Singular* means "single," or "one." In English grammar, nouns, pronouns, and verbs can take singular forms. For example, *car* is a singular noun, *he* or *she* is a singular pronoun, and *climbs* is a singular verb in the present tense.

subject—The subject of a sentence tells who or what a sentence is about. For example, in the sentence *Stephen ran into the parking lot, Stephen* is the subject of the sentence.

supporting idea—Supporting ideas are the details that develop the main idea of a paragraph. They can be definitions, explanations, illustrations, opinions, evidence, and examples. They usually come after the topic sentence and make up the body of a paragraph.

tense—Tenses indicate time. Sometimes tenses are formed by changes in the verb, as in *He sings* (present tense) and *He sang* (past tense). At other times, tenses are formed by adding modals, or helping verbs. For example: *He will give me fifty dollars* (future tense); *He has given me fifty dollars* (perfect tense).

thesis—The thesis or thesis statement of an essay states what will be discussed in the whole essay. It offers your reader a quick and easy summary of the essay. A thesis statement usually consists of two parts: your topic and what you are going to say about the topic. Thesis statements are supported by main ideas.

topic sentence—The topic sentence states the main idea of a paragraph. It tells your reader what the paragraph is about. An easy way to make sure your reader understands the topic of a paragraph is to put your topic sentence near the beginning of the paragraph. (This is a good general rule for less experienced writers, although it is not the only way to do it.)

transition word or phrase—Transition words and phrases are used to connect ideas and signal relationships between them. For example, *first* can be used to signal the first of several points; *thus* can be used to show a result.

transitive verb—Transitive verbs require an object. For example, in the sentence *He mailed the letter, mailed* is a transitive verb, and *letter* is its object.

verb—A verb is an "action" word (for example, *climb, jump, run, eat*). English verbs also express time. (For example, past tense verbs such as *climbed, jumped, ran,* and *ate* show that the action happened in the past.) Verbs also show states of being—"to be" words—mentioned earlier in the chapter.

verb phrase—A verb phrase is a phrase (or a group of words) that consists of a main verb (for example, *climb, jump, run, eat*) plus one or more helping verbs (for example, *may, can, has, is, are*). Examples of verb phrases are *She may go,* and *The students will receive certificates.*

Performance Feedback for Test Takers

The scores you receive on the *TOEFL iBT*® test indicate your performance level in each of the four skill areas: reading, listening, speaking, and writing. This appendix provides descriptions of what test takers can typically do at each score level, as well as advice about how test takers at each level can improve their skills.

Only the "Your Performance" descriptions appear on test taker score reports. The "Advice for Improvement" is only a sample of the advice available. More extensive advice is available on the *TOEFL*® test website, www.ets.org/toefl.

TOEFL iBT® Reading Section Performance Descriptors

Advanced
(Score range 24–30, CEFR Level C1)

Test takers who receive a Reading section score at the **ADVANCED** level typically understand academic passages in English at the introductory university level. These passages are dense with propositions and information and can include difficult vocabulary, lengthy, complex sentences and paragraphs, and abstract or nuanced ideas that may be presented in complex ways.

Test takers who score at the Advanced level typically can

- Understand a range of academic and low-frequency vocabulary as well as less common meanings of words.
- Understand explicit connections among pieces of information and make appropriate inferences, even when the passage is conceptually dense and the language is complex.
- Recognize the expository organization of a passage and the purpose that specific information serves within the larger context, even when the purpose of the information is not marked and the passage is conceptually dense.
- Follow a paragraph-length argument involving speculation, qualifications, counterevidence, and subtle rhetorical shifts.
- Synthesize information in passages that contain complex language and are conceptually dense.

Read as much and as often as possible. Make sure to include academic texts on a variety of topics written in different genres and with different degrees of conceptual density as part of your reading.

- Read major newspapers, such as the *New York Times* or *Science Times*, and websites (National Public Radio [NPR] or the BBC).
- Write summaries of texts, making sure they incorporate the organizational pattern of the originals. Continually expand your vocabulary.

Practice using new words you encounter in your reading. This will help you remember both the meaning and correct usage of the new words.

High-Intermediate

(Score range 18–23, CEFR Level B2)

Test takers who receive a Reading section score at the **HIGH-INTERMEDIATE** level typically understand the main ideas and important details of academic passages in English at the introductory university level, but they may have an incomplete or incorrect understanding of parts of passages that are especially dense with propositions and information, or are complex in their presentation of ideas and information.

Test takers who score at the High-Intermediate level typically can

- Understand common academic vocabulary, but sometimes have difficulty with low-frequency words or less common meanings of words.
- Understand explicit connections among pieces of information and make appropriate inferences, but may have difficulty in parts of a passage that contain low-frequency vocabulary or that are conceptually dense, rhetorically complex, or abstract.
- Distinguish important ideas from less important ones.
- Often recognize the expository organization of a passage and the purpose of specific information within a passage, even when such information is not explicitly marked.
- Synthesize information in a passage, but may have difficulty doing so when the passage is conceptually dense, rhetorically complex, or abstract.

ADVICE FOR IMPROVEMENT

Read as much and as often as possible. Study the organization of academic texts and overall structure of reading passages. Read an entire passage from beginning to end.

- Pay attention to the relationship between the **main ideas** and the **supporting details**.
- Outline the text to test your understanding of the structure of the reading passage.

- Write a summary of the entire passage.
- If the text is a comparison, be sure that your summary reflects that. If the text argues two points of view, be sure both points of view are reflected in your summary. Continually expand your vocabulary by developing a system for recording unfamiliar words.
- Group words according to topic or meaning and study the words as a list of related words.
- Study **roots**, **prefixes**, and **suffixes**; study word families.
- Use available vocabulary resources, such as a good thesaurus or a dictionary of collocations (words commonly used together).

Low-Intermediate

(Score range 4–17, CEFR Level B1)

Test takers who receive a Reading section score at the **LOW-INTERMEDIATE** level typically understand some main ideas and important information presented in academic passages in English, but their overall understanding is limited. They are able to understand connections across two or more sentences when the relationships are clear and simple, such as a claim followed by a supporting example. However, they have difficulty following denser or more complex parts of a passage.

Test takers who score at the Low-Intermediate level typically can

- Understand texts with basic grammar, but have inconsistent understanding of texts with complex grammatical structures.
- Understand high-frequency academic vocabulary, but often have difficulty with lower-frequency words.
- Locate information in a passage by matching words or relying on high-frequency vocabulary, but their limited ability to recognize paraphrases results in incomplete understanding of the connections among ideas and information.
- Identify an author's purpose when that purpose is explicitly stated or easy to infer from the context.
- Recognize major ideas in a passage when the information is clearly presented, memorable, or illustrated by examples but have difficulty doing so when the passage is more demanding.

ADVICE FOR IMPROVEMENT

Read as much and as often as possible. Develop a system for recording unfamiliar words.

- Group words into lists according to topic or meaning and review and study the words on a regular basis so that you remember them.
- Increase your vocabulary by analyzing word parts; study **roots**, **prefixes**, and **suffixes**; study **word families**. Study the organization of academic texts

and overall structure of a reading passage. Read an entire passage from beginning to end.

- Look at connections between sentences; look at how the end of one sentence relates to the beginning of the next sentence.
- Look for the **main ideas** and **supporting details** and pay attention to the relationship between them.
- Outline a text to test your understanding of the structure of a reading passage.
- Begin by grouping paragraphs that address the same concept.
- Write one sentence summarizing the paragraphs that discuss the same idea.
- Write a summary of the entire passage.

Below Low-Intermediate

(Score range 0-3)

Test takers with a Reading section score below 4 have not yet demonstrated proficiency at the Low-Intermediate level.

TOEFL iBT® Listening Section Performance Descriptors

Advanced
(Score range 22–30, CEFR Level C1)

Test takers who receive a Listening section score at the **ADVANCED** level typically understand conversations and lectures that take place in academic settings. The conversations and lectures may include difficult vocabulary, abstract or complex ideas, complex sentence structures, various uses of intonation, and a large amount of information, possibly organized in complex ways.

Test takers who score at the Advanced level typically can

- Understand main ideas and explicitly stated important details, even if not reinforced.
- Distinguish important ideas from less important points.
- Keep track of conceptually complex (and sometimes conflicting) information over extended portions of a lecture.
- Understand how information or examples are being used (for example, to provide evidence for or against a claim, to make comparisons or draw contrasts, or to express an opinion or a value judgment) and how pieces of information are connected (for example, in a cause-effect relationship).
- Understand different ways that speakers use language for purposes other than to give information (for example, to express an emotion, to emphasize a point, to convey agreement or disagreement, or to communicate an intention).
- Synthesize information, even when it is not presented in sequence, and make appropriate inferences on the basis of that information.

ADVICE FOR IMPROVEMENT

Further develop your listening ability with daily practice in listening in English and by challenging yourself with increasingly lengthy listening selections and more complex listening material.

- Listen to different kinds of materials on a variety of topics:
  - Focus on topics that are new to you.
  - Listen to academic lectures and public talks.
  - Listen to audio and video material on TV, radio, and the Internet.
  - Listen to programs with academic content, such as NOVA, BBC, and NPR broadcasts.
  - Listen to conversations, phone calls, and phone recordings.
  - Take live and audio-recorded tours (for example, tours of museums).
- Listen actively:
  - Take notes as you listen for main ideas and important details.
  - Make predictions about what you will hear next.
  - Summarize.
  - Write down new words and expressions.

For the more difficult material you have chosen to listen to, listen several times:

1. First listen for the main ideas and key details;
2. Then listen again to fill in gaps in your understanding; to understand the connections between ideas, the structure of the talk, and the speaker's attitude; and to distinguish fact from opinion.

High-Intermediate
(Score range 17–21, CEFR Level B2)

Test takers who receive a Listening section score at the **HIGH-INTERMEDIATE** level typically understand the main ideas and important details of conversations and lectures that take place in academic settings. The conversations and lectures may include difficult vocabulary, abstract or complex ideas, complex sentence structures, various uses of intonation, and information that must be tracked across sequences of utterances. However, lectures and conversations that are dense with information may present difficulty if the information is not reinforced.

Test takers who score at the High-Intermediate level typically can

- Understand main ideas and explicitly stated important details that are reinforced (by repetition, paraphrase, or indirect reference).
- Distinguish main ideas from other information.
- Keep track of information over an extended portion of an information-rich lecture or conversation, and recognize multiple, possibly conflicting, points of view.
- Understand how information or examples are being used (for example, to provide support for a claim) and how pieces of information are connected (for example, in a narrative explanation, a compare-and-contrast relationship, or a cause-effect chain).
- Understand, though perhaps not consistently, ways that speakers use language for purposes other than to give information (for example, to emphasize a point, express agreement or disagreement, express opinions, or convey intentions indirectly), especially when the purpose is supported by intonation.
- Synthesize information from adjacent parts of a lecture or conversation and make appropriate inferences on the basis of that information, but may have difficulty synthesizing information from separate parts of a lecture or conversation.

ADVICE FOR IMPROVEMENT

Practice listening in English daily. Gradually increase the amount of time that you spend listening, the length of the listening selections, and the difficulty of the material.

- Listen to different kinds of materials on a variety of topics:
  - Start with familiar topics; then move to topics that are new to you.
  - Listen to audio and video material on CD/DVD or recorded from TV, radio, and the Internet.
  - Listen to programs with academic content, such as NOVA, BBC, and NPR broadcasts.
  - Listen to conversations and phone recordings.
- Listen actively:
  - Take notes as you listen for main ideas and important details.
  - Ask yourself about basic information. (Who? What? When? Where? Why? How?)
  - Make predictions about what you will hear next.
  - Summarize.
  - Write down new words and expressions.

For more difficult material, listen several times:

1. First listen with English subtitles, if they are available;
2. Then, without subtitles, listen for the main ideas and key details;
3. Then listen again to fill in gaps in your basic understanding and to understand the connections between ideas.

Low-Intermediate

(Score range 9–16, CEFR Level B1)

Test takers who receive a Listening section score at the **LOW-INTERMEDIATE** level typically understand the main idea and some important details of conversations and lectures that take place in academic settings. These conversations and lectures can include basic academic language, abstract or complex ideas that are significantly reinforced, complex sentence structures, certain uses of intonation, and a large amount of information that is repeated or significantly reinforced.

Test takers at the Low-Intermediate level typically can

- Understand main ideas, even in complex discussions, when the ideas are repeatedly referred to, extensively elaborated on, or illustrated with multiple examples.
- Understand explicitly stated important details but may have difficulty understanding details if they are not reinforced (such as through repetition or with an example) or marked as important, or if they are conveyed over several exchanges among different speakers.
- Understand some ways that speakers use language to express an opinion or attitude (for example, agreement, disagreement, surprise), especially when the opinion or attitude is related to a central theme, clearly marked as important, or supported by intonation.
- Understand connections between important ideas, particularly if the ideas are related to a central theme or are repeated and can make appropriate inferences from information expressed in one or two sentences, especially when that information is reinforced.

Practice listening in English daily. Gradually increase the amount of time that you spend listening, as well as the length of the individual listening selections.

- Listen to different kinds of materials on a variety of topics:
  - recordings on topics that are familiar to you
  - recordings of English lessons
  - audio and video material on CD/DVD or recorded from TV
  - short programs with some academic content conversations
- Listen actively:
  - Take notes as you listen for main ideas and important details.
  - Ask yourself about basic information. (Who? What? When? Where? Why? How?)
  - Make predictions about what you will hear next.
  - Summarize.
  - Write down new words and expressions.

Listen several times to each recording:

1. First listen with English subtitles, if they are available.
2. Then, without subtitles, listen for the main ideas and key details.
3. Then listen again to fill in gaps in your basic understanding and to understand the connections between ideas.

Below Low-Intermediate

(Score range 0–8)

Test takers with a Listening section score below 9 have not yet demonstrated proficiency at the Low-Intermediate level.

TOEFL iBT® Speaking Section Performance Descriptors

Advanced

(Score range 25–30, CEFR Level C1)

Test takers who receive a Speaking section score at the **ADVANCED** level are typically able to communicate fluently and effectively on a wide range of topics with little difficulty.

Test takers who score at the Advanced level typically can

- Speak clearly and use intonation to support meaning so that speech is generally easy to understand and follow; any minor lapses do not obscure meaning.
- Speak with relative ease on a range of general and academic topics, demonstrating control of an appropriate range of grammatical structures and vocabulary; any minor errors may be noticeable, but do not obscure meaning.
- Convey mostly well-supported summaries, explanations, and opinions, including both concrete and abstract information, with generally well-controlled organization and cohesion; lapses may occur, but they rarely impact overall comprehensibility.

ADVICE FOR IMPROVEMENT

Look for opportunities to build your fluency in English.

- Take risks and engage others in conversation in English whenever possible.
- Join an Internet chat room.

Record yourself and then listen and transcribe what you said.

- Read a short article from a newspaper or textbook. Record yourself summarizing the article.
- Transcribe the recording and review the transcription. Think about other ways to say the same thing.

High-Intermediate

(Score range 20–24, CEFR Level B2)

Test takers who receive a Speaking section score at the **HIGH-INTERMEDIATE** level are typically able to communicate effectively on most general or familiar topics, and to make themselves understood when discussing more complex or academic topics.

Test takers who score at the High-Intermediate level typically can

- Speak clearly and without hesitancy on general or familiar topics, with overall good intelligibility; pauses and hesitations (to recall or plan information) are sometimes noticeable when more demanding content is produced, and any mispronunciations or intonation errors only occasionally cause problems for the listener.
- Produce stretches of speech that demonstrate control of some complex structures and a range of vocabulary, although occasional lapses in precision and accuracy may obscure meaning at times.
- Convey sufficient information to produce mostly complete summaries, explanations, and opinions, but some ideas may not be fully developed or may lack elaboration; any lapses in completeness and cohesion may at times affect the otherwise clear progression of ideas.

ADVICE FOR IMPROVEMENT

Practice speaking in English about everyday topics that are important to students' lives. This will develop your fluency and confidence.

- Find a speaking partner. Set aside time each week to practice speaking with your partner in English.
- If you cannot find a native English speaker, find a friend who wants to practice speaking English and promise to speak only English for a certain period.
- Read articles from campus newspapers that can be found on the Internet. Practice speaking for a limited time on different academic topics.

Practice speaking for a limited time on different academic topics.

- Read a short article from a newspaper or a textbook. Write down key content words from the article.
- Write down two or three questions about the article that include the content words
- Practice answering the questions aloud. Try to include the content words in your response
- After practicing, record your answers to the questions.

Low-Intermediate

(Score range 16–19, CEFR Level B1)

Test takers who receive a Speaking section score at the **LOW-INTERMEDIATE** level are typically able to talk about general or familiar topics with relative ease.

Test takers who score at the Low-Intermediate level typically can

- Speak clearly with minor hesitancies about general or familiar topics; longer pauses are noticeable when speaking about more complex or academic topics, and mispronunciations may obscure meaning at times.

- Produce short stretches of speech consisting of basic grammatical structures connected with "and", 'because" and "so"; attempts at longer utterances requiring more complex grammatical structures may be marked by errors and pauses for grammatical planning or repair; use vocabulary that is sufficient to discuss general or familiar topics, but limitations in range of vocabulary sometimes result in vague or unclear expression of ideas.
- Convey some main points and other relevant information but summaries, explanations, and opinions are sometimes incomplete, inaccurate, and/or lack detail; long or complex explanations may lack coherence. Basic Score range 10–15 CEFR Level A2 Test takers who receive a Speaking section score at the BASIC level are typically able to communicate limited information about familiar, everyday topics. Test takers who score at the Basic level typically can
- Speak slowly and carefully so that they make themselves understood, but pronunciation may be strongly influenced by the speaker's first language and at times be unintelligible; speech may be marked by frequent pauses, reformulations, and false starts.
- Produce mostly short utterances, connecting phrases with simple linking words (such as "and") to make themselves understood; grammar and vocabulary are limited, and frequent pauses may occur while searching for words.
- Convey some limited information about familiar topics; supporting points and/or details are generally missing, and main ideas may be absent, unclear, or not well connected.

ADVICE FOR IMPROVEMENT

Develop friendships with people who want to speak English with you. Interaction with others will improve your speaking ability. If you cannot find a native speaker, find a friend who wants to practice speaking English and promise to speak only English for a certain period.

- Read a short article from a newspaper or a textbook. Write down key content words from the article.
- Write down two or three questions about the article that include the content words.
- Practice answering the questions aloud. Try to include the content words in your response.
- After practicing, record your answers to the questions.

Practice speaking about current events.

- Read newspaper articles, editorials, and information about cultural events in English. Share the information that you read with a friend in English.
- Visit a university class and take notes in the class. Then use your notes to tell a friend about some of the information you heard in English.
- Develop your academic vocabulary. Write down important new words that you come across while reading or listening and practice pronouncing them.
- Listen to a weather report and take notes on what you heard. Then give the weather report to a friend in English.

Below Low-Intermediate

(Score range 0–8)

Test takers with a Speaking section score below 10 have not yet demonstrated proficiency at the Basic level.

ADVICE FOR IMPROVEMENT

Take a conversation class. This will help improve your fluency and pronunciation in English.

Increase your vocabulary and improve your grammar in your speech.

- Study basic grammar rules so that your speech is grammatically correct.
- As you learn new words and expressions, practice pronouncing them clearly. Record yourself as you practice.

TOEFL iBT® Writing Section Performance Descriptors

Advanced

(Score range 24–30, CEFR Level C1)

Test takers who receive a Writing section score at the **ADVANCED** level are typically able to write in English on a wide range of academic and non-academic topics with confidence and clarity.

Test takers who score at the Advanced level typically can

- Produce clear, well-developed, and well-organized text; ungrammatical, unclear, or unidiomatic use of English is rare.
- Express an opinion on a controversial issue and support that opinion with appropriate details and explanations in writing, demonstrating variety and range of vocabulary and grammatical structures.
- Select important information from multiple sources, integrate it, and present it coherently and clearly in writing, with only occasional minor imprecision in the summary of the source information.

ADVICE FOR IMPROVEMENT

Continue to improve your ability to relate and convey information from two or more sources. For example, practice analyzing reading passages in English.

- Read two articles or chapters on the same topic or issue, write a summary of each, and then explain the ways they are similar and the ways they are different.
- Practice combining listening and reading by searching for readings related to talks and lectures with a teacher or a friend.

Continue to improve your ability to express opinions by studying the ways that published writers express their opinions.

- Read articles and essays written by professional writers that express opinions about an issue (for example, a social, environmental, or educational issue).
- Identify the writer's opinion or opinions.
- Notice how the writer addresses possible objections to the opinions, if the writer discusses these.

High-Intermediate

(Score range 17-23, CEFR Level B2)

Test takers who receive a Writing section score at the **HIGH-INTERMEDIATE** level are typically able to write in English well on general or familiar topics. When writing about complex ideas or ideas on academic topics, they can convey most of the main ideas.

Test takers who score at the High-Intermediate level typically can

- Produce summaries of multiple sources that include most of the main ideas; some important ideas from the sources may be missing, unclear, or inaccurate.
- Express an opinion on an issue clearly; some ideas and explanations may not be fully developed and lapses in cohesion may at times affect a clear progression of ideas.
- Write with some degree of facility; grammatical mistakes or vague/incorrect uses of words may make the writing difficult to follow in some places.

ADVICE FOR IMPROVEMENT

Practice finding main points.

- Record news and informational programs in English from the television or radio or download talks or lectures from the Internet.
- Listen and take notes. Stop the recording about every 30 seconds to write out a short summary of what you heard.
- Replay the recording to check your summary. Mark places where you are not sure if you have understood what was said or where you are not sure if you have expressed yourself well

Write a response to an article or essay in English, taking the opposite viewpoint.

- Outline your response.
- Note the methods you use to support your ideas. Reread what you have written.
- Make sure your supporting ideas are clearly related to your main point.
- Note what method you use to develop each of your supporting points.
- Make sure you have developed each of your points in detail. Is there anything more you could have said to strengthen your points?

Low-Intermediate

(Score range 13-16, CEFR Level B1)

Test takers who receive a Writing section score at the LOW-INTERMEDIATE level are typically able to produce simple written texts in English on general or familiar topics.

Test takers who score at the Low-Intermediate level typically can

- Produce a simple text that expresses some ideas on an issue, but the development of ideas is limited because of insufficient or inappropriate details and explanations.
- Summarize some relevant information from multiple sources, but important ideas from the sources are omitted or significantly misrepresented, especially ideas that require unfamiliar vocabulary or are complex.
- Write with limited facility, with language errors obscuring connections or meaning at key junctures between ideas in the text.

Read and listen to academic articles and other material in your own language. Take notes about what you read and hear.

- Begin by taking notes in your own language and then take notes in English.
- Summarize the points in complete English sentences.
- Ask your teacher to review your writing and help you correct your errors.
- Gradually decrease the time it takes you to read the material and write the summaries.
- Practice typing on a standard English (QWERTY) keyboard.

Study the organization of good paragraphs and essays. A good paragraph discusses one main idea. This idea is usually written in the first sentence, which is called the topic sentence. In essay writing, each paragraph should discuss one aspect of the main idea of an essay.

- Write paragraphs in English that focus on one main idea and contain several complete sentences that explain or support that idea.
- Ask your teacher to review your paragraphs for correctness.

Basic

(Score range 7-12, CEFR Level A2)

Test takers who receive a Writing section score at the BASIC level are typically able to communicate very basic information in written English.

Test takers who score at the Basic level typically can

- Produce some text that is related to the topic, but with little detail and/or lack of organization.
- Convey some information from the sources or some ideas on an issue, but grammatical errors, unclear expressions, and/or poor sentence structure make their writing difficult to comprehend.

ADVICE FOR IMPROVEMENT

- Practice English language comprehension and writing skills, increasing your vocabulary and improving your grammar.
- As your comprehension and writing skills improve, follow the suggestions for the Low-Intermediate level above.

Below Basic

(Score range 0-6)

Test takers with a Writing section score below 7 have not yet demonstrated proficiency at the Basic level.

Notes

Notes

Notes